terra australis 45

Terra Australis reports the results of archaeological and related research within the south and east of Asia, though mainly Australia, New Guinea and island Melanesia — lands that remained terra australis incognita to generations of prehistorians. Its subject is the settlement of the diverse environments in this isolated quarter of the globe by peoples who have maintained their discrete and traditional ways of life into the recent recorded or remembered past and at times into the observable present.

List of volumes in Terra Australis

terra australis 45

New Perspectives in Southeast Asian and Pacific Prehistory

Edited by Philip J. Piper, Hirofumi Matsumura
and David Bulbeck

Australian
National
University

PRESS

ANU PRESS

Published by ANU Press
The Australian National University
Acton ACT 2601 Australia
Email: anupress@anu.edu.au
This title is also available online at press.anu.edu.au

National Library of Australia Cataloguing-in-Publication entry

Title:	New perspectives in Southeast Asian and Pacific prehistory / edited by Philip J. Piper, Hirofumi Matsumura, David Bulbeck.
ISBN:	9781760460945 (paperback) 9781760460952 (ebook)
Series:	Terra Australis ; 45.
Subjects:	Archaeology--Southeast Asia.
	Archaeology--Pacific Area.
	Antiquities, Prehistoric--Southeast Asia.
	Antiquities, Prehistoric--Pacific Area.
	Paleoanthropology--Southeast Asia.
	Paleoanthropology--Pacific Area.

Other Creators/Contributors:
Piper, Philip J., editor.
Matsumura, Hirofumi., editor.
Bulbeck, David, editor.

Terra Australis Editorial Board: Sue O'Connor, Jack Golson, Simon Haberle, Sally Brockwell, Geoffrey Clark.

Cover design and layout by ANU Press. Cover photograph by Mariko Yamagata.

This edition © 2017 ANU Press

Contents

Contributors

Noboru Adachi

Department of Legal Medicine, Interdisciplinary Graduate School of Medicine and Engineering, University of Yamanashi, Yamanashi, Japan

Karina Arifin

Fakultas Ilmu Pengetahuan Budaya, Departemen Arkeologi, Universitas Indonesia, Depok, Indonesia

Robert Blust

Department of Linguistics, University of Hawai'i, Honolulu, USA

David Bulbeck

Department of Archaeology and Natural History, College of Asia and the Pacific, The Australian National University, Canberra, Australia

Judith Cameron

Department of Archaeology and Natural History, College of Asia and the Pacific, The Australian National University, Canberra, Australia

Zhang Chi

School of Archaeology and Museology, Peking University, Beijing, China

Gang He

The Cultural Relics and Archeological Research Institution in Hunan Province, China

Helen Heath

Department of Anthropology and Archaeology, University of Otago, North Dunedin, New Zealand

Charles Higham

Department of Anthropology and Archaeology, University of Otago, North Dunedin, New Zealand

Mark J. Hudson

Mt Fuji World Heritage Centre for Mountain Research, Shizuoka, Japan
Museum of Natural and Environmental History, Shizuoka, Japan

Hsiao-chun Hung

Department of Archaeology and Natural History, College of Asia and the Pacific, The Australian National University, Canberra, Australia

Michiko Intoh

Department of Social Research, National Museum of Ethnology, Osaka, Japan

Timothy A. Jinam

Division of Population Genetics, National Institute of Genetics, Shizuoka, Japan

Hideaki Kanzawa-Kiriyama

Department of Anthropology, National Museum of Nature and Science, Tokyo, Japan

Nguyen Kim Dung

The Vietnamese Institute of Archaeology, Hanoi, Vietnam

Nguyen Lan Cuong

The Vietnamese Institute of Archaeology, Hanoi, Vietnam

Tracey L.-D. Lu

Department of Anthropology, the Chinese University of Hong Kong, Hong Kong, China

Hirofumi Matsumura

Faculty of Health Science, Sapporo Medical University, Sapporo, Japan

Armand Salvador Mijares

Archaeological Studies Program, University of the Philippines, Quezon City, Philippines

Sofwan Noerwidi

Balai Arkeologi Yogyakarta, Yogyakarta,
Indonesia

Andrew Pawley

Centre for Research on Language Change,
College of Asia and the Pacific, The Australian
National University, Canberra, Australia

Philip J. Piper

School of Archaeology and Anthropology,
College of Arts and Social Sciences,
The Australian National University,
Canberra, Australia

Naruya Saitou

Division of Population Genetics, National
Institute of Genetics, Shizuoka, Japan

Department of Genetics, School of Life
Science, Graduate University for Advanced
Science (SOKENDAI), Kanagawa, Japan

Department of Biological Sciences, Graduate
School of Science, University of Tokyo,
Tokyo, Japan

Carmen Sarjeant

School of Archaeology and Anthropology,
College of Arts and Social Sciences,
The Australian National University,
Canberra, Australia

Ken-ichi Shinoda

Department of Anthropology, National
Museum of Nature and Science,
Tsukuba, Japan

Truman Simanjuntak

Center for Prehistoric and Austronesian
Studies, National Center for Archaeology,
Jawa Barat, Indonesia

Glenn R. Summerhayes

Department of Anthropology and
Archaeology, University of Otago,
North Dunedin, New Zealand

Katsushi Tokunaga

Department of Human Genetics, Graduate
School of Medicine, University of Tokyo,
Tokyo, Japan

Mariko Yamagata

Center for Cultural Resource Studies,
Kanazawa University, Kanazawa, Japan

Ya-feng Zhao

The Cultural Relics and Archeological
Research Institution in Hunan Province,
China

Comment from Ian Lilley

This collection is dedicated to a remarkable figure in Indo-Pacific archaeology. I first came across Peter Bellwood's work when rapidly preparing myself for an unexpected trip to New Britain in 1980 with Jim Specht. I bought a copy of Peter's magisterial *Man's Conquest of the Pacific*, as there was nothing else even remotely similar that would bring me up to speed on the state of the art as we then understood it. It cost a lot for a student, but it was worth every cent! It is still on my bookshelf and I still periodically refer to it, if only to remind myself how far we have come (or not).

Since then, Peter has produced a number of other indispensable reference works as well as a multitude of papers, reports and the like. He also ran the Indo-Pacific Prehistory Association (IPPA), which I usually describe as the peak professional body in the region. He took up the reins, initially as Secretary and Editor, at IPPA's Pune congress in India in 1978, the same year *Man's Conquest* appeared, and handed over to me as Secretary General 21 years later, after IPPA's Hanoi meeting in Vietnam in 2009.

What a record of service! In that time, IPPA grew from a tiny group of colleagues to one that now has hundreds of members around the world, and brought almost 1,000 delegates together at the last congress held in Siem Reap, Cambodia, in early 2014. Peter continues to provide the elected members of the IPPA Executive and me with very welcome advice and support while also advancing his fieldwork in various parts of IPPA's domain. Long may he carry on! With that, I commend to you the work that follows, in recognition of Peter's extraordinary contribution to Indo-Pacific archaeology.

Ian Lilley
Leiden (2016)

Preface

This volume was created to celebrate the achievements of Professor Peter Bellwood, who has spent a successful and distinguished career of almost 50 years researching the prehistory of Southeast Asia and the Pacific. No other individual has had such a profound impact on our understanding of the archaeology of the region. Peter's extensive knowledge of Southeast Asian prehistory is embedded in decades of fieldwork across the Indo-Pacific, from the Society and Marquesas Islands in the east to Vietnam in the west. His five books, *Man's Conquest of the Pacific* (1978), *The Polynesians* (1978), *Prehistory of the Indo-Malayan Archipelago* (1985), *First Farmers* (2005) and *First Migrants* (2013), not to mention the numerous journal articles, monographs and book chapters, have been extremely influential, and his passion for understanding the past has inspired more than a generation of archaeologists. Peter is probably one of the few archaeologists working in Southeast Asia and the Pacific who has embraced a multidisciplinary approach to unravelling the prehistoric past by integrating historical linguistics with archaeology and anthropology. His firm belief in the farming/language dispersal hypothesis has often courted controversy and stimulated considerable literary debate in both the fields of archaeology and linguistics. Indeed, several of the chapters in this book challenge one or other aspects of his hypotheses on the migration of farming communities across Southeast Asia.

Another noteworthy achievement of Peter's career was his role in consolidating the Indo-Pacific Prehistory Association (IPPA), of which he remained the Secretary and General Editor (or Secretary General and Editor) between the late 1970s and late 2000s. During his stewardship of the society, Peter headed the organisation of nine Indo-Pacific Prehistory congresses, always held in India, Taiwan or Southeast Asian countries. The congresses provided a unique opportunity for archaeologists from South Asia to China, Australia and the Pacific to share their interests, experience and research. Peter was instrumental in organising funds for Asian archaeologists to attend the congresses and have their contributions prepared for publication for the international audience in the *Bulletin of the Indo-Pacific Prehistory Association*. This journal continues to serve (now as the *Journal of India-Pacific Archaeology*) as a useful outlet for the publication of other contributions such as student thesis summaries, papers from other Asia-Pacific conferences, and miscellaneous contributions ready for submission by the call-up due date. Peter's famously encyclopaedic knowledge of archaeological sites and finds are a result of his commitment to reading and editing the research work of Southeast Asian and other colleagues. Peter's achievements as the General Secretary of IPPA was acknowledged by a session in his honour during the 2009 Hanoi conference and the succeeding proceedings published as a Special Issue in *Antiquity* 2011 Vol. 85(328).

In addition to his outstanding contribution to research and international collaboration, Peter has demonstrated an inexhaustible commitment to the advancement and training of aspiring young researchers from across Southeast Asia. Many of the archaeologists who obtained their Master's and PhD degrees under Peter's supervision have continued on to become research leaders in their own rights, and many have contributed to this volume. Some within senior academic and cultural heritage administration positions sadly could not find the time to contribute to this volume when approached by the editors. However, it has been possible to include a wide variety of chapters by colleagues with whom Peter has productively engaged over the years.

The research herein reflects the broad diversity of Peter's interests, and is a product of multidisciplinary efforts in archaeology, biological anthropology and linguistics to understand cultural developments in the prehistory of Southeast Asia and the Pacific.

This volume was refereed by two independent reviewers who commented on each of the individual chapters. We are grateful to all the authors for their participation in this endeavour and the referees and manuscript readers.

Publication was possible through financial assistance from The Australian National University grant and Grant in Aid by JSPS (Nos 23247040 and 16H02527). Thanks are also due to Chikako Ogawa who assisted in formatting chapter pages.

Philip J. Piper
Hirofumi Matsumura
David Bulbeck

List of Figures

List of Tables

1

Professor Peter Bellwood's Ongoing Journey in Archaeology

Hsiao-chun Hung

I will always remember the hard digging down the deepest trenches, the hoping and hoping for something special, the fine sieving, the heat and dust, and conversely the heat and rainforest humidity, and of course the local workers, the graduate students, and the many colleagues and past teachers … (interview with Peter Bellwood, 2011).

A brief introduction

Peter Bellwood is known for his decades of contributions to Asian and Pacific archaeology, responsible for formulating the fundamental chronological sequences of the region and situating these findings within broader contexts of human migrations, the 'farming/language dispersal hypothesis', origins and spread of Austronesian cultures, and interdisciplinary approaches to prehistory. The worldwide impact of Peter's work is evident in more than 300 academic publications since 1967, translations and updated revised editions of his major books, more than 50 invitations as a key speaker in international conferences, and as supervisor to more than 30 graduate students who have filled professional positions in Australia, USA, Brunei, Malaysia, Indonesia, the Philippines, Laos, Thailand, Japan, Hong Kong, China and Taiwan (see list of students this chapter).

Many of Peter's colleagues link his name with The Australian National University (ANU) and with the Indo-Pacific Prehistory Association (IPPA), which indeed comprised two of his chief occupations for some decades, among several other activities. Peter's tenured posts began as Lecturer in Prehistory at University of Auckland in 1967–1972, followed by a succession of positions at ANU as Lecturer in Prehistory (1973–1975), Senior Lecturer in Prehistory (1976–1983), Reader in Archaeology (1984–1999), Professor of Archaeology (2000–2013), and currently as Emeritus Professor of Archaeology since September 2013. Concurrent with his employment duties at ANU, Peter devoted many sustained years of service as the Secretary or Secretary General of the IPPA (Figure 1.1) while also acting as editor of the Association's publication *Bulletin of the Indo-Pacific Prehistory Association*, 1978–2009. Further, Peter has been a Fellow of the Australian Academy of the Humanities since 1983, a Corresponding Fellow of the British Academy since 2016, a member of editorial boards of journals such as *Antiquity*, *Asian Perspectives*, and *Journal of Archaeological Method and Theory*, and he is the Honorary Editor of *Journal of Austronesian Studies*.

Figure 1.1 Peter Bellwood (centre) attending the 15th Congress of the Indo-Pacific Prehistory Association at Chiang Mai, Thailand, in 1994, with (from left to right) Trinh Nang Chung, Ha Van Tan, Vu The Long, Nguyen Kim Dung, Hoang Xuan Chinh and Bui Vinh.

Source: Courtesy of Peter Bellwood.

Born in Leicester, England, in 1943, Peter followed his interest in archaeology from a young age. He completed his academic degrees at the University of Cambridge (Figure 1.2), including a BA in 1966, MA in 1969, and PhD by publication in 1980. By the time of receiving his PhD, Peter had already published an impressive roster of works that continue to influence archaeological research today. His first academic publication in 1967 was concerning 'A Roman dam in the Wadi Caam, Tripolitania', printed in *Libya Antiqua* (IV: 41–44). Ever since then, Peter's published work has been based on his years of research in Asia and the Pacific, including his pioneering directions in cross-regional syntheses and interdisciplinary coordination of archaeology with historical linguistics, human biology, and other perspectives.

Figure 1.2 The 1964 Cambridge Limes Tripolitanus Expedition, photographed in Cambridge; Peter Bellwood is standing at the far right.
Source: Courtesy of Peter Bellwood.

One of the hallmarks of Peter's career has involved seeing the 'big picture' of regional and cross-regional archaeology, augmented by his direct field experience in New Zealand, the Cook Islands, the Marquesas Islands, the Talaud Islands, Brunei, western Malaysia, India, Sabah, Sarawak, Maluku, the Batanes Islands, northern Vietnam, southern Vietnam, northern Luzon, Taiwan, Bali, and Kalimantan. As early as 1975, Peter had already established his reputation as a grand synthesiser with the publication of an influential research article 'The Prehistory of Oceania' in *Current Anthropology* (16: 9–28). This early success was magnified with the publication of two books in 1978. *The Polynesians* (Thames and Hudson, 1978) was later translated into French (1983) and Japanese (1985). *Man's Conquest of the Pacific* (Collins, 1978) proposed a novel integration of Southeast Asian and Pacific archaeology, later re-printed by Oxford University Press (1979) and translated into Russian (1986) and Japanese (1989). Yet his major regional synthesis was *Prehistory of the Indo-Malaysian Archipelago*, first published by Academic Press in 1985 and subsequently undergoing a number of reprints, revised editions, and language translations, with the latest fourth edition currently (2017) in production by Wiley-Blackwell as *First Islanders: Prehistory and Human Migration in Island Southeast Asia*.

Peter's insights into the interlinking of Asian and Pacific archaeology have been tied to the recognition of the widespread Austronesian-speaking communities, their language histories, and the connections between those language histories and archaeological evidence of the pan-regional spread of farming societies. This work has made Austronesian prehistory in the Asia-Pacific into one of the world's classic textbook examples of human migrations attested in archaeology. It has further been associated with the 'farming/language dispersal hypothesis', concerning how the world's major patterns of language groups reflect the migrations of farming societies in antiquity. Perhaps the broadest recognition of Peter's output regarding the Austronesian synthesis began with his 1991 research article 'The Austronesian dispersal and the origin of languages' (*Scientific American* 265/1: 88–93), followed in 1995 by the edited volume (with James Fox and Darrell Tryon) *The Austronesians: Historical and Comparative Perspectives* (published by Department of Anthropology, Research School of Pacific and Asian Studies, ANU). Related to larger issues of human migrations, Peter co-edited (with Colin Renfrew) *Examining the Farming/ Language Dispersal Hypothesis* (2002, McDonald Institute for Archaeological Research), and he most recently edited *The Global Prehistory of Human Migration* (2015, Wiley-Blackwell), in addition to his sole-authored monographs such as *First Farmers* (2005, Blackwell) and *First Migrants* (2013, Wiley-Blackwell). Without exaggeration, these products can be said to have changed the picture of world archaeology, noting that *First Farmers* received the Society for American Archaeology Book Award as well as the Association for American Publishers Award for Excellence in Professional and Scholarly Publishing, and so far it has been translated into Japanese (2008) and Vietnamese (2010). A special section of *Antiquity* was published in Peter's honour in 2011 (vol. 85).

As someone who has produced so much material, with broad regional coverage and touching on enduring central research themes of world archaeology, Peter has been no stranger to controversy at different points in his career. Admirably, he has revised and updated his work according to new developing ideas and datasets, not the least of which have included his own efforts. The ever-improving nature is evident from looking at Peter's earlier work in comparison to later editions and newer products, which simultaneously have proven the long-term value of Peter's primary contributions and have served as inspiration for generations of scholars.

As any student or colleague working with Peter can affirm, his legendary knowledge of Asian and Pacific archaeology is matched only by his enthusiastic support of others. Peter's years of teaching and major funded research projects have provided life-changing opportunities for countless students and professional colleagues internationally, as seen at least partially in the chapters of this book. This volume illustrates just a sample of the depth and breadth of Peter's impact and influence. Undoubtedly, we can expect to see more, as Emeritus Professor Peter Bellwood remains an active and leading figure in archaeology.

Interview with Peter Bellwood

In 2011, Professor Shuicheng Li of Peking University in Beijing invited Hsiao-chun Hung to conduct an interview with Professor Peter Bellwood, as part of the 'World Distinguished Scholar Series' of *Journal of Cultural Relics in Southern China (Nanfang Wenwu)*. Twelve questions were asked by Hung about Peter's student life, research career, current work, and the role of Chinese archaeology. The completed version of the 2011 interview was translated by Hung into Chinese and then published by the journal in China during the same year (Bellwood and Hung 2011). In the interview, Peter talked about his study of ancient Austronesian migration, the development and testing of the 'farming/language dispersal hypothesis', and the significance of Neolithic farmers in worldwide perspective. He additionally gave valuable advice for students who are interested in studying archaeology. The following interview record is based on the 2011 version, with a few new questions added in January 2015.

Q1: You have been known as the representative figure of research on Southeast Asian and Pacific archaeology since the 1970s. Could you please tell us how your interest started in this region?

I became interested in archaeology at age 17 in 1960, through reading popular books on the topic. At this time, I was an apprentice shoe machinery worker in Leicester, England, my city of birth. After finishing my university entrance studies I was able to get a State Scholarship to Cambridge University (King's College) in 1963, where I studied Roman and European archaeology for my

BA degree (1966) (Figure 1.3). The professor at that time was Grahame Clark, an authority on economic archaeology and the European Mesolithic. I was also taught by Edmund Leach (social anthropology), Glyn Daniel (European Neolithic), John Coles (European archaeology), Eric Higgs (economic archaeology), Brian Hope-Taylor (Anglo-Saxon archaeology) and Joan Liversidge (Roman archaeology). As a student I was able to take part in archaeological field projects in Tunisia, Libya, France, Denmark, Turkey and Iran, as well as on Roman and Medieval excavations in England.

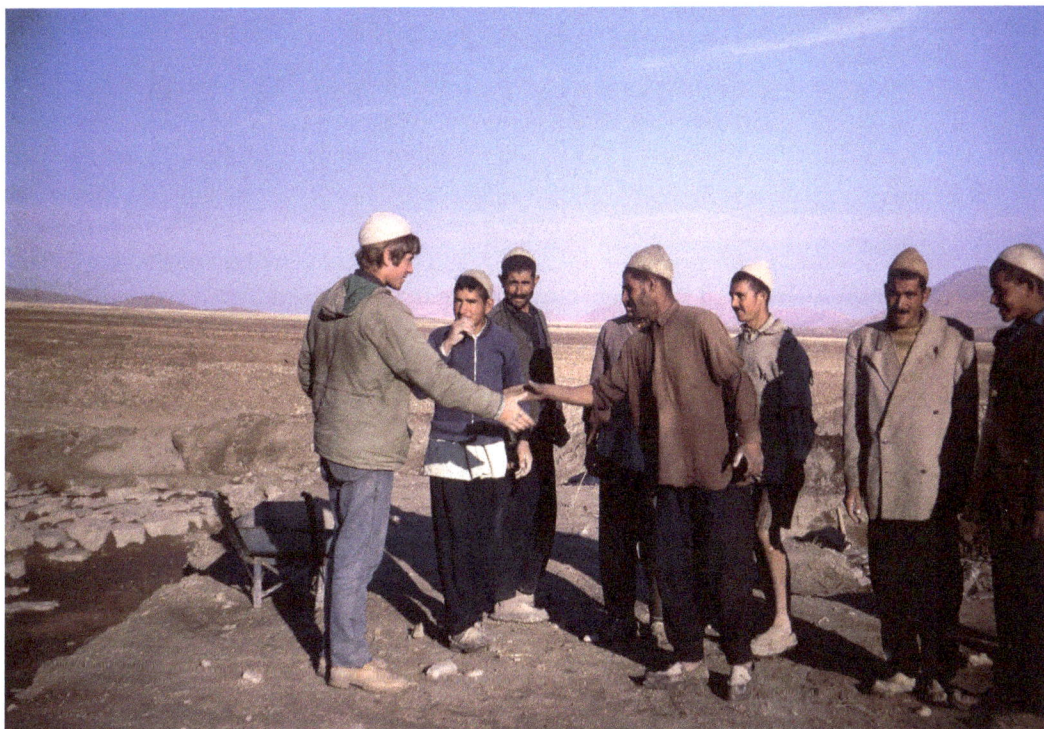

Figure 1.3 Peter Bellwood (left) at Bābā Jān Tepe, northeastern Luristan, Iran, in 1966.
Source: Courtesy of Peter Bellwood.

My Cambridge archaeology background always kept me interested in the relations between archaeology, history and human culture. I was still an undergraduate student when the 'New Archaeology' hit American and British archaeology in the mid-1960s, but I was never able to develop an interest in the more mechanistic aspects of this rather anti-historical approach to the human past. History, evolution and migration always remained my central interests, as they are today. As a student I became very interested in the archaeology of Polynesia, through reading the writings of the pioneer archaeologist Robert Suggs. Polynesia in the 1960s was a very romantic place, and the scene of a great human migration that had puzzled Western minds for over 200 years. In 1966, I applied for a job as a lecturer in archaeology at Auckland University in New Zealand, and emigrated from England to New Zealand in early 1967, then aged 23 and still without a PhD. At that time, the expansion of universities in the British Commonwealth was so strong that people with specialised bachelor degrees from Oxford and Cambridge were able to get tenurable teaching positions. This would be unthinkable nowadays, and a PhD is rightly essential for all advancement. I received my PhD from Cambridge in 1980, after submitting four of my books and monographs in lieu of writing a thesis (Cambridge University had special regulations to allow this for its former students who, like me, had full-time teaching positions and hence were unable to devote three years to writing a specialist thesis).

I spent six years at Auckland University, and during this time I came to understand the importance of historical linguistics in reconstructing the past, via my colleagues Roger Green and Andrew Pawley. I carried out fieldwork in Polynesia (Figure 1.4), in New Zealand itself from 1967–1970, in the Society and Marquesas Islands in 1967–1968 (with Yosihiko Sinoto of the Bishop Museum in Honolulu), and in the Cook Islands from 1968–1972. In 1972, I was invited by Professor John Mulvaney to apply for a lectureship in a new Department of Prehistory that he had just founded in The Australian National University in Canberra. I moved there in 1973, and am still there now (but it is now called the School of Archaeology and Anthropology, College of Arts and Social Sciences).

During my time in Auckland a distant relative, Peter Lewin, who worked as a publisher's agent in London, contacted me. Peter was very helpful because he suggested I apply for contracts to write books for international publishers. By 1978 I had my first two books published – *Man's Conquest of the Pacific* (Collins, Auckland, and Oxford University Press, New York) and *The Polynesians* (Thames and Hudson, London). During this time, between about 1970 and 1978, I was thinking broadly about the whole prehistory of Southeast Asia and the Pacific, in terms of the archaeology, the biological anthropology, and the comparative linguistics. At that time, comparative linguistics was actually quite far ahead of both archaeology and biological anthropology in its power to interpret Austronesian population history (the modern science of population genetics was only in its infancy then, and had little useful to say on such issues). Because of this, I discovered the tremendous importance of the linguistic population that we today term 'the Austronesians', and of the archaeological record that can putatively be associated with their remote ancestors.

Figure 1.4 Peter Bellwood during research at Huahine in the Society Islands, French Polynesia, in 1967.
Source: Courtesy of Peter Bellwood.

Q2: We learned from your publications that you have worked on many sites in many countries. Could you tell us how your research focus has changed over the last decades?

Due to my growing interest in Austronesian prehistory, and in the expansion history of Neolithic populations in general, I ceased my Polynesian research in 1972 and moved into Island Southeast Asia, continuing my research over many years in eastern Indonesia (Talaud Islands and northern Moluccas), East Malaysia (Sabah, northern Borneo), and the Batanes Islands (northern Philippines). It was obvious then, as now, that Polynesia was simply the end of the line for ancient Oceanic voyaging, despite its huge extent and the vast distances between islands. The Austronesians had not evolved their foundation of cultural and linguistic characteristics in Polynesia, but far to the west in southern China and Island Southeast Asia (an earlier idea that ancestral Polynesians arrived via the Americas was no longer held seriously by the 1970s). Since 1974, most of my fieldwork has therefore been focused within Southeast Asia

Figure 1.5 Peter Bellwood (right) at Tingkayu, Sabah, Malaysia, in 1982.
Source: Courtesy of Peter Bellwood.

Many of my students during the period from 1978 onwards also came from Indonesia, Malaysia, Brunei, the Philippines and Taiwan, and all carried out valuable fieldwork in these regions (Figures 1.5 and 1.6). Since 2004 my research and fieldwork interests have also moved into Vietnam, but my interests have always remained most strongly focused on the Neolithic. Of course, I have worked on the archaeology of many other periods as well – Palaeolithic in Indonesia, Hoabinhian in Malaysia, Indian contact in Indonesia at *ca.* 2,000 years ago, Bronze Age in northern Vietnam, ceramic trade in recent prehistory in Island Southeast Asia – but my central interest has always remained the history of early food-producing populations, their economies and their languages.

Today, my research focus has moved into worldwide issues with the first being the expansions of early food-producing populations in all continents, which I discussed in my 2005 book *First Farmers*. More recently, I have published my book *First Migrants* (Wiley-Blackwell 2013), which covers the prehistory of human migration everywhere, from African hominins at 2 million years ago to eastern Polynesians at only 800 years ago. I have also edited *Global Prehistory of Human Migration* for Wiley-Blackwell (2015), a book that contains over 50 chapters by many authors on all aspects of ancient human migration from archaeological, linguistic and genetic perspectives.

Figure 1.6 Peter Bellwood (centre) at Reranum, Itbayat Island, Philippines, in 2006.
Source: Courtesy of Hsiao-chun Hung.

Q3: What are some of the more memorable places where you have conducted field research?

My earliest experiences remain most strongly in my mind. These include my first pre-university excavations as a volunteer and site supervisor at Cirencester and Leicester (both Roman cities) in England in 1961–1963; as a volunteer at Herculaneum in Italy in 1963; tracing archaeological remains with my Cambridge contemporary Norman Hammond along a Roman road in Tunisia and Libya in 1964; excavating a *tepe* in the province of Luristan, western Iran, with Clare Goff in 1966; excavating rock shelters in the Marquesas Islands in French Polynesia with Yoshihiko Sinoto in 1967; and then starting my own research projects with my own students in New Zealand and the Cook Islands in 1967 and 1968. In 1974 I carried out my first research in Southeast Asia with Indonesian archaeologist I Made Sutayasa in the remote Talaud Islands of northeastern Indonesia, and then commenced a project with David McReady and the Sabah Museum in 1978 in the southeastern rainforests of Sabah, northern Borneo. In 1990 I began another project with Geoffrey Irwin and Gunadi Nitihaminoto in the northern Moluccas in Indonesia, and then in the late 1990s, due to growing social unrest in this region, I moved my research interests into the Batanes Islands in the northern Philippines, commencing there with Atholl Anderson and Bong Dizon in 2002. Since 2004 I have been also excavating sites in both northern and southern Vietnam, with Judith Cameron, Marc Oxenham, Philip J. Piper and many Vietnamese colleagues (Figure 1.7).

Since my pre-student days, in 1961, I have taken part in archaeological fieldwork in no less than 20 countries, much of it with graduate students undertaking surveys and excavations for their Master's and PhD projects. I will always remain grateful for all this opportunity, which has shown me how varied are the populations of the world, and how important are the prehistories of everyone, not just of the dominant cultures and conquest civilisations.

Figure 1.7 Peter Bellwood (right) in discussion with Nguyen Kim Dung (left) and Bui Chi Hoang (centre) at Rach Nui, Long An Province, Vietnam, in 2012.

Source: Courtesy of Philip Piper.

In terms of those fieldwork 'sensations' that are hard to forget, I will always remember the hard digging down the deepest trenches, the hoping and hoping for something special, the fine sieving, the heat and dust, and conversely the heat and rainforest humidity, and of course the local workers, the graduate students, and the many colleagues and past teachers, some of whom are no longer with us. Naturally, from time to time, discoveries of an immediate material nature came to light – a gold ring down a Roman drain in Leicester, a Dong Son (Iron Age) boat with locked mortise and tenon construction in northern Vietnam, an earring of Taiwan jade in the Batanes Islands, even small pieces of obsidian that travelled more than 3,000 km, more than 3,000 years ago, from the Bismarck Archipelago in Melanesia to the site of Bukit Tengkorak in Sabah (East Malaysia). There are also discoveries of a much deeper nature that have taken lots of analysis and thought to reach, and it is these deeper discoveries that have informed most of my books and articles over the years.

Q4: *What have been some of your most important research findings?*

I think my most important research finding, which I was approaching in the late 1970s and early 1980s, has been that the expansions of major language families have gone hand in hand in many cases with the expansions of early populations of food producers (Neolithic in European terminology, or Formative in the Americas). Colin Renfrew was working on this theme in Cambridge at the same time, but on Indo-European and the European Neolithic, whereas I was considering Austronesian and the Southeast Asian Neolithic. So we were working independently. My Austronesian experience up to the mid-1980s gradually made it clear to me that a linked farming and language explanation was the only conceivable one to explain most of their dispersal, via population growth, but of course with maritime skills contributing as well in this instance. Linked food producer and language family expansion worked not just for Austronesian but for many of the other major agriculturalist language families of the world, although such explanations do not necessarily imply population replacement – a much more gradual process of demic diffusion and population mixing has always been, in my view, far more likely in all regions of the world where farmers have spread, including China. Some of my opponents claim from time to time that I favour a virtual extermination of hunter-gatherers by farmers, but most of them do not read my writings in detail and make blanket assumptions.

In terms of excavation discoveries, I cannot claim to have uncovered any ancient cultures or fossils that have revolutionised understanding of human history. But I think some of my fieldwork has led to new insights into a number of locally significant issues. For instance, my late 1960s excavations of Maori fortifications in New Zealand revealed substantial information about the internal organisation and defences of such sites. The 1990s excavations in the northern Moluccas revealed a 40,000-year-old Palaeolithic culture on one of the migration routes to New Guinea and Australia, and my excavations here and in the Talaud Islands (in 1974) led me to recognise the importance of a very widespread Neolithic tradition of red-slipped pottery, especially in the Philippines and eastern Indonesia. The 2000 BP Dong Xa boat, discovered in northern Vietnam in 2004, revealed possible contacts with the Mediterranean. My work in the Batanes Islands has revealed important data on the early movement of Austronesian-speaking populations between Taiwan and the Philippines. Finally, our current excavations with Vietnamese archaeologists in southern Vietnam are revealing the presence there of peoples growing *japonica* rice (of Yangzi origin, presumably), and keeping pigs and dogs and making fine pottery, commencing about 4,000 years ago. These Vietnam discoveries relate very closely to discoveries made in recent years in central and northeastern Thailand.

Q5: *The quality of your book* First Farmers *was recognised with an award for the best book by the Society for American Archaeology (SAA) in 2005, and this book's success prompted translation into multiple languages (such as Vietnamese and Japanese). Could you please tell us how you developed the idea for this book?*

After many years of research on the Austronesians, drawing the conclusion that their expansion had begun with Neolithic populations in southern China and Taiwan, I felt myself drawn into considering other regions of the world. Colin Renfrew in the 1980s was working on the suggestion that speakers of Indo-European languages had entered Europe during the early Neolithic, migrating as farmers from Anatolia. Luca Cavalli-Sforza and Albert Ammerman had also examined the same idea for the European Neolithic from an archaeological and genetic perspective, but without considering the languages. It remained to consider all three areas of research together – languages, genes and archaeology – and when this was done it became ever more clear that the pre-colonial distributions of other major language families, such as Austroasiatic, Afroasiatic, Bantu, Sino-Tibetan, Uto-Aztecan and Iroquoian, could be explained from a similar perspective. Of course, not all language families expanded to great extents, and those that have expanded have not all done so due to early agricultural population growth, but it was never my intention to apply the farming/language hypothesis to all situations. However, it seems to work for many, and in 2003 I was invited by Jared Diamond to join him in preparing a paper on the topic for the journal *Science*. I also organised a conference on the theme with Colin Renfrew in the McDonald Institute for Archaeological Research in Cambridge in 2001.

Q6: *Concerning the farming/language dispersal issues in general, what is your current thinking?*

Early on in my research, I perhaps tended to assume that farming dispersal began very soon after the initial shift from hunting and gathering to farming in many parts of the world. But new work is showing that the development of full agriculture with domesticated crops and animals took several millennia to advance from the early phases of cultivating wild plants and taming of wild animals. In the Middle East, China and Mesoamerica, these developments took perhaps 3,000 years – for instance, from Natufian to the end of the Pre-Pottery Neolithic B in the Levant and Anatolia, or from Shangshan to the Songze culture in the lower Yangzi Basin in China. This means that the very first 'farmers', however we might wish to define them in economic terms, did not commence the major migrations. They began later when large populations were already dependent on food production, and became more intensive as these populations began to impact heavily on their home environments, encouraging them to look for new resources and land elsewhere, especially in terrain only hitherto occupied by hunters and gatherers. I feel that current results from archaeology, genetics and comparative linguistics are supporting this farming/language viewpoint very strongly, especially for highly significant regions of early farming such as the Middle East, northern Sub-Saharan Africa, China, Mesoamerica, and the central Andes and Amazonia. The farming/language dispersal viewpoint has many enemies, but I rarely find their arguments well informed or watertight. More often they seem to reflect a natural tendency to avoid using migration as an explanation for any significant patterning in human prehistory, except for the presumed migration that brought modern humans out of Africa in the first place.

My views have also changed over the years on the degree to which indigenous populations contributed genes and even perhaps some cultural knowledge to incoming populations of farmers. I find it hard to accept that indigenous foraging populations would ever have adopted farming unless substantial numbers of farmers had already entered their territory. But we have many cases – I called them 'friction zones' in my *First Farmers* – in which the incoming farming populations did not enjoy any very significant demographic advantages over the indigenous foragers. Such situations might initially have developed in regions where farming was rather marginal for various climatic or other environmental reasons, but the fact remains that large populations of mainly indigenous forager ancestry could have adopted farming in such areas, increased their populations, and begun their own expansions.

I think the greatest significance of the farming/language model for Neolithic expansion is that it can explain the pre-colonial racial distributions of mankind so very clearly. By 'racial' I refer only to phenotypic surface characters, which vary with latitude and geography. No one believes any more that races are fixed and clearly bounded entities, and all intergrade as a result of the enormous number of human movements that have occurred in both prehistory and history. But, even so, clear racial differences do exist between populations such as Africans, Europeans, Asians, Australians and Melanesians. These differences in skin colour and hair form undoubtedly evolved initially in the Paleolithic, after modern humans spread from Africa, but they have not remained fossilised in distribution according to the pattern that might have existed 30,000 years ago. Instead, the modern distributions of Africans south of the Sahara, Eurasians north of the Sahara and in western and central Eurasia, and Asians in East and Southeast Asia, in my view, reflect very greatly the expansions that occurred during the Neolithic. The Americas were of course settled long before farming developed, but farming expansions occurred there too, as in Melanesia and New Guinea.

Q7: Specifically concerning the topic of Austronesian origins and dispersals, what is your current thinking?

The ancestors of the Austronesian-speaking people clearly migrated from some homeland region right across the Pacific in ancient times, taking their genes, languages, material culture and food-producing economies with them. I could never agree with the idea that languages simply moved without human migration, and still do not now, even though I find many of my colleagues are rather eager to adopt this most unrealistic scenario. 'Language shift', as linguists call it when people abandon their own native language and adopt an incoming one, has always been a localised process in human affairs, although colonial states have certainly increased its significance in the past 500 years. But language shift alone does not explain the distributions of major language families such as Austronesian. The early Austronesians were real people, undergoing real canoe-borne migrations into the Pacific. But from where, when, and in which directions? In 1978, when I wrote *Man's Conquest of the Pacific*, the answers to these questions were not as clear as they are now, and while I still agree with most of what I published at that time, I have developed my thoughts greatly in subsequent years on the deeper prehistory of the Austronesians, and indeed of humanity in general. The geographical region known as 'China' now bulks much larger in my thinking about Southeast Asia and the Pacific than it did in 1978, and this is attributable to the developments alluded to in the previous sections, especially amongst the Neolithic populations of the Yangzi Basin and southern China.

But the early Austronesians were not 'Chinese' – they did not speak Sinitic languages or have any obvious direct connections with the roots of Chinese culture in the Yellow River Valley (although I should add here that linguist Laurent Sagart believes there were such connections during the Neolithic, and to me this possibility is extremely interesting). Before 2,500–2,000 years ago, China was a kaleidoscope of many very diversified Neolithic (and some Bronze Age) populations, many of whom have descendants in Southeast Asia and Oceania nowadays, and of whom many were ultimately to be incorporated into the expanding Chinese cultural world. Linguists today refer to these populations of Southeast Asia and Oceania as Tai, Austroasiatic, Austronesian and Tibeto-Burman – all can, to some degree, be traced to origins in southern China, allowing for the obvious factor of intermixing with native populations in all regions.

As far as the early Austronesians are concerned, my opinion over many years has been that their Pre-Austronesian ancestors moved as Neolithic and probably rice- and millet-cultivating populations from Fujian to Taiwan between 5,000 and 6,000 years ago. In Taiwan, they developed what linguists reconstruct today as 'Proto-Austronesian' (no Austronesian speakers ever inhabited southern China according to linguistic records, but Pre-Austronesian ones obviously did), and honed their coastal economies for more than a millennium before moving on into the Batanes Islands and the northern Philippines at about 4,000 years ago, carrying with them traditions of making red-slipped pottery, ornaments of Taiwan (Fengtian) jade, polished and sometimes stepped stone adzes, domesticated crops, pigs and dogs, and of course a well-developed maritime tradition of fishing and canoe construction, using sails. The prehistory of the Austronesian world is far too complex to summarise here, but it is important to remember that it took more than 3,000 years for colonists to spread gradually, from island to island, until they finally reached New Zealand around AD 1250, via the islands of central and eastern Polynesia. As I have stated, I do not agree with some current views that Austronesian languages spread through Island Southeast Asia without human migration, and I regard food production as being just as important as maritime knowledge in fuelling the expansion. Naturally, early colonists found many wild resources in previously uninhabited islands, especially sea mammals and birds, so amongst these early colonists we can expect the importance of agriculture to have declined a little, and temporarily, as we see in early Maori ('Moa-Hunter') New Zealand. But this does not negate the overall significance of food production, without which many small Oceanic islands would not have been habitable by humans over the long term.

Q8: In the past two years, you have published two books about ancient human migrations (First Migrants ***and*** The Global Prehistory of Human Migration, ***both with Wiley-Blackwell). As we know, migration is always a major theme in your research. However, as you have mentioned, 'when I was a student of archaeology in the 1960s, migration was becoming an uncomfortable concept for many archaeologists, and home-grown independence or multiregionalism was becoming the favoured perspective on the past in both human evolution and archaeology'. In fact, I myself encountered a similar feeling from many other archaeologists when I was a PhD student (in 2004–2008). Nonetheless, it seems that since 2010, the issue of migration in archaeology has become popular again. How do you see these waves and changes in thinking in the discipline, and what do you propose that archaeology can contribute to this topic?***

In my *First Migrants* I examine all major episodes of human migration from early hominin movements out of Africa to the spreads of modern humans and later on of food producers, in all regions of the world. I see migration as one of the most significant aspects of human behaviour, one which can spread new forms of human biology and culture over vast distances and thus allow the forces of mutation, selection and drift that drive evolution to work on new canvases. Migration as an event has waxed and waned in significance over the millennia, and it was certainly more important during certain transitions in human history than in others. Migration as a concept within archaeology has also waxed and waned in its perceived significance. This might be a reflection of the simplistic way in which the concept was used on some occasions in the past to explain trivial changes in the archaeological record, and there is an undoubted level of guilt amongst educated people in the world today about human rights and the oppression of colonised populations during the colonial era. But, regardless of what might be contained within the archaeological record, I think it is imperative that modern archaeologists be aware of debates within other disciplines, such as linguistics, within which the issue of whether language families spread through migration of speakers or through 'elite dominance' is often of great significance (my answers usually favour migration of speakers, for reasons that I discuss in my book *First Migrants*).

More to the point, however, are the current remarkable developments in human genetics and the extraction of ancient DNA from bones. Geneticists can now survey whole human genomes in terms of the polymorphic nucleotide positions that reveal their deep ancestries and histories of admixture. I have just attended (January 2015) a genetics conference at Harvard University where the power of these new techniques has exposed a migration from the Russian steppes into central Europe about 4,500 years ago (Laziridis et al. 2014 provide preliminary data), a migration that I would associate with the spread of the Baltic- and Slavic-linguistic populations within the Indo-European language family. In many ways, it may be no longer relevant in such cases if some archaeologists wish to deny that a migration occurred since the genetic evidence is so clear and incontrovertible, as it is in the case of another recent analysis in which the very high importance of a Formosan ancestry component in the genomes of modern Austronesian language speakers has been clearly demonstrated (Lipson et al. 2014). Of course, archaeology still holds the power to provide a definite chronology and to illuminate the cultural contexts that allowed such migrations to occur, but it is time for all archaeologists to acknowledge the significance of multidisciplinary approaches and to cease burying themselves myopically in their own data sets.

Q9: In your research career, you received continued accolades from your colleagues, but sometimes you also faced criticism. How did you handle those criticisms, especially those that you might have regarded as unfair at the time?

Criticism is important for all of us, and I hold the view that if one receives no criticism then no one is reading one's published work. Citations are important to me, and citations often reflect the intensity of discussion about a given topic, and by definition the existence of criticism. However, I become resentful when the criticism is couched in *ad hominem* and sometimes mildly insulting terminology – I hardly need to give examples! The late Roger Green, a Pacific archaeologist I much admired, once said to me that critics often fail because 'they haven't done their homework' (Figure 1.8). He was right – doing homework is an endless and greatly time-consuming task, especially if one is trying to keep up with the new electronic literature in more than one discipline. Of course, criticism if one is actually wrong is another matter, but I enjoy well-informed criticism and try to modify my views whenever I feel it is truly necessary. When I receive criticism that I consider unfair or poorly informed, I reply immediately in print and try to keep my temper under control.

Figure 1.8 Peter Bellwood (left) at the 14th Congress of the Indo-Pacific Association in Yogyakarta, Indonesia, in 1990 with Roger Green (centre) and R.P. Soejono (right).
Source: Courtesy of Peter Bellwood.

Q10: In your opinion, what are some of the more interesting challenges facing Southeast Asian and Pacific archaeology research today and in the near future?

The most important historical and population questions will always revolve around issues such as the timing of modern human arrival, the timing and directions of the main agriculturalist expansions, and the nature of the later religious and trading contacts with external civilisations, such as those of India and China, after about 2,500 years ago. As far as modern human origins in the region are concerned, archaeologists face the problem that the normally accepted 'markers' of modern humanity, such as blade tools, projectile points and use of ochre are rare to absent [in Southeast Asia] in the period of time termed 'the Upper Palaeolithic', although new dating of rock art in Sulawesi to about 40,000 years ago must surely alter our perspectives a little (Aubert et al. 2014). Nevertheless, modern human behaviour in the Java Palaeolithic in Indonesia is not clearly distinguishable from the archaic human behaviour of *Homo erectus* in terms of the lithics that survive for archaeological inspection. Indeed, it is now becoming clearer in the western Old World generally that modern and archaic human behaviours cannot always be distinguished from each other, even in Africa. This means, of course, that archaeologists cannot interpret questions of modern human migration without paying serious attention to the results from biological anthropology and ancient DNA in bone.

Likewise, understanding of Neolithic developments nowadays can only proceed with attention to fields of research parallel to archaeology, such as comparative linguistics, and again the biological aspects. The days have long gone when archaeologists can assert that only they can study the past directly, and those who continue to assert this will soon find their works ignored by the growing torrent of research in ancient DNA, palaeoanthropology, and linguistic reconstruction.

There is another very important challenge, which I discover frequently whenever I have organised conferences of the Indo-Pacific Prehistory Association. There is a kind of 'tyranny of language' in archaeological scholarship, in that all of us must from time to time deal with archaeological reports from countries whose published internal literature is often beyond our direct reading ability. Busy archaeologists cannot be expected to be fluent in several languages, although some certainly try to be, and it is not fair to expect everyone to have to learn English, or any other major language such as Mandarin, just so that they can read archaeological reports. In my view, the main long-term solution to this problem will come with more efficient methods of computer translation from one language to another. Fortunate students can often improve their foreign language skills by studying abroad, but this option is not open to everyone, and I know that many people who choose to study in a foreign country will often find it hard to enter the job queue in their home country, and can even be actively excluded from following a career at home. There are no simple answers to these problems, but one way to improve the access of local scholars to worldwide knowledge is to organise research projects with international personnel.

Q11: Nowadays, it seems that many archaeologists are becoming increasingly specialised, although we always will need to be aware of general knowledge. What is your advice for students who want to balance specialisation with a general approach? What is your advice for students who wish to engage in long-term archaeological research and seek a career in archaeology?

The best way to maintain a broad generalised approach to any research field is to teach it to undergraduates since the material has to be put into summary form and statements must be made as to its overall significance. Specialisation is essential if research is to proceed, but not at the expense of a broad and balanced perspective. Archaeologists have long argued over the merits and demerits of 'bottom up' approaches derived from actual field data, versus 'top down' approaches based on the testing of broad hypotheses derived from comparative and multidisciplinary research. I suggest both approaches be followed, not just one at the expense of the other, even though much of my own research has been top down in this regard.

The best way to become involved in long-term archaeological research is to join a large cooperative research project that has funding for several years and that can support postdoctoral researchers (having a PhD first is essential nowadays for a research career in archaeology or any other science). Many students do this through their PhD supervisors, and in Australia the funds come from the Australian Research Council (or the National Science Foundation in the USA). However, my experience in this regard is based in Australia, where virtually all significant archaeological research is undertaken by universities. In many countries, government-funded research institutes play this role and provide funding – for instance, the Institute of Archaeology in Beijing and the many provincial institutes in China; Academia Sinica in Taipei; the National Museum in Manila; and the Thai Fine Arts Department in Bangkok. But I would presume that the same advice still holds – join a large project and try to develop a specialisation that will place your skills in demand!

Q12: What other research topics would you like to address in the future, and do you have plans for upcoming field projects?

In 2014, with my colleagues Hsiao-chun Hung, Philip J. Piper and Mike Carson, I received another three-year grant from the Australian Research Council to continue our project on the Neolithic of Southeast Asia. We have excavations planned at the site of Thach Lac in Ha Tinh Province in north-central Vietnam, in eastern Taiwan, in the Cagayan Valley in the northern Philippines, and in the Mariana Islands, in each case excavating sites that give evidence for the earliest developments of Neolithic cultures. Our aim is to examine the widespread occurrence of Neolithic cultures in the centuries around 2000 BC from the perspectives of their material cultures and economies, especially seeking evidence for food production through animal domestication and through archeobotany, the latter in collaboration with the Institute of Archaeology in London. Our plans are to continue with this research into 2017, after which I will probably have retired to something a little less strenuous (Figure 1.9)!

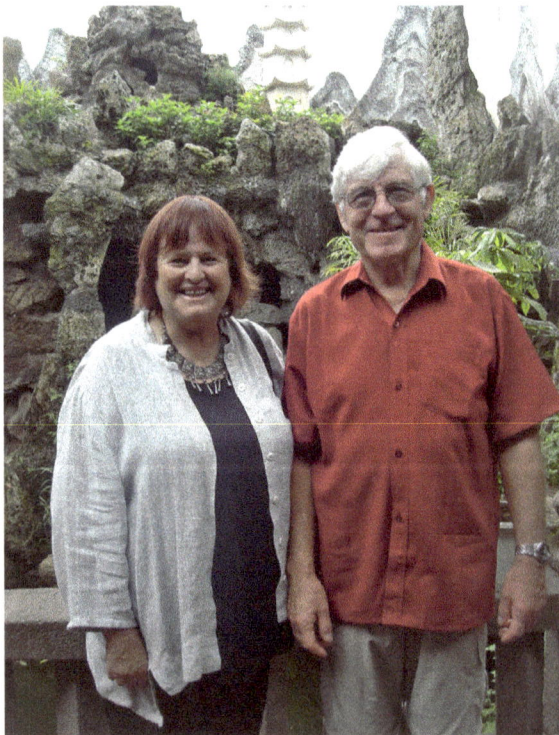

Figure 1.9 Peter Bellwood at Fuzhou, China, in 2010 with wife Claudia Morris.
Source: Courtesy of Peter Bellwood.

References

Aubert, M., A. Brumm, R. Ramli, T. Sutikna et al. 2014. Pleistocene cave art from Sulawesi, Indonesia. *Nature* 514: 223–227.

Bellwod, P. and Hung, H.-c. 2011. Professor Peter Bellwood's reflections on archaeological research. *Cultural Relics of South China (Nanfang Wenwu)* 2011(3): 22–29 (in Chinese).

Laziridis, I., N. Patterson, A. Mittnik, G. Renaud et al. 2014. Ancient human genomes suggest three ancestral populations for present-day Europeans. *Nature* 513: 409–413.

Lipson, M., P-R. Loh, N. Patterson, P. Moorjani et al. 2014. Reconstructing Austronesian population history in Island Southeast Asia. *Nature Communications* 5: 4689.

Major field projects undertaken during Peter's professional career, 1967–2013

1967 Skipper's Ridge, New Zealand – excavation.

1967–1968 Society and Marquesas Islands (with Y. Sinoto) – 5 months survey and excavation.

1968 Otakanini pa, New Zealand – excavation.

1968–1970 Mangakaware, New Zealand – excavation (several short seasons).

1968–1972 The Cook Islands – survey and excavation (one year of fieldwork).

1974 Talaud Islands and Minahasa region, Northern Sulawesi, Indonesia – survey and excavation (with Dr I.M. Sutayasa).

1977–1978 Brunei (with Mr Matussin bin Omar) – 2 months excavation.

1979 Gua Cha, Kelantan, West Malaysia (with Adi Haji Taha) – excavation.

1984 Reconnaissance in the Sanjai valley, Bihar, India, with A.K. Ghosh and staff of the Department of Anthropology, University of Calcutta.

1980–1987 Sabah, Malaysia – 8 months of fieldwork and excavation.

1989 Sarawak (with Ipoi Datan) – excavation.

1990, 1994, 1995–1996 Halmahera, Morotai, Gebe and Kayoa islands, northern Maluku, Indonesia-survey and excavations, with G.J. Irwin of Auckland University, Indonesian archaeologists from Yogyakarta (Universitas Gadjah Mada, DPP Sejarah Purbakala and Balai Arkeologi) and two graduate students (Mahirta and Daud Tanudirjo, MA and PhD respectively).

1994 The caves of Gua Bukit Chawas and Gua Peraling, Kelantan, Malaysia – fieldwork, with Adi Haji Taha.

2001–2007 Fieldwork and excavation in the Batanes Islands, northern Luzon, Vietnam and Taiwan. Feb–March 2002 (Batanes: Batan Island), Sept–Oct 2002 (Ilocos Norte), Feb–March 2003 (Batanes: Batan, Sabtang Islands), Feb–March 2004 (Batanes: Itbayat, Batan Islands), June–July 2005 (Itbayat Island), May–June 2007 (Cagayan Valley and Sabtang Island). With Eusebio Dizon, Marc Oxenham, Janelle Stevenson, Armand Mijares and Hsiao-chun Hung.

2004 Excavation at Dong Xa and Yen Bac, northern Vietnam (with Judith Cameron, Nguyen Viet and Bui Van Liem).

2009 April–May: Excavation in the Neolithic site of An Son, Long An Province, southern Vietnam, with Bui Chi Hoang, Nguyen Kim Dung, and Marc Oxenham.

2009 November: excavation in the Neolithic site of Nagsabaran, Cagayan Valley, Philippines, with Hsiao-chun Hung, Marc Oxenham and Eusebio Dizon.

2012 March–April: Excavation in the Neolithic site of Rach Nui, Long An Province, Vietnam, with Marc Oxenham, Philip J. Piper and Nguyen Khanh Trung Kien.

2012 May: Excavations at Sembiran and Pacung, northern Bali, with Ambra Calo.

2013 March: Excavation of Loc Giang Neolithic mound, Long An Province, southern Vietnam, with Philip J. Piper and Nguyen Khanh Trung Kien.

2013 November: Excavation of Diang Balu cave in the headwaters of the Kapuas River (interior Borneo) with Vida Kusmartono.

Although Peter retired in 2013, he has continued field research in the Asia-Pacific region. For instance, he was part of the Loc Giang excavation in southern Vietnam during March–April 2014, and then he participated in the excavations at Ru Diep and Thach Lac in central Vietnam with Philip J. Piper and Lam Thi My Dung during April–May 2015. More recently, during October 2016, he was in Saipan, Northern Mariana Islands, western Micronesia with Mike Carson and Hsiao-chun Hung for excavations at the Bapot Site, where he discovered a beautiful shell ornament linked with previous findings in Southeast Asia.

Publications by Peter Bellwood (until July 2016)

These are classified under the following headings: A. Books and monographs; B. Edited volumes; C. Singled-authored journal articles; D. Singled-authored chapters in edited books; E. Jointly written articles in journals and edited books; F. Book reviews, letters to editors and other minor contributions.

A. Books and monographs

1.　1972. *A Settlement Pattern Survey of Hanatekua Valley, Hiva Oa, Marquesas Islands*. Honolulu: Bishop Museum: Pacific Anthropological Records Vol. 17, 50 pages.

2.　1978. *Man's Conquest of the Pacific*. Auckland and London: Collins. North American edition published by Oxford University Press, New York, 1979.

　　—— 1986. Russian translation of *Man's Conquest of the Pacific* (Покорение человеком Тихого океана), published by Nauka, Moscow.

　　—— 1989. Japanese translation of *Man's Conquest of the Pacific* (太平洋―東 南アジアとオセアニアの人類史), published by Hosei University Press, Tokyo.

3.　1978. *The Polynesians*. London: Thames and Hudson.

　　—— 1983. French translation of *The Polynesians* (*Les Polynésiens*), published by Les Editions du Pacifique, Papeete, Tahiti.

　　—— 1985. Japanese translation of *The Polynesians* (ポリネシア), published by Taimeido, Tokyo.

4.　1978. *Archaeological Research in the Cook Islands*. Pacific Anthropological Records No. 27. Honolulu: Bishop Museum.

5. 1978. *Archaeological Research at Lake Mangakaware, Waikato, 1968-1970.* Volume 12, University of Otago Studies in Prehistoric Anthropology. New Zealand Archaeological Association, Monograph 9.

6. 1985. *Prehistory of the Indo-Malaysian Archipelago.* Sydney: Academic Press.

7. 1987. *The Polynesians.* Revised edition. London: Thames and Hudson.

8. 1988. *Archaeological Research in South-eastern Sabah.* Kota Kinabalu: Sabah Museum Monograph no.2.

9. 1997. *Prehistory of the Indo-Malaysian Archipelago* (2nd edition). Honolulu: University of Hawaii Press. Republished online in 2007 by ANU E Press, Canberra.

    —— 2000. Indonesian translation of *Prehistory of the Indo-Malaysian Archipelago* (*Presejarah Kepulauan Indo-Malaysia*) (2nd edition). PT Gramedia Pustaka Utama, Jakarta.

10. 2005. *First Farmers: The Origins of Agricultural Societies.* Oxford: Blackwell.

    —— 2008. Japanese translation of *First Farmers* (農耕起源の人類史), published by Kyoto University Press, Kyoto.

    —— 2010. Vietnamese translation of *First Farmers* (*Những Nhà Nông Đầu Tiên*), published by The Gioi Publishing House, Hanoi.

11. 2013. *First Migrants: Ancient Migration in Global Perspective.* Chichester, Boston and Oxford: Wiley-Blackwell.

    —— 2016. Greek translation of *First Migrants* (*Protoi Metanastes*), published by Eikostou Protou, Athens.

12. In press. *First Islanders: The Prehistory and Human Migration in Island Southeast Asia.* Chichester, Boston and Oxford: Wiley-Blackwell.

B. Edited volumes

1. *Bulletin of the Indo-Pacific Prehistory Association.* Peter Bellwood was the main editor for every issue of this journal between 1982 (volume 3) and 2009 (volume 29).

2. 1985. *Recent Advances in Indo-Pacific Prehistory*, edited by Virendra N. Misra and Peter Bellwood. New Delhi: Oxford and IBH.

3. 1988. Proceedings of 'Origin and expansion of the Austronesians', edited by Peter Bellwood and Wilhelm G. Solheim II. *Asian Perspectives*, vol. 26, no. 1 (issue dated 1984–1985).

4. 1992. *Man and his Culture: A Resurgence*, edited by Peter Bellwood, Asok Datta, P.G. Chatterjee and A.K. Sen. New Delhi: Books and Books.

5. 1995. *The Austronesians: Historical and Comparative Perspectives*, edited by Peter Bellwood, James Fox and Darrell Tryon. Department of Anthropology, Research School of Pacific and Asian Studies, ANU.

6. 1992–1997. Peter Bellwood served as general editor (with Dr Ian Glover) of a book series entitled *Peoples of Southeast Asia and the Pacific*, published by Basil Blackwell of Oxford. (Six volumes published: V.T. King, *The Peoples of Borneo*, 1993; Ian Mabbett and David Chandler, *The Khmers*, 1995; Angela Hobart, Urs Ramseyer and Albert Leemans, *The Peoples of Bali*, 1996; Christian Pelras, *The Bugis*, 1996; Patrick Vinton Kirch, *The Lapita Peoples*, 1997; Matthew Spriggs, *The Island Melanesians*, 1997). Anthony Milner, *The Malays*, was published by Wiley-Blackwell as a final contribution to this series in 2008.

7. 2002. *Examining the Farming/Language Dispersal Hypothesis*, edited by Peter Bellwood and Colin Renfrew. Cambridge: McDonald Institute for Archaeological Research.

8. 2004. *Southeast Asia: From Prehistory to History*, edited by Ian Glover and Peter Bellwood. London: RoutledgeCurzon. Paperback edition published 2005.

9. 2013. *4000 years of Migration and Cultural Exchange: The Archaeology of the Batanes Islands, Northern Philippines*, edited by Peter Bellwood and Eusebio Dizon. Terra Australis 40. Canberra: ANU E Press.

10. 2013. *The Encyclopedia of Global Human Migration, Volume 1: Prehistory*, edited by Peter Bellwood. Boston, USA and Chichester, UK: Wiley-Blackwell Publishers (Vol. 1 of a 5-volume series, general editor Immanuel Ness).

11. 2015. *The Global Prehistory of Human Migration*, edited by Peter Bellwood. Chichester: Wiley-Blackwell (separate paperback publication of the previous item, volume 1).

C. Single-authored journal articles

1. 1967. A Roman dam in the Wadi Caam, Tripolitania. *Libya Antiqua* IV: 41–44.

2. 1969. Excavations at Skipper's Ridge, Opito Bay, Coromandel Peninsula, North Island of New Zealand. *Archaeology and Physical Anthropology in Oceania* IV: 198–221.

3. 1969. Pa excavations at Otakanini, South Kaipara and Lake Mangakaware, Waikato. *New Zealand Archaeological Association Newsletter* 12: 38–49.

4. 1969. Archaeology on Rarotonga and Aitutaki, Cook Islands. *Journal of the Polynesian Society* 78: 517–530.

5. 1970. Dispersal centres in East Polynesia, with special reference to the Society and Marquesas Islands. *Pacific Anthropological Records* 11: 93–104. Honolulu: Bishop Museum.

6. 1971. Otakanini pa, South Kaipara. *NZAA Newsletter* 12: 74–76.

7. 1971. Archaeological research at Lake Mangakaware, Waikato: A summary of results. *New Zealand Archaeological Association Newsletter* 14: 113–125.

8. 1971. Fortifications and economy in prehistoric New Zealand. *Proceedings of the Prehistoric Society* 37, Part 1: 56–95.

9. 1971. Varieties of ecological adaptation in the southern Cook Islands. *Archaeology and Physical Anthropology in Oceania* 6, no. 2: 145–169.

10. 1972. Excavations at Otakanini Pa, South Kaipara Harbour. *Journal of the Royal Society of New Zealand* 2: 259–291.

11. 1974. Lapita potters' families. *Hemisphere* 18, no. 7: 17–21.

12. 1974. Prehistoric contacts in the Cook Islands. *Mankind* 9: 278–280.

13. 1975. Report on archaeological research in Sulawesi Utara. *Far Eastern Prehistory Association Newsletter* 4: 30–36.

14. 1975. The prehistory of Oceania. *Current Anthropology* 16: 9–28.

15. 1975. The atoll dwellers. *Hemisphere* 19, no. 11: 19–23.

16. 1976. Archaeological research in Minahasa and the Talaud Islands, north-eastern Indonesia. *Asian Perspectives* 19, Part 2: 240–288.

17. 1976. Review article on The Pacific Islanders, by W.W. Howells. *Asian Perspectives* 19, Part 2: 295–300.

18. 1977. Less mysterious now. *Hemisphere* 21, no. 3: 36–41.

19. 1977. Diversity galore. *Hemisphere* 21, no. 12: 16–20.

20. 1978. City planning, B.C. *Hemisphere* 22, no. 6: 30–33.

21. 1978. The sultanate of Brunei. *Hemisphere* 22, no. 11: 18–21.

22. 1979. The real pioneers. *Hemisphere* 23, no. 6: 370–374.

23. 1980. The peopling of the Pacific. *Scientific American* 243/5: 174–85, November, 1980 (UK edition pp. 138–147).

24. 1981. Le peuplement du Pacifique. *Pour La Science*, January 1981, pp. 90–102. (French translation of the above article).

25. 1980. Comment on D. Rindos, 'Symbiosis, instability, and the origins and spread of agriculture'. *Current Anthropology* 21/6: 765–766.

26. 1980. Indonesia, the Philippines and Oceanic prehistory. *Journal de la Société des Océanistes* 66–67 (vol. 36): 148–155.

27. 1980. The Buidane Culture of the Talaud Islands, North-eastern Indonesia. *Bulletin of the Indo-Pacific Prehistory Association* 2: 69–127.

28. 1983. The ancient peoples of North Borneo. *Hemisphere* 28, no. 1: 48–52.

29. 1983. New perspectives on Indo-Malaysian prehistory. *Bulletin of the Indo-Pacific Prehistory Association* 4: 71–83. Also published in *Archaeology at ANZAAS 1983* (Smith M. ed.), pp. 5–17. Perth: Western Australian Museum, 1983.

30. 1983. On 'Diffusionists' and legitimate aims in Polynesian prehistory. *Asian Perspectives* 23/2: 323–325 (volume dated 1980, published 1983).

31. 1983. The great Pacific Migration. *(Encyclopaedia Britannica) Yearbook of Science and the Future* for 1984, pp. 80–93.

32. 1984. Comment on M. Marshall, 'Structural patterns of sibling classification in Island Oceania', *Current Anthropology* 25/5: 625.

33. 1984. Archaeological research in the Madai-Baturong region, Sabah. *Bulletin of the Indo-Pacific Prehistory Association* 5: 38–54.

34. 1984. The 12th Congress of the Indo-Pacific Prehistory Association. *Bulletin of the Indo-Pacific Prehistory Association* 5: 1–13.

35. 1984–1985. A hypothesis for Austronesian origins. *Asian Perspectives* 26 (1988): 107–117.

36. 1987. The prehistory of Island Southeast Asia: a multidisciplinary review of recent research. *Journal of World Prehistory* 1, no. 2: 171–224.

37. 1987. The impact of sea level changes on Pacific prehistory. *Journal of Pacific History* 22/2: 106–108.

38. 1987. Comment on P.V. Kirch and R.C. Green, 'History, phylogeny and evolution in Polynesia', *Current Anthropology* 28: 443–444.

39. 1988. Affluence and ranking, Southeast Asian style. *Quarterly Review of Archaeology* 9/3, Fall: 4–5.

40. 1989. Archaeological investigations at Bukit Tengkorak and Segarong, southeastern Sabah. *Bulletin of the Indo-Pacific Prehistory Association* 9: 122–162.

41. 1990. Foraging towards farming; a decisive transition or a millennial blur? *Review of Archaeology* 11/2: 14–24.

42. 1991. The Austronesian dispersal and the origin of languages. *Scientific American* 265/1: 88–93.

43. 1991. La dispersion et l'origine des langues austronesiennes. *Pour La Science* 167: 48–53 (French translation of the above article).

44. 1994. Chinese translation of the above article. *Minzu Yicong* 3: 29–34.

45. 1991. The implications of the South Chinese Neolithic for the history of language families. *Guang Dong Wen Bo* (Guangdong Provincial Museum Journal) 15–16: 13–19 (in Chinese).

46. 1992. Early Burmese urbanization: Inspired independence or external stimulus? *Review of Archaeology* 13/2: 1–7.

47. 1992. The prehistory of Borneo. *Borneo Research Bulletin* 24: 7–15.

48. 1993. Smokescreens? (reply to Stargardt, see item 46). *Review of Archaeology* 41/2: 33–35.

49. 1993. Cultural and biological differentiation in Peninsular Malaysia: The last 10,000 years. *Asian Perspectives* 32: 37–60.

50. 1994. An archaeologist's view of language macrofamily relationships. *Oceanic Linguistics* 33(2): 391–406. Also published with minor modifications in *Bulletin of the Indo-Pacific Prehistory Association* 13: 46–60, 1993.

51. 1994. Colonizing the limits. *Review of Archaeology* 15 (1): 16–23. Reprinted in *RA* 20/2, Fall 1999, pp. 23–28 (Retrospective Issue: from the Archives).

52. 1995. Language families and human dispersal. *Cambridge Archaeological Journal* 5/2: 271–275.

53. 1995. Archaeological research in the Northern Moluccas 1991–1994: A preliminary report. *Southeast Asian Archaeology International Newsletter* 7: 3–12.

54. 1995. Comment on 'Predicting similarity in material culture among New Guinea villages' by Roberts, J.M. et al., *Current Anthropology* 36: 776–777.

55. 1996. Phylogeny vs reticulation in prehistory. *Antiquity* 70: 881–890.

56. 1997. Ancient seafarers. *Archaeology* March/April: 20–22.

57. 1997. The Austronesian dispersal. *Newsletter of Chinese Ethnology* 35: 1–26. Taipei: Ethnological Society of China.

58. 1997. Comment on Terrell, Hunt and Gosden, 'Social life in the Pacific', *Current Anthropology* 38: 175–176.

59. 1997. Taiwan and the prehistory of the Austronesian-speaking peoples. *Review of Archaeology* 18/2: 39–48.

60. 1999. Comment on Helen Leach, Intensification in the Pacific. *Current Anthropology* 40: 324–325.

61. 1999. (Who were the statue carvers of Easter Island?). Text and illustrations for two double-page spreads in the Japanese graphic science magazine *Newton* vol. 19 no. 3, pp. 68–71 (in Japanese).

62. 2000. Some thoughts on understanding the human colonization of the Pacific. *People and Culture in Oceania* 16: 5–17.

63. 2001. Early agriculturalist population diasporas? Farming, languages and genes. *Annual Review of Anthropology* 30: 181–207.

64. 2001. Comment on Terrell, Kelly and Rainbird, Foregone conclusions? *Current Anthropology* 42: 107–108.

65. 2002. Review Article: Phylogeny in action. *Cambridge Journal of Archaeology* 12: 174–176.

66. 2002. Lapita ascendant. *Review of Archaeology* 23, Part 1: 1–5.

67. 2004. Comment on Colledge et al., Archaeobotanical evidence for the spread of farming in the eastern Mediterranean. *Current Anthropology* 45: S47–48.

68. 2004. The origins of Afroasiatic (response to Ehret et al., commenting on Diamond and Bellwood 2003). *Science* 306: 1681.

69. 2005. Mind the Gap. *Asian Perspectives* 44: 247–248.

70. 2005. New Guinea, and its place in world prehistory. *Review of Archaeology* 26/2: 10–17.

71. 2007. 'Overview' and 'Reply' in review feature on *First Farmers. Cambridge Archaeological Journal* 17: 88–91, 102–106. (Authors Bellwood, Gamble, Le Blanc, Pluciennik, Richards and Terrell).

72. 2007. May the revolution prosper. *Review of Archaeology* 28: 68–71.

73. 2007–2008. Understanding the Neolithic in northern India. *Pragdhara* 18: 331–346 (Journal of the Uttar Pradesh State Archaeology Department, India).

74. 2009. The dispersals of established food-producing populations. *Current Anthropology* 50: 621–626, with comments pp. 707–708.

75. 2010. Comment on Heggarty and Beresford-Jones, Agriculture and language dispersals, *Current Anthropology* 51: 182–183.

76. 2010. Comment on Donohue and Denham, Farming and language in Island Southeast Asia, *Current Anthropology* 51: 240–241.

77. 2011. Holocene population history in the Pacific region as a model for world-wide food producer dispersals. *Current Anthropology* 52, no. S4: 363–378.

78. 2011. (interviewed and translated by Hsiao-chun Hung). Professor Peter Bellwood's reflections on archaeological research. *Cultural Relics in Southern China (Nanfang Wenwu)*, vol. 2011(3), pp. 22–29 (in Chinese).

79. 2011. The checkered prehistory of rice movement southwards as a domesticated cereal – from the Yangzi to the Equator. *Rice* 4: 93–103.

80. 2011. Comment on P. Sheppard, Lapita colonization across the Near/Remote Oceania boundary. *Current Anthropology* 52: 819–820.

81. 2011. Comment on E. Holman et al., Automated dating of the world's language families based on lexical similarity. *Current Anthropology* 52: 863–864.

82. 2011. Dá mới ở Việt Nam, văn hóa Sa Huỳnh, và tiền sử Đông Nam Á (The Vietnam Neolithic, the Sa Huynh culture, and Southeast Asian prehistory). *Thông Báo Khoa Học (Bulletin of Science)* for 2011, pp. 16–38. Hanoi: National Museum of Vietnamese History (Bảo Tàng Lịch Sử Việt Nam). In Vietnamese.

83. 2013. Interview entitled 'New ideas in migration', in online forum *Thinking in Practice: Exploring New Thinking and Theory*, vol. 15.

84. 2015. Ban Non Wat: crucial research, but is it too soon for certainty? *Antiquity* 89: 1224–1226.

D. Single-authored chapters in edited books

1. 1972. A prehistoric Maori settlement – Lake Mangakaware, Te Rore. In D.H. Goodall (ed.), *The Waikato: Man and his Environment*, pp. 27–29. Hamilton: N.Z. Geographical Society.

2. 1976. Prehistoric plant and animal domestication in Austronesia. In G. de G. Sieveking, I.H. Longworth and D.E. Wilson (eds), *Problems in Economic and Social Archaeology*, pp. 153–168. London: Duckworth.

3. 1976. The significance of excavated bronze objects and casting moulds from the Talaud Islands, northeastern Indonesia. In N. Barnard (ed.), *Ancient Chinese Bronzes and Southeast Asian Metal and Other Archaeological Artefacts*, pp. 413–420. Melbourne: National Gallery of Victoria.

4. 1979. Chapters entitled 'The Oceanic context' and 'Settlement patterns'. In J.D. Jennings (ed.), *The Prehistory of Polynesia*, pp. 6–26, 308–322. Harvard University Press.

5. 1978. Entries on Easter Island and New Zealand. In G.E. Daniel (ed.), *The Illustrated Encyclopaedia of Archaeology*. London: Macmillan.

6. 1980. Plants, climate and people; the early horticultural prehistory of Indonesia. In J.J. Fox (ed.) *Indonesia: the Making of a Culture*, pp. 57–74. Research School of Pacific Studies, ANU, Canberra.

7. 1983. 184 separate entries on the prehistory of Southeast Asia and Oceania. In R. Whitehouse (ed.), *The Macmillan Dictionary of Archaeology*. London: Macmillan.

8. 1984. Foreword. In *An Archaeological Perspective of Panay Island, Philippines*, by Peter J.F. Coutts. Cebu City: San Carlos Publications.

9. 1985. Holocene flake and blade industries of Wallacea and their predecessors. In V.N. Misra and P. Bellwood (eds), *Recent Advances in Indo-Pacific Prehistory*, pp. 197–205. New Delhi: Oxford and IBH.

10. 1986. Recent archaeological research in Sabah, and its implications for Indo-Malaysian prehistory. In *Pertemuan Ilmiah Arkeologi IV, Volume 1: Evolusi Manusia, Lingkungan Hidup dan Teknologi*, pp. 305–335. Jakarta: Pusat Penelitian Arkeologi Nasional.

11. 1988. Texts for 'The settlement of Polynesia,' 'Islands of Polynesia' and 'Maori New Zealand'. In C. Scarre (ed.), *Past Worlds: The Times Atlas of World Archaeology*, pp. 200–201, 268–270. London: Times Books.

12. 1989. The colonization of the Pacific; some current hypotheses. In A.V.S. Hill and S.W. Serjeantson (eds), *The Colonization of the Pacific; a Genetic Trail*, pp. 1–59. Oxford: Clarendon Press.

13. 1990. From Late Pleistocene to Early Holocene in Sundaland. In C. Gamble and O. Soffer (eds), *The World at 18000 BP*, vol. 2; Low Latitudes, pp. 255–263. London: Unwin Hyman.

14. 1990. The Tingkayu industry of Late Pleistocene Sabah. In I. Glover and E. Glover (eds), *Southeast Asian Archaeology 1986*. BAR International Series 561, pp. 1–10. Oxford.

15. 1990. Hunters, gatherers and navigators. In T.A. Volkman and I. Caldwell (eds), *Sulawesi*, pp. 24–27. Berkeley: Periplus.

16. 1991. Fils du Pleistocene. In A. Guerreiro and P. Couderc (eds), *Bornéo; des 'Chasseurs de Têtes' aux Ecologistes*, pp. 164–171. Paris: Autrement (Série 'Monde' HS 52).

17. 1991. 'Java Man' and later migrations. In E. Oey (ed.), *Java*, pp. 30–31. Berkeley: Periplus.

18. 1991. Bronze drums, migrations and megaliths. In. D. Pickell (ed.), *East of Bali*, pp. 26–27. Berkeley: Periplus.

19. 1991. From flaked glass to iron and bronze. In E. Oey (ed.), *Sumatra*, pp. 28–29. Berkeley: Periplus.

20. 1992. The antiquity of equatorial rainforest occupation in Southeast Asia. In P. Bellwood et al. (eds), *Man and his Culture: A Resurgence*, pp. 67–78. New Delhi: Books and Books.

21. 1992. Southeast Asia before history. In N. Tarling (ed.), *The Cambridge History of Southeast Asia*, vol. 1, pp. 55–136. Cambridge: Cambridge University Press.

22. 1992. New discoveries in Southeast Asia relevant for Melanesian (especially Lapita) prehistory. In J.C. Galipaud (ed.), *Poterie Lapita et Peuplement*, pp. 49–66. Nouméa: ORSTOM.

23. 1993. The origins of Pacific peoples. In M. Quanchi and R. Adams (eds), *Culture Contact in the Pacific*, pp. 2–14. Melbourne: Cambridge University Press.

24. 1993. Cave dwellers and forest foragers. In M. Wendy (ed.), *West Malaysia and Singapore*, pp. 24–25. Singapore: Periplus.

25. 1993. Crossing the Wallace Line – with style. In M. Spriggs et al. (eds), *A Community of Culture*, pp. 152–163. Canberra: Dept. Prehistory RSPacS, ANU, Occasional Papers in Prehistory 21.

26. 1994. Contributed text on Sumerian civilization for textbook *Environmental Science*, pp. 140–142, Australian Academy of Science.

27. 1995. Early agriculture, language history and the archaeological record in China and Southeast Asia. In C.-T. Yeung and W.-L. Li (eds), *Archaeology in Southeast Asia*, pp. 11–22. Hong Kong: University Museum and Art Gallery, University of Hong Kong.

28. 1995. Austronesian prehistory in Southeast Asia: Homeland, exodus and transformation. In P. Bellwood, J. Fox and D. Tryon (eds), *The Austronesians: Historical and Comparative Perspectives*, pp. 96–111. Canberra: Dept. Anthropology RSPAS, ANU.

29. 1996. Early agriculture and the dispersal of the Southern Mongoloids. In T. Akazawa and E. Szathmary (eds), *Prehistoric Mongoloid Dispersals*, pp. 287–302. Oxford: Oxford University Press.

30. 1996. Three entries on Indonesian prehistory for J. Miksic (ed.), *Indonesian Heritage: Ancient History*, pp. 28–33. Singapore: Didier Millet.

31. 1996. The origins and spread of agriculture in the Asian-Pacific region. In D. Harris (ed.), *The Origins and Spread of Agriculture and Pastoralism in Eurasia*, pp. 465–498. London: University College Press.

32. 1996. Hierarchy, founder ideology and Austronesian expansion. In J. Fox and C. Sather (eds), *Origin, Ancestry and Alliance*, pp. 18–40. Canberra: Department of Anthropology, Comparative Austronesian Project, ANU.

33. 1996. Entries on 'Hoabinhian' and 'Origins of food production in the Pacific Islands'. In B. Fagan (ed.), *The Oxford Companion to Archaeology*, pp. 305, 549–550.

34. 1996. The Pacific. In J. Herrmann and E Zurcher (eds), *History of Humanity: Scientific and Cultural Development*, vol. III, pp. 435–438. Paris: Unesco.

35. 1997. Prehistoric cultural explanations for the existence of widespread language families. In P. McConvell and N. Evans (eds), *Archaeology and Linguistics: Aboriginal Australia in Global Perspective*, pp. 123–134. Melbourne: Oxford University Press.

36. 1998. Between Southeast Asia and Oceania: preceramic occupation in the northern Moluccas and associated mysteries. In S. Atmosudiro (ed.), *Jejak-Jejak Budaya II: Persembahan untuk Prof. Dr. R.P. Soejono*, pp. 323–369. Yogyakarta: Asosiasi Prehistorisi Indonesia Rayon II.

37. 1998. Human dispersals and colonizations in prehistory – the Southeast Asian data and their implications. In K. Omoto and P.V. Tobias (eds), *The Origins and Past of Modern Humans – Towards Reconciliation*, pp. 188–205. Singapore: World Scientific.

38. 1998. La dispersion des Austronésians. In D. Newton (ed.), *Arts des Mers du Sud*, pp. 8–17. Paris: Société Nouvelle Adam Biro.

39. 1998. The archaeology of Papuan and Austronesian prehistory in the northern Moluccas, Indonesia. In R. Blench and M. Spriggs (eds), *Archaeology and Language, Volume 2: Correlating Archaeological and Linguistic Hypotheses*, pp. 128–140. One World Archaeology Series, Routledge, London.

40. 1998. Several entries in N.H.S.N. Abdul Rahman (ed.), *Early History*. vol. 4 of *The Encyclopaedia of Malaysia*, pp. 10, 20, 26–28, 44. Singapore: Archipelago Press.

41. 1998. From Bird's Head to bird's eye view: Long term structures and trends in Indo-Pacific Prehistory. In J. Miedema, C. Odé and R. Dam (eds), *Perspectives on the Bird's Head of Irian Jaya, Indonesia*, pp. 951–975. Amsterdam: Rodopi.

42. 1999. Commemorative Speech: 'Dispersal of people in the Pacific: past, present and future'. Published in *International Ocean Symposium 1998: The Ocean, Can She Save Us?* pp. 63–80 (Japanese text), 177–191 (English text). Tokyo: Nippon Foundation.

43. 1999. Archaeology of Southeast Asian hunters and gatherers. In R.B. Lee and R. Daly (eds), *The Cambridge Encyclopaedia of Hunters and Gatherers*, pp. 284–288. Cambridge: Cambridge University Press.

44. 2000. The time depth of major language families: an archaeologist's perspective. In C. Renfrew, A. McMahon and L. Trask (eds), *Time Depth in Historical Linguistics*, pp. 109–140. Cambridge: McDonald Institute for Archaeological Research (Papers in the Prehistory of Languages).

45. 2000. Footsteps from Asia: The peopling of the Pacific. In B. Lal and K. Fortune (eds), *The Pacific Islands: An Encyclopaedia*, pp. 53–58. Honolulu: University of Hawai'i Press.

46. 2000. Formosan prehistory and Austronesian dispersal. In D. Blundell (ed.), *Austronesian Taiwan*, pp. 337–365. Berkeley CA: Phoebe A. Hearst Museum of Anthropology.

47. 2001. Southeast Asia Neolithic and Early Bronze. In P. Peregrine and M. Ember (eds), *Encyclopaedia of Prehistory. Volume 3: East Asia and Oceania*, pp. 287–306. New York: Kluwer/Plenum.

48. 2001. Archaeology and the historical determinants of punctuation in language family origins. In A. Aikhenvald and R. Dixon (eds), *Areal Diffusion and Genetic Inheritance: Problems in Comparative Linguistics*, pp. 27–43. Oxford: Oxford University Press.

49. 2001. Archaeology and the history of languages. *International Encyclopaedia of the Social and Behavioral Sciences*, vol. 1, pp. 617–622. Amsterdam: Pergamon (2nd edition in 2015).

50. 2001. Cultural evolution: Phylogeny versus reticulation. *International Encyclopaedia of the Social and Behavioral Sciences*, vol. 5, pp. 3052–3057. Amsterdam: Pergamon (2nd edition in 2015).

51. 2001. Keynote address: Polynesian prehistory and the rest of mankind. In C.M. Stevenson, G. Lee and F.J. Morin (eds), *Pacific 2000*, pp. 11–25. Los Osos, California: Easter Island Foundation.

52. 2002. Southeast Asian prehistory and archaeology at the turn of the millennium. In B. Cunliffe, W. Davies, and C. Renfrew (eds), *Archaeology: The Widening Debate*, pp. 318–334. Oxford: Oxford University Press.

53. 2002. Foreword, and Concluding Observations. In P. Bellwood and C. Renfrew (eds), *Examining the Farming/language Dispersal Hypothesis*, pp. xiii–xiv, 467–469. Cambridge: McDonald Institute for Archaeological Research.

54. 2002. Farmers, foragers, languages, genes: The genesis of agricultural societies. In P. Bellwood and C. Renfrew (eds), *Examining the Farming/language Dispersal Hypothesis,* pp. 17–28. Cambridge: McDonald Institute for Archaeological Research.

55. 2004. Colin Renfrew's emerging synthesis: Farming, languages and genes as viewed from the Antipodes. In M. Jones (ed.), *Traces of Ancestry: Studies in Honour of Colin Renfrew*, pp. 31–41. Cambridge: McDonald Institute for Archaeological Research.

56. 2004. The origins and dispersals of agricultural communities in Southeast Asia. In I. Glover and P. Bellwood (eds), *Southeast Asia: From Prehistory to History*, pp. 21–40. London: RoutledgeCurzon.

57. 2004. Aslian, Austronesian, Malayic: suggestions from the archaeological record. In V. Paz (ed.), *Southeast Asian Archaeology: Wilhelm G. Solheim II Festschrift*, pp. 347–365. Diliman: University of the Philippines Press.

58. 2004. Austronesiani. In *Enciclopedia Italiana: Americhe Oceania, Parte Seconda, Oceania*, p. 900. Roma: Istituto della Enciclopedia Italiana.

59. 2005. 18 entries on Philippine, Indonesian and Malaysian archaeology, translated into Italian, for *Enciclopaedia Archaeologica*, pp. 797–826. Roma: Istituto della Enciclopedia Italiana.

60. 2005. Examining the language/farming dispersal hypothesis in the East Asian context. In L. Sagart, R. Blench and A. Sanchez-Mazas (eds), *The Peopling of East Asia: Putting Together Archaeology, Linguistics and Genetics*, pp. 17–30. London: RoutledgeCurzon.

61. 2005. Keynote paper: Coastal South China, Taiwan, and the prehistory of the Austronesians. In C.-Y. Chen and J.-G. Pan (eds), *The Archaeology of the Southeast Coastal Islands of China*, pp. 1–22. Taiwan: Executive Yuan, Council for Cultural Affairs.

62. 2006. Early Pacific Voyagers. In R. Hanbury-Tenison (ed.), *The Seventy Great Journeys in History*, pp. 26–28. London: Thames and Hudson.

63. 2006. Asian farming diasporas? Agriculture, languages, and genes in China and Southeast Asia. In M.T. Stark (ed.), *Archaeology of Asia*, pp. 96–118. Malden: Blackwell.

64. 2006. The dispersal of Neolithic cultures from China into Island Southeast Asia: Standstills, slow moves, and fast spreads. In Institute of Archaeology, Chinese Academy of Social Sciences (ed.), *Prehistoric Archaeology of South China and Southeast Asia*, pp. 223–234. Beijing: Cultural Relics Publishing House.

65. 2006. Borneo as the homeland of Malay? The perspective from archaeology. In J. Collins and A. Sariyan (eds), *Borneo and the Homeland of the Malays: Four Essays*, pp. 45–63. Kuala Lumpur: Dewan Bahasa dan Pustaka.

66. 2006. The early movements of Austronesian-speaking peoples in the Indonesian region. In T. Simanjuntak, I. Popoh and M. Hisyam (eds), *Austronesian Diaspora and the Ethnogeneses of People in Indonesian Archipelago*, pp. 61–82. Jakarta: Indonesian Institute of Sciences (LIPI).

67. 2007. Southeast China and the prehistory of the Austronesians. In T. Jiao (ed.), *Lost Maritime Cultures: China and the Pacific*. Honolulu: Bishop Museum Press.

68. 2007. Tracing ancestral connections across the Pacific. In J.X. Li (ed.), *Across Oceans and Time: Art in the Contemporary Pacific*, pp. 32–40 (including translations into Chinese and French). Kaohsiung Museum of Fine Arts, Taiwan.

69. 2008. Archaeology and the origins of language families. In A. Bentley, H. Maschner and C. Chippindale (eds), *Handbook of Archaeological Theories*, pp. 225–243. Lanham: Altamira.

70. 2008. Die erste reiche Ernte ('History's first bountiful harvest'). In J.A. Robinson and K. Wiegandt (eds), *Die Ursprünge der modernen Welt*, pp. 166–213. Frankfurt-am-Main: Fischer Taschenbuch Verlag.

71. 2009. Early farmers: Issues of spread and migration with respect to the Indian Subcontinent. In T. Osada (ed.), *Linguistics, Archaeology and Human Past in South Asia*, pp. 55–69. New Delhi: Manohar.

72. 2010. La diffusion des populations d'agriculteurs dans le monde. In J-P. Demoule (ed.), *La Revolution Neolithique dans le Monde*, pp. 239–262. Paris: CNRS Editions.

73. 2010. Language families and the history of human migration. In J. Bowden, N. Himmelmann and M. Ross (eds), *A Journey through Austronesian and Papuan Linguistic and Cultural Space: Papers in Honour of Andrew K. Pawley*, pp. 79–93. Canberra: Pacific Linguistics.

74. 2011. La dispersione dei primi agricoltori e delle famiglie linguistiche in Estremo Oriente. In R. Ciarla and M. Scarpari (eds), La Cina, vol. 1, *Preistoriae Origini della Civilta Cinese*, pp. 369–396. Roma: Einaudi.

75. 2012. How and why did agriculture spread? In P. Gepts, R. Bettinger, S. Brush, T. Famula, P. McGuire, C. Qualset and A. Damania (eds), *Biodiversity in Agriculture: Domestication, Evolution, and Sustainability*, pp. 160–189. Cambridge: Cambridge University Press.

76. 2013. Austronesian migration, 3500 BC to AD 1500. In C. de Monbrisson (ed.), *Philippines: An Archipelago of Exchange*, pp. 40–49. Paris: Coédition musée du quai Branly/ Actes Sud.

77. 2015. Prehistoric migration and the rise of humanity. In P. Bellwood (ed.), *The Encyclopedia of Global Human Migration*, pp. 1–6. Chichester, UK: Wiley-Blackwell Publishers.

78. 2015. Neolithic migrations: food production and population expansion. In P. Bellwood (ed.), *The Encyclopedia of Global Human Migration*, pp. 79–86. Chichester, UK: Wiley-Blackwell.

79. 2015. Human migrations and the histories of major language families. In P. Bellwood (ed.), *The Encyclopedia of Global Human Migration*, pp. 87–95. Chichester, UK: Wiley-Blackwell.

80. 2015. Southeast Asian islands: Archaeology. In P. Bellwood (ed.), *The Encyclopedia of Global Human Migration*, pp. 284–292. Chichester, UK: Wiley-Blackwell.

81. 2015. Migration and the origins of *Homo sapiens*. In Y. Kaifu, M. Izuho, T. Goebel, H.Sato and A. Ono (eds), *Emergence and Diversity of Modern Human Behavior in Paleolithic Asia*, pp. 51–58. College Station: Texas A&M University Press.

82. 2015. Vietnam's place in the prehistory of Eastern Asia – a multidisciplinary perspective on the Neolithic / Vị trí của Việt Nam trong tiến sử Đông Á –một hướng tiếp cận đa ngành về thời kỳ đồ đá mới. In A. Reinecke (ed.), *Perspectives on the Archaeology of Vietnam*, pp. 47–70. Published in Bonn by the LWL-Museum for Archaeology, Herne, the Reiss-Engelhorn-Museums in Mannheim, the State Museum of Archaeology of Chemnitz, and the German Archaeological Institute (in English and Vietnamese).

83. 2015. Language Families, Archaeology and History of. In J.D. Wright (ed.), *International Encyclopedia of the Social & Behavioral Sciences* (2nd edition), vol. 13, pp. 337–343. Oxford: Elsevier.

84. 2015. Cultural evolution: phylogeny versus reticulation. In J.D. Wright (ed.), *International Encyclopedia of the Social & Behavioral Sciences*, 2nd edition, vol. 13, pp. 394–400. Oxford: Elsevier.

E. Jointly written articles in journals and edited books

1. 1970. Neolithic comments (with others). *Antiquity* XLIV: 105–114.

2. 1972. Armitage, G.C., R.D. Reeves and P. Bellwood. Source identification of archaeological obsidians in New Zealand. *New Zealand Journal of Science* 15: 408–420.

3. 1980. Farrington, I.S. and P. Bellwood. Prehistoric irrigation hydrology of pondfield taro: Two case studies from Polynesia. *Archaeology and Physical Anthropology in Oceania*. 15: 120–127.

4. 1980. Bellwood, P. and M.b. Omar. Trade patterns and political developments in Brunei and adjacent areas, A.D. 700–1500. *Brunei Museum Journal* 4/4: 155–179.

5. 1981. Bellwood, P. and A.H. Taha. A home for ten thousand years. *Hemisphere* 25, no. 5: 310–313.

6. 1987. Chinese translation of the above article published *Yunnan Wenwu*, 1986, pp. 201–209.

7. 1984. Ghosh, A.K., R. Ray, P. Chatterjee, P. Nanda and P. Bellwood. Archaeological reconnaissance in the Sanjai Valley, Singhbhum District, Bihar. *Bulletin of the Indo-Pacific Prehistory Association* 5: 24–28.

8. 1989. Bellwood, P. and P. Koon. 'Lapita colonists leave boats unburned!' The question of Lapita links with Island Southeast Asia. *Antiquity* 63: 613–622.

9. 1991. Ardika, I.W. and P. Bellwood. Sembiran: the beginnings of Indian contact with Bali. *Antiquity* 247: 221–232.

10. 1991. Datan, I. and P. Bellwood. Recent research at Gua Sireh (Serian) and Lubang Angin (Gunung Mulu National Park), Sarawak. *Bulletin of the Indo-Pacific Prehistory Assn.* 10: 386–405. This paper was later reprinted in *Sarawak Museum Journal* 44 (n.s. 65), pp. 93–111, 1993.

11. 1991. Endicott, K. and P. Bellwood. The possibility of independent foraging in the rain forest of Peninsular Malaysia. *Human Ecology* 19: 151–186.

12. 1992. Bellwood, P., R. Gillespie, G.B. Thompson, I.W. Ardika and Ipoi Datan. New dates for prehistoric Asian rice. *Asian Perspectives* 31/2: 161–170.

13. 1993. Bellwood, P., A. Waluyo, Gunadi, Gunadi Nh. and G. Irwin. Archaeological research in the northern Moluccas; interim results, 1991 field season. *Bulletin of the Indo-Pacific Prehistory Association* 13: 20–33.

14. 1993. Bellwood, P. and G. Barnes. Stone age farmers in southern and eastern Asia. In G. Burenhult (ed.), *People of the Stone Age (The Illustrated History of Humankind, vol. 2)*, pp. 123–127, 129–131, 138–139. San Francisco: Harper.

15. 1993. Ardika, I.W., P. Bellwood, R. Eggleton and D. Ellis. A single source for South Asian export-quality Rouletted Ware? *Man and Environment* XVIII(1): 101–109. Pune.

16. 1994. Bellwood, P. and Earl of Cranbrook. Human prehistory. In Earl of Cranbrook and D.S. Edwards (eds), *Belalong: A Tropical Rainforest*, pp. 336–337. London: Royal Geographical Society.

17. 1995. Bellwood, P., J.J. Fox and D. Tryon. The Austronesians in history: Common origins and diverse transformations. In P. Bellwood, J. Fox and D. Tryon (eds), *The Austronesian: Historical and Comparative Perspectives*, pp. 1–16. Canberra, Dept. Anthropology RSPAS, ANU.

18. 1995. Flannery, T., P. Bellwood, J.P. White, A. Moore, Boeadi and G. Nitihaminoto. Fossil marsupials (Macropodidae, Peroryctidae) and other mammals of Holocene age from Halmahera, North Moluccas, Indonesia. *Alcheringa* 19: 17–25.

19. 1997. Ardika, I.W., P. Bellwood, I.M. Sutaba and C. Yuliathi. Sembiran and the first Indian contacts with Bali: An update. *Antiquity* 71: 193–195.

20. 1998. Flannery, T., P. Bellwood, J.P. White, T. Ennis, G. Irwin, K. Schubert and S. Balasubramanian. Mammals from Holocene archaeological deposits on Gebe and Morotai Islands, Northern Moluccas, Indonesia. *Australian Mammalogy* 20/3: 391–400.

21. 1998. Bellwood, P., G., Nitihaminoto, G., Irwin, Gunadi, A., Waluyo, D. Tanudirjo. 35,000 years of prehistory in the northern Moluccas. In G.-J. Bartstra (ed.), *Bird's Head Approaches*, pp. 233–275. *Modern Quaternary Research in Southeast Asia* 15. Rotterdam: Balkema.

22. 1999. Irwin, G., P. Bellwood, Gunadi Nitihaminoto, Daud Tanudirjo and Joko Siswanto. Prehistoric relations between Island Southeast Asia and Oceania: recent archaeological investigations in the Northern Moluccas. In J-C. Galipaud and I. Lilley (eds), *The Pacific from 5000 to 2000 BP*, pp. 363–374. Paris: Institut de Recherche pour le Développement.

23. 2000. Bellwood, P., Gunadi Nitihaminoto, Gunadi, Agus Waluyo and G. Irwin. The Northern Moluccas as a crossroads between Indonesia and the Pacific. In Sudaryanto

and A.H. Rambadeta (eds), *Antar Hubungan Bahasa dan Budaya di Kawasan Non-Austronesia*, pp. 195–254. Yogyakarta: Pusat Studi Asia Pasifik.

24. 2000. Bellwood, P. and T. Sayavongkhamdy. Recent archaeological research in Laos. *Bulletin of the Indo-Pacific Prehistory Assn* 19: 101–110.

25. 2001. Peregrine, P. and P. Bellwood. Southeast Asia Upper Palaeolithic. In P. Peregrine and M. Ember (eds), *Encyclopaedia of Prehistory. Volume 3: East Asia and Oceania*, pp. 307–309. New York: Kluwer/Plenum.

26. 2003. Diamond, J. and P. Bellwood. Farmers and their languages: The first expansions. *Science* 300: 597–603.

27. 2003. Bellwood, P., J. Stevenson, A. Anderson and E. Dizon. Archaeological and palaeoenvironmental resesarch in Batanes and Ilocos Norte Provinces, northern Philippines. *Bulletin of the Indo-Pacific Prehistory Association* 23: 141–161.

28. 2003. Szabo, K., H. Ramirez, A. Anderson and P. Bellwood. Prehistoric subsistence strategies on the Batanes Islands, northern Philippines. *Bulletin of the Indo-Pacific Prehistory Association* 23: 163–171.

29. 2004. Glover, I. and P. Bellwood. Introduction. In I. Glover and P. Bellwood (eds), *Southeast Asia: From Prehistory to History*, pp. 1–3. London: RoutledgeCurzon.

30. 2004. Bellwood, P. and I. Glover. Southeast Asia: Foundations for an archaeological history. In I. Glover and P. Bellwood (eds), *Southeast Asia: From Prehistory to History*, pp. 4–20. London: RoutledgeCurzon.

31. 2004. Glover, I. and P. Bellwood. Retrospect and prospect. In I. Glover and P. Bellwood (eds), *Southeast Asia: From Prehistory to History*, pp. 337–345. London: RoutledgeCurzon.

32. 2004. Pasveer, J. and P. Bellwood. Prehistoric bone artefacts from the northern Moluccas, Indonesia. *Modern Quaternary Research in Southeast Asia* 18: 301–359.

33. 2004. Mahirta, K. Aplin, D. Bulbeck, W. Boles and P. Bellwood. Pia Hudale Rockshelter: A terminal Pleistocene occupation site on Roti Island, Nusa Tenggara Timur, Indonesia. *Modern Quaternary Research in Southeast Asia* 18: 361–394.

34. 2005. Bellwood, P. and P. Hiscock. Australia and the Austronesians. In C. Scarre (ed.), *The Human Past*, pp. 264–305. London: Thames and Hudson.

35. 2005. Bellwood, P. and A. Sanchez-Mazas. Human migrations in continental East Asia and Taiwan: Genetic, linguistic and archaeological evidence. *Current Anthropology* 46: 480–484.

36. 2005. Bellwood, P. and P. White. Domesticated pigs in eastern Indonesia (response to Larson et al.). *Science* 309: 381.

37. 2005. Bellwood, P. and J. Diamond. On explicit 'replacement' models in island Southeast Asia – a reply to Stephen Oppenheimer. *World Archaeology* 37: 503–506.

38. 2005. Bellwood, P. and E. Dizon. The Batanes Archaeological Project and the 'Out of Taiwan' hypothesis for Austronesian dispersal. *Journal of Austronesian Studies* (Taitung, Taiwan) 1: 1–33.

39. 2005. Iizuka, Y., P. Bellwood, H.-c. Hung and E. Dizon. A non-destructive mineralogical study of nephritic artifacts from Itbayat Island, Batanes, northern Philippines. *Journal of Austronesian Studies* (Taitung, Taiwan) 1: 83–108.

40. 2005. Iizuka, Y., P. Bellwood, I. Datan and H.-c. Hung. Mineralogical studies of the Niah West Mouth *lingling-o. Sarawak Museum Journal* 61 (n.s. 82): 19–29.

41. 2006. Hung, H.-c., Y. Iizuka and P. Bellwood. Taiwan jade in the context of Southeast Asian archaeology. In E. Bacus, I. Glover and V. Pigott (eds), *Uncovering Southeast Asia's Past*, pp. 203–215. London: British Museum.

42. 2007. Bellwood, P., J. Cameron, V.V. Nguyen and V.L. Bui. Ancient boats, boat timbers, and locked mortise and tenon joints from Bronze Age northern Vietnam. *International Journal of Nautical Archaeology* 36: 2–20.

43. 2007. Iizuka, Y., H.-c. Hung and P. Bellwood. A noninvasive mineralogical study of nephritic artifacts from the Philippines and surroundings: the distribution of Taiwan nephrite and implications for Island Southeast Asian archaeology. In J. Douglas, P. Jett and J. Winter (eds), *Scientific Research on the Sculptural Arts of Asia*, pp. 12–19. Freer Gallery of Art/Arthur M. Sackler Gallery, Smithsonian Institution, Washington DC, USA.

44. 2007. Szabo, K., A. Brumm and P. Bellwood. Shell artefact production at 32,000 BP in Island Southeast Asia: thinking across media? *Current Anthropology* 48: 701–724.

45. 2007. Hung, H.-c., Y. Iizuka, P. Bellwood, K.D. Nguyen, B. Bellina, P. Silapanth, E. Dizon, R. Santiago, I. Datan and J. Manton. Ancient jades map 3000 years of prehistoric exchange in Southeast Asia. *Proceedings of the National Academy of Sciences (USA)* 104: 19745–19750.

46. 2008. Bellwood, P. and E. Dizon. Austronesian cultural origins: out of Taiwan, via the Batanes Islands, and onwards to western Polynesia. In A. Sanchez-Mazas, R. Blench, M.D. Ross, I. Peiros and M. Lin (eds), *Past Human Migrations in East Asia: Matching Archaeology, Linguistics and Genetics*, pp. 23–39. London: Routledge.

47. 2008. Bellwood, P. and M. Oxenham. The expansions of farming societies and the role of the Neolithic Demographic Transition. In J.-P. Bocquet-Appel and O. Bar-Yosef (eds), *The Neolithic Demographic Transition and its Consequences*, pp. 13–34. Dordrecht: Springer.

48. 2008. Bellwood, P., J. Stevenson, E. Dizon, A. Mijares, G. Lacsina and E. Robles. Where are the Neolithic landscapes of Ilocos Norte? *Hukay* 13: 25–38. Manila.

49. 2009. Bellwood, P. and P. Hiscock. Holocene Australia and the Pacific Basin. In C. Scarre (ed.), *The Human Past*. 2nd revised edition, pp. 264–305. London: Thames and Hudson.

50. 2009. Cameron, J., P. Bellwood, V.L. Bui and V.V. Nguyen. (Study results of Dong Son cultural textiles from Dong Xa site (Hung Yen) in the first joint Australian Vietnamese Archaeology Project). *Khao Co Hoc* (Hanoi), no. 2 for 2009, pp. 20–25 (in Vietnamese with English abstract).

51. 2009. Piper, P., H.-c. Hung, F. Campos, P. Bellwood and R. Santiago. A 4000 year-old introduction of domestic pigs into the Philippine Archipelago: Implications for understanding routes of human migration through Island Southeast Asia and Wallacea. *Antiquity* 83: 687–695.

52. 2010. Mijares, A., F. Détroit, P. Piper, R. Grün, P. Bellwood, M. Aubert, G. Champion, N. Cuevas, A. De Leon, E. Dizon. New evidence for a 67,000-year-old human presence at Callao Cave, Luzon, Philippines. *Journal of Human Evolution* 59: 123–132.

53. 2010. Hung, H.-c. and P. Bellwood. Movement of raw materials and manufactured goods across the South China Sea after 500 BCE: From Taiwan to Thailand, and back. In B. Bellina, L. Bacus, O. Pryce and J. Wisseman Christie (eds), *50 Years of Archaeology in Southeast Asia: Essays in Honour of Ian Glover*, pp. 234–243. Bangkok: River Books.

54. 2011. Bellwood, P. and Hung, H.-c. Professor Peter Bellwood's reflections on archaeological research. *Cultural Relics of South China (Nanfang Wenwu)* 2011(3): 22–29 (in Chinese).

55. 2011. Bellwood, P., H.-c. Hung and Y. Iizuka. Taiwan jade in the Philippines: 3000 years of trade and long-distance interaction. In P. Benitez-Johannot (ed.), *Paths of Origins: Austronesia in the Collections of the National Museum of the Philippines, the Museum Nasional Indonesia, and the Netherlands Rijksmuseum voor Volkenkunde*, pp. 30–41. Manila: ArtPostAsia.

56. 2011. Bellwood, P., G. Chambers, M. Ross and H.-c. Hung. Are 'cultures' inherited? Multidisciplinary perspectives on the origins and migrations of Austronesian-speaking peoples prior to 1000 BC. In B. Roberts and M. Van der Linden (eds), *Investigating Archaeological Cultures: Material Culture, Variability and Transmission*, pp. 321–354. Dordrecht: Springer.

57. 2011. Nguyen, K.D., M. Yamagata, S. Watanabe and P. Bellwood. The Man Bac burial pottery – an illustrated corpus of the whole vessels from the burials in Cultural Unit III. In M. Oxenham, H. Matsumura and K.D. Nguyen (eds), *Man Bac: The Excavation of a Late Neolithic Site in Northern Vietnam: Biological Research*, pp. 169–85. Terra Australis 33. Canberra: ANU E Press.

58. 2011. Hung H.-c., M.T. Carson, P. Bellwood, F. Campos, P. Piper, E. Dizon, M. Bolunia, M. Oxenham and C. Zhang. The first settlement of Remote Oceania: Luzon to the Marianas. *Antiquity* 85: 909–926.

59. 2011. Bellwood, P., M. Oxenham, B.C. Hoang, K.D. Nguyen, A. Willis, C. Sarjeant, P. Piper, H. Matsumura, K. Tanaka, N. Beavan, T. Higham, Q.M. Nguyen, N.K. Dang, K.T.K. Nguyen, T.H. Vo, N.B. Van, T.K.Q. Tran, P.T. Nguyen, F. Campos, Y.-I. Sato, L.C. Nguyen and N. Amano. An Son and the Neolithic of southern Vietnam. *Asian Perspectives* 50: 144–175 (published in 2013).

60. 2012. Hung, H.-c., M.T. Carson and P. Bellwood. Earliest settlement in the Marianas – a response. *Antiquity* 86: 910–914.

61. 2013. Bellwood, P. and P. Hiscock. Australia and the Pacific Basin during the Holocene. In C. Scarre (ed.), *The Human Past* (third edition), pp. 264–305. London: Thames and Hudson.

62. 2013. Carson, M.T., H.-c. Hung, G. Summerhayes and P. Bellwood. The pottery trail from Southeast Asia to Remote Oceania. *Journal of Coastal and Island Archaeology* 8: 17–36.

63. 2013. Amano, N., P. Piper, H.-c. Hung and P. Bellwood. Introduced domestic animals in the Neolithic and Metal Age of the Philippines and evidence of human subsistence strategies and behavior at Nagsabaran, Northern Luzon. *Journal of Coastal and Island Archaeology* 8: 317–335.

64. 2013. H.-c. Hung, K.D. Nguyen, P. Bellwood and M.T. Carson. Coastal connectivity: Long-term trading networks across the South China Sea. *Journal of Coastal and Island Archaeology* 8: 384–404.

65. 2013. Bellwood, P. and H.-c. Hung. The dispersals of early food producers from Southern China into Southeast Asia. In Y. Yang (ed.), *Hemudu Culture International Forum*, pp. 160–175. Beijing: China Modern Economic Publishing House.

66. 2014. T. Pryce, S. Baron, B.H.M. Bellina, P. Bellwood, N. Chang and 18 others. More questions than answers: The Southeast Asian Lead Isotope Project 2009–2012. *Journal of Archaeological Science* 42: 273–294.

67. 2014. Piper, P., F. Campos, D.N. Kinh, M. Oxenham, B.C. Hoang, P. Bellwood and A. Willis. Early evidence for pig and dog husbandry from the site of An Son, Southern Vietnam. *International Journal of Osteoarchaeology* 24: 68–78.

68. 2014. Anggraeni, T. Simanjuntak, P. Bellwood and P. Piper. Neolithic foundations in the Karama valley, West Sulawesi, Indonesia. *Antiquity* 88: 740–756.

69. 2015. Oxenham, M., P. Piper, P. Bellwood, C.H. Bui, K.T.K. Nguyen, Q.M. Nguyen, F. Campos, C. Castillo, R. Wood, C. Sarjeant, N. Amano, A. Willis and J. Ceron. Emergence and diversification of the Neolithic in southern Vietnam: insights from coastal Rach Nui. *Journal of Island and Coastal Archaeology* 10(3): 309–338. DOI: 10.1080/15564894.2014.980473.

70. 2015. Calo, A., B. Prasetyo, P. Bellwood, J.W. Lankton, B. Gratuze, T.O. Pryce, A. Reinecke, V. Leusch, H. Schenk, R. Wood, R.A. Bawono, I D.K. Gede, Ni L.K.C. Yuliati, J. Fenner, C. Reepmeyer, C. Castillo and A. Carter. Sembiran and Pacung on the north coast of Bali: a strategic crossroads in early trans-Asiatic exchange. *Antiquity* 89: 378–396.

F. Book reviews, letters to editors and other minor contributions

Anthropological Forum (Perth WA), vol. VIII, nos 1 and 2, pp. 97–100, 1998.

Anthropological Science (Japan), vol. 103–104, pp. 403–404, 1995.

Antiquity, vol. 51: 97–8 (1977); vol. 70: 999–1001 (1996); vol. 74: 968–969 (2000); vol. 89: 235–236 (2015).

ANU Reporter, vol. 14/8, 10 June 1983, p. 6; vol. 26/14, 16 August 1995, p. 6.

Archaeology in Oceania, vol. 21, no. 2, 1986, p. 154; vol. 34, no. 2, pp. 88–89, 1999.

Asian Perspectives, vol. 11, 1970, pp. 197–198; vol. 30/2, 1991, pp. 269–270; vol. 51, 2012, pp. 128–129.

Asian Studies Association of Australia Review, vol. 6, no. 3, pp. 115–116, 1983.

Asian Studies Review, vol. 31, pp. 79–81, 2007.

Australian Academy of Science: Contributed text on Sumerian civilization for textbook *Environmental Science*, pp. 140–142, published 1994.

Borneo Research Bulletin vol. 27, p. 38, 1996.

Canberra Anthropology vol. 14, no. 2, p. 101, 1991; vol. 21, no. 1, pp. 115–116, 1998.

Environmental Archaeology vol. 16, no. 2, 171–172, 2011.

Hemisphere, book reviews in January and December 1974, January and March 1975, September–October 1981.

Institute of Archaeology Bulletin, vol. 18, 1981, pp. 298, 302–303.

Journal of Anthropological Research 70: 136–138, 2014; 70: 625–626, 2014.

Journal of Field Archaeology vol. 19, pp. 255–256, 1992.

Journal of Human Evolution, vol. 14, 1985, pp. 217–218.

Journal of Interdisciplinary History, vol. VI (1), 1975, pp. 154–157.

Journal of Pacific History, vol. 11, 1976, pp. 253–257; vol. 13, 1978, pp. 247–249; vol. 14, 1979, p. 120; vol. 20, 1985, p. 104; vol. 30, 1995, pp. 121–122.

Journal of the Polynesian Society, vol. 76, 1967, pp. 249–250; vol. 77, 1968, pp. 451–454; vol. 79, 1970, pp. 437–440; vol. 81, 1972, pp. 277–279; vol. 82, 1973, pp. 310–311; vol. 84, 1975, pp. 244–245; vol. 85, 1976, pp. 397–399; vol. 86, 1977, pp. 137–138, 421–423; vol. 88, 1979, pp. 22–23; vol. 92, 1983, pp. 417–418; vol. 95, 1986, pp. 131–134.

Man, vol. 25, no. 1, 1990, pp. 148–149.

Mankind, vol. 9/1, 1973, pp. 57–58; vol. 12/1, 1979, pp. 85–87; vol. 12/2, 1979, pp. 185–188; vol. 12/3, pp. 278–279, 1981.

New Zealand Archaeological Association Newsletter, vol. 10, 1967, pp. 143–150; vol. 11, 1968, pp. 88–92, 175–176; vol. 12, 1969, pp. 230–231; vol. 13, 1970, pp. 88, 92–96, 122; vol. 15, 1972, pp. 123–124; vol. 16, 1973, pp. 173–174; vol. 22, 1979, pp. 188–189.

Pacific Studies, vol. 4, no. 2, 1981, pp. 186–189; vol. 9, no. 3, 1986, pp. 182–184; vol. 11, no. 1. 1987, pp. 163–166.

Review of Archaeology 14/2, Fall 1993, pp. 33–35 (reply to Janice Stargardt).

Review of Indonesian and Malaysian Affairs 31/1: 294, 1997.

Scientific American, February 1992, p. 10.

The Chameleon (Centre for Research on Language Change, ANU), invited editorial, edition 7, July 2005.

The Times (London), 'Pacific man: early cultural achievements,' 17/8/73.

Conferences organised by Peter Bellwood (Peter retired from conference organisation in 2009)

1975 ANZAAS (Australian and New Zealand Association for the Advancement of Science), Canberra. Secretary of Section 25A (Archaeology).

1978 10th Congress of the Indo-Pacific Prehistory Association, Poona, India. Publication editor. See V.N. Misra and P. Bellwood (eds), 1985, *Recent Advances in Indo-Pacific Prehistory*.

1980 3rd National Conference, Asian Studies Association of Australia, Brisbane. Panel organiser; Prehistory and Archaeology in Asia.

1985 12th Congress of the Indo-Pacific Prehistory Association, Penablanca, Luzon, Philippines (with Professor Jack Golson). See *Asian Perspectives*, vol. 26, no. 1 (issue dated 1984–1985).

1990 Conference entitled 'The Austronesians in history: Common origins and diverse transformations', held at ANU under the auspices of the Comparative Austronesian Project, November 1990. See Peter Bellwood, James Fox and Darrell Tryon (eds), 1995, *The Austronesians: Historical and Comparative Perspectives*.

1990 14th Congress of the Indo-Pacific Prehistory Association, Yogyakarta, Indonesia, 200 delegates from around 20 countries. *IPPA Bulletins* 10–13, 1990–1993.

1994 15th Congress of the Indo-Pacific Prehistory Association, Chiang Mai, Thailand, around 200 delegates from 20 countries. *IPPA Bulletins* 14–16, 1995–1996.

1998 16th Congress of the Indo-Pacific Prehistory Association, Melaka, Malaysia, July 1–7, around 250 delegates from 35 countries. See *IPPA Bulletins* 17 to 22, 1997–2002, edited or co-edited by Bellwood.

2001 Conference on Origins and Dispersals of Agricultural Societies and Language Families, co-organised with Professor Colin Renfrew, McDonald Institute for Archaeological Research, University of Cambridge, UK, 24–27 August 2002. See P. Bellwood and C. Renfrew (eds), 2002, *Examining the Farming/Language Dispersal Hypothesis*.

2002 17th Congress of the Indo-Pacific Prehistory Association, Institute of History and Philology, Academia Sinica, Taipei, Taiwan, 9–15 September 2002, 300 delegates from 35 countries. See *IPPA Bulletins* 23–27, 2003–2007.

2004 2-day workshop on The Asian Fore-Arc Project: Results and Prospects from the Philippines and Taiwan. Research School of Pacific and Asian Studies, ANU, 5–6 August 2004.

2006 18th Congress of the Indo-Pacific Prehistory Association, University of the Philippines, Diliman, Manila, 20–26 March, 350 delegates from 35 countries. See report in *Science* 312: 360–361, 21 April 2006, and *IPPA Bulletins* 26–29, 2006–2009.

2009 19th Congress of the Indo-Pacific Prehistory Association, Vietnam Academy of Social Sciences and Institute of Archaeology, Hanoi, Vietnam, 29 Nov to 5 Dec 2009, 600 delegates from about 30 countries world-wide.

MA, MPhil and PhD students supervised by Peter Bellwood (as chair of the supervisory panel) and their research topics

Matussin bin Omar (Brunei)
MA 1978, Archaeological Excavations in Protohistoric Brunei.

Adi bin Haji Taha (Malaysia)
MA 1981, The Re-excavation of the Rockshelter of Gua Cha, Ulu Kelantan, West Malaysia.
PhD 2000, Archaeological Investigations in Ulu Kelantan, Peninsular Malaysia.

I. Wayan Ardika (Indonesia)
MA 1987, Bronze Artefacts and the Rise of Complex Society in Bali.
PhD 1991, Archaeological Research in Northeastern Bali, Indonesia.

Somsuda Rutnin (Thailand)
PhD 1988, The Prehistory of Western Udon Thani and Loei Provinces, Northeast Thailand.

Dianne Tillotson (Autralia)
MA 1989, The Graves of the Rice Ancestors: Changing Mortuary Patterning in Island Southeast Asia.
PhD 1994, Who Invented the Dayaks? Historical Case Studies in Art, Material Culture and Ethnic Identity from Borneo.

Ida Ayu Mediani (Indonesia)
MA 1989, Wet-Rice Cultivation in Bali: The Continuity of Technology and Social Organisation from the 9th Century to the Present.

Ipoi Datan (Malaysia)
MA 1990, Archaeological Excavations at Gua Sireh (Serian) and Lubang Angin (Gunung Mulu National Park), Sarawak, Malaysia.

Karina Arifin (Indonesia)
MA 1990, Social Aspects of Pottery Manufacture in Boera, Papua New Guinea.
PhD 2004, Early Human Occupation of the East Kalimantan Rainforest (the Upper Birang River Region, Berau).

Daud Tanudirjo (Indonesia)
MA 1991, Some Behavioural Aspects of the Bomo-Teleng Stone Adze Workshop Site in East Java (Indonesia).
PhD 2001, Islands in Between: Prehistory of the Northeastern Indonesian Archipelago.

Francis David Bulbeck (Autralia)
PhD 1992, A Tale of Two Kingdoms: The Historical Archaeology of Gowa and Tallok, South Sulawesi, Indonesia.

Widya Nayati (Indonesia)
MA 1994, The Archaeology of Trading Sites in the Indonesian Archipelago in the Sixteenth and Seventeenth Centuries: Possibilities and Limitations of the Evidence.

Mark Hudson (UK)

PhD 1995, Ruins of Identity: Ethnogenesis in the Japanese Islands, 400 B.C. to A.D. 1400.

Mahirta (Indonesia)

MA 1997, The Development of the Mare Pottery Tradition in the Northern Moluccas.

PhD 2005, Human Occupation on Rote and Sawu Island, Nusa Tenggara Timur, Indonesia.

Tracey Lie Dan Lu (China)

PhD 1998, The Transition from Foraging to Farming and the Origin of Agriculture in China.

Anggraeni (Indonesia)

MA 1999, The Introduction of Metallurgy into Indonesia: A Comparative Study with Special Reference to Gilimanuk.

PhD 2012, The Austronesian Migration Hypothesis as Seen from Prehistoric Settlements on the Karama River, Mamuju, West Sulawesi.

Djoko Nugroho Witjaksono (Indonesia)

MA1999, Study of Prehistoric Iron Objects in Western Indonesia in the Context of Contacts between India and the Indo-Malaysian Archipelago.

David G. Campbell (Australia)

MA 1999, Na Vu-ni-valu: 'The Root of War' in Fiji, Samoa & Tonga.

Judith Cameron (Australia)

PhD 2002, Textile Technology in the Prehistory of Southeast Asia.

Andrew Barram (Australia)

MA 2004, Dating 'Dvaravati'.

Mimi Savitri (Indonesia)

MA 2005, The Spatial Organisation of the Kedhaton in Kraton Surakarta, from the Reigns of Paku Buwana X to Paku Buwana XII (1883–2004).

Shawna Yang (Taiwan)

MA 2006, Fishing Sinkers in the Batanes Islands (Philippines) and Taiwan, and Further Relationships with East Asia.

Armand Salvador B Mijares (Philippines)

PhD 2006, Unravelling Prehistory: The Archaeology of North-Eastern Luzon.

Michael Tracey (Australia)

PhD 2007, Wooden Ships, Iron Men and Stalwart Ladies: The TSS Douglas Mawson Saga.

Hsiao-chun Hung (Taiwan)

PhD 2008, Migration and Cultural Interaction in Southern Coastal China, Taiwan and the Northern Philippines, 3000 BC to AD 100: The Early History of the Austronesian-Speaking Populations.

Po-yi Chiang (Taiwan)

MPhil 2008, Han Cultural and Political Influences in the Transformation of the Shizhaishan Cultural Complex.

PhD 2015, Pottery Production and Social Complexity on the Chengdu Plain, Sichuan, China, 2500 to 800 BC.

Mandy Mottram (Australia)

PhD 2010, Continuity versus Cultural Markers: Results of the Controlled Surface Collection of Tell Halula, North Syria.

Carmen Sarjeant (New Zealand)

PhD 2012, The Role of Potters at Neolithic An Sơn, Southern Vietnam.

Nicholas Skopal (Australia)

MA 2015, Explaining Harappan Fortifications (Pakistan and India).

Vida Pervaya Rusianti Kusmartono (Indonesia)

MA 2005, The Sandong of the Ngaju: Mortuary Variability in Southern Kalimantan.

Current PhD thesis title: Cave Archaeology and Rainforest Occupation in Central Kalimantan, Indonesia.

Chris Carter (Australia)

Current PhD thesis title: Prehistoric Maritime Societies in Northern Chile.

Apppendix

Figure 1.10 Peter Bellwood on a 1965 medieval excavation at Grafton Regis, Northamptonshire, England.

Source: Courtesy of Peter Bellwood.

Figure 1.11 Peter Bellwood in 1975 at Rano Raraku, Rapa Nui (Easter Island), Chile.
Source: Courtesy of Peter Bellwood.

Figure 1.12 Peter Bellwood in 1982 at Tingkayu, Sabah, Malaysia.
Source: Courtesy of Peter Bellwood.

Figure 1.13 Peter Bellwood in 1985 at the International Conference on Anthropological Studies of the Taiwan Area, National Taiwan University, Taipei (with K.C. Chang and Wen-hsun Sung).
Source: Courtesy of Peter Bellwood.

Figure 1.14 Peter Bellwood in 1986 at Londa village, Tana Toraja, Sulawesi, Indonesia.

Source: Courtesy of Peter Bellwood.

Figure 1.15 Peter Bellwood (seated right) at Nagsabaran, northern Luzon, Philippines, in 2009; Standing (left to right) Jonathan de Asis, Marc Oxenham and Eusebio Dizon; Seated (left to right) Mary Jane Louise A. Bolunia (Owis), Tony Peñarosa, Yi-lin Elaine Chen, Philip Piper, Hirofumi Matsumura, Juliet Meyer, Anna Willis, Hsiao-chun Hung and Peter Bellwood.

Source: Courtesy of Hsiao-chun Hung.

Figure 1.16 Peter Bellwood with Truman Simanjuntak in Peter's office at ANU in 2013.

Source: Courtesy of Truman Simanjuntak.

Figure 1.17 Siem Reap Cambodia IPPA (Indo-Pacific Prehistory Association) Congress Symposium 'Human dispersals and interactions in Asia and Oceania', 2014; front left to right: Emiri Miyama, Mariko Yamagata, Ian Glover, Peter Bellwood, Naruya Saitou; rear left to right: Ken-ichi Shinoda, Hirofumi Matsumura, Hsiao-chun Hung, Michiko Intoh, Sofwan Noerwidi.

Source: Courtesy of Hirofumi Matsumura.

2

Initial Movements of Modern Humans in East Eurasia

Naruya Saitou, Timothy A. Jinam, Hideaki Kanzawa-Kiriyama and Katsushi Tokunaga

This contribution discusses three topics touching on the initial movements of modern humans in East Eurasia using genetic data:

1. *The emergence of modern humans including the establishment of the 'Sahulian' inhabitants of the Pleistocene continent of Australia and adjacent islands.*
2. *Negritos as remnants of the initial dispersal to the Southeast Asian region.*
3. *The descendants of ancient human migration to the Japanese Archipelago.*

From the emergence of modern humans to the establishment of Sahulians

Anatomically modern humans (AMH) are now distributed all over the inhabited planet, and are genetically divided into six major groups: African, West Eurasian, East Eurasian, Sahulian, Northern American, and Southern American (Saitou 1995). It has now been established that AMH originated in Sub-Saharan Africa. Nei and Roychoudhury (1974) estimated the divergence times of three human populations (African, East Eurasian, and West Eurasian) as *ca*. 120,000 BP for the African and Eurasian split and *ca*. 55,000 BP for the East Eurasian–West Eurasian divergence. Later, Nei and Ota (1991) obtained essentially the same divergence time estimates from the allele frequency data of 181 loci.

More recently, Gronau et al. (2011) estimated somewhat different divergence times from a comparison of six personal genomes; 38,000–64,000 BP years for African and Eurasian divergence, and 31,000–40,000 BP for West Eurasian and East Eurasian divergence. Although the rooted tree topology is the same, the divergence time estimates between Africans and non-Africans based on classic markers and genome data are rather different. Gronau et al. (2011) also estimated the divergence time of San (bushman) and Yoruba in Nigeria as *ca*. 150,000 BP when the human–chimpanzee divergence was assumed as 7.6 Mya, and migration between these two populations after their divergence was surmised. If this estimate of human–chimpanzee divergence is a close approximation then the emergence of modern humans would also date to at least *ca*. 150,000 BP.

Human movements during the 'Out-of-Africa' dispersal possibly started via coastal routes (e.g. Macaulay et al. 2005). If we connect the coastlines in present-day Tanzania and the northern reaches of Australia, the total length across land is less than 40,000 km. If AMH migrated along this coastal route using raft-like boats, they could have arrived at present-day Australia within 110 years, assuming an average forward movement of 1 km per day. If they encountered any reason to halt progressive movement and abandon the fringes of occupied territory, they could have simply backtracked to their homeland by following the same coastline. The adventurous colonists who continued to move south and east would have passed down the Thai-Malay Peninsula and overland across 'Sundaland' as far as Borneo and Bali, and then traversed the islands of eastern Indonesia before eventually settling in Sahul. Their descendants became Australian Aborigines and Melanesians (including some of the present-day inhabitants of New Guinea, the islands of the Bismarck and Solomon archipelagos, Australia and Tasmania).

Negritos as remnants of secondary dispersal within the Indo-Pacific Ocean area

Until the Holocene (starting *ca*. 11,000 BP), the present-day islands of Sumatra, Java and Borneo were joined together with the Asian mainland, forming a landmass known as Sundaland (Bellwood and Glover 2004). Sundaland was separated from Sahulland by multiple islands referred to as Wallacea. Several human populations with characteristic morphological features in the Andaman Islands, the Philippines, and Peninsular Malaysia are collectively known as 'Negritos'. These Negritos may be remnants of early AMH dispersals within Island Southeast Asia postdating the initial colonisation of Sahulland.

Omoto and his collaborators studied Philippine Negritos using classic genetic polymorphism markers such as blood groups, red cell enzymes, and serum proteins (Omoto et al. 1978; Omoto 1981, 1985). A phylogenetic tree shown in Omoto (1981) suggests that the Philippine Negritos diversified after the Sahulians split off from Eurasians but before the majority of East Eurasian lineages diversified. Omoto (1985) also demonstrated that the Mamanwa, a Negrito population found on Mindanao Island, appear to be quite different from other Negrito groups in the Philippines. We are now conducting genome-wide SNP data analysis of these Philippine Negritos typed by one of us (Katsushi Tokunaga) as well as those for Malaysian and Andamanese Negritos, and have found some shared components among these populations (Jinam et al. 2013).

Jinam et al. (2012) conducted a genetic analysis of Southeast Asian populations using SNP data from PASNP (HUGO Pan-Asian Consortium 2009) and HGDP-CEPH panel database (www.cephb.fr/), together with newly generated complete mitochondrial DNA (mtDNA) sequences in four indigenous Malaysian groups, and compared them with other populations. These include three Austronesian groups (Temuan, Seletar, and Bidayuh) and a Negrito group (Jahai). Negritos in the Thai-Malay Peninsula currently speak Austro-Asiatic languages, but this is attributed to 'language switch' following the mid-Holocene incursion of early Austro-Asiatic populations into the Peninsula. Complete mtDNA sequences were newly determined from 86 individuals (24 Jahai, 18 Temuan, 21 Seletar and 23 Bidayuh). These sequence data are available from the DDBJ/EBA/GenBank International Nucleotide Sequence Databases accession nos AP012346–AP012431. All individuals were assigned to specific haplogroups belonging to M and N macro-haplogroups by following the nomenclature in these databases (www.phylotree.org).

Principal Component Analysis (PCA) was performed using haplogroup frequencies from this study and from selected populations available in the literature. The PCA plot shown in Figure 2 of Jinam et al. (2012) shows that Negrito populations (Jahai, Kensiu, Batek and Mendriq) and one non-Negrito population in the Thai-Malay Peninsula (Temuan) are clearly separated from other Southeast Asian populations in terms of their PC1 coordinates. Interestingly, the population closest to this 'Peninsula Negrito' cluster is Papuan. This suggests some level of shared ancestry between Peninsula Negritos and Papuans. Five other (non-Papuan) populations, which are close to the 'Peninsula Negrito' cluster, are non-Negrito populations in the Thai-Malay Peninsula and the Philippine Negrito Mamanwa. This result also suggests some level of shared ancestry between Peninsula and Philippine Negrito populations.

Phylogenetic trees of M and N mtDNA macro-haplogroups are shown in Figures 3A and 3B of Jinam et al. (2012), and the coalescence time estimates of selected haplogroups based on mtDNA coding-region sequences are shown in Table 3 of Jinam et al. (2012). These results show that the mtDNA lineages of all three populations living in the Thai-Malay Peninsula coalesce with mtDNA sequences found from other geographical areas, and their coalescence time estimates are older than 10,000 years ago.

Jinam et al.'s (2012) study included the first description of mtDNA diversity in four indigenous Thai-Malay Peninsula populations using complete sequence data from all sampled individuals. This is in contrast to most studies in which complete mtDNA sequencing was performed only on selected haplotypes based initially on control region diversity. Such biased sampling can lead to exaggerated results in some analyses as demonstrated by Gunnarsdottir et al. (2011).

Jinam et al. (2012) also analysed genome-wide (~50,000 SNP) data for 17 human populations that are mainly located in Southeast Asia. Those data were retrieved from the Pan-Asian SNP database (www4a.biotec.or.th/PASNP) based on the paper by HUGO Pan-Asian SNP Consortium (2009). PC1 of the PCA plot shown in Figure 4A of Jinam et al. (2012) clearly separates Melanesian from the other populations. The Alorese in east Indonesia are closest to Melanesian, suggesting some gene flow between them if we consider their geographical propinquity. Philippine Negritos lie between Alorese and other populations, and this suggests some degree of shared common ancestry. Thai-Malay Peninsula Negritos are quite different from all other populations in terms of PC2 coordinates. When these four outlier populations (Melanesians, Alorese, Philippine Negritos, and Peninsula Negritos) are eliminated from comparison, the remaining 13 populations are now well scattered in a circular structure as shown in Figure 4B of Jinam et al. (2012). The Bidayuh in Borneo and the Temuan in the Thai-Malay Peninsula both show a 'comet-like' pattern (named by Jinam et al. 2012), which suggests recent admixture with surrounding populations. The locations of the other 11 populations on this PCA plot are as follows (counter-clockwise): Indigenous Taiwanese, Filipino, Mentawai, Sulawesi, Sumatran, Malay, Dayak, Javanese, Cambodian, Thai, and South Chinese. This constellation of populations is more or less consistent with the 'Out-of-Taiwan' model for the origins of people who speak Austronesian languages (Bellwood 2005, 2007).

A phylogenetic network of 17 human populations mainly from Southeast Asia, which was drawn by using Neighbor-Net (Bryant and Moulton 2004), is shown in Figure 2.1 (modified from Figure 5B of Jinam et al. 2012). Consistent with the PCA plot (Figure 4A of Jinam et al. 2012), Melanesians fall well apart from all other populations, although Alorese are closest to Melanesians because they are separated from the other 15 populations at split 'a'. Interestingly, split 'b' links Melanesians and Philippine Negritos. Splits 'a' and 'b' are incompatible with each other, and a parallelogram is formed to represent the reticulated structure. These splits suggest different types of shared ancestry or outcomes of recent Alorese-Melanesian admixture and Philippine Negrito-Melanesian admixture. Splits 'c' and 'd' are also incompatible, as the former indicates genetic similarity between the Temuan and Peninsula Negritos, while the latter clusters Peninsula Negritos, Philippine Negritos, Alorese, and Melanesians. The dichotomy of populations suggested by split 'd' may correspond to two major waves of human dispersals to Southeast Asia and Oceania.

The paper by Jinam et al. (2013), which was included in the special *Human Biology* issue on Negritos (Endicott 2013), analysed admixture patterns between two Peninsula Negrito groups (the Jahai and Kensiu) and surrounding populations. It found traces of recent admixture in both Negrito populations, particularly the Jahai. It also identified significantly differentiated non-synonymous SNPs and haplotype blocks related to intracellular transport, metabolic processes, and detection of stimulus. These results highlight the different levels of admixture experienced by the two Malaysian Negrito populations.

If we examine external edge lengths for each population in Figure 2.1, most of the populations with large population size have short lengths, such as Southern Chinese, Thai, Javanese, Malays and Filipinos. In contrast, populations with small population sizes tend to have long exterior edge length, such as Aboriginal Taiwanese, Mentawai in Sumatra, Dayak and Bidayuh in Borneo, Temuan in Malay Peninsula, and Peninsula and Philippine Negritos. A possible exception is Cambodians; although they have a large population size, their exterior edge length is quite long. This suggests a unique history of the Cambodian population. It should also be noted that populations who experienced admixture in the past, such as the Japanese of Japan's central islands, also tend to have short external edge lengths, as indicated by the Japanese Archipelago Human Population Genetics Consortium (2012).

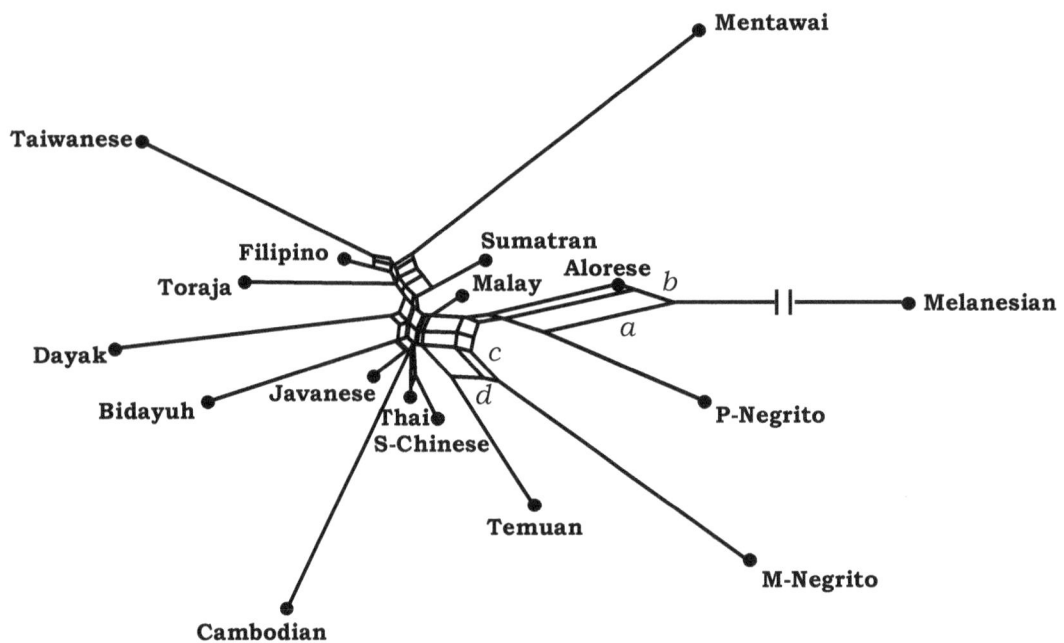

Figure 2.1 A phylogenetic network of 17 human populations based on genome-wide SNP data.
Source: Modified from Jinam et al. 2012.

Descendants of ancient human migrants to the Japanese Archipelago

After modern humans initially migrated into Sundaland and then Sahulland, their movements northward reached the Japanese Archipelago, which has been populated for more than 40 Kya (Imamura 1996). The Jomon people were Neolithic hunter-gatherers who inhabited the Japanese Archipelago from *ca.* 16,000 BP to 3000 BP (Harunari and Imamura 2004). The Jomon culture is defined by the presence of cord-marked ('jomon' in Japanese) pottery, and ranged geographically from Hokkaido to the Okinawa islands, stretching over 4,000 km from north to south. The archipelago was essentially disconnected from continental East Eurasia, by the end of the last glacial period, from *ca.* 12,000 BP. The Jomon people were probably genetically isolated from continental East Eurasians after that time. Craniofacial data suggests that the ancestors of the Jomon came from somewhere in Southeast Asia (Hanihara 1991), while classic genetic marker data (Omoto and Saitou 1997) and mtDNA sequence data (Adachi et al. 2011) suggest a northern origin. Interestingly, the so-called Jomon mtDNA haplotypes (M7a and N9b) are rarely observed in other modern East Eurasians (Adachi et al. 2011). Therefore, the origins of the Jomon people and their genetic relationship with other modern humans are still unclear.

Kanzawa-Kiriyama et al. (2013) determined the mtDNA haplotypes of four individuals excavated from the Sanganji shell mound in Fukushima, Tohoku district, Japan, dating to the late and final Jomon Period, between 4000–2500 BP. The haplogroup frequencies were 50 per cent for N9b and 50 per cent for M7a2. Haplogroup N9b had previously been observed at high frequencies in other Tohoku Jomon fossils and Hokkaido Jomon fossils, as well as the Okhotsk and Ainu peoples, whereas its frequency is reported to be low in Kanto Jomon fossils and the modern Japanese of the central islands. Sub-haplogroup M7a2 has previously been reported in Hokkaido Jomon fossils, and the Okhotsk and modern Udegey peoples, but not amongst Kanto Jomon fossils, or the Ainu or Ryukyu peoples.

Kanzawa-Kiriyama et al. (2013) also compared mtDNA haplogroup frequencies of Jomon fossils from three areas (Tohoku, Hokkaido, and Kanto) and 15 present-day East Asians. The phylogenetic network using Neighbor-Net (Bryant and Moulton 2004) based on Fst values is shown in Figure 2.2 (from Figure 4 of Kanzawa-Kiriyama et al. 2013). Interestingly, the Tohoku and Hokkaido Jomon populations appear to be closely related, while the Kanto Jomons are obviously distinct. The Udegey of Southern Siberia, who live near the Japan Sea, are relatively closer to Tohoku and Hokkaido Jomon. The reticulation suggests that the Udegey represent an admixture of southern Siberian populations and the northern Jomon people.

It should be noted that mtDNA is a single locus, and its genetic information is very limited even if its complete genomic sequence is obtained. We have therefore proceeded to determine nuclear DNA sequences that are much larger than mtDNA. The results (Kanzawa-Kiriyama et al. 2017) clearly indicate that the present-day Japanese have inherited the DNA of Jomon people, as best represented by the Ainu who are direct descendants of the Jomon. This confirms Hanihara's (1991) dual structure model and the conclusion of Japanese Archipelago Human Population Genetics Consortium (2012).

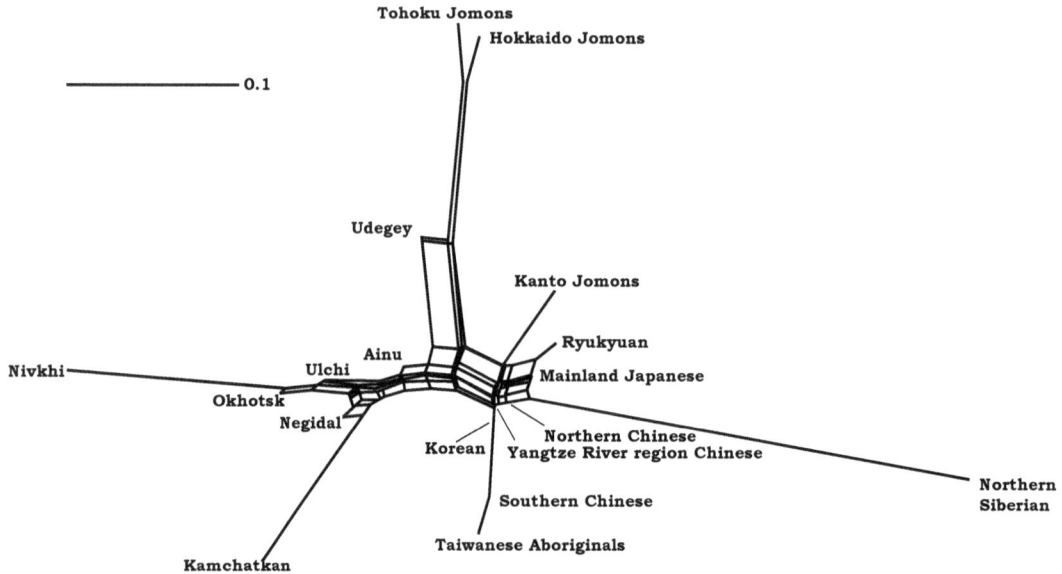

Figure 2.2 A phylogenetic network of three ancient Jomon populations and 15 present-day populations based on mtDNA haplotype frequencies. Scale bar represents the genetic distance between populations based on mitochondrial DNA haplotype frequencies.

Source: From Kanzawa-Kiriyama et al. 2013; published with the permission of the Anthropological Society of Nippon.

Acknowledgements

This study is supported by a SOKENDAI strategic research grant given to Naruya Saitou and in part by a Grant-in-Aid in 2011–2015 (no. 23247040) and 16H02527 (P.I. of both grants are Hirobumi Matsumura) from the Japan Society for the Promotion of Science.

Authors are grateful to Dr Hirofumi Matsumura who gave us the opportunity to contribute this paper to this book.

References

Adachi, N., K.-i Shinoda, K. Umetsu, T. Kitano, H. Matsumura, R. Fujiyama, J. Sawada and M. Tanaka. 2011. Mitochondrial DNA analysis of Hokkaido Jomon skeletons: remnants of archaic maternal lineages at the southwestern edge of former Beringia. *American Journal of Physical Anthropology* 146: 346–360.

Bellwood, P.S. 2005. *First Farmers: The Origins of Agricultural Societies*. Malden, MA: Blackwell.

———. 2007. *Prehistory of the Indo-Malaysian Archipelago*. 3rd edition. Canberra: ANU E Press.

Bellwood, P. and I. Glover. 2004. Southeast Asia: Foundations for an Archaeological History. In I. Glover and P. Bellwood (eds), *Southeast Asia: from Prehistory to History*, pp. 4–20. Oxford, UK: Routledge.

Bryant, D. and V. Moulton. 2004. Neighbor-net: an agglomerative method for the construction of phylogenetic networks. *Molecular Biology and Evolution* 21: 255–265. doi.org/10.1093/molbev/msh018.

DDBJ/EBA/GenBank International Nucleotide Sequence Databases www.phylotree.org.

Endicott, P. (ed.). 2013. Special issue on revisiting the 'Negrito' Hypothesis. *Human Biology* vol. 85, issues 1–3.

Foundation Jean Dausset, Le panel HGDP-CEPH (Human Genome Diversity Panel-Centre d'Etude du Polymorphisme Humain), www.cephb.fr/.

Gronau, I., M.J. Hubisz, B. Gulko, C.G. Danko and A. Siepel. 2011. Bayesian inference of ancient human demography from individual genome sequences. *Nature Genetics* 43: 1031–1035. doi. org/10.1038/ng.937.

Gunnarsdottir, E.D., M. Li, M. Bauchet, K. Finstermeier and M. Stoneking. 2011. High throughput sequencing of complete human mtDNA genomes from the Philippines. *Genome Research* 21: 1–11. doi.org/10.1101/gr.107615.110.

Hanihara, K.1991. Dual structure model for the population history of the Japanese. *Japan Review* 2: 1–33.

Harunari, H. and M. Imamura (eds). 2004. *Real Age of Yayoi Period.* Tokyo: Gakusei Sha (in Japanese).

HUGO Pan-Asian SNP Consortium. 2009. Mapping human genetic diversity in Asia. *Science* 326: 1541–1545. doi.org/10.1126/science.1177074.

Imamura, K. 1996. *Prehistoric Japan: New Perspectives on Insular East Asia.* Honolulu: University of Hawaii Press.

Japanese Archipelago Human Population Genetics Consortium (Consortium members: Jinam, T., N. Nishida, M. Hirai, S. Kawamura, H. Oota, K. Umetsu, R. Kimura, J. Ohashi, A. Tajima, T. Yamamoto, H. Tanabe, S. Mano, Y. Suto, T. Kaname, K. Naritomi, K. Yanagi, N. Niikawa, K. Omoto, K. Tokunaga and N. Saitou). 2012. The history of human populations in the Japanese Archipelago inferred from genome-wide SNP data with a special reference to the Ainu and the Ryukyuan populations. *Journal of Human Genetics* 57: 787–795. doi.org/10.1038/jhg.2012.114.

Jinam, T.A., L.-C. Hong, M.A. Phipps, M. Stoneking, M. Ameen, J. Edo, Pan-Asian SNP Consortium, and N. Saitou. 2012. Evolutionary history of continental South East Asians: 'early train' hypothesis based on genetic analysis of mitochondrial and autosomal DNA data. *Molecular Biology and Evolution* 29: 3513–3527. doi.org/10.1093/molbev/mss169.

Jinam, T.A., M.A. Phipps and N. Saitou. 2013. Admixture patterns and genetic differentiation in Negrito groups from West Malaysia estimated from genome-wide SNP data. *Human Biology* 85(1): Article 8. doi.org/10.3378/027.085.0308.

Kanazawa-Kiriyama H., A. Soso, G. Susa and N. Saitou. 2013. Ancient mitochondrial DNA sequences of Jomon teeth samples from Sanganji, Tohoku district, Japan. *Anthropological Science* 121: 89–103. doi.org/10.1537/ase.121113.

Kanzawa-Kiriyama H., K. Kryukov, T.A. Jinam, K. Hosomichi, A. Saso, G. Suwa, S. Ueda, M. Yoneda, A. Tajima, K. Shinoda, I. Inoue and N. Saitou. 2017. A partial nuclear genome of the Jomons who lived 3,000 years ago in Fukushima, Japan. *Journal of Human Genetics* 62(2): 213–221. doi. org/10.1038/jhg.2016.110.

Macaulay, V., C. Hill, A. Achilli, C. Rengo, D. Clarke, W. Meehan, J. Blackburn, O. Semino, R. Scozzari, F. Cruciani, A. Taha, N.K. Shaari, J.M. Raja, P. Ismail, Z. Zainuddin, W. Goodwin, D. Bulbeck, H.J. Bandelt, S. Oppenheimer, A. Torroni and M. Richards. 2005. Single, rapid coastal settlement of Asia revealed by analysis of complete mitochondrial genomes. *Science* 308: 1034–1036. doi.org/10.1126/science.1109792.

Nei, M. and A. Roychoudhury. 1974. Genetic variation within and between the three major races of man, Caucasoids, Negroids, and Mongoloids. *American Journal of Human Genetics* 26: 421–443. doi. org/10.1007/978-4-431-68302-5_26.

Nei, M. and T. Ota. 1991. Evolutionary relationships of human populations at the molecular level. In S. Osawa and T. Honjo (eds), *Evolution of life*, pp. 415–428. New York: Springer-Verlag.

Omoto, K. 1981. The genetic origins of the Philippine Negritos. *Current Anthropology* 22: 421–422. doi. org/10.1086/202696.

——. 1985. The Negritos: genetic origins and microevolution. In R. Kirk and E. Szathmary (eds), *Out of Asia: Peopling the Americas and the Pacific*, pp. 123–131. Canberra: The Journal of Pacific History.

Omoto, K. and N. Saitou. 1997. Genetic origins of the Japanese: A partial support for the 'dual structure hypothesis'. *American Journal of Physical Anthropology* 102: 437–446. doi.org/10.1002/(SICI)1096-8644(199704)102:4<437::AID-AJPA1>3.0.CO;2-P.

Omoto, K., S. Misawa, J.S. Sumpaico, P. M. Medado and H. Ogonuki. 1978. Population genetic studies of the Philippine Negritos. I. A pilot survey of red cell enzyme and serum protein groups. *American Journal of Human Genetics* 30: 190–201.

Saitou, N. 1995. A genetic affinity analysis of human populations. *Human Evolution* 10: 17–33. doi. org/10.1007/BF02437511.

van Oven, M., M. Kayser. 2009. Updated comprehensive phylogenetic tree of global human mitochondrial DNA variation. *Hum Mutat* 30(2): E386-E394, www.phylotree.org. doi.org/10.1002/humu.20921.

3

Ancient DNA Analysis of Palaeolithic Ryukyu Islanders

Ken-ichi Shinoda and Noboru Adachi

Ishigaki Island is one of the westernmost islands in Japan. Due to its geographical location, it is considered to have played a significant role in the migration route from Southern Asia to the Japanese archipelagos. Recently, human remains were excavated from Shiraho-Saonetabaru Cave, constituting the first physical evidence of human occupation on Ishigaki Island. In order to investigate the genetic makeup of the ancient Ishigaki people and to assess their genetic relationship with other Asian populations at a molecular level, we analysed the single nucleotide polymorphisms of the coding region of mtDNA that defines the haplogroups of these individuals. Because of the poor quality of the DNA extracted from the ancient material, it was not possible to analyse all samples. Among the 10 samples considered in this study, ancient DNA data was successfully extracted from five individuals. MtDNA haplogroups show geographic specificity within Asia; the existence of haplogroup B4e and M7a in this population hints at their linkage with Southeast Asia and the Late Pleistocene Ryukyu Islands.

Introduction

Steady progress in DNA analytical techniques since the late twentieth century has revolutionised the field of physical anthropology. This has meant that instead of relying solely on morphometrical studies of the human skeleton it has been possible to use DNA to analyse genetic variations in the human gene and determine with greater resolution the origins and migration routes of anatomically modern human populations. Conclusions drawn from DNA research have prompted the review of existing views and inspired new theories in human origins research.

While most of the research regarding local population events is based on modern DNA analysis, straightforward retrogressive projection of modern genetic composition and distribution has its inherent limitations. Currently, ancient DNA analysis is the next logical step after obtaining excavated remains from the regional population. Advances in molecular biology techniques in the last 20 years have allowed for the analysis of DNA extracted from ancient bone samples, making it possible to obtain information on lineage, with significantly higher probabilities of accuracy (e.g. Shinoda and Kanai 1999; Maca-Mayer et al. 2005; Melchior et al. 2008).

DNA analysis of ancient materials currently focuses on mitochondrial DNA (mtDNA) owing to its special characteristics such as small size, matrilineal inheritance, high copy number, and fast mutation rate. During the course of human migration across the world, mutations created new types of mtDNA. Further mutation of these types increased the variation. The resultant types are grouped under a single lineage, namely, 'haplogroup'. Relationships within and between haplogroups provide important clues to help reconstruct the history of human migration (e.g. Kivisild et al. 2002). Currently, DNA-based studies determine the origin of a given population through comparisons of haplogroup compositions with that of neighbouring populations. This approach has led to more detailed data collection, which, in turn, has yielded more sophisticated scenarios regarding human migration.

This approach is restricted not only because of its matrilineal succession, but also by poor preservation, small sample size, and contamination in the case of ancient samples. Further, it depends on successful extraction and analysis of minute quantities of mtDNA. In spite of these difficulties, mtDNA analysis of ancient bones and teeth samples recovered by regionally based archaeological projects offers an effective means of understanding local and/or regional population history and dynamics in Japan (e.g. Adachi et al. 2011).

The genesis of the modern Japanese population is an area of intense study in anthropology, archaeology, and genetics in East Asia. In this context, because of its geographical location, Ishigaki Island is thought to have played a significant role in the migration route from Taiwan and Southeast Asia to the Ryukyu and Japanese archipelagos. According to archaeological evidence, the Sakishima area (Figure 3.1), consisting of the Miyako and Yaeyama island groups, including Isigaki Island, formed a different cultural area from the main island of Okinawa until the twelfth century AD. There was no influence from the mainland of Japan (Jomon and Yayoi cultures), and from archaeological remains, the Sakishima area seems to have a lot in common with the southeastern regions of Asia. Perhaps the sea lying between the main islands of Okinawa and Sakishima was the boundary of the expansion of Japanese culture to the south (Takamiya 2005) and possibly Austronesian expansion from Taiwan towards the north (see Hudson, Chapter 10, this volume).

Due to its complex history, it is not surprising that the Ryukyu Islands have often attracted the interest of population geneticists (e.g. Jinam et al. 2012). Nevertheless, very little is known about the genetic history of their human population. To learn more about the genetic characteristics of the first inhabitants of this westernmost island of Japan, we analysed mtDNA from human remains that were excavated from an archaeological site belonging to the Late Paleolithic period.

Materials and methods

Human skeletal remains from the archaeological site of Shiraho-Saonetabaru Cave on the east coast of Ishigaki Island were analysed for this project (Figure 3.1). As a part of an airport construction project, Shiraho-Saonetabaru Cave was excavated between 2010 and 2013. In total, 10 individuals were sampled for DNA. Eight were directly radiometrically dated using ^{14}C to between 27,000–4000 BP (Table 3.1). For two others the ages were extrapolated from their stratigraphic and chronological relationships with known age samples. The dating indicates that the human remains excavated from Siraho-Saonetabaru Cave belong to the Late Pleistocene to early modern periods (Yoneda 2014). These are the oldest directly radiocarbon dated human skeletal remains from Japan, and these bones constitute the first physical evidence of human occupation on the Ishigaki Island in the Late Pleistocene period.

A study has shown that tooth enamel forms a natural barrier to exogenous DNA contamination – teeth appear to lack most of the inhibitors that prevent the enzymatic amplification of ancient DNA (Woodward et al. 1994). Therefore, tooth samples from the collagen-bone-dated skeletons were the first choice in the present study. When tooth samples were not available, bone samples from other skeletal fragments were used. Results of dating indicated that all the samples were not related to each other.

When ancient DNA is analysed, it is necessary to exclude false-positive results caused by contamination with contemporary DNA (Sampietro et al. 2006). In order to prevent contamination during excavation, the remains were handled using gloves and were not touched with bare hands. Bone samples were wrapped in aluminium foil and stored in a refrigerator at 4°C until DNA extraction. Standard precautions were practised to avoid contamination, such as separation of pre- and post-polymerase chain reaction (PCR) experimental setups, use of disposable laboratory gear and filter-plugged pipette tips, treatment with DNA contamination removal solution (DNA Away; Molecular Bio Products, San Diego, CA, USA), ultraviolet (UV) irradiation of equipment and benches, and negative extraction and PCR controls (Shinoda et al. 2006).

DNA was extracted from the skeletal samples, according to previously published protocols (Adachi et al. 2009). The tooth and bone samples were dipped in DNA contamination removal solution for 15 min, rinsed with DNase-/RNase-free distilled water, and allowed to air-dry. The outer surface of the samples was removed using a dental drill, and the samples were again rinsed with DNase-/RNase-free distilled water and allowed to air-dry under UV irradiation. Then the tooth samples were encased in silicone rubber and the dentin around the *cavitas dentis* and the dental pulp was powdered and extracted through the cut plane of the root tip, as described by Gilbert et al. (2003). The bone samples were pulverised using a mill (Multi-beads shocker; Yasui Kikai, Osaka, Japan).

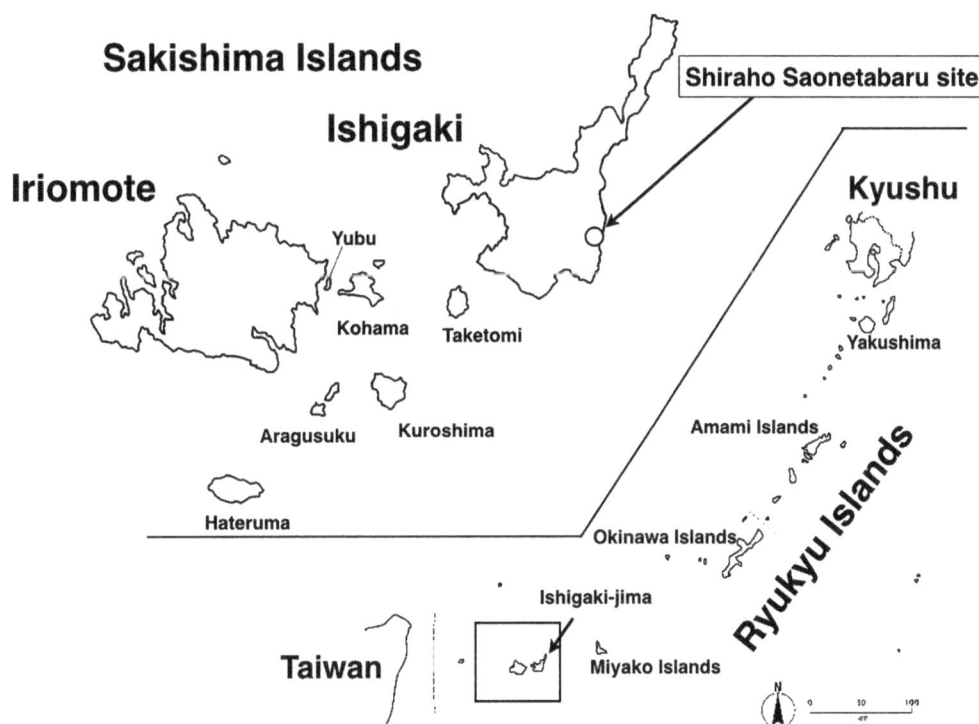

Figure 3.1 The geographic distribution of the islands in the Ryukyu Archipelago, and the location of Shiraho-Saonetabaru on Ishigaki Island.

Source: Ken-ichi Shinoda.

Table 3.1 Radiocarbon dates on collagen and dentine from samples of the
Shiraho-Saonetabaru skeletons.

Sample No.	Code	Skeletal Element	C14 date (uncalibrated) BP	C14 datenn (calibrated) BP**	Laboratory codes
1	SRH 12	Right Humerus	20160±108	24558-23997 (95.4%)	MTC-14189
2	SRH 13	Rib	20761±163	25521-24558 (95.4%)	MTC-14196
3	SRH 15	Rib	24556±205	29097-28142 (95.4%)	MTC-14197
4	SRH 94	Right Humerus	16170±60	19767-19341 (95.4%)	PLD-19660
5	SRH 166	Femur	19723±61	24040-23575 (95.4%)	PLD-19658
6	SRH 181	Isolated teeth	16573±51	20238-19842 (95.4%)	PLD-19692
7	SRH 188	Left Humerus	3970±30	4574-4452 (95.4%)	PLD-19659
8	SRH 214	Left Femur	18071±62	22196-21711 (95.4%)	PLD-19657
9	SRH 242	Left Fibula	*20000		
10	SRH 292	Femur	*9000–16000		

* The age of these two samples were assumed through association with bones from the same layers that were chronometrically C14 dated.

**The dates calibrated using OxCal 4.2, IntCal 13.

Source: Ken-ichi Shinoda.

The powdered samples (approximately 0.4 g) were decalcified with 10 ml of 0.5 M EDTA (pH 8.0) at 20°C for three days and lysed in 500 µ l of Fast Lyse (Genetic ID, Fairfield, IA) with 30 µ l of 20 mg/ml Proteinase K at 60°C for 4 h. DNA was extracted from the lysate using a FastDNA™ Extraction kit (Genetic ID), as per the manual. Finally, 100 µ l of DNA extract was obtained from each sample.

Segments of hypervariable regions of mtDNA (HVRs; nucleotide positions 16121–16238, HVR1-1; 16209–16291, HVR1-2; and 160289–16366; HVR1-3) of mtDNA, as per the revised Cambridge reference sequence (Andrews et al. 1999), were sequenced in all samples. Aliquots (2 µ l) of the extracts were used as templates for PCR. Amplifications were carried out in a reaction mixture (total volume, 15 µ l) containing 1 unit of Taq DNA polymerase (HotStarTaqTM DNA polymerase; Qiagen, Germany), 0.1 M of each primer, and 100 mM of deoxyribonucleoside triphosphates in 1×PCR buffer provided by the manufacturer. The PCR conditions were as follows: incubation at 95°C for 15 min; followed by 40 cycles of heat treatment at 94°C for 20 s; 50–56°C for 20 s, and 72°C for 15 s; and final extension at 72°C for 1 min.

The PCR products were separated by agarose gel electrophoresis on a 1.5 per cent gel and were recovered by using a QIAEX II agarose gel extraction kit (Qiagen, Germany). Aliquots of the samples were prepared for sequencing on a BigDye cycle sequencing kit Ver.3.1 (Life Technologies, Foster City, CA, USA), which was performed using forward and reverse primers. The primers used in PCR amplification were also used in the sequencing reaction. Sequencing was performed in both directions to enable identification of polymorphisms or ambiguous bases by using a single primer. The sequencing reactions were performed on a DNA Sequencer (ABI model 3130) equipped with SeqEd software (ABI).

To confidently assign mtDNA samples to relevant haplogroups, 24 haplogroup-diagnostic single nucleotide polymorphisms (SNPs), including a 9 bp repeat variation in the non-coding cytochrome oxidase II/tRNALys intergenic region, that defines major haplogroups found in Japanese and East Asian populations, were analysed by multiplex APLP (Umetsu et al. 2005). SNPs that defined major haplogroups were detected by using suspension array technology (Luminex 100) at the laboratory of G&G Science, Fukushima. The methodology for genotyping and primer sequences has been described in detail elsewhere (Itoh et al. 2005; Shinoda et al. 2012). Moreover, 26 haplogroup-diagnostic SNPs and a 9 bp repeat variation were analysed by another multiplex APLP, as described previously (Adachi et al. 2009).

Results and discussion

Table 3.2 shows the results of PCR amplification and genotyping of polymorphisms. Both negative extraction and PCR controls consistently showed negative results throughout the study. Because of the poor quality of the mtDNA extracted from the ancient material, it was not possible to amplify all samples. Five samples failed to amplify any portion of mtDNA, and no DNA was recovered. Using multiplex single nucleotide polymorphism (SNP) typing, five of the 10 samples were successfully typed to the smallest named haplogroup they belonged to (Figures 3.2 and 3.3). Thus, three samples were assigned to haplogroup M7a and the other samples to haplogroups B4 and R. In the case where D-loop sequence was revealed, we classified them further based on the mutations observed in these regions. Therefore, we assigned the B4 samples to haplogroup B4e. More detailed data has been previously described by Shinoda and Adachi (2014). Owing to the small sample size, it was difficult to verify genetic characteristics by statistical methods, although the existence of these haplogroups is noteworthy.

Table 3.2 Result of the analysis. N.D. denotes 'not determined'.

No.	Sample	Sequence 16209-16366 (16000+)	SNP PCR-Luminex	APLP analysis	Haplogroup
1	No. 12	217 223 291	B4	N.D.	B4e
2	No. 13	311	R	N.D.	R
3	No. 15	N.D.	N.D.	N.D.	N.D.
4	No. 94	N.D.	N.D.	N.D.	N.D.
5	No. 166	N.D.	N.D.	N.D.	N.D.
6	No. 181	N.D.	N.D.	N.D.	N.D.
7	No. 188	N.D.	N.D.	M7a	M7a
8	No. 214	N.D.	N.D.	N.D.	N.D.
9	No. 242	N.D.	N.D.	M7a	M7a
10	No. 292	N.D.	N.D.	M7a	M7a

Source: Ken-ichi Shinoda.

A: Examination of M7a

B: Examination of M7a1

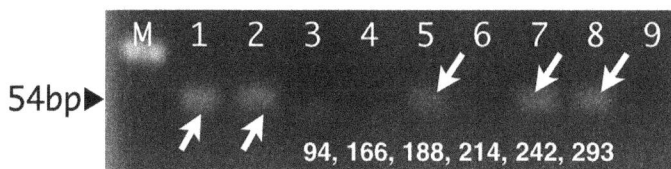

Figure 3.2 Results of PCR-luminex analysis. Number of each lane shows the sample number. Lane 1 and 2 are positive controls and lane 9 is negative control.

A: 63 base pair amplified products indicates haplogroup M7a.
B: 54 base pair products indicates haplogroup M7a1.
M: size marker.
Source: Ken-ichi Shinoda.

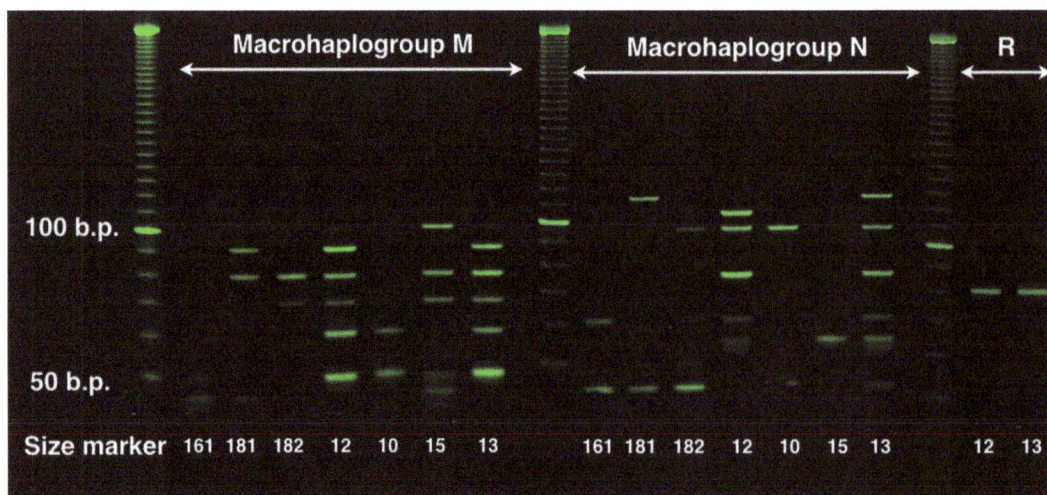

Figure 3.3 Results of amplified product length polymorphism (APLP) analysis. Number of each lane shows the sample number.

Source: Ken-ichi Shinoda.

Though small in number, the distribution of mtDNA haplogroups in this period provides insights into regional population history. Haplogroups B4 and R are the most prevalent in Southeast Asia, especially in the coastal region (Trejaut et al. 2005), indicating that this haplogroup may have been introduced to Japan from Southeast Asia. Interestingly, haplogroup B was also found in ancient Chinese samples (Fu et al. 2012). It seems that the ancestral population of coastal East Asia and Island Southeast Asia was enriched by the founder lineages of haplogroup B4, and the Ryukyu Islands may be one of the northernmost regions where this population arrived in the Palaeolithic period. This finding indicates that the southeast influx into the ancient Ryukyu population affected their genetic makeup and that the ancestors of the Aboriginal Taiwanese or Asian coastal region populations might be the main source of this haplogroup in the Ryukyu Islands.

The geographic specificity of haplogroup M7a is the most intriguing result of this study. Its ancestral haplogroup M7, although a characteristic of East Asian populations, was not found in the northeast region of the continent (Torroni et al. 1993; Derenko et al. 2007). Haplogroup M7a is absent or scarce in the East and Southeast Asian populations outside Japan. Moreover, M7a is one of the prevailing haplogroups not only among modern Japanese, including Honshu, Okinawa islanders, and Ainu populations (Tanaka et al. 2004), but also in the Jomon population (Adachi et al. 2011). The frequency of haplogroup M7a among modern Japanese is highest in the Okinawa islanders (23.3 per cent; Umetsu et al. 2005) – gradually decreasing towards the northern part of Honshu (Shinoda 2007). This finding indicates that this haplogroup may have a southern origin. Moreover, the age of haplogroup M7a was calculated to be *ca.* 23,000 BP, and the age likely falls within the onset of the Last Glacial Maximum (LGM; Adachi et al. 2011).

Our results confirm that the haplogroup M7a entered Japan, with the earliest settlers more than 20,000 years ago from Southeast Asia or the southern region of the Asian continent. The fact that positive proof of human occupation by haplogroup M7a on Ishigaki Island appears about 30,000–20,000 BP fits this scenario.

The peopling in Japan can be seen as a complex process, as the earliest settlements and recent migrations affected the resident populations differently. Although we can draw limited conclusions from this study, our results of ancient mtDNA analysis help to shed light on late Palaeolithic human migrations to, and within, the Japanese archipelagos from Southeast Asia.

Since hot and humid conditions are unfavourable for DNA preservation, there is a low possibility of finding well-preserved DNA in regions with a tropical climate, like the Ryukyu Islands. However, the present study shows that sufficient amounts of DNA were available in the human skeletal samples from the late Palaeolithic period obtained from the Ryukyu Islands because the remains were protected within caves. It seems that caves are favourable burial sites from the viewpoint of DNA preservation (Fehren-Schmitz et al. 2011). However, further studies are necessary to obtain more details on the human skeletal remains excavated from this region.

Acknowledgements

We wish to thank Dr Naomi Doi from the University of Ryukyu and members of the Center for Buried Cultural Properties, Okinawa prefecture for permitting us to use the skeletal materials, and for their valuable advice. Financial support for the research by Ken-ichi Shinoda was provided by the Japan Society for the Promotion of Science KAKENHI, grant number 25251043 and 23247040 from the Japan Society for the Promotion of Science (JSPS) (Representation; Dr Hirofumi Matsumura of Sapporo Medical School).

References

Adachi, N., K. Shinoda, K. Umetsu and H. Matsumura. 2009. Mitochondrial DNA analysis of Jomon skeletons from the Funadomari Site, Hokkaido, and its implication for the origin of native Americans. *American Journal of Physical Anthropology* 138: 255–265. doi.org/10.1002/ajpa.20923.

Adachi, N., K. Shinoda, K. Umetsu, T. Kitano, H. Matsumura, R. Fujiyama, J. Sawada and T. Masashi. 2011. Mitochondrial DNA analysis of Hokkaido Jomon skeletons: remnants of archaic maternal lineages at the southwestern edge of former Beringia. *American Journal of Physical Anthropology* 146: 346–360. doi.org/10.1002/ajpa.21561.

Andrews, R.M., I. Kubacka, P.F. Chinnery, R.N. Lightowlers, D.M. Turnbull and N. Howell. 1999. Reanalysis and revision of the Cambridge reference sequence for human mitochondrial DNA. *Nature Genetics* 23: 147. doi.org/10.1038/13779.

Derenko, M., M. Boris, G. Tomasz, D. Galina, D. Irina, P. Maria, D. Choduraa, L. Faina, K.L. Hong, V. Tomas, V. Richard and I. Zakharov. 2007. Phylogeographic analysis of mitochondrial DNA in northern Asian populations. *American Journal of Human Genetics* 81(5): 1025–1041. doi.org/10.1086/522933.

Fehren-Schmitz, L., O. Warnberg, M. Reindel, V. Seidenberg, J. Isla, E. Tomasto, S. Hummel, and B. Herrmann. 2011. Diachronic investigations of mitochondrial and Y-chromsomal genetic markers in pre-Columbian Andean Highlanders from South Peru. *Annals of Human Genetics* 75: 266–283.

Fu, Q., M. Matthias, G. Xing, S. Udo, A.B. Hernán, J. Kelso, and S. Pääbo. 2012. DNA Analysis of an early modern human from Tianyuan Cave, China. *Proceedings of the National Academy of Sciences of the United States of America* 110: 2223–2227. doi.org/10.1073/pnas.1221359110.

Gilbert, M.T.P., E. Willerslev, A.J. Hansen, I. Barnes, L. Rudbeck, N. Lynnerup and C. Alan. 2003. Distribution patterns of postmortem damage in human mitochondrial DNA. *American Journal of Human Genetics* 72: 32–47. doi.org/10.1086/345378.

Itoh, Y., N. Mizuki, T. Shimada, F. Azuma, M. Itakura, K. Kashiwase, E. Kikkawa, K.J. Kulski, M. Satake and H. Inoko. 2005. High-throughput DNA typing of HLA-A, -B, -C, and -DRB1 loci by a PCR-SSOP-Luminex method in the Japanese population. *Immunogenetics* 57: 717–729. doi.org/10.1007/s00251-005-0048-3.

Jinam, T., N. Nishida, M. Hirai, S. Kawamura, H. Oota, K. Umetsu, R. Kimura, J. Ohashi, A. Tajima, T. Yamamoto, H. Tanabe, S. Mano, Y. Suto, T. Kaname, K. Naritomi, K. Yanagi, N. Niikawa, K. Omoto, and N. Saitou. 2012. The history of human populations in the Japanese Archipelago inferred from genomewide SNP data with a special reference to the Ainu and the Ryukyuan Populations. *Journal of Human Genetics* 57: 787–795. doi.org/10.1038/jhg.2012.114.

Kivisild, T., H.V. Tolk, J. Parik, Y. Wang, S.S. Papiha, H.J. Bandelt, and V. Richard. 2002. The emerging limbs and twigs of the East Asian mtDNA Tree. *Molecular Biology and Evolution* 19(10): 1737–1751. doi.org/10.1093/oxfordjournals.molbev.a003996.

Maca-Mayer, N., V.M. Cabrera, M. Arnay, C. Flores, R. Fregel, A.M. Gonzalez and J.M. Larruga. 2005. Mitochondrial DNA diversity in 17th–18th century remains from Tenerife (Canary Islands). *American Journal of Physical Anthropology* 127: 418–426. doi.org/10.1002/ajpa.20148.

Melchior, L., M.T.P. Gilbert, T. Kivisild, N. Lynnerup and J. Dissing. 2008. Rare mtDNA haplogroups and genetic differences in rich and poor Danish Iron-Age villages. *American Journal of Physical Anthropology* 135: 206–215. doi.org/10.1002/ajpa.20721.

Sampietro, M.L., M.T.P. Gilbert, O. Lao, D. Caramelli, M. Lari, J. Bertranpetit and C. Lalueza-Fox. 2006. Tracking down human contamination in ancient human teeth. *Molecular and Biological Evolution* 23: 1801–1807. doi.org/10.1093/molbev/msl047.

Shinoda, K. 2007. *People Who Became the Ancestor of the Japanese*. Tokyo: Nihon Housou Syuppan Kyoukai (in Japanese).

Shinoda, K. and N. Adachi. 2014. DNA Analysis of Skeletal Remains from the Shiraho Saonerabaru Site In Ishigaki Island. *Excavation report of Center for buried cultural properties of Okinawa prefecture* (in Japanese).

Shinoda, K. and S. Kanai. 1999. Intracemetry genetic analysis at the Nakazuma Jomon site in Japan by mitochondrial DNA sequencing. *Anthropological Science* 107: 129–140. doi.org/10.1537/ase.107.129.

Shinoda, K., N. Adachi, S. Guillen and I. Shimada. 2006. Mitochondrial DNA analysis of ancient Peruvian Highlanders. *American Journal of Physical Anthropology* 131: 98–107. doi.org/10.1002/ajpa.20408.

Shinoda, K., T. Kakuda and N. Doi. 2012. Mitochondrial DNA polymorphisms in Late Shell Midden Period skeletal remains excavated from two archaeological sites in Okinawa. *Bulletin of the National Museum of Nature and Science Series D* vol. 38, pp. 51–61.

Takamiya, H. 2005. *Prehistory of the Okinawa Islands*. Naha, Okinawa: Border Inc. (in Japanese).

Tanaka, M., V.M. Cabrera, A.M. González J.M. Larruga T. Takeyasu N. Fuku, L.J. Guo, R. Hirose, Y. Fujita, M. Kurata, K. Shinoda, K. Umetsu, Y. Yamada, Y. Oshida, Y. Sato, N. Hattori, Y. Mizuno, Y. Arai, N. Hirose, S. Ohta, O. Ogawa, Y. Tanaka, R. Kawamori, M. Shamoto-Nagai, W. Maruyama, H. Shimokata, R. Suzuki and H. Shimodaira. 2004. Mitochondrial genome variation in East Asia and the peopling of Japan. *Genome Research* 74: 1832–1850. doi.org/10.1101/gr.2286304.

Torroni, A., R.I. Sukernik, T.G. Schurr, Y.B. Starikovskaya, M.F. Cabell, M.H. Crawford, A.G. Comuzzie and C.W. Douglas. 1993. mtDNA Variation of aboriginal Siberians reveals distinct genetic affinities with Native Americans. *American Journal of Human Genetics* 53: 591–608.

Trejaut, J.A., T. Kivisild, J.H. Loo, C.L. Lee, C.L. He, C.J. Hsu, Z.Y. Li and L. Marie. 2005. Traces of archaic mitochondrial lineages persist in Austronesian-speaking Formosan populations. *PLoS Biology* 3: e247. doi.org/10.1371/journal.pbio.0030247.

Umetsu, K.M. Tanaka, I. Yuasa, N. Adachi, A. Miyoshi, S. Kashimura, S.P. Kyung, Y.H. Wei, G. Watanabe and M. Osawa. 2005. Multiplex amplified product-length polymorphism analysis of 36 mitochondrial single-nucleotide polymorphisms for haplogrouping of East Asian populations. *Electrophoresis* 26: 91–98. doi.org/10.1002/elps.200406129.

Woodward, S.R., J.K. Marie, M.C. Nancy, J.K. Marvin, and C.W. Griggs. 1994. Amplification of Ancient Nuclear DNA from Teeth and Soft Tissues. *Genome Research* 3: 244–247. doi.org/10.1101/gr.3.4.244.

Yoneda, M. 2014. *Carbon Dating Of Shiraho Saonetabaru Site In Ishigaki Island.* Excavation Report of Center for Buried Cultural Properties of Okinawa Prefecture (in Japanese).

4

Mid-Holocene Hunter-Gatherers 'Gaomiao' in Hunan, China: The First of the Two-layer Model in the Population History of East/Southeast Asia

Hirofumi Matsumura, Hsiao-chun Hung, Nguyen Lan Cuong, Ya-feng Zhao, Gang He and Zhang Chi

Gaomiao, the eponymous archaeological site of the Gaomiao Culture (ca. 7500–5500 BP) has produced evidence of a unique hunter-gatherer society in Hunan Province, China, that produced fine decorated pottery. The human remains unearthed from this site provided an excellent opportunity to assess phenotypic and biological relationships between the Gaomiao and prehistoric and modern human populations that have inhabited East/Southeast Asia over the past ca. *10,000 years through cranial morphometrics. The assessment of morphometric affinity presented here addresses the peopling of East Asia, particularly in the context of the 'two-layer' hypothesis describing the population history of this region. The results suggest that the Gaomiao skeletons inherited genetic signatures from early colonising populations of Late Pleistocene southern Eurasian origin to a certain extent, and might share a common ancestry with present-day Australian Aboriginal and Melanesian people.*

Introduction

The study of the population history of East Asia remains complex due to various migration processes and intermixing of populations throughout prehistory, poor archaeological sample sizes and limited radiometric dating. In general terms, East Asia is thought to have been originally inhabited by (to use the classic term) 'Mongoloid' peoples from the Late Pleistocene onwards. In the Late Pleistocene and early Holocene of Southeast Asia, several sets of human remains exhibit Australo-Melanesian characteristics, and it has been argued that an indigenous population possessing this morphological form occupied Southeast Asia. These skeletal data demonstrated significant genetic discontinuity between pre- and post-agricultural populations, suggesting that dramatic agriculturally driven demic expansion occurred in Mainland Southeast Asia (MSEA) beginning in the Neolithic period (see Matsumura and Zuraina 1999; Matsumura and Hudson 2005; Matsumura 2006; Matsumura et al. 2008a, 2008b, 2011a, 2011b; Oxenham et al. 2011; Matsumura and Oxenham 2013a, 2013b, 2014, 2015). This population history scenario for Southeast Asia is known as the 'two-layer' or 'immigration' model, a scenario of human population movement that was first postulated in the middle of the last century (q.v., Jacob 1967).

Given this perspective overview in MSEA, problems have arisen as to whether pre-existing indigenous hunter-gatherers in more northerly East Asia, as well as early settlers of Southeast Asia, were genealogically akin to present-day Australian Aboriginal and Melanesian populations, whether there was an agriculturally driven mass population movement, and whether they were replaced by the migrating agriculturalists who shared a suite of features with Northeast Asians (archetypically referred as 'Mongoloid').

The discovery of human skeletal remains at the site of Gaomiao provides a rare opportunity to apply cranial morphometrics to compare the skeletal affinities of these hunter-gatherers with other prehistoric and modern human populations in the region, and to evaluate the strengths of the 'two-layer' hypothesis in Mainland East Asia. This paper introduces the skeletal morphology of Gaomiao and presents results pertaining to the cranial affinity, based on craniometric data, in comparison with early and modern population samples from the area covering East/Southeast Asia and the Western Pacific.

Archaeological background and context

Gaomiao is located on the northern bank of the Yuan River in Yanli Village of Chatou in Hongjiang City (formerly named as Qianyang County) in Hunan Province (Figure 4.1). The site was excavated three times (in 1991, 2004 and 2005) by the Cultural Relics and Archeological Research Institution in Hunan Province (He 2006a, 2006b). It consists of large shell mounds produced by the human discard of abundant freshwater molluscs, and aquatic and terrestrial fauna, including some pigs identified as domestic (He 2006a). Evidence for agriculture is currently sparse with no rice phytoliths or macrobotanicals having been identified so far. Rice grain impressions have been identified in three sherds and rice husk in another at Gaomiao, but the source of this pottery is unclear (Gu and Zhao 2009). Overall, it is considered that the site occupants were hunter-gatherers rather than agriculturalists (He 2006a). A unique feature of the Gaomiao site is its pottery decoration. Despite the deep antiquity, the early pottery forms exhibit very fine decoration, including cord impressions and dentate stamping, the latter forming animal faces, phoenixes, waves, trapezoids, circles and band-like motifs on the surfaces of vessels, jars, plates and bowls. Furthermore, it is noteworthy that the pottery with the phoenix motif probably embodied certain religious beliefs (He 2006a, 2006b). This finding has led archaeologists to realise the mutual and remote influences of cultural and artistic accomplishments from Gaomiao on various later regional cultures in ancient China. Gaomiao appears to have been a unique hunter-gatherer subsistence society associated with a well-developed material culture (Zhang and Hung 2012; Figure 4.2).

Figure 4.1 The locality of Gaomiao in southern China.
Source: H. Matsumura.

Figure 4.2 The representative pottery from Gaomiao.
Source: G. He.

From the Gaomiao site, two major burial assemblages were exposed, containing more than 30 burials. The earliest individuals were interred in a flexed position without grave goods (see Figure 4.3), whereas in the later-phase burials shifted to the extended type with abundant grave goods, including pottery and jade. The later burial sequence, though lacking *Oryza sativa* rice, was likely influenced by a neighbouring agricultural society; for example, the Daxi culture (*ca.* 6500–5000 BP) around the Dongting Lake area in Hunan Province. Nevertheless, only three inhumation burials produced well-preserved skeletal remains, all of which were found in the flexed position of the earlier sequence.

Figure 4.3 The human skeleton M-02 from Gaomiao.

Source: H. Matsumura.

These three individuals provided AMS carbon-14 dates based on tooth dentine collagen, of approximately 6500 BP (see Table 4.1, dated by the Beta Analytic laboratory in the USA).

Table 4.1 Gaomiao radiocarbon dating results gained from this study.

Beta Sample No.	Human remains	Measured radiocarbon age (years BP)	$^{13}C/^{12}C$ ratio (‰)	Conventional age (years BP)	Calibrated years BP (2-Sigma)
328354	Gaomiao M-01 child	5690±40	-20.8	5760±40	6659–6464 (94.6%) or 6459–6453 (0.8%)
328353	Gaomiao M-02 adult	5500±40	-19.2	5600±40	6452–6300 (95.4%)
333225	Gaomiao M-20 unknown age	5680±30	-12.6	5880±30	6777–6764 (3.1%) or 6752–6640 (92.3%)

Source: H.-c. Hung.

Cranial preservation and morphological remarks

Of the three skeletal individuals unearthed at Gaomiao, one (no. M-01) was a child around 12–14 years old, currently exhibited at the Haihua (懷化) City Museum. Another child specimen, numbered M-20, is very fragmentary and housed at the Cultural Relics and Archeological Research Institution in Changsha City (長沙市). The M-02 skeleton alone, currently displayed at the Hongjiang City (洪江市) Museum, is of an adult individual in a good state of preservation. In this study, we reconstructed only this adult cranium for morphometric analysis.

The M-02 individual was estimated to be a mature male over 60 years old based on the extent of tooth attrition, antemortem tooth loss, cranial suture closures, and severity of osteoarthritis. Figure 4.4 displays various aspects of his reconstructed skull. Although the cranium had fragmented through *in situ* crushing, almost all parts of the specimen could be reconstructed. The greater and lesser wings of the sphenoid bone are missing from the cranial vault.

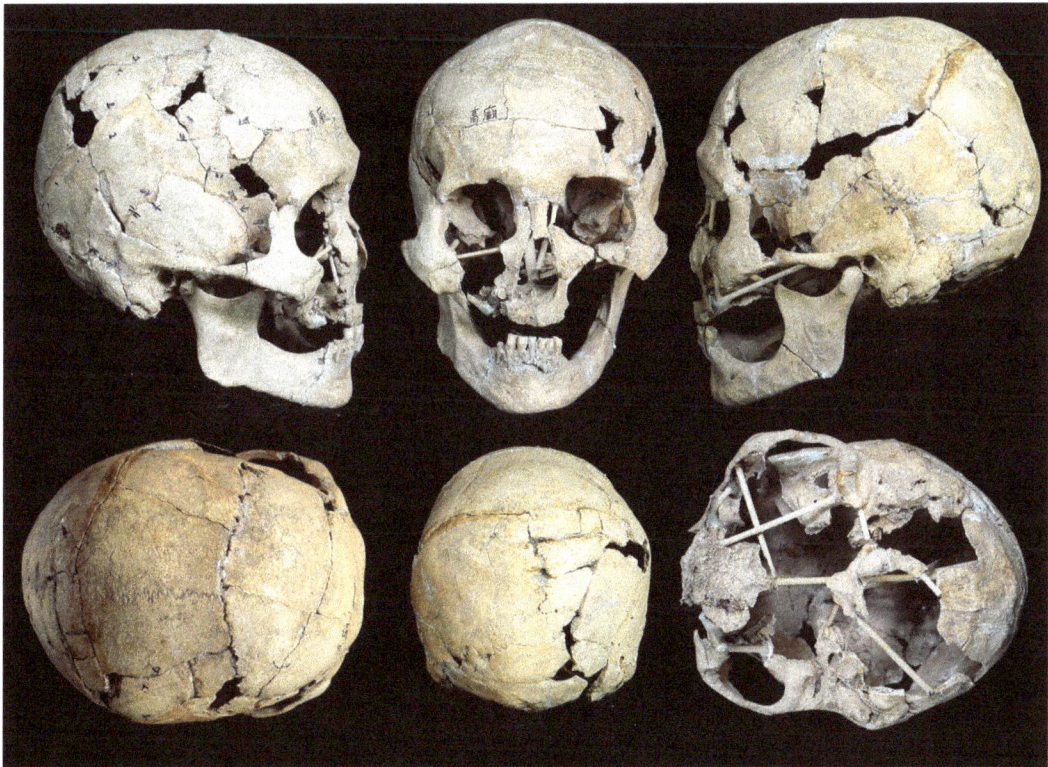

Figure 4.4 The reconstructed skull of M-02 from Gaomiao.
Source: H. Matsumura.

The face of the skeleton lacks some parts of the maxilla, and the ethmoid and lachrymal bones, and the inferior conchae and vomer, which together form the inside of the orbits and the inner portion of the nasal cavity.

The cranial shape is ovoid in superior view and the vault is mesocephalic (cranial index 79.1). The external occipital protuberance is well protruding, and the superior nuchal line is clearly defined with a well-developed nuchal plane, indicating that this person possessed strong neck muscles. The temporal line, to which the temporal muscles attach, is marked in the frontal region but becomes weak towards the posterior end of the temporal bones. The glabella region is large and prominently protruding compared with the majority of modern East Asian males, although the supercilliary arch is relatively flat. The frontal bone leans well back, clearly exhibiting male characteristics. The facial skeleton is low and wide (upper facial index 47.1, upper facial height was estimated as described in the section on the recoding system for cranial measurements). The orbital margins are straight at the superior line, and the nasal root is moderately concave. The coronal, sagittal, and lambdoidal sutures are completely fused ecto- and endocranially. The mandible expresses alveolar prognathism. Frontal nerve incisures and superior orbital foramina are absent on both sides of the frontal bone. The supramastoid crest is weak, and the mastoid process is moderate in size.

The mandibular body is relatively small and low, while the muscle attachments are moderately developed. The mental eminence is weakly projecting. The mylohyoid line is well angulated. The mandibular ramus is wide with a weakly concave mandibular notch. The preangular *incisula* is shallow and the lateral prominence is small at the gonial angle. The attachment area of the medial pterygoid muscles is well developed.

The following teeth are present in the maxilla and mandible.

/	/	X	X	/	X	X	X	X	X	X	/	/	/	M2	/
X	X	X	X	0	0	I2	I1	I1	I2	C	X	X	X	X	X

X = tooth lost antemortem and alveolus remodelled
0 = tooth lost post-mortem and alveolus not remodelled
/ = tooth lost post-mortem and alveolus damaged

The maxilla lacked almost all teeth, and the mandible had also lost most posterior teeth antemortem. The occlusal surfaces of the remaining teeth were heavily worn, with enamel remaining only on the outer rim, the entire occlusal surface of the crown being lost and secondary dentine visible on every tooth. To carry out mitochondrial DNA analysis, the left maxillary second molar was taken out for sampling.

Recording system for cranial measurements and statistical procedures

Thirty-two cranial measurements and some representative cranial indices were recorded following Martin's definitions (Bräuer 1988), as given in Table 4.2. The upper facial height and the basion-prosthion length are estimated values, as the measurement landmark of the prosthion was missing due to the antemortem loss of maxillary incisors, which eroded the edge of the maxillary alveolar bone. In this study, the prosthion was estimated to be at the point extending 5 mm from the alveolar margin. This estimation was based on the average height of the missing portion in representative samples such as Jomon and Japanese crania.

Using the data sets of cranial metrics, multivariate statistical procedures were used to explore the population affinities between the Gaomiao sample and ethnically and chronologically different groups. The comparative samples are listed in Tables 4.3 and 4.4 and this summary also includes archaeological specimens from East/Southeast Asia, as well as modern samples from East/Southeast Asia and the Pacific. Similarities in cranial proportions were estimated by Q-mode correlation coefficients (Sneath and Sokal 1973) using the cranial measurements. The cranial data set selected for this calculation were a subset of 16 measurements (Martin's method number: M1, M8, M9, M17, M43(1), M43c, M45, M46b, M46c, M48, M51, M52, M54, M55, M57, M57a), as these were the most commonly available among the comparative samples. The neighbor-net split method (the software package 'Splits Tree Version 4.0' provided by Hudson and Bryant 2006) was applied to the distance matrix of the Q-mode correlation coefficients to aid in the interpretation of inter-sample phenotypic affinities.

Table 4.2 Cranial measurements (mm) and indices for the human skull from Gaomiao site.

Martin no. and measurement	(mm)	Martin no. and measurement	(mm)
1 Maximum cranial length	191	54 Nasal breadth	24
5 Basion-nasion length	107	55 Nasal height	55
8 Maximum cranial breadth	151	60 Upper alveolar length	-
9 Minimum frontal breadth	98	61 Upper alveolar breadth	-
10 Maximum frontal breadth	125	66 Bigonial breadth	105
12 Maximum occipital breadth	125	68 Mandibular length	81
17 Basion-bregma height	151	69 Symphyseal height	39
29 Frontal chord	117	70 Ramus height	60
30 Parietal chord	121	71 Ramus breadth	34
31 Occipital chord	107	8:1 Cranial index	79.1
40 Basion-prosthion length	98	48:45 upper facial index	47.1
43 Upper facial breadth	110	43(1) Frontal chord	104
45 Bizygomatic breadth	153	43c Frontal subtense	19.4
46 Bimaxillary breadth	117	57 Nasal cord	8.5
48 Upper facial height	72	57a Nasal subtense	1.5
51 Orbital breadth	44	46b Bimaxillary cord	119
52 Orbital height	35	46c Nasospinale sabutense	32.9

Source: H. Matsumura.

Table 4.3 Comparative prehistoric population samples from across East and Southeast Asia.

Sample	Locality	Period	Remarks	Data Source	Storage
Pre-Neolithic Samples					
Liujinag 柳江	China	Late Pleistocene	Individual, Site in Guangxi Prov. 広西壮族自治省	Woo 1959; measurements of M43(1), 43c, 46b, 46c by H.M (cast).	
Lang Gao	Vietnam	Hoabinhian	Averages of two individuals (nos 17 and 19), Site in Hoa Binh Prov., N Vietnam (Cuong 2007)	H.M.	MHO
Lang Bon	Vietnam	Hoabinhian (ca. 7000 BP)	Individual, Site in Thanh Hoa Prov., N Vietnam (Cuong 2007)	H.M.	MHO
Mai Da Nuoc	Vietnam	Hoabinhian (ca. 8000 BP)	Individual, in Thanh Hoa Prov., N Vietnam (Cuong 1986, 2007)	H.M.	IAH
Hoabinhian (average)	Vietnam	Hoabinhian (ca. 11,000–8000 BP)	6 specimens including fragmental remains from above 4 sites and 1 from Mai Da Dieu site in Thanh Hoa Prov. (Cuong 2007)	H.M.	MHO, IAH
Bac Son	Vietnam	Epi-Hoabinhian (ca. 8000–7000 BP)	Sites of Pho Binh Gia, Cua Git, Lang Cuom, and Dong Thuoc in N Vietnam (Mansuy and Colani 1925)	H.M.	MHO
Con Co Ngua	Vietnam	Da But Culture (ca. 6000 BP)	Site in Than Hoa Prov., N Vietnam	Thuy 1990; Cuong 2003; measurements of M43(1), 43c, 46b, 46c by H.M.	IAH
Gua Cha	Malaysia	Hoabinhian (ca. 8000–6000 BP)	Individual Sample no. H12, Site in Kelantan Prov. (Sieveking 1954)	H.M.	CAM
Tam Hang	Laos	Early Holocene	Hua Pan Province, N Laos (Mansuy and Colani 1925; Huard and Saurin 1938; Demeter et al. 2009)	H.M.	MHO
Zengpiyan 甑皮岩	China	Mesolithic (ca. 8000 BP)	Site in Guangxi Prov. 広西壮族自治省	IACAS, ATGZM, ZM, and ATGC, 2003	
Neolithic Samples					
Man Bac	Vietnam	Late Neolithic (ca. 3800–3500 BP)	Site in Ninh Binh Prov., N Vietnam (Oxenham et al. 2011)	Matsumura 2011	
An Son	Vietnam	Late Neolithic (ca. 3800 BP)	Site in Long An Prov., S Vietnam (Nishimura and Dung 2002; Cuong 2006; Bellwood et al. 2013)	H.M.	LAPM
Ban Chiang	Thailand	Neolithic-Bronze Age (ca. 3500–1800 BP)	Site in Udon Thani Prov. (Gorman and Charoenwongsa 1976; Pietrusewsky and Douglas 2002)	Pietrusewsky and Douglas 2002; measurements of M43(1), 43c, 46b, 46c by H.M.	UHW, SAC
Non Nok Tha	Thailand	Neolithic-Bronze Age (ca. 3500–3000 BP)	Site in Khok Kaen Prov. (Bayard 1971)	H.M.	UNLV
Weidun 圩墩	China	Neolithic (ca. 7000–5000 BP, Majiabang Culture 馬家浜文化)	Sites in Jiangsu Prov. 江蘇省 Central China	Nakahashi and Li 2002	

Sample	Locality	Period	Remarks	Data Source	Storage
Jiahu 賈湖	China	Neolithic (*ca.* 9000 BP)	Site in Henan Prov. 河南省 Central China (HPIAC 1989, 1998)	H.M.	HEPICA
Xipo 西坡	China	Neolithic (*ca.* 5300 BP, Yangshao Culture 仰韶文化)	Site in Henan Prov. 河南省 Central China (IACAS and HPIAC 2010)	H.M.	HEPICA
Hemudu 河姆渡	China	Neolithic (*ca.* 6300 BP, Hemudu Culture 河姆渡文化)	Site in Zhejiarg Province 浙江省, Yangzi Delta region (ZCARI 2003)	H.M.	HEMSM
Baikal	Russia	Neolithic (*ca.* 8000–4000 BP)	Lake Baikal (Debets 1951).	Ishida 1997	
Jomon	Japan	Neolithic (*ca.* 5000–2300 BP)	Over almost the entire Japanese archipelago	Hanihara 1993, 2000	
Bronze – Iron Age Samples					
Anyang 安陽	China	Yin (Shan) Period (*ca.* 3500–3027 BP)	Site in Henan Prov. 河南省 Central China (IHIA and CASS 1982)	Han and Qi 1985; measurements of M43(1), 43c, 46b, 46c by H.M.	AST
Rach Rung	Vietnam	Bronze Age (*ca.* 2800 BP)	Site in Moc Hoa District, Laong An Prov., Sth Vietnam (The and Cong 2001)	H.M.	LAPM
Giong Ca Vo	Vietnam	Iron Age (*ca.* 2300–2000 BP)	Site in Ho Chi Minh (Dang and Vu 1997)	Cuong 2007; measurements of M43(1), 43c, 46b, 46c by H.M.	HCHM
Go O Chua	Vietnam	Iron Age (*ca.* 2300–2000 BP)	Site in Long An Prov., S Vietnam (Reinecke 2008)	Cuong in press	LAPM
Hoa Diem	Vietnam	Iron Age (Hoa Diem 2=*ca.* 2150 BP; Hoa Diem 1 =*ca.* 2000–1700 BP)	Site of Hoa Diem in Khanh Hoa Prov., Central Vietnam (Yamagata 2013)	Matsumura et al. 2013	
Dong Son	Vietnam	Dong Son Period (*ca.* 3000–1700 BP)	Sites of Dong Son Culture in N Vietnam (Cuong 1996)	Cuong 1996, partially by H.M.	IAH, CSPH
Phum Snay	Cambodia	Iron Age (*ca.* 2350–1800 BP)	Site in Preah Neat Orey District, W Cambodia	Matsumura et al. 2010	
Yayoi	Japan	Yayoi Period (*ca.* 2800–1700 BP)	Sites of Doigahama, Nakanohama, Kanenokuma and others in Northern Kyushu and Yamaguchi Districts, W Japan	Nakahashi 1993	

Source: H. Matsumura

Table 4.4 Comparative population samples of historic and modern times.

Sample	Remarks	Data Source	Storage
Oceania and Indian Sea			
Andaman		Howells 1989; M43(1),43c,46b,46c,48,51,55,57,57a by H.M	BMNH, CAM
Australia		Hanihara 1993; M43(1),43c,46b,46c,57,57a by H.M.	BMNH
Melanesia		Hanihara 1993, 2000	
Loyalty Islands, New Britain, New Guinea Tolai, Veddah, Nicobal		H.M.	CAM, USYD, MHO
Southeast and East Asia			
Laos		Cuong 1996; M43(1),43c,46b,46c,57,57a by H.M.	MHO
La Lo Philippines	ca. 800 BP Site of La Lo in Northern Luzon island	H.M.	NMP
Aeta Negrito	Philippines	H.M.	MHO
Atayal, Bunun	Taiwan Aborigines	Pietrusewsky and Chang 2003; M43(1),43c,45,46b,46c,48,51,55,57,57a by H.M.	NTW
Cambodia, Vietnam		Matsumura et al. 2010	
Celebes, Java, Myanmar, South Moluccas, Sumatra		Pietrusewsky 1981; Hanihara 2000; M17,45,48,51 by H.M.	BMNH, CAM
Thailand	Residents in Bangkok	Sangvichien 1971; Hanihara 2000	
Philippines	Non-Negrito	Suzuki et al. 1993; M43(1),43c,46b,46c,57,57a by H.M.	NMP
Dayak	Sarawak in Borneo Island	Yokoh 1940; Hanihara 2000	
Semang Negrito	Malaysia	H.M.	BMNH
Wasi Yunnan 雲南	Ancient Yunnan, South China	Ji et al. 2005	
Hainan 海南	Hainan Island, South China	Howells 1989; M43(1),43c,46b,46c,48,51,55,57,57a by H.M	
South China	Residents in Hong Kong	H.M.	CAM
Jiangnan 江南	Lower Basin of Yangtze River, Eastern Zhou – Former Han Periods (2770–1992 BP) in China	Nakahashi and Li 2002	

Sample	Remarks	Data Source	Storage
Northeast Asia			
Japan, North China, North China 2	North China from Manchuria (North China) and Kirin (North China 2)	Hanihara 1993, 2000	
Okhotsk	*ca.* 1600–1000 BP	Ishida 1996	
Aleut, Asian Eskimo, Buryat, Chukchi, Ekven, Evenki, Hokkaido Ainu, Mongol, Nanay, Negidal, Nivkh, Oroch, Sakhalin Ainu, Troitskoe, Ulch, Yakut, Yukagir	Siberia in Russia and N Japan	Ishida 1990, 1997	

H.M. = current author Hirofumi Matsumura, M = Martin's measurement definition number.

Storage: institutions whose materials were studied by Matsumura for unpublished data: AST=Academia Sinica of the Republic of China in Taipei; BMNH=Department of Paleontology, Natural History Museum, London; CAM=Department of Biological Anthropology, University of Cambridge; CSPH=Center for South East Asian Prehistory, Hanoi; HCHM=Ho Chi Minh Historical Museum; HEMSM=Hemudu Site Museum; HEPICA=Henan Provincial Institute of Cultural Relics and Archaeology; IAH=Department of Anthropology, Institute of Archaeology, Hanoi; LAPM=Long An Provincial Museum, Vietnam; MHO=Laboratoire d'Anthropologie Biologique, Musée de l'Homme, Paris; NMP=Department of Archaeology, National Museum of the Philippines, Manila; NTW=Department of Anatomy, National Taiwan University; SAC=Princess Maha Chakri Sirindhorn Anthropology Centre, Bangkok; UHW=Department of Anthropology, University of Hawai'i, UNLV: Department of Anthropology, University of Nevada, USA.

Source: H. Matsumura.

Results of cranial metric analysis

Figure 4.5 depicts the results from the neighbor-net split analysis applied to the distances of the Q-mode correlation coefficients based on 16 cranial measurements from Gaomiao and comparative population samples. The unrooted network tree diagram resulting from this analysis branches into two major clusters at the right and left sides. These include: 1) East Asians and many Southeast Asians ranging from the Neolithic to modern times; and 2) Australo-Melanesians and early Holocene Southeast Asians, including the Hoabinhian and Mesolithic (see Bellwood 2014 on the use of term 'Mesolithic' for Southern China and Northern Southeast Asian archaeology), respectively. The Gaomiao specimen branched out relatively close to the cluster consisting of Australo-Melanesian and Hoabinhian samples.

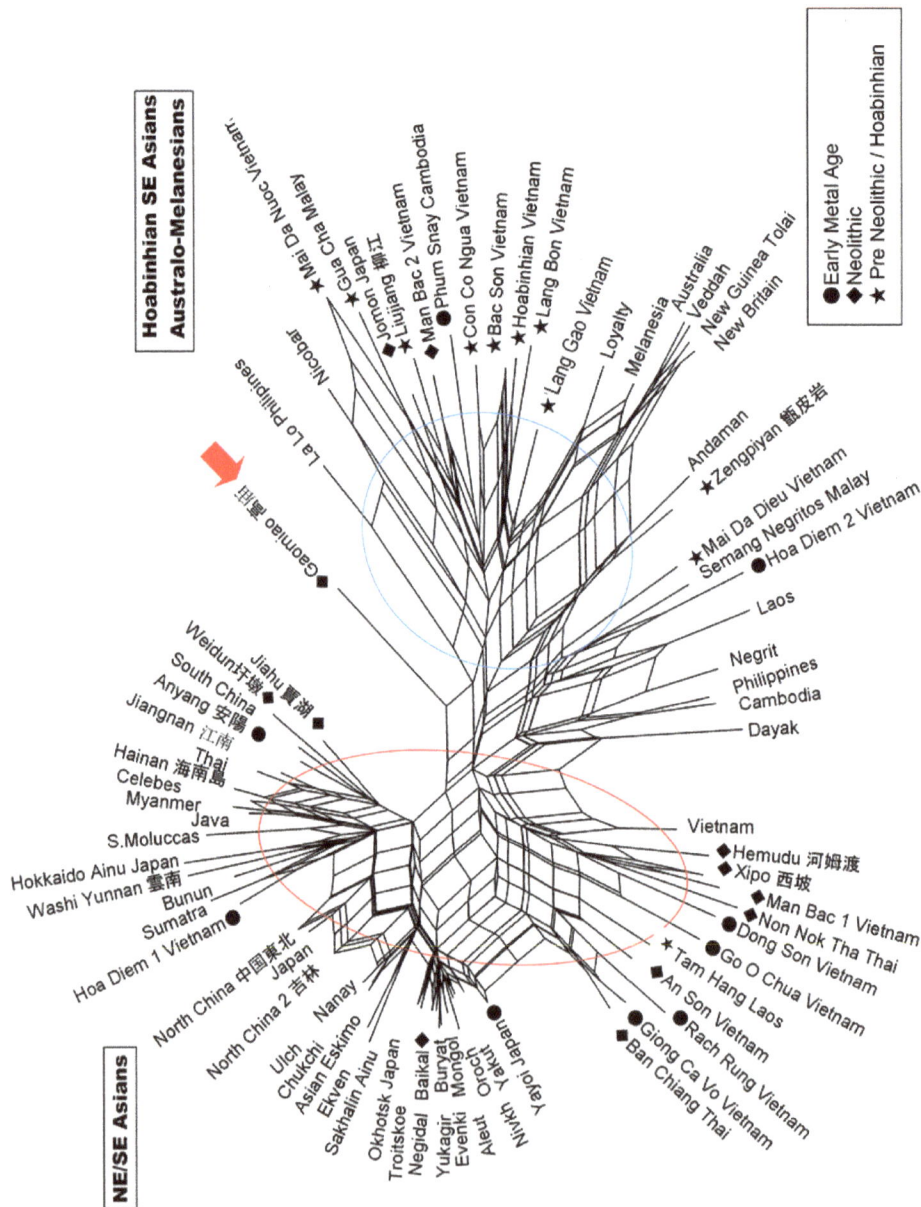

Figure 4.5 Net split tree generated from Q-mode correlation coefficients based on 16 cranial measurements.

Source: H. Matsumura.

Discussion and conclusion

In comparing the Gaomiao specimen with ethnically, chronologically and geographically different population samples, dissimilarities from the majority of comparative East and Northeast Asian samples, including other Neolithic samples from China such as those from Jiahu (賈湖), Xipo (西坡), Hemudu (河姆渡) and Weidun (圩墩), are apparent in the cranial morphology. The interpretation of this difference is a crucial issue in the discussion of the population history of this region. With regard to Hoabinhian/Mesolithic foragers, which were widely distributed over Mainland Southeast Asia during the Late Pleistocene and early Holocene, the majority of analyses of skeletal materials have demonstrated cranial morphology with Australo-Melanesian characteristics (Callenfels 1936; Mijsberg 1940; Jacob 1967). These skeletons of the preceramic period may represent some of the early indigenous settlers of Southeast Asia who were possibly the first modern human colonisers of MSEA, and the subcontinental Sahul, who were ancestral to present-day Australo-Melanesians in the region. Based on these findings, Southeast Asia is thought to have been initially occupied by such indigenous people who later exchanged or admixed genes with immigrants from North and/or East Asia, leading to the formation of present-day populations. This is known as the 'two-layer' hypothesis, and is a common hypothesis used to explain the population history of this region. Most recent studies based on the morphological analysis of new skeletal discoveries, as well as dental characteristics, strongly support the two-layer hypothesis (Matsumura and Hudson 2005; Matsumura 2006; Matsumura et al. 2008a, 2008b, 2011a, 2011b). This hypothesis has gained theoretical support from the fields of historical linguistics and archaeology, which have linked the dispersal of language families, including Austronesian, Austroasiatic, Daic, Tai-Kadai, Miao-Yao, etc., with the expansion of rice farming societies during the Neolithic period (Bellwood 1987, 1991, 2005; Higham 1998, 2001; Bellwood and Renfrew 2003; Diamond and Bellwood 2003; Zhang and Hung 2010). These studies of historical linguistics and archeology suggest that south China was a major center of linguistic diversification and appears to have been the ultimate source of the language families.

The morphometric analysis of this early phase Gaomiao individual suggests it has cranial features more closely aligned with Hoabinhian/Mesolithic groups of MSEA than with modern East Asian and Northeast Asian populations (so-called 'Mongoloid' samples). Taking this cranial affinity into consideration, it may be concluded that the early phase Gaomiao hunter-gatherers (*ca.* 6500 BP), who inhabited the region prior to major interaction with farming communities, were less affected by substantial gene flow via diffusion from northern and eastern peripheral areas than other contemporary Neolithic Chinese such as the Jiahu (賈湖), Xipo (西坡) and Hemudu (河姆渡) peoples. It may be worth mentioning in passing that the early Holocene Zengpiyan (甑皮岩) skull from Guangxi Province is also affiliated with early indigenous aggregation (see Figure 4.5), suggesting that the Gaomiao people had genetic material inherited from such early settlers of southern China. Thus far, the long debate concerning the two-layer hypothesis has targeted the population history of Southeast Asia. Our current morphometric analyses of the Gaomiao skeleton may expand adoption of the two-layer scenario to the area of inland China by elucidating the genealogical affinity of the early indigenous populations before diffusion of the rice farming peoples phenotypically possessing Northeast Asian features into the region.

Acknowledgements

We express sincere gratitude to Dr Wei Xing-tao (Henan Provincial Institute of Archaeology), Professor Li Xin-wei (Institute of Archaeology, Chinese Academy of Social Science in Beijing), Director Huang Wei-jin (Hemudu Museum in Zhejiang) and Professor Sun Guo-ping (Zhejiang Provincial Institute of Archaeology) for their collaboration and permission to study the Chinese Neolithic skeletal remains.

This study was supported in part by KAKENHI in 2012–2015 (nos 2347040 and 16H02527) from the Japan Society for the Promotion of Science (JSPS) and ARC Discovery Project in 2011–2013 (ID: DP 110101097) from the Australian Research Council (ARC) Grant Aid in Australia .

References

Bayard, D.T. 1971. Non Nok Tha: The 1968 Excavation, procedure, stratigraphy, and summary of the evidence. *University of Otago Studies in Prehistoric Anthropology*, vol. 4. Dunedin: University of Otago.

Bellwood, P. 1987. The prehistory of Island Southeast Asia: a multidisciplinary review of recent research. *Journal of World Prehistory* 1: 171–224. doi.org/10.1007/BF00975493.

——. 1991. The Austronesian dispersal and the origin of languages. *Scientific American* 265: 88–93. doi.org/10.1038/scientificamerican0791-88.

——. 2005. Examining the farming/language dispersal hypothesis in the East Asian context. In L. Sagart, R. Blench and A. Sanchez-Mazas (eds), *The Peopling of East Asia: Putting Together Archaeology, Linguistics and Genetics*, pp. 17–30. London: Routledge. doi.org/10.4324/9780203343685_chapter_1.

——. 2014. The human populations and archaeology of Southern China and Northern Southeast Asia: pre-Neolithic into Neolithic. Paper presented at 2014 From Matsu Archipelago to Southeast Coast of Asia: International Symposium on the Studies of Prehistoric Cultural and Physical Remains, 27–28 September 2014, Academia Sinica, Taipei.

Bellwood, P. and C. Renfrew (eds). 2003. Examining the Farming/Language Dispersal Hypothesis. McDonald Institute for Archaeological Research, Cambridge.

Bellwood, P., M. Oxenham, C.H. Bui, T.K.D. Nguyen, A. Willis, C. Sarjeant, P.J. Piper, H. Matsumura, K. Tanaka, M. Beavan, T. Higham, Q.M. Nguyen, N.K. Dan, K.T.K. Nguyen, T.H. Vo, VNB, T.K.Q. Tran, P.T. Nguyen, F. Campos, Y.I. Sato, L.C Nguyen and N. Amano. 2013. An Son and the Neolithic of Southern Vietnam. *Asian Perspectives* 50: 144–175.

Bräuer, G. 1988. Osteometrie. In R. Martin, and K. Knussmann (eds), *Anthropologie*, pp. 160–232. Stuttgart: Gustav Fisher.

Callenfels, V.S. 1936. The Melanesoid civilizations of Eastern Asia. *Bulletin of the Raffles Museum 1* (Series B): 41–51.

Cuong, N.L. 1986. Two early Hoabinhian crania from Thanh Hoa province, Vietnam. *Zeitschrift fur Morphologie und Anthropologie* 77: 11–17.

——. 1996. Anthropological Characteristics of Dong Son Population in Vietnam. Hanoi: Social Sciences Publishing House (in Vietnamese with an English title and summary).

——. 2003. Ancient human bones in Da But Culture – Thanh Hoa Province. *Khao Co Hoc* (Vietnamese Archaeology) 3-2003: 66–79 (in Vietnamese with an English title and summary).

——. 2006. About the ancient human bones at An Son (Long An) through the third excavation. *Khao Co Hoc* (Archaeology) 6-2006: 39–51 (in Vietnamese with an English title and summary).

——. 2007. Paleoanthropology in Vietnam. *Khao Co Hoc* (Vietnamese Archaeology) 2-2007: 23–41.

——. in press. Anthropological Study on the Origin of Vietnamese People (in Vietnamese with an English title and summary).

Dang, V.T and Q.H. Vu. 1997. Excavation of Giong Ca Vo site (Can Gio District, Ho Chi Minh City). *Journal of Southeast Asian Archaeology* 17: 30–44.

Debets G.F. 1951. Anthropological studies in the Kamchatka region. *Trudy Institute of Ethnography*, 17 (New Series): 1–263 (in Russian).

Demeter, F.T., E. Sayavongkhamdy, A.S. Patole-Edoumba, A.M. Coupey, J. Bacon, C. DeVos, B. Tougard, P. Bouasisengpaseuth, Sichanthongtip and P. Duringer. 2009. Tam Hang rockshelter: Preliminary study of a prehistoric site in northern Laos. *Asian Perspectives* 48: 291–308. doi. org/10.1353/asi.2009.0000.

Diamond, J. and P. Bellwood. 2003. Farmers and their languages: The first expansions. *Science* 300: 597–603. doi.org/10.1126/science.1078208.

Gorman, C.F. and P. Charoenwongsa. 1976. Ban Chiang: A mosaic of impressions from the first two years. *Expedition* 18: 14–26.

Gu, H.B. and Z.J. Zhao. 2009. Study on carbonized rice from different cultural phases in Hunan. Dongfang Kaogu 6: 358–365 (in Chinese).

Han K.X. and P.F. Qi. 1985. The study of the human bones of the middle and small cemeteries of Yin sites, Anyang. In Institute of History and Institute of Archaeology (IHIA)(eds), *Contributions to the Study on Human Skulls from the Shang Sites at Anyang*, pp. 50–81. Beijing: Cultural Relics Publishing House (in Chinese).

Hanihara, T. 1993. Craniofacial features of Southeast Asians and Jomonese: A reconsideration of their microevolution since the late Pleistocene. *Anthropological Science* 101: 25–46. doi.org/10.1537/ase.101.25.

——. 2000. Frontal and facial flatness of major human populations. *American Journal of Physical Anthropology* 111: 105–134. doi.org/10.1002/(SICI)1096-8644(200001)111:1<105::AID-AJPA7>3.0.CO;2-O.

He, G. 2006a. Reappearance of prehistoric religious and ritual scenario—the Neolithic Gaomiao site in Hongjiang, Hunan. Paper presented at the archaeology forum of the Chinese Academy of Social Sciences: new discoveries in Chinese archaeology in 2005, *Chinese Academy of Social Science*, Beijing, 10 January 2006 (in Chinese).

——. 2006b. The big discovery of Hongjiang Gaomiao site in Hunan. *China Cultural Relics News* 6 January 2006: 1 (in Chinese).

Higham, C.F.W. 1998. Archaeology, linguistics and the expansion of the East and Southeast Asian Neolithic. In R. Blench and M. Spriggs (eds), *Archaeology and Language II: Archaeological Data and Linguistic Hypotheses*, pp. 103–114. London: Routledge. doi.org/10.4324/9780203202913_chapter_3.

——. 2001. Prehistory, language and human biology: is there a consensus in East and Southeast Asia? In L. Jin, M. Seielstad, and C.J. Xiao (eds), Genetic, *Linguistic and Archaeological Perspectives on Human Diversity in Southeast Asia,* pp. 3–16. Singapore: World Scientific. doi. org/10.1142/9789812810847_0001.

Howells, W.W. 1989. *Skull Shapes and the Map: Cranio-Metric Analysis in the Dispersion of Modern Homo.* Papers of the Peabody Museum of Archaeology and Ethnology, vol. 79. Cambridge: Harvard University Press.

HPIAC (Henan Provincial Institute of Archaeology and Cultural Relics). 1989. Henan Wuyang Jiahu Xiangshiqi Shidai Yizhi Di Erci Zhi Di Liuci Fajue Jianbao (Excavations of the Neolithic sites at Jiahu in Wuyang, Henan [2nd–6th seasons]). Wenwu: *Cultural Relics* 1: 2–20 (in Chinese).

——. 1998. Wuyang Jiahu (Jiahu Site at Wuyang). Beijing: Science Press (in Chinese).

Huard, P. and E. Saurin. 1938. État Actuel de la Craniologie Indochinoise. *Bulletin du Service Géologique de l'Indochine* XXV (in French).

Hudson, D.H. and D. Bryant. 2006. Application of phylogenetic networks in evolutionary studies. *Molecular Biology and Evolution* 23: 254–267. doi.org/10.1093/molbev/msj030.

IACAS (Institute of Archaeology, Chinese Academy of Social Science) and HPIAC (Henan Provincial Institute of Archaeology and Cultural Relics) (eds). 2010. *Xipo Cemetery in Lingbao.* Beijing: Cultural Relics Publishing House (in Chinese with English summary).

IACAS (Institute of Archaeology, Chinese Academy of Social Science), ATGZM (Archaeological Team of the Guangxi Zhuang Municipality), ZM (Zengpiyan Museum) and ATGC (Archaeological Team of Guilin City). 2003. *Zengpiyan – a Prehistoric Site in Guilin.* Archeological Monograph Series Type D no. 69. Beijing: Cultural Relics Publishing House (in Chinese with an English title and abstract).

IHIA (Institute of History and Institute of Archaeology) and CASS (Chinese Academy of Social Science) (eds). 1982. *Contributions to the Study on Human Skulls from the Shang Sites at Anyang.* Beijing: Cultural Relics Publishing House (in Chinese with an English summary).

Ishida, H. 1990. Cranial morphology of several ethnic groups from the Amur basin and Sakhalin. *Journal of the Anthropological Society of Nippon* 98: 137–148. doi.org/10.1537/ase1911.98.137.

——. 1996. Metric and nonmetric cranial variation of the prehistoric Okhotsk people. *Anthropological Science* 104: 233–258. doi.org/10.1537/ase.104.233.

——. 1997. Craniometric variation of the Northeast Asian populations. *Homo* 48: 106–124.

Jacob, T. 1967. Some Problems Pertaining to the Racial History of the Indonesian Region. Unpublished PhD dissertation, University of Utrecht, Utrecht.

Ji, X., M. Nakayama, K. Han, X. Liu, H. Liu, and O. Kondo. 2005. Unique biological affinity of the hanging coffin people in ancient China based on craniometry of two skulls from Yunnan province. *Anthropological Science* 113: 259–271. doi.org/10.1537/ase.040805.

Mansuy, H. and M. Colani. 1925. Contribution à l'étudede la préhistoire de l'Indochine VII. Néolithique inférieur (Bacsonien) et Néolithique supérieur dans le Haut-Tonkin. *Bulletin du Service Géologique de l'Indochine* 12: 1–45.

Matsumura, H. 2006. The population history of Southeast Asia viewed from morphometric analyses of human skeletal and dental remains. In M. Oxenham, and N. Tayles (eds), *Bioarchaeology of Southeast Asia,* pp. 33–58. Cambridge: Cambridge University Press. doi.org/10.1017/CBO9780511584220.004.

——. 2011. Quantitative cranio-morphology at Man Bac. In M.F. Oxenham, H. Matsumura and N.K. Dung (eds), *Man Bac: The Excavation of a Late Neolithic Site in Northern Vietnam*, pp. 21–32. Terra Australis 33. Canberra: ANU E Press.

Matsumura, H. and M.J. Hudson. 2005. Dental perspectives on the population history of Southeast Asia. *American Journal of Physical Anthropology* 127: 182–209. doi.org/10.1002/ajpa.20067.

Matsumura, H. and M.F. Oxenham. 2013a. Eastern Asia and Japan: human biology. In I Ness (ed.), *The Encyclopedia of Global Human Migration*. Wiley-Blackwell. DOI: 10.1002/9781444351071. doi.org/10.1002/9781444351071.

——. 2013b. Population dispersal from East Asia into Southeast Asia: Perspectives from prehistoric human remains, in K. Pechenkina and M.F. Oxenham (eds), *Bioarchaeological Perspectives on Migration and Health in Ancient East Asia*, pp. 179–212. Florida: University of Florida.

——. 2014. Demographic transitions and migration in prehistoric East/Southeast Asia: Through the lens of nonmetric dental traits. *American Journal of Physical Anthropology* 155: 45–65. doi.org/10.1002/ajpa.22537.

—— .2015. Eastern Asia and Japan: human biology. In P. Bellwood, (ed.), *The Global Prehistory of Human Migration*, pp. 217–223 New York: Wiley-Liss.

Matsumura, H. and M. Zuraina. 1999. Metric analyses of an early Holocene human skeleton from Gua Gunung Runtuh, Malaysia. *American Journal of Physical Anthropology* 109: 327–340. doi.org/10.1002/(SICI)1096-8644(199907)109:3<327::AID-AJPA4>3.0.CO;2-5.

Matsumura, H., M. Yoneda, Y. Dodo, M.F. Oxenham, N.K. Thuy, N.L. Cuong, L.M. Dung, V.T. Long, M. Yamagata, J. Sawada, K. Shinoda and W. Takigawa. 2008a. Terminal Pleistocene human skeleton from Hang Cho cave, northern Vietnam: implications for the biological affinities of Hoabinhian people. *Anthropological Science* 116: 135–148. doi.org/10.1537/ase.070405.

Matsumura, H., M.F. Oxenham, Y. Dodo, K. Domett, N.L. Cuong, N.K. Thuy, N.K. Dung, D. Huffer and M. Yamagata. 2008b. Morphometric affinity of the late Neolithic human remains from Man Bac, Ninh Binh Province, Vietnam: Key skeletons with which to debate the 'two layer' hypothesis. *Anthropological Science* 116: 135–148. doi.org/10.1537/ase.070405.

Matsumura, H., K. Domett and D. O'Reilly. 2011a. On the origin of pre-Angkorian peoples: Perspectives from cranial and dental affinity of the human remains from Iron Age Phum Snay, Cambodia. *Anthropological Science* 119: 67–79. doi.org/10.1537/ase.100511.

Matsumura, H., M.F. Oxenham, K.T. Nguyen, L.C. Nguyen, and K.D. Nguyen. 2011b. The population history of mainland Southeast Asia: Two layer model in the context of Northern Vietnam. In N. Enfield (ed.), *Dynamics of Human Diversity: the Case of Mainland Southeast Asia*, pp. 153–178. Canberra: Pacific Linguistics.

Matsumura, H., N.L. Cuong and M. Yamagata. 2013. The origin of Hoa Diem people: Perspectives from cranial and dental morphometric Analysis. In M. Yamagata, and V.T. Hoang (eds), *The Excavation of Hoa Diem in Central Vietnam*, pp. 241–260. Tokyo: Showa Womens University.

Matsumura, H., M.F. Oxenham and N.L. Cuong. 2015. Hoabinhian: Key Population with which to debate the peopling Southeast Asia, T. Goebel and Y. Kaifu (eds), *Emergence and Diversity of Modern Human Behavior in Palaeolithic Asia*, pp. 117–132. Texas: Texas A&M University Press.

Mijsberg, W.A. 1940. On a Neolithic Paleo-Melanesian lower jaw found in kitchen midden at Guar Kepah, Province Wellesley, Straits Settlements. Proceedings of 3rd Congress of Prehistorians of the Far East, Singapore, pp. 100–118.

Nakahashi, T. 1993. Temporal craniometric changes from the Jomon to the modern period in western Japan. *American Journal of Physical Anthropology* 90: 409–425. doi.org/10.1002/ajpa.1330900403.

Nakahashi, T. and M. Li (eds). 2002. *Ancient People in the Jiangnan Region, China*. Fukuoka: Kyushu University Press.

Nishimura, M. and N.K. Dung. 2002. Excavation of An Sơn: a Neolithic site in the middle reach of the Vam Co Dong River, southern Vietnam. *Bulletin of the Indo-Pacific Prehistory Association* 22: 101–109.

Oxenham, M.F., H. Matsumura and N.K. Dung (eds). 2011. *Man Bac: The Excavation of a Late Neolithic Site in Northern Vietnam*. Terra Australis 33. Canberra: ANU E Press.

Pietrusewsky, M. 1981. Cranial variation in early metal age Thailand and Southeast Asia studied by multivariate procedures. *Homo* 32: 1–26.

Pietrusewsky, M. and M.T. Douglas. 2002. *Ban Chiang, a Prehistoric Village Site in Northeast Thailand I: The Human Skeletal Remains*. Philadelphia: University of Pennsylvania, Museum of Archaeology and Anthropology.

Pietrusewsky, M. and C. Chang. 2003. Taiwan aboriginals and peoples of the Pacific–Asia region: multivariate craniometric comparisons. *Anthropological Science* 111: 293–332. doi.org/10.1537/ase.111.293.

Reinecke, A. 2008. Briquetage und Gräber in Go O Chua (Vietnam): Zeugnisse der Prä-Funan- bis Angkor-Periode im Mekong-Delta: *Zeitschrift für Archäologie Außereuropäischer Kulturen Bd.* 2-2007: 395–402.

Sangvichien, S. 1971. *Physical Anthropology of the skull of Thai* .Unpublished PhD dissertation, Faculty of Medicine Siriraj Hospital, Mahidol University, Bangkok, no. 2514.

Sieveking, G.G. 1954. Excavations at Gua Cha, Kelantan, Part 1. *Federation Museums Journal* 1: 75–143.

Sneath, P.H. and R.R. Sokal. 1973. *Numerical Taxonomy*. San Francisco: WH Freeman and Co.

Suzuki, H., Y. Mizoguchi and E. Conese. 1993. Craniofacial measurement of artificially deformed skulls from the Philippines. *Anthropological Science* 101: 111–127. doi.org/10.1537/ase.101.111.

The, N.K. and D.N. Cong. 2001. *Archeology in Long An Province*. Long An: Long An Provincial Museum.

Thuy, N.K. 1990. Ancient human skeletons at Con Co Ngua. *Khao Co Hoc* 3: 37–48 (in Vietnamese with an English summary).

Woo, J. 1959. Human fossils found in Liukiang, Kwangsi, China. *Vertebrata Palasiatica* 3: 108–118.

Yamagata, M. and V.T. Hoang (eds). 2013. *The excavation of Hoa Diem in central Vietnam*. Tokyo: Showa Women's University.

Yokoh, Y. 1940. Beiträge zur kraniologie der Dajak. *Japanese Journal of Medical Science, Part I Anatomy* 8: 1–354.

ZCARI (Zhejiang Cultural Relics Archaeological Research Institute). 2003. Hemudu-Xishiqishidai yizhi kaogu fajüe baogao Hemudu [Report on the Excavation of the Neolithic Hemudu Site]. Beijing: Wenwu (in Chinese).

Zhang, C. and H.-c. Hung. 2010. The emergence of agriculture in southern China. *Antiquity* 84(323): 11–25. doi.org/10.1017/S0003598X00099737.

——. 2012. Later hunter-gatherers in Southern China, 18000–3000BC. *Antiquity* 86(331): 11–25. doi.org/10.1017/S0003598X00062438.

5

Using Dental Metrical Analysis to Determine the Terminal Pleistocene and Holocene Population History of Java

Sofwan Noerwidi

The Song Keplek 5 burial from Java, initially dated to the early Holocene from charcoal in the grave fill, has now been directly dated to around 3000 BP. Bivariate and multivariate analyses of its lower premolar and molar diameters demonstrates affinities with recent Javanese and Malays, whereas other Java burials dated to between the terminal Pleistocene and mid-Holocene have greater dental metrical similarities with recent Australians and Melanesians. This finding is consistent with Peter Bellwood's argument that the major component of the late Holocene gene pool of Indo-Malaysians can be attributed to a migration of Austronesian-speaking 'southern Mongoloids' from Taiwan into Island Southeast Asia at around 4000 BP. However, there may also have been later exogenous inputs into the gene pool of the Javanese, as suggested by their Y-chromosome diversity and implied here by analysis of the lower dental metrics of some of the Batujaya burials from Java's protohistorical period.

Introduction

Java is of strategic importance for registering the dispersal of anatomically modern humans across the region that is today Island Southeast Asia (ISEA) and further on into the Pacific. Prior to the Holocene rise in sea levels that separated Java from Sumatra, the Malay Peninsula and Kalimantan (Borneo), Java was part of the Late Pleistocene subcontinent known as Sundaland. The *Homo sapiens* fossil record in Java may date back to as early as 125,000 BP, based on the proposed dating for the Punung (Gunung Sewu) rainforest fauna (Sémah et al. 2006; Westaway et al. 2007), which includes a human premolar crown with diameters of *H. sapi*ens rather than *H. erectus* size (Storm et al. 2005). More definitive evidence of early *H. sapiens* in Java is presented by the Wajak burials, minimally dated to 28,000 BP (Storm et al. 2013), still somewhat younger than the *ca.* 35,000 BP directly dated human remains from Niah (Borneo), and the colonisation of Australia and Melanesia between *ca.* 50,000 and 60,000 BP (Reynolds et al. 2013). Fossil remains of the terminal Pleistocene to mid-Holocene hunter-gatherer occupants of Java are preserved within the habitation sequences of the Gunung Sewu caves and Gua Pawon. Late Holocene colonisation events associated with the dispersal of Austronesian languages across ISEA and much of the Pacific, and the introduction of Indic culture to protohistorical Java, are potentially registered in the human remains from cemetery sites such as Batujaya and Plawangan.

There has been considerable debate over the origins of the Austronesian languages and the significance of the dispersal of these languages for the gene pool of present-day Island Southeast Asians. Lexicostatistical analysis by Isidore Dyen originally suggested an origin in Melanesia, and John Terrell has perpetuated the notion of Melanesia's importance for understanding developments in ISEA with his proposal that the two regions constitute an 'entangled bank' (see Chambers 2006). Solheim (2006: 90–92) noted that shell tools were reconstructed by linguists as an aspect of proto-Austronesian material culture, and accordingly located the proto-Austronesian homeland in the northern Moluccas, the centre of distribution of shell adzes extending from the Bismarcks into eastern Indonesia, the Ryukyus and Western Micronesia. This view is consistent with the craniometric analysis of Pietrusewsky (2006), which finds that Southeast Asians constitute a discrete, homogeneous group. However, the most widely accepted proposal is that the Austronesian languages originated in Taiwan, prior to their dispersal across ISEA and the smaller and more remote islands of the Pacific, facilitated by their advanced watercraft and fuelled by the agricultural component of their subsistence economy (Blust 1976; Bellwood 1995). Bellwood (1997) further proposes that the ancestors of the proto-Austronesians were agricultural 'Mongoloids' located in southern China, and their absorption of the indigenous ISEA foragers resulted in ISEA's 'Southern Mongoloid' racial type. According to Bellwood's 'Out of Taiwan' theory, initial expansion from Taiwan commenced at about 4000 BP and extended across ISEA by 3000 BP, as registered by the appearance of Neolithic sites and associated material culture.

A more complicated scenario has recently been proposed by Karafet et al. (2010) based on their analysis of Indonesian Y-chromosome diversity. There were two Late Pleistocene colonisation events into Sundaland, an 'A' event associated with the dispersal of *H. sapiens* from Africa to Australia and Melanesia at around 50,000 BP, and a 'B' event in which terminal Pleistocene foragers from Mainland Southeast Asia migrated south into Sundaland. The 'C' and 'D' events in Indonesia's population history correspond to the 'Out-of-Taiwan' migration, and to protohistorical inputs from India into Sumatra and Java and from North Vietnam into Borneo, respectively.

Figure 5.1 Map of Java showing locations of the studied specimens. Blue: Pre-Neolithic sites, Red: Palaeometallic sites.

Source: Google Maps with modification by S. Noerwidi.

One of the critical burials for testing the various scenarios described above is Song Keplek 5 from the Gunung Sewu caves in Java (Figure 5.1). Initially it was dated to 7020±180 BP on charcoal from the grave fill, but the features of the skull pointed to a Mongoloid affinity (Détroit 2002; Widianto 2006). The Mongoloid identification conflicted with the 'Australo-Melanesian' morphology described for other early to mid-Holocene human remains from ISEA, and also cast doubt on scenarios that associated a Mongoloid presence in ISEA with the late Holocene migration of Austronesian speakers from Taiwan. However, as detailed below, direct dating of the Song Keplek 5 burial places it within the timeframe for the 'Out-of-Taiwan' migration and not within the mid-Holocene prehistory of the island. Accordingly, one of the key predictions of the 'Out-of-Taiwan' theory – a dichotomy between Australo-Melanesians dating to the mid-Holocene and earlier, and Mongoloids dating to the late Holocene – retains its viability for testing against the Java human skeletal record. For further details on the study presented here, see the author's Erasmus Mundus Master's thesis (Noerwidi 2011/12), from which this contribution is extracted and adapted.

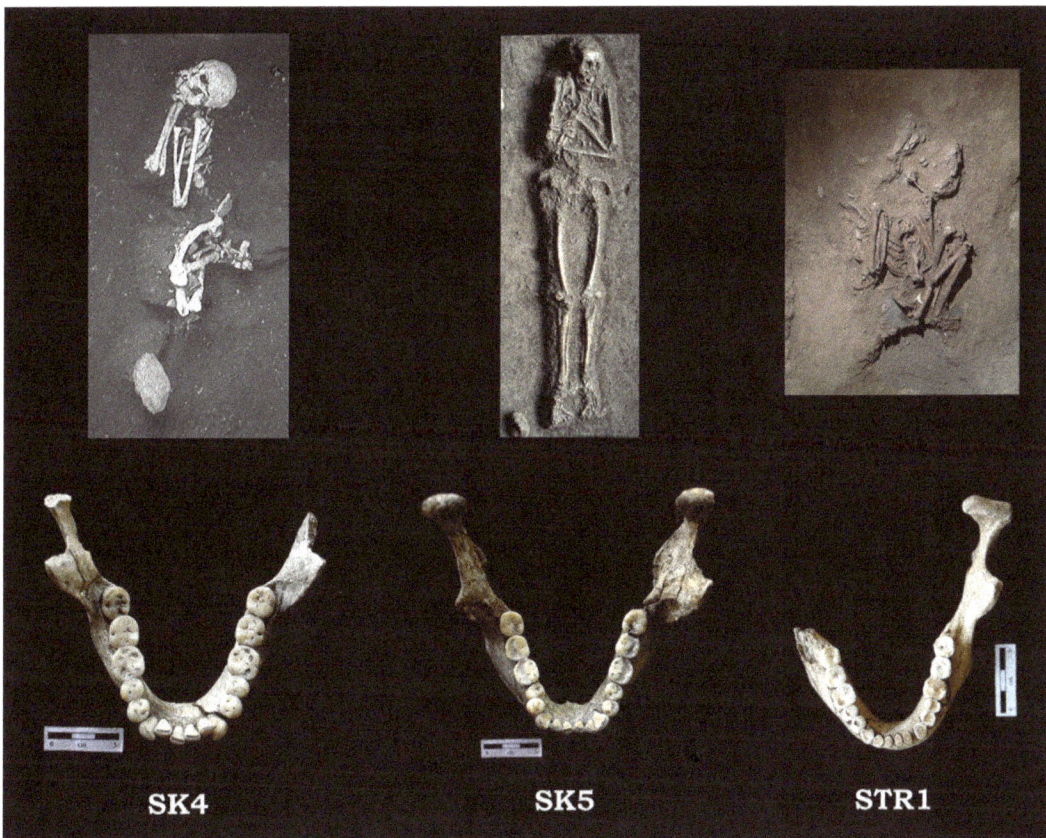

Figure 5.2 Human remains with the mandibles discovered at Song Keplek and Song Tritis sites.
Source: Photographs of SK4, SK5 and STR1 *in situ* by Détroit (2002); kind permission by H.T. Simanjuntak and F. Détroit, others by S. Noerwidi.

Materials and methods

The author's original study (Noerwidi 2011/12) focused on Song Keplek 5 and in particular its mandible and lower teeth, which are the best preserved parts of the skull (Figure 5.2). The critical comparisons lie with other specimens from Java's human skeletal record, which led to the decision to include a focus on the premolars and first and second molars, as these are usually better preserved than the other lower teeth. As described below, the Java archaeological specimens available for comparison are dated to between the terminal Pleistocene and the early centuries AD (Table 5.1). To test the predicted Australo-Melanesian affinities of the pre-3500 BP Java fossils, versus the predicted Southern Mongoloid affinities of the post-3500 BP archaeological specimens, the lower premolars and molars were also recorded for 51 recent Australian, Melanesian and ISEA mandibles collected by seventeenth- to nineteenth-century French naturalists. These mandibles, held at the Paris Museum of Natural History, include four Tasmanians, four mainland Australians, three Torres Strait Islanders, one Papuan, six Solomon Islanders and three Fijians (21 Australo-Melanesians), as well as 20 Javanese and 10 Malays (30 Southeast Asians).

In addition to Song Keplek 5, four other specimens from four sites in the Gunung Sewu region of East Java were available for analysis (Figure 5.1). None of them are directly dated and this attaches some doubt to the reliability of their age indicated in Table 5.1, when we consider that direct dating of Song Keplek 5 reduced its antiquity by approximately 4,000 years compared to its age as implied by charcoal from the grave fill. However, from the available age estimates, Song Tritis 1 would be predicted to align with Song Keplek 5 in showing Southern Mongoloid affinities, whereas Song Keplek 4, Song Terus 1 (Figure 5.2) and Gua Braholo 5 should show Australo-Melanesian affinities. An Australo-Melanesian affinity would also be expected for two specimens from Gua Pawon, in West Java, which *are* directly dated to the terminal Pleistocene and early Holocene, respectively. Fifteen specimens dated to within the last 2,000 years or so together represent the two open-air cemetery sites of Baturaja and Plawangan on Java's north coast. Their predicted affinities would be predominantly Southern Mongoloid, although the pronounced, early Indian influence documented at Batujaya (Manguin and Indradjaja 2011) makes the skeletal remains of particular interest for registering the 'D' event in the multi-stage colonisation scenario of Karafet et al. (2010).

Table 5.1 Archaeological specimens from Java (Figure 5.1) used in this study.

ID	Specimen	Dating	Calibrated date cal.BP (at 2 s.d)	Laboratory/Literature reference
BHL5	Gua Braholo 5	13,290±400 BP (charcoal at same stratigraphic level)	17,328–14,768 (95%)	P3G 1998 (Simanjuntak 2002)
ST1	Song Terus 1	9330±90 BP (shellfish in grave fill)	Calibration inappropriate	Beta 124011 (Sémah et al., 2004)
SK4	Song Keplek 4	4510±90 BP (charcoal in grave fill)	5378–4921 (90.5%) or 5498–5437 (4.9%)	Beta 69689 (Simanjuntak 2002)
SK5	Song Keplek 5	3053±65 BP (direct date on human bone)	3450–3116 (95.4%)	AA96775 (Noerwidi 2011/12)
STR1	Song Tritis 1	ca. 3000 BP (estimated age based on material culture)	No dates	Widianto 2001
Paw5	Gua Pawon 5	9525±200 BP (direct date on human bone)	11,342–10,301 (95.4%)	P3TIR, BATAN 2004 (this paper)
Paw4	Gua Pawon 4	7320±180 BP (direct date on human bone)	8510–7839 (94.9%)	P3TIR, BATAN 2004 (this paper)
Bat	Batujaya; 8 specimens	1998±34 (charcoal from cemetery)	2060–1923 (92.8%) or 2091–2071 (2.6%)	Wk-21319 (Manguin and Indradjaja 2011)
Pla	Plawangan; 7 specimens	Early centuries AD (estimated from associated material culture)	No reliable dates	Bintarti 2000

Source: Dates calibrated with Intcal 13 (Oxcal 4.2; Bronk Ramsey 2014).

The tooth measurements collected for this study and analysed here are the maximum mesio-distal (M-D) length and bucco-lingual (B-L) breadth of the left-side premolars and the first and second molars. Recent Australo-Melanesians have larger average tooth size than recent Southeast Asians, including Malays and Javanese, as well as 'shape' differences in the relative size of the tooth diameters to each other, after removing the size difference effects (Matsumura and Hudson 2005). Principal Components Analysis (PCA) is a useful statistical tool to detect patterns in both tooth size and shape as it compresses the data by reducing the number of dimensions with little loss of information. In particular, the first principal component usually reflects size differences when biological data are analysed, while the other components reflect different, statistically independent aspects of shape (Joliffe 2002). However, the PCA results produce scattergrams that do not clearly specify the relationships of the studied specimens to each other. To achieve that outcome, the Euclidean distances between each pair of specimens were calculated and the specimens were grouped together using hierarchical, agglomerative clustering.

This particular procedure groups the most similar specimens into pairs, and then either groups other similar specimens with these pairs or else groups together similar pairs, progressively adding less similar specimens or groups until all of the original specimens have been included within a single large cluster (Holland 2006).

Two caveats should be mentioned that may obscure complete confirmation of the hypothesised expectations (see Snell 1949; Brown 1989). The first caveat is that males tend to have larger teeth than females. Accordingly, male and female samples of groups with larger teeth and groups with smaller teeth will tend to overlap more with each other than if the compared samples were restricted just to males or females. In the present study, male and female samples were used because of the unreliability of assigning sex to mandibles, even though this contributes sex-based variability to the tooth sizes of the compared groups. The second caveat is that tooth wear during life includes a component known as interstitial wear, caused by the friction between adjacent teeth in the tooth-row, which pares back the mesio-distal lengths of the adjacent teeth. Particularly in the case of elderly individuals from populations that experienced heavy wear – notably, populations that practised traditional foraging – the mesio-distal lengths are systematically reduced compared with the bucco-lingual widths. The implications for the present analysis are the potential for specifically reduced tooth lengths and decreased overall tooth size for some of the forager specimens.

Accordingly, Bellwood's (1997) scenario of Southern Mongoloid immigration into ISEA after 3500 BP entails the four, following testable predictions for the tooth measurements collected for this study.

1. When the M-D and B-L diameters for the premolars and molars are graphed, these should tend to be larger for the pre-Neolithic Java fossils and recent Australo-Melanesians than the Neolithic to recent Javanese and Malays.

2. This difference in tooth-size trends should also be revealed by the first principal component of the PCA.

3. The second and third components of the PCA should reveal tooth-size shape differences distinguishing pre-Neolithic Java fossils and recent Australo-Melanesians from Neolithic and later Javanese and Malays.

4. The cluster analysis should identify discrete clusters of pre-Neolithic Java and recent Australo-Melanesian specimens on the one hand and Neolithic to recent Javanese and Malays on the other hand.

Results

Bivariate Analyses

In Figures 5.3 to 5.6, the left mesio-distal diameters of the lower first premolar (P_3), second premolar (P_4), first molar (M_1) and second molar (M_2) are plotted on the X-axis, and the left bucco-lingual diameters are plotted on the Y-axis. In three of the plots (Figures 5.3, 5.4 and 5.6), there are recent Australo-Melanesians with larger teeth than any recorded for recent Southeast Asians, and recent Southeast Asians with smaller teeth than any recorded for recent Australo-Melanesians. There is also considerable overlap between the Australo-Melanesian and Southeast Asian ranges of variation, but this is presumably due in part to comparing female Australo-Melanesians with male Southeast Asians. However, the overlap is so pronounced for the first molar (Figure 5.5) that it is difficult to ascertain whether the recent Australo-Melanesians and Southeast Asians recorded for this study show any apparent difference in first lower molar size.

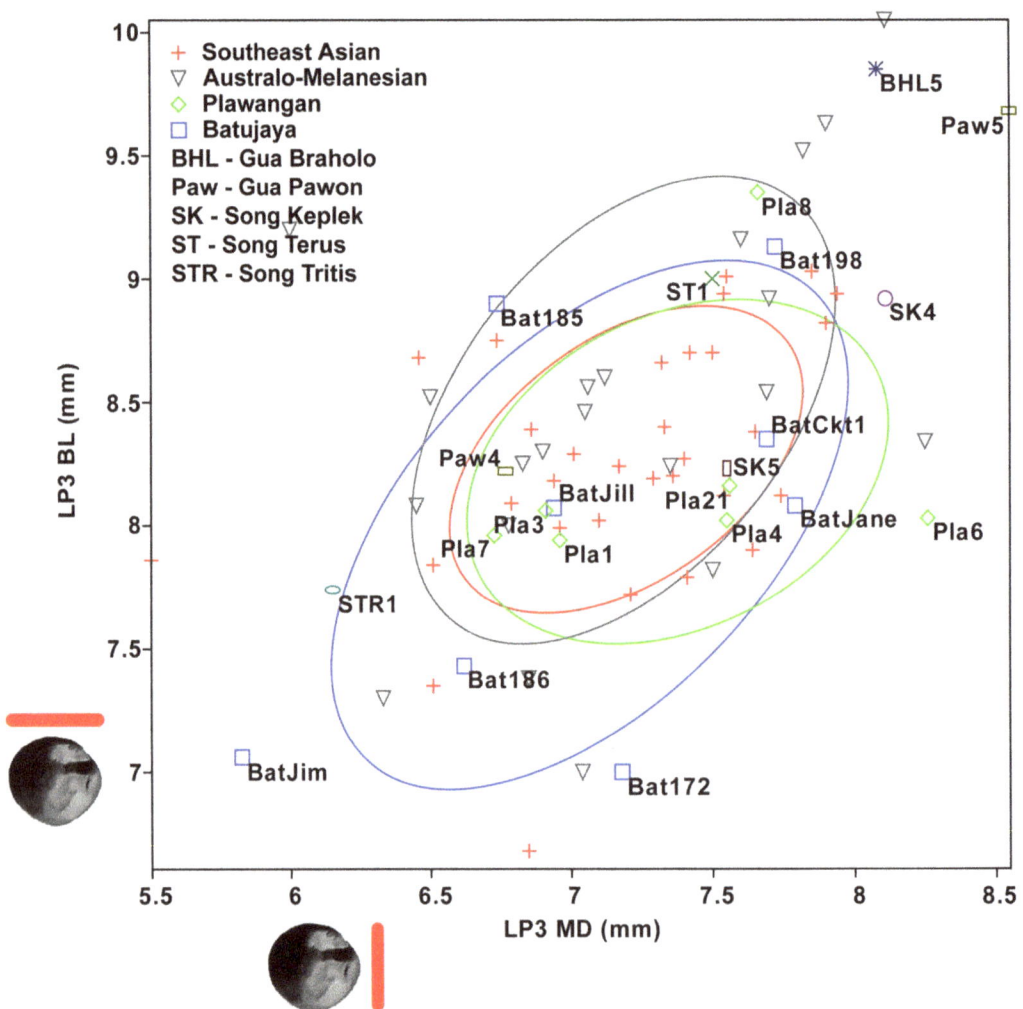

Figure 5.3 Bivariate plot of mesio-distal versus bucco-lingual measurements for LP$_3$.
Source: S. Noerwidi.

Most of the pre-Neolithic Java specimens show large premolars and/or molars. Paw5 has tooth diameters that fall above the recent Southeast Asian range or, in the case of the fourth premolar (Figure 5.4), just within it. ST1 and SK4 have molar diameters that fall above the recent Southeast Asian range and premolar diameters that are large by recent Southeast Asian standards, albeit within the range. BLH5 has premolar diameters that fall above the recent Southeast Asian range, although its molar diameters would be typical by recent Southeast Asian standards. It may also be noted that these pre-Neolithic Java specimens have tooth diameters that consistently fall within the recent Australo-Melanesian range, except for the first molar, where the diameters of SK4 and Paw5 are actually larger than any recorded here for Australo-Melanesians. However, it should be noted that one of the pre-Neolithic Java specimens, Paw4, has tooth diameters that either fall within the recent Southeast Asian range or, in the case of the first molar, lie very close (Figures 5.3 to 5.6).

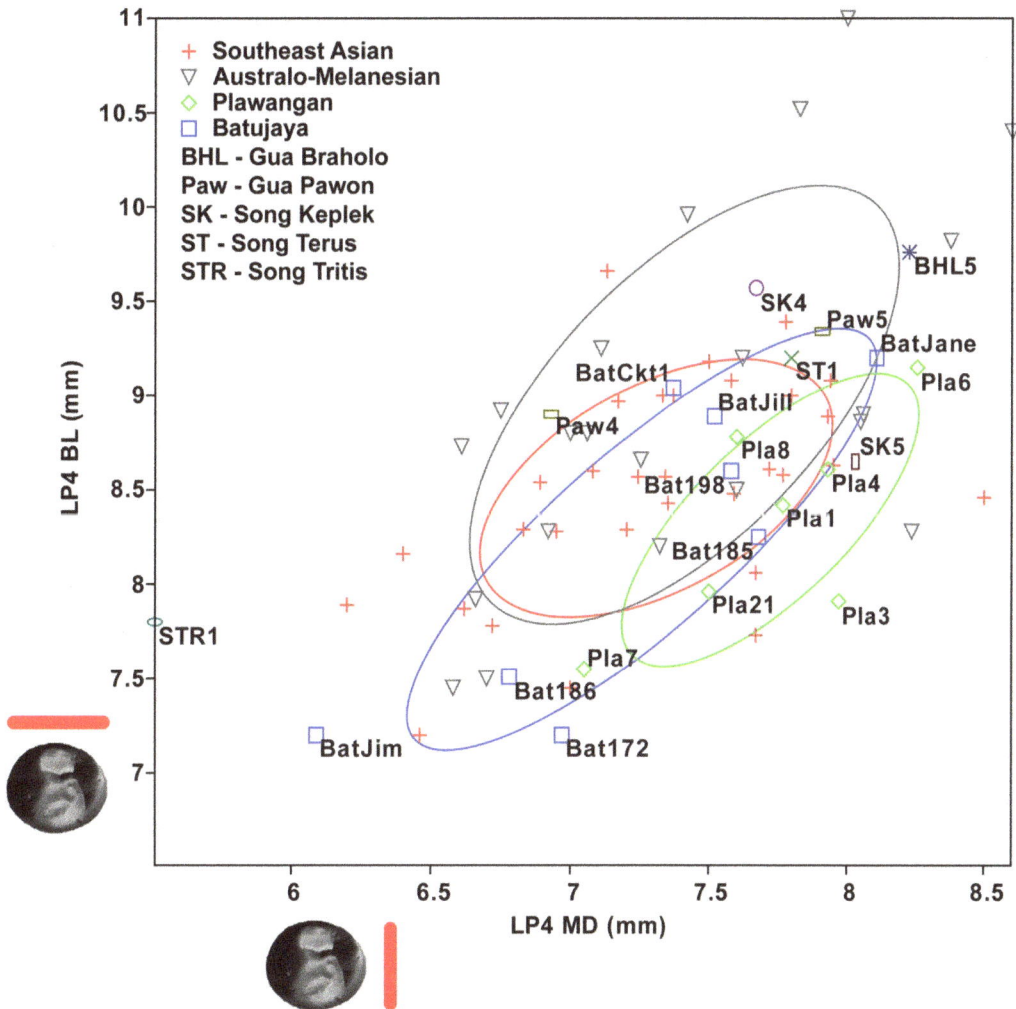

Figure 5.4 Bivariate plot of mesio-distal versus bucco-lingual measurements for LP$_4$.

Source: S. Noerwidi.

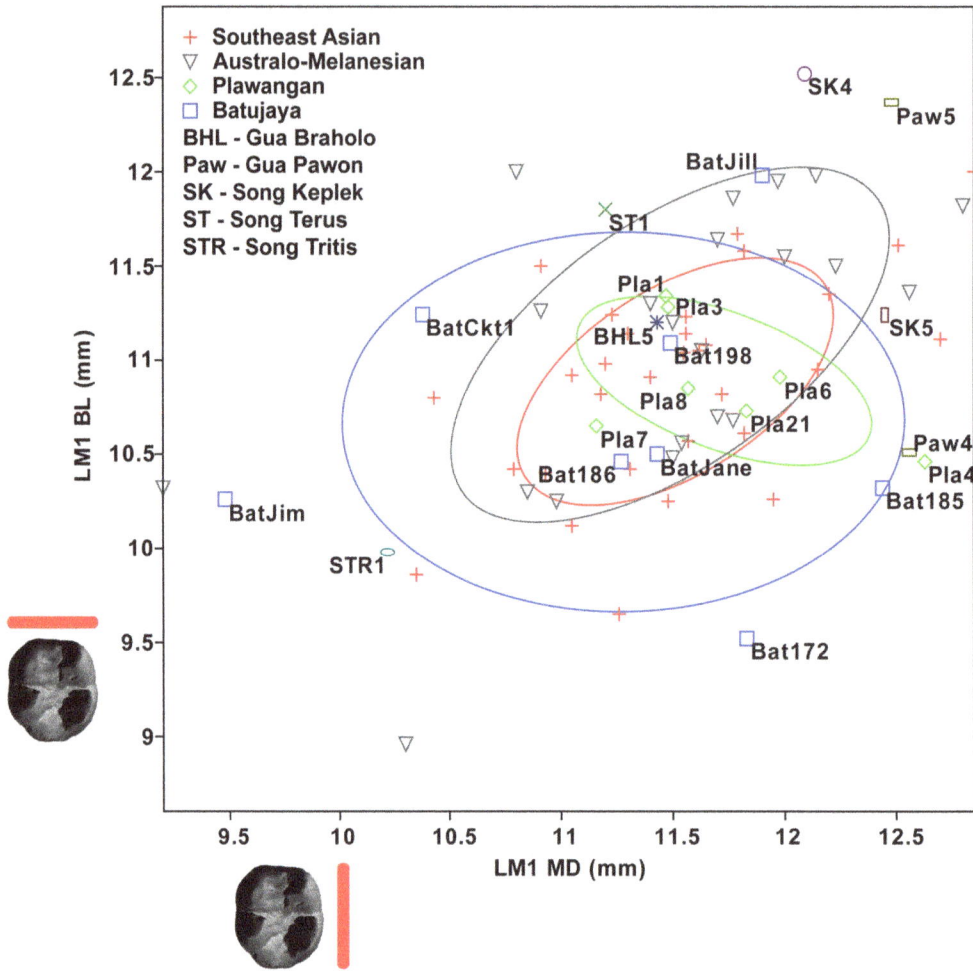

Figure 5.5 Bivariate plot of mesio-distal versus bucco-lingual measurements for LM$_1$.

Source: S. Noerwidi.

In contrast to their pre-Neolithic counterparts, the two Neolithic Java specimens have tooth diameters that are either typical by recent Southeast Asian standards (SK5) or small (STR1). STR1 from Song Tritus has remarkably small teeth, especially the lengths, which are consistently less than those recorded here for any recent Southeast Asian.

Finally, the Palaeometallic teeth from Batujaya and Plawangan are best described as similar in size to recent Southeast Asian teeth. Some show a tendency to be comparatively large, notably Pla6, which has lengths and/or breadths that put it outside of the recent Southeast Asian range except on its first molar. However, the specimens that possess remarkably small teeth, notably BatJim for whom the premolars and the first molar are smaller than those of any recent Southeast Asian recorded here, balance this.

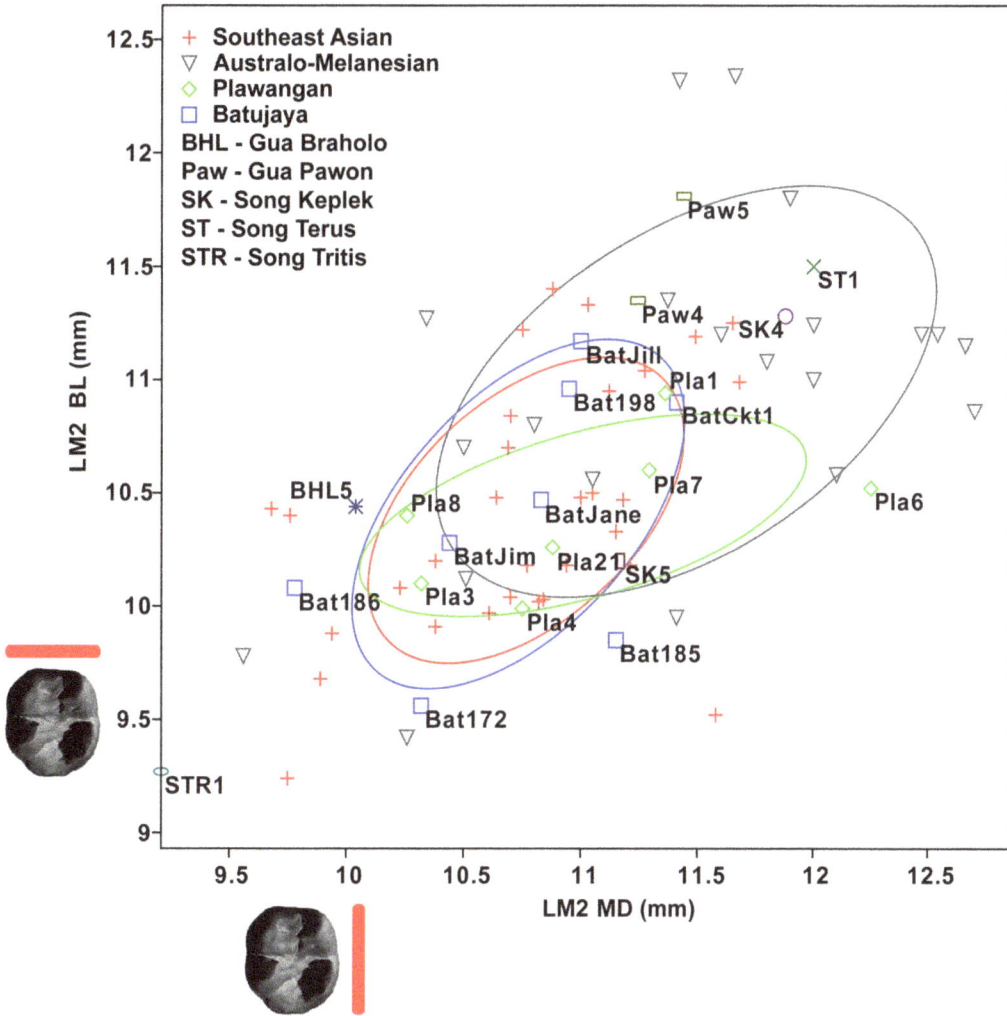

Figure 5.6 Bivariate plot of mesio-distal versus bucco-lingual measurements for LM$_2$.
Source: S. Noerwidi.

In summary, prediction 1 of Bellwood's Southern Mongoloid immigration scenario is clearly confirmed, due to the relatively large tooth size of recent Australo-Melanesians and especially the pre-Neolithic Java fossils compared with Neolithic and later specimens from Southeast Asia.

Principal Components Analysis

Before presenting the results from the PCA, we need to assess how many principal components (PCs) to include for analysis. A rule of thumb is to include all of the PCs with an eigenvalue greater than 1; that is, PCs that account for a larger proportion of the total variance than the average variance accounted for by the measurements originally entered into the PCA (Joliffe 2002). As there are eight measurements in the original data, the eigenvalues cumulatively sum to 8, and for each of the eight PCs, the percentage it contributes to the total variance can be calculated (Table 5.2).

Table 5.2 Eigenvalue and percentage of variance in PCA.

PC	Eigenvalue	% variance	Cumul. eigenvalue	Cumul. % variance
1	4.04	50.50	4.04	50.50
2	1.11	13.85	5.15	64.35
3	0.85	10.56	5.99	74.91
4	0.66	8.20	6.65	83.11
5	0.44	5.56	7.09	88.67
6	0.42	5.23	7.51	93.90
7	0.31	3.85	7.82	97.75
8	0.18	2.25	8.00	100.00

Source: S. Noerwidi.

PC1 accounts for about half of the total variance, while PC2 and PC3 together account for about half of the remaining half. The decision was made to include all of PC1 to PC3 for analysis even though PC2 and PC3 are marginal in terms of the rule of thumb stated by Joliffe (2002).

Table 5.3 presents the loadings that the eight measurements have on each of the eight axes (PCs). All of the loadings are positive on Axis 1, which shows that PC1 is a size component that usefully summarises overall tooth size. Axis 2 has negative loadings on all of the bucco-lingual breadths and positive loadings on all of the mesio-distal lengths, except for the second molar length, which has a negative loading. Thus, the overall distinction is drawn between relatively short, broad teeth (registered by a negative PC2 score) and relatively narrow teeth (registered by a positive PC2 score). As noted previously, advancing interstitial wear tends to shorten teeth, decreasing the value of a positive PC2 score or making a negative PC2 score more strongly negative. Finally, Axis 3 has negative loadings on the premolar diameters and positive loadings on the molar diameters. Accordingly, a positive PC3 score registers a specimen with relatively large molars while a negative PC3 score registers a specimen with relatively large premolars.

Table 5.3 Value number of PCA correlation.

	Axis 1	Axis 2	Axis 3	Axis 4	Axis 5	Axis 6	Axis 7	Axis 8
P_3 MD	0.34	0.46	-0.25	0.19	0.54	-0.58	0.02	-0.08
P_3 BL	0.38	-0.09	-0.46	0.13	-0.01	0.35	-0.70	0.04
P_4 MD	0.36	0.21	-0.06	0.50	-0.68	-0.15	0.09	0.15
P_4 BL	0.38	-0.16	-0.45	-0.13	-0.01	0.37	0.69	-0.05
M_1 MD	0.28	0.38	0.61	-0.45	0.13	0.35	-0.09	0.24
M_1 BL	0.40	-0.23	0.25	-0.50	-0.29	-0.31	-0.12	-0.59
M_2 MD	0.31	-0.47	0.37	0.45	0.36	0.31	0.08	-0.32
M_2 BL	0.36	-0.55	0.25	-0.16	0.09	-0.27	0.05	0.67

Source: S. Noerwidi.

A strong positive score for PC1 reflects large teeth overall, while a strong negative score reflects small teeth overall. Thus, PC1 in Figures 5.7 and 5.8 shows the great variability of Australo-Melanesians in their tooth size, with some specimens presenting larger teeth than those recorded for any recent Southeast Asian but other specimens presenting teeth as small as those of any recent Southeast Asian. As for the pre-Neolithic Java specimens, three (Paw5, SK4 and ST1) resemble the larger-toothed of the Australo-Melanesians in overall tooth size, and lie beyond the recent Southeast Asian range. BHL5 also has large teeth, at the upper limit of the recent Southeast Asian range, whereas Paw4 is typical by recent Southeast Asian standards. The Neolithic and later Java specimens together show a variability, which matches that of recent Southeast Asians on PC1, except STR1 and BatJim (Batujaya) whose overall tooth size is slightly smaller than that of any of the recent Southeast Asians recorded here

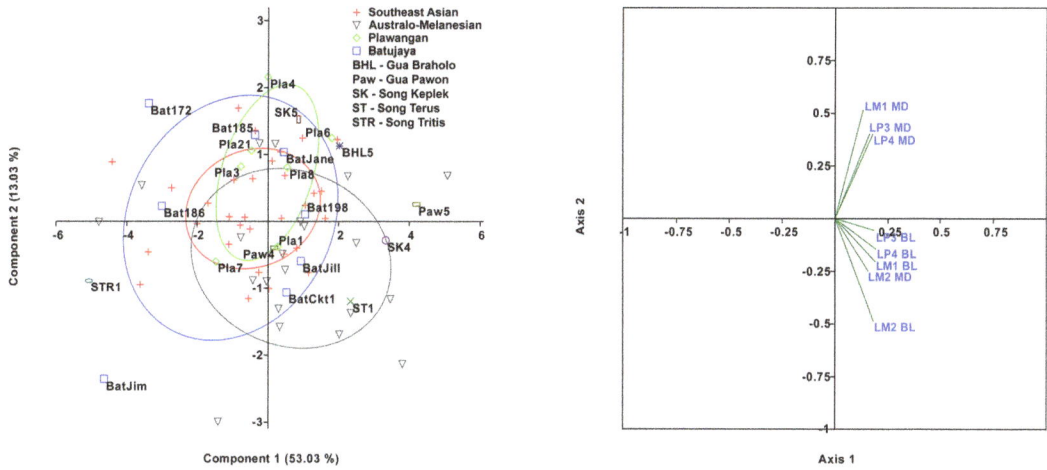

Figure 5.7 Biplot Graph of PC 1–2 for LP$_3$–LM$_2$ and Map of Axis 1 versus Axis 2.

Source: S. Noerwidi.

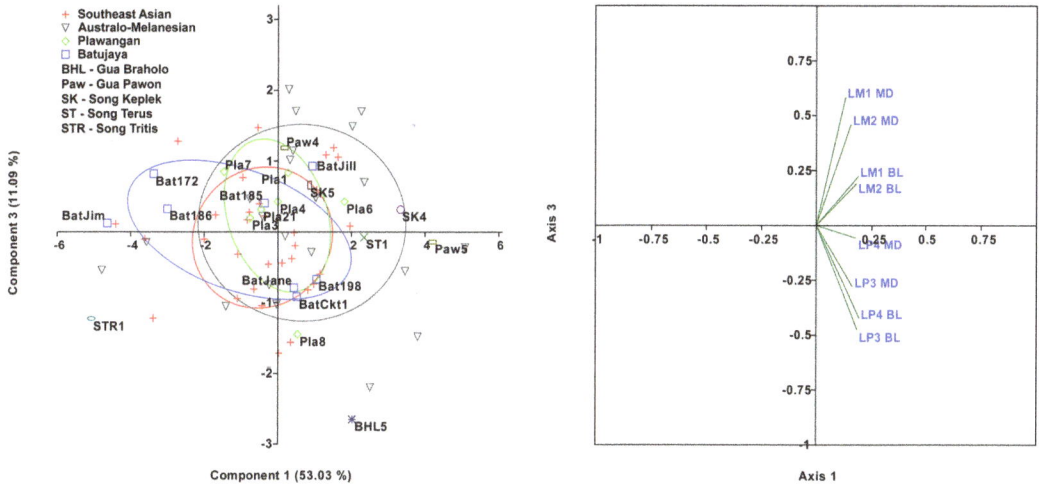

Figure 5.8 Biplot Graph of PC 1–3 for LP$_3$–LM$_2$ and Map of Axis 1 versus Axis 3.

Source: S. Noerwidi.

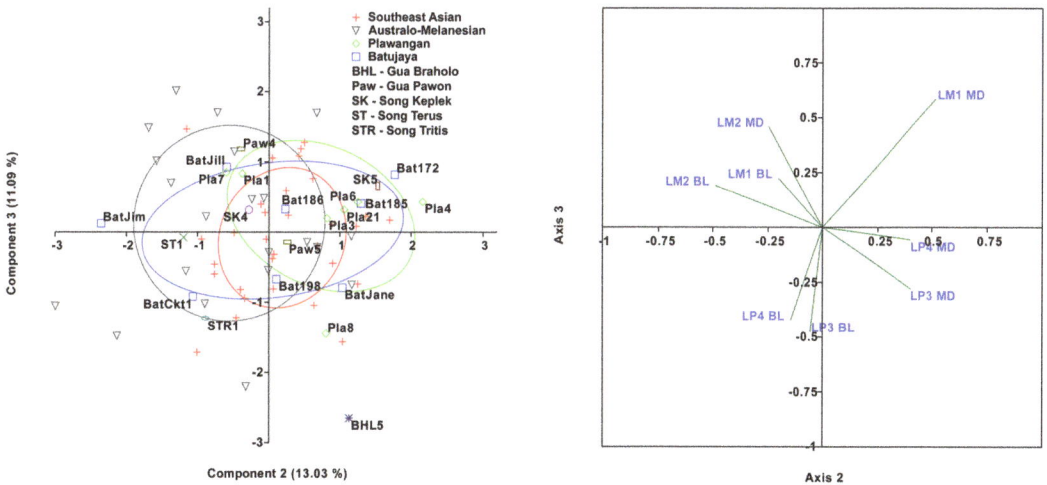

Figure 5.9 Biplot Graph of PC 2–3 for LP$_3$–LM$_2$ and Map of Axis 2 versus Axis 3.

Source: S. Noerwidi.

The graphs that include PC2 (Figures 5.7 and 5.9) reveal a moderate degree of overlap of Australo-Melanesians and recent Southeast Asians in their PC2 scores. However, some of the former are distinct from the latter on account of their relatively broader teeth and, conversely, some recent Southeast Asians have relatively more narrow teeth than recorded here for any Australo-Melanesian. The BatJim specimen has the relatively broad teeth otherwise shown only by Australo-Melanesians and falls well away from recent Southeast Asians in this regard. On the other hand, Pla4 (Plawangan) has slightly more narrow teeth (relatively speaking) than recorded here for any recent Southeast Asian.

The graphs that include PC3 (Figures 5.8 and 5.9) suggest extensive overlap between Australo-Melanesians and recent Southeast Asians in their PC3 scores, distinguished only by Australo-Melanesians' greater variability. The Pre-Neolithic BLH5 fossil has unusually large premolars compared to its molar size, and so is distinguished from every other specimen on its strongly negative PC3 score.

In summary, PC1 demonstrates a larger tooth size for three to four of the pre-Neolithic Java fossils (Paw5, SK4, ST1, and marginally BLH5) than recorded for any of the Neolithic to recent Java and Malay specimens. Similarly large teeth are otherwise recorded only amongst Australo-Melanesians. This result clearly confirms prediction 2 of Bellwood's Southern Mongoloid immigration scenario. The inferences that can be drawn from the shape comparisons (PC2 and PC3) are more equivocal and cannot reasonably be stated as confirmation of Bellwood's prediction 3. However, this may be because such a large proportion of the total variance – just over half – is explained by overall tooth size, whereas both PC2 and PC3 are of marginal value for retention in the PCA presented here.

Cluster analysis

The cluster analysis (Figure 5.10) identified three main clusters. Cluster 1 includes specimens with large teeth, whereas clusters 2 and 3 include specimens with middle-sized and small teeth respectively. These summary descriptions of the clusters are clear from which of the previously discussed Java archaeological specimens are found in which cluster, and from the particular importance of size (rather than any shape aspect) in accounting for the measurements' variability (see PCA results, above). Clusters 1 and 2 join with each other before an isolated Australian specimen joins this super-cluster, with the final join made by Cluster 3.

Cluster 1 includes 10 specimens, four pre-Neolithic Java fossils (SK4, Paw5, ST1 and BLH5) and six Australo-Melanesians (interestingly, all from Tasmania and the Solomon Islands). While one pre-Neolithic Java fossil (Paw4) is included in Cluster 2, so are 12 Australo-Melanesians, four of them in the same sub-cluster as Paw4. Accordingly, the tooth-size difference between Paw4 and the other pre-Neolithic Java fossils is hardly indicative of different 'racial groups', but is instead consistent with the expected tooth-size variability to be found within a single group.

The 52 specimens with middle-sized teeth assigned to Cluster 2 include the majority (26) of the 30 recent Southeast Asians, just over half of the Batujaya specimens (5/8), all seven Plawangan specimens and SK5. Notwithstanding the inclusion of 12 Australo-Melanesians, noted above, Cluster 2 is predominantly a Southern Mongoloid cluster, suggesting that this status applies to SK5.

The 11 small-toothed specimens in Cluster 3 include three of the eight Batujaya specimens, STR1, five recent Southeast Asians and two Australo-Melanesians. The quite strong representation of Batujaya specimens in this cluster suggests a possible role of India as a source for very small-toothed immigrants to Java. The smaller tooth size of Indians compared with Southern Mongoloids is demonstrated by Hanihara (2005: Figure 1). However, this could not be an explanation for the very small teeth of STR1, whose antiquity predates Indian influence on Java, or the two Australo-Melanesians whose very small teeth were also apparent from the PCA.

In summary, the cluster analysis results confirm prediction 4 of Bellwood's Southern Mongoloid immigration scenario. They reveal a cluster of large-toothed specimens restricted to pre-Neolithic Java and Australo-Melanesians, and a cluster of specimens with middle-sized teeth dominated by Neolithic to recent Java and Malay specimens. The latter cluster also includes the pre-Neolithic Java Paw5 fossil and 12 of the 21 Australo-Melanesians, reflecting some combination of the inclusion of small-toothed females in the analysis and intraracial tooth-size variability unrelated to sexual dimorphism.

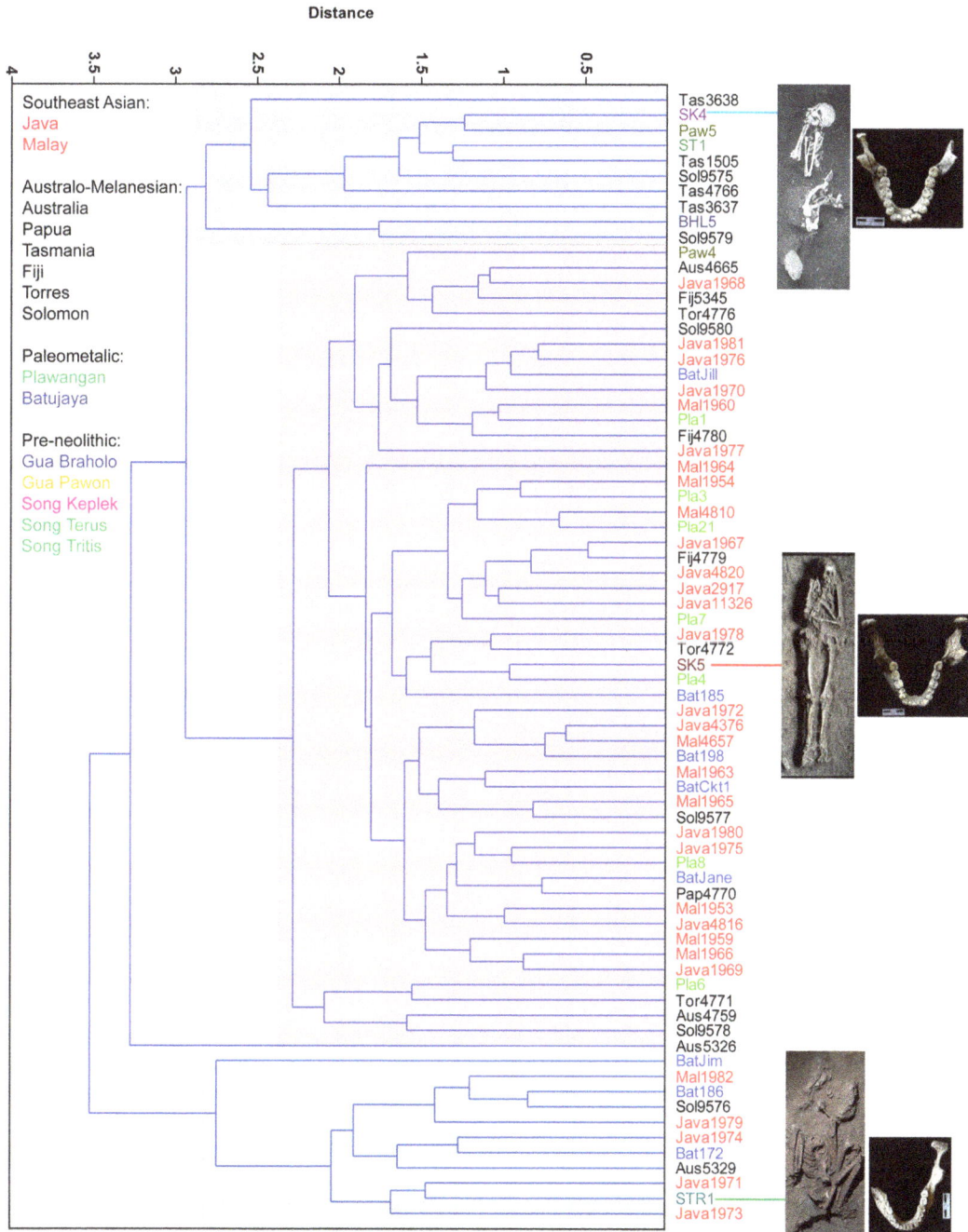

Figure 5.10 Cluster analysis on LP_3-LM_2 from all specimens by Euclidean Distance Method.
Source: S. Noerwidi.

Discussion

Java was part of the Pleistocene subcontinent of Sundaland and its human fossil record has long attracted the attention of anthropologists interested in the colonisation of the region. Initial occupation of Java by *Homo erectus* occurred almost two million years ago. The multiregional hypothesis on modern human origins proposed a deeply rooted ancestry of Australo-Melanesians in Java *Homo erectus*, whereas the ultimate roots of the Mongoloids lay with *Homo erectus* in China (see Wolpoff 1999). There has been an accumulation of fossil and genetic evidence for the Late Pleistocene origins of anatomically modern humans in Africa, leading to widespread rejection of the multiregional hypothesis, but not of all of the associated concepts. For instance, the colonisation of Australia and Melanesia would have occurred via Sundaland, undertaken by colonists with Australo-Melanesian biological affinities. And according to the 'two-layer hypothesis', the populations across Southeast Asia retained these Australo-Melanesian affinities until approximately 4000 BP, when there was a southward expansion of Mongoloid populations from the early agricultural heartlands of southern and central China (Matsumura and Oxenham 2014). Bellwood's (1997) hypothesised expansion of Austronesian-speaking Southern Mongoloids from Taiwan across ISEA after 4000 BP represents the component of the two-layer hypothesis relevant to Java's population history.

The dental metrical analysis performed here is consistent with the points described above. There is a basic distinction between the pre-Neolithic Java fossils, with tooth sizes otherwise recorded for Australo-Melanesians, and the Neolithic and Palaeometallic specimens with tooth sizes similar to those of recent Southeast Asians. The 'Australo-Melanesian' dentitions in Java are dated to contexts spanning the terminal Pleistocene (BHL5) and Pleistocene-Holocene boundary (Paw5) to the early Holocene (ST1) and mid-Holocene, *ca*. 5000 cal. BP (SK4). One of the pre-Neolithic Java fossils (Paw4) cannot be distinguished from recent Southeast Asians on the basis of tooth size, but this is also the case with many Australo-Melanesians. The 'Southern Mongoloid' archaeological dentitions in Java include the SK5 and STR1 Neolithic specimens dated to approximately 3000 BP, and the Batujaya and Plawangan specimens dated to approximately 2000 BP. None of these dentitions are large by recent Southeast Asian standards, and their variability is expressed in the particularly small tooth size of STR1 and some of the Batujaya specimens. In summary, the tooth-size results clearly confirm Bellwood's 'Out-of-Taiwan' scenario.

As observed in the Introduction, Karafet et al. (2010) have proposed a more complicated population history for ISEA that would have involved four colonisation events, two in the Late Pleistocene and two in the late Holocene. However, the data and analytical framework employed in the present study do not allow for a test of the scenario of two Late Pleistocene colonisation events. This is because both events would have involved Australo-Melanesians, and so the Australo-Melanesian affinity of the pre-Neolithic Java fossils would be the expected consequence of either event. On the other hand, there is the potential to test for a protohistorical influence from India, as proposed by Karafet et al. (2010), on top of the Neolithic immigration from Taiwan. The cluster of specimens with very small teeth (Cluster 3 in Figure 5.10) includes an unexpectedly high proportion from Batujaya and none from Plawangan. The difference between these two burial populations, which are geographically and chronologically close, suggests an exogenous genetic contribution to Batujaya, consistent with the site's Indian cultural influences as recorded archaeologically (Manguin and Indradjaja 2011). If there had been an exogenous genetic influence on the Plawangan population, it may have been from northern Vietnam during the early centuries AD. According to Bintarti (2000), Dong Son (protohistorical northern Vietnam) cultural influences can be seen on the Plawangan mortuary assemblage. In this context, it is worth noting that Dong Son Vietnamese tooth size was comparable to that of recent Javanese and Malays (Matsumura and Hudson 2005).

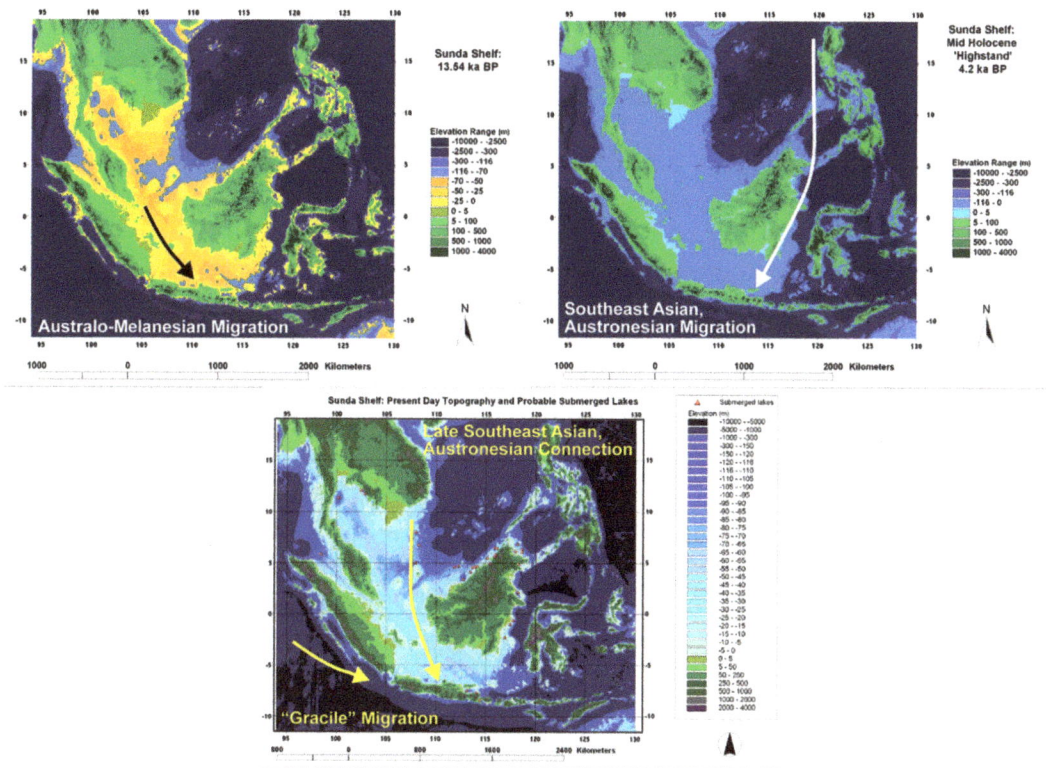

Figure 5.11 The multiple migrations hypothesis: Australo-Melanesian (Latest Pleistocene), Southeast Asian or 'Southern Mongoloid' (Austronesian, 3000 BP), and 'gracile' (early AD, perhaps from India).
Map sources: Sathiamurthy and Voris 2006.

These suggested protohistorical contributions to the recent Javanese gene pool can be regarded as elaborations of the 'two-layer hypothesis'. Note also that proponents of this hypothesis envisage the persistence of the Australo-Melanesian substratum till today amongst the populations of ISEA, albeit to varying degrees, rather than complete replacement by the immigrant Mongoloids. Jacob (1967), Bellwood (1997: 92), Matsumura and Hudson (2005), Hanihara (2006: 100), Matsumura et al. (2011) and Matsumura and Oxenham (2014), amongst others, have all advocated dual inheritance. Further, based on his study of the Gunung Sewu and other ISEA fossil skulls, Détroit (2002) proposed that ISEA has long been an 'inter-population hybridisation zone', with more complex population movements during the pre-Neolithic than the blanket term 'Australo-Melanesian' necessarily conveys. While Détroit's proposal was partly based on the early Holocene dating of SK5 that he had at his disposal – a dating that has now been revised to around 3300 cal. BP – it is consistent with the proposal by Karafet et al. (2010) of a terminal Pleistocene colonisation event from what is now Mainland Southeast Asia into Sundaland.

Conclusions

The Java archaeological specimens covered here correspond in time to the terminal Pleistocene to late Holocene colonisation events proposed by Karafet et al. (2010), and analysis produces compatible results (see Figure 5.11). Their Layer B would have involved a terminal Pleistocene, migration overland from the north by populations with Australo-Melanesian affinities. The pre-Neolithic Java fossils show large teeth overall, which is more an Australo-Melanesian than a Southern Mongoloid trait. Their Layer C corresponds to the 'Out-of-Taiwan', Mongoloid migration, which is the hallmark of the 'two layer hypothesis' in an ISEA context. The Neolithic and Palaeometallic Java specimens all demonstrate small to moderate tooth size, which characterises recent Southeast Asians. This study confirms that Song Keplek 5 has premolar and molar dimensions that place it within Layer C, grouped with those individuals with Southern Mongoloid dental traits. Finally, their Layer D includes protohistorical genetic contributions on ISEA from India and northern Vietnam, and the first of these may be reflected in the particularly small teeth of several Batujaya specimens. The results of the present analysis are particularly strong in their support for Bellwood's 'Out-of-Taiwan' scenario, including his view that a considerable Australo-Melanesian genetic inheritance has persisted across ISEA.

Acknowledgements

The author acknowledges the advice of Peter Bellwood on the 'Out-of-Taiwan' hypothesis and his help in utilising the IPPA–Arizona AMS Outreach Program to obtain a direct date on the Song Keplek 5 burial (provided by Greg Hodgkins of the NSF-Arizona AMS Laboratory). He also thanks his supervisors Florent Détroit, Dominique Grimaud-Hervé, Truman Simanjuntak, Harry Widianto and François Sémah for their advice on the archaeological sites. Thanks are also due to Truman Simanjuntak, Harry Widianto, Etty Indriaty, Rusyad Adi Suriyanto, Pierre-Yves Manguin, Lutfi Yondri, Siswanto and Desril Riva Shanti for permission to record the Java archaeological dental remains.

References

Bellwood, P. 1995. Austronesian prehistory in Southeast Asia: Homeland, expansion and transformation. In P. Bellwood, J.J. Fox and D. Tryon (eds), *The Austronesians: Historical and Comparative Perspectives*, pp. 96–111. Canberra: The Australian National University.

———. 1997. *Prehistory of the Indo-Malaysian Archipelago*. 2nd edition. Hawai'i: University of Hawaii Press.

Bintarti, D.D. 2000. More on urn burials in Indonesia. *Indo-Pacific Prehistory Association Bulletin* 19: 73–76.

Blust, R. 1976. Austronesian culture history: some linguistic inferences and their relations to the archaeological record. *World Archaeology* 8: 19–42. doi.org/10.1080/00438243.1976.9979650.

Bronk Ramsey, C. 2014. Oxcal 4.2 manual. c14.arch.ox.ac.uk/oxcal.html.

Brown, P. 1989. *Coobool Creek: A Morphological and Metrical Analysis of the Crania, Mandibles and Dentitions of a Prehistoric Australian Human Population*. Terra Australis 13. Canberra: The Australian National University.

Chambers, G.K. 2006. Polynesian genetic and Austronesian prehistory. In T. Simanjuntak, I.H.E. Pojoh and M. Hisyam (eds), *Austronesian Diaspora and the Ethnogenesis of People in Indonesian Archipelago*, pp. 299–319. Jakarta: LIPI Press.

Détroit, F. 2002. Origine et évolution des Homo sapiens en Asie du Sud-Est: Descriptions et analyses morphométrique de nouveaux fossils. Unpublished PhD thesis, Muséum National d'Histoire Naturelle, Paris.

Hanihara, T. 2005. Metric dental variation of major human populations. *American Journal of Physical Anthropology* 128: 287–298. doi.org/10.1002/ajpa.20080.

——. 2006. Interpretation of craniofacial variation and diversification of East and Southeast Asians. In M. Oxenham and N. Tayles (eds), *Bioarchaeology of Southeast Asia*, pp. 91–111. Cambridge: Cambridge University Press. doi.org/10.1017/CBO9780511584220.006.

Holland, S.M. 2006. Cluster analysis. strata.uga.edu/6370/lecturenotes/clusterAnalysis.html.

Jacob, T. 1967. *Some Problems Pertaining to the Racial History of the Indonesian Region*. Utrecht: Bureau of Technical Assistance.

Joliffe, I.T. 2002. *Principal Component Analysis*. 2nd edition. New York: Springer.

Karafet, T.M., H. Brian, P.C. Murray, H. Sudoyo, S. Downey, J.S. Lansing and M.F. Hammer. 2010. Major east–west division underlies Y chromosome stratification across Indonesia. *Molecular Biology and Evolution* 27: 1833–1844. doi.org/10.1093/molbev/msq063.

Manguin, P.-Y. and A. Indradjaja. 2011. The Batujaya site: new evidence of early Indian influence in West Java. In P.-Y. Manguin, A. Mani and G. Wade (eds), *Early Interactions between South and Southeast Asia*, pp. 113–136. Singapore: Southeast Asian Studies.

Matsumura, H. and M.J. Hudson. 2005. Dental perspectives on the population history of Southeast Asia. *American Journal of Physical Anthropology* 127: 182–209. doi.org/10.1002/ajpa.20067.

Matsumura, H. and M.F. Oxenham. 2014. Demographic transitions and migration in prehistoric East/Southeast Asia through the lens of nonmetric dental traits. *American Journal of Physical Anthropology* 155: 45–65. doi.org/10.1002/ajpa.22537.

Matsumura, H., M.F. Oxenham, K.T. Nguyen, L.C. Nguyen, and K.D. Nguyen. 2011. The population history of mainland Southeast Asia: Two layer model in the context of northern Vietnam. In N. Enfield (ed.), *Dynamics of Human Diversity: The Case of Mainland Southeast Asia*, pp. 153–178. Canberra: Pacific Linguistics.

Noerwidi, S. 2011/12. The Significance of the Holocene Human Skeletal Song Keplek 5 in the History of Human Colonization of Java: A Comprehensive Morphological and Morphometric Study. *Master Erasmus Mundus en Quaternaire et Préhistoire*. Paris: Muséum National d'Histoire Naturelle. hopsea. mnhn.fr/pc/thesis/M2%20Noerwidi_S.pdf.

Pietrusewsky, M. 2006. The initial settlement of Remote Oceania: The evidence from physical anthropology. In T. Simanjuntak, I.H.E. Pojoh and M. Hisyam (eds), *Austronesian Diaspora and the Ethnogenesis of People in Indonesian Archipelago*, pp. 320–347. Jakarta: LIPI Press.

Reynolds, T., G. Barker, H. Barton, G. Cranbrook, L. Farr, C. Hunt, L. Kealhofer, V. Paz, A. Pike, P.J. Piper, R.J. Rabett, G. Rushworth, C. Stimpson and K. Szabó. 2013. The first modern humans at Niah, c. 50,000–35,000 years ago. In G. Barker (ed.), *Rainforest Foraging and Farming in Island Southeast Asia*, pp. 135–172. Cambridge: McDonald Institute for Archaeological Research.

Sathiamurthy, E. and H.K. Voris. 2006. Maps of Holocene sea level transgression and submerged lakes on the Sunda Shelf. *The Natural History of Chulalongkorn University Supplement* 2: 1–43.

Sémah, F., A-M. Sémah, C. Falguères, F. Détroit , X. Gallet, S. Hameu, A-M. Moigne, and H.T. Simanjuntak. 2004. The significance of the Punung karstic area (eastern Java) for the chronology of the Javanese Palaeolithic, with special reference to the Song Terus cave, *Mod. Quaternary Research in Southeast Asia 18: Quaternary Research In Indonesia*, pp. 45-62. Leiden: A.A. Balkema

Sémah, F., A.-M. Sémah and M. Chacornac-Rault. 2006. Climate and continental record in Island South East Asia since the Late Pleistocene: Trends in current research, relationship with the Holocene human migration wave. In T. Simanjuntak, I.H.E. Pojoh and M. Hisyam (eds), *Austronesian Diaspora and the Ethnogenesis of People in Indonesian Archipelago*, pp. 15–29. Jakarta: LIPI Press.

Simanjuntak, T. (ed.). 2002. *Gunung Sewu in Prehistoric Times*. Yogyakarta: Gadjah Mada University Press.

Snell, C.A.R.D. 1949. Human skeletal remains from Gol Ba'it, Sungai Siput, Perak, Malaya Peninsula. *Acta Neerlandica Morphologica Normalis et Pathologicae* 6: 353–377.

Solheim, W.G.II. 2006. *Archaeology and Culture in Southeast Asia: Unraveling the Nusantao*. Quezon City: The University of Philippines Press.

Storm, P., F. Aziz, J. de Vos, D. Kosasih, S. Baskoro, Ngaliman and L.W. van den Hoek Ostende. 2005. Late Pleistocene *Homo sapiens* in a tropical rainforest fauna in East Java. *Journal of Human Evolution* 49: 536–545. doi.org/10.1016/j.jhevol.2005.06.003.

Storm, P., R. Wood, C. Stringer, A. Bartsiokas, J. de Vos, M. Aubert, L. Kinsley and R. Grün. 2013. U-series and radiocarbon analyses of human and faunal remains from Wajak, Indonesia. *Journal of Human Evolution* 64: 356–365. doi.org/10.1016/j.jhevol.2012.11.002.

Westaway, K.E., M.J. Morwood, R.G. Roberts, A.D. Rokus, J.-X. Zhao, P. Storm, F. Aziz, G. van den Burgh, P. Hadi, Jatmiko and J. de Vos. 2007. Age and biostratigraphic significance of the Punung rainforest fauna, East Java, Indonesia, and implications for *Pongo* and *Homo*. *Journal of Human Evolution* 53: 709–717. doi.org/10.1016/j.jhevol.2007.06.002.

Widianto, H. 2001. Laporan Penelitian Song Tritis. *Laporan Penelitian Arkeologi*. Yogyakarta: Balai Arkeologi.

——. 2006. Austronesia prehistory from the perspective of skeletal anthropology. In T. Simanjuntak, I.H.E. Pojoh and M. Hisyam (eds), *Austronesian Diaspora and the Ethnogenesis of People in Indonesian Archipelago*, pp. 174–185. Jakarta: LIPI Press.

Wolpoff, M.H. 1999. *Paleoanthropology*. 2nd edition. Boston: McGraw-Hill.

6

Terminal Pleistocene and Early Holocene Human Occupation in the Rainforests of East Kalimantan[1]

Karina Arifin

This paper presents results of archaeological excavations at two rock shelters and a cave in the Berau region of East Kalimantan. The investigations produced significant new evidence for the occupation of tropical rainforest environments along the Upper Birang River by human foragers from at least the end of the Last Glacial Period. The substantial bone assemblages, human burials and material culture recovered during excavation have provided important insights into modes of subsistence, burial traditions and technological innovations from the terminal Pleistocene through the Holocene. The observed patterns in human cultural and ideological behaviour correspond well with evidence from elsewhere in Borneo and across Island Southeast Asia.

Introduction

The island of Borneo has produced significant Palaeolithic archaeological deposits encompassing much of the Late Pleistocene and Holocene, from as early as 50,000 years ago. Most well documented archaeological investigations have focused on Sarawak and Sabah in the west, in Malaysian Borneo. Of these, probably the most significant excavations have concentrated on the Niah Caves, Sarawak, where Tom and Barbara Harrisson identified a deep, well-stratified sequence of archaeological deposits spanning the Late Pleistocene to sub-recent, and recovered anatomically modern human remains dated to ca. 35,000 BP (Harrisson, 1957, 1958, 1970; Brothwell 1960; Bellwood 1997: 172; Barker et al. 2007; Barker 2013). Subsequent excavations have illustrated the complexities of human frequentation of the caves, the diverse foraging strategies employed, changes in lithic artefact repertoires with the increasing utilisation of plant processing technologies and the emergence of burial traditions in the early to mid-Holocene (Zuraina Majeed-Lowee 1981; Rabett et al. 2013). Other notable archaeological investigations that have enhanced our knowledge of Bornean and Southeast Asian prehistory have been conducted at Lubang Angin and Gua Sireh (Datan 1993), Madai and Baturong caves (Bellwood 1988), Bukit Tengkorak (Bellwood 1989; Chia 1997) and Tingkayu (Bellwood 1997: 177–180). Some research has been undertaken in Kalimantan, for example, Chazine (1994, 2005), Chazine and Ferrié (2008) and Widianto et al. (1997) have all reported on excavations at various caves and rock shelters that have produced evidence of flexed burials typical of the early to mid-Holocene.

---

1   An earlier version of this paper was presented at the 17th Congress of the Indo Pacific Prehistory Association, Taipei, 2002.

However, the potential of these large limestone karst landscapes to provide new and significant data on human occupation and adaptation to humid tropical rainforest environments in the region is yet to be fully realised.

This paper addresses some of the outstanding questions regarding Palaeolithic human occupation of eastern Kalimantan. Archaeological excavations were conducted at two cave sites and a rock shelter: Liang Gobel, Lubang Payau and Kamanis in the Berau region along the Upper Birang River. The investigations demonstrate that Eastern Kalimantan possesses a rich Late Pleistocene and Holocene archaeological record comparable with that discovered to the west in Sarawak and Sabah, and provide significant new insights into human occupation of the region, technological innovation and cultural and ideological developments.

The archaeological investigations

Units of Analysis: Each trench in the various cave and rock shelter entrances was excavated using 5 cm, or in the case of LPY/D5 10 cm, spits. For accuracy in analyses, assemblages from each excavation pit were 'grouped' into different analytical units, which represent hypothetical units of activity, or phases of occupation. The 'boundaries' of each analytical unit were delineated by observations of the stratigraphic sequence excavated, and by the characteristics of recovered archaeological assemblages such as content and density of material culture. Thus, an analytical unit generally consisted of several 5 cm spits and straddled more than one stratigraphic unit. By distinguishing analytical units in this way it became possible to clearly determine spatial and temporal changes in the archaeological record at both the intra- and inter-site levels (Table 6.1).

Table 6.1 A summary of number of units recorded for Kimanis trenches KMS/C4, KMS/C8, KMS/TP and Lubang Payau LPY/C3; the numbers within the columns represent the spits and their depths below modern ground level allocated to each of the analytical units recorded for each site.

Unit	Spit/Depth (cm)			
	KMS/TP	KMS/C4	KMS/C8	LPY/C3
I	1–10 (0<x≤50 cm)	1–10 (0<x≤50 cm)	1–10 (0<x≤50 cm)	1–8 (0<x≤40 cm)
II	11–21 (50<x≤105 cm)	11–23 (50<x≤105 cm)	11–27 (50<x≤135 cm)	9–18 (40<x≤90 cm)
III	-	24–34 (105<x≤160 cm)	-	19–32 (90<x≤160 cm)
IV	-	35–42 (160<x≤200 cm)	-	-
V	-	43–61 (200<x≤295 cm)	-	-

Source: K. Arifin.

The following information is primarily drawn from Arifin (2004). Archaeological investigations were conducted at three cave and rock shelter sites in a limestone massif in the tropical rainforest in the upper reaches of the Birang River, about 60 km in a straight line from the east coast of Borneo (Figure 6.1). The three sites investigated were Liang Gobel, Lubang Payau and Kimanis.

Figure 6.1 Map of Borneo illustrating the location of the Upper Birang and other key archaeological sites across the island.

Source: After Arifin 2004: 9.

Liang Gobel was the smallest rock shelter (8 m long by 5 m wide) excavated in this study. It is situated on a 5 m high limestone wall, at 205 m above sea level (asl) and just a few metres from a path that leads to the site of Lubang Payau, no more than a few hundred metres away. A test pit (1 m x 2 m) labeled LGB/TP was excavated in the middle of the site. It possessed one unit split into three layers, consisting of loose brown ashy silts. Combined, the total depth of deposit was no more than 0.2 m. The excavations produced a small number of earthenware sherds, some lithics and some vertebrate and invertebrate remains.

Lubang Payau is a commercial bird's nesting cave with two tunnels leading to an underground river. The cave is situated at 206 m asl and has a chamber that covers approximately 10 m x 20 m with a flat platform at the entrance, before gradually sloping towards the interior. Two test pits were excavated in the middle of the entrance gallery. Trench LPY/C3 was the closest of the trenches to the cave entrance. It was excavated at the highest point in the cave floor and measured 1 m x 2 m with the long axis orientated east–west. This trench produced the most informative sequence of occupation in Lubang Payau, extending to a total depth of 1.6 m. LPY/C3 could be divided into three units consisting of sandy silts (Unit I) overlying the silts and silty clays of Units II and III. Unit I had a depth of *ca.* 0.4 m and consisted of a sequence of thin deposits that contained earthenware pottery. Unit II comprised two stratigraphic layers of total depth *ca.* 0.45 m, with the upper containing the greatest density of archaeological materials, and concentrations diminishing towards the base of the unit. The upper of the two stratigraphic layers assigned to Unit III (total depth *ca.* 0.7 m) was really an extension of Unit II, but contained fewer cultural remains. The basal deposits were devoid of any evidence of human activity. Earthenware pottery was only recorded in the upper layers (Unit I) along with three shell scrapers manufactured from the mangrove bivalve *Geloina erosa*, most of the animal bones and shell. Stone artefacts were recovered throughout the archaeological sequences but with a concentration within Unit II. Although isolated human bones were recovered, no distinctive burials were identified.

Trench LPY/D5 was situated towards the interior of the cave, *ca.* 2 m to the northeast of Trench LPY/C3, and measured 2 m x 2 m. LPY/D5 had a total depth of 0.5 m, but only the upper 0.3 m contained any archaeological materials (below this was sterile sandy silts). Within this single activity unit all but Spit 6 possessed earthenware pottery, with lithics, animal bone and shell to the base.

Three samples were dated from Lubang Payau using radiocarbon, one on charcoal and two on freshwater shell, all from LPY/C3 (Table 6.2). The two dates, one on charcoal, the other on freshwater shell, both from Spit 6 (Unit II), emphasise the problem of potential 'old carbon' uptake during the construction of the calcium carbonate shell in limestone karst regions (ANU-11152 and ANU-11260). This conclusion is supported by Bellwood (1988: 120) and Datan (1993: 17), who have suggested that at Madai Cave in Sabah and Gua Sireh in Sarawak, respectively, freshwater shell dates were approximately 500 years older than those on charcoal from the same stratigraphic layers. Spriggs (1989: 598) has argued that 'old carbon' in shell can result in unpredictable ages, potentially greater than 1,500 years older than those recorded for charcoal from corresponding deposits. In the case of the Upper Birang samples the error is probably even greater than this. For example, in Kimanis trench KMS/C4, a freshwater shell dated to 13,860±180 (ANU-11258) was derived from the same layer (Spit 24, 105–110 cm below the surface) as charcoal dated to 10,030±260 BP (ANU-11150) suggesting a potential 3,000 year deviation (see Table 6.2). As a result, only the charcoal dates from Lubang Payau and Kimanis are considered reasonably reliable in this study. Therefore, the only trustworthy sample from Lubang Payau is the charcoal from Unit II that produced a date of 5637–5081 cal. BP (ANU-11152). This date implies that pottery was introduced to the region after *ca.* 5000 BP, and that Unit II at Lubang Payau is of similar age to the upper sequence in the same unit at Kimanis (ANU-11148; see below and Table 6.2).

Kimanis is a large cave with an overhang at the entrance that forms a rock shelter. It is located at 2°27'4"N/117°24'38"E and 206 m asl, about 160 m west of Lubang Payau. The rock shelter forms a spacious dry area, with its surface sloping slightly to the west, towards the entrance of the cave. The habitable area under the rock shelter covers approximately 22 m x 8 m. Three trenches were excavated.

Test pit KMS/TP, measured 1 m² and was located furthest east and the greatest distance from the cave entrance. The five stratigraphic deposits were divided into two cultural units (Units I and II). Unit I consisted of several layers of brown or yellowish-brown ashy soil totaling between 0.5 m–0.7 m thick. This unit contained earthenware sherds, substantial amounts of bat bone, some stone artefacts, and damar. The lowest excavated layer of Unit II (recorded as Layer E) was excavated to between 0.4 m and 0.7 m depth. Excavation ceased when a flexed burial was encountered at 1.3 m below modern ground surface. Layer E contained some animal bone and shell but no earthenware pottery.

Table 6.2 A list of the radiocarbon dates from Lubang Payau and Kimanis.

Square/Spit	Unit/Depth (cm)	Material	Lab No.	Conventional Age (BP)	Calibrated Date (cal.BP) OxCal 4.2/ IntCal 13
LPY/C3 Spit 6	Unit II/ 25–30	Charcoal	ANU-11152	4610±110	5637-5081 (92.4%)/5069-5026 (3%)
LPY/C3 Spit 6	Unit II/ 25–30	Freshwater shell	ANU-11260	13,100±140	Not calibrated
LPY/C3 Spit 23	Unit III/ 110-115	Freshwater shell	ANU-11261	17,730±250	Not calibrated
KMS/C4 Spit 8	Unit I/ 35-40	Charcoal	ANU-11311	1270±240	1685-776 (94.1%)/1746-1697 (1.3%)
KMS/C4 Spit 11	Unit II/ 50-55	Charcoal	ANU-11148	4650±90	5639-5308 (79.8%)/5240-5105 (13.5%) / 5302-5282 (1.3%)
KMS/C4 Spit 20	Unit II/ 98	Charcoal	ANU-11149	8840±250	10,638-9452 (95.1%)
KMS/C4 Spit 24	Unit III/ 105-110	Charcoal	ANU-11150	10,030±260	12,582-11,116 (91.4%)/11,017-10,843 (3.7%)
KMS/C4 Spit 24	Unit III/ 105-110	Freshwater shell	ANU-11258	13,860±180	Not calibrated
KMS/C4 Spit 34	Unit III/ 155-160	Charcoal	ANU-11151	11,270±220	13,543-10,774 (94.7%)
KMS/C4 Spit 59	Unit V/ 280-285	Freshwater shell	ANU-11259	23,630±480	Not calibrated

Source: Following Arifin (2004: 104), except the recalibration using OxCal vers.4.2 (Bronk Ramsey 2009) IntCal 13 (Reimer et al. 2013).

Trench KMS/C4 was located 1.5 m west of KMS/TP and 6 m east of KMS/C8 in the rock shelter, relatively close to the south wall. The trench measured 1 m x 2 m with the long axis orientated north–south and was excavated to a maximum depth of 3 m below modern ground level. At *ca.* 1.5 m depth a flexed burial was uncovered in the northern portion of the trench, and only the southern half was excavated to rock fall. Nine layers of deposit varying in colour and texture from dark brown ashy silt to reddish-yellow ashy silt could be divided into five activity units (Figure 6.2). Unit I was the only phase of activity to contain pottery. The preceding Unit II (0.5 m–1.05 m) contained relatively few animal bones and a considerable amount of roof collapse. Unit III (1.05 m–1.6 m) produced by far the greatest number of stone tools, animal bones and molluscs, reflecting the most intensive occupation of the site. Unit IV (1.6 m–2 m) possessed fewer vertebrate remains and stone artefacts than Unit III, but still relatively high concentrations of shells. Unit V was excavated to a depth of 2.95 m before large rock fall finally prevented deeper investigation. This unit contained much fewer animal bones, lithics and shells than the overlying units, but several notable lenses of ash.

All seven radiocarbon dates for Kimanis are from KMS/C4. Excluding the freshwater shell dates, the remaining five charcoal assays suggest occupation from at least the end of the glacial period at *ca.* 13,000 cal. BP, and perhaps considerably earlier based on the freshwater shell date of 23,630±460 (ANU-11259) in Unit V, until less than 2,000 cal. BP. A date of *ca.* 5600–5300 cal. BP from Unit II indicates that the introduction of pottery certainly post-dates this date. If the Unit I date of 1685–776 cal. BP (ANU-11311) is considered representative, pottery might not have been introduced to the region until within the last 2,000 years.

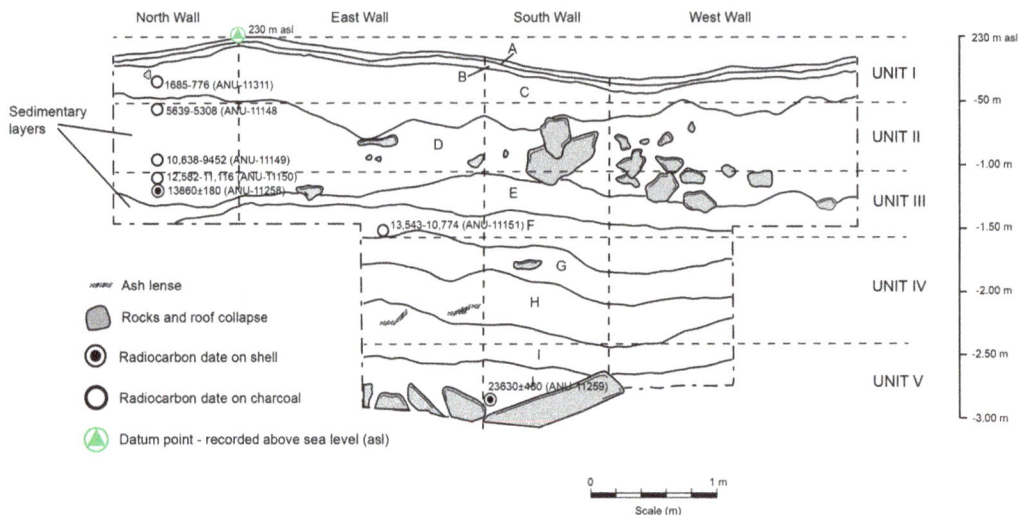

Figure 6.2 An illustration of the four walls of Trench KMS/C4 showing the different archaeological layers and units excavated, and the approximate locations of radiocarbon dates.

Source: After Arifin 2004: 85; the dates have been recalibrated using OxCal vers.4.1 (Bronk Ramsey 2009) IntCal.13 (Reimer et al. 2013).

Trench KMS/C8 measured 1 m x 2 m and was dug to a depth of 1.3 m. Two units with layers of brown and yellowish-brown silts with ash very similar to those recorded in KMS/C4 were identified. Unit I was 0.5 m deep and was the only phase of activity to contain pottery, with relatively small amounts of animal bone, stone artefacts and invertebrates. Unit II was excavated to a maximum depth of 1.3 m. This phase of activity produced higher concentrations of vertebrate and invertebrate remains than Unit I, as well as sizable amounts of roof collapse.

As Kimanis produced the richest archaeological record with the greatest temporal range, the following discussion will be heavily weighted towards interpretation of this site, with a lesser focus on Liang Gobel and Lubang Payau.

Subsistence strategies

1. Vertebrate remains

Vertebrate remains from all the Upper Birang archaeological sites are very fragmented. This is typical for cave sites in Southeast Asia and probably results from a combination of anthropic taphonomic processes such as butchery and bone breakage for marrow extraction, considerable human foot traffic within the confines of cave entrances and rock shelters, and natural processes like roof collapse (see Piper and Rabett 2016). As a result the majority (greater than 50 per cent) of small bone fragments remain anatomically and taxonomically unidentified (Table 6.3). Of the remainder, levels of taxonomic identification are dependent on a number of variables that include the degree of preservation, survival of diagnostic anatomical features and the complexity and diversity of the family and/or genus the skeletal element is likely to belong to. For example, the Malay tapir (*Tapirus indicus*) is the sole survivor of its genus in the Late Pleistocene of SEA, and any bone fragments attributable to the tapir almost certainly come from this species. In contrast, the complex diversity of rodent murids (Muridae) makes it difficult to confidently differentiate the majority of anatomical elements recovered from the archaeological record beyond family level (Tables 6.4 and 6.5).

Table 6.3 Summary of the vertebrate remains recovered from the Upper Birang River sites recorded by trench, weight, number of identifiable taxa, Number of Identifiable Specimens (NISP) and Minimum Number of Individuals (MNI).

SITE	EXCAVATION PIT	UNIDENTIFIED SPECIMEN		IDENTIFIABLE SPECIMENS							
		WEIGHT	%	TAXA	%	NISP	%	WEIGHT	%	MNI	%
KIMANIS	KMS/C4	6815.9	64.9	36	78.3	6040	72	5690.2	72	290	61
	KMS/C8	1999	19.1	37	80.4	1763	21	1608.98	20	125	26
	Total	8814.9	84	42	91.3	7803	93	7299.18	92	415	87
LUBANG PAYAU	LPY/C3	1173.9	11.2	21	45.7	315	3.8	249.6	3.2	31	6.5
	LPY/CD5	433.5	4.1	18	39.1	208	2.5	261.1	3.3	19	4
	Total	1607.4	15.3	29	63	523	6.3	510.7	7	50	10
LIANG GOBEL	LGB/TP	64.7	0.7	12	26.1	52	0.7	95	0.7	13	3
TOTAL		10,487	100	46	100	8378	100	7905.38	100	478	100

Source: K. Arifin.

Table 6.4 The minimum numbers (MNI) of different taxa recovered from the various excavation trenches at Liang Gobel, Lubang Payau and Kimanis; those numbers in parentheses and question marks represent uncertain identifications; *Suidae – probably the bearded pig *Sus barabatus* but there is the possibility of introduced *S. scrofa*, especially in the later phases.

Class	Order	Family	Taxon	Archaeological Trench				
				KMS/C4	KMS/C8	LPY/C3	LPY/D5	LGB/TP
Actinopterygii			Ray-finned fishes	2	2		1	
Amphibia	Anura		Frogs and toads				?	
Reptilia			Reptiles	3	1			
	Testudines	Geoemydidae	Hardshell turtles	12?	4	2	?	1
		Trionychidae	Softshell turtles	4?	?			
	Squamata	Colubridae	Snakes		1			
			Snakes	3?	?			
		Pythonidae	Python sp.	4?	2		1	
		Varanidae	Monitor lizards	6	4	1	1	
		Agamidae	Iguanian lizards	3	1			

Class	Order	Family	Taxon	Vernacular	Archaeological Trench				
					KMS/C4	KMS/C8	LPY/C3	LPY/D5	LGB/TP
Aves	Galliformes			Birds	1				
				Pheasants, junglefowl etc.			1		
Mammalia	Dermoptera	Cynocephalidae	Cynocephalus variegatus	Colugo or flying lemur	1	1			
	Megachiroptera (Suborder)			Fruit bats		1			
	Microchiroptera (Suborder)			Insectivorous bats	169	62	6	2	1
	Primates	Cercopithecidae	Presbytis sp(p).	Leaf monkeys (Langurs)	7	2			
			Trachypithecus cristatus	Silvered langur	1	1	1		
			cf. Nasalis larvatus	Proboscis monkey	1				
			Macaca fascicularis	Long-tailed macaque	2	2			
			Macaca sp(p).	Macaques	4	3		1	
				Langurs and/or macaques	12	4	2	1	1
		Hylobatidae	Hylobates muelleri	Bornean gibbon	2		1		
		Hominidae	Pongo pygmaeus	Orangutan	3(1)	1	1		
	Rodentia	Muridae		Rats and mice	4	6	1		
		Sciuridae		Squirrels	2	3		1	
		Hystricidae		Porcupines	3	2		1	
				Rodents unident.	3	2	2		1
	Carnivora	Ursidae	Helarctos (Ursus) malayanus	Sun bear	6	2	1	1	2
		Mustelidae		Weasels, badgers and otters	2	3	1		
		Viverridae	Viverra tangalunga	Malay civet	2				
			Arctictis binturong	Binturong			1		
				Mongoose/civet unident.	3	1		1	
				Carnivores unident.	5	2	1	2	1
	Perissodactyla	Rhinocerotidae		Rhinoceros		1	1		
		Tapiridae	Tapirus indicus	Malay tapir	2	1		1	
	Artiodactyla	*Suidae	Sus sp(p).	*Pig	7	5	4	2	3
		Tragulidae	Tragulus sp(p).	Mouse deer		1	1		

Class	Order	Family	Taxon	Vernacular	Archaeological Trench				
					KMS/C4	KMS/C8	LPY/C3	LPY/D5	LGB/TP
		Cervidae	Muntiacus muntjac	Common barking deer	1				
			cf. Rusa unicolor	Sambar deer	1				
				Deer	5	2	2	1	1
		Bovinae		Cattle	5	1	1	1	1
				Unident. medium-sized mammal	7	?		13	
				TOTALS MNI	299	125	31	19	13

Source: K. Arifin.

Table 6.5 The Number of Individual Specimens (NISP) and Minimum Numbers (MNI) of different taxa recovered from within the various 'activity units' in Kimanis trench KMS/C4; those numbers in parentheses represent uncertain identifications; *Suidae – the most likely representative is the bearded pig *Sus barabatus* but there is the possibility of introduced *S. scrofa*, especially in the later phases.

Class	Order	Family	Taxon	Vernacular	UNIT 1		UNIT 2		UNIT 3		UNIT 4		UNIT 5		TOTALS	
					NISP	MNI	NISP	MNI	NISP	MNI	NISP	MNI	NISP	MNI	NISP	MNI
Actinopterygii				Ray-finned fishes	4	1	2	1							6	2
Reptilia				Reptiles			1	1	2	2					3	3
	Testudines	Geoemydidae		Hardshell turtles	73	1	224	1	641	8	12	1	6	1	956	12
		Trionychidae		Softshell turtles	4	1	8	1	87	1			1	1	100	4
	Squamata			Snakes												
		Colubridae		Snakes	3	1	11	1	18	1					32	3
		Pythonidae	Python sp.	Python	12	1	37	1	154	1	3	1			206	4
		Varanidae		Monitor lizards	7	1	42	3	76	2					125	6
		Agamidae		Iguanian lizards			1	1	3	2					4	3
Aves				Birds			1	1							1	1
Mammalia	Dermoptera	Cynocephalidae	Cynocephalus variegatus	Colugo or flying lemur					1						1	1
	Microchiroptera (Suborder)			Insectivorous bats	1419	46	1555	88	143	30	1	1	142	4	3260	169

Class	Order	Family	Taxon	Vernacular	UNIT 1		UNIT 2		UNIT 3		UNIT 4		UNIT 5		TOTALS	
					NISP	MNI	NISP	MNI	NISP	MNI	NISP	MNI	NISP	MNI	NISP	MNI
	Primates	Cercopithecidae	Presbytis sp(p).	Leaf monkeys (Langurs)			2	2	15	5					17	7
			Trachypithecus cristatus	Silvered langur	1	1									1	1
			cf. Nasalis larvatus	Proboscis monkey	1	1									1	1
			Macaca fascicularis	Long-tailed macaque					1(1)	1(1)					1(1)	1(1)
			Macaca sp(p).	Macaques	2	1	8	1	14	2					24	4
				Langurs and/or macaques	11	1	27	1	270	8	10	1	2	1	320	12
		Hylobatidae	Hylobates muelleri	Bornean gibbon			1	1	1	1					2	2
		Hominidae	Pongo pygmaeus	Orangutan	0(1)	0(1)			10	1			3	2	13(1)	3(1)
	Rodentia	Muridae		Rats and mice	1	1	1	1	4	2					6	4
		Sciuridae		Squirrels					2	1	1	1			3	2
		Hystricidae		Porcupines	1	1	1	1	1	1					3	3
				Rodents unident.	3	1	4	1	11	1					18	3
	Carnivora	Ursidae	Helarctos (Ursus) malayanus	Sun bear	4	1	2	1	38	2	1	1	2	1	47	6
		Mustelidae		Weasels, badgers and otters	4	1	8	1							12	2
		Viverridae	Viverra tangalunga	Malay civet					2	2					2	2
				Mongoose/civet unident.			3	1	13	2					16	3
				Carnivores unident.			2	1	5	3	1	1			8	5
		Tapiridae	Tapirus indicus	Malay tapir			3	1	1	1					4	2

Class	Order	Family	Taxon	Vernacular	UNIT 1 NISP	UNIT 1 MNI	UNIT 2 NISP	UNIT 2 MNI	UNIT 3 NISP	UNIT 3 MNI	UNIT 4 NISP	UNIT 4 MNI	UNIT 5 NISP	UNIT 5 MNI	TOTALS NISP	TOTALS MNI
	Artiodactyla	*Suidae	*Sus sp(p).*	*Pig	12	1	45	1	495	3	13	1	10	1	575	7
		Cervidae	*Muntiacus muntjac*	Common barking deer					2	1					2	1
			cf. *Rusa unicolor*	Sambar deer					1	1					1	1
				Deer			10	1	96	2	5	1	2	1	113	5
		Bovinae		Cattle	3	1	7	1	40	2	4	1			54	5
				Unident. Medium-sized mammal	3	1	9	1	77	3	10	1	2	1	101	7
				TOTALS INCL Microchiroptera	1568	65	2015	116	2225	92	61	11	170	13	6040	299
				TOTALS EXCL Microchiroptera	149	19	460	28	2082	62	60	10	28	9	2780	130

Source: K. Arifin.

Although a systematic analysis of butchery was not conducted on the bone assemblages from the Upper Birang sites, the presence of burnt bones and the strong similarities between these bone accumulations and those recovered from sites such as Niah where a thorough examination of human exploitation was undertaken (see Piper and Rabett 2016) strongly suggests that most, if not all, the remains of large and medium-sized mammals and reptiles were accumulated by people. Some animals, especially bats and rodents may have died in, or been brought back into, the caves and rock shelters by carnivores. The vertebrate assemblages include a diverse range of taxa that occupied a variety of ecological niches. By far the most abundant taxa recorded (MNI) in the Upper Birang sites were insectivorous bats, particularly at Kimanis. Although many species of bat are trogloxenes and would have inhabited the dark recesses of the caves and probably represent part of the caves' natural death assemblage, some could also have been hunted. For example, Stimpson (2016) identified the hunting of particular species of at Niah Caves, Sarawak from at least 40,000 years ago. However, close examination of the spatial distribution of bats compared to the main animal bone accumulations at Kimanis indicates that the Chiroptera bones amassed in the later phases of activity (Units I and II), whereas large and intermediate-sized mammals and reptiles were recovered primarily from Unit III. This perhaps indicates natural rather than anthropic modes of accumulation for bats. In fact, if bats are excluded in KMS/C4, approximately 75 per cent of all mammals and reptiles were recorded in Unit III (Table 6.5) and probably date to the terminal Pleistocene, between 13,000–11,000 cal. BP.

A broad diversity of arboreal and terrestrial mammals and reptiles appear to have been hunted or captured during the terminal Pleistocene and early Holocene at Kimanis and Lubang Payau, including a variety of carnivores, monitor lizards (*Varanus* sp(p).), softshell (Trionychidae) turtles, sun bear (*Helarctos* (*Ursus*) *malayanus*), cattle (Bovinae) and tapirs (*Tapirus indicus*). Large deer, probably Sambar appears to have been relatively common in the environments of the Upper Birang. However, in KMS/C4 pigs (*Sus* cf. *barbatus*), primates and hardshell turtles (Geoemydidae) dominate the hunted vertebrate communities in the terminal Pleistocene. Several primates are represented in the assemblages including habitual arboreal taxa such as the Bornean gibbon (*Hylobates muelleri*) and the orangutan (*Pongo pygmeaus*). The most common primates though are the macaques (*Macaca* sp(p).) and leaf monkeys (*Presbytis* sp(p).).

The presence of both the silvered langur (*Trachypithecus cristatus*) and proboscis monkey (*Nasalis larvata*) in Unit I are intriguing. Both these species are most commonly found in coastal mangrove swamp forests or peat forests, though they do also frequent riverine forests (Meijaard et al. 2008). Indeed, Arifin (2004: 127) reports that the proboscis monkey is the most common species of primate encountered along the Birang River today.

2. Osseous artefacts

Bone artefacts were not common in the Upper Birang sites only being found in the upper units at Kimanis (N=7) and Lubang Payau (N=5). Provisional analysis suggests they were all manufactured from longitudinally split fragments of mammalian long bone. These had then been modified through oblique grinding to produce points (unipoint or bipoint) or spatulae (see Rabett 2002 for terminology). Preliminary observations (no systematic microscopic analysis was undertaken) indicated that some artefacts possessed smooth and/or polished surfaces near the tip suggesting use-wear perhaps as piercing implements or awls. Generally speaking though, the small overall number of bone artefacts recovered from within large bone accumulations would perhaps indicate that other organic materials such as bamboo, rattan and palm as well as stone provided substantially more raw materials for artefact production than bone.

The osseous artefacts from Kimanis were all recovered from below the ceramic horizons in deposits with abundant animal bones and shell and likely date to the terminal Pleistocene/ early Holocene. In Lubang Payau bone implements were recorded from within and below the ceramic levels.

3. Invertebrates and shell artefacts

In all sites, the mollusc assemblages were dominated by the freshwater snails *Brotia* sp. (Table 6.6). These were present in small numbers from the basal deposits of KMS/C4 to contemporary ground surface in Lubang Payau. In trenches KMS/C4 and KMS/C8, *Brotia* sp. accounted for 95.6 per cent of the total MNI counted (6399/287; Table 6.7). Trench KMS/C4 indicated that the densest accumulations were within Units III and IV, and associated with the largest concentrations of animal bone dated to *ca.* 13,000–11,000 cal. BP. A high proportion of the shells were missing the apex, a pattern of deliberate human breakage of the natural vacuum within the gastropod that enables easier removal of the fleshy body.

In LPY/C3, the greatest numbers of *Brotia* sp. were concentrated in Unit II and the basal deposits of Unit I, just below a radiocarbon date of 5637–5081 cal. BP (ANU-11152). This suggests that the majority of shells were collected in the mid-Holocene. The accumulations peter out below layers containing pottery. In contrast, *Brotia* sp. was common throughout the deposits of LPY/D5, to modern surface. Overall, this suggests differential periods of intermittent collection and shell dumping within these two caves' entrances, but the practice of freshwater snail consumption continued from the late Pleistocene through the Holocene. *Brotia* sp. can be found close to the archaeological sites in the Birang River and are still being eaten by the contemporary inhabitants of the region today.

Several other freshwater, terrestrial and arboreal snails likely found within the local environments around the caves were identified including *Paludomus* sp(p)., *Cycloporids* and *Amphidromus* sp(p). Of more interest is the small number of 'exotic' marine Mollusca identified in the assemblages (Tables 6.6 and 6.7). The coast is now some 60 km in a straight line from the Upper Birang sites, and even if sea level change potentially increased (in the Pleistocene) or shortened (during the Holocene high sea stand) that gap, it would still mean transportation over a considerable distance from coast to cave. The species collected and returned to the sites also derive from different ecological zones. For example, *Cypraea* spp. (cowry shell) is commonly found in shallow/deep marine environments, whereas the bivalve *Geloina erosa* and gastropods *Terebralia* and *Telescopium* inhabit mangrove swamps.

At Kimanis cowry shells were found throughout the ceramic and upper preceramic layers. The oldest specimen was from Unit III and potentially associated with a date of 12,582–11,116 cal. BP (ANU-11150). The dorsal surfaces of the shells had been removed and the edges ground flat, and probably strung for ornamental purposes. It was clear from the fragmentary remains of the *Geloina erosa* valves that they had been modified and probably used as tools. Close examination of the margins indicated that they had either been retouched and/or showed evidence of use wear (Figure 6.3). It is possible that these artefacts were used for either scraping or cutting functions. Edge damage and step fractures indicate that the shell tools might have been used on relatively hard materials, and possibly over a considerable length of time. Shell implements were primarily found in ceramic-bearing deposits, but the deepest and potentially oldest specimen was recovered from Kimanis Unit II in association with a date of 10,638–9452 cal. BP (ANU-11149).

Table 6.6 The various Mollusca and Arthropods recovered during excavation at Liang Gobel, Lubang Payau and Kimanis listed by environmental preference, minumum number of individuals (MNI) and weight in grams; *species with a preference of mangrove swamps; **Brachyura = true crabs.

Environment	Class	Family	Taxon	KMS/C4		KMS/C8		LPY/C3		LPY/D5		LGB/TP	
				MNI	Weight (g)	MNI	Weight (g)	MNI	Weight (g)	MNI	Weight (g)	MNI	Weight (g)
Freshwater	Gastropoda	Unionidae	Brotia sp(p).	5968	28186.1	431	2260.8	3922	16851.5	1638	5345	206	1025.5
		Thiaridae	Paludomus broti	4	2	9	5	646	997	273	430	69	86
			Paludomus vondenbuschianus	13	18	15	7.7	7	68	1	5	0	0
	Malacostraca	**Brachyura (Infraorder)		71	31.5	5	2.7	5	9.2	4	2.6	1	1.8
Land	Gastropoda	Cyclophoridae	Cyclophorus borneense	41	67.2	22	184	181	560.5	192	670	166	465
			Cyclophorus sp(p).	0	0	0	0	20	19.5	3	?	0	0
			Pterocyclus termilabiatus	7	3.3	2	1	0	0	0	0	0	0
			Leptopoma geotrochiforme	0	0	2	1	4	4	0	0	0	0
		Ariophantidae	Naninia sp.	3	8.2	0	0	7	9	0	0	0	0
		Camaenidae	Amphidromus sp(p).	13	38.6	19	192.1	38	147	11	65.5	27	72
Marine/Estuarine	Bivalvia	*Corbiculidae	Geloina erosa	12	33.6	33	57.6	18	71.5	15	76	1	1.9
		Arcidae	Arca granulosa	0	0	0	0	1	11.8	0	0	0	0
			Anadara granosa	0	0	0	0	11	85	15	127.2	0	0
	Gastropoda	Nautilidae	Nautilus sp.	1	0.5	2	0.6	0	0	0	0	0	0
		*Potamididae	Terebralia sulcata	0	0	0	0	1	3	2	10.3	0	0
			Telescopium telescopium	0	0	0	0	0	0	1	26.7	0	0
		Cypraeidae	Cypraea moneta	6	5.3	7	6.5	0	0	0	0	0	0
		Muricidae	Chicoreus capucinus	0	0	0	0	0	0	1	4.4	0	0

Source: K. Arifin.

Table 6.7 The Minimum Number (MNI) of different genera and species of Mollusca recorded from each unit within trench KMS/C4.

Environment	Class	Family	Taxon	UNIT 1 MNI	UNIT 2 MNI	UNIT 3 MNI	UNIT 4 MNI	UNIT 5 MNI	TOTALS MNI
Freshwater	Gastropoda	Unionidae	Brotia sp(p).	55	106	3090	2301	416	5968
		Thiaridae	Paludomus broti			4			4
			Paludomus vondenbuschianus			12		1	13
Land	Gastropoda	Cyclophoridae	Cyclophorus borneense	27	3	10		1	41
			Pterocyclus termilabiatus		4	1	2		7
		Ariophantidae	Naninia sp.		1	2			3
		Camaenidae	Amphidromus sp(p).		4	5		4	13
Marine/Estuarine	Bivalvia	*Corbiculidae	Geloina erosa		1?	1?			2?
	Gastropoda	Nautilidae	Nautilus sp.			1			1
			TOTALS	82	119	3125	2303	422	6050

Source: After Arifin 2004: 136.

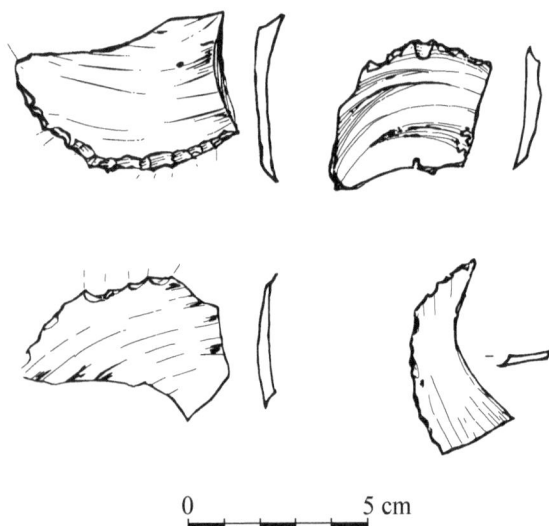

Figure 6.3 An example of retouched fragments of shell artefact from the Upper Birang River sites.
Source: After Arifin 2004: 248.

4. Stone artefacts

A total of 1,319 stone artefacts weighing 43 kg were analysed from the Upper Birang sites. In total, more than 70 per cent of the lithic assemblage came from Kimanis, 27 per cent from Lubang Payau and only 1 per cent from Liang Gobel. Kimanis also produced more than 94 per cent of the stone artefacts by weight. This was primarily due to the number of calcareous sandstone implements manufactured and/or utilised from shattered roof fall from the cave roof.

All three archaeological sites produced stone artefacts manufactured on similar raw materials. Overall they consisted of 42 per cent chert, 16 per cent volcanic rocks, 12 per cent calcareous sandstone and 9 per cent unidentified sedimentary rock, while 5 per cent consisted of miscellaneous microgranodiorite, limestone, crystalline limestone, sandstone, calcareous siltstone, milky quartz and quartzite. There appeared to be little spatial or temporal change in raw material preference or types of tool manufactured throughout the archaeological sequences that might have indicated, amongst other things, technological change. The only exception to this general rule was the introduction of milky quartz artefacts in the upper activity units (Units I and II), coinciding with the first appearance of bipolar flaking (bipolar flakes and cores).

Aside from implements produced on calcareous sandstone, all raw materials must have been derived from somewhere other than the limestone caves in which they were found. Remnant cortex on some artefacts indicated that most, if not all had been manufactured from river pebbles. Observations on the stone within the Upper Birang River close to the archaeological sites showed that the stone in the riverbed close to the rock shelters and cave consisted of small pieces of siltstone. The likelihood is that raw materials for tool production were acquisitioned from further upstream in rivers nearby.

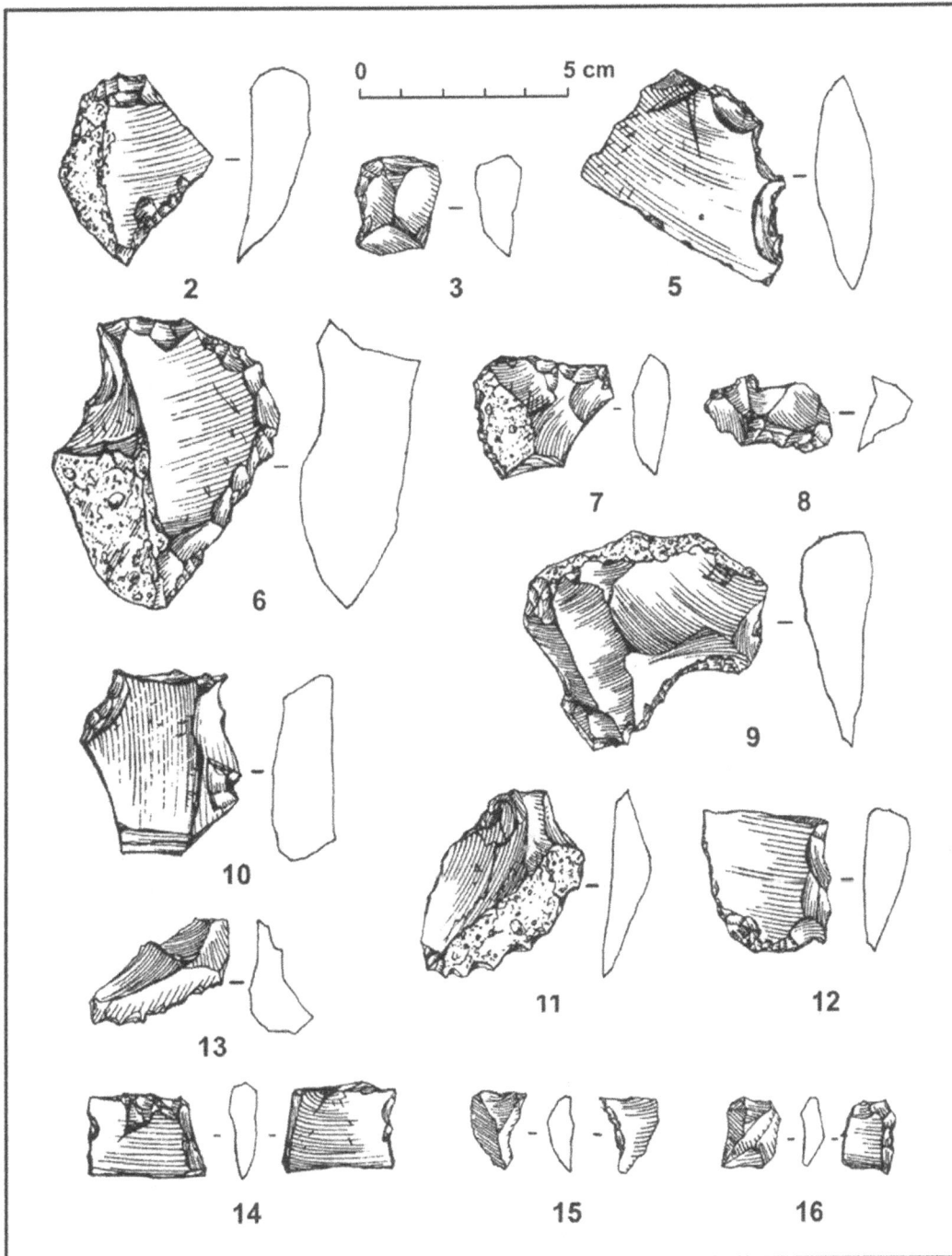

Figure 6.4 Lithic implements from KMS/C4: utilised flakes (2 & 3), retouched flakes (5 & 6), and utilised and retouched flakes (7–16).

Source: After Arifin 2004: 443.

Twenty different types of artefact/artefact fragment could be identified, with flakes (37 per cent of the total stone items analysed), followed by shatters (20 per cent), flake fragments (15 per cent), flake shatters (10 per cent), and heat shatters (9 per cent) dominating. Other specimens included bipolar flakes, érailure flakes, retouched flakes, retouched cores, unidirectional cores, multidirectional cores, bipolar cores and core fragments. The presence of primary flaking and cores suggests that pebble reduction and artefact production were occurring on site.

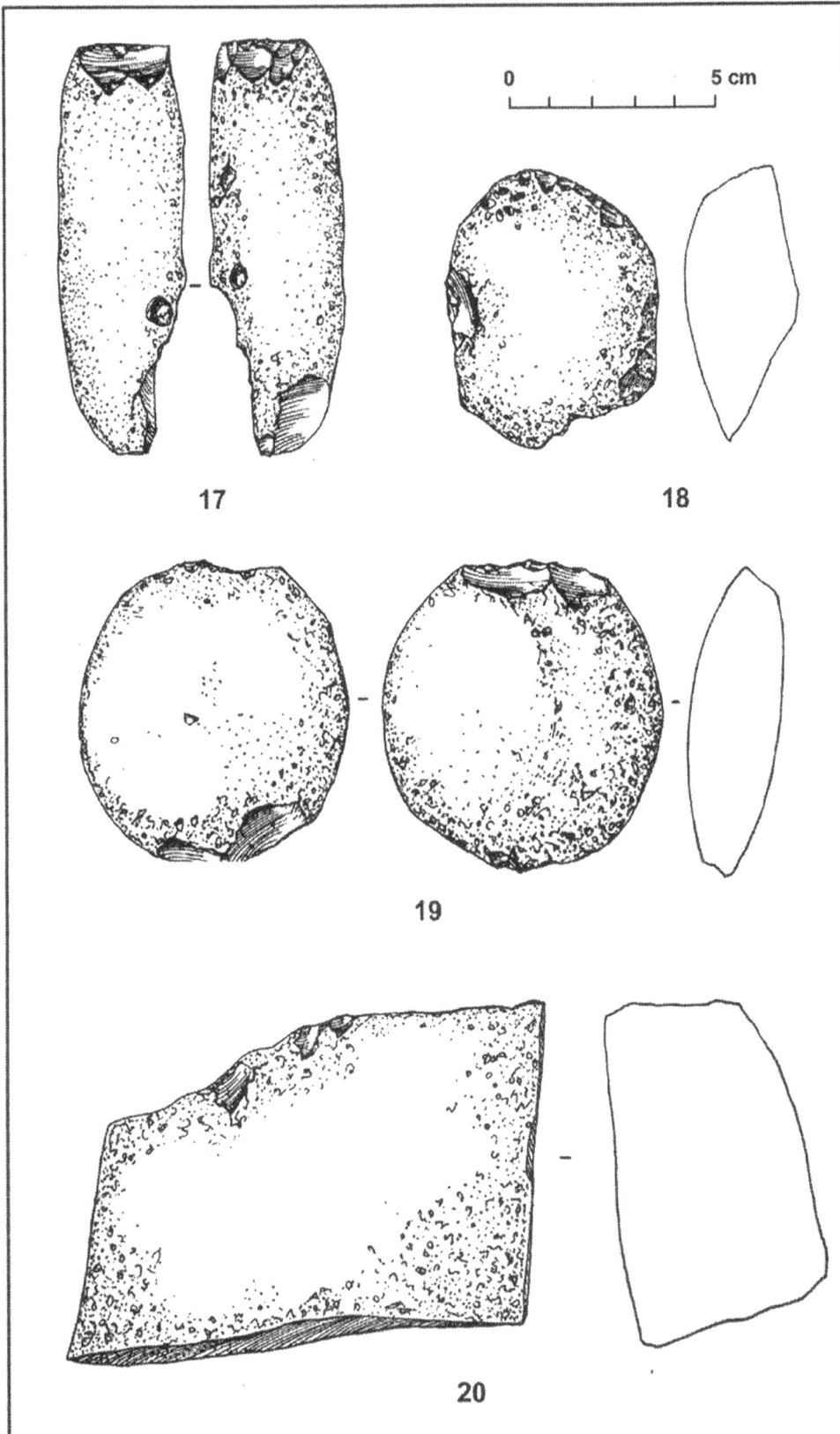

Figure 6.5 Lithic implements from KMS/C4: hammerstone fragments (17 & 18), hammerstone and grindstone (19), and grindstone fragment (20).

Source: After Arifin 2004: 444.

Of these, 41 stone implements were recorded, accounting for just 3 per cent of the total lithic assemblage. Most of these had been produced using the hard hammer technique flaking pebble cores. Represented were lost or discarded utilised flakes, utilised and retouched flakes, retouched flakes, retouched cores, hammerstones and hammerstone fragments, and grindstone fragments (Figures 6.4 and 6.5).

In total, 13 different types of activity involving stone tool use could be discerned within the lithic assemblages (Table 6.8). For example, use-wear analysis showed that several implements possessed use scars with bending initiation and step terminated fractures, as well as edge rounding between use fractures, characteristic of scrapers used on resistant materials, such as hard wood or bone (Kamminga 1982: 69). The existence of highly reflective silica polish on some implements perhaps indicates utilisation in processes such as the stripping rattan, palm leaves or bamboo, or the manufacture of basketry. In some instances, non-silica polish on the working edge of implements suggested functional use in activities such as hide working or butchery. On one artefact, the presence of bending fractures is reminiscent of damage reported by Kamminga (1982: 34) to have resulted from cutting fresh meat. Other artefacts have concave working edges suggestive of tools used to produce and/or maintain cylindrical objects, such as wooden shafts.

Table 6.8 Activities undertaken in Upper Birang sites according to the evidence of lithic items.

No.	Activity	Categories of artefacts
1	Non-specific stone knapping	Flake or flake fragment
		Core or core fragment
		Flake shatter
2	Bipolar flaking	Bipolar flake
		Bipolar core
		Utilised and retouch flake with one of the lateral margins removed by bipolar blow
3	Pressure flaking?	Hammerstone fragment
4	Retouching	Retouched flake
		Retouched core
		Utilised and retouched flake
5	Backing retouch	Utilised and retouched flake
6	Light duty hammering	Hammerstone
		Hammerstone fragment
7	Use and discard of non-specific implement	Utilised flake
		Retouched flake
		Retouched core
		Utilised and retouched flake
8	Use and discard of implement for maintenance activity such as making wooden object	Utilised flake
		Utilised and retouched flake
9	Use and discard of implement for light duty activity, such as butchering and cutting	Utilised flake
		Utilised and retouched flake
10	Use and discard of implement for stripping palm leaves, bamboo or rattan to make mat or basketry	Utilised flake
11	Use and discard of grindstone for ochre grinding and other material	Grindstone fragment with ochre stain
12	Use and discard of implement with ochre stain	Retouched flake
13	Burning activities	Heat shatter

Source: After Arifin 2004: 233.

Amongst the retouched artefacts is a small implement of crystalline quartz from KMS/C4 Unit III dating to the terminal Pleistocene or early Holocene. This specimen had deliberate 'backing' retouch along the left lateral margin, a characteristic of implements that have been hafted (Figure 6.4, no. 16). In fact, the very tiny size of all the crystalline quartz implements might indicate they were specifically designed for hafting. Other evidence of possible hafting includes utilised flakes from KMS/C4 and KMS/C8 Unit I with a black substance coating the artefact surfaces that could represent remnant-hafting mastic. Other implements were more likely handheld, especially between the thumb, index and middle fingers.

Two grindstones, one of white quartzite from KMS/C4 Unit III and the other a fragment of crystalline limestone from Unit II of the same excavation square are notable. The specimen from Unit III was a flattened oval pebble with both surfaces moderately convex and smooth (Figure 6.5, no. 19). Subsequent use as a hammerstone had resulted in the removal of a flake from each end of the artefact. The Unit II specimen was a flat stone that retained a thin layer of ochreous residue in depressions suggesting it was used as a pallet (Figure 6.5, no. 20). These specimens probably date to the terminal Pleistocene and mid-Holocene respectively.

Burnt and heat-shattered stone was a relatively common modification observed in almost all the stone assemblages from the three archaeological sites.

5. Pottery

All the ceramics recorded from the Upper Birang archaeological sites were within the upper units of excavation. Two dates of 5637–5081 cal. BP (ANU-11152) from LPY/C3 and 5639–5308 cal. BP (ANU-11148) from Kimanis indicate that all pottery was derived after the mid-sixth millennium BP. If a date of 1685–776 cal. BP (ANU-11311) from within the Unit I pottery-bearing deposits of Kimanis is considered reliable then the introduction of ceramics to the Upper Birang might not have occurred until after 2,000 years ago.

All the pottery was made by hand through modelling and the use of the paddle and anvil technique. The majority of sherds were plain, but a few (with the greater number at Lubang Payau) possessed simple paddle-impressed, cord-marked or incised decoration (Figure 6.6). Based on rim shapes, diameters, carinations and base fragments, it is likely that most of the pottery consisted of globular cooking pots very similar to ethnographic examples in Sarawak (Morrison 1954–1955; Freeman 1957) and the cooking pots of the Kenyah Lepo' Ké or Apau Ping of Kecamatan Long Pujungan, East Kalimantan (Arifin and Sellato 1999). None of the sherds possessed red-slipped exteriors characteristic of the Neolithic pottery from sites such as Bukit Tengkorak in Sabah (Bellwood 1989).

A few of the potsherds have inclusions of rice husk as temper. This implies that the visitors to the caves and rock shelters of the Upper Birang either belonged to, or had direct or indirect contact with, agricultural communities within the last two millennia or so.

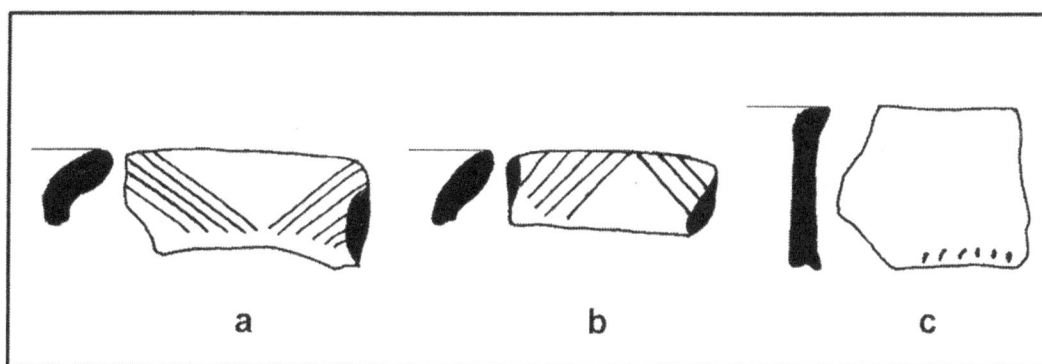

Figure 6.6 Incised rim sherds from Lubang Payau.
Source: After Arifin 2004: 257.

Discussion

Archaeological excavations in the Upper Birang have demonstrated that initial human occupation of this region of East Kalimantan can be dated to the Late Pleistocene. Until recently, Kimanis had the deepest and oldest archaeological record in the region with the earliest reliable date coming from the base of Unit III at 13,543–10,774 cal. BP (ANU-11151). However, the archaeological record extends into Unit V and perhaps indicates initial colonisation by at least the end of the Last Glacial Maximum.

Kimanis is situated at *ca.* 200 m asl and it is likely that the cooler, drier climates that existed at the end of the Pleistocene in Borneo had a significant impact on the local and regional environment (see Bird et al. 2005; Würster et al. 2010). A provisional study of the phytolith samples from Unit V by Bowdery (in Arifin 2004: 374) seems to support this conclusion, in that a number of (undefined) tree species seem to be absent from the floral record, compared to the later phases of cave sediment deposition, possibly as a result of changes in the levels of forest cover. At Niah, systematic pollen analysis has demonstrated that during the Late Pleistocene there was relatively rapid climate-driven environmental change, from extremes of warm, moist dense tropical rainforest to much cooler climates when a diverse mixture of submontane and lowland woodland predominated within ecological communities with no modern parallels (Hunt et al. 2007; Barton et al. 2013). At Kimanis the presence of arboreal taxa such as leaf monkeys, orangutan and the sun bear in lower Unit IV and Unit V would suggest that forest cover of some sort was maintained, if only periodically, during the final stages of the Late Pleistocene in the Upper Birang.

Evidence of human activity in the earliest recorded phases at Kimanis is relatively scant and consists of a few stone flakes and flake fragments manufactured primarily from chert. This might indicate that frequentation of the cave was intermittent and over a short duration by small mobile forager groups. In addition to primates the Late Pleistocene foragers appear to have hunted pig and deer, and caught or trapped hardshell turtles. There is no evidence for the persistence of members of the now extinct middle Pleistocene megafauna such as the giant pangolin (*Manis* cf. sp. *Palaeojavanica*), a species that was recorded in the *ca.* 40,000 BP deposits at Niah (Hoojier 1960; Cranbrook 2000; Piper et al. 2007).

In the upper layers of Unit IV and in Unit III there is a significant increase in density of human activity at Kimanis. This intensification in occupation coincides with dates of 13,543–10,774 cal. BP (ANU-11151) and 12,582–11,116 cal. BP (ANU-11150). A similar pattern of increased cave frequentation and magnitude of habitation at the end of the Pleistocene has been recorded at Niah (Rabett et al. 2013), at Song Terus (Sémah and Sémah 2012) and Song Gupuh (Morwood et al. 2008) in Java and at Ille Cave on Palawan (Lewis et al. 2008). It has been argued that this reflects the movement of human populations inland from coastlines as the marine incursion disrupted ecological systems and reduced resource predictability (Piper and Rabett 2014).

Dense forest cover during the terminal Pleistocene close to Kimanis is suggested by the diversity of arboreal taxa represented in the hunted assemblage such as the flying lemur (*Cynocephalus variegatus*), squirrels (Sciuridae) and sun bear.

The human communities appear to have engaged in broad spectrum foraging using a variety of capture techniques to trap various small carnivores, aquatic softshell turtles and monitor lizards, hunt cattle and deer and collect shellfish from local rivers.

The most abundant prey taxa are pigs, leaf monkeys and macaques – a hunting pattern similar to that observed at Niah during the terminal Pleistocene and Holocene (Piper and Rabett 2009). Rabett and Piper (2012) argued that the significant increase in hunting of arboreal primates at the end of the Pleistocene in Borneo and Java was possibly related to a combination of closure of the tropical rainforests resulting in larger monkey populations, and/or advances in technology as indicated by the appearance of bone projectile points as proxy evidence for the introduction of range weaponry. Although no osseous projectile points were identified at Kimanis, the presence of small stone tools suitable for hafting from Unit III onwards suggests that hafting technology was already present at the site from this period onwards.

The presence of Malay tapir in the Upper Birang region of East Kalimantan is an important new biogeographic record. In all likelihood this species is now extinct in Borneo but has been recorded in several archaeological assemblages in Sarawak from the Late Pleistocene to sub-recent times (Medway 1960; Cranbrook and Piper 2013; Piper and Cranbrook 2007). At Kimanis the oldest tapir bones were recovered from a layer between two radiocarbon dates of 13,543–10,774 cal. BP (ANU-11151) and 12,582–11,116 cal. BP (ANU-11150). The most recent record is from within the pottery-bearing deposits at Lubang Payau, which suggests the Malay tapir was still present in the late Holocene. The records from Sarawak and now East Kalimantan would suggest that the Malay tapir was formerly widespread across Borneo from the east to west coasts of the island. The presence of rhinoceros in the terminal Pleistocene also extends the known range of this large browser to the east coast of Borneo during the early and/or mid-Holocene. The Upper Birang remains may represent the Sumatran rhinoceros (*Dicerorhinus sumatrensis*) that is clinging to survival in Tabin National Park in Sabah (van Strien et al. 2008) and/or the Javan rhinoceros (*Rhinoceros sondaicus*) that is now extinct on Borneo, but has been identified in the archaeological record of Niah Cave (see Cranbrook 1986; Cranbrook and Piper 2007).

Another key feature of the late Pleistocene onwards in SEA is the emergence and spread of bone technologies. Van Es (1930) was the first to document the presence of osseous artefacts in layers predating ceramic horizons at the site of Gua Lawa, close to the village of Sampung in East Java. Subsequently, further investigations in the region resulted in the discovery of similar bone technologies within comparable stratigraphic locations just below the ceramic horizon at 19 other cave and rock shelter sites, and they probably all date to the early and/or mid-Holocene. Currently, the earliest records of bone technology come from the West Mouth of Niah Cave (Reynolds et al. 2013), Lang Longrien in the Thai Peninsula (Anderson 1990), Song Terus in East Java (Kusno 2006) and Matja Kuru II East Timor (O'Connor et al. 2014) variously dated to between 45,000 and 30,000 BP. By the early to mid-Holocene, osseous artefacts are relatively common across all of Mainland and ISEA (Rabett and Piper 2012). The earliest osseous artefacts recovered from Kimanis appear to coincide neatly with the observed rise in bone technologies at other sites across ISEA in the terminal Pleistocene/early Holocene. As at Kimanis and Lubang Payau bone tools appear to have served a variety of locally required functions, including piercing implements.

The repertoire of stone debitage and other artefacts suggests the inhabitants of the Upper Birang region produced tools locally to undertake a variety of different tasks that included plant processing, butchery and hide working. The majority of lithic implements appear to have been produced expediently, utilised and discarded. However, use wear analysis also demonstrated that some artefacts were manufactured in order to shape wooden shafts for durable implements that would have been hafted.

There is evidence for the increasing use of pounders, grindstones and pestles and mortars for plant processing and grinding resins and minerals such as haematite across SEA in the early Holocene (Bellwood 1997: 181; Rabett et al. 2013; Simanjuntak 2002). The crystalline limestone pebble with evidence of ochre processing from Unit II falls within this category of artefact and probably dates to the mid-Holocene. The hammerstone reused as a grindstone from Unit III might imply that grinding technology extends back to the terminal Pleistocene in the Upper Birang region.

At least two burials were recorded in KMS/C4 Unit III and at the base of Unit II in KMS/TP. Though these burials could have been dug into preceding archaeological deposits from later phases of activity, the presence of tightly flexed inhumations in the terminal Pleistocene and early Holocene is consistent with other records across SEA. The emergence of these burial traditions seems to be linked to the regional development of complex new ideologies that, amongst other things, involved belief in the afterlife. At Niah, the two oldest interments recorded within the terminal Pleistocene/early Holocene burial grounds are both flexed, and date to 11,270–11,698 cal. BP (OxA-15157) and 8354–8454 cal. BP (OxA-16161) and are probably of a similar age to those discovered at Kimanis. The methods by which burials were treated at Niah were diverse and included flexion, seated inhumations, flexed decapitations and secondary burial. Cremation is another ritual behavior recorded at Niah (Lloyd-Smith 2012; Rabett et al. 2013). Several cremation burials have also been recovered at Ille Cave, Palawan Island in the Philippines. Samples of bone from Burial 758 produced dates of 9260–9006 cal. BP (OxA-16020) and 9425–9280 cal. BP (OxA-15982; Lewis et al. 2008). Close examination of bone surfaces indicated that this individual had been de-fleshed, dismembered and the long bones shattered prior to being burnt. Further examples of early to mid-Holocene (mostly flexed) burials include those from Gua Braholo, Song Keplek, Song Terus and Pawon on Java (Simanjuntak 2002; Détroit, 2006: 199; Noerwidi 2011/2012) and at Gua Cha, Gua Teluk Kelawar and Gua Peraling in Peninsular Malaysia (Zuraina Majid 2005).

During the mid-Holocene (KMS/C4, KMS/C8 and LPY/C3), foragers frequenting the Upper Birang continued to hunt and capture a diverse range of forest mammals and reptiles and collect *Brotia* sp. and freshwater crabs in rivers close to the caves and rockshelters. Contact with the coast is evident through the presence of several mangrove and marine species of mollusc that were utilised as decorative ornaments (*Cypraea* spp.) or as cutting or scraping tools (*Geloina erosa*). Similar tools have been found in caves and rockshelters in East Java such as Bale, Pawon, Peturon, Gede and Suruh in the northern Limestone Massif of Tuban (Willems 1939; van Heekeren 1972). Scrapers manufactured from *Geloina erosa* have also been reported from coastal and inland sites in East Timor like Lie Seri (Glover 1986: 75).

Use of forest plant products is evident through the presence of damar resin in Units I and II of LPY/C3, which indicates that this secreted resin was being used as an illuminant or a sealant. A small fragment of candlenut (*Aleurites moluccana*) from KMS/C8 might reflect use of this nut for its rich oil (Arifin 2004: 150–151).

Pottery first occurs in the archaeological record after 5000 cal. BP, and possibly as late as 2,000 years ago. All the pottery appears to have had a utilitarian function and consisted primarily of globular cooking pots. Fragments of rice chaff were identified in some of the pottery fabrics, suggesting that the visitors to the Upper Birang were either associated with or in contact with communities that produced or had access to rice agricultural products. However, none of the other material culture such as quadrangular stone adzes or stone and shell ornamentation associated with the regional appearance of Malayo-Polynesian speaking populations that have been identified at sites like Bukit Tengkorak in Sabah or the northern Philippines were recovered from the three Upper Birang archaeological sites. Thus, it is perhaps more likely that the communities inhabiting the rugged limestone regions of Berau maintained a forager lifestyle but had access to traded pottery from inhabitants of sedentary settlements nearby (Arifin 2006). Bulbeck (in Arifin 2004: 391) reached much the same conclusion through analysis of the teeth of the individuals recovered from preceramic (N=7) and ceramic (N=3) layers in the Upper Birang cave sites. He argued that the limited calculus build-up and absence of caries in both the terminal Pleistocene/early to mid-Holocene individuals, and those from the pottery-bearing horizons suggested that they all had a similar forager diet. The expansion of agriculture in the region might be quite a recent phenomenon.

Conclusion

The excavations of Liang Gobel, Lubang Payau and Kimanis have demonstrated that the limestone karst formations of the Berau region of Eastern Kalimantan possess cave and rockshelter sites with significant Late Pleistocene and Holocene archaeological records comparable with those recorded in Sabah and Sarawak. The investigations have shown that human frequentation of the Upper Birang River is evident from the terminal Pleistocene onwards, and potentially extends back at least as far as the end of the Last Glacial Maximum. Evidence for increased cave utilisation by larger human populations over prolonged periods along with a broadening of subsistence strategies and the proliferation in the hunting and trapping of arboreal taxa such as primates is a feature of human adaptation across Java and Borneo at the end of the Pleistocene. The increasing use of bone as a raw material from the Late Pleistocene onwards reflects similar trends observed across Mainland and ISEA, and the discovery of flexed inhumations and burnt human remains indicates that the local forager populations of Eastern Kalimantan were integrated into the social, cultural and ideological networks that were emerging across the region in the early Holocene.

Acknowledgements

This contribution is an excerpt from my PhD thesis research, which was funded by The Australian National University and UNESCO. I would like to thank my supervisor, Peter Bellwood, and various people for helping me with the analysis (Rokhus Due Awe, Colin Groves, Ken Aplin and Erik Meijaard (vertebrate faunal identifications), Ian Loch (mollusc identifications), John Seelley (geoarchaeological analysis), Peter Hiscock and Jo Kamminga (lithics analysis), Doreen Bowdery (phytolith identifications), Glenn Summerhayes (pottery analysis) and David Bulbeck (human remains identifications)) and drawings (Dubel Driwantoro and Mudjiono).

References

Anderson, D.D. 1990. *Lang Longrien Rockshelter: A Pleistocene-Early Holocene Archaeological Site from Krabi, Southwestern Thailand.* University Museum Monograph 71. Philadelphia: University of Pennsylvania University Museum.

Arifin, K. 2004. Early Human Occupation of the East Kalimantan Rainforest. Unpublished PhD thesis, The Australian National University, Canberra.

——. 2006. The Austronesian in Borneo. In T. Simanjuntak, I. Pojoh and M. Hisyam (eds) *Austronesian Diaspora and the Ethnogenesis of People in Indonesian Archipelago*, pp. 146–162. Jakarta: Indonesian Institute of Science.

Arifin, K. and B. Sellato. 1999. Gerabah Kalimantan terakhir yang tradisional: deskripsi ringkas tentang teknologinya. In C. Eghenter and B. Sellato (eds), *Kebudayaan dan Pelestarian Alam: Penelitian Interdisipliner di Pedalaman Kalimantan*, pp. 523–532. Jakarta: WWF Indonesia.

Barker, G. (ed.). 2013. *Rainforest foraging and farming in Island Southeast Asia: The archaeology of Niah Caves Project Monographs Vol.1*, Cambridge: McDonald Institute Monographs.

Barker, G., H. Barton, M. Bird, P. Daly, I. Datan, A. Dykes, L. Farr, D.D. Gilbertson, B. Harrisson, C.O. Hunt, T. Higham, J. Krigbaum, H. Lewis, S. McLaren, V. Paz, P.A. Pike, P. Piper, P. Pyatt, R. Rabett, T.E.G. Reynolds, J. Rose, G. Rushworth, M. Stephens, C. Stringer and G. Thompson. 2007. The 'human revolution' in lowland tropical Southeast Asia: the antiquity and behaviour of anatomically modern humans at Niah Cave (Sarawak, Borneo). *Journal of Human Evolution* 52: 243–261. doi. org/10.1016/j.jhevol.2006.08.011.

Barton, H., G. Barker, D. Gilbertson, C. Hunt, L. Kealhofer, H. Lewis, V. Paz, P.J. Piper, R.J. Rabett, T. Reynolds and K. Szabó. 2013. Later Pleistocene foragers *c.* 35,000–11,500 years ago. In G. Barker (ed.), *Rainforest Foraging and Farming in Island Southeast Asia: The Archaeology and Environmental History of the Niah Caves, Sarawak,* pp. 173–216. Niah Cave Project Monographs vol. 1. Cambridge: McDonald Institute Monograph Series.

Bellwood, P. (ed.). 1988. *Archaeological Research in South-Eastern Sabah.* Kota Kinabalu: Sabah Museum Monograph 2.

——. 1989. Archaeological excavations at Bukit Tengkorak and Segarong, South-Eastern Sabah. *Bulletin of the Indo-Pacific Prehistory Association* 9: 122–162.

——. 1997. *Prehistory of the Indo-Malaysian Archipelago.* 2nd edition. Honolulu: University of Hawaii Press.

Bird, M., D. Taylor and C. Hunt. 2005. Palaeoenvironments of insular Southeast Asia during the last glacial period: A savanna corridor in Sundaland? *Quaternary Science Reviews* 24: 2228–2242. doi. org/10.1016/j.quascirev.2005.04.004.

Bronk Ramsey, C. 2009. Bayesian analysis of radiocarbon dates. *Radiocarbon* 51: 337–360. doi. org/10.1017/S0033822200033865.

Brothwell, D.R. 1960. Upper Pleistocene human skull from Niah Caves, Sarawak. *Sarawak Museum Journal* 9 (n.s. 15–16): 323–349.

Bulbeck, D. 2004. Human remains from Kimanis Rockshelter and Lubang Payau, Kalimantan, Indonesia. Appendix 8.1 in K. Arifin, Early Human Occupation of the East Kalimantan Rainforest, pp. 376–398. Unpublished PhD thesis, The Australian National University, Canberra.

Chazine, J-M. 1994. New archaeological perspectives for Borneo and especially Kalimantan Provinces. Paper presented in the IPPA Conference, Chiang Mai, 1994.

——. 2005. Rock art, burials, and habitations: Caves in East Kalimantan. *Asian Perspectives* 44(1): 219–230. doi.org/10.1353/asi.2005.0006.

Chazine, J.-M. and J.-G. Ferrié. 2008. Recent archaeological discoveries in East Kalimantan, Indonesia. *Bulletin of the Indo-Pacific Association* 28: 16–22. doi.org/10.7152/bippa.v28i0.12011.

Chia, S. 1997. The prehistory of Bukit Tenkgorak, Sabah, Malaysia. *Journal of Southeast Asian Archaeology* 21: 146–159.

Cranbrook, Earl of. 1986. A review of fossil and prehistoric remains of rhinoceros of Borneo. *Sabah Museum and Archives Journal* 1 (n.s. 1): 50–110.

——. 2000. Northern Borneo environments of the past 40,000 years: archaeozoological evidence. *Sarawak Museum Journal* 55 (n.s. 76): 61–109.

Cranbrook, Earl of and P.J. Piper. 2007. The Javan Rhinoceros *Rhinoceros sondaicus* in Borneo. *The Raffles Bulletin of Zoology* 55(1): 229–232.

——. 2013. Paleontology to policy: The Quaternary history of South-east Asian tapirs (Tapiridae) and a proposal for the re-introduction of Malayan tapir *Tapirus indicus* to Borneo. *Integrative Zoology* 8: 95–120.

Datan, I. 1993. Archaeological excavations at Gua Sireh (Serian) and Lubang Angin (Gunung Mulu National Park), Sarawak, Malaysia. Kuching: *Sarawak Museum Journal*. Special Monograph no. 6.

Détroit, F. 2006. *Homo sapiens* in Southeast Asian archipelagoes: The Holocene fossil evidence with special reference to funerary practices in East Java. In T. Simanjuntak, I. Pojoh & M. Hisyam (eds), *Austronesian Diaspora and the Ethnogenesis of People in Indonesian Archipelago*, pp. 186–204. Jakarta: Indonesian Institute of Science.

Freeman, J.D. 1957. Iban pottery. *Sarawak Museum Journal* 8 (n.s. 10): 153–176.

Glover, I.C. 1986. *Archaeology in Eastern Timor, 1966–67*. Terra Australis 11. Canberra: Department of Prehistory, Research School of Pacific Studies.

Harrisson, T. 1957. The Great Cave of Niah: a preliminary report on Bornean prehistory. *Man* 57: 161–166. doi.org/10.2307/2795279.

——. 1958. The Cave of Niah: A history of prehistory. *Sarawak Museum Journal* 8 (n.s. 12): 549–595.

——. 1970. The prehistory of Borneo. *Asian Perspectives* 13: 17–45.

Hooijer, D.A. 1960. The giant extinct Pangolin (*Manis palaeojavanica* Dubois) from Niah. *Sarawak Museum Journal* 9 (n.s. 15–16): 350–355.

Hunt, C.O., D.D. Gilbertson and G. Rushworth. 2007. Modern humans in Sarawak, Malaysian Borneo, during oxygen isotope stage 3: palaeoenvironmental evidence from the Great Cave of Niah. *Journal of Archaeological Science* 34(11): 1953–1969. doi.org/10.1016/j.jas.2007.02.023.

Kamminga, J. 1982. *Over the Edge: Functional Analysis of Australian Stone Tools*. Occasional Papers on Anthropology no. 12. St Lucia, Brisbane: University of Queensland Anthropology Museum.

Kusno, S. F. 2006. L'industrie osseouse de l'horizon Keplek, Holocène de la grotte de Song Terus, Punung, Java Est (Indonésie). Mémoire de Master. Paris: Muséum national d'Histoire naturelle.

Lewis, H., V. Paz, M. Lara, H. Barton, P. Piper, J. Ochoa, T. Vitales, A.J. Carlos, T. Higham, L. Neri, V. Hernandez, J. Stevenson, E.C. Robles, A. Ragragio, R. Padilla, W. Solheim II and W. Ronquillo 2008. Terminal Pleistocene to mid-Holocene occupation and an early cremation burial at Ille Cave, Palawan, Philippines, *Antiquity* 82: 318–335. doi.org/10.1017/S0003598X00096836.

Lloyd-Smith, L. 2012. Early Holocene burial practice at Niah Cave, Sarawak. *Journal of Indo-Pacific Archaeology* 32: 54–69.

Meijaard, E., Nijman, V. and Supriatna, J. 2008. *Nasalis larvatus*. The IUCN Red List of Threatened Species. Version 2015.2. www.iucnredlist.org. Downloaded on 30 June 2015.

Medway, Lord. 1960. The Malay tapir in late Quaternary Borneo. *Sarawak Museum Journal* 9 (n.s. 15–16): 356–360.

Morrison, A. 1954–1955. Murut pottery. *Sarawak Museum Journal* 6 (n.s. 5): 295–296.

Morwood, M.J., T. Sutikna, E.W. Saptomo, K.E. Westaway, Jatmiko, R. Awe Due, M.W. Moore, Dwi Yani Yuniawati, P. Hadi, J.-X. Zhao, C.S.M. Turney, K. Fifield, H. Allen and R.P. Soejono. 2008. Climate, people and faunal succession on Java, Indonesia: evidence from Song Gupuh. *Journal of Archaeological Science* 35(7): 1776–1789. doi.org/10.1016/j.jas.2007.11.025.

Noerwidi, S. 2011/2012. The Significance of the Human Skeleton Song Keplek 5 in the History of Human Colonization of Java: A Comprehensive Morphological and Morphometric Study. Unpublished Master's thesis, Muséum National d'Histoire Naturelle, Paris.

O'Connor, S., G. Robertson and K.P. Aplin. 2014. Are osseous artefacts a window to perishable material culture? Implications of an unusually complex bone tool from the Late Pleistocene of East Timor. *Journal of Human Evolution* 67: 108–119. doi.org/10.1016/j.jhevol.2013.12.002.

Piper, P.J. and Earl of Cranbrook. 2007. The potential for large protected areas for the secure re-introduction of Borneo's lost 'Megafauna': A case for the Malay tapir *Tapirus indicus*. In R.B. Stuebing, J. Unggang, J. Ferner, J. Ferner, B. Giman and Kee Kum Ping (eds), *Proceedings of the Regional Conference: Biodiversity Conservation in Tropical Planted Forests in South East Asia*, pp. 161–168. Kuching: Forest Department, Sarawak Forest Corporation & Grand Perfect Sdn Bhd. doi.org/10.1002/oa.1046.

Piper, P.J. and R.J. Rabett. 2009. Hunting in a tropical rainforest: evidence from the terminal Pleistocene at Lobang Hangus, Niah Caves, Sarawak. *International Journal of Osteoarchaeology* 19(4): 551–565.

——. 2014. Late Pleistocene subsistence strategies in Southeast Asia and their implications for understanding the development of modern human behaviour. In R. Dennell and M. Porr (eds), *Southern Asia, Australasia and the Search for Modern Human Origins*, pp. 118–134. Cambridge: Cambridge University Press.

——. 2016. Vertebrate fauna from the Niah Caves. In G. Barker and L. Farr (eds), *The Archaeology of the Niah Caves, Sarawak*, vol. 2, pp. 401–438. Cambridge: McDonald Institute for Archaeological Research.

Piper, P.J., R.J. Rabett and Earl of Cranbrook. 2007. New discoveries of an extinct giant pangolin (*Manis* cf. *palaeojavanica* Dubois) at Niah Cave, Sarawak, Borneo: Biogeography, palaeoecology and taxonomic relationships. *Sarawak Museum Journal* 63 (n.s. 84): 207–226.

Rabett, R.J. 2002. Bone Technology and Subsistence Variability in Prehistoric Southeast Asia. Unpublished PhD thesis, University of Cambridge, Cambridge. doi.org/10.1017/S0959774312000030.

Rabett, R.J. and P.J. Piper. 2012. The emergence of bone technologies at the end of the Pleistocene in Southeast Asia: Regional and evolutionary implications. *Cambridge Archaeological Journal* 22(1): 37–56.

Rabett, R.J., G. Barker, H. Barton, C. Hunt, L. Lloyd-Smith, V. Paz, P.J. Piper, R. Premathilake, G. Rushworth, M. Stephens and K. Szabó. 2013. Landscape transformations and human responses, *c*. 11,500–*c*. 4500 years ago. In G. Barker (ed.), *Rainforest Foraging and Farming in Island Southeast Asia: The Archaeology and Environmental History of the Niah Caves, Sarawak*, pp. 217–254. Niah Cave Project Monographs vol. 1. Cambridge: McDonald Institute Monograph Series.

Reimer, P.J., E. Bard, A. Bayliss, J.W. Beck, P.G. Blackwell, C. Bronk Ramsey, C.E. Buck, H. Cheng, R.L. Edwards, M. Friedrich, P.M. Grootes, T.P. Guilderson, H. Haflidason, I. Hajdas, C. Hatté, T.J. Heaton, D.L. Hoffmann, A.G. Hogg, A.G., Hughen, K.F. Kaiser, B. Kromer, S.W. Manning, M. Niu, R.W. Reimer, D.A. Richards, E.M. Scott, J.R. Southon, R.A. Staff, C.S.M. Turney, and J. van der Plicht. 2013. IntCal13 and Marine13 radiocarbon age calibration curves 0-50,000 years cal BP. *Radiocarbon* 55 (4): 1869–1887. doi.org/10.2458/azu_js_rc.55.16947.

Reynolds, T., G. Barker, H. Barton, G. Cranbrook, L. Farr, C. Hunt, L. Kealhofer, V. Paz, A. Pike, P.J. Piper, R.J. Rabett, G. Rushworth, C. Stimpson and K. Szabó. 2013. The first modern humans at Niah *c.* 50,000–35,000 years ago. In G. Barker (ed.), *Rainforest Foraging and Farming in Island Southeast Asia: The Archaeology and Environmental History of the Niah Caves, Sarawak,* pp. 135–172. Niah Cave Project Monographs vol. 1. Cambridge: McDonald Institute Monograph Series.

Sémah, A.-M. and F. Sémah. 2012. The rain forest in Java through the Quaternary and its relationships with humans (adaptation, exploitation and impact on the forest). *Quaternary International* 249: 120–128. doi.org/10.1016/j.quaint.2011.06.013.

Simanjuntak, T. (ed.). 2002. *Gunung Sewu in Prehistoric Times*. Yogyakarta: Gadjah Mada University Press.

Spriggs, M. 1989. The dating of the Island Southeast Asian Neolithic: an attempt at chronometric hygiene and linguistic correlation. *Antiquity* 63: 587–613. doi.org/10.1017/S0003598X00076560.

Stimpson, C. 2016. Bird and bat bones from the Great Cave: taphonomic assessment. In G. Barker and L. Farr (eds), *The Archaeology of the Niah Caves, Sarawak,* vol. 2, pp. 439–454. Cambridge: McDonald Institute for Archaeological Research.

van Es, L.J.C. 1930. The prehistoric remains in the Sampoeng Cave, Residency of Ponorogo, Java, *Proceedings of the Fourth Pacific Science Congress, Java, 1929.* vol. III, Biological Papers, pp. 329–340. Batavia and Bandoeng: Pacific Science Association.

van Heekeren, H.R. 1972. *The Stone Age of Indonesia*. 2nd edition. The Hague: Martinus Nijhoff.

van Strien, N.J., Manullang, B., Sectionov, Isnan, W., Khan, M.K.M, Sumardja, E., Ellis, S., Han, K.H., Boeadi, Payne, J. and Bradley Martin, E. 2008. *Dicerorhinus sumatrensis*. The IUCN Red List of Threatened Species. Version 2015.2. www.iucnredlist.org. Downloaded on 3 July 2015.

Widianto, H, T. Simanjuntak and B. Toha. 1997. Ekskavasi situs Gua Babi, Kabupaten Tabalong, Propinsi Kalimantan Selatan. *Berita Penelitian Arkeologi Balai Arkeologi Banjarmasin* no. 1.

Willems, W. 1939. Merkwaardige praehistorische schelpartefacten van Celebes en Java. *Cultureel Indië* 1: 181–185.

Würster, C.M., M.I. Bird, I.D. Bull, F. Creed, C. Bryant, J.A.J. Dungait and V. Paz. 2010. Forest contraction in north equatorial Southeast Asia during the last glacial period. *Proceedings of the National Academy of Sciences* 107(35): 15508–15511. doi.org/10.1073/pnas.1005507107.

Zuraina Majid-Lowee, Z. 1981. *The West Mouth, Niah in the Prehistory of Southeast Asia*. PhD thesis, Yale University, 1979. Michigan: University Microfilm International.

Zuraina Majid (ed.). 2005. *Perak Man and Other Prehistoric Skeletons of Malaysia*. Penang: Universiti Sains Malaysia.

7

Understanding the Callao Cave Depositional History

Armand Salvador Mijares

This paper presents a soil micromorphological analysis of the stratigraphic sequence of sediments recorded in the antechamber of Callao Cave, northern Luzon. The study builds on our understanding of the depositional and post-depositional history of the cave sediments and elucidates further our knowledge of human occupation at Callao. The results confirm three in situ *periods of human frequentation in the antechamber. The most recent recognisable archaeological horizon dates to ca. 3600 BP and represents a Neolithic occupation layer with ceramics, flake tools, a spindle whorl, faunal remains and human burials. Below this is a layer of volcanic sediment that forms a hiatus in cultural deposition, preceded by a habitation at ca. 25,000 BP characterised by hearths, abundant charcoal and burnt sediments and associated chert flake tools. Below a further ca. 2 m of almost sterile deposit is the lowest cultural horizon, comprising breccia containing faunal bones and a human metatarsal, dated by uranium series to ca. 67,000 BP. The study demonstrates that Callao Cave was only intermittently and irregularly occupied over the last 70 millennia.*

Introduction

The author has intermittently investigated the Callao Limestone Formation in the Municipality of Peñablanca, Cagayan Province, northern Luzon, since 1999 (Mijares 2001; Figure 7.1). From 2003 onwards, and as part of my PhD supervised by Peter Bellwood, I implemented a more intensive and sustained research program at Callao. The initial project was primarily focused on Neolithic occupation of northern Luzon and comparisons between burial and habitation sites in the Callao karstic formations and the contemporaneous open-air settlement sites of the Cagayan River valley (Mijares 2007). Following the completion of my PhD, I returned to Callao Cave itself to investigate the deeper, older sedimentary sequences that potentially lay undiscovered in the main cave entrance (Mijares et al. 2010).

Callao is the largest cave complex in the Callao karstic formation, with seven chambers and three collapsed roof holes that open to the sky. Since 1979, the antechamber of the cave has been the focus of several periods of archaeological research (Figure 7.2; Cuevas 1980, 1982). My initial excavation at Callao in 2003 focused on the eastern section of the antechamber, close to the eastern cave wall. Deposits were excavated to a depth of 1.3 m and resulted in the discovery of Palaeolithic and Neolithic activities in the cave (Mijares 2005a). In 2007, inspired by the work of Mike Morwood at Liang Bua, Flores (Morwood and van Ostersee 2007), I went back to Callao and excavated my original trenches to a greater depth with the hope of finding evidence of early hominin activity. It was during these excavations that we were able to recover a human third metatarsal, dated by Uranium Series to *ca.* 67,000 BP, and recognised as potentially one of the oldest *Homo sapiens* bones discovered in Southeast Asia (Mijares et al. 2010; Heaney et al. 2011).

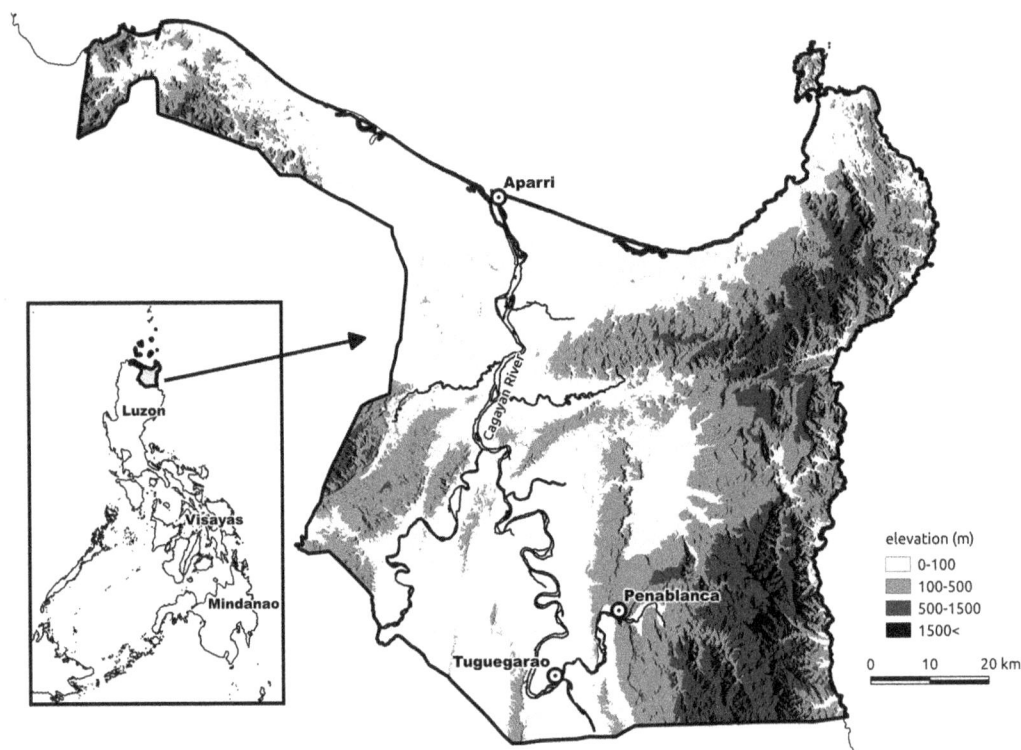

Figure 7.1 The location of Peñablanca karst formations in northern Luzon, Philippines.
Source: E. Robles and A. Mijares.

Since 1979, a total of eight trenches have been excavated within the Callao antechamber and one of the outstanding issues has been correlation of the sedimentary and stratigraphic sequences across the cave entrance. As Anderson (1997: 614) has noted with respect to Lang Rongrien cave in southern Thailand, a particularly difficult problem is correlating occupational debris from one part of a cave with deposits and materials from another part, without physically connecting stratigraphic units by a single excavated profile. In this paper, soil micromorphology, corroborated by macroscopic observations, phytolith analysis, SEM-EDXA analysis and pH testing are used to correlate the layers within the different excavation units in the antechamber of Callao Cave. The data presented here are from excavations carried out in 2003, 2007 and 2009, plus a re-excavation of one unfinished square from the 1979–1980 excavation seasons. Linking the stratigraphic sequences across the cave entrance has provided insights into the depositional histories of accumulating sediments and correlation of human activity throughout the antechamber.

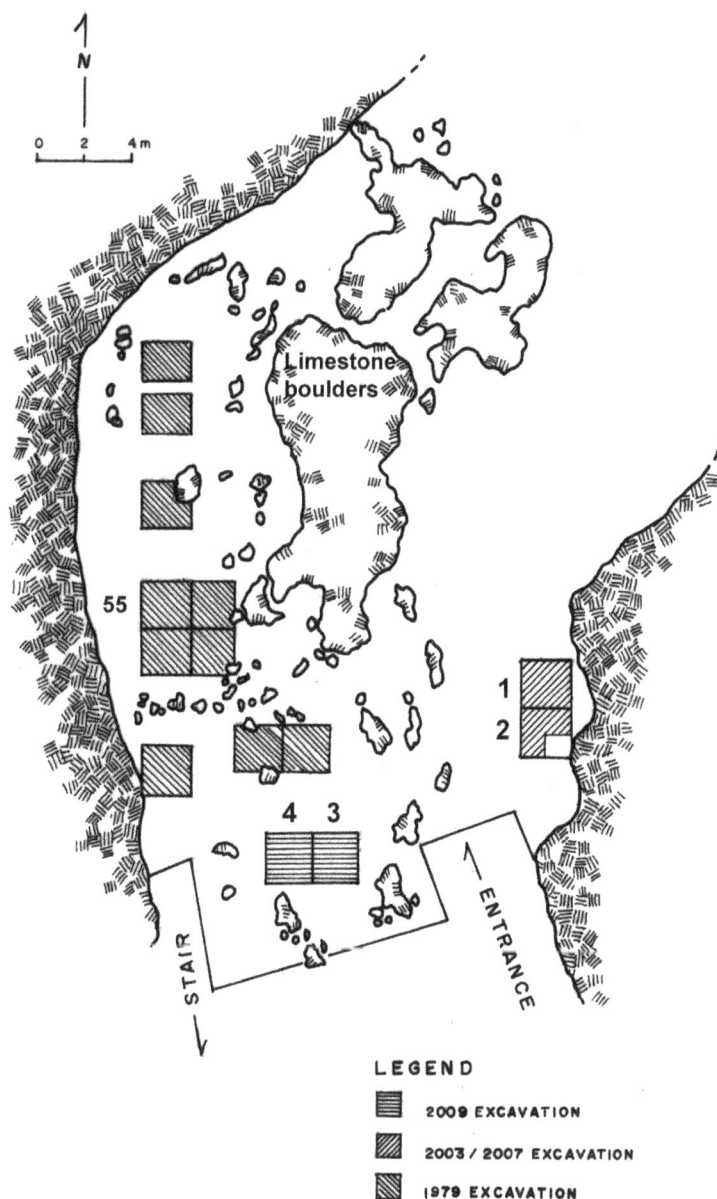

Figure 7.2 The locations of the Callao Cave excavation units.
Source: A. Mijares.

Archaeological background

A team from the National Museum of the Philippines led by M. Cuevas first excavated Callao Cave in 1979–1980. The archaeologists excavated a 4 m² trench (containing squares numbered 45, 46, 55 and 56) to a depth of 1.9 m below modern ground surface (bms; Cuevas 1980). In 1980–1982, research continued with the excavation of squares 17, 25, 27, 28, 73, 96 and 108, to an average depth of 2 m bms (Cuevas 1982). In 2003, Mijares (2005a) excavated an 8 x 4 m trench near the eastern wall of the antechamber by the cave entrance. This was divided into two 4 m² squares, termed squares 1 and 2 (Figure 7.2), and excavated to a depth of 1.3 m below the surface. In 2007, the same trench was excavated further, to bedrock, at 3.8 m. The trench yielded 11 soil micromorphology samples (Figure 7.3), of which five were collected from the northern wall of the excavation trench in 2003, and the remaining six from the eastern wall in 2007.

In 2009, part of the 1979–1980 square 55 was further excavated to 7.5 m depth in a 1 m² trench in the northwest corner. The original stratigraphic description of Square 55 was checked and forms the basis for comparison with the results of the 2003 and 2007 excavations. Also in 2009, another 8 x 4 m trench (Squares 3 and 4) was excavated towards the cave entrance, near a large boulder located under the drip-line. This trench reached a maximum depth of 4 m bms.

To understand the depositional history of the Callao antechamber the stratigraphic profiles in sample squares 55, 1/2, and 3/4 were studied and correlated.

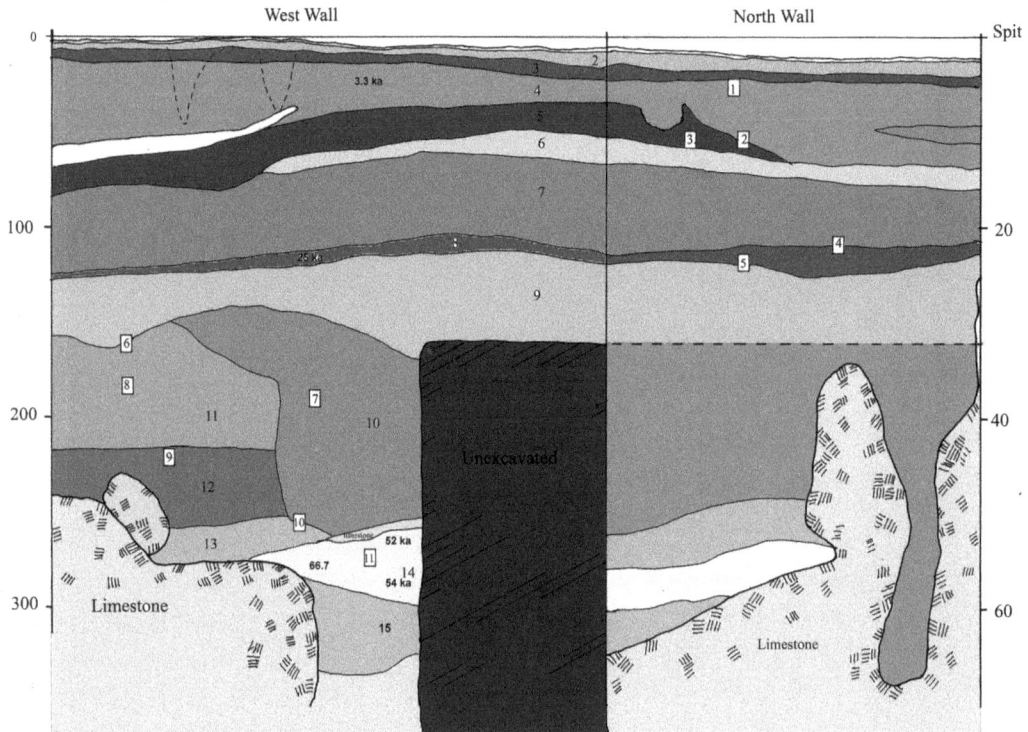

Figure 7.3 Sections of the west and north walls of Squares 1 and 2 showing the locations of the micromorphological soil samples (white boxes).
Source: A. Mijares.

Soil micromorphology

Soil micromorphology, the study of undisturbed soil and sediment samples in thin section, is often used to conduct fine-grained analysis of site formation processes (e.g. Courty et al. 1989). In Southeast Asia, its application to archaeological sites has steadily increased in recent years. It was first applied in Malaysia, particularly in the Tingkayu site complex in Sabah (Magee 1988), at Gua Gunung Runtuh (Zauyah 1994) in the Malay Peninsula and more recently in Niah Cave, Sarawak (Lewis 2003, 2004; Stephens et al. 2005). In the Philippines, soil micromorphology has been employed at Tabon and Ille Caves on Palawan (Lewis 2004, 2007), and in Eme and Dalan Serkot Caves in the Cagayan Valley of northern Luzon (Mijares and Lewis 2009). The approach has also been applied to an alluvial deposit sealed beneath a shell midden at the site of Nagsabaran, also in the Cagayan Valley (Mijares 2005b).

Samples for this study were recovered from standing profiles and taken as blocks in tins driven into the sections. The samples were air dried, then impregnated with crystic resin and hardened to form solid blocks from which 'slices' (thin sections) were cut (4 x 6 x 0.8 cm). The samples were then mounted on glass slides and ground to produce 25 μm thin sections, which were observed under plane and crossed polar light at 40 and 100 X magnifications (Tables 7.1 and 7.2). The following bibliographic resources were consulted to describe the observed features: Adams and Mackenzie 2001, Adams et al. 1984, Bullock et al. 1985, Courty et al. 1989, Fitzpatrick 1984, Mackenzie and Adams 1994, Stoops 2003.

Results

Stratigraphic description

The cave deposits at Callao are generally undulating, varying in depth within and between excavation trenches. Excavation of the sedimentary sequences generally proceeded by removing layers in 5 cm spits and following the natural contours of different deposits (where possible). All the excavation trenches at Callao produced a relatively similar sequence of upper deposits to a depth of 1.5 m, albeit with sediments of varying thickness across the antechamber.

Layer 1 (Spit 1) was a thin, loose surface deposit containing modern materials. Layer 2 (Spit 2) is more compact and contains Chinese glass beads, earthenware sherds, bones and lithic debris.

Layer 3 (Spits 3–4), was a yellowish-red clay sediment of late Neolithic date (*ca.* 3000 BP) containing shell beads, clay *lingling-o* earrings, brown, red-slipped and black earthenware sherds, flake tools, human bones and teeth, bat bones, riverine and land snail shells, and a single spindle whorl recovered during the 1980 excavations (Cuevas 1980). In addition, 38 tubular shell beads were recovered, measuring 3 to 6 mm in length and 1 to 4 mm in diameter. The perforations seem to have been drilled from both sides using a lithic implement that produced the typical hourglass shape, with diameters ranging from 1.5 to 2.5 mm. Disarticulated and fragmentary human bones suggest disturbance that might have occurred during prehistoric times. Within this level a calcium carbonate cemented deposit occurred in the west central part of two squares, making excavation and recovery difficult (Mijares 2005a).

Layer 4 (Spits 5–8) was also a yellowish-red clay deposit that still contained earthenware pottery with brown, red-slipped and black surface finishes, but this layer yielded no *lingling-o* earrings or shell beads. A red-slipped carinated sherd, with double parallel incisions enclosing a triangle with punctate in-filling similar in shape, decoration and form to the earthenware from the *ca.* 3500–3000 BP Magapit Hill site near the main Cagayan River (Aoyagi et al. 1993), was recovered (Mijares 2005a). Human bones, stone flakes, riverine and terrestrial gastropod shells were collected. Four deer teeth, a wild boar tusk and nine other pig teeth were also found. One AMS radiocarbon determination on charcoal dates this layer to 3335±34 uncal. BP (Wk-17010) or 3693–3527 cal. BP (using Oxcal 4.2 Intcal.13; Bronk Ramsey et al. 2010). Layer 4b was a distinctive reddish and loose sandy silt loam that forms an intermediary layer in the northeast corner of Square 1 (Mijares 2005a).

Layer 5 (Spits 8–10) was a black sandy deposit devoid of cultural remains. Though no artefacts were recovered, phytolith identification showed grass to be dominant in this layer, accounting for 53 per cent of the microfossils recorded. Other phytoliths identified were palm (Arecaceae), bamboo and sedge (Cyperaceae) (Mijares 2007).

Layers 6 (Spits 10–13) and 7 (Spits 14–20) were geogenic deposits devoid of cultural materials. Both contain inter-bedded layers of cemented as well as extremely loose sand. Layer 7 had a reddish hue suggesting that it had undergone oxidation. An Energy Dispersive X-ray Analysis (EDXA) on impregnated sediment from this layer was conducted using a Jeol 6400 SEM.

The EDXA result shows that the grains are high in silica (Si) and aluminium (Al), suggesting that the deposit derives from volcanic ash. Minerals identified include plagioclase, quartz, ilmenite and possible garnet (almandine) (Mijares 2007).

In Layer 8 (Spit 21), chert flake tools were recovered. A probable hearth was also observed at the south end of Square 1 and fragmentary burnt cervid bones were recovered. An AMS radiocarbon determination on charcoal collected from an *in situ* hearth from this layer is 25,968±373 uncal. BP (Wk-14881) or 28,980–27,420 cal. BP (using Oxcal 4.2 Intcal.13; Bronk Ramsey et al. 2010). The silt loam Layer 9 (Spits 26–32) was devoid of cultural remains apart from a few sparsely distributed burnt bones.

In 2007 the team reduced the size of the 2003 excavation trench at a depth of 160 cm below surface and only excavated the adjacent southern end of Square 1 and northern end of Square 2. There were two distinct sedimentary deposits in the excavation area. The yellowish-brown clay at the north end designated Layer 10 (Spits 31–50) was devoid of cultural materials. At the southern end, an olive-brown clay designated Layer 11 (Spits 31 to 43), produced a flake tool, a chert core and faunal remains, mostly deer. Layer 10 is stratigraphically younger than Layer 11 and seems to be the infilling of a gully that was eroded and truncated during the deposition of Layer 9. Layer 12 (Spits 44–50) was a silty clay loam containing several large bones including a deer scapula, the proximal end of a humerus, and a broken antler (Piper and Mijares 2007).

In Spits 51–53 of the clay Layer 13 the bones and teeth of deer were widespread. In Spit 54 (270 cm below the surface), the team encountered a cemented carbonate-rich breccia (Layer 14; Spits 54–59). This produced 533 faunal bone fragments, mostly deer, pig and bovine (Piper and Mijares 2007). A number of small mammal fossils were also recovered and identified as murid rodents belonging to the genera *Batomys* and *Apomys* (Heaney et al. 2011). It was also within this layer that the hominin third metatarsal (MT3) was recovered. The dating of two cervid teeth and the hominin MT3 by U-series ablation produced minimum ages of 52,000, 54,000 and 66,700 BP respectively, from depths between 275 and 295 cm (Mijares et al. 2010).

Layer 15 (Spits 60–68) below Layer 14 consisted of interbedded, loose and cemented sediment. One cervid antler fragment was recovered from this layer at a depth of 345 cm. Below this was bedrock.

Description of the soil micromorphology samples

The qualitative and semi-quantitative descriptions of the samples are summarised in Tables 1 and 2. The following are the specific descriptions of each sample. Callao 1 (Figure 7.4, no. 1) was taken from the upper boundary of Layer 4, underlying Layer 3, and is characterised by an assemblage of earthenware pottery, human skeletal remains and a few flake tools. The sample shows heavily bioturbated sediments, with frequent channels and circular poroids made by faunal activity, and a crumb microstructure. Clay coatings were seen on void walls and grains, as well as in aggregates, and micrite impregnates the groundmass, as well as coating some bone fragments. A zone of depletion in the mid-section of the slide shows the loss of iron-rich minerals, probably due to water or faunal activity. Anthropogenic deposits observed in the thin section included small fragments of earthenware, abundant charcoal and charred plant residue, mostly wood.

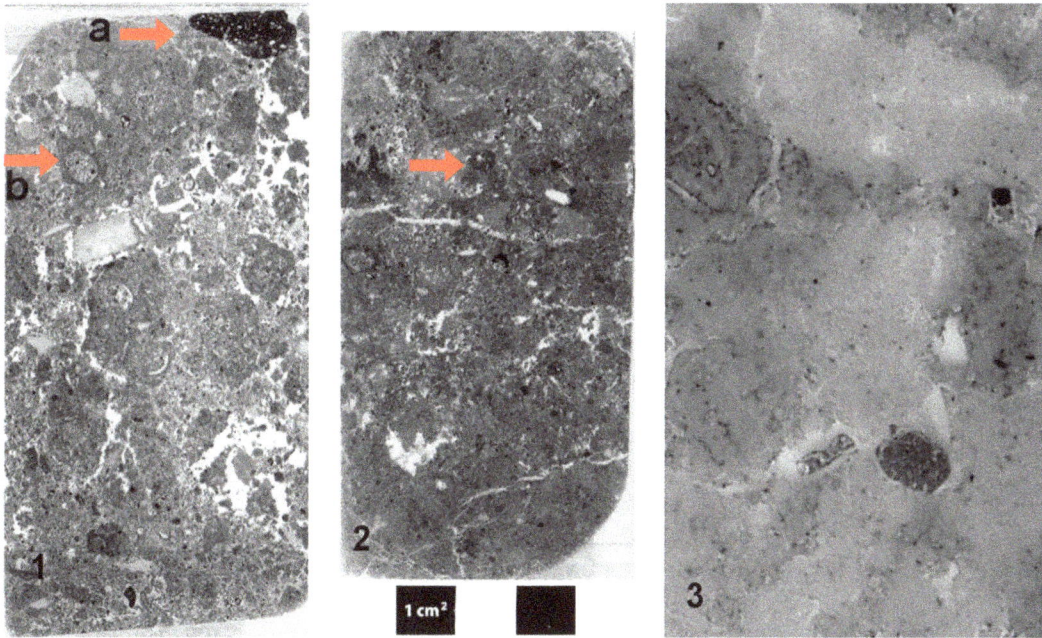

Figure 7.4 Sample thin sections from Callao Cave.

1. Sample 1, with arrow 'a' showing a fragment of a pot, and arrow 'b' showing faunal activity.
2. Sample 4, with arrow showing fragments of burnt sediment in the 26 ka layer.
3. Sample 11, from the 67 ka breccia layer.

Scale bar 1 cm.

Source: A. Mijares.

Callao 2 was taken from the lower boundary of Layer 4 (over Layer 5). Localised burning produced abundant charcoal and had oxidised the sediment, turning it a reddish colour; these features are probably related to a hearth event. Deposition of leached clay was observed in the coatings on grains, aggregates and bones. Precipitation of calcium carbonate was also observed, with the pseudomorphising and coating of bones with micrite and sparite.

Callao 3 was taken from Layer 5. While the layer was devoid of cultural materials, the thin section did contain burnt organic material (Figure 7.5B), probably of grass and sedge, and phytoliths.

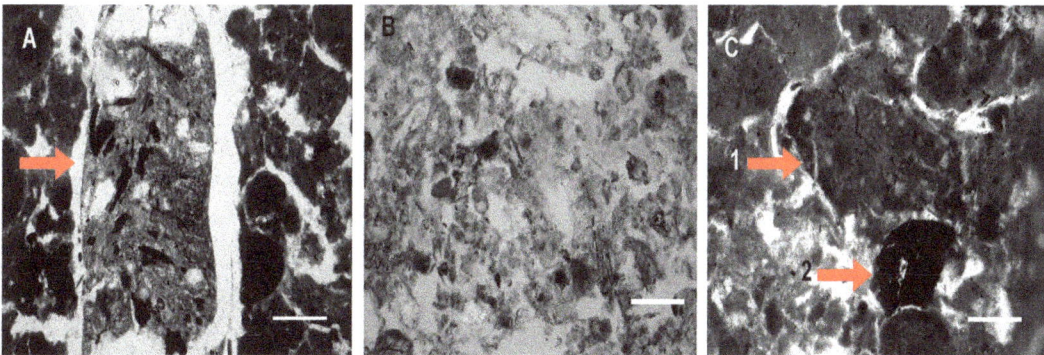

Figure 7.5 Sample thin sections from Callao Cave.

A. Arrow showing faunal excrement (Sample 4).
B. Biological remains in Layer 5 (Sample 3).
C. Arrow 1 showing a rubified ped and arrow 2 showing charcoal (Sample 5).

Scale bar 200 µm.

Source: A. Mijares.

Callao 4 and 5 were taken from Layer 8 (Figure 7.4, no. 2). In thin section that deposit has a mixed blocky and crumb structure, with evidence of bioturbation that is also observed in the large horizontal channels partially infilled with faunal excrement (Figure 7.5A). Remains of roots were also observed (Figure 7.5B). The layer was evidently subjected to wetting and drying events, as characterised by its blocky structure, granostriated fabric and high iron nodule content. Precipitation of calcium carbonate in the form of micritic coatings and infilling of voids is evident. During excavation a probable hearth was observed in this layer, which contained oxidised reddish sediment and charcoal (Figure 7.5C). The thin section also showed burning features including charcoal, other burnt plant residues and possible ash aggregates. A dark reddish-brown fabric pedofeature observed in the thin section could be oxidised sediment related to the hearth event.

Callao 11 was taken from Layer 14 (Figure 7.4, no. 3). The sample was highly impregnated with micrite, particularly in the central area. The sediment has angular blocky structure with moderately developed pedality. The observed voids consisted of planes with partially accommodated walls and vughs (small rock or vein cavities).

Callao 6 was taken between Layers 9 and 11. The upper portion (Layer 9) contains many inclusions of limestone measuring 10 to 20 mm. The lower portion (Layer 11) has a silty clay matrix. This sediment has a sub-angular structure with moderately developed pedality. Coatings of peds and void walls with clay and sparite infillings of pores were recorded. Reddish-orange rounded nodules, which appear to be of 'dirty' clay, were also observed. Callao 7 was taken from Layer 10 and is massive, but can be divided into two by a break near the mid-section. The walls of the break are accommodating, which might signify that it is recent. The sediment consists of a silty-clay with angular blocky structure and weak pedality. The only organic matter observed was charcoal fragments with a size range of 50–300 μm, and 2 per cent frequency. No bone or shell was observed. Orange-red limpid clay was recorded in rounded aggregates with a size range of 50–200 μm. There were also sub-angular, strongly impregnated typic nodules. Excrements of rounded to oblong shape and 500 μm in size were seen filling channels.

Callao 8 was taken in the middle of the massive Layer 11. The lower part contained gravel size sub-angular limestone bioclasts (molluscs) (Figure 7.6A). This sample has a sub-angular blocky structure with moderately developed pedality. Sparite crystals were observed infilling voids and coating channel walls. Oblong-shaped excrements 600 μm in diameter were also observed in channels.

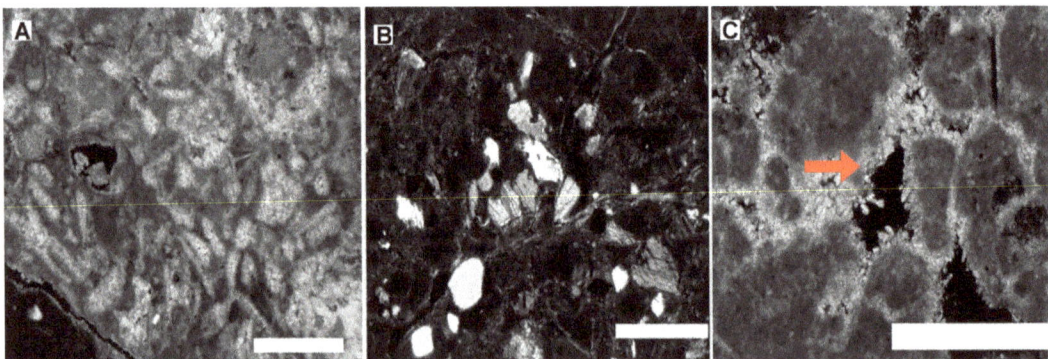

Figure 7.6 Sample thin sections from Callao Cave.

A. Limestone fragment with bioclast (mollusc) inclusions (Sample 8).

B. Volcanic minerals in a clay matrix (Sample 9).

C. Arrow pointing to equant calcite of meteoric phreatic origin (Sample 11).

Scale bar 1000 μm.

Source: A. Mijares.

Table 7.1 Semi-quantitative description of soil micromorphology features.

Site/section	Cultural	Organic	Bone and shells	Minerals	Pedofeatures					
					micrite coating	limpid clay	clay coating	iron nodules	burnt soil	excrement
Callao 1	ch (2), pt (1)	pr (2)	b (1), s(1)	ad (1), bl (1), lm (2), o (1), pl (3), a (2), cl (2), py (2), ch (1), q (4)	2	3	2	4		2
Callao 2	ch (3), Bt (2)	pr (3)	b (1)	ad (1), lm (2), a (2), py (2), ch (1), cl (2)	2	2	3	2	2	
Callao 3	ch (3), ph (2)	pr (3)	b (2)	q (2), a (2), py (1), ch (1)	2	2	2	2		
Callao 4	ch (3), ws (2), bt (2)	pr (1)		q (2), pl (2), a(1), ch(1)	2	2	2	3	4	2
Callao 5	ch (3)	pr (1)	b (1)	q (2), ch (2), pl (2), a (1)	2	1	2	2	4	2
Callao 6	ch (2)		b (1)	pl (3), q (3), a (2), bt (2)	2	2	2	2		
Callao 7	ch (1)			q (3), py (2), pl (2), a (2), ad (1)		2	2	2		2
Callao 8	ch (2)			lm (3), q (2), pl (2), a (2), ad (2)	2					1
Callao 9	ch (1)			q (2), pl (2), a (2), o (91), ad (1)			2			
Callao 10	ch (1)		b (2)	q (2), pl (2), a (2), py (2), ad (1)		2	2	3		
Callao 11	ch (2)		b (1)	lm (3), ad (1), pl (2), q(2), a(2)	4	2				2

Legend

1=very few	pt=pottery	pl=plant residue	b=bone	q=quartz	1=rare
2=few	ch=charcoal	r=roots	s=shell	pl=plagioclase	2=occasional
3=common	ws=wood ash			a=amphibole	3=many
4=dominant	ph=phytoliths			bt=biotite	4=abundant
5=very dominant	Bt=burnt soil			py=pyroxene	5=very abundant
	pt=pottery			o=olivine	
				m=muscovite	
				lm=limestone	
				cl=calcite	
				ch=radiolarian chert	
				ad=andesite	
				bl=basalt	

Source: A. Mijares.

Table 7.2 Description of soil micromorphology features.

Site/section	Cultural	Organic	Bone and shells	Minerals	Pedofeatures					
					micrite coating	limpid clay	clay coating	iron nodules	burnt soil	excrement
Callao 1	ch (2), pt (1)	pr (2)	b (1), s(1)	ad (1), bl (1), lm (2), o (1), pl (3), a (2), cl (2), py (2), ch (1), q (4)	2	3	2	4		2
Callao 2	ch (3), Bt (2)	pr (3)	b (1)	ad (1), lm (2), a (2), py (2), ch (1), cl (2)	2	2	3	2	2	
Callao 3	ch (3), ph (2)	pr (3)	b (2)	q (2), a (2), py (1), ch (1)	2	2	2	2		
Callao 4	ch (3), ws (2), Bt (2)	pr (1)		q (2), pl (2), a (1), ch (1)	2	2	2	3	4	2
Callao 5	ch (3)	pr (1)	b (1)	q (2), ch (2), pl (2), a (1)	2	1	2	2	4	2
Callao 6	ch (2)		b (1)	pl (3), q (3), a (2), bt (2)	2	2	2	2		
Callao 7	ch (1)			q (3), py (2), pl (2), a (2), ad (1)		2	2	2		2
Callao 8	ch (2)			lm (3), q (2), pl (2), a (2), ad (2)	2					1
Callao 9	ch (1)			q (2), pl (2), a (2), o (91), ad (1)			2			
Callao 10	ch (1)		b (2)	q (2), pl (2), a (2), py (2), ad (1)		2	2	3		
Callao 11	ch (2)		b (1)	lm (3), ad (1), pl (2), q (2), a (2)	4	2				2

Legend					
1=very few	pt=pottery	pr=plant residue	b=bone	q=quartz	1=rare
2=few	ch=charcoal	r=roots	s=shell	pl=plagioclase	2=occasional
3=common	ws=wood ash			a=amphibole	3=many
4=dominant	ph=phytoliths			bt=biotite	4=abundant
5=very dominant	Bt=burnt soil			py=pyroxene	5=very abundant
				o=olivine	
				m=muscovite	
				lm=limestone	
				cl=calcite	

Source: A. Mijares.

Callao 9 was taken just below the border of Layer 11, within Layer 12 (Figure 7.6B). The layer is a massive deposit macroscopically, with large channels. The thin section sample has a sub-angular blocky structure with moderate pedality and a silty clay loam texture. Hypo-coating of channel walls was observed.

Callao 10 was taken from a massive deposit between Layers 10 and 13. It has a large (3 mm wide) channel at the mid-section that divides the sample; this could be a recent break. The sediment has subangular blocky structure with moderate pedality. The groundmass, which has a silty clay loam texture, is poorly sorted. Dark reddish nodules of fine matrix were observed as well as limpid clay aggregates. Clay coatings were also identified.

The matrix of Callao 11 Layer 14 was moderately sorted with a silty clay loam texture, and is cemented with equant calcite of meteoric phreatic origin (Figure 7.6C). Limestone fragments between 250 µm to 8 mm in size are the dominant mineral inclusions. Volcanic rock fragments and minerals are also present. This deposit also contained rounded yellow orange aggregates (125–250 µm) of possible limpid clay and excrements of ellipsoid and cylinder shapes containing organic minerals (1,500–2,500 µm).

Discussion

The following interpretation of depositional history in the Callao antechamber begins from the lowest known layer upwards, and emphasis is placed on those archaeological layers with evidence of human activity (Table 7.3, Figure 7.7).

Table 7.3 Stratigraphic correlation between Squares 1 and 2, 3 and 4, and 55.

Square 1/2	Square 3/4	Square 55	Descriptions
L1	L1		Modern debris
L3/L4	L2	L1/L2	3 3 ka (Neolithic)
L5	missing	L3	Organic layer
missing	L3	L4/L5	Sterile layer
L6	L4	L7/L8	volcanic
L7	missing	L9	Sterile layer
L8	missing	L10	25 ka occupation layer
L9–13	L5	L11–16	Few animal bones
L14	L6	L17	66.7 ka, human and animal bones

Note: Correlation is based on field observation, texture and colour of the sediments. Missing layers could be due to erosion or the material was not deposited such as organic materials (Layer 5).

Source: A. Mijares.

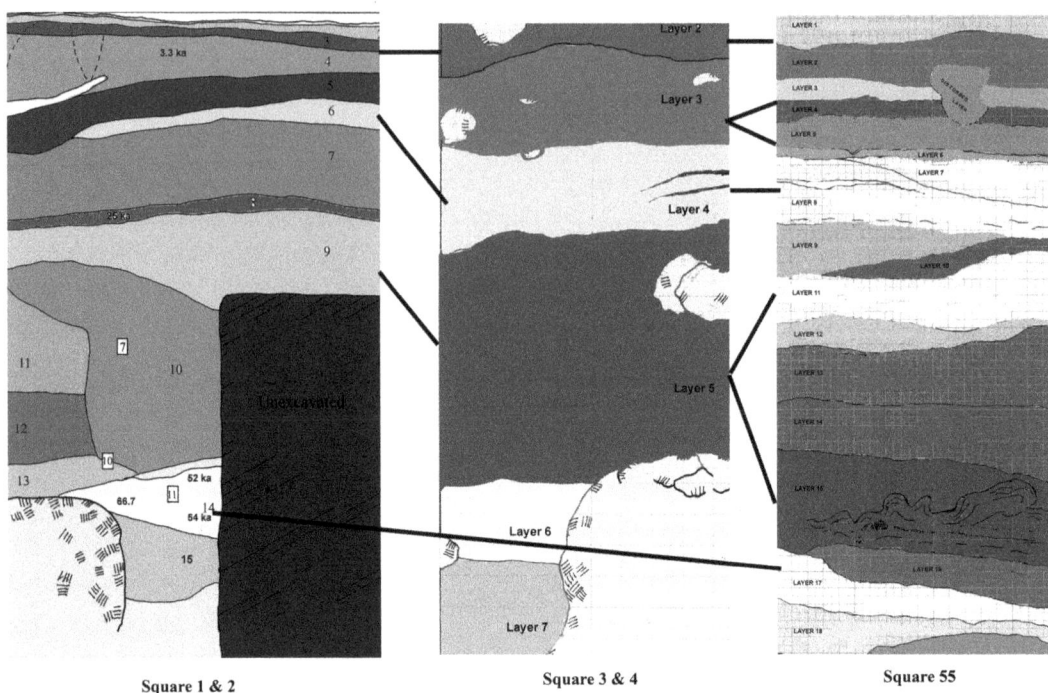

Figure 7.7 Stratigraphic correlations between Squares 1 and 2, 3 and 4, and 55.
Source: A. Mijares.

The 1979–1980 excavations of Square 55 reached a depth of *ca.* 7.5 m below surface (BS) before exposing what the excavator deemed to be bedrock (Cuevas 1980). Cuevas (1980) identified a total of six layers in the sedimentary sequence, with the lowest archaeological layer recorded at 3.5 m below ground surface. During re-excavation and re-analysis of Square 55 in 2009, a total of 27 layers were identified.

The stratigraphic sequence in the upper 4 m of 1979–1980 Square 55 can be correlated with Squares 1–2 and 3–4 from the more recent excavations, though not all the layers were observed in all units (Figure 7.7; Table 7.3). The lower layers of Square 55 stand alone as representing the lowest deposits of the antechamber excavated. Unfortunately, neither micromorphological nor biological samples were collected from the lowest levels of Square 55 and their composition cannot be assessed. But from Layer 19 (*ca.* 4 m BS) to Layer 27 at 7.3 m BS the sediments are clays with colours ranging from dark yellowish-brown to yellowish-brown. Layer 21 at 4.65 m BS is the lowest volcanic ash deposit found in the cave. No evidence of hominin activity was recorded in any of these lower deposits.

Layer 14 in Square 1–2, there is a hominin and other bone-bearing breccia that can be correlated with Layer 6 in Squares 3–4 and Layer 17 in Square 55 (Figure 7.7). The sediment is a silty clay loam with microscopic charcoal fragments (50–1,000 μm) that might be associated with human activity. The breccia results from impregnation of the matrix with micrite. The identification of equant calcite of meteoric phreatic origin could mean that some of the sediments were deposited in a phreatic (hydrological) environment and subsequently reworked when exposed to subaerial conditions and secondary movement (Adams and Mackenzie 2001). The faunal bones have surface polishing and rounding that could have been caused by erosion and water transport (Mijares et al. 2010). The lower layers in Square 55 could also have been deposited initially in a phreatic environment. The spatial distribution of the faunal bone within this deposit shows linear concentrations extending from the entrance of the cave towards the interior. This implies water transport and post-depositional redistribution of vertebrate remains from the entrance towards the interior within a possible low energy flow channel.

The deposits in Layers 9–13 in Squares 1–2, Layer 5 in Squares 3–4 and Layers 11–16 in Square 55 are yellowish-brown silt loams that contain sporadic faunal bones, mostly Cervidae. The sediment is impregnated with calcium carbonate and might have come from different sources, including decomposing limestone (as indicated by the limestone bioclasts), volcanic sediments (as indicated by the presences of volcanic minerals and rock fragments), and authigenic (generated *in situ*) carbonates. Some of the faunal remains again show polishing, rounding and abrasion (Piper and Mijares 2007), which could mean that the sediment has undergone some reworking and secondary deposition.

Layer 8 in Square 1–2 was also identified in Square 55 as Layer 10, but was not observed in Square 3–4. Instead, Square 3–4 has a 26,000 BP human occupation layer with a distinctly reddish-brown colour. *In situ* hearth deposits were observed in Square 3–4, and disturbed deposits apparently related to burning were identified in thin section. This deposit also produced a considerable number of lithic artefacts (Mijares 2007). The absence of this deposit in Squares 3–4 might be due to post-depositional erosion of deposits close to the cave entrance or the occupants of the cave did not utilise this area quite so intensively.

Layers 6 and 7 in Square 1–2, Layer 4 in Square 3–4, and Layers 7 and 8 in Square 55 represent a 10–50 cm thick volcanic ash layer observed across the antechamber. No archaeological remains were recovered from these layers and the actual volcanic source still needs to be identified. Geochemical analysis of the ash might help with provenance.

Above the volcanic ash was a thick, dark layer rich in biological remains (Layer 5 in Squares 1–2 and Layer 3 in Square 55) but with an absence of archaeological materials. This was not observed in Squares 3–4, which lie closer to the mouth of the antechamber. Phytolith and micromorphological analyses show that some of the biological remains were burnt. It is currently unclear whether these deposits represent a natural burning event or resulted from anthropogenic activity. If people were involved, then the absence of cultural remains would suggest that their main activities were beyond the cave entrance.

Layers 3 and 4 in Squares 1–2, Layer 2 in Squares 3–4, and Layers 1 and 2 in Square 55 represent the *ca.* 3600–3500 BP Neolithic activity within the cave entrance. The deposit is composed of a sandy silt loam and soil micromorphological analysis shows that the layer has been highly bioturbated by faunal activity, with a crumb structure. There is also some evidence of burning from the reddened sediment and a high charcoal content with pottery and other material culture. The presence of numerous fragmented human bones and teeth indicates that the antechamber was also utilised for burial during this period.

Conclusions

Cave sites have complicated depositional and post-depositional histories and require a detailed approach to understanding formation processes. The case of Callao Cave clearly shows the importance of conducting a fine-grained analysis of soil and sediment to determine the processes involved in sediment deposition. Callao Cave, with its important archaeological findings, has greatly benefited from a multidisciplinary approach anchored by contextual information from soil micromorphological analysis.

At Callao, the depositional history of the antechamber reveals multiple sources of sediment accumulation, from the lower material deposited under phreatic conditions, through a period of reworking and mixing with in-washed sediments, and then a deposition of volcanic ash and authigenic carbonate formation. Other processes observed include bioturbation by soil fauna, cementation with micrite and sparite crystals, oxidation, coating of peds and infilling of voids.

A number of anthropogenic features within at least three phases of human activity were also identified. This included evidence of burning, charcoal, as well as bones and artefacts. The earliest phase of activity occurred between 67,000–54,000 BP and resulted in the deposition of faunal and human bone. The re-deposition of bone fragments towards the interior of the cave suggests that most (if not all) of the activity occurred close to or within the entrance of the cave. Movement of bone appears to have been facilitated by their deposition within a shallow flow-channel that drained from the entrance of the cave into the antechamber close to the east wall. The second phase of habitation occurred during the Late Pleistocene around 28,980–27,420 cal. BP and is evidenced through the identification of an *in situ* hearth and a lithic scatter close to the east wall of the antechamber. The local presence of people was also inferred in Layer 5, through the identification of high concentrations of burnt plant remains. This was succeeded by cave occupation and burial following the introduction of pottery and other material culture associated with the arrival of Austronesian-speaking peoples in northern Luzon dating to about 3693–3527 cal. BP at Callao. Each phase of human activity was preceded and succeeded by long hiatuses in human activity that suggest only intermittent and sporadic visitations to Callao Cave across many millennia.

Acknowledgements

I am grateful for the support of the National Museum of the Philippines, the Cagayan Provincial Government, and the Peñablanca Protected Area Management Board. Funding for this research came from an Australian Research Council Discovery Grant to Peter Bellwood and a University of the Philippines Research Grant to Armand Mijares. Funding for processing of the thin sections was partially provided by a New Initiative Grant from the Centre for Archaeological Research at The Australian National University.

References

Adams, A.E. and W.S. Mackenzie. 2001. *A Colour Atlas of Carbonate Sediments and Rocks Under the Microscope*. Manson London: Publishing.

Adams, A.E., W.S. Mackenzie and C. Guilford. 1984. *Atlas of Sedimentary Rocks under the Microscope*. Harlow: Prentice Hall.

Anderson, D. 1997. Cave archaeology in Southeast Asia. *Geoarchaeology* 12: 607–638. doi.org/10.1002/(SICI)1520-6548(199709)12:6<607::AID-GEA5>3.0.CO;2-2.

Aoyagi, Y., M. Aguilera, H. Ogawa and K. Tanaka. 1993. Excavation of Hill Top Site, Magapit Shell Midden in Lal-lo Shell Middens, Northern Luzon, Philippines. *Man and Culture in Oceania* 9: 127–155.

Bronk Ramsey, C., M. Dee, S. Lee, T. Nakagawa and R. Staff. 2010. Developments in the calibration and modelling of radiocarbon dates *Radiocarbon* 52(3): 953–961. doi.org/10.1017/S0033822200046063.

Bullock, P., N. Fedoroff, A. Jongerius, G. Stoops and T. Tursina. 1985. *Handbook for Soil Thin Section Description*. England: Waine Research Publication.

Courty, M.A., P. Goldberg and R. Macphail. 1989. *Soils and Micromorphology in Archaeology*. Cambridge: Cambridge University Press.

Cuevas, M. 1980. Preliminary Report on the Archaeological Excavation conducted at Callao Caves. Manila: Manuscript of the National Museum.

———. 1982. Progress Report on the Archaeological Activities conducted at Callao Caves (November 1980–August 1982). Manila: Manuscript of the National Museum.

Fitzpatrick, E.A. 1984. *Micromorphology of Soils*. London: Chapman and Hall Ltd. doi.org/10.1007/978-94-009-5544-8.

Heaney, L., P. Piper and A.S.B. Mijares. 2011. The first fossil record of endemic murid rodents from the Philippines: a late Pleistocene cave fauna from northern Luzon, Philippines. *Proceedings of the Biological Society of Washington* 124(3): 234–247. doi.org/10.2988/10-32.1.

Lewis, H. 2003. The potential of soil micromorphology in Southeast Asian archaeology: Preliminary work at Niah Cave Sarawak, Malaysia, and Ille Cave, Palawan, Philippines. *Hukay* 5: 60–72.

———. 2004. The soil micromorphological potential of cultural sediments from cave sites in Island Southeast Asia: progress report on work at Niah, Ille and Tabon Caves. Unpublished report for the Evans Fund, the Society of Southeast Asian Studies, and the Niah Cave Project (AHRB).

———. 2007. Preliminary soil micromorphology studies of landscape and occupation history at Tabon Cave, Palawan, Philippines. *Geoarchaeology* 22: 685–708. doi.org/10.1002/gea.20182.

Mackenzie, W.S. and A.E. Adams. 1994. *A Colour Atlas of Rocks and Minerals in Thin Section*. London: Manson Publishing.

Magee, J. 1988. Oriented soil samples from Tingkayu Basin. In P. Bellwood (ed.), *Archaeological Research in South-eastern Sabah*. pp. 31–37. Sabah: Sabah Museum Monograph 2.

Mijares, A. 2001. An expedient lithic technology in Northern Luzon Philippines. *Lithic Technology* 26(2): 138–152. doi.org/10.1080/01977261.2001.11720983.

———. 2005a. The archaeological excavation of Eme, Callao and Dalan Serkot Caves, Northern Luzon, Philippines. *Journal of Austronesian Studies* 1: 65–93.

———. 2005b. The Nagsabaran Shell Midden Site: A soil micromorphology approach. *Hukay* 8: 1–12.

———. 2007. *Unearthing Prehistory: The Archaeology of Northeastern Luzon, Philippine Islands*. BAR International Series 1613. Oxford: John and Erica Hedges Ltd.

Mijares, A. and H. Lewis. 2009. Cave sites in Northeastern Luzon, Philippines: A preliminary soil micromorphology study. *Asian Perspectives* 48: 98–118. doi.org/10.1353/asi.0.0010.

Mijares, A., F. Détroit, P. Piper, R. Grün, P. Bellwood, M. Aubert, G. Champion, N. Cuevas, A. De Leon and E. Dizon. 2010. New evidence for a 67,000-year-old human presence at Callao Cave, Luzon, Philippines. *Journal of Human Evolution* 59: 123–132. doi.org/10.1016/j.jhevol.2010.04.008.

Morwood, M. and P. van Osterzee. 2007. *The Discovery of the Hobbit*. Sydney: Random House Australia.

Piper, P. and A. Mijares. 2007. *A Preliminary Report on a Late Pleistocene Animal Bone Assemblage from Callao Cave, Penablanca, Northern Luzon, Philippines*. Archaeological Studies Program, Quezon City: University of the Philippines.

Stephens, M., J. Rose, D. Gilbertson and M. Canti. 2005. Micromorphology of cave sediments in the humid tropics: Niah Cave Sarawak. *Asian Perspectives* 44: 42–55. doi.org/10.1353/asi.2005.0014.

Stoops, G. 2003. Guidelines for the Analysis and Description of Soil and Regolith Thin Section. Wisconsin: Soil Science Society of America, Inc.

Zauyah, S. 1994. Characteristic of Soil Layers in Gua Gunung Runtuh. In M. Zuraina (ed.), *The Excavation of Gua Gunung Runtuh and the Discovery of the Perak Main in Malaysia*, pp. 123–140. Kuala Lampur: Department of Museums and Antiquity Malaysia.

8

Traditions of Jars as Mortuary Containers in the Indo-Malaysian Archipelago

David Bulbeck

Earthenware and imported ceramic jars were from time to time used as mortuary containers across a large swathe of the Indo-Malaysian Archipelago. As noted by Peter Bellwood, this deployment of earthenwares has Neolithic origins, and burgeoned during approximately the first millennium AD. The assemblages were frequently dominated by disposals in mortuary jars but these were one of a variety of mortuary practices at other sites. Defining a jar-burial tradition as a potentially independent development of the use of jars as mortuary containers, we may provisionally identify 14 geographically discrete jar-burial traditions within the archipelago.

Introduction

In his textbook on the prehistory of the Indo-Malaysian Archipelago, Peter Bellwood (1997) dealt at length with the use of jars as mortuary containers, which he assigned to a tradition best regarded 'as an indigenous development in Island Southeast Asia' (p. 306). He traced the tradition's origins to late Neolithic contexts, noting, however, that many more sites date to the Palaeometallic or Early Metal Phase. He also stated that the recorded sites appeared to be particularly a feature of the triangular area in between the Philippines, Borneo and Sumba (p. 296). Implicitly, Bellwood referred to the use of jars not as grave goods but as mortuary containers, even if this specific use of the recovered pottery is inferred rather than directly observed at certain sites, such as Leang Buidane (see below). The examples he discussed also exclude sites with jars buried for rituals that were probably non-mortuary, considering the lack of associated human remains in conditions that should be conducive to preservation of bone – for instance, the Palaeometallic jars buried at Makabog in the Philippines (Henson 1992), Leang Balangingi in the Talaud Islands (Bellwood 1976) and Batu Ejaya in southwest Sulawesi (Bulbeck 1996–1997).

In this review of the sites covered by Bellwood (1997) as well as more recently documented sites, I shall summarise the evidence in broad support of Bellwood's chronology. However, the area with a concentrated use of jars as mortuary containers can now be revised as the trapezoidal belt of islands from the Philippines in the north to southern Sumatra in the southwest and Sumba and the Moluccas in the southeast (Figure 8.1). In addition, I shall propose that the mourners' choice of jars rather than some other container, or indeed the disposal of container-free mortuary remains, cannot be related in any simple way to socioeconomic factors or reconstructible belief systems.

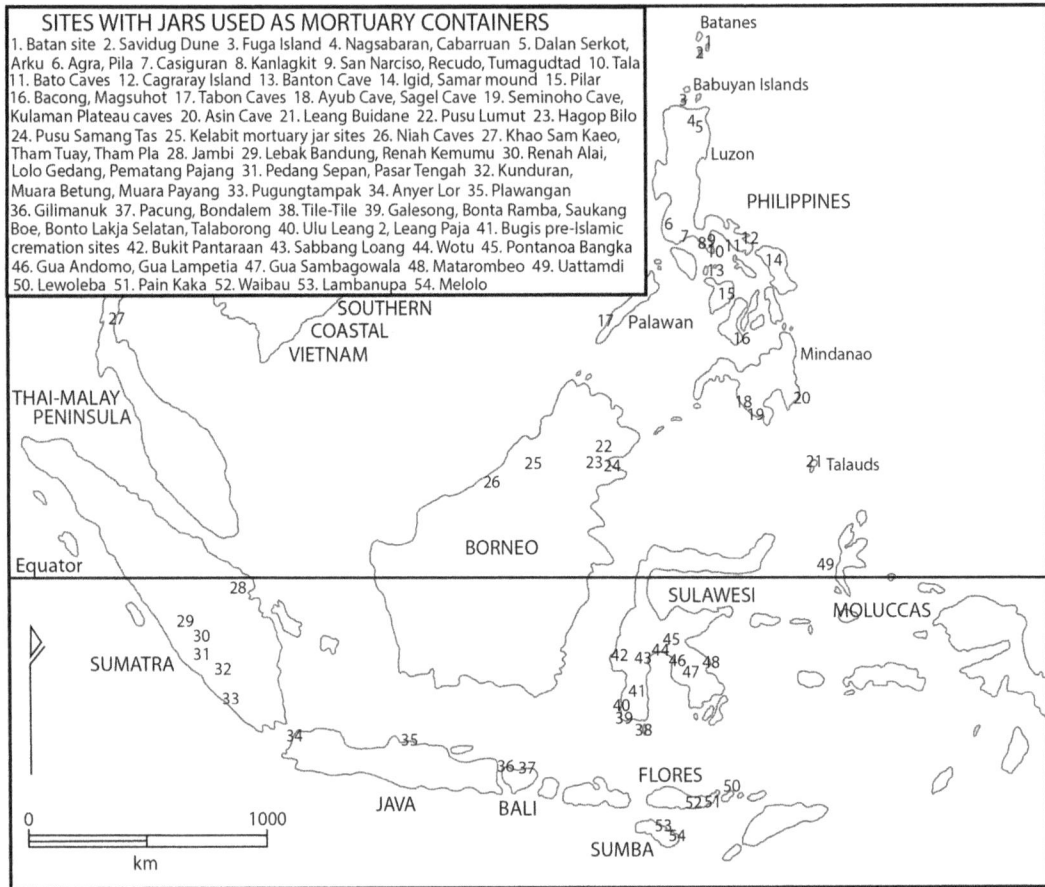

SITES WITH JARS USED AS MORTUARY CONTAINERS
1. Batan site 2. Savidug Dune 3. Fuga Island 4. Nagsabaran, Cabarruan 5. Dalan Serkot, Arku 6. Agra, Pila 7. Casiguran 8. Kanlagkit 9. San Narciso, Recudo, Tumagudtad 10. Tala 11. Bato Caves 12. Cagraray Island 13. Banton Cave 14. Igid, Samar mound 15. Pilar 16. Bacong, Magsuhot 17. Tabon Caves 18. Ayub Cave, Sagel Cave 19. Seminoho Cave, Kulaman Plateau caves 20. Asin Cave 21. Leang Buidane 22. Pusu Lumut 23. Hagop Bilo 24. Pusu Samang Tas 25. Kelabit mortuary jar sites 26. Niah Caves 27. Khao Sam Kaeo, Tham Tuay, Tham Pla 28. Jambi 29. Lebak Bandung, Renah Kemumu 30. Renah Alai, Lolo Gedang, Pematang Pajang 31. Pedang Sepan, Pasar Tengah 32. Kunduran, Muara Betung, Muara Payang 33. Pugungtampak 34. Anyer Lor 35. Plawangan 36. Gilimanuk 37. Pacung, Bondalem 38. Tile-Tile 39. Galesong, Bonta Ramba, Saukang Boe, Bonto Lakja Selatan, Talaborong 40. Ulu Leang 2, Leang Paja 41. Bugis pre-Islamic cremation sites 42. Bukit Pantaraan 43. Sabbang Loang 44. Wotu 45. Pontanoa Bangka 46. Gua Andomo, Gua Lampetia 47. Gua Sambagowala 48. Matarombeo 49. Uattamdi 50. Lewoleba 51. Pain Kaka 52. Waibau 53. Lambanupa 54. Melolo

Figure 8.1 Sites in the Indo-Malaysian Archipelago with jars used as mortuary containers.

Source: Compiled and drawn by D. Bulbeck.

On the question of whether jar burials in the Indo-Malaysian Archipelago should be assigned to a single (Bellwood 1997) or multiple traditions (Lloyd-Smith and Cole 2010), we should first define the term 'tradition'. According to Fagan (1994: 420), the term implies cultural continuity of the subject of the tradition (such as an artefact type) over lengthy periods of time by cultures that may vary in other ways. Valentin et al. (2015) interpret the concept of a single Indo-Malaysian jar-burial tradition to mean a single shared belief system on issues related to handling the deceased. However, in terms of Fagan's definition, all that would be required is continuity of jar burials as a practice tracing back to its original source. This source would be Neolithic Taiwan, where jar burials date back to at least 1000 cal. BC; and its transmission to Indo-Malaysia would have been undertaken by the southward expansion of early Austronesian (Malayo-Polynesian) speakers, according to Valentin et al. (2015) as well as Bellwood (as reported by Cuevas and de Leon 2008: 19). Thus, despite their explicit support for multiple traditions in Indo-Malaysia, and a separate but related tradition at Teouma in Vanuatu, Valentin et al. (2015) actually endorse a single tradition. This may also be the same tradition that resulted in jar burials postdating Teouma (and mostly dating to the second millennium AD) in various other Pacific Islands where Austronesian languages were spoken ethnographically or the inhabitants were in contact with Austronesian speakers (Bedford and Spriggs 2007).

Instead, the touchstone for recognising multiple traditions would be to show that one or more independent developments of the practice of jar burials is a more reasonable scenario than continuity of the original practice. In addition, if multiple independent developments of jar burials appears likely, then geographical proximity of sites with a similar range of jar-burial practices would provide the empirical grounds to be confident in assigning these sites to a single tradition. On that basis, as detailed below, 14 traditions could be posited to cover the diversity documented across the archipelago.

The concept of 'horizon', which may be used to 'link a number of phases in neighboring areas that have rather general cultural patterns in common' (Fagan 1994: 420), is also useful for reviewing the archaeological evidence. A horizon could mark the appearance of a new jar-burial tradition(s) or it could signify the shared transformation of previously established jar-burial traditions.

The broad chronological scheme for Indo-Malaysian prehistory outlined by Bellwood (1997) is employed here, with the Neolithic (defined by the appearance of pottery and polished stone tools) dating to between *ca.* 2000 and 200 cal. BC, and the Palaeometallic to approximately the first millennium AD. The latter largely corresponds to the early appearance of metals and exotic items of glass and semi-precious stone, but the date of their earliest appearance varied across the archipelago. Accordingly, their absence from an assemblage is no guarantee that the assemblage predates 200 BC, particularly if it is not large.

Neolithic foundations

Niah Caves

The oldest intact jar burials in the archipelago were excavated in the Neolithic cemeteries at the Niah Caves, predominantly the West Mouth but also several from the smaller Lobang Jeragan cemetery (Table 8.1). The term 'Neolithic' is qualified by the occurrence of three small bronze items amongst the sparse assemblage of grave goods, two inside jar burials and the third found with an extended burial. Dating all three bronzes to earlier than 500 cal. BC – making them the archipelago's oldest dated bronzes – is conservative in view of the 1500–1414 cal. BC and 812–559 cal. BC determinations on the two dated burials with bronze (Lloyd-Smith et al. 2013). Moreover, the appearance of bronze – undocumented for Taiwan sites of this antiquity (Valentin et al. 2015) – raises a legitimate question of whether the source for the Niah jar burials should be traced to Mainland Southeast Asia, where sites such as Ban Non Wat, Ban Lum Khao and Nong Nor included jar burials by the second millennium BC and bronze by the end of the millennium (Bulbeck 2011; Higham 2011).

All of the Niah burial jars were at least partially interred, with full burial noted for three of the 12 West Mouth examples (Lloyd-Smith and Cole 2010). The Niah Caves jar burials are notable for their sparse occurrence (some 5–10 per cent of burials) over a long period of time between *ca.* 1150 and 300 cal. BC (Lloyd-Smith et al. 2013). They are remarkable for their diversity in terms of the nature of the jars used as containers, the treatment of the bone (variably cremated and/or haematite-stained), the interred individuals' demographics and whether single or multiple burials were interred (Table 8.1). Their sparseness and diversity suggest a recurrent practice 'reinstantiated' to meet particular ritual needs, with the use of the jars – rather than one of the other Niah burial modes (Table 8.2) – as a marker of attained wealth and social status (Lloyd-Smith and Cole 2010). Significantly, another Niah cemetery, Gan Kira, had no jar burials for either its Neolithic or its Palaeometallic stage (Szabó et al. 2013).

Table 8.1 Published jar burials from the Niah Caves.

Burial number	Nature/size of jar	Number of individuals	Status of bone	Grave goods	Date
West Mouth B159	Large (69.5 cm high, 67 cm diameter)	5 (2 women, 3 children)	Cleaned and redeposited	Small jar, wooden stick	1226±105 BC, 1731–1132 cal. BC (GX-1428); 940±29 BC, 1195–977 cal. BC (OxA-20995)
West Mouth B69	Medium (30 cm diameter)	2 (1 man, 1 child)	Unburnt	None	ca. 1050–750 cal. BC
West Mouth B18	Large (41 cm diameter)	2 adults	Cremated & unburnt	Bronze hook/clasp	628±33 BC, 812–564 cal. BC (OxA-22058)
West Mouth B96/85a	Small (16.5 cm high, 26 cm diameter)	2 (1 woman, 1 child)	Cremated & unburnt, haematite-stained	None	626±25 BC, 809–596 cal. BC (OxA-18560)
West Mouth B198	Medium (28 cm high and diameter), in ramie basket	3 (including 1 man)	Cremated, haematite-stained	None	549±27 BC, 775–521 cal. BC (OxA-18360)
West Mouth B63	Fragments from 2 large jars	1 adult	Haematite-stained	Bronze knife	ca. 750–550 cal. BC
West Mouth B85	Small (25 cm diameter)	1 adult	Cremated, haematite-stained	None	ca. 750–550 cal. BC
West Mouth B100	Container a bowl, cover a jar fragment	3 (1 adult, 2 children)	Cremated & unburnt	None	ca. 450–250 cal. BC
West Mouth B221	Deliberately collapsed	Mixed unburnt and cremated	Secondary	None	ca. 450–250 cal. BC
West Mouth B190	Large (like B159 jar)	5 (including 1 woman)	Unburnt	Shell fish hook	359±35 BC, 477–209 cal. BC (OxA-11548)
West Mouth B154	Small (13.5 cm high, 19.5 cm diameter)	1 infant	Haematite-stained, cremated?	2 shell earrings	ca. 450–250 cal. BC
West Mouth B233	Medium (37.5 cm high, 36 cm diameter)	1	Cremated, haematite-stained	None	Neolithic
Lobang Jeragan	Various	Various?	Cremated & unburnt, some haematite-stained	Marine conch ring in 1 jar	ca. 950–550 cal BC

Sources: Harrisson 1958, 1967; Lloyd-Smith and Cole 2010; Lloyd-Smith et al. 2013. Calibrations (95.4 per cent confidence interval) undertaken by the author using Oxcal 4.2 (Bronk Ramsey 2014).

Table 8.2 Indo-Malaysian sites and complexes with both mortuary disposals in jars and other mortuary disposal modes.

Site/complex	Proportion placed in jars	Other recorded mortuary disposal modes
Niah Caves, Sarawak (Lloyd-Smith and Cole 2010; Lloyd-Smith et al. 2013)	Between 5 and 10% of burials	Highly diverse; predominantly extended burials, some in wooden coffins or bamboo caskets, and secondary burials interred directly into the deposit
Tabon Jar Burial Complex, Palawan (Fox 1970)	Majority	Direct inhumations, a surface disposal wrapped in a mat, and skull disposals unassociated with jars
Arku Cave, Luzon (Thiel 1986–1987)	6–7/57 individuals	Secondary inhumations, some burnt, some others haematite-stained
Batan Island jar-burial site (Solheim 1960)	Unclear	3 primary flexed burials
Kanlakgit, southern Luzon (Paz et al. 2013)	Unclear	Extended inhumations
Tumagudtad, southern Luzon (Solheim 1960)	13/16 burials	2 extended and 1 secondary burial
Igid, Samar (Solheim 1960; Henson 1992)	Jar burials holding children	Supine extended adult burials, some with iron weapons and glass beads
Bacong, Negros (Henson 1992)	2/5 burials	2 multiple interments, 1 primary burial
Leang Buidane, Talaud Islands (Bellwood 1976)	5/36 individuals	5 skulls beneath the jar-burial layer
Melolo, Sumba (Bintarti 2000)	Great majority	Poorly preserved burials outside of the jars
Lambanupa, Sumba (Bintarti 2000)	Majority	3 human skeletons lacking jars
Pain Haka, Flores (Valentin et al. 2015)	Not all	Primary interments
Lewoleba, Lembata Island (Bintarti 2000)	Minority	Direct burials
Pacung, Bali (Calo et al. 2015)	2/19 burials	Primary inhumations with flexed legs
Bondalem, Bali (Ardika 2000)	1/8 burials	Primary inhumations, 5 extended and 1 flexed
Gilimanuk, Bali (Aziz 2012)	8/216 individuals	60 primary inhumations in various positions and 148 secondary inhumations, plus 2 empty stone sarcophagi
Anyer Lor, Java (Van Heekeren 1956)	Small minority	Primary flexed and extended prostrate inhumations
Plawangan, Java (Soegondho 1995)	Less than half	Primary and secondary inhumations
Cagraray Island, Luzon (Fox and Evangelista 1957b)	Memanoso Cave (ca. AD 1500), both jar and non-jar burials	Pre-sixteenth-century disposals included wooden coffins and skulls either directly buried or placed inside rock-face cavities
Lake Towuti caves, Sulawesi (Grubauer 1913)	Elite adults only	Secondary storage of commoner adults in wooden coffins; secondary disposal of subadults directly on cave floor
Borneo ethnohistorical (Winzeler 2004)	Proportion undocumented	Boat-shaped wooden coffins could be used instead of ceramic jars

The Philippines

Several Philippine sites have yielded Neolithic jar burials although a larger number date to the Palaeometallic. Their coverage presented here should be considered in the context of the Neolithic and Palaeometallic Philippine burials that did not involve mortuary jars, including Callao Cave (Mijares 2005) and some of the Lal-lo shell middens (Ogawa 2004) in Luzon, and Sa'gung (Kress 2004), Ille Cave (Szabó et al. 2004) and Leta Leta (Szabó and Ramirez 2009) in Palawan. The Neolithic grave goods, in particular, show strong parallels with Taiwan Neolithic material culture (Valentin et al. 2015).

Table 8.3 Dates for Philippine mortuary jar sites.

Site	Summary description of mortuary jars	Dating
Dalan Serkot (Mijares 2005)	Thick jar sherds associated with fragmentary human remains	1581±34 BC (Wk-15648), 1947–1753 cal. BC
Manunggul A, near Tabon (Fox 1970)	Frequently decorated, medium-sized jars containing secondary disposals; grave goods (including pots and nephrite, agate and shell jewellery) placed inside or near the jars	891±80 BC (UCLA-992A), 1222–827 cal. BC 711±80 BC (UCLA-992B), 1014–544 cal. BC
Manunggul B (Fox 1970)	Plain medium-sized jars containing secondary disposals; grave goods now including iron, carnelian and glass jewellery	191±100 BC (UCLA-992C), 396 cal. BC–cal. AD 49
Arku Cave, Luzon (Thiel 1986–1987)	4 small to medium-sized jars containing secondary disposals, some burnt, some others haematite-stained; grave goods within jars include a small jar and ochre	471±80 BC (ISGS-495), 780–405 cal. BC
Bato Cave 1, Luzon (Fox and Evangelista 1957a)	Large to medium-sized jars containing secondary disposals; grave goods of shell and indurated shale, 1 polished stone axe	331±250 BC (M-727A) on marine shell (Crane and Griffin 1959), 694 cal. BC–cal. AD 546
Nagsabaran, Luzon (Piper et al. 2009)	Medium-sized jars containing crania, perhaps removed from flexed inhumations; associated with glass and iron	150 cal. BC–cal. AD 450 (multiple dates) for the midden deposit containing the burials
Ayub Cave, Mindanao (Bacus 2004)	100–200 large jars (some anthropomorphic, some others also decorated) with secondary disposals and grave goods such as decorated small jars, and ornaments of earthenware, shell and glass	AD 30±50 (Beta-83316), 38 cal. BC–cal. AD 217 AD 120±160 (Beta-83315), cal. AD 55–339 (Ronquillo 2003)
Savidug Dune, Batanes (Bellwood and Dizon 2013a)	Large jars probably containing flexed primary burials	AD 195±25 (ANU 33938), cal. AD 222–378
Seminoho Cave, Mindanao (Cuevas and de Leon 2008)	Large jars (some anthropomorphic, some others also decorated) holding secondary disposals and grave goods such as small jars, carnelian beads, and ornaments of earthenware, shell, brass and iron	AD 585±85 on human bone, cal. AD 436–882
Banton Cave, Visayas (Barnes and Kahlenburg 2010)	Medium-sized jar containing human remains wrapped in Indian textile	Thirteenth-century AD on human bone
Pilar, Panay (Anon. 2009)	24 jar burials containing clay, glass beads and iron spearhead	AD 1460±180 (Coutts 1983), cal. AD 1161–1950

Source: Calibrations (95.4 per cent confidence interval) undertaken by the author using Oxcal 4.2 (Bronk Ramsey 2014).

The antiquity of jar burials in the Philippines may reach back to the beginnings of the Neolithic, if Mijares (2005) is correct in his interpretation of Dalan Serkot as a cave for the secondary burial of the deceased in mortuary jars, dated to the early second millennium BC (Table 8.3). Arku Cave, near Dalan Serkot, produced a rich, late Neolithic mortuary assemblage dated to approximately 1300–1 cal. BC (Spriggs 1989), with grave goods that included jewellery of shell, fired clay, nephrite and other stone, as well as polished stone adzes, bone points, tattooing chisels of horn and clay spindle whorls (Thiel 1986–1987). About one-ninth of the represented individuals can be clearly identified as jar burials, distinguished from the other burials by the modest quality of the grave goods (Tables 8.2 and 8.3). Jar burials at Arku Cave, then, would appear to have been reserved for a residue of individuals of low socioeconomic status, unless the act of burial within a jar signified an elevated status in itself.

Fox (1970; Winters 1974) nominated the term 'Tabon Jar Burial Complex' for the 29 Palawan sites with mortuary ceramics near Tabon Cave. The jars had been placed on or within the cave surfaces, which rules out dating the jars with samples from cave deposits except where the cave had no other documented utilisation. There are three such dates, on charcoal, which together indicate pre-metallic mortuary disposals in Manunggul Chamber A during the first half of the first millennium BC, and Palaeometallic mortuary disposals in Manunggul Chamber B during the last centuries BC (Table 8.3). Winters identified a minimum of 14–19 individuals from the human remains in the 20–30 burial jars at Duyong Cave, and 16 individuals from the Uyaw Cave human remains. His analysis confirms Fox's inference that the Tabon complex mortuary jars generally contained single individuals, including infants and one apparent primary child burial. Fox also noted that the human remains were sometimes painted with haematite, and that the jars sometimes contained just the skull or, in one case, the teeth of multiple individuals. The majority but not all of mortuary disposals were placed inside jars (Table 8.2).

Palaeometallic mortuary-jar container sites (*ca.* 200 BC to AD 1200)

Most Palaeometallic jar-burial sites have been assigned to this period based on the nature of their grave goods, but in some cases the assignment relies on radiometric dating. For instance, on Sabtang Island at the far north of the Philippines, Bellwood and Dizon (2013a) uncovered a cluster of 14 large jars dating to the early centuries AD, but lacking any grave goods (Table 8.3). A similar antiquity may apply to the large jar burials excavated on nearby Batan Island, although the fact these jars were looted might suggest the original presence of grave goods (Solheim 1960). Also, the Bato Caves in Luzon produced 18 jar burials associated with Neolithic grave goods and no trace of metals (Fox and Evangelista 1957a), despite their dating to around the time of Christ based on the only associated radiocarbon date (Table 8.3).

Of possibly similar age is the 'Neolithic' pottery with 'Kalanay'-style painted and incised decorations at Asin Cave, southeastern Mindanao, suspected to date before Christ. Solheim et al. (1979) estimated the burial of about 20 large jars holding the skull and other human bones, probably secondarily disposed, in association with 80 bowls and small jars, and a stone jar cover. Similar stone covers are reported for the jar burials from Kanlagkit, San Narciso, Recudo and Tumagudtad, Luzon (Paz et al. 2013) and the burial jars containing juveniles at the open site of Igid, Samar (Henson 1992). The Igid extended burials and the Recudo and Tumagudtad jar burials were associated with iron implements and other Palaeometallic grave goods.

Other Philippine jar-burial sites with glass and/or metal grave goods include most of the secondary jar-burial sites on Cagraray Island in southern Luzon (Fox and Evangelista 1957b), the Casiguran and other northwest Sorsogan jar burials from southern Luzon, the 60 jar burials from a mound on Samar, and the Bacong jar burials on Negros (Henson 1992). At Magsuhot, near Bacong, two large burial jars containing glass and iron grave goods were excavated, one also holding the remains of an adult female and two subadults, along with three empty burial jars (Bacus 2004). The Nagsabaran jar burials in northern Luzon, dated to around 2,000 years ago, are of particular interest, in that they appear to have held the crania removed from the flexed inhumations in the same level (Piper et al. 2009). A similar practice of decapitating the corpse, with the skull sometimes stored inside a jar, appears to have been adopted at the Neolithic cemetery at Teouma in Vanuatu (Valentin et al. 2015).

Also of considerable interest are the large, anthropomorphic burial jars in southern Mindanao, dated to the first millennium AD at Ayub Cave and at Seminoho Cave (Table 8.3), one of the numerous such sites (more than 1,000 recorded mortuary jars) on the Kulaman Plateau. However, not all southern Mindanao jar-burial sites with Palaeometallic burial goods include anthropomorphic jars, as indicated by their absence from Sagel Cave, which lies near Ayub Cave (Cuevas and de Leon 2008).

To the south of Mindanao lie the Talaud Islands, where the Leang Buidane rockshelter yielded mortuary pottery and scattered human remains whose chronology is suspected to span much of the first millennium AD. Interpretation of the excavated materials as a jar-burial assemblage is strengthened by the match between the minimum numbers of 36 interred individuals and 32 large jars. The rich assemblage of mortuary goods includes beads and bracelets of shell, semi-precious stone and glass, as well as bronze and iron, and three baked-clay casting moulds, one with a thermoluminescence date of AD 1000±130 (Bellwood 1976, 1997).

Three jar-burial assemblages of similar nature, age, pottery decorations and associated grave goods have also been excavated in southeastern Sabah, Borneo (Bellwood 1988a, 1988b, 1988c). Hagop Bilo yielded fragmentary human remains associated with iron fragments (including one from a bushknife) and decorated pottery with affinities to the Leang Buidane and Manunggul A pottery, to a depth of 15 cm. Its estimated antiquity is AD 450–850. Pusu Lumut contained a 30 cm thick layer with pottery similar to the Hagop Bilo mortuary pottery and was associated with human fragments and a variety of grave goods, including small stone adzes, pottery-making burnishing stones or anvils, a socketed copper/bronze axe, an axe-casting valve, an iron spearhead and two stone or glass beads. The assemblage has a quite wide estimated age range (AD 450–1450). Pusu Samang Tas also contained a 30 cm thick sedimentary layer with fragmentary human remains associated with grave goods (five glass beads and two iron knives). Bellwood (1988c) estimates its age as AD 950–1450 based on the similarity of its mortuary pottery to Pusu Lumut and also to Pilar in the Visayas. Both Pusu Lumut and Pusu Samang Tas would overlap in age with the log coffin from the nearby site of Agop Atas, radiocarbon-dated to around AD 1000 (Bellwood 1988b).

Another similar site, according to Bellwood et al. (1998), is the Uattamdi rockshelter (Kayoa Island, North Moluccas) with jar burials associated with glass beads, iron and bronze fragments, dated to the first millennium AD. However, Uattamdi differs from the Sabah sites in that the only skeletal remains associated with its two massive jars are two human crania. Indeed, Uattamdi evidently combines a previously established tradition of secondary skull burials, recorded at the nearby site of Tanjung Pinang, with the locally derived 'invention' of using the jars as mortuary containers rather than grave furniture (Bulbeck submitted).

Five sites with jar burials, at least four also containing direct interments (Table 8.2), are recorded for Nusatenggara. Melolo is an extensive urn field with hundreds of large globular jars covered by a smaller upside-down pot, most containing just a single skull, but others containing skulls of multiple individuals and/or a few limb bones. The site is renowned for its burnished *kendi* flasks with incised human faces, interred as grave goods along with a range of shell ornaments, stone axes and beads, spindle whorls, glass items and bronze fragments (Van Heekeren 1972; Bintarti 2000). Bellwood (1997) interprets *kendi* flasks as a widely distributed Palaeometallic chronological marker, also recorded at Leang Buidane, Hagop Bilo, as well as Gunung Piring on Lombok and Liang Bua on Flores (where jar burials have not been documented), and Anyer Lor in Java (see below).

Table 8.4 Open jar-burial sites from southern Sumatra.

Site/s	Description	Dating evidence
Jambi city (Bintarti 2000)	3 urns, 30.5 cm high and 24.5 cm mouth diameter	85 beads including 8 Indo-Pacific orange glass beads
Lebak Bandung, Jambi (Bonatz et al. 2006)	Large jars	Grave goods include glass beads and iron knives
Renah Kemumu, Kerinci highlands (Bonatz et al. 2006; Tjoa-Bonatz 2012)	35 jars 0.6–1.2 m diameter, human remains dissolved in acidic soil, small pots as grave goods	AD 813±128 (OSL), burial jar AD 1039±124 (OSL), burial jar AD 1560±51 (OSL), small pot grave good AD 1140±120 (cal. AD 994–1396)
Pematang Pajang, Renah Alai, unnamed site—Kerinci highlands (Tjoa-Bonatz 2012)	At least 6 jars at Renah Alai	Information not found
Lolo Gedang, Kerinci highlands (Bonatz 2012; Tjoa-Bonatz 2012)	Large jars containing broken bones, iron and bronzes including miniature drums	AD 690±90 (TL, CUDaM Lab. code D2248) AD 890±120 (cal. AD 692–1211) AD 1140±120 (cal. AD 954–1396)
Pedang Sepan, Pasar Tengah—Bengkulu (Bonatz et al. 2006)	Information not found	Information not found
Kunduran, Muara Betung, Muara Payang—Lintang, South Sumatra, 200–1,000 m asl (Soeroso 1997; Guillaud et al. 2006)	Large jars taking primary or secondary burials	Grave goods include a *kendi* flask at Kunduran, metal fragments at Muara Betung, and polished adzes of jasper and chalcedony
Pugungtampak, Lampung (Bintarti 2000)	No information	No information

Source: Calibration of radiocarbon dates (95.4 per cent confidence interval) undertaken by the author using Oxcal 4.2 (Bronk Ramsey 2014).

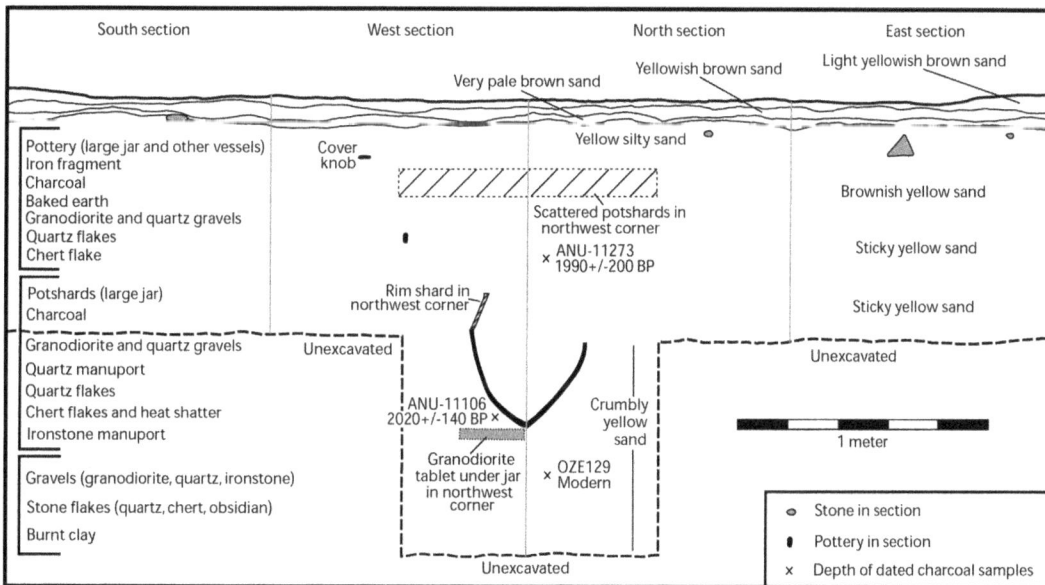

Figure 8.2 Stratigraphic section and contents of Sabbang Loang 1999 test burial jar in northwest corner.

Source: Drawn by D. Bulbeck based on excavation reports and author's laboratory studies; presented in Do 2013: Figure 20.

Figure 8.3 Large earthenware burial jar at Gua Lampetia sketched by Ambra Calo after its exposure in test pit.

Source: Photograph Jack Fenner, published here with his kind permission.

Lambanupa, also on Sumba, contained burial jars 30–70 cm in height and 20–30 cm in diameter, covered by an upside-down pot (as at Melolo). The interred remains included complete skeletons as well as skulls accompanied by postcranial bones, and the burial goods included pottery flasks, shells, beads and stone adzes (Bintarti 2000). Pain Haka, in Flores, is a similar site, with six jar burials including two that only contain adult skulls and others with primary infant burials and multiple burials, and rare grave goods including shell beads and a small pottery flask (Valentin et al. 2015). Lewoleba and Waibau, to the northeast, may be similar sites, with fragmentary human remains inside jars and, in the case of Lewoleba, burial goods that included shell artefacts and pottery (Bintarti 2000). Southwest Sulawesi, lying to the northwest of Nusatenggara, had highly variable mortuary practices during the Palaeometallic. These include the burial of numerous teeth with barely any associated pottery at the Leang Codong rockshelter and the direct interment of burnt and unburnt human fragments in the Leang-Leang caves of Maros (Bulbeck 1996–1997). Leang-Leang also has two jar-burial sites, Ulu Leang 2 and Leang Paja, that are similar to Leang Buidane. The surface collection at Ulu Leang 2 included numerous earthenware sherds interpreted as the remnants of large mortuary containers, associated with glass beads and iron fragments, and the unburnt remains of at least 50 individuals. The Leang Paja surface collection yielded medium-sized to large jars, along with ornate covers and bowls, and numerous unburnt human fragments (Flavel 1997, 2006). Open-air burial sites to the south of Leang-Leang include Takbuncinik with its suspected primary burials in large jars, Bonto Ramba with its reported association of a Heger IA bronze kettle drum alongside cremations in burial jars, and Papanlohea where a Heger IA kettle drum appears to have been used as a burial container (Table 8.4).

Further north in Sulawesi, three burial jars were excavated at Bukit Pantaraan on the Karama River, associated with ornaments of iron, bronze, gold, glass and polished stone (no preserved human remains). The charred residues from some apparently associated potsherds date to the early to middle first millennium BC, so either the association is spurious or the date is too old (Anggraeni 2012). The three earthenware jars recovered from Pontanoa Bangka, on the northern shore of Lake Matano, stratified above a charcoal sample dating to cal. AD 900–1190, probably contained cremated human remains in association with twelfth- to fourteenth-century glass beads (Bulbeck and Caldwell 2000). In addition, a field of 11 large jars was excavated in 1938 at Sabbang Loang, where a river critical for trade with the hinterland meets the coastal plain. Re-excavations in 1998–1999 recovered an additional jar from this field of around 1 m high and wide (Figure 8.2) and isolated examples of similar jars across a 2 hectare area uphill from the urn field. The acidic soils explain the lack of human remains in the jars, which evidently lacked grave goods, but they can be dated to the early centuries AD based on a consistent series of five charcoal dates from the associated, Palaeometallic habitation deposits (Bulbeck and Caldwell 2000).

Table 8.5 Open jar-burial sites from Selayar and South Sulawesi's southwest coastal plain.

Site	Summary description of mortuary jars	Dating evidence
Takbuncinik, Galesong (Bulbeck 1996–1997, 2010)	10 egg-shaped jars, 29–86 cm high and 27–58 cm girth, containing flexed primary burials of children and adults	Palaeometallic beads of copper and semi-precious stone in separate jar
Manjalling, Galesong (Bulbeck 1996–1997)	2 potsherd clusters interpreted as earthenware burial jar bases	6 stone beads (Palaeometallic?)
Bonto Ramba (Bulbeck 1996–1997)	Low-fired sherds from reported cluster of burial jars containing burnt bone	Reported Heger IA kettle drum containing necklace beads and gold jewellery
Galoggoro, near Bonto Ramba (Bulbeck 1996–1997)	4 reported earthenware burial jars containing fragmented human bone	Reported iron spearhead
Tile-Tile, Selayar (Bulbeck 1996–1997)	3 earthenware urns, 1 containing broken human bone and grave goods	Bronze jewellery, gold leaf, semi-precious stone beads
Papanlohea, Selayar (Bulbeck 1996–1997)	Possible use of bronze kettle drum as burial container	Heger IA kettle drum
Matoanging, near Galesong (Bulbeck 1996–1997)	Reported earthenware burial jars containing cremated remains	Abundant gold jewellery (no imported ceramics)
Saukang Boe (Bulbeck 1992)	Large buried earthenware jar, reportedly containing 2 gold rings and iron sword, associated with a cremated corpse	AD 1500±220 (ANU-5923) on human bone, cal. AD 1189–1950
Talaborong (Bulbeck 1992)	Cremated human remains buried in jars, associated with eleventh- to fourteenth-century Chinese ceramics	AD 1030±170 (ANU-5924) on human bone, cal. AD 720–1392
Bonto Lakja Selatan (Bulbeck 1992)	Cluster of Chinese martavans buried in acidic soil (no extant human remains)	Tenth to fourteenth centuries AD (Chinese martavans' chronology)

Source: Calibration (95.4 per cent confidence interval) undertaken by the author using Oxcal 4.2 (Bronk Ramsey 2014).

In Southeast Sulawesi, excavations at Gua Lampetia cave yielded a single jar similar to the Sabbang Loang jars (Figure 8.3), but up to a millennium later, based on the thermoluminescence dates of AD 1140±60 for the jar and 1050±120 for the cover. The *ca.* 60 cm tall jar, which was coated with dammar tree resin, contained the commingled remains of five adult and subadult individuals, a bone pendant and a ring of marine shell from the coast. Both at Gua Lampetia and two nearby caves, there was an earlier or contemporary mortuary practice of extended inhumations (Bulbeck et al. 2016). Large earthenware mortuary jars are also reported as surface finds at the Rukuo and Anawai caves in the Matarombeo Massif to the east of Gua Lampetia, but no information has been provided as to their likely antiquity (Fage 2014).

Southwest of Sulawesi, in the southwest corner of the archipelago, the northern beaches of Bali and Java have revealed five Palaeometallic cemeteries that evidently represent a shared tradition. These cemeteries, Pacung, Bondalem, Gilimanuk (Bali), Anyer Lor and Plawangan (Java), are distinguished by a predominance of extended inhumations and the minority presence of jar burials (Table 8.2). A sixth cemetery on the coastal plain, at Batujaya in West Java (early centuries AD), is currently documented with just nine extended inhumations (Widianto 2006), though it too may also reveal a minority presence of jar burials with future excavations.

Pacung, dated to between the late second millennium BC and first century AD, includes a primary infant burial and an adult skull burial in locally made jars that had been cut to admit the human remains, and then covered with local imitations of Indian-style dishes (Calo et al. 2015). Bondalem was heavily eroded before it could be recorded, and so it is not known whether the beads and bronzes collected from the site were grave goods (Ardika 2000). At Gilimanuk, the jar burials involved secondary interments of infants, children and young adults (but no older adults) with similar Palaeometallic grave goods to the wider range documented for the Gilimanuk direct interments. The cemetery's period of use started contemporarily with Pacung but lasted till late in the first millennium AD (Aziz 2012).

Anyer Lor included two large earthenware urns, a disturbed jar that reportedly contained a primary adult burial, and a 76 cm tall jar (73 cm girth) with a secondary adult burial and some carnelian beads (Van Heekeren 1956). At Plawangan, the burial jars were cylindrical jars measuring 22–60 cm tall and up to 90 cm in girth, including one 'double jar burial' involving two cylindrical jars stacked rim to rim. All of the jar burials were secondary, and the grave goods included beads of glass and carnelian and items of iron and bronze. The richest burial, associated with gold and earthenware pots, was interred inside a Heger IA kettle drum (Soegondho 1995). Interestingly, the use of a Heger IA kettle drum as a burial container, in this case cut open to admit the corpse, is also recorded from Manikliyu in inland Bali (Sutaba 2006).

Survey and excavation in southern Sumatra have recorded 13 open sites with earthenware burial jars and Palaeometallic grave goods. These sites have a documented chronological range between the seventh and sixteenth centuries AD (Table 8.5), and evidently represent a local tradition that continued into the eleventh century when megaliths started to become a prominent feature within the local settlements (Bonatz et al. 2006).

To date, jar burials have not been reported from the northern half of Sumatra nor the Thai-Malay Peninsula south of the Isthmus of Kra. However, immediately north of the Isthmus of Kra, at the northwest margin of the archipelago, Khao Sam Kaeo (KSK) yielded a burial jar with the cremated remains of two children directly dated to 260–50 cal. BC. The burial is contemporary with the main occupation phase of KSK as a massive fortified site involved in the production of ironware and glass and stone ornaments as well as the maritime trade of these and other luxury goods (Bellina-Pryce and Silapanth 2006). Presumably, the burial had been part of a larger cemetery subsequently destroyed by riverine erosion. Decorated pottery similar to that at KSK has been recovered from the disturbed mortuary cave sites of Tham Tuay (associated with a charcoal date of 156±34 BC, Wk-3088) and Tham Pla, with closest external parallels to Hoa Diem and other Sa Huynh sites of southern coastal Vietnam (Bellina et al. 2012). The Sa Huynh culture features numerous jar burials and other mortuary disposals associated with a rich array of Palaeometallic grave goods, and marked the occupation of this stretch of Vietnam by the ancestors of the Cham, the only documented Malayo-Polynesian speakers on Mainland Southeast Asia (Dzung 2011). Thus, the mortuary sites directly north of the Isthmus of Kra may be assigned to a tradition related to coastal Vietnam.

Later mortuary jar disposals (*ca.* AD 1200 onwards)

The examples covered in the previous section include traditions that continued after AD 1200, at southeastern Sabah (based on the estimated chronologies), Sumatra (Table 8.5), and the Makasar-speaking region of South Sulawesi (Saukang Boe, Talaborong and probably Bonto Lakja Selatan, Table 8.4). Makasar mortuary practices generally switched over to extended inhumations during the late pre-Islamic period between the fourteenth and seventeenth centuries, whereas their Bugis neighbours interred the cremated remains of their deceased in large imported ceramic jars, especially coarse stoneware 'martavans', as did the Wotu and Lemolang speakers at the northeast of the Bugis range (Bulbeck and Caldwell 2000; Druce et al. 2005). The Bugis practice of cremation potentially reflects cultural influence from classical Java (Bulbeck 1996–1997), but the use of jars as mortuary containers was already well established in southwest Sulawesi (Table 8.4).

Storage in caves of locally made stone mortuary jars is reported for two Kulaman Plateau sites in Mindanao. Noting an eighteenth-century coin in one of these jars, Maceda (1964) interpreted them as a continuation of an older practice of manufacturing earthenware mortuary jars. An orderly transition from Palaeometallic to later times is also evident for the mortuary jars on Fuga Island to the immediate north of Luzon. These jars were buried in the ground or in coral, or placed inside coral cairns, without grave goods (Solheim 1960). The larger jars, designed for primary disposals, included martavans as well as earthenware vessels, while both imported stoneware and earthenware jars were used as smaller containers for secondary disposals. Solheim reported an early first millennium AD dating for the imported jars, but such an early dating has not been repeated in later publications. As Solheim (1960) noted, the use of jars as mortuary containers could have continued till quite recently on Fuga Island, especially as the practice reportedly persisted on the Batanes until the eighteenth century.

In the Visayas, jar-burial sites postdating AD 1200 include Pilar and Banton Cave. The 24 jar burials excavated at Pilar included typically 'Palaeometallic' grave goods whereas the Banton jar burial was associated with Indian textiles (Table 8.3). In Luzon, the use of imported ceramics as mortuary containers includes thirteenth- to fourteenth-century martavans containing cremated remains at Agra and Pila (Tenazas 1968), an early Ming jar holding bone fragments at Tala (Paz et al. 2013), two sites on Cagraray Island (Fox and Evangelista 1957b) and Cabarruan in northern Luzon (Henson 1992). However, between the thirteenth century and the seventeenth century, when Christianity was widely adopted in the Philippines, direct inhumations and secondary burials in pits were the dominant mortuary disposals, with the tempayans and other high-fired, imported ceramics interred as grave goods (Clark 2013; Dueppen 2013; Sinopoli 2013).

Near Lake Towuti in Southeast Sulawesi, Grubauer (1913) recorded a recently practised tradition that involved the secondary disposal of deceased, aristocratic adults in martavans. These jars were carried in wooden litters to the same caves where the commoner adults (secondarily stored in wooden coffins) were also taken, as well as the disinterred remains of children (aristocratic and commoner) for secondary disposal. Of the numerous caves near Lake Towuti with visible remains consistent with this tradition, Gua Andomo, Gua Lampetia and Gua Sambagowala were excavated. These yielded imported ceramics dating approximately between the fifteenth and nineteenth centuries, which would appear to be the time range for the tradition, along with personal adornments such as glass beads and ornaments of bronze and brass (Bulbeck et al. 2016). This tradition is unique in Sulawesi ethnography, although the Gua Lampetia earthenware burial jar and Bugis/Wotu ceramic jar burials are potential antecedents.

The uniqueness of the Lake Towuti tradition in Sulawesi ethnography prompted Grubauer (1913) to speculatively associate it with a tribal immigration from Borneo. Certainly, the use of martavans as mortuary containers is recorded ethnographically amongst the Ngaju of the Central Kalimantan uplands, some of the Iban of Sarawak and Sabah (Harrisson 1990), and the Kajang, Melanau, Berawan, Kelabit and Lun Dayeh of Sarawak (Winzeler 2004). In Sarawak, the jars served both as containers to hold the corpse while the soft tissues decomposed, and as the final repository where the bones were stored after collection and cleaning. The jars were then displayed either on wooden funerary monuments (Winzeler 2004) or (as recorded for the Kelabit) in rockshelters, or atop megalithic constructions, which also included stone jars holding the remains of the deceased (Lloyd-Smith et al. 2010). The chronology of this tradition based on typological dating of the jars is the sixteenth to early twentieth centuries (Harrisson 1990; Lloyd-Smith et al. 2010).

Discussion and conclusions

Indo-Malaysian jar-burial horizons

Three jar-burial horizons can be discerned for the Indo-Malaysian Archipelago. These horizons are identifiable from their rapid, initial appearance across a considerable portion of the archipelago, although in some cases they appear to have formed the basis for traditions of considerable longevity within designated parts of Indo-Malaysia.

The oldest horizon involved mortuary jars of variable size, used for primary disposals only for subadults, which co-occurred with other burial modes within the same cemetery. Neolithic examples of this horizon include Niah West Mouth in Borneo and the Manunggul A and Arku caves in the Philippines (Tables 8.1 to 8.3), as well as Teouma in Vanuatu (Valentin et al. 2015). According to Valentin et al. (2015), the cultural basis for this horizon may have been a predilection for complex mortuary rituals, which may well have emerged specifically in Indo-Malaysia. Thus, recognising that certain sites represent the same horizon need not imply a single source of external influence for their shared practice of jar burials.

There is a geographic distinction between the predominantly paddle-impressed Neolithic pottery of the western archipelago (including Niah) and the frequently red-slipped Neolithic pottery of the eastern archipelago (Bulbeck 2008), which may respectively relate to early immigration of Austroasiatic speakers from Mainland Southeast Asia and Austronesian speakers from Taiwan (Simanjuntak, Chapter 1, this volume). The case for these separate origins of the Niah and Philippines jar-burial traditions is further supported by the early appearance of bronze at Niah, as noted earlier in this chapter.

Table 8.6 Proposed Indo-Malaysian Archipelago mortuary jar container traditions.

Tradition name	Geographical area	Chronology	Sites contain other disposal modes?	Contemporary sites lacking mortuary jars?	Basis for recognising tradition	Comments
Far northern Philippines	Batanes and Babuyan Islands	First and second millennia AD	Not documented	Not documented	Large jars lacking grave goods	
Middle Philippines	Luzon to Palawan and Visayas	(Late?) Neolithic to mid-second millennium AD	Many do	Yes, Luzon and Palawan	Frequent recurrence would allow for continuity of cultural transmission. Predominantly secondary disposals with associated grave goods	The Agra and Pila cremations in tempayans stand apart from other sites, and may reflect separate external influence
Western Mindanao	Southwestern Mindanao	First and second millennia AD	Not documented	Not documented	Large jars, some with special treatment (anthropomorphic or made of stone)	Variable presence of associated grave goods
Sulawesi Island/Sea	Eastern Mindanao to southwest Sulawesi (Figure 8.4)	First and second millennia AD	Not documented	Yes, in Sabah and southwest Sulawesi	Scatters of human remains, sherds from large jars, and ceramics and other grave goods in caves	Southwest Sulawesi extension overlaps with other traditions
Niah	Niah Caves, Sarawak	Neolithic, ca. 1150–300 BC	Most burials not jar burials	Gan Kira, Niah Caves	Geographically isolated concentration of jar burials	Highly diverse, chronologically sparse
Isthmus of Kra	Southern Thai Peninsula	Last centuries BC	Poorly documented	Not known	Geographically isolated concentration of jar-burial sites	Southern extension of Sa Huynh influence?
Southern Sumatra	Southern Sumatra	ca. AD 700–1500	Not on current evidence	Not on current evidence	Open-air burials of typically large jars	Provisionally documented
North Java/Bali	North coasts of Java and Bali	ca. first millennium AD	Most burials not jar burials	Batujaya, West Java (on current data)	Beach/coastal jar burials associated with direct inhumations	Reflects maritime connections along north Java/Bali
Sulawesi large jars	Southwest and Southeast Sulawesi	ca. AD 200–1200	Gua Lampetia	Certainly in Southeast Sulawesi	Large earthenware jars, sometimes in fields	Three included sites may be independent developments

Tradition name	Geographical area	Chronology	Sites contain other disposal modes?	Contemporary sites lacking mortuary jars?	Basis for recognising tradition	Comments
Sulawesi secondary burials	Karama River, Lake Matano, southwest Sulawesi	First millennium to seventeenth century AD	Not on current evidence	Yes, e.g. Makasar extended inhumations	Broken, cremated or missing bones in jars	Jars may be locally made or imported (including Dong Son kettle drum?)
North Moluccas	North Moluccas	First millennium AD	Later secondary direct burials	Directly buried skulls	Geographically isolated jar-burial site	Skull burials in jars
Nusatenggara	Lembata, Flores, Sumba	ca. first millennium AD	Yes (3 documented sites)	Not documented	Geographically isolated concentration of jar-burial sites	Sumba sites distinguished by stacked jar burials
Sulawesi ethnohistorical	Lake Towuti, Southeast Sulawesi	ca. AD 1400–1900	Jars reserved for elite adults	Apparently not	Secondary disposal of elite adults in tempayans stored in caves	Good example of a unified tradition
Borneo ethnohistorical	Sarawak, west Sabah, Central Kalimantan	ca. AD 1500–1950	Yes (wooden coffins)	Yes	Geographically isolated zone of similar practices	Variety of predominantly secondary disposals

The second horizon involved the specialism of large burial jars, usually of pottery, but including the use of covers and sometimes jars of stone in the southern half of the Philippines. This horizon covers sites securely dated to the early centuries AD in the Batanes Islands, Mindanao (Table 8.3) and Sulawesi (Sabbang Loang), as well as various *ca.* first millennium AD sites in the Talaud Islands (Leang Buidane), the Moluccas (Uattamdi), Sumba (Melolo and Lambanupa), and especially Sumatra (Table 8.5). The widespread distribution of this horizon corresponds well with Bellwood's (1997) overview of the Palaeometallic as a time of expanding trade linkages across the archipelago. That said, it was also a time of intensified cultural contact between the western archipelago and South Asia (e.g. Calo et al. 2015) and between the Batanes and Taiwan (Bellwood and Dizon 2013b). Accordingly, the fact that large jars dominate the jar burials of southern Sumatra and the Batanes, at opposite ends of the Archipelago, may reflect their status as independent developments inspired, respectively, by influence from South Asia and Taiwan. The case for Taiwan as the source for the Batanes large mortuary jars is strengthened by the prevailing use of the Taiwan mortuary jars for primary burials (Valentin et al. 2015).

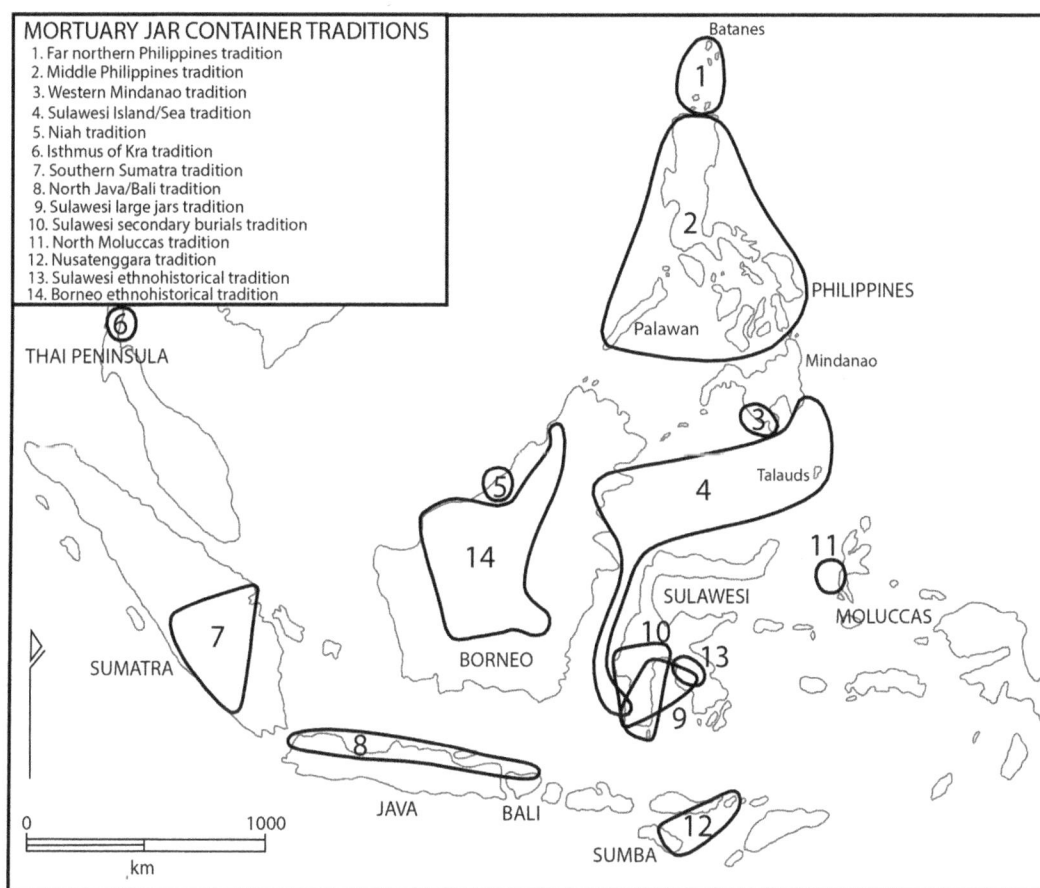

Figure 8.4 Twelve Indo-Malaysian traditions using jars as mortuary containers.

Source: Compiled and drawn by D. Bulbeck, based on Table 8.6.

The most recent horizon involved the use of large imported jars, especially martavans, for holding the cremated remains of the deceased. The geographic extent of this horizon reached from Fuga Island in the north to Borneo in the west and Sulawesi in the south. In the case of southwest Sulawesi, there appears to have been a switch from earthenware to stoneware and porcelain burial jars when the latter became readily available through maritime trade at around the fourteenth century AD (Bulbeck 1996–1997). However, in the case of Borneo, there are no immediate earthenware antecedents for the use of martavans as large mortuary containers.

Indo-Malaysian jar-burial traditions

The preceding review of the archaeological evidence refers on several occasions to local traditions covering similar mortuary assemblages found across a definable area. These imply a strong case for cultural continuity in terms of the vertical inheritance and horizontal transmission of beliefs on the appropriate treatment of the deceased. Taking this approach to its logical conclusion, we may propose a schema of 14 traditions to cover all of the previously reviewed sites with jars used as mortuary containers (Figure 8.4, Table 8.6). The purpose of this schema is not to produce a rigid classification of the archipelago's mortuary-jar sites – other interpretations involving a smaller or larger number of traditions are certainly possible – but to illustrate that the variability is productively managed through the recognition of multiple traditions. In addition, the assignment of sites to separate traditions need not imply the absence of contacts reflected by the jar-burial horizons. For instance, haematite staining of a proportion of the Niah, Tabon and Arku Cave burials may reflect shared adoption of an ancillary mortuary practice between Sarawak and Luzon during the late Neolithic and early Palaeometallic.

The least convincing of my traditions is arguably the 'middle Philippines' tradition, recognised essentially on the basis of a reasonable likelihood of these islands' jar-burial sites tracing back to early colonisation by Austronesian speakers. In contrast, the 'Sulawesi ethnohistorical' tradition satisfies all the requirements of a tradition, being documented for numerous sites and appearing to be the only mortuary practice in operation around Lake Towuti between *ca.* AD 1500 and 1900. It evidently crossed three language groups whose common adoption of the tradition can be attributed to participation in the burgeoning local trade in dammar resin (Bulbeck et al. 2016). The 'North Java/Bali' tradition also works well as a tradition, even if one of the distinguishing features is the minority presence of jar burials in these similar cemetery sites. The shared mortuary practices can be attributed to the persistence of this coastal stretch as a node for a maritime trade network that extended to the eastern archipelago (e.g. Calo 2014). The 'Borneo ethnohistorical' tradition can also be understood in terms of a trade network, in this case the high esteem placed on imported, large ceramic jars across much of Borneo. This is a critical context for understanding the mortuary use of these jars, which were also ritually important for the fermentation of rice for festivals and strategic displays of prestige (Harrisson 1990). In addition, the appearance of jar burials in southeastern Sabah, as well as general similarities in pottery production, apparently relates to Palaeometallic interactions across the Sulawesi Sea (Bellwood 1988b), an interaction sphere suggested here to have extended to southwest Sulawesi (Figure 8.4).

Cultural implications

The Niah Neolithic cemeteries are interpreted as corporate mortuary centres where the dispersed local communities, whose subsistence basis probably depended more on foraging than farming, displayed their broader social relations through the collective burial of the deceased (Lloyd-Smith et al. 2013). Similarly, Bonatz (2012) suggests that the Sumatra highland jar-burial sites served as ritual centres for the dispersed communities settled on the ridges to commemorate their perception of a collective ancestry in the hinterland valleys. Many of the Philippine sites would also be open to interpretation as cemeteries for the ancestors recognised by multiple communities as the basis for their corporate interests transcending the local community, although at least one site, Tumagudtad, was directly associated with a single settlement (Solheim 1960). A similar situation may apply to the southwest Sulawesi prehistoric sites, where Sabbang Loang and Galesong would appear to have been trading centres that proclaimed their independence through their jar-burial fields, whereas the communal ossuaries (including Leang Codong, which lacks mortuary jars) appear to have symbolised a collective claim to prime agricultural land (Bulbeck 2010).

One advantage of recognising multiple traditions (Table 8.6) is the demonstration of the contrast between those where most, if not all, of the disposals of human remains were contained by jars (e.g. the southern Sumatra tradition) and those with only a small minority inside jars (e.g. the Niah and North Java/Bali traditions). Also, where jar containers were in the minority, they were sometimes associated with higher-status individuals (Niah and Sulawesi ethnohistorical traditions) and sometimes with lower-status (Arku Cave) or younger individuals (Gilimanuk). Where the deceased person was a child or reduced to fragments through preliminary mortuary rites, then the sorts of jars in common domestic use would have been large enough for deployment as mortuary containers. However, where large jars were used, these would have required considerable potting skill to be robust enough to hold their contents for the duration of the mortuary ceremony, and would have depended on sufficient personal wealth for their acquisition (especially with the imported jars). Accordingly, locally available technological skills and/or community social status may have been factors that affected whether there was no use, occasional deployment or thoroughgoing reliance on jars as mortuary containers – within a complex web of ancestor-worship beliefs that would have varied greatly from place to place and time to time.

Acknowledgements

The author acknowledges the Australian Research Council for funding 'The Archaeology of Sulawesi: A Strategic Island for Understanding Modern Human Colonisation and Interactions across our Region' project (DP110101357) to Sue O'Connor, Jack Fenner, Janelle Stevenson and Ben Marwick. The Gua Lampetia burial jar was excavated and photographed (Figure 8.3) as part of this project.

References

Anggraeni. 2012. The Austronesian Migration Hypothesis as seen from Prehistoric Settlements on the Karama River, Mamuju, West Sulawesi. Unpublished PhD thesis, Department of Archaeology and Anthropology, The Australian National University, Canberra.

Anon. 2009. Early Philippine society, culture & history. www.studymode.com/essays/Phil-Society_And_Ci_Thulture-24113.html, viewed 25 October 2014.

Ardika, I.W. 2000. Archaeological research at Bondalem, northeastern Bali. *Bulletin of the Indo-Pacific Prehistory Association* 19: 81–83.

Aziz, F.A. 2012. Archaeology-demography studies at Gilimanuk site (Bali). In E. Sedyawati and I.W. Ardika (eds), *Recent Studies in Indonesian Archaeology*, pp. 17–48. Delhi: B.R. Publishing Corporation.

Bacus, E.A. 2004. The archaeology of the Philippine Archipelago. In I. Glover and P. Bellwood (eds), *Southeast Asia from Prehistory to History*, pp. 257–281. London: RoutledgeCurzon.

Barnes, R. and M. Hunt Kahlenburg (eds). 2010. *The Mary Hunt Kahlenburg Collection: Five Centuries of Indonesian Textiles*. Munich: DelMonico Books.

Bedford, S. and M. Spriggs. 2007. Birds on the rim: A unique Lapita carinated vessel in its wider context. *Archaeology in Oceania* 42: 12–21. doi.org/10.1002/j.1834-4453.2007.tb00010.x.

Bellina, B., G. Epinal and A. Favereau. 2012. Caracterisation préliminaire des poteries marqueurs d'échanges en mer de Chine méridionale à la fin de la préhistoire. *Archipel* 84: 7–33. doi. org/10.3406/befeo.2006.6039.

Bellina-Pryce, B. and P. Silapanth. 2006. Weaving cultural identities on trans-Asiatic networks: Upper Thai-Malay Peninsula – an early socio-political landscape. *Bulletin de l'École Française d'Êxtreme-Orient* 93: 257–293.

Bellwood, P. 1976. Archaeological research in Minahasa and the Talaud islands, northeastern Indonesia. *Asian Perspectives* 19(2): 240–288.

——. 1988a. Cultural remains in the Baturong and Madai caves. In P. Bellwood (ed.), *Archaeological Research in South-Eastern Sabah*, pp. 128–131. Kota Kinabalu: Sabah Museum Monograph vol. 2.

——. 1988b. Madai and Baturong since 1000BC: Comparative perspectives and cultural trends. In P. Bellwood (ed.), *Archaeological Research in South-Eastern Sabah*, pp. 245–258. Kota Kinabalu: Sabah Museum Monograph vol. 2.

——. 1988c. The prehistoric earthenwares and other small finds of the Atas and Idahan periods. In P. Bellwood (ed.), *Archaeological Research in South-Eastern Sabah*, pp. 173–244. Kota Kinabalu: Sabah Museum Monograph vol. 2.

——. 1997. *Prehistory of the Indo-Malaysian Archipelago*. 2nd edition. Honolulu: University of Hawaii Press.

Bellwood, P. and E. Dizon. 2013a. Archaeological investigations at Savidug, Sabtang Island. In P. Bellwood and E. Dizon (eds), *4000 Years of Migration and Cultural Exchange: The Archaeology of the Batanes Islands, Northern Philippines*, pp. 47–65. Terra Australis 40. Canberra: ANU E Press.

——. 2013b. The Batanes Islands and the prehistory of Island Southeast Asia. In P. Bellwood and E. Dizon (eds), *4000 Years of Migration and Cultural Exchange: The Archaeology of the Batanes Islands, Northern Philippines*, pp. 235–241. Terra Australis 40. Canberra: ANU E Press.

Bellwood, P., N. Goenadi, G. Irwin, A.W. Gunadi and D. Tanudirjo. 1998. 35,000 years of prehistory in the northern Moluccas. In G-J. Bartstra (ed.), *Bird's Head Approaches*, pp. 233–275. Modern Quaternary Research in Southeast Asia 15. Rotterdam: A.A. Balkema.

Bintarti, D.D. 2000. More on urn burials in Indonesia. *Bulletin of the Indo-Pacific Prehistory Association* 19: 73–77.

Bonatz, D. 2012. A highland perspective on the archaeology and settlement history of Sumatra. *Archipel* 84: 35–81.

Bonatz, D., J.D. Neidel and M.L. Tjoa-Bonatz. 2006. The megalithic complex of highland Jambi: An archaeological perspective. *Bijdragen tot de Taal-, Land- en Volkenkunde* 162(4): 490–522. doi.org/10.1163/22134379-90003664.

Bronk Ramsey, C. 2014. Oxcal 4.2 manual. c14.arch.ox.ac.uk/oxcal.html.

Bulbeck, F.D. 1992. A Tale of Two Kingdoms: The Historical Archaeology of Gowa and Tallok, South Sulawesi, Indonesia. Unpublished PhD thesis, Department of Archaeology and Anthropology, The Australian National University, Canberra.

——. 1996–1997. The Bronze-Iron Age of South Sulawesi, Indonesia: mortuary traditions, metallurgy and trade. In F.D. Bulbeck and N. Barnard (eds), *Ancient Chinese and Southeast Asian Bronze Age Cultures* vol. II, pp. 1007–1076. Taipei: Southern Materials Center Inc.

——. 2008. An integrated perspective on the Austronesian diaspora: the switch from cereal agriculture to maritime foraging in the colonisation of Island Southeast Asia. *Australian Archaeology* 67: 31–51. doi.org/10.1080/03122417.2008.11681877.

——. 2010. Uneven development in southwest Sulawesi, Indonesia during the Early Metal Phase. In B. Bellina, E.A. Bacus, T.O. Pryce and J. Wisseman Christie (eds), *50 Years of Archaeology in Southeast Asia: Essays in Honour of Ian Glover*, pp. 152–169. Bangkok: River Books.

——. 2011. Biological and cultural evolution in the population and culture history of Malaya's anatomically modern inhabitants. In N. Enfield (ed.), *Dynamics of Human Diversity: The Case of Mainland Southeast Asia*, pp. 207–255. Pacific Linguistics 627. Canberra: The Australian National University.

——. Submitted. Bioarchaeological analysis of the Northern Moluccan excavated human remains. For P. Bellwood (ed.), *Archaeology in the Northern Moluccas, Indonesia.*

Bulbeck, D. and I. Caldwell. 2000. *Land of Iron: The Historical Archaeology of Luwu and the Cenrana Valley*. Hull: University of Hull Centre for South-East Asian Studies.

Bulbeck, D., F.A. Aziz, S. O'Connor, A. Calo, J.N. Fenner, B. Marwick, J. Feathers, R. Wood and S. Prastiningtyas. 2016. Mortuary caves and the dammar trade in the Towuti-Routa region, Sulawesi, in an Island Southeast Asian context. *Asian Perspectives* 55(2): 148–183. doi.org/10.1353/asi.2016.0017.

Calo, A. 2014. *Trails of Bronze Drums across Early Southeast Asia – Exchange Routes and Connected Cultural Spheres*. Singapore: Institute of Southeast Asian Studies.

Calo, A., B. Prasetyo, P. Bellwood, J.W. Lankton, B. Gratuze, T.O. Pryce, A. Reinecke, V. Leusch, H. Schenk, R. Wood, R.A. Bawono, I.D.K. Gede, N.L.K.C. Yuliati, J. Fenner, C. Reepmeyer, C. Castillo and A. Carter. 2015. Sembiran and Pacung on the northern coast of Bali: A strategic crossroads for early trans-Asiatic exchange. *Antiquity* 344: 378–396. doi.org/10.15184/aqy.2014.45.

Clark, J.L. 2013. The distribution and cultural context of artificial cranial modification in the central and southern Philippines. *Asian Perspectives* 52(1): 28–42. doi.org/10.1353/asi.2013.0003.

Coutts, P.J. 1983. *An Archaeological Perspective of Panay Island, Philippines*. Cebu City: University of San Carlos.

Crane, H.R. and J.B. Griffin. 1959. University of Michigan radiocarbon dates IV. *Radiocarbon* 1: 173–198. doi.org/10.1017/s0033822200020452.

Cuevas, N. and A. de Leon. 2008. Archaeological investigations of Sagel Cave at Maitum, Sarangani Province, Southern Mindanao, Philippines. *Hukay* 13: 1–24.

Do, M. 2013. Iron-Nickel Smelting Production in Luwu, South Sulawesi during the pre-Islamic Period. Unpublished MSc dissertation, Institute of Archaeology, University College of London. Available at: www.oxis.org/theses/misol-2103.pdf.

Druce, S., D. Bulbeck and I. Mahmud. 2005. A transitional Islamic Bugis cremation in Bulubangi, South Sulawesi: Its historical and archaeological context. *Review of Indonesian and Malaysian Affairs* 39(1): 1–22.

Dueppen, S. 2013. Temporal variability in Southeast Asian dragon jars: A case from the Philippines. *Asian Perspectives* 52(1): 75–118. doi.org/10.1353/asi.2013.0004.

Dzung, L.T.M. 2011. Central Vietnam during the period from 555 BCE to CE 500. In P.-Y. Manguin, A. Mani and G. Wade (eds), *Early Interactions between South and Southeast Asia: Reflections of Cross-Cultural Exchange*, pp. 17–45. Singapore: Institute of Southeast Asian Studies.

Fagan, B. 1994. *In the Beginning: Introduction to Archaeology*. 8th edition. New York: HarperCollins.

Fage, L.-H. 2014. Rapport préliminaire: prospection archéologique Massif de Matarombeo, Sulawesi Central, octobre 2014. kalimanthrope.com/sulawesi2014/RAPPORT%20SULAWESI-2014-OK. pdf, viewed 24 June 2015.

Flavel, A. 1997. Sa-Huynh Kalanay? Analysis of the Prehistoric Decorated Earthenware of South Sulawesi in an Island Southeast Asian Context. Unpublished BSc (Hons) thesis, Centre for Archaeology, University of Western Australia, Perth.

———. 2006. Sa-Huynh Kalanay: Analysis of the prehistoric decorated earthenware of South Sulawesi in an Island Southeast Asian context. In W.G. Solheim II and contributors, *Archaeology and Culture in Southeast Asia: Unravelling the Nusantao*, pp. 193–237. Quezon City: University of Philippines Press.

Fox, R. 1970. *The Tabon Caves*. Manila: Monographs of the National Museum 1.

Fox, R. and A. Evangelista. 1957a. The Bato Caves, Sorsogon Province, Philippines: A preliminary report of a jar burial-stone tool assemblage. *Journal of East Asiatic Studies* 6(1): 49–56.

———. 1957b. The cave archaeology of Cagraray Island, Albay Province, Philippines: A preliminary report of exploration and excavations. *Journal of East Asiatic Studies* 6(1): 57–68.

Grubauer, A. 1913. *Unter Kopfjägern in Central-Celebes: Ethnologische Streifzüge in Sudost- und Central-Celebes*. Leipzig: R. Voigtlander.

Guillaud, D., H. Forestier, A. Romsan and B. Prasetyo. 2006. Bab 2-Daerah pengunungan: Sebuah pendekatan arkeogeografis untuk mengetengahkan zaman protosejarah. In D. Guillaud (ed.), *Menyelusuri Sungai, Menurut Waktu: Penelitian Arkeologi di Sumatera Selatan*, pp. 35–47. Jakarta: Pusat Penelitian Arkeologi Nasional Paris: Institut de Recherche pour le Développement.

Harrisson, B. 1958. Niah's Lobang Tulang ('Cave of Bones'). *Sarawak Museum Journal* 8 (n.s. 12): 596–610.

———. 1967. A classification of Stone Age burials from Niah Great Cave, Sarawak. *Sarawak Museum Journal* 15 (n.s. 30–31): 126–200.

———. 1990. *Pusaka: Heirloom Jars of Borneo*. Singapore: Oxford University Press.

Henson, F.G. 1992. Jar burial excavations in the Philippines. In I. Glover, P. Suchitta and J. Villiers (eds), *Early Metallurgy, Trade and Urban Centres in Thailand and Southeast Asia*, pp. 213–225. Bangkok: White Lotus.

Higham, C. 2011. The Bronze Age of Southeast Asia: New insight on social change from Ban Non Wat. *Cambridge Archaeological Journal* 21: 365–389. doi.org/10.1017/S0959774311000424.

Kress, J.H. 2004. The necrology of Sa'gung rockshelter and its place in Philippine prehistory. In V. Paz (ed.), *Southeast Asian Archaeology Wilhelm G. Solheim II Festschrift*, pp. 239–275. Quezon City: University of the Philippines Press.

Lloyd-Smith, L. and F. Cole. 2010. The jar-burial tradition in the West Mouth of Niah Cave, Sarawak. In B. Bellina, E.A. Bacus, T.O. Pryce and J. Wisseman Christie (eds), *50 Years of Archaeology in Southeast Asia: Essays in Honour of Ian Glover*, pp. 114–127. Bangkok: River Books.

Lloyd-Smith, L., G. Barker, H. Barton, I. Datan, C. Gosden, B. Nyíri, M. Janowski and E. Preston. 2010. The Cultured Rainforest project: Archaeological investigations in the third (2009) season of fieldwork in the Kelabit highlands of Sarawak. *Sarawak Museum Journal* 67 (88): 57–104.

Lloyd-Smith, L., G. Barker, H. Barton, J. Cameron, F. Cole, P. Daly, C. Doherty, C. Hunt, J. Krigbaum, H. Lewis, J. Manser, V. Paz, P.J. Piper, R.J. Rabett, G. Rushworth and K. Szabó. 2013. 'Neolithic' societies c. 4000–2000 years ago: Austronesian farmers? In G. Barker (ed.), *Rainforest Foraging and Farming in Island Southeast Asia: The Archaeology of the Niah Caves, Sarawak*, vol. 1, pp. 255–298. Cambridge: McDonald Institute for Archaeological Research.

Maceda, M.N. 1964. Preliminary report on ethnographic and archaeological field work in the Kulaman Plateau, Island of Mindanao, Philippines. *Anthropos* 59: 75–82.

Mijares, A.S.B. 2005. The archaeology of the Peñablanca cave sites, northern Luzon, Philippines. *Journal of Austronesian Studies* 1(2): 65–93.

Ogawa, H. 2004. Chronological context of nondecorated black pottery phase from Lal-lo shell middens, Cagayan Province, Philippines. In V. Paz (ed.), *Southeast Asian Archaeology Wilhelm G. Solheim II Festschrift*, pp. 184–208. Quezon City: University of the Philippines Press.

Paz, V., A. Ragragio and J. Medrana. 2013. Preliminary archaeological survey of the Municipality of Catanauan, Bondoc Peninsula, Quezon Province. catanauanproject.com/index.php/publications/finish/255-catanauan-site-reports/1691-preliminary-archaeological-survey-of-the-municipality-of-catanauan-bondoc-peninsula-quezon-province/, viewed 15 November 2014.

Piper, P.J., F.Z. Campos and H.-c. Hung. 2009. A study of the animal bone recovered from pits 9 and 10 at the site of Nagsabaran in northern Luzon, Philippines. *Hukay* 14: 47–90.

Ronquillo, W. 2003. Philippine earthenware pottery from the early prehistoric period. In M. John (ed.), *Earthenware in Southeast Asia*, pp. 32–38. Singapore: Singapore University Press.

Sinopoli, S.M. 2013. New research on an old collection: Studies of the Philippine Expedition ('Guthe') Collection of the Museum of Anthropology, University of Michigan. *Asian Perspectives* 52(1): 1–11. doi.org/10.1353/asi.2013.0000.

Soegondho, S. 1995. *Tradisi Gerabah di Indonesia*. Jakarta: Himpunan Keramik Indonesia.

Soeroso, M. 1997. Recent discoveries of jar burials in South Sumatra. *Bulletin de l'École française d'Extrême-Orient* 84: 418–422. doi.org/10.3406/befeo.1997.3825.

Solheim, W.G. II. 1960. Jar burial in the Babuyan and Batanese Islands and in Central Philippines, and its relationship to jar burial elsewhere in the Far East. *Philippine Journal of Science* 8–9: 115–148.

Solheim, W.G. II, A.M. Legaspi and J.S. Neri. 1979. *Archaeological Survey in Southeastern Mindanao*. Monograph no. 8. Manila: National Museum of the Philippines.

Spriggs, M. 1989. The dating of the Island Southeast Asian Neolithic: An attempt at chronometric hygiene and linguistic correlation. *Antiquity* 63: 587–613. doi.org/10.1017/S0003598X00076560.

Sutaba, I.M. 2006. Recently discovered burial systems at Manikliyu, Bali. In T. Simanjuntak, M. Hisyam, B. Prasetyo and T.S. Nastiti (eds), *Archaeology: Indonesian Perspective, R.P. Soejono's Festschrift*, pp. 303–316. Jakarta: Indonesian Institute of Science.

Szabó, K. and H. Ramirez. 2009. Worked shell from Leta Leta Cave, Palawan. *Archaeology in Oceania* 44: 150–159. doi.org/10.1002/j.1834-4453.2009.tb00059.x.

Szabó, K., M.C. Swete Kelly and A. Peñalosa. 2004. Preliminary results from excavations in the eastern mouth of Ille Cave, northern Palawan. In V. Paz (ed.), *Southeast Asian Archaeology Wilhelm G. Solheim II Festschrift*, pp. 209–224. Quezon City: University of the Philippines Press.

Szabó, K., F. Cole, L. Lloyd-Smith, G. Barker, C. Hunt, P.J. Piper and C. Doherty. 2013. The 'Metal Age' at the Niah Caves, c. 2000–500 years ago. In G. Barker (ed.), *Rainforest Foraging and Farming in Island Southeast Asia: The Archaeology of the Niah Caves, Sarawak*, vol. 1, pp. 288–340. Cambridge: McDonald Institute for Archaeological Research.

Tenazas, R.C.P. 1968. A Report on the Archaeology of the Locsin-University of San Carlos Excavations in Pila, Laguna. books.google.com.au/books/about/A_Report_on_the_Archaeology_of_the_Locsi. html?id=M3ZzPQAACAAJ&redir_esc=y, viewed 2 October 2015.

Thiel, B. 1986–1987. Excavations at Arku Cave, Northeast Luzon, Philippines. *Asian Perspectives* 28(1): 61–81.

Tjoa-Bonatz, M.L. 2012. More than 3400 years of earthenware traditions in highland Jambi on Sumatra. In M.L. Tjoa-Bonatz, A. Reinecke and D. Bonatz (eds), *Connecting Empires and States: Selected Papers from the 13th International Conference of the European Association of Southeast Asian Archaeologists*, vol. 2, pp. 16–31. Singapore: National University of Singapore Press.

Van Heekeren, H.R. 1956. Note on a proto-historic urn-burial site at Anjar, Java. *Anthropos* 51: 194–201.

——. 1972. *The Stone Age of Indonesia*. 2nd edition. Verhandelingen van het Koninklijk Instituut voor Taal-, Land- en Volkenkunde 61. The Hague: Martinus Nijhoff.

Valentin, F., J.-i. Choi, H. Lin, S. Bedford and M. Spriggs. 2015. Three-thousand-year-old jar-burials at the Teouma cemetery (Vanuatu): A Southeast Asian–Lapita connection? In C. Sand, S. Chiu and N. Hogg (eds), *The Lapita Cultural Complex in Time and Sapce: Expansion Routes, Chronologies and Typologies*, pp. 81–101. Noumea: Institut d'archéologie de la Nouvelle-Calédonie et du Pacifique.

Widianto, H. 2006. Cranio-morphological aspects of the recent discovery of human remains from Batujaya, West Java. In T. Simanjuntak, M. Hisyam, B. Prasetyo and T.S. Nastiti (eds), *Archaeology: Indonesian Perspective, R.P. Soejono's Festschrift*, pp. 124–135. Jakarta: Indonesian Institute of Science.

Winters, N.J. 1974. An application of dental anthropological analysis to the human dentition of two Early Metal Age sites, Palawan, Philippines. *Asian Perspectives* 17(1): 28–35.

Winzeler, R.L. 2004. *The Architecture of Life and Death in Borneo*. Honolulu: University of Hawai'i Press.

9

An Son Ceramics in the Neolithic Landscape of Mainland Southeast Asia

Carmen Sarjeant

Most comparative studies of pottery and other material culture in Mainland Southeast Asia (MSEA) have emphasised well-researched sites in Thailand, with little attention to the archaeological record from southern Vietnam. Recent excavations at An Son provide new opportunities to redress this disparity through comparative research between Neolithic sites in southern Vietnam and those in other parts of MSEA. This research employed systematic methods for data collection and statistical analysis in order to compare the ceramic assemblages and additional material culture at An Son, in the Mekong delta region of southern Vietnam, with 14 other sites in MSEA. The aim of this study was to place An Son and southern Vietnam within the context of Neolithic developments in MSEA at around the second millennium BC by determining regional relationships in the geographic distribution of material cultural traits and identifying regional patterns of connectivity and possible routes of migration that led to the appearance of the Neolithic community at An Son. The analysis suggests that sites in northeast and central Thailand have ancestral links with An Son, with the implication that Neolithic populations perhaps settled An Son via major tributaries of the Mekong River. Additionally, there are strong parallels between the material culture at sites in southeastern Cambodia and southern Vietnam, which suggests continuing contact during the Neolithic.

Introduction

This paper builds on previous research on the relationships between Neolithic sites in Mainland Southeast Asia (MSEA) based on ceramic comparisons (e.g. Rispoli 2007; Wiriyaromp 2007, 2011). It draws upon specific comparisons with the site of An Son, focusing on the 2009 excavation material, in order to place southern Vietnam in the wider context of Neolithic developments in Southeast Asia, *ca.* 3500 to 2000 BP. A correspondence analysis (CA) is utilised to compare a broad range of sites in MSEA chosen for their Neolithic occupational evidence and accessible excavation reports.

The Neolithic of MSEA has been most intensively researched in central and northeast Thailand (e.g. Higham and Bannanurag 1990; Ciarla 1992; Rispoli 1992; Higham and Thosarat 1998a; Nguyen 2006; Higham and Kijngam 2009; Oxenham et al. 2011). Over the past two decades, research, surveys and excavations have increased in southern Vietnam along the Vam Co Dong and Vam Co Tay Rivers, adjacent to the Dong Nai and Sai Gon River valleys. Many date to the Bronze and Iron ages (3000–1500 BP), but the Vam Co Dong has a concentration of tested

Neolithic sites dating to the late third and second millennia BC, including An Son in Long An Province, nearby Loc Giang, and Dinh Ong further upstream in Tay Ninh Province (Figure 9.1; Nishimura 2002; Nishimura and Nguyen 2002).

An Son is so far the most comprehensively excavated site in southern Vietnam with a Neolithic sequence. An Australian Research Council Discovery Grant awarded to Peter Bellwood, Marc Oxenham and Janelle Stevenson, entitled 'The Creation of Southeast Asian Peoples and Cultures, 3500 BC to AD 500' (DP0666607), funded an excavation at An Son in 2009 in collaboration with the Institute of Archaeology, Hanoi and Nguyen Kim Dung and the Centre for Archaeological Studies, Southern Institute of Social Sciences, Ho Chi Minh City and Bui Chi Hoang (Bellwood et al. 2011). This excavation was intended to address the origins of rice agriculture in southern Vietnam and Southeast Asia in general, and to obtain information on the inhabitants from their interment practices and human remains. Within the context of this new research, previous overviews of cultural sequences for Southeast Asia (e.g. Higham 1996: 4; fig. 1.2) could be reworked to include southern Vietnam.

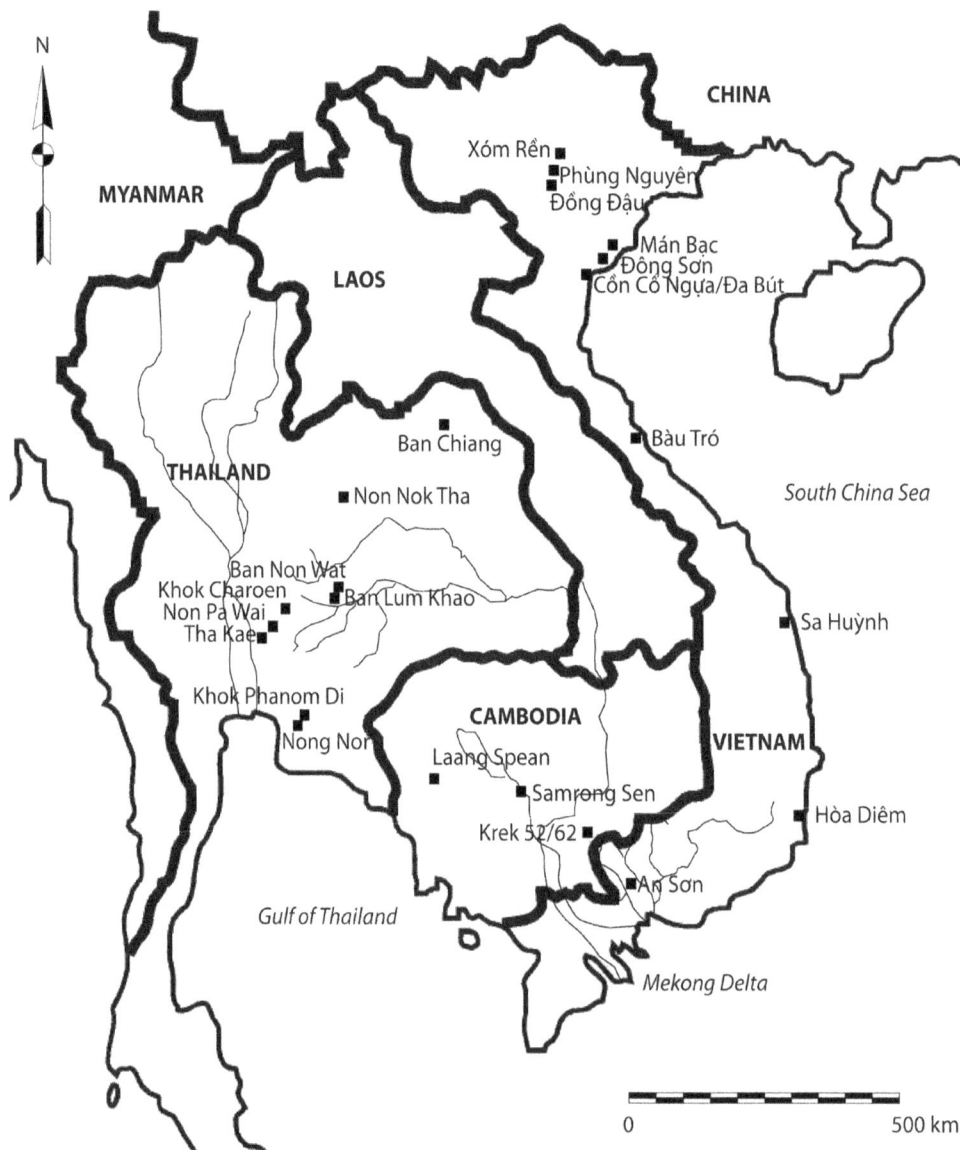

Figure 9.1 Map of An Son and other sites analysed in this contribution.
Source: C. Sarjeant.

The An Son mound is located in An Ninh Tay Commune, Duc Hoa District at coordinates 10°59'19"N/106°17'41"E, close to the northern border of Long An Province where the Vam Co Dong River approaches the Cambodian border (Figure 9.1; Bellwood et al. 2011). It is situated on a slightly raised natural levee overlooking extensive rice fields about 300 m east of the Vam Co Dong and *ca.* 85 km from the coast (Nishimura and Nguyen 2002: 101). An Son was initially reported by Louis Malleret and Paul Levy (Malleret 1963: 94–95). The first excavations at An Son were initiated in 1978 on the top of the mound. Little information exists with regards to this excavation, except that the excavators uncovered *ca.* 4 m of prehistoric deposits and recovered a substantial collection of cultural remains that are now housed in Long An Provincial Museum.

Further investigations through the mound in 1997 identified three major depositional events. The upper, Unit 1 consisted of disturbed sediments associated with the construction of the modern pagoda atop the archaeological site. Preceding this was Unit 2, which contained a complex sequence of hard-compacted 'earthen' surfaces alternating with soft humic deposits containing high concentrations of pottery and bone and hearth features (Nishimura and Nguyen 2002). Nishimura and Nguyen (2002) interpreted the stratigraphy as representing a series of sequential floor surfaces that had built up through time. Unit 3, the basal mound deposits below Unit 2, consisted of greyish sandy soil truncated by postholes and rich in potsherds. Although the site is located on a river levee of silt, there was little evidence of fluvial sediments in Unit 3. They concluded that Unit 3 had been deliberately brought to the site as a foundation deposit.

In 2004 and 2007, excavations focused on areas eastern edge of the main mound where burials were located. The investigators uncovered 25 extended inhumations. In 2009, excavations by a joint Australian/Vietnamese team positioned their trenches adjacent to the 2004 trenches, with the intention of uncovering more extended burials. A small test square was also opened at the western side of the mound. The excavations produced a further six individuals (Bellwood et al. 2011).

The 2009 excavations at An Son also revealed evidence for a mixed economy, including domestic pig and dog, the *Oryza japonica* subspecies of rice (as husks in pottery), fish and shellfish from brackish estuarine rivers, and hunted animals. Some of the earliest layers contained domestic dog, but it is uncertain whether the earliest pig remains were domesticated or wild (Piper et al. 2014). Rice chaff was not identified in pottery tempers from the earliest layers of An Son, but appeared shortly after. Other material culture at An Son includes ground and polished stone tools, shell beads, bone fishhooks and worked bone/ivory, ceramic roundels or counters, and baked clay pellets (Bellwood et al. 2011).

The lack of an established chronology for southern Vietnam, largely resulting from insecure radiocarbon dates and lack of stratigraphic understanding, led Nishimura (2002: 50–51) to formulate four periods for the Neolithic occupation of southern Vietnam based on ceramic form and decoration. Period I represented the lowest layers at An Son and Da Kai, beginning around 4000 BP. This period possessed a minimal variety in ceramic forms with cord-marking, red paint, and incised wavy motifs. Period II was estimated to date to 4000–3500 BP and exhibited the first appearance of fibre or rice chaff tempered ceramics and a development of earlier incised motifs on ceramics. Period III dated to 3500–3000 BP and had ceramics with zigzag and impressed decorations. Period IV was estimated to date to 3000 BP and had a greater variety of ceramic forms and of impressed decorations. Temporal distinctions are reported for some ceramic features (Bellwood et al. 2011); however, full resolution of the Neolithic sequence in southern Vietnam will require further excavation and an increased understanding of the relationships between sites.

Neolithic occupation in MSEA

In keeping with recent research in Vietnam (Oxenham and Tayles 2006; Matsumura and Oxenham 2011), the Neolithic in MSEA is here tentatively applied to 'food-producing communities that lacked evidence for metal'. On that basis, the MSEA Neolithic is thought to have commenced in the late third to early second millennium BC. There are two models for the development of Neolithic occupation in the region (Bellwood and Oxenham 2008; Higham 2011a: 1): the first is an expansionist model whereby farmers from the north moved into areas occupied by indigenous hunter-gatherers; the second prioritises the ability of indigenous groups to adopt cultivated subsistence and technological traits as Neolithic farmers entered the region.

Neolithic sites in MSEA are predominantly distributed either along or near present and former coastlines and rivers, in environments that provided the natural flooding and rainfall required for rice cultivation. Rivers and their tributaries were likely to have been of great importance to the movement of people and ideas in the past. The Neolithic occupation of Vietnam exhibits evidence of contact with China and other regions of MSEA, leading to suggestions that agricultural practices travelled from the north via rivers and/or along the coast (Fuller et al. 2010; Higham et al. 2011). The Neolithic sites exhibit the oldest evidence of cultivation in MSEA, including rice and other crops, supplemented by a hunter-gatherer-fisher economy. Domestic pigs and dogs and shared aspects of ceramic traditions, ground and polished stone assemblages, and bone and shell technologies were evident in sedentary village habitation sites. Recent radiocarbon chronologies suggest that some sites were occupied for more than 1,000 years, whilst others appear to have remained in existence for just a few hundred. An Son has been identified as a Neolithic site due to its late third to second millennium BC where many generations of sedentary inhabitants were occupied in rice cultivation and animal husbandry, and utilised ceramic, stone, shell and bone technologies (Bellwood et al. 2011; Piper et al. 2014).

For the purposes of comparing An Son with other MSEA Neolithic sites, only those with evidence from premetal contexts, both early and late Neolithic, are included, even though only some of these have secure radiocarbon-dated chronologies. Examples with clear and established Neolithic sequences include Ban Non Wat and Man Bac (Higham and Higham 2009a; Oxenham et al. 2011). Tha Kae exhibited Neolithic evidence in the lowest occupational layer 5, while Khok Charoen has one secure date from a burial of 2853 BP and the site is associated with Neolithic material culture (Ciarla 1992; Bulbeck 2011; Ciarla n.d.). Charles Higham suggests Khok Phanom Di and Nong Nor (Phase 1) are hunter-gatherer-fisher sites since there is no secure evidence that the occupants ever cultivated rice. There were some rice remains at Khok Phanom Di but they appear to reflect trade with Neolithic rice cultivators located inland, whereas Nong Nor proceeded directly from a hunter-gatherer site during Phase 1 to a Bronze Age site in Phase 2 (Charles Higham, pers. comm.). Nevertheless, Khok Phanom Di and Nong Nor (Phase 1) are included in the comparison due to similar dates with An Son, so as to represent the coastal region of central Thailand at the time.

The additional sites of Samrong Sen, Laang Spean, early Ban Lum Khao (its early Layer 3 and Mortuary Phase 1, which are considered Neolithic), Ban Chiang (Initial to Early Period I–II), Non Nok Tha (Early Period), Krek, Bau Tro and Xom Ren are also included, even though the contextual information and chronologies for these sites are not particularly secure. In attempting to cover a wide geographic area (Figure 9.1) for a period of time spanning some 1,000 years, a certain allowance for archaeological estimation is unavoidable. The sites compared with An Son are summarised in Table 9.1.

Table 9.1 Sites in Mainland Southeast Asia with Neolithic sequences included in the comparative study with An Son with dates of occupation and cited publications for the archaeological research.

	Location	Date	References
Ban Chiang (Initial Period to Early Period I-II)	Northeast Thailand	*ca.* 4000 BP (Gorman and Charoenwongsa 1976)	Gorman and Charoenwongsa 1976; Bayard 1977; McGovern et al. 1985; see also Bubpha 2003
Ban Lum Khao (Neolithic Layer 3 and Mortuary Phase 1)	Northeast Thailand	Neolithic occupation: *ca.* 3450–3000 BP (T.F.G. Higham in Higham and Thosarat 2004b: 5)	Chang 2004; Higham and Thosarat 2004a, 2004b
Ban Non Wat (Neolithic Phases 1 and 2)	Northeast Thailand	Neolithic occupation: *ca.* 3750–3500 cal. BP Neolithic Phase 1 burials: *ca.* 3450–3350 cal. BP Neolithic phase 2 burials: *ca.* 3350–3150 cal. BP (Higham and Higham 2009a, 2009b)	Wiriyaromp 2007; Higham 2009a, 2009b, 2009c; Higham and Kijngam 2011; Higham and Wiriyaromp 2011a, 2011b
Bau Tro	Central Vietnam	*ca.* 4000–3500 BP (Pham 1997)	Patte 1924; Pham 1997
Khok Charoen	Central Thailand	2980±450 BP, 3180±300/3080±300 BP (pottery, thermoluminescence) (Watson 1979), 2853±33 BP (burial) (Bulbeck 2011)	Watson 1979; Ho 1984; Higham 2011b
Khok Phanom Di	Coastal central Thailand	4000–3500 BP (Higham and Bannanurag 1990)	Higham and Bannanurag 1990; Higham and Thosarat 2004c; Vincent 2004
Krek	Cambodia	Neolithic material culture (Dega 1999)	Albrecht *et al.* 2000; Dega 2002
Laang Spean	Cambodia	Possible Neolithic deposits: *ca.* 4050 BP (Mourer and Mourer 1970)	Mourer and Mourer 1970
Man Bac	Northern Vietnam	4000–3500 cal. BP (Oxenham et al. 2008)	Nguyen 2006; Oxenham *et al.* 2011
Non Nok Tha (Early Period)	Northeast Thailand	*ca.* 4000 BP (Gorman and Charoenwongsa 1976)	Gorman and Charoenwongsa 1976; Bayard 1977; Rispoli 1997; Bayard and Solheim 2009
Nong Nor (Phase 1)	Coastal central Thailand	4500–4100 cal. BP (Higham and Hogg 1998)	Higham and Thosarat 1998a, 1998b; O'Reilly 1998
Samrong Sen	Cambodia	3230±120 BP (Carbonnel and Delebrias 1968)	Mourer 1977; Vanna 2002; Heng 2007
Tha Kae (Layer 3)	Central Thailand	Neolithic occupation: end of the third millennium BC to the beginning of the second millennium BC, based on ceramic typologies (Rispoli 1992, 1997; Ciarla n.d.)	Ciarla n.d., 1992; Rispoli 1992, 1997
Xom Ren	Northern Vietnam	Phung Nguyen phase/early Bronze Age (Nguyen 2006)	Nguyen 2006; Hán 2009

Source: C. Sarjeant.

Methodology for the correspondence analysis

Comparison of ceramic assemblages has traditionally relied on classifications using the type-variety system coupled with pottery seriation, stratigraphic analysis and, until chronometric dating techniques became widely available, culture-historical approaches (Dunnell 1986). More recent research often extends beyond classificatory approaches, including rigorous and systematic methods of analysis that study 'phenotypic change as a result of variation and selective retention' in order to overcome the untestable nature of the inferences that might otherwise result (Neff 1993: 39). Such systematic and intensive comparative methods, employing many cases and many variables, additionally facilitate an understanding of variation over time and space (Caramani 2009: 15; Smith and Peregrine 2012).

There are many factors that affect comparative studies: sample size, sample selection, contextualisation, spatial and temporal scale, synchronic versus diachronic perspectives, whether the data are primary or secondary, whether the data are archaeological or historical, how the data are interpreted, and stage in research trajectory (Smith and Peregrine 2012). Within this comparative study, the sample size and selection are impacted upon by the nature of the excavation and the recording, analysis, interpretation and publication of the material, especially as so many different researchers across such a wide region are included. This study is presented as a preliminary, systematic and intensive comparison that can be expanded upon as additional information for Southeast Asian contexts becomes available.

Correspondence Analysis (CA) is an exploratory analytical technique that is essentially a principal component analysis of tables of categorical data, and the results are illustrated in a graphical plot of the relationship between the rows and columns of a table (Baxter 2003: 137). The CA undertaken here aims for a systematic comparison of the ceramics and other material culture between sites in southern Vietnam, and MSEA in general, improving on the broad descriptive approaches and illustrative data presentations on which past comparisons have relied. The data employed here result from personal observations of some collections but other collections are represented only by their published documentation. Further, to relate the chronology of the analysed sites to the sequence at An Son, the material culture at An Son was divided into a burial phase and early, middle and late phases of occupation.

In the present study, each material-culture trait was treated separately as a single variable. This is to account for and manage the high variability of material culture when a wide geographic area is examined. Further, each variable was scored as present (1) or absent (0), because reliable quantitative data are not available for most of the sites. Absence was assigned when no information for that variable was available; this may not always mean that the variable concerned was not present, but that there is no evidence for its presence. The CA was conducted with GenStat software (VSN International 2011).

The identified variables for the CA included the major ceramic vessel forms, modes of decoration and surface treatment, location of decoration on ceramic vessels, ceramic temper when possible, and the presence (or absence) of animal bones, specific stone tools, other stone and bone/ivory tools and ornaments, and ceramic/clay items like roundels and pellets at An Son and the other 14 assessed sites. A total of 131 cultural variables were included in the CA, of which 73 were ceramic vessel variables and the remaining 58 were other material-culture variables (Table 9.2).

The CA resulted in values for a number of dimensions, of which two were then plotted. The correspondence scores for the sites and variables were plotted to identify the sites that are most similar or different in terms of material culture, and also the material culture variables that resulted in these similarities and differences. Two plots are presented for each analysis, one of the material-culture variables and one of the sites. The scale on these plots reflects the variability of the total analysed sample (Figure 9.2).

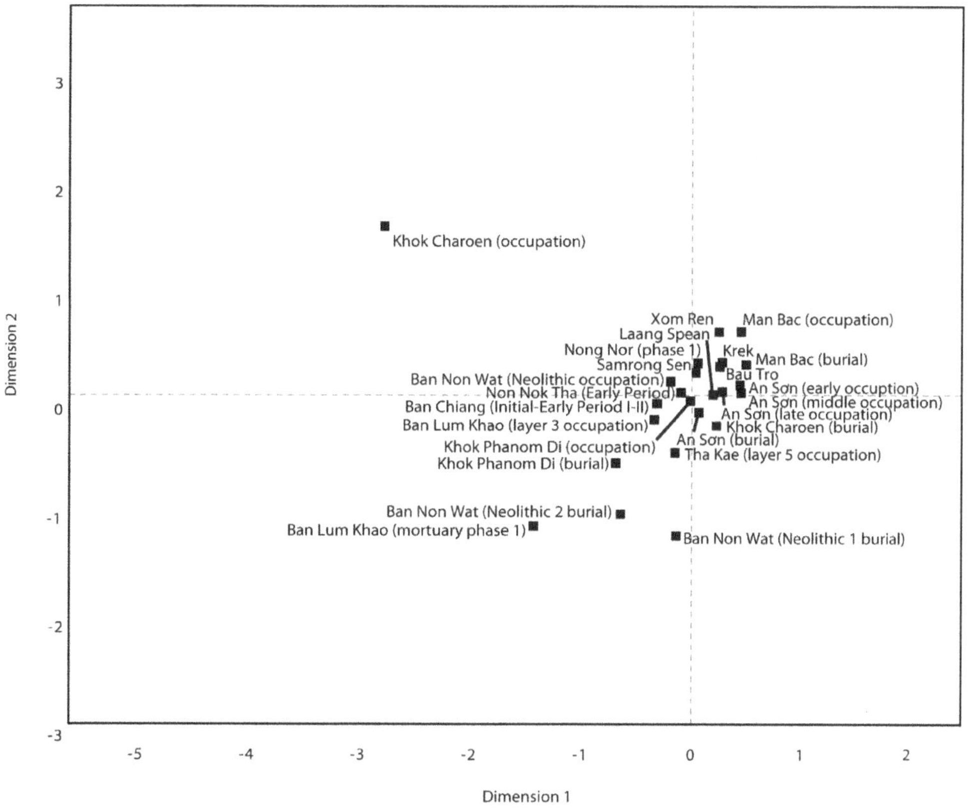

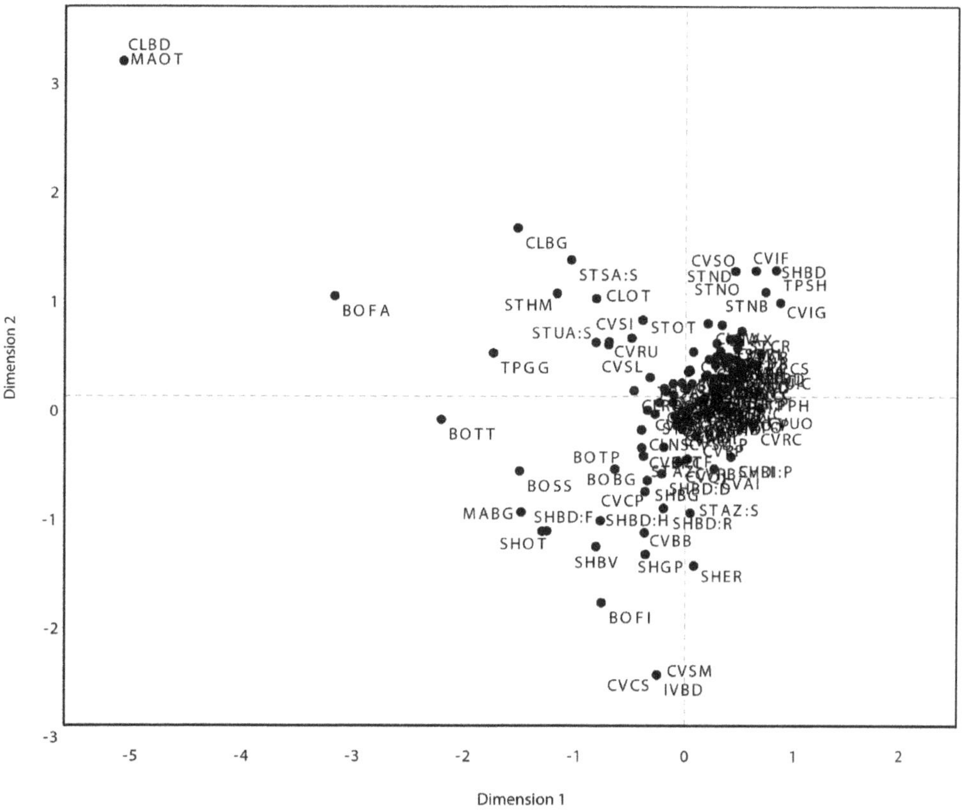

Figure 9.2 CA plots for the Southeast Asian Neolithic cultural variables. Occupation and burial data separated. Top: sites; bottom: variables. Refer to Table 9.2 for variable codes.

Source: C. Sarjeant.

Results

Two CAs are presented here, one that separates the occupational and burial phases for each site when possible (Figure 9.2), and one that combines this data for each site except An Son (Figure 9.3). The variables are coded with an abbreviation, as summarised in Table 9.2. When the sites are separated into occupation and burial phases, the CA plot (Figure 9.2) shows a main cluster of sites that crosses the various regions of MSEA, unrelated to chronology. This main cluster includes Nong Nor, Samrong Sen, Krek, Bau Tro, Man Bac (burial), An Son (early, middle and late occupation), Laang Spean, Ban Non Wat (occupation), Non Nok Tha, Ban Chiang, Khok Phanom Di (occupation), An Son (burial), Khok Charoen (burial), and Ban Lum Khao (occupation); in summary, northern, central and southern Vietnam and Cambodia, together with the occupation phases from the northeast and southern coastal Thailand sites.

The An Son burials cluster more closely with the late occupation than the early or middle occupation, which is concordant with the dates for the burials. The occupation assemblages from Ban Non Wat and Khok Phanom Di may also have predominantly predated their burials, which may explain why these occupation phases do not cluster with these sites' burial phases but instead cluster with the An Son occupation phases. Finally, the majority of the variables are associated with this main cluster of sites.

Lying slightly outside of the main cluster, Man Bac (occupation) and Xom Ren are closely related to each other. This is because they share the presence of nephrite artefacts, shell temper in the ceramics, and geometric impressions, scroll incisions and eye-shaped incisions (pottery decorations). Outliers of the CA plot included Khok Charoen (occupation), because of the presence of clay beads and marble items; Ban Lum Khao (burial), because of its absence of artefact variability; Ban Non Wat Neolithic burial Phases 1 and 2, because of the presence of a range of shell, ivory and marble ornaments and curvilinear incisions and painting on the ceramic vessels; Tha Kae, because of the presence of painted curvilinear designs; and Khok Phanom Di (burial), because of the presence of a wide range of shell items.

Table 9.2 Analysed variables and codes.

Code	Variables
BOAW	bone awl
BOBG	bone bangle
BOBO	cattle remains
BOCA	dog remains
BOFA	other faunal remains
BOFH	bone fishhook
BOFI	fish remains
BOOT	bone worked
BOPT	bone tool/weapon point
BOSS	pig remains
BOTP	tooth pendant
BOTT	turtle/tortoise remains
CLAV	clay anvil
CLBD	clay bead
CLBG	clay bangle
CLCO	clay counter/roundel
CLNS	clay net sinker/weight
CLOT	clay artefact

Code	Variables
CLPL	clay pellet
CLRO	clay roller
CLSW	clay spindle whorl
CVAI	applique and incision on top
CVAP	applique
CVBB	black burnish/surface
CVBO	decoration on body
CVBS	decoration on base
CVCB	combed
CVCC	coarse cord-marking
CVCI	curvilinear incision with impressed fill
CVCM	cord-marking
CVCO	ceramic vessel concave rim independent restricted
CVCO:P	ceramic vessel concave rim independent restricted:pedestal
CVCP	curvilinear painting
CVCS	curvilinear incision with paint/slip/burnish fill
CVDI	ceramic vessel direct independent restricted
CVDI:P	ceramic vessel direct independent restricted:pedestal
CVDS	dentate stamping
CVEI	ceramic vessel everted independent restricted
CVEI:C	ceramic vessel everted independent restricted:carinated
CVEI:P	ceramic vessel everted independent restricted:pedestal
CVFI	fingernail impression
CVHI	horizontal incision
CVIC	incised
CVIF	geometric eye-shape incision with impressed or incised fill
CVIG	geometric impressed
CVII	incised and impressed
CVIP	impressed
CVLP	decoration at lip
CVNI:C	ceramic vessel inverted independent restricted:carinated
CVPC	punctate stamping: circular
CVPD	decoration on pedestal
CVPH	punctate stamping: hollow circular/large circular
CVPI	paddle impression
CVPQ	punctate stamping: quadrangular/triangular
CVQI	geometric quadrangular incision with impressed fill
CVQO	geometric quadrangular incision
CVRB	red burnish
CVRC	roulette stamping: zigzag line continuous
CVRD	roulette stamping: dotted linear
CVRM	decoration on rim
CVRP	red paint
CVRS	roulette stamping: square
CVRT	roulette stamping: dotted zigzag line continuous
CVRU	roulette stamping: unspecified

Code	Variables
CVRZ	roulette stamping: zigzag lines
CVSD	decoration on pronounced shoulder
CVSH	decoration on shoulder
CVSI	S'/scroll shape incision with impressed fill
CVSL	red slip
CVSM	shell impressed
CVSO	S'/scroll shape incision
CVSR	ceramic vessel simple restricted
CVSR:C	ceramic vessel simple restricted:carinated
CVSR:P	ceramic vessel simple restricted:pedestal
CVSU	ceramic vessel simple unrestricted
CVSU:C	ceramic vessel simple unrestricted:carinated
CVSU:P	ceramic vessel simple unrestricted:pedestal
CVTF	geometric triangular/diamond incision with diagonal incision fill
CVTI	geometric triangular/diamond incision with impressed fill
CVTO	geometric/diamond triangular incision
CVUI	geometric circular/semi-circular incision with impressed fill
CVUO	geometric circular/semi-circular incision
CVVI	vertical incision
CVWL	white lime
CVWV	wavy incision
CVXI	criss-cross incision
CVZZ	zigzag incision
IVBD	ivory bead
IVBG	ivory bangle
MABG	marble bangle
MAOT	marble other
SHBD	shell bead
SHBD:D	shell bead:disc shape
SHBD:F	shell bead:funnel shape
SHBD:H	shell bead:H-shape
SHBD:R	shell bead:rectangular/barrel/cylindrical-shape
SHBG	shell bangle
SHBV	shell bivalve
SHER	shell earring
SHGP	shell gastropod
SHOT	shell worked
SHRI	shell ring
STAX	stone axe
STAZ	stone adze
STAZ:S	stone adze:small
STBD	stone bead
STBG	stone bangle
STBL	stone blade
STBS	stone burnishing
STCH	stone chisel

Code	Variables
STCR	stone core
STFL	stone flake
STHM	stone hammerstone
STNB	stone nephrite bangle
STND	stone nephrite bead
STNO	stone nephrite other
STOT	stone other
STRO	stone red ochre
STSA	stone shouldered adze
STSA:S	stone shouldered adze:small
STSS	stone polishing/sandstone/coarse grained
STUA	stone unshouldered adze
STUA:S	stone unshouldered adze:small
STWH	stone whetstone/grinding stone/fine grained
TPCL	other calcareous temper
TPCS	coarse sand temper
TPFB	fibre/rice chaff temper
TPGG	grog temper
TPPH	phosphate temper
TPSA	sand temper
TPSH	shell temper

Source: C. Sarjeant.

Further commentary for Figure 9.2 is provided as the second CA plot reveals clearer relationships between the sites. This is achieved by combining the occupation and burial phases so as to increase the number of variables that can be recorded as present for each site (Figure 9.3). It emphasises the differences between sites that clustered together in Figure 9.2 despite known marked differences in material culture between the sites. Seven apparent groups can be identified in the second CA plot (Figure 9.3), and the corresponding variables shared by the sites within each group are summarised in Table 9.3. Some of these groups correspond closely with those in Figure 9.2, such as group 6 (Xom Ren and Man Bac), while others correspond loosely, such as Group 7 (Laang Spean, Samrong Sen and Krek). Ban Lum Khao and An Son (burial) are the main outliers, although An Son (burial) also corresponds with Group 1, particularly the late occupation phase at An Son.

While ceramic vessel forms are highly variable and difficult to compare in such an analysis and ceramic temper sequences for most sites in the region are incompletely documented, Rispoli's (as previously analysed by Rispoli 1997, 2007) disentangling of the incised and impressed designs that predominate in the decorative modes of the assemblages has added to our understanding of the movements of these designs during the Neolithic. This extends to the relationship between these motifs and other material cultural variables within Southeast Asia. The distributions of selected analysed variables in the CAs, intended to be open-ended areas rather than to have rigid boundaries, are presented in Figures 9.4, 9.5 and 9.6. The absence of central Vietnamese sites in this comparative study is a notable deficiency, and hinders interpretation for MSEA as a whole. Further research across MSEA is needed to add to the currently available perspective.

Table 9.3 The CA plots and contributing variables for groups in Figures 9.2 and 9.3.

Group number	Corresponding sites	Corresponding variables
1	Bau Tro An Son (early occupation) Nong Nor (Phase 1) An Son (middle occupation) An Son (late occupation)	Shell rectangular beads Circular and semi-circular incisions on ceramic vessels Shouldered and unshouldered adzes, varying sizes Concave rim ceramic vessels
2	An Son (burial)	Concave rim ceramic vessels with pedestal
3	Ban Lum Khao (Neolithic Layer 3 and Mortuary Phase 1)	Absence of artefact variability
4	Ban Non Wat (Neolithic Phases 1 and 2) Khok Charoen	Shell artefacts Marble artefacts Ivory artefacts Small adzes Curvilinear incision and painting on ceramic vessels
5	Ban Chiang (Initial-Early Period I-II) Tha Kae (Layer 5 neolithic) Non Nok Tha (Early Period) Khok Phanom Di	Shell artefacts Ivory artefacts Unshouldered adzes Zigzag incision on ceramic vessels Black surface treatment on ceramic vessels Curvilinear incision and painting on ceramic vessels S-shaped incision with impressed fill on ceramic vessels
6	Xom Ren Man Bac	Nephrite artefacts Geometric impression on ceramic vessels Shell temper in ceramic fabrics Scroll incisions on ceramic vessels Eye-shaped incisions on ceramic vessels
7	Laang Spean Samrong Sen Krek	Flake and core stone tool artefacts Hollow circle punctate stamping on ceramic vessels

Source: C. Sargeant.

Comparison between An Son and MSEA material culture

Many of the material culture variables studied in the CA are influenced by chronology. This may explain why An Son displays its greatest correspondence with two other early Neolithic sites, Nong Nor (Phase 1) and Bau Tro, in the CA (Figure 9.3). The particularly strong affinities between An Son and Nong Nor (Phase 1) include the band designs on the shoulders of ceramic vessels. One difference is the rarity of shell artefacts at An Son and their greater variety and abundance at Nong Nor (Phase 1), but this may be due to, respectively, restricted and ready access to a marine environment with suitable shells.

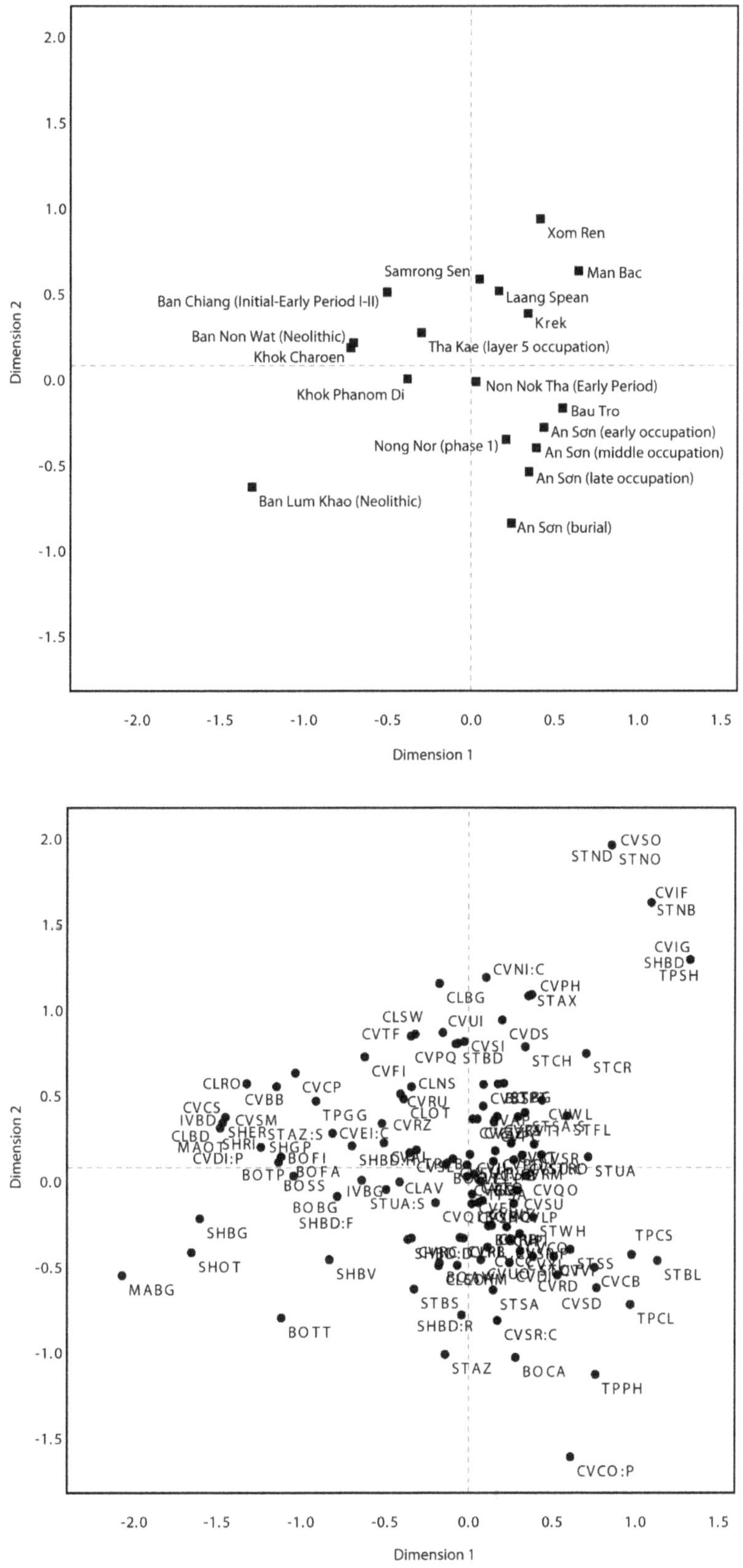

Figure 9.3 CA plots for the Southeast Asian Neolithic cultural variables. Occupation and burial data combined, except for An Son. Top: sites; bottom: variables. Refer to Table 9.2 for variable codes.

Source: C. Sarjeant.

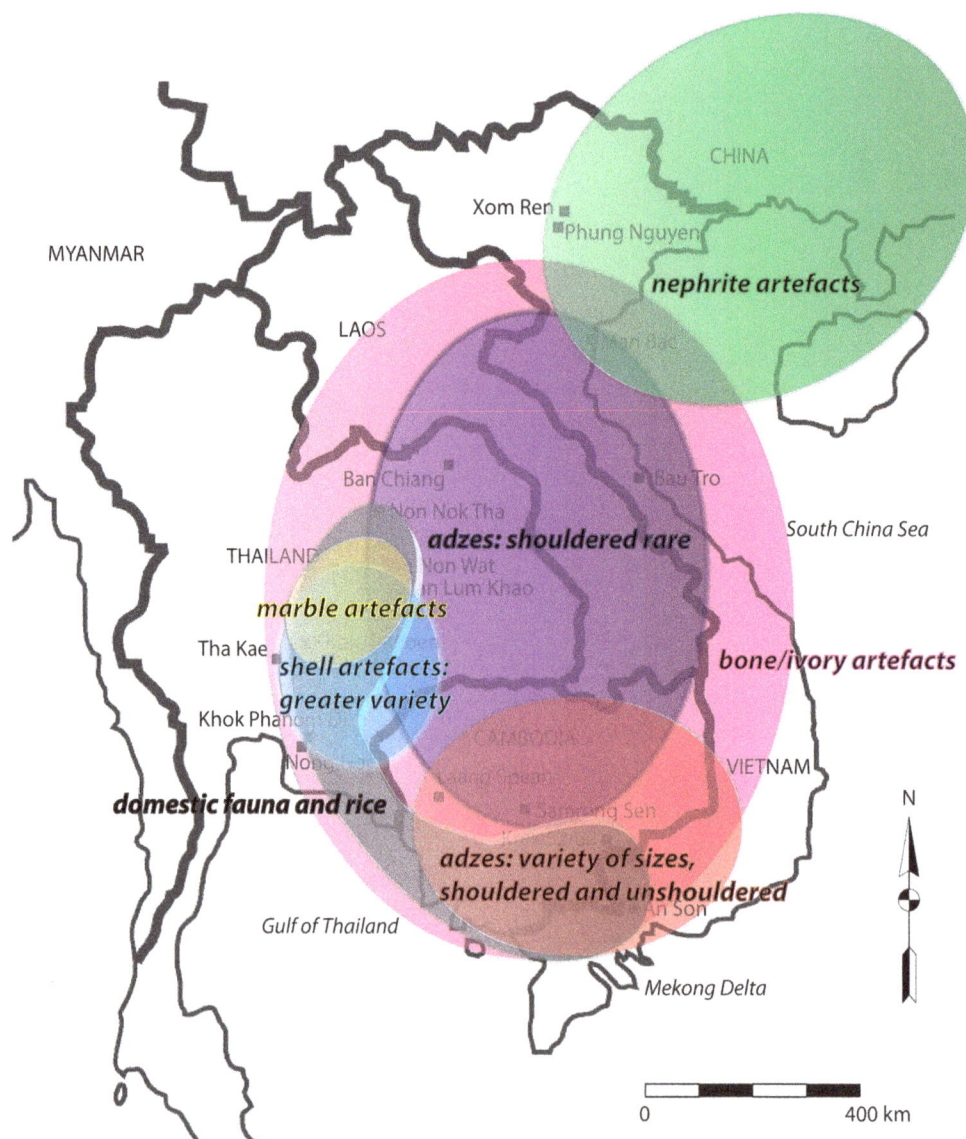

Figure 9.4 Distribution of notable non-ceramic material culture in Mainland Southeast Asia.
Source: C. Sarjeant.

However, not all early MSEA Neolithic sites are similar to An Son in their material culture. Khok Phanom Di is a case in point on account of its more variable and abundant bone and shell artefacts compared with An Son, and its presence of marble artefacts (absent from An Son). However, Khok Phanom Di would have had ready access to marine shell, potentially explaining this difference from An Son. An Son was also the more distant site from limestone and marble deposits, which in MSEA are located in the Lopburi region, and near Man Bac, Bau Tro, Samrong Sen and Laang Spean (Fromaget et al. 1971; Vimuktanandana 1999). Overland exchange of Lopburi marble a short distance south to Khok Phanom Di and a longer distance north to the Khorat Plateau is the likely explanation for the presence of marble artefacts at Khok Phanom Di and the Khorat Plateau sites.

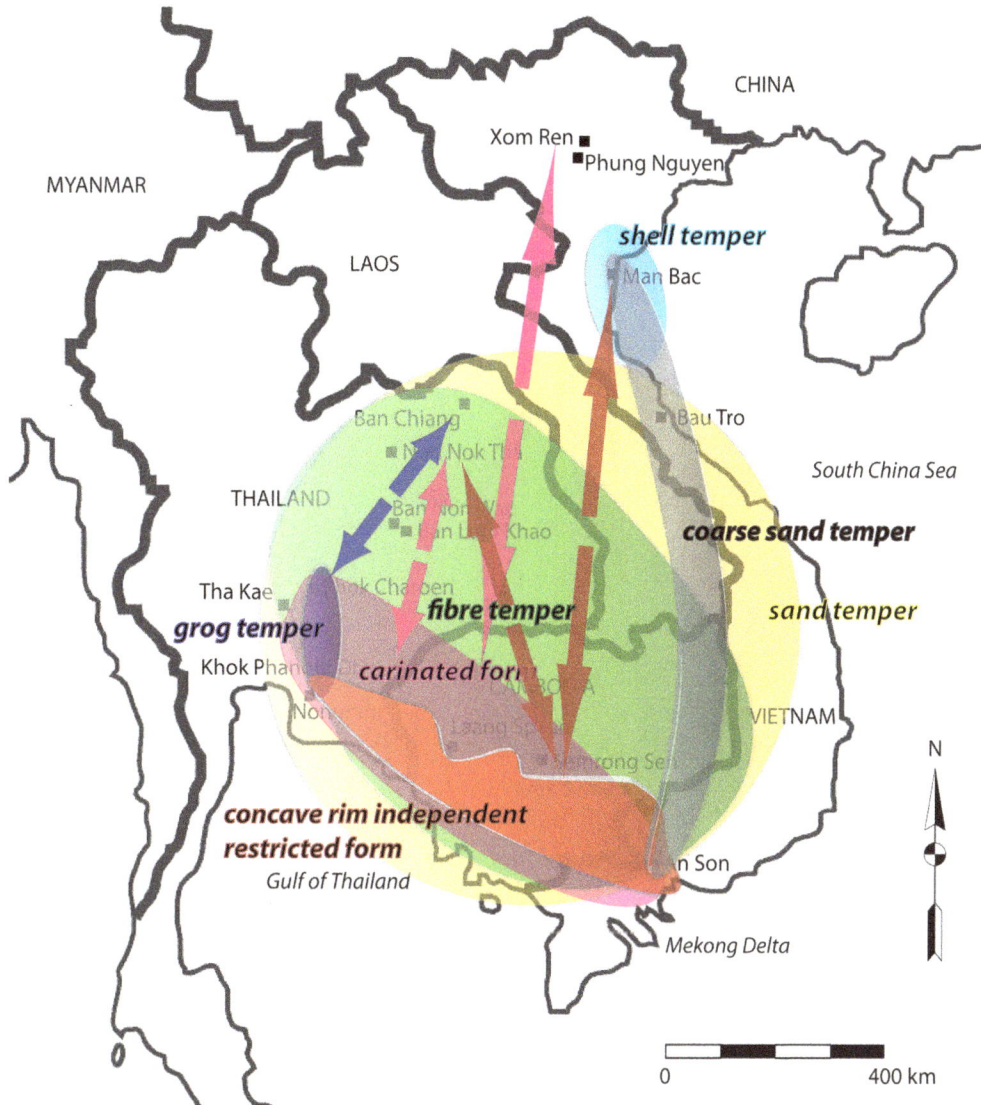

Figure 9.5 Distribution of notable An Son ceramic vessel forms and dominant tempers in Mainland Southeast Asia. The arrows point to sites beyond the coloured sphere with the specified variable.

Source: C. Sarjeant.

Suitable stone sources for adze production include basalt outcrops in Dong Nai Province, southeastern Cambodia and the Khorat Plateau in northeast Thailand, and granite outcrops near Khok Phanom Di and Nong Nor (Fromaget et al. 1971; Vimuktanandana 1999). The Dong Nai basalt was the closest significant source to An Son. The shape of the An Son adzes was probably related to the rectangular-sectioned adze technology based in the Dong Nai region, with the tools reduced and reworked at An Son to result in their notable variation in size. The southern Vietnam adze technology was unrelated to the technology of small, ovoid-sectioned basalt adzes in northeast Thailand.

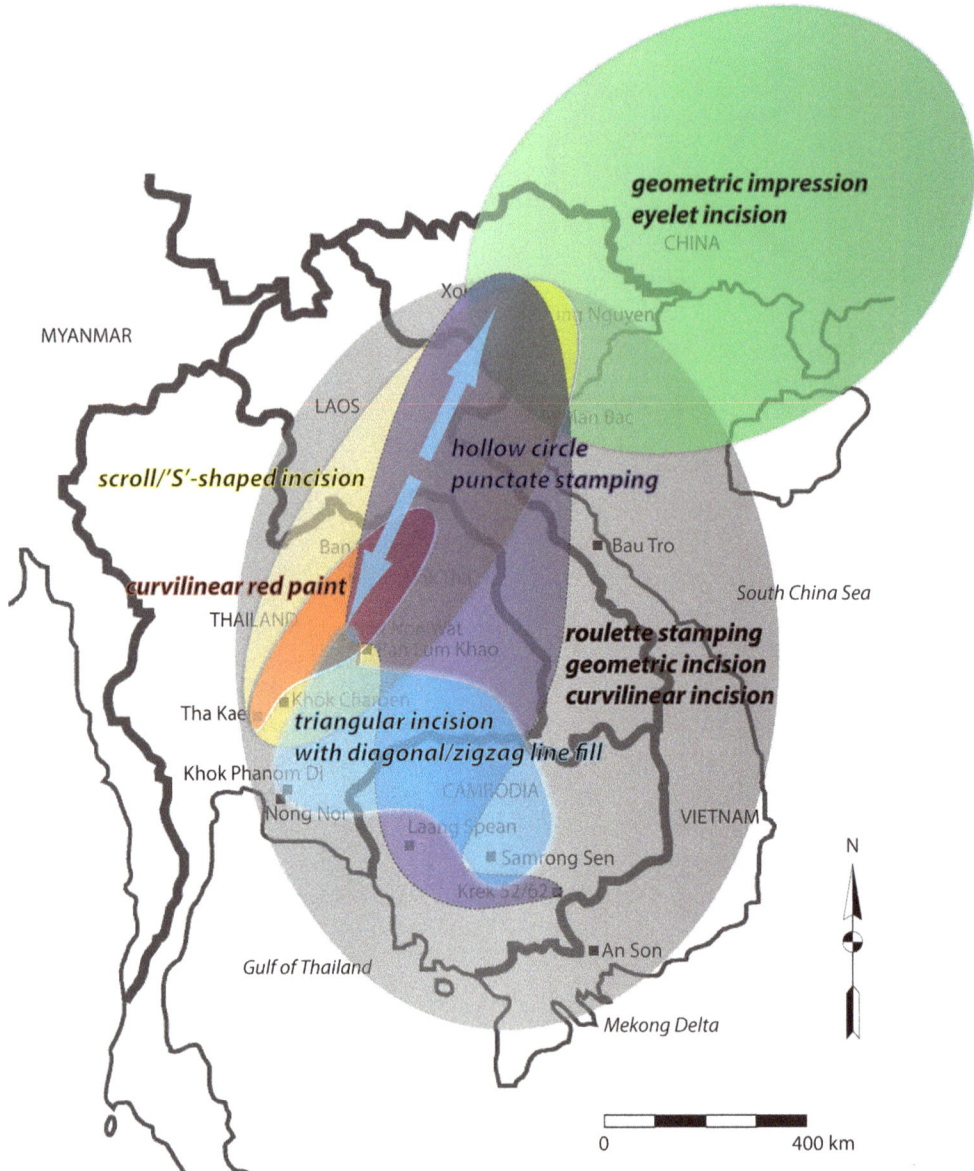

Figure 9.6 Distribution of notable modes of decoration on ceramic vessels in Mainland Southeast Asia. The arrows point to sites beyond the coloured sphere with the specified variable.

Source: C. Sarjeant.

Strong parallels have been established between the ceramic vessel forms of An Son and those at other Neolithic sites in southern Vietnam (Sarjeant 2012, 2014), but such parallels were limited in this study. Of the archaeological assemblages available for this study, the dominant restricted vessel form with a concave rim at An Son was restricted to the southern sites (including Khok Phanom Di and Krek), apart from some variations of this form observed at Man Bac. The concave rim forms were associated with band designs on the shoulder, typically roulette stamping between two horizontal incised lines. Roulette stamping, also known as rocker stamping, was formed by rolling a stamp with an impressed or relief motif around a vessel. The stamps could have been created by carving a cylindrical item, perhaps wood, or adhering plant weaving or knotted cord around a cylindrical item. While roulette stamping was highly sophisticated, detailed and varied at An Son, it was in fact a widespread mode of decoration in MSEA.

Roulette stamping appeared alongside many other modes of incised and impressed motifs during the Neolithic at other MSEA sites (see Rispoli 1997) where, also unlike at An Son, many decorated vessels had incised and impressed motifs that extended onto the body below the shoulder. In addition, painted motifs and 'S'-shaped incised motifs were restricted to northern Vietnam and northeast and central Thailand, and were never manifested in southern Vietnam. The limited variation in decorative mode at An Son, with a focus on variation within a single mode of decoration (roulette stamping) on one frequently produced vessel form, reflects an intensity in the ceramic manufacture of concave rim form vessels. While An Son was part of the incised and impressed tradition of Neolithic Southeast Asia, it was evidently not exposed to numerous decorative elaborations that held sway further north.

While the occurrence of roulette stamping is not unique to MSEA, and does not necessarily stipulate contact between sites from its presence alone, the overall combination of Neolithic features at An Son (domestic rice, dog and pig, polished stone technology, and incised and impressed ceramic vessels) implies an associated transference of this mode of decoration with Neolithic settlement. At the point of transference to southern Vietnam, certain material cultural variables were adopted and others were omitted. Those variables that were initially adopted developed locally over time, but contacts did not extend into the wider Neolithic world inclusive of ornate shell and marble ornaments, painted ceramics and increasingly variable incised ceramics. An Son was one of the sites at the 'end of the line' in terms of MSEA Neolithic traditions. It contrasts with centrally located sites like Ban Non Wat which received goods and technological ideas from both the south and north, visible in its shell and marble artefacts and its ceramics.

The likely immediate source for the An Son Neolithic was northeast and central Thailand, particularly in view of the specific parallels between An Son and Nong Nor (Phase 1) in the CA. There are also clear similarities between An Son and Krek in their material culture. While these are less clearly reflected in the CA, this could at least partly reflect taphonomic factors, because the local soil conditions at Krek did not allow for the preservation of bone and shell artefacts. In summary, there is evidence for long-lasting and widespread Neolithic traditions that extended to southern Vietnam, but little sign of direct contact between An Son and sites further north during the 1,000 years of occupation at An Son, when contact via material culture was limited to the more immediate vicinity of southern Vietnam and southeastern Cambodia.

Towards a characterisation of Neolithic An Son

Whilst there is general acceptance for a Neolithic transference from southern China to MSEA, with a potentially ultimate origin in the Yangtze River, its timing, events and routes via river courses or coastal lowlands continue to be discussed (Higham 2002; Rispoli 2007; Fuller et al. 2010; Nakamura 2010; Zhang and Hung 2010; Zhao 2010; Bellwood 2011; Castillo 2011; Higham et al. 2011; Lu 2011). Increasingly, more interpretations posit multiple movements over a period of time and the adoption of selected traits in the transition to agriculture (Zhang and Hung 2010). Rispoli (2007) proposes that particular traits were chosen or rejected as material culture was moved from the Yangtze into southern and southeastern China, and then into MSEA. Fuller (2011) hypothesises that distinct movements with taro and rice millet cultigens occurred at different times and may have overlaid former routes.

The ceramic evidence is consistent with hypotheses that propose riverine (as opposed to coastal) origins for Austroasiatic speakers, and specifically their movement down the Mekong (Sidwell and Blench 2011). This could be responsible for the appearance of a similar Neolithic expression, inclusive of incised and impressed decoration on the ceramics, alongside rivers in MSEA (Higham 2004; Bellwood 2005: 131–134; Rispoli 2007). While there is archaeobotanical evidence for the dispersal of rice cultivation along coastal lowlands and coastlines in Southeast Asia (Fuller et al. 2010; Fuller et al. 2011), there is currently a lack of ceramic evidence to support this. On the other hand, particularly if multiple waves of cultigens entered Southeast Asia (Fuller 2011), there may be no reason to expect a direct correspondence between rice and ceramic origins.

At An Son, the introductions of rice, domestic animals, polished stone tools and ceramics occurred together at or shortly after the initiation of the settlement. Thus, by the time cultivation and domestic animals reached southern Vietnam, there is evidence of a collective package associated with Neolithic occupation. This rapid adoption of a developed Neolithic culture was probably well-established in MSEA (Zhang and Hung 2010). However, the onset of this widespread Neolithic culture in southern Vietnam led to regionalisation and innovation at a local level almost immediately after settlement. Long-lasting traditions of ceramic manufacture, observed all over MSEA, were maintained as new ones were established at a local and regional level. The potters at An Son actively maintained ceramic traditions that connected southern Vietnam with the wider MSEA Neolithic, whilst also investing in new traditions that exhibited a local material identity.

The research into Neolithic MSEA presented here illustrates both consistency and discontinuity in terms of interaction with the Neolithic landscape:

1. An Son belongs to a cultural lineage connected to the sites of coastal central Thailand and Cambodia.

2. A more distant, perhaps ancestral, relationship is evident between southern Vietnam and northeast Thailand; however, a number of northeast Thailand traits did not reach southern Vietnam.

3. There is no clear relationship between the sites of southern Vietnam and northern Vietnam, which display distinct ceramic affinities.

4. More generally, there is evidence for separate northern and southern Neolithic traditions, whose components intermingled only in the area of northeast and inland central Thailand and northern Cambodia.

Distinct affinities are exhibited by the sites of northern and southern Vietnam and, while the northern Vietnam ceramic practices are evident in central and northeast Thailand, it appears that some of these never reached southern Vietnam. Thus, regardless of the actual date and route for the initial Neolithic occupation of southern Vietnam, its sites evidently belonged to a major tradition that appears to have followed the Mekong River and its major tributaries. This is suggestive of interactions and movements of Neolithic peoples from Cambodia and northeast Thailand into southern Vietnam, and also across land and/or coastlines from central Thailand, through Cambodia, to southern Vietnam.

Acknowledgements

I would firstly like to thank my PhD supervisor, Professor Peter Bellwood, and his continuing support of my research on the Neolithic occupation of Southeast Asia. I would also like to thank Philip J. Piper and Hsiao-chun Hung for inviting me to contribute to Peter's Festschrift. I thank Dougald O'Reilly at The Australian National University for his supervision. I also would like to thank Marc Oxenham at ANU, Bui Chi Hoang of the Centre for Archaeological Studies, Southern Institute of Social Sciences, Ho Chi Minh City, and Nguyen Kim Dung of the Institute of Archaeology, Hanoi. The excavations at An Son were funded by a Discovery Grant from the Australian Research Council (DP0666607). My own research was funded by an Australian Postgraduate Award. There are a number of individuals who assisted during the An Son ceramic sorting process at the Long An Provincial Museum: Nguyen Khanh Trung Kien, Nguyen Manh

Quoc, Dang Ngoc Kinh, Nguyen Khai Quynh, Le Hoang Phong, Nguyen Phuong Thao, Tran Thi Kim Quy, Vo Thanh Huong, and Van Ngoc Bich. I would like to sincerely thank Nguyen Khanh Trung Kien for his help in accessing museums in southern Vietnam. The comparative sites were supported by information provided by Peter Bellwood, Charles Higham, Nigel Chang, Fiorella Rispoli and Roberto Ciarla, Helmut Loofs-Wissowa, Hubert Forestier and Heng Sophady, Nguyen Kim Dung and Nishimura Masanari.

References

Albrecht, G., M. Noel Haidle, C. Sivleng, L.H. Heang, S. Heng, T. Heng, S. Mao, K. Sirik, S. Som, C. Thuy and L. Vin. 2000. Circular earthwork Krek 52/62: Recent research on the prehistory of Cambodia. *Asian Perspectives* 39(1–2): 20–46. doi.org/10.1353/asi.2000.0002.

Baxter, M. 2003. *Statistics in Archaeology*. London: Arnold.

Bayard, D.T. 1977. Phu Wiang pottery and the prehistory of Northeastern Thailand. *Modern Quaternary Research in Southeast Asia* 3: 57–102.

Bayard, D.T. and W.G. Solheim, II. 2009. Archaeological Excavations at Non Nok Tha, Thailand. guampedia.com/archaeological-excavations-at-non-nok-tha-thailand, viewed 23 November 2011.

Bellwood, P. 2005. *First Farmers: The Origins of Agricultural Societies*. Malden, MA: Blackwell.

——. 2011. The checkered prehistory of rice movement southwards as a domesticated cereal-from the Yangzi to the Equator. *Rice* 4(3): 93–103.

Bellwood, P. and M. Oxenham. 2008. The expansions of farming societies and the role of the Neolithic Demographic Transition. In B-A. Jean-Pierre and B.-Y. Ofer (eds), *The Neolithic Demographic Transition and its Consequences*, pp. 13–34. Netherlands: Springer Netherlands. doi.org/10.1007/978-1-4020-8539-0_2.

Bellwood, P., M. Oxenham, C.H. Bui, K.D. Nguyen, A. Willis, C. Sarjeant, P. Piper, H. Matsumura, K. Tanaka, T. Higham, M.Q. Nguyen, N.K. Dang, K.T.K. Nguyen, T.H. Vo, N.B. Van, T.K.Q. Tran, P.T. Nguyen, F. Campos, Y. Sato, L.C. Nguyen and N. Amano. 2011. An Son and the Neolithic of Southern Vietnam. *Asian Perspectives* 50: 144–174. doi.org/10.1353/asi.2011.0007.

Bubpha, S. 2003. A comparative study of ceramic petrography from Ban Don Thong Chai and Ban Chiang. *Bulletin of the Indo-Pacific Prehistory Association* 23(1): 15–18.

Bulbeck, D. 2011. Biological and cultural evolution in the population and culture history of *Homo sapiens* in Malaya. In N. Enfield (ed.), *Dynamics of Human Diversity: The Case of Mainland Southeast Asia*, pp. 207–255. Canberra: Pacific Linguistics.

Caramani, D. 2009. *Introduction to the Comparative Method with Boolean Algebra*. Los Angeles: Sage. doi.org/10.4135/9781412984690.

Carbonnel, J.P. and G. Delebrias. 1968. Premiere datations absolues de trois gisements neolithiques cambodgiens (First absolute dates of three Neolithic Cambodian deposits). *Comptes Rendus de l'Academie des Sciences* 267: 1432–1434 (in French).

Castillo, C. 2011. Rice in Thailand: The archaeobotanical contribution. *Rice* 4(3): 114–120. doi.org/10.1007/s12284-011-9070-2.

Chang, N. 2004. The personal ornaments. In C.F.W. Higham and R. Thosarat (eds), *The Excavation of Ban Lum Khao*, pp. 217–230. Bangkok: The Thai Fine Arts Department.

Ciarla, R. 1992. The Thai-Italian Lopburi regional archaeological project: preliminary results. In G. Ian, (ed.), *Southeast Asian Archaeology 1990: Proceedings of the 3rd Conference of the European Association of Southeast Asian Archaeologists*, pp. 111–128. Hull: Center for South-East Asian Studies, University of Hull.

——. n.d. The Thai-Italian 'Lopburi Regional Archaeological Project' – LoRAP: A preliminary report of fifteen years of activities. Unpublished report. Italian Institute for Africa and the Orient, Rome.

Dega, M.F. 1999. Circular settlements within eastern Cambodia. *Indo-Pacific Prehistory Association Bulletin* 18: 181–190. doi.org/10.7152/bippa.v18i0.11713.

——. 2002. *Prehistoric Circular Earthworks of Cambodia*. Oxford: Archaeopress (British Archaeological Reports).

Dunnell, R.C. 1986. Methodological issues in Americanist artifact classification. In S. Michael (ed.), *Advances in Archaeological Method and Theory*, pp. 149–207. New York: Academic Press. doi. org/10.1016/B978-0-12-003109-2.50007-6.

Fromaget, J., E. Saurin and H. Fontaine. 1971. *Geological Map of Vietnam, Cambodia and Laos*. 3rd edition. Dalat: National Geographic Directorate of Vietnam.

Fuller, D.Q. 2011. Pathways to Asian civilizations: Tracing the origins and spread of rice and rice cultures. *Rice* 4(3): 78–92. doi.org/10.1007/s12284-011-9078-7.

Fuller, D.Q., Y. Sato, C. Cristina, L. Qin, A. Weisskopf, E. Kingwell-Banham, J. Song, S.M. Ahn and J. van Etten. 2010. Consilience of genetics and archaeobotany in the entangled history of rice. *Archaeological and Anthropological Sciences* 2(2): 115–131. doi.org/10.1007/s12520-010-0035-y.

Fuller, D.Q., J. van Etten, K. Manning, C. Castillo, E. Kingwell-Banham, A. Weisskopf, L. Qin, Y. Sato and R.J. Hijmans. 2011. The contribution of rice agriculture and livestock pastoralism to prehistoric methane levels: An archaeological assessment. *The Holocene* 21(5): 743–759. doi. org/10.1177/0959683611398052.

Gorman, C.F. and P. Charoenwongsa. 1976. Ban Chiang: A mosaic of impressions from the first two years. *Expedition* 18(4): 14–26.

Hán, V.K. 2009. *Xom Ren: Mot di tich khao co dac biet quan trong cua thoi dai do dong Viet Nam (Xom Ren: The Archaeological Importance of Bronze Age Vietnam)*. Hanoi: Nha Xuat Ban Dai Hoc Quoc Gia Ha Noi (in Vietnamese).

Heng, S. 2007. A Study of Polished Stone Tools from Samrong Sen, Cambodia: the French Museum Collections. Unpublished Master of Arts thesis. Departement de Prehistoire, Museum National d'Histoire Naturelle, Paris.

Higham, C.F.W. 1996. *The Bronze Age of Southeast Asia*. Cambridge: Cambridge University Press.

——. 2002. Languages and farming dispersal: Austroasiatic languages and rice cultivation. In P. Bellwood and C. Renfrew (eds), *Examining the Farming/Language Dispersal Hypothesis*, pp. 223–232. Cambridge: McDonald Institute for Archaeological Research.

——. 2004. Mainland Southeast Asia from the Neolithic to the Iron age. In I. Glover and P. Bellwood (eds), *Southeast Asia: From Prehistory to History*, pp. 41–67. London and New York: RoutledgeCurzon.

——. 2009a. Layer five. In C.F.W. Higham and A. Kijngam (eds), *The Excavation of Ban Non Wat. Part One: Introduction*, pp. 27–31. Bangkok: The Thai Fine Arts Department.

——. 2009b. Layer four. In C.F.W. Higham and A. Kijngam (eds), *The Excavation of Ban Non Wat. Part One: Introduction*, pp. 33–50. Bangkok: The Thai Fine Arts Department.

——. 2009c. Summary. In C.F.W. Higham and A. Kijngam (eds), *The Excavation of Ban Non Wat. Part One: Introduction*, pp. 251–257. Bangkok: The Thai Fine Arts Department.

——. 2011a. Introduction. In C.F.W. Higham and A. Kijngam (eds), *The Excavation of Ban Non Wat. Part Two: The Neolithic Occupation*, pp. 1–3. Bangkok: The Thai Fine Arts Department.

——. 2011b. Summary and conclusions. In C.F.W. Higham and A. Kijngam (eds), *The Excavation of Ban Non Wat. Part Two: The Neolithic Occupation*, pp. 199–212. Bangkok: The Thai Fine Arts Department.

Higham, C.F.W. and R. Bannanurag. 1990. *The Excavation of Khok Phanom Di, a Prehistoric Site in Central Thailand. Volume I: Excavation, Chronology and Human Burials*. London: The Society of Antiquaries of London.

Higham, C.F.W. and T. Higham. 2009a. The chronology. In C.F.W. Higham, and A. Kijngam (eds), *The Excavation of Ban Non Wat. Part One: Introduction*, pp. 17–25. Bangkok: The Thai Fine Arts Department.

——. 2009b. A new chronological framework for prehistoric Southeast Asia, based on a Bayesian model from Ban Non Wat. *Antiquity* 83: 125–144. doi.org/10.1017/S0003598X00098136.

Higham, C.F.W. and A. Kijngam (eds). 2009. *The Excavation of Ban Non Wat: Introduction*. Bangkok: The Thai Fine Arts Department.

——. 2011. *The Excavation of Ban Non Wat. Part Two: The Neolithic Occupation*. Bangkok: The Thai Fine Arts Department.

Higham, C.F.W. and R. Thosarat (eds). 1998a. *The Excavation of Nong Nor: A Prehistoric Site in Central Thailand*. Dunedin: Department of Anthropology, University of Otago.

——. 1998b. Section three: The first occupation phase. In C.F.W. Higham and R. Thosarat (eds), *The Excavation of Nong Nor: A Prehistoric Site in Central Thailand*, pp. 91–92. Dunedin: Department of Anthropology, University of Otago.

——. 2004a. The burials from mortuary phase 1. In C.F.W. Higham, and R. Thosarat (eds), *The Excavation of Ban Lum Khao*, pp. 23–32. Bangkok: The Thai Fine Arts Department.

——. 2004b. *The Excavation of Ban Lum Khao*. Bangkok: The Thai Fine Arts Department.

——. 2004c. *The Excavation of Khok Phanom Di, a Prehistoric Site in Central Thailand. Volume VII: Summary and Conclusions*. London: The Society of Antiquaries.

Higham, C.F.W. and W. Wiriyaromp. 2011a. Neolithic phase one. In C.F.W. Higham and A. Kijngam (eds), *The Excavation of Ban Non Wat. Part Two: The Neolithic Occupation*, pp. 15–64. Bangkok: The Thai Fine Arts Department.

——. 2011b. Neolithic phase two. In C.F.W. Higham and A. Kijngam (eds), *The Excavation of Ban Non Wat. Part Two: The Neolithic Occupation*, pp. 65–92. Bangkok: The Thai Fine Arts Department.

Higham, T.F.G. and A. Hogg. 1998. The radiocarbon chronology. In C.F.W. Higham and R. Thosarat (eds), *The Excavation of Nong Nor: A Prehistoric Site in Central Thailand*, pp. 23–25. Dunedin: Department of Anthropology, University of Otago.

Higham, C.F.W., X. Guangmao and L. Qiang. 2011. The prehistory of a Friction Zone: first farmers and hunters-gatherers in Southeast Asia *Antiquity* 85(328): 529–543.

Ho, C.M.W. 1984. The Pottery of Kok Charoen and Its Farther Context. Unpublished PhD thesis, Institute of Archaeology, University of London, London.

Lu, T.L-D. 2011. Early pottery in South China. *Asian Perspectives* 49(1): 1–42. doi.org/10.1353/asi.2010.0003.

Malleret, L. 1963. *L'Archeologie du delta du Mekong, tome quatrieme, Le Cisbassac (The Archaeology of the Mekong Delta, the fourth volume, The Cisbassac)*. Paris: École française d'Extrême-Orient (in French).

Matsumura, H. and M.F. Oxenham. 2011. Introduction: Man Bac biological research objectives. In M.F. Oxenham, H. Matsumura and K.D. Nguyen (eds), *Man Bac: The Excavation of a Neolithic Site in Northern Vietnam: The Biology*, pp. 1–8. Terra Australis 33. Canberra: ANU E Press.

McGovern, P.E., W.V. Watson, and C.W. Joyce. 1985. Ceramic technology at prehistoric Ban Chiang, Thailand: Physiochemical analyses. *MASCA Journal* 3(4): 104–113.

Mourer, C. and R. Mourer. 1970. The prehistoric industry of Laang Spean, Province Battambang, Cambodia. *Archaeology and Physical Anthropology in Oceania* 5: 128–146.

Mourer, R. 1977. Laang Spean and the prehistory of Cambodia. *Modern Quaternary Research in Southeast Asia* 3: 29–56.

Nakamura, S. 2010. The origin of rice cultivation in the Lower Yangtze Region, China. *Archaeological and Anthropological Sciences* 2(2): 107–113. doi.org/10.1007/s12520-010-0033-0.

Neff, H. 1993. Theory, sampling, and analytical techniques in the archaeological study of prehistoric ceramics. *American Antiquity*: 23–44. doi.org/10.1017/S0002731600056079.

Nguyen, K.D. 2006. Preliminary report on the Vietnamese-Japanese-Australian archaeological excavation at Man Bac site. Unpublished report. Anthropological and Archaeological Study on the Origin of Neolithic People in Mainland Southeast Asia, Hanoi.

Nishimura, M. 2002. Chronology of the Neolithic Age in the southern Vietnam. *Journal of Southeast Asian Archaeology* 22: 25–57.

Nishimura, M. and K.D. Nguyen. 2002. Excavation of An Son: A Neolithic mound site in the middle reach of the Vam Co Dong River, Southern Vietnam. *Bulletin of the Indo-Pacific Prehistory Association* 22: 101–109.

O'Reilly, D.J.W. 1998. The ceramic analysis. In C.F.W. Higham, and R. Thosarat (eds), *The Excavation of Nong Nor: A Prehistoric Site in Central Thailand*, pp. 97–118. Dunedin: Department of Anthropology, University of Otago.

Oxenham, M. and N. Tayles. 2006. *Bioarchaeology of Southeast Asia*. Cambridge: Cambridge University Press. doi.org/10.1017/CBO9780511584220.

Oxenham, M., H. Matsumura, K. Domett, K.T. Nguyen, K.D. Nguyen, L.C. Nguyen, D. Huffer and S. Muller. 2008. Health and the experience of childhood in late neolithic Viet Nam. *Asian Perspectives* 47(2): 190–209. doi.org/10.1353/asi.0.0001.

Oxenham, M., H. Matsumura, and K.D. Nguyen (eds). 2011. *Man Bac: The Excavation of a Neolithic Site in Northern Vietnam: The Biology*. Terra Australis 33. Canberra: ANU E Press.

Patte, E. 1924. Le Kjokkenmodding neolithique du Bau Tro a Tam-toa pres de ng-hi (Annam) (The Neolithic of Bau Tro). *Bulletin de l'Ecole Francaise D'Extreme-Orient* 24(1): 521–561 (in French). doi.org/10.3406/befeo.1924.3013.

Pham, T.N. 1997. Bau Tro culture; characteristic features and regional variants. *Journal of Southeast Asian Archaeology* 17(6): 7–16.

Piper, P., F. Campos, N.K. Dang, N. Amano, M. Oxenham, C.H. Bui, P. Bellwood and A. Willis. 2014. Early evidence for pig and dog husbandry from the Neolithic site of An Son, southern Vietnam. *International Journal of Osteoarchaeology* 24: 68–72. doi.org/10.1002/oa.2226.

Rispoli, F. 1992. Preliminary report on the pottery from Tha Kae, Lopburi, central Thailand. In I. Glover (ed.), *Southeast Asian Archaeology: Proceedings of the Third Conference of the European Association of Southeast Asian Archaeologists*, pp. 129–142. Hull: Centre for South-East Asian Studies.

——. 1997. Late third-mid second millennium BC pottery traditions in central Thailand: some preliminary observations in a wider perspective. In R. Ciarla and F. Rispoli (eds), *Southeast Asian Archaeology 1992: Proceedings of the Fourth International Conference of the European Association of the South-East Asian Archaeologists*, pp. 59–97. Rome: Instituto Italiano per l'Africa e L'Oriente.

——. 2007. The incised & impressed pottery style of mainland Southeast Asia: following the paths of Neolithisation. *East and West, a quarterly published by the Istituto Italiano per l'Africa e l'Oriente* 57(1–4): 235–304.

Sarjeant, C. 2012. The Role of Potters at Neolithic An Son, Southern Vietnam. Unpublished PhD thesis, School of Archaeology and Anthropology, The Australian National University, Canberra.

——. 2014. *Contextualising the Neolithic Occupation of Southern Vietnam: The Role of Ceramics and Potters at An Son*. Terra Australis 42. Canberra: ANU Press.

Sidwell, P. and R. Blench. 2011. The Austroasiatic Urheimat: the southeastern riverine hypothesis. In N.J. Enfield (ed.), *Dynamics of Human Diversity: the case of mainland Southeast Asia*, pp. 315–343. Canberra: Pacific Linguistics.

Smith, M.E. and P. Peregrine. 2012. Approaches to comparative analysis in archaeology. In Michael E. Smith (ed.), *The Comparative Archaeology of Complex Societies*, pp. 4–20. Cambridge. Cambridge University Press.

Vanna, L. 2002. The Archaeology of Shell Matrix Sites in the Central Floodplain of the Tonle Sap River, Central Cambodia (The Shell Settlement Site of Samrong Sen and its Cultural Complexity). Unpublished PhD thesis, Sophia University, Tokyo.

Vimuktanandana, S. 1999. *Geological Map of Thailand*. Geological Survey Division, Bangkok: Department of Mineral Resources.

Vincent, B.A. 2004. *The Excavation of Khok Phanom Di, a Prehistoric Site in Central Thailand. Volume VI: The Pottery, Other Ceramic Materials and their Cultural Role. The Material Culture (Part II)*. London: The Society of Antiquaries of London.

VSN International. 2011. GenStat for Windows. 14th Edition. VSN International, Hemel Hempstead, UK. www.GenStat.co.uk, viewed 8 April 2011.

Watson, W. 1979. Kok Charoen and the early Metal Age of central Thailand. In R.B. Smith and W. Watson (eds), *Early South East Asia: Essays in Archaeology, History and Geographical Geography*, pp. 53–62. New York and Kuala Lumpur: Oxford University Press.

Wiriyaromp, W. 2007. The Neolithic Period in Thailand. Unpublished PhD thesis, Department of Anthropology, University of Otago, Dunedin.

——. 2011. The wider relationships of the Neolithic 1 ceramics. In C.F.W. Higham and A. Kijngam (eds), *The Excavation of Ban Non Wat. Part Two: The Neolithic Occupation*, pp. 108–123. Bangkok: The Thai Fine Arts Department.

Zhang, C. and H.-c. Hung. 2010. The emergence of agriculture in southern China. *Antiquity* 84: 11–25. doi.org/10.1017/S0003598X00099737.

Zhao, Z. 2010. New data and new issues for the study of origin of rice agriculture in China. *Archaeological and Anthropological Sciences* 2(2): 99–105. doi.org/10.1007/s12520-010-0028-x.

10

The Ryukyu Islands and the Northern Frontier of Prehistoric Austronesian Settlement

Mark J. Hudson

The origins and dispersals of Austronesian peoples have been widely discussed in Pacific archaeology. There is broad agreement that Taiwan was the primary source for the initial expansion of these human populations in the second half of the third millennium BC. From Taiwan, these Neolithic populations migrated into the Philippines, and then to Indonesia and the Marianas. Rice and pottery disappeared as Austronesians moved further into the Pacific, but agriculture, long-distance voyaging, and an ideology of exploration were widely shared hallmarks of the migration and colonisation.

While numerous studies have examined the movement of Austronesian-speaking peoples from Taiwan to the south and east, little attention has so far been given to expansions to the Ryukyu Islands, situated 110–320 km northeast of Taiwan. This paper argues that the southern Ryukyu Islands should be included within the Austronesian cultural sphere from the fourth millennium BP until the beginning of the second millennium AD. The prehistory of the southern Ryukyus is important to Austronesian studies because their proximity to Taiwan can help test models of Austronesian origins and early expansions. The southern Ryukyus form part of the northern frontier of settlement in the North Pacific, a frontier that followed a remarkably uniform line between latitudes 23–27°N. In the Ryukyus this frontier was maintained despite the existence of further habitable islands only 250 km to the north.

Introduction

The archaeology of the Pacific Ocean in the late Holocene can be divided into two strikingly different cultural zones. Predominantly agricultural populations speaking languages derived from a common ancestor and displaying numerous commonalities in social and cultural traditions colonised the North Pacific, as far as Hawai'i and the Marianas as well as much of the South Pacific. In contrast, the North Pacific coasts and islands above Hawai'i and the Marianas were populated by diverse cultures and languages possessed by peoples who were almost exclusively hunter-gatherers. The border between these two zones traversed a remarkably consistent line of latitude between 23 and 27°N. This paper will examine this frontier in more detail and will discuss the position of the southern Ryukyu Islands in Austronesian prehistory.

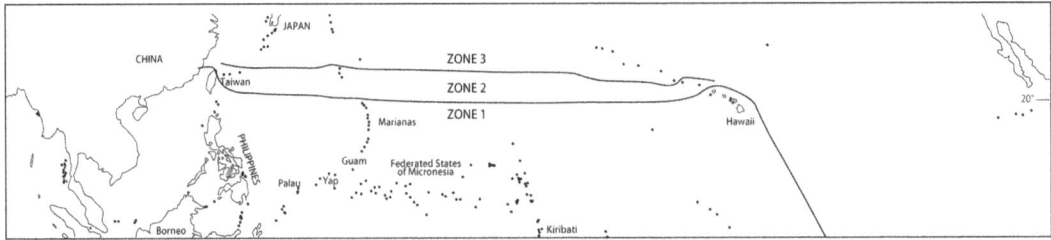

Figure 10.1 Austronesian settlement zones in the North Pacific.
Source: Drawn by J. Uchiyama using Peter Bellwood/ANU Cartography base map.

Austronesian frontiers and the north Pacific

In writing about the historical geography of borders, it is useful to distinguish between 'boundaries' that take the form of a *line* and 'frontiers' that comprise a broader *zone* (Batten 2003). The three archipelagoes that form the northern geographic limit of Austronesian colonisation are Hawai'i, the Marianas/Ogasawaras, and – I argue here – the Ryukyus, between latitudes 23 and 27°N. These archipelagoes form a frontier in that, in all three cases, there was an area of permanent Austronesian settlement (Zone 1), a zone of once inhabited but later abandoned 'mystery islands' (Bellwood 1978; Zone 2), and a line beyond which Austronesians seem to have never settled (Zone 3; Figure 10.1). For example, in Hawai'i, the large, agriculturally productive island of Kaua'i (nicknamed the 'Garden Isle') marked the northern extent of Zone 1 at 22°13'N. To the northwest, Zone 2 comprised the rocky islets of Nihoa and Necker, which have numerous archaeological sites, including ritual platforms (Emory 1928). These islands were, however, uninhabited when first visited by Europeans and may not have been permanently settled for long periods (Kirch 1985). Beyond Necker at 23°34'N stretches a series of small islands and atolls as far as Kure Atoll at 28°25'N that could potentially have been colonised, but there is no archaeological evidence that these Zone 3 islands were visited in prehistory (Rauzon 2001). In the Marianas, Zone 1 included almost all the islands of the Northern Marianas, except perhaps the small, barren Farallon de Medinilla north of Saipan and the active volcanic island of Uracas at 20°N, in the far north of the archipelago (Russell 1998). According to a 1673 Jesuit report, Uracas was periodically visited to hunt sea birds, which were salted and distributed down the Northern Marianas chain (Coomans 1997). North of Uracas there is an almost 600 km wide stretch of ocean before the next island of Minami Iwo Jima is reached. Evidence for Zone 2 here comprises a number of finds of stone adzes and shell artefacts on landmasses in the Ogasawara (Bonin) Islands. These islands were all uninhabited when the Japanese reported on them in the seventeenth century (Oda 1981, 1990). Only one archaeological site on one of these islands, Ishino on Kita Iwo Jima (25°26'N), has been excavated (Tokyo Board of Education 2005). The excavation produced two large stone concentrations with 163 earthenware sherds, 22 chipped stone axes, a small (3.3 cm long) *Tridacna* adze and two *Tridacna* adze blanks. An incised drawing was found on a rock in the northern stone concentration. The stone concentrations were covered by thick vegetation but not buried in the soil. A single ^{14}C date on carbonised material attached to a potsherd from a test excavation between the two stone concentrations produced a result of 2855 cal. BP (IAAA-41487). In the Ogasawaras, the northern limit of Zone 2 would seem to have been Chichijima (Peel Island) at 27°4'N. Further north, the Izu chain as far south as Hachijo Island (33°6'N) was part of the Jōmon cultural zone (Oda 1981, 1990). The southern Ryukus would appear to have had intermittent occupation in prehistory and can be considered a Zone 2-type Austronesian colonisation.

The archaeology of the southern Ryukyus

The Ryukyu Islands were incorporated as Japanese territory in 1879 and are now split administratively between Kagoshima and Okinawa Prefectures. The islands in Okinawa Prefecture are usually divided into three cultural zones: the Amami Islands in the north near Kyushu, the Okinawa Islands in the centre, and the Sakishima Islands to the south closest to Taiwan (Figure 10.2). In the north, the Amami and Okinawa Islands as far south as Okinawa Main Island were settled by at least 6000 BP by Jōmon populations originating on Kyushu Island (Takemoto 2003; Pearson 2013; Takamiya et al. 2016). To the south, the Sakishima Islands were inhabited by quite different cultures that will be discussed in more detail below. Although archaeological research in the southern Ryukyus began as early as 1904 and at least 77 prehistoric sites are now known in these islands (Shimabukuro 2011), many aspects of the archaeology of the southern Ryukyus remain poorly understood. Nevertheless, two Holocene-era prehistoric cultural phases are currently recognised in the southern Ryukyus (Ōhama 1999; Shimabukuro 2011; Pearson 2013). The earliest known Neolithic sites date to *ca.* 4200 BP (or several centuries earlier) and are only found south of Miyako Island (Summerhayes and Anderson 2009). The initial Neolithic colonists of the southern Ryukyu Islands produced low-fired pottery known as the Shimotabaru type. The succeeding Late Neolithic began around 2800 BP. This phase lacks pottery and is characterised by *Tridacna* shell adzes. Many archaeologists have assumed that the early and late Neolithic phases of activity reflect colonisation of the islands by two different human populations, and that there was a hiatus between the two phases of occupation between 3500–2800 BP. So far, no archaeological sites that can be clearly dated to this hiatus period have been identified, implying that it might reflect real island abandonment and recolonisation. In the eleventh to twelfth centuries AD, the Gusuku Culture spread down the Ryukyu chain from Japan, bringing agriculture, the contemporary Ryukyuan languages and new cultural items such as iron and Chinese ceramics (Hudson 1994; Miyagi 2012; Pearson 2013; Pellard 2015; Takamiya 2004; Yamamoto 2008). On Miyako there is no archaeological evidence for interaction between Late Neolithic and incoming Gusuku populations. However, a few sites on Ishigaki, Taketomi and Hateruma islands have produced Gusuku period ceramics from the upper layers of Late Neolithic sites (Kin 1994), suggesting some overlap and interaction between pre-existing cultural groups and the Gusuku colonists.

The origins of Neolithic culture in the southern Ryukyus

The Neolithic cultures of the southern Ryukyus have four possible origins. In order of geographical proximity, these are: (1) Taiwan, (2) the Ryukyu Jōmon cultures of Okinawa, (3) mainland China, and (4) the Philippines. Of these four, there is no archaeological evidence for (2) or (3). No sites in the southern Ryukyus have produced Jōmon-type remains and no Shimotabaru pottery, shell adzes or other features of southern Ryukyus prehistory have been found further north, beyond the Sakishima Islands. This clear division between the archaeological cultures of the central and southern Ryukyus would seem to rule out a Jōmon origin for the latter. The southern Ryukyus are approximately 500 km from the Chinese coast where the Neolithic and later cultures of Zhejiang and Fujian provinces have been extensively studied. However, the only archaeological finds from the southern Ryukyus that could possibly be linked with China are a number of Tang dynasty (AD 618–906) coins from Late Neolithic deposits. Such coins were widely distributed across East Asia and did not necessarily come directly from China.

Figure 10.2 Map of the Ryukyu Islands showing the location of the Nagabaka site, Miyako Island.
Source: M. Hudson.

Several archaeologists have proposed the Philippines as a possible source for the southern Ryukyu Neolithic, based on morphological similarities of shell adzes (Pearson 1969; Asato 1991). Shell adzes from the Philippines, however, are much older and fewer in number than in the Ryukyus. Almost 300 shell adzes are known from 43 sites the southern Ryukyus (Anzai 2009). In the Philippines, shell adzes have only been discovered at a 'few sites', including Duyong, Leta-leta, Balobok and Kamuanan (Ronquillo 1998: 63). Pawlik et al. (2015) have recently published a careful study of the problems of dating shell adzes in the Philippines. However, their analysis of the shell adze from the Bubog I site confirms that such adzes were present in the Philippines by the early Middle Holocene. Early dates and the 'scarcity' (Ronquillo 1998: 63) of shell adzes in the Philippines do not necessarily rule out connections with the Ryukyus, and Pawlik et al. (2015) follow several earlier scholars in arguing that shell adzes spread through discrete inter-regional contact between Island Southeast Asia, the Moluccas and Island Melanesia. However, the absence of other material culture parallels and the great distance involved suggest prehistoric links between the Philippines and the southern Ryukyus are unlikely.

Figure 10.3 Peter Bellwood excavating at the Nagabaka site in 2008.
Source: M. Hudson.

Taiwan is geographically the closest potential source area, lying only *ca.* 110 km from Yonaguni Island. Despite this proximity, the prehistoric cultures of Taiwan and the southern Ryukyus were rather different in many respects (Hung and Carson 2014). The main aspects of material culture that suggest connections between the two areas that have been proposed are pottery and stone adzes (Pearson 1969). Early Neolithic Shimotabaru type pottery from the southern Ryukyus is a low-fired earthenware with flat-bottomed vessels, sometimes with lug handles, and made using local clays (Summerhayes and Anderson 2009). Shimotabaru pottery lacks most of the vessel forms and decorative designs found in Neolithic ceramics from Taiwan. However, flat-bottom vessels with lug handles are known from Middle Neolithic (4500–3500 BP) sites on Taiwan such as Yanliao and Huagangshan (Summerhayes and Anderson 2009; Lu 2012). Decoration involving lines of circular perforations is also found at both Huagangshan and in Shimotabaru wares (Lu 2012). Many scholars including Pearson (1969) and Summerhayes and Anderson (2009) have discussed the similarities in morphology of stone axes and adzes from Taiwan and the southern Ryukyus. Lu (2012) has recently emphasised similarities in style but differences in technique, especially the absence of 'saw-polishing' in the Ryukyus. Shimotabaru pottery and stone adzes from the southern Ryukyus seem to have been locally made 'poor imitations' of those found in Taiwan (Summerhayes and Anderson 2009: 87). Nevertheless the most parsimonious explanation for the origins of the peoples that arrived in the southern Ryukyus at the end of the third millennium BC is from Taiwan.

Recent finds of slate artefacts from the site of Nagabaka on Miyako Island may provide further evidence of a link with Taiwan. Nagabaka is a rock shelter and shell midden excavated by the author since 2006 (Figure 10.3). The site dates from around 4200 BP to at least the tenth century AD (Nagabaka Archaeological Project 2013). Excavations inside the rock shelter in 2013 produced two slate artefacts. Morphologically, these artefacts are similar to sickles and reaping knives known in Neolithic Taiwan. The 'sickle' is a 44 mm long distal fragment from a longer blade with a maximum width and thickness of 17 and 2 mm, respectively (Figure 10.4). The 'reaping knife' is 61 mm long, 36 mm wide and 6 mm thick and appears similar to the knife from Tapenkeng, Taiwan illustrated in Chang (1967: Plate 92, P; Figure 10.5). Although there is a slate source on Ishigaki Island, no other slate artefacts have been identified in the southern Ryukyus. Slate from Okinawa Island was used to make artefacts in the central Ryukyus, but the absence of contacts between the southern and central Ryukyus in prehistory suggests a source in Taiwan is possible for the two artefacts in Nagabaka. This possibility of a Taiwan source requires further research and analysis.

Figure 10.4 Slate sickle from Nagabaka.
Source: M. Hudson.

Figure 10.5 Slate reaping knife from Nagabaka.
Source: M. Hudson.

Austronesians and the southern Ryukyus

If Okinawa and China can be ruled out as sources for the prehistoric cultures of the southern Ryukyus, then an origin to the south is almost certain. While Taiwan seems the most probable source, other possibilities such as the Philippines or even Micronesia were all areas where Austronesian languages were the dominant or only language spoken at this time. It thus seems extremely likely that the southern Ryukyus were also home to Austronesian languages in the Neolithic. There is no historical or linguistic evidence that Austronesian languages were ever spoken in the southern Ryukyus (Pellard 2015). The historic languages of these islands are part of the Ryukyuan branch of Japonic, which spread down the Ryukyu chain from Japan in the medieval period (tenth to twelfth centuries AD) in association with the spread of farming, a process that presumably involved the replacement of earlier languages in the islands (Hudson 1994, 1999; Pellard 2015). Evidence from biological anthropology supports this medieval immigration into the Ryukyus (Pietrusewsky 2010) and the southern Ryukyus would appear to be an unusual example of Austronesian languages being replaced by a later farming/language dispersal.

Another possibility, suggested to me by Peter Bellwood himself, is that the Neolithic people of the southern Ryukyus were speakers of a pre-Austronesian language who were pushed out of Taiwan by expanding Austronesians. Based on evidence from Qing period historical records and from Aboriginal folklore, it is sometimes suggested that pre-Austronesians in Taiwan were a so-called 'Negrito' people (e.g. Chai 1968). This pre-Austronesian theory certainly warrants further consideration since, as discussed below, the Neolithic cultures of the southern Ryukyus display some striking differences from other prehistoric Austronesian cultures in Southeast Asia and the Pacific.

Despite its proximity to Taiwan and probable origins on that island, the Neolithic of the southern Ryukyus is quite different from the Neolithic cultures of Taiwan, the Batanes Islands and other regions of the Philippines, which are usually linked with early Austronesian expansions. Archaeological components of these expansions included rice cultivation, domesticated pigs and dogs, red-slipped pottery, earthenware spindle whorls, stone adzes, Taiwan slate and nephrite, notched pebble sinkers, stone bark cloth beaters, fishhooks and a variety of shell artefacts (Bellwood 2011: S369). Of these, only the dog and 'poor imitations' (see above) of Taiwanese pottery and stone adzes have been found in the southern Ryukyus, although the two slate artefacts from Nagabaka mentioned above may be another possible link. While agricultural expansion is the most widely favoured explanation for the spread of the Austronesians, the prehistoric sites of the southern Ryukyus offer no evidence of cultivated plants and all known sites appear to have had a foraging economy. Water flotation has been conducted at the Arafu site on Miyako as well as at Nagabaka, but has produced no evidence for rice or other cultigens (Takamiya 2003). The use of root crops such as taro is a possibility but there is no direct evidence from the prehistoric period yet (Matthews et al. 1992). Pigs were common and were certainly transported to smaller islands such as Hateruma, but there is no evidence for domestication. The chicken is not found in the southern Ryukyus until the medieval era. An isotope analysis of the Late Neolithic human femur from Amitori produced results consistent with evidence for heavy reliance on reef fish and shellfish (Hōjō and Yoshida 2007).

Fishing adaptations in the southern Ryukyus were also very different from those reconstructed for Taiwan, the Batanes and the Marianas, where offshore species such as dolphinfish and marlin were commonly taken (Hung et al. 2011: 921). Inshore parrotfish comprised 80 per cent (on MNIs) of the Nagabaka sample (Najima 2013), but only reached 3 per cent (on weight) at Eluanbi II in southern Taiwan (Li 2001). In contrast to Taiwan, the Philippines, and most of Oceania, no fishhooks are known from the Neolithic of the southern Ryukyus.

These significant differences in subsistence do not necessarily contradict the basic model of farming dispersals for the early Austronesian expansion. Growing Neolithic population densities on Taiwan encouraged groups to fission off in search of new land and opportunities. While the net result was the spread of agriculture, when geographical conditions were not appropriate for farming or where other, abundant resources were available it can be presumed that the groups concerned would have forfeited agriculture in favour of other resources (cf. Anderson 1996). One problem here, of course, is how the southern Ryukyu people apparently managed to maintain a 'strandlooper' (Groube 1971) subsistence strategy for thousands of years while elsewhere in the Pacific population growth led quickly to the re-adoption of agriculture. The high productivity of the coral reef foraging adaptation in the prehistoric Ryukyus was potentially a key factor here (Takamiya et al. 2016).

The archaeological record from the southern Ryukyus provides no support for alternative views of Austronesian expansions as part of maritime trade networks (cf. Bulbeck 2008; Goodenough 1996; Oppenheimer and Richards 2002; Solheim 1975, 2007). The Ryukyus are, in fact, a good place to test such ideas about the role of maritime trade networks since they are geographically close to the states and trading centres of East and Southeast Asia. By the Late Neolithic period in the southern Ryukyus, Southeast Asia had already been incorporated into trading networks that linked China, India, and even West Asia. The southern Ryukyus, however, have produced only a handful of iron objects and Tang coins – all from Late Neolithic deposits – that could conceivably be linked with such trade. The archaeology of the southern Ryukyus islands provides no evidence to support the hypothesis that maritime trading networks were a major motivating factor behind the dispersal of Austronesian peoples. In contrast, extreme cultural isolation seems to be a defining feature of the southern Ryukyu Neolithic.

The northern frontier of the Austronesian world

If, as argued above, a case can be made that the southern Ryukyus were part of the northern frontier of the Austronesian world, what if any common factors can be discerned between the Ryukyus, the Marianas and Hawai'i? If the southern Ryukyus were a 'Zone 2' area of settlement, then they differ from the northwestern Hawaiian and Ogasawara Islands in forming home to a zone of apparently stable prehistoric settlement that continued for at least 2,000 years. Here the northern limit of Zone 2 was northern Miyako (24°56'N). Previous studies on the Pacific 'mystery islands' have identified island size, cultural isolation, low ecological diversity and low rainfall as factors leading to island abandonment in Polynesia (Anderson 2001, 2002). These factors seem to apply to Hawai'i and the Ogasawaras. In Hawai'i, a stormy passage between Kaua'i and Nihoa limited voyaging in that direction and the northwestern Hawaiian Islands are extremely small, isolated, and generally unsuitable for permanent settlement (Rauzon 2001). In the Ogasawaras, the 600 km sea gap between these islands and the northern Marianas was probably a major factor limiting exploration and settlement to the north. If Hawai'i and the Ogasawaras thus seem to fit the causal factors previously suggested for island abandonment in Polynesia, the Ryukyus are clearly a separate case. The apparent failure of Austronesians to expand north beyond Miyako cannot be explained by geographical isolation, island size or ecological diversity. The next island from Miyako, Okinawa Island, is only 250 km distant, has a surface area of over 1,200 km^2 and a similar natural environment to the southern Ryukyus. Prehistoric populations on both sides of this ocean gap possessed remarkably similar subsistence adaptations, yet both groups seem to have remained in their respective cultural worlds, eschewing the exploration and interaction that was so common elsewhere in the Pacific.

References

Anderson, A.J. 1996. Adaptive voyaging and subsistence strategies in the early settlement of East Polynesia. In T. Akazawa and E.J.E. Szathmáry (eds), *Prehistoric Mongoloid Dispersals*, pp. 359–373. Oxford: Oxford University Press.

——. 2001. No meat on that beautiful shore: The prehistoric abandonment of subtropical Polynesian islands. *International Journal of Osteoarchaeology* 11: 14–23. doi.org/10.1002/oa.542.

——. 2002. Faunal collapse, landscape change and settlement history in Remote Oceania. *World Archaeology* 33: 375–390. doi.org/10.1080/00438240120107431.

Anzai, E. 2009. Sakishima shotō shutsudo no shakogai-sei kaifu ni tsuite [The Tridacna adzes excavated from the Sakishima islands]. In Ishigaki City (eds), *Ishigaki shishi kōko visual-ban* [A visual history and archaeology of Ishigaki City], vol. 3, pp. 61–64. Ishigaki: Ishigaki City.

Asato, S. 1991. The distribution of Tridacna shell adzes in the southern Ryukyu islands. *Bulletin of the Indo-Pacific Prehistory Association* 10: 282–291. doi.org/10.7152/bippa.v10i0.11319.

Batten, B.L. 2003. *To the Ends of Japan: Premodern Frontiers, Boundaries, and Interactions*. Honolulu: University of Hawai'i Press.

Bellwood, P. 1978. *Man's Conquest of the Pacific*. London: Collins.

——. 2011. Holocene population history in the Pacific region as a model for worldwide food producer dispersals. *Current Anthropology* 52: S363–378. doi.org/10.1086/658181.

Bulbeck, D. 2008. An integrated perspective on the Austronesian diaspora: The switch from cereal agriculture to maritime foraging in the colonization of Island Southeast Asia. *Australian Archaeology* 67: 31–51. doi.org/10.1080/03122417.2008.11681877.

Chai, C.-K. 1968. *Taiwan Aborigines: A Genetic Study of Tribal Variations*. Cambridge, MA: Harvard University Press; and Taipei: Bookcase Shop.

Chang, K.-C. 1967. *Fengpitou, Tapenkeng, and the Prehistory of Taiwan*. New Haven: Department of Anthropology, Yale University.

Coomans, P. 1997. *History of the Mission in the Mariana Islands, 1667–1673*. Occasional Historical Papers no. 4. Saipan: Division of Historic Preservation.

Emory, K.P. 1928. *Archaeology of Nihoa and Necker islands*. Honolulu: Bishop Museum Bulletin 53.

Goodenough, W.H. 1996. Introduction. In W.H. Goodenough (ed.), *Prehistoric Settlement of the Pacific*, pp. 1–10. Philadelphia: American Philosophical Society. doi.org/10.2307/1006617.

Groube, L. 1971. Tonga, Lapita pottery, and Polynesian origins. *Journal of the Polynesian Society* 80: 278–316.

Hōjō, Y. and K. Yoshida. 2007. Dōitai bunseki kekka kara mita senshi jidaijin to kinsei Amitori-jin. In Tōkai University (eds), *Amitori iseki, Katura kaizuka no kenkyū*, pp. 263–268. Hiratsuka: Tōkai University.

Hudson, M.J. 1994. The linguistic prehistory of Japan: Some archaeological speculations. *Anthropological Science* 102: 231–255. doi.org/10.1537/ase.102.231.

——. 1999. *Ruins of Identity: Ethnogenesis in the Japanese Islands*. Honolulu: University of Hawaii Press.

Hung, H.-c., M.T. Carson, P. Bellwood, F.Z. Campos, P.J. Piper, E. Dizon, M.J.L.A. Bolunia, M. Oxenham and Z. Chi. 2011. The first settlement of Remote Oceania: The Philippines to the Marianas. *Antiquity* 85: 909–926. doi.org/10.1017/S0003598X00068393.

Hung, H.-c. and Carson, M.T. 2014. Foragers, fishers and farmers: Origins of the Taiwanese Neolithic. *Antiquity* 88: 1115–1131. doi.org/10.1017/S0003598X00115352.

Kin, M. 1994. Doki→mudoki→doki: Yaeyama kōko hennen shian. *Nantō Kōko* 14: 83–92.

Kirch, P.V. 1985. *Feathered Gods and Fishhooks: An Introduction to Hawaiian Archaeology and Prehistory.* Honolulu: University of Hawaii Press.

Li, K.-T. 2001. Prehistoric marine fishing adaptation in southern Taiwan. *Journal of East Asian Archaeology* 3(1–2): 47–74.

Lu, J.-C. 2012. The Neolithic cultures in southern Ryukyu and eastern coast of Taiwan. Paper presented at the Fifth World Conference of the Society for East Asian Archaeology, Fukuoka, June 2012.

Matthews, P.J., E. Takei and T. Kawahara. 1992. *Colocasia esculenta* var. *aquatilis* on Okinawa island, southern Japan: The distribution and possible origins of a wild diploid taro. *Man & Culture in Oceania* 8: 19–34.

Miyagi, H. (ed.). 2012. *Sakishima chi'iki ni okeru senshi jidai no shūen to suku iseki shutsugen ni kansuru kenkyū* [Research on the end of prehistory and the appearance of Suku sites in the Sakishima region]. Mitsubishi Foundation Grant Report for the Humanities no. 31.

Nagabaka Archaeological Research Project (eds). 2013. *Pai-mmi-nu-Nagabaka iseki chōsa kenkyū 1.* Kanzaki: University of West Kyushu.

Najima, Y. 2013. Nagabaka iseki shutsudo no gyorui itai (2008 nendo chōsa shutsudo shiryō) [Fish remains excavated from the Nagabaka site (Materials from the 2008 season)]. In Nagabaka Archaeological Research Project (eds), *Pai-mmi-nu-Nagabaka iseki chōsa kenkyū 1* [Pai-mmi-nu-Nagabaka, vol. 1], pp. 83–105. Kanzaki: University of West Kyushu.

Oda, S. 1981. The archaeology of the Ogasawara islands. *Asian Perspectives* 14: 111–138.

——. 1990. A review of archaeological research in the Izu and Ogasawara Islands. *Man & Culture in Oceania* 6: 53–79.

Ōhama, E. 1999. *Yaeyama no kōkogaku.* Ishigaki: Sakishima Bunka Kenkyūjo.

Oppenheimer, S. and M. Richards. 2002. Polynesians: Devolved Taiwanese rice farmers or Wallacean maritime traders with fishing, foraging and horticultural skills? In P. Bellwood and C. Renfrew (eds), *Examining the Farming/Language Dispersal Hypothesis*, pp. 287–297. Cambridge: McDonald Institute.

Pawlik, A.F., P.J. Piper, R. Wood, K.A.A. Lim, M.G.P.G. Faylona, A.S.B. Mijares, A.S.B. and M. Porr. 2015. The direct dating and analysis of an early middle Holocene shell adze from Ilin Island, Mindoro, Philippines and its implications for understanding shell tool technology in Island Southeast Asia. *Antiquity* 89(344): 292–308. doi.org/10.15184/aqy.2015.3.

Pearson, R.J. 1969. *Archaeology of the Ryukyu Islands.* Honolulu: University of Hawaii Press.

——. 2013. *Ancient Ryukyu: An Archaeological Study of Island Communities.* Honolulu: University of Hawai'i Press.

Pellard, T. 2015. The linguistic archaeology of the Ryūkyū Islands. In P. Heinrich, S. Miyara and M. Shimoji (eds), *Handbook of the Ryukyuan Languages.* pp. 13–37. Amsterdam: DeGruyter Mouton.

Pietrusewsky, M. 2010. A multivariate analysis of measurements recorded in early and more modern crania from East Asia and Southeast Asia. *Quaternary International* 211: 42–54. doi.org/10.1016/j.quaint.2008.12.011.

Rauzon, M.J. 2001. *Isles of Refuge: Wildlife and History of the Northwestern Hawaiian Islands*. Honolulu: University of Hawai'i Press.

Ronquillo, W.P. 1998. Tools from the sea. In G.S. Casal, E.Z. Dizon, W.P. Ronquillo and C.G. Salcedo, *Kasaysayan: The Story of the Filipino People Vol. 2: The Earliest Filipinos*, pp. 63–75. Manila: Asia Publishing.

Russell, S. 1998. Gani revisited: A historical overview of the Mariana archipelago's northern islands. *Pacific Studies* 21(4): 83–105.

Shimabukuro, A. 2011. Sakishima shotō no senshijidai. In H. Takamiya and S. Itō (eds), *Senshi, genshi jidai no Ryūkyū rettō: hito to keikan* [The prehistoric and protohistoric Ryukyu islands: People and landscapes], pp. 267–289. Tokyo: Rokuichi Shobō.

Solheim, W.G. 1975. The Nusantao and South China. *Journal of the Hong Kong Archaeological Society* 6: 108–115.

——. 2007. *Archaeology and Culture in Southeast Asia: Unraveling the Nusantao*. Honolulu: University of Hawai'i Press.

Summerhayes, G.R. and A. Anderson. 2009. An Austronesian presence in southern Japan: Early occupation in the Yaeyama Islands. *Bulletin of the Indo-Pacific Prehistory Association* 29: 76–91. doi.org/10.7152/bippa.v29i0.9481.

Takamiya, H. 2003. Arafu iseki shutsudo no shokubutsu itai [Plant remains from the Arafu site]. In T. Egami (ed.), *Arafu iseki chōsa kenkyū I* vol. 1, pp. 105–106. Tokyo: Rokuichi Shobō.

——. 2004. Population dynamics in the prehistory of Okinawa. In S.M. Fitzpatrick (ed.), *Voyages of Discovery: The Archaeology of Islands*, pp. 111–128. Westport, CT: Praeger.

Takamiya, H., M.J. Hudson, H. Yonenobu, T. Kurozumi and T. Toizumi. 2016. An extraordinary case in human history: Prehistoric hunter-gatherer adaptation to the islands of the Central Ryukyus (Amami and Okinawa arhipelagos), Japan. *The Holocene* 26: 408–422. doi.org/10.1177/0959683615609752.

Takemoto, M. 2003. Jōmon jidai [Jōmon period]. In Okinawa Prefecture (eds), *Okinawakenshi kakuron-hen 2: kōko*, pp. 97–182. Naha: Okinawa Prefecture Board of Education.

Tokyo Board of Education. 2005. *Kitaiojima Ishino iseki*. Tokyo: Tokyo Board of Education.

Yamamoto, M. 2008. The Gusuku period in the Okinawa islands. *Acta Asiatica* 95: 1–17.

11

The Western Route Migration: A Second Probable Neolithic Diffusion to Indonesia

Truman Simanjuntak

The emergence of the Neolithic is considered to be a pivotal event in the history of human occupation of the Indonesian archipelago as it brought significant changes in numerous aspects of livelihood. Indonesia's Neolithic was characterised by sedentary living, plant and animal domestication, polished stone tools, pottery, jewellery, bark cloth and ancestor worship. The Neolithic in Indonesia is generally traced to the culture of Austronesian-speaking people who migrated from Taiwan and entered the archipelago at ca. 4000 BP. However, new data from various disciplines reveal another probable Neolithic diffusion from Mainland Southeast Asia, probably by Austroasiatic-speaking people. Current dating results indicate this westerly migration route reached western Indonesia earlier than the eastern route migration from Taiwan, thus before 4000 BP. The subsequent dispersal of Austronesian-speaking people into the western parts of Indonesia influenced the Neolithic cultures there and resulted in the replacement of the local Austroasiatic languages.

Introduction

One of Peter Bellwood's great archaeological interests is in the emergence and expansion of food production and the Neolithic, which he initially investigated across the Pacific and Southeast Asia (Bellwood 1978) before focusing on Island Southeast Asia (Bellwood 1984–1985, 1985) and then moving onto a worldwide perspective (Bellwood 2005). In Island Southeast Asia (ISEA) Peter's research has focused on the relationship between the migration of early farming communities and the origins of the Austronesian language families spoken ethnographically by large numbers of people across the region. He wavered on the question of whether or not there may have been some involvement of early Austoasiatic speakers from Mainland Southeast Asia (MSEA) in the Neolithic foundations of ISEA (Bellwood 1997, 2006). For example, Bellwood (1997: 237) noted that the material culture recovered from the site of Gua Sireh in Sarawak, Malaysian Borneo, had more in common with the Peninsular Malaysian and southern Thai Neolithic than it did with eastern Indonesia, and that the archaeological record correlated neatly with Adelaar's (1995) argument for a substratum of Austroasiatic in the Land Dayak languages of western Sarawak. The possible migration of Neolithic Austroasiatic populations from MSEA into western Indonesia is the topic that this contribution explores.

Neolithic and Austronesian

The development of Neolithic culture brought immense changes to people's daily life across numerous aspects of technology, economy and social organisation, and is considered to be a major event in the pathways to civilisation (Simanjuntak 1992). The main factor that triggered this development is sedentary lifeways. By establishing permanent settlements, people were able to dedicate time to experimenting with new ideas and enriching their material culture and developing economic strategies. For instance, the concept of ensuring a reliable food supply led to strategic plant and animal domestication. Likewise, the concept of using more effective equipment in daily activities encouraged the use of tough, resistant stone that required polishing in lieu of flaking to produce stone tools. Social mechanisms for internal harmony allowed larger social groupings to reside together for longer periods of time. Furthermore, the idea that individuals retained their identity after death fostered the notion that the ancestors maintained a watchful eye over the present-day community, as manifested in respectful treatment of the dead. The rapid changes in cultural behaviour, economies and associated ideologies led Gordon Childe to coin the term the 'Neolithic Revolution' (Childe 1936).

How about the Neolithic in Indonesia? When, by whom, from where it emerged and how it developed constitute a set of intriguing questions that have not been fully and conclusively answered in our efforts to fully understand more about Indonesia's ancestors and their culture. The following discussion and interpretation is preliminary, and based on our current understanding of available linguistic, genetic and archaeological data.

Indonesia's distinctive culture is characterised by sedentary life in communities that also domesticated certain animals and plants; making polished stone tools, pottery, jewellery from various materials and bark cloth; adherence to metaphysical beliefs manifested in the burial systems; and the ability to sail, which facilitated settlement across the large area of the archipelago. I link 'Indonesia's ancestors' with the Neolithic because the Neolithic forebears brought this distinctive culture with them when they entered the archipelago thousands of years ago, and then have continued to occupy the archipelago up to the present. Briefly, I would say that the Neolithic is the real foundation stone of contemporary Indonesian culture. It is worth noting that the bearers of the Neolithic culture in Indonesia are generally associated with Austronesian-speaking people (hereafter named Austronesians). This 'Mongoloid' people entered the archipelago at *ca*. 4000 BP (Simanjuntak 2008).

This view is based on the 'Out-of-Taiwan' model explaining the migration of Austronesians and their Neolithic culture to ISEA (Bellwood 1984–1985, 1997; Bellwood et al. 1995), utilising archaeological and linguistic data, following similar views proposed by Blust (1984–1985) and Chang (1964) on the origin of the Austronesians in Taiwan. Their ancestors lived in Neolithic communities in Fujian or Zhejiang, South China, in about 7000–6000 BP. In *ca*. 6000–5500 BP they migrated to Taiwan and brought grain and tuber agriculture, pig and dog domestication, and knowledge of water navigation. In *ca*. 4500–4000 BP some of them moved southward to the northern Philippines and gave rise to the Proto-Malayo-Polynesian language, bringing with them agriculture, more advanced sailing technology and red-slipped pottery. The southward movement went via the southern Philippines, reached Kalimantan (Borneo) and Sulawesi and then continued to Java, Sumatra, Malay Peninsula, southern Vietnam and Madagascar (all areas that are linguistically Western Malayo-Polynesian). An eastward movement through the Moluccas to reach the Lesser Sundas (linguistically Central Malayo-Polynesian), and through Halmahera (linguistically Eastern Malayo-Polynesian) to reach Island Melanesia and Polynesia (linguistically Oceanic). In Western Melanesia, Austronesians moved mainly along the coast and never penetrated deeply into the interior of larger islands, at least partly due to the prior establishment of agricultural or arboricultural communities.

The 'Out-of-Taiwan' model outlined above would invoke Sulawesi as an initial point of arrival for Austronesians into the modern sociopolitical region of Indonesia. There is archaeological evidence to support this view, in the form of early Neolithic sites such as Minanga Sipakko on a bank of the Karama River at Kalumpang, West Sulawesi. Minanaga Sipakko, characterised by an abundance of red-slipped potsherds in the lower occupation layer and the most richly decorated pottery in Southeast Asia in the upper layer (Bulbeck and Nasruddin 2002; Simanjuntak 2008; Anggraeni et al. 2014), was occupied by Austronesians between *ca.* 3800 BP (3446 ± 51 BP or cal. 3834–3572 BP (Wk-14651)) and *ca.* 2500 BP. It is possible that Austronesians entered Sulawesi as early as *ca.* 4000 BP, considering the location of Minanga Sipakko in a mountainous area in the hinterland of Sulawesi. Several other early sites in the region are Leang Tuwo Mane'e in the Sangihe-Talaud Islands, North Sulawesi, *ca.* 3600 BP (Tanudirjo 2001) and cave sites in the Maros-Pangkep area, *ca.* 3500 BP (Bulbeck 1996/1997). From Sulawesi, the Austronesians dispersed to other islands and by *ca.* 2500 BP occupied most of the Indonesian archipelago.

Western Route Migration evidence

Until recently, there were some views on the homeland of Austronesian that opposed the 'Out-of-Taiwan' model (see Anceaux 1965; Tanudirjo and Simanjuntak 2004). These included Isidore Dyen's (1965) lexico-statistical analysis, which suggested a homeland in Melanesia; a proposal for the northeast Indonesia-Southern Philippines areas (Solheim 1984–1985); the former Pleistocene sub-continent of Sundaland (Oppenheimer 1998; Oppenheimer and Richards 2001); and the triangle of Taiwan-Sumatra-Timor (Meacham 1984–1985). This debate appears to have been resolved in favour of unanimous scholarly acceptance of Taiwan as the place of origin of the Austronesians. However, what is less clear is whether the Austronesians were the only people to introduce the Neolithic to Indonesia.

An important consideration is that ancient migration routes may be more complicated than single unidirectional pathways. Routes of migration could have had several departure and arrival points and been used multiple times, perhaps even involving movement back and forth, though to explain the wide geographic distributions of language families such as Austronesian there must have been some overall directionality away from the point of origin. In ISEA there is now evidence to suggest another route of migration besides the 'Out-of-Taiwan' model, from MSEA, and Vietnam, through Peninsular Malaysia and entering western Indonesia via Sumatra, before expanding into Borneo and Java (Figure 11.1; see also Anderson 2005). I will refer to this migration as the Western Route Migration (WRM) in order to distinguish it from the Eastern Route Migration (ERM) from Taiwan. Blench (2010) traces the WRM from northern Vietnam through Borneo and Palawan, before proceeding to Peninsular Malaysia and Sumatra. Regardless of which route is accurate (further research is required), those proposals recognise another route besides that from Taiwan.

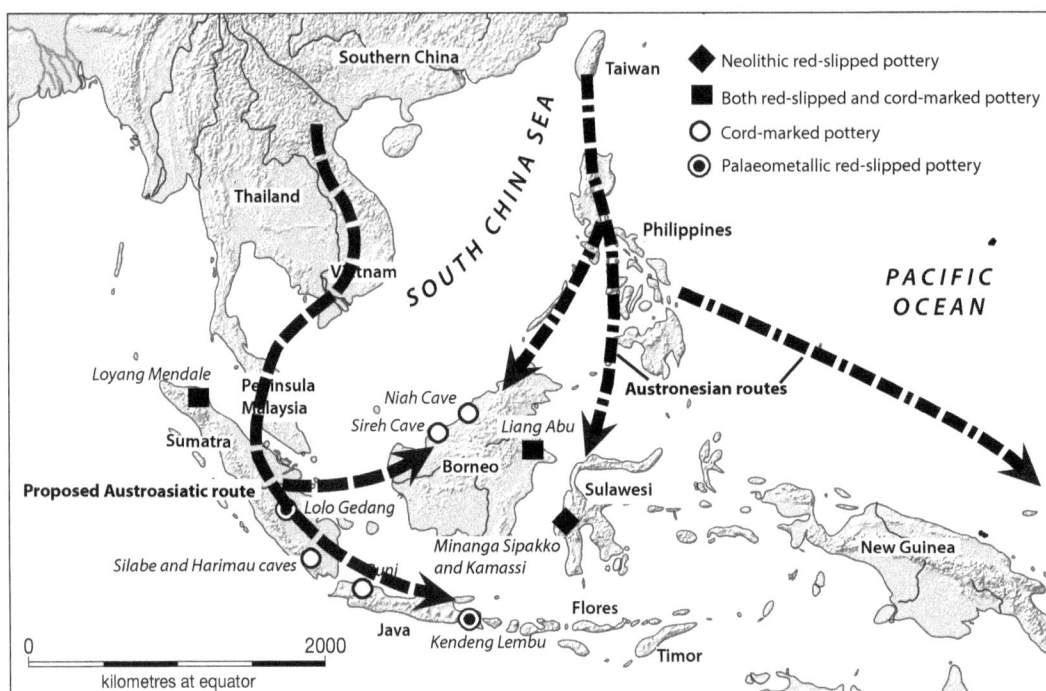

Figure 11.1 The proposed route of Austroasiatic and Austronesian migration into Indonesia and the geographic distribution of sites that have produced red-slipped and cord-marked pottery discussed in the text.

Source: Base map Peter Bellwood/ANU Cartography; Illustration courtesy of Philip Piper.

In a sense, the WRM is not a new idea, it was first proposed by scholars as early as the late nineteenth century, but without well-grounded empirical support. For example, in 1889 Hendrik Kern, a linguist, assigned the languages of the archipelago and remote Pacific to a Malayo-Polynesian group, with an ancestral homeland in MSEA, western Indonesia or South China (see Anceaux 1965). A decade later, W. Schmidt introduced the term 'Austronesian' to substitute for Kern's term 'Malayo-Polynesian', and traced the origins of Austronesian specifically to the Asia mainland. According to Schmidt, an ancestral Austric language, spoken on mainland Asia, split into the Austroasiatic languages spoken by mainland Asians (Mon-Khmer in Indo-China and Munda in India) and the Austronesian languages spoken by Indonesian and Pacific Islanders (Anceaux 1965). The proposals of these linguists were corroborated by archaeologists, such as van Stein Callenfels (1926), Heine-Geldern (1945) and Duff (1970). Heine-Geldern for instance claimed that the dispersal of quadrangular adzes might have originated in South China, and then moved southward through Indochina and the Malay Peninsula before reaching Indonesia at *ca*. 4000 BP.

This perspective proposed by early scholars regained its popularity with the support of new evidence from recent studies of various disciplines. Similarities in material culture, language and human biology reveal interconnections between MSEA and Sumatra, Kalimantan and Java in western Indonesia (Simanjuntak 2013). The archaeological evidence includes the geographic distribution of paddle-impressed pottery, especially the use of textile-wrapped paddles to produce what is often referred to as cord-marked pottery – one of the markers of the early Neolithic. This particular type of decoration is essentially limited to western Indonesia, including Loyang Mendale cave in Aceh (Wiradnyana and Taufikurrachman 2011), the Silabe and Harimau Caves in South Sumatra (Simanjuntak 2013), Buni on the north coast of West Java (Sutayasa 1972), and Liang Abu and some other sites in Kalimantan (Plutniak et al. 2014), extending to Gua Sireh and the Niah Caves in Sarawak, Malaysia. To date there are no reports of the presence of cord-marked pottery in eastern Indonesian Neolithic sites. To the north, cord-marked pottery is found in Neolithic sites in Vietnam (Masanari and Dung 2002), Peninsular Malaysia (Jaafar 2003), South China (Jiao 2004), Hong Kong (Meacham 1999) and Taiwan (Chang 1970). In contrast, red-slipped pottery, the marker of the 'Out-of-Taiwan' migration, is commonly found in Neolithic sites in or near the eastern parts of Indonesia (Spriggs 1989, 2011; Bellwood et al. 1998; Simanjuntak 2008; Galipaud et al. 2010; Simanjuntak et al. 2012; Anggraeni et al. 2014; O'Connor 2015). Red-slipped pottery is also found in the western parts of Indonesia, but so far limited to Palaeometallic and historical sites. Some archaeological sites containing red-slipped pottery are Kendenglembu in East Java (Noerwidi 2009), Liang Abu in Kalimantan (Plutniak et al. 2014) and Lolo Gedang in Jambi (Aziz 2009). Several examples are also reported from Loyang Mendale Cave, Aceh found together with three-coloured pottery (Wiradnyana and Taufiqurrahman 2011), but their stratigraphic associations still need verification.

It is important to note that the finding of both cord-marked and red-slipped pottery at the sites of Liang Abu and Loyang Mendale might suggest possible contacts between the two cultural streams. Indeed, proposals that would link the decorated pottery in Vietnam and eastern ISEA have a lengthy history in Southeast Asian archaeology. According to Heekeren (1950), Heine-Geldern viewed Samrong Sen in Cambodia as the closest parallel for the decorated pottery at Kamassi, a Neolithic settlement near Minanga Sipakko in the Karama Valley region of Sulawesi. For his part, Heekeren (1972) concluded that the pottery designs at Kamassi were derived from the Sa-Huynh culture of Central Vietnam. Kamassi is now dated to *ca.* 3500 BP (Anggraeni et al. 2014) and clearly much older than Sa Huynh. Solheim (e.g. 1984–1985) noted further systematic similarities that the decorated pottery from the southern Philippines and Kalimantan exhibit with the decorated pottery from Vietnam and several parts of Thailand, which he attributed to a widespread 'Sa-Huynh Kalanay' tradition. Solheim further proposed that this shared tradition reflected the formation of a 'Nusantao' trading network in operation in the area of the South China Sea since 7000 BP, but this dating seems very early in the light of current archaeological evidence, and the Sa-Huynh Kalanay tradition is perhaps best viewed as reflecting an intensification of maritime trade during the late Neolithic and Palaeometallic (Bellwood 1997).

Apart from pottery comparisons, there are other similarities in material culture that support the WRM. The edge-ground stone tools at the Niah Caves, Sarawak, resemble those from Bacsonian sites in northern Vietnam, both dating back to the early Holocene (Bulbeck 2008; Rabett et al. 2013). Indonesia's Neolithic adzes include the pick-adze and shield-shaped types that are typical of western Indonesia and the shouldered-adze, stepped-adze, and violin-shaped types of eastern Indonesia (Heekeren 1972). In addition, ethnographic data reveal similar mouth organs in the western part of Kalimantan and MSEA, especially Vietnam. This type of instrument is considered indigenous to Southeast Asia, as it is not found in any other part of the world (Blench 2010).

Linguistic data provide another indication of the western migration route. Adelaar (1995) noted that the Aslian languages of Peninsular Malaysia, which belong to the Austroasiatic family, resemble the Land Dayak languages of Kalimantan in two ways: sharing an unusual phonological feature known as preplosion and sharing cognate words for dying and bathing. His preferred explanation for these similarities is that Land Dayak originated as the result of a language shift from Aslian to Austronesian or that both of the languages have a common sub-stratum inherited from an unknown language. Blench (2010) strengthened this perspective by noting further similarities between Aslian and the Dayak languages of Sarawak. Without ignoring the possibility of a shared legacy from ancestral Austric, we can note that neither Adelaar nor Blench advocated this explanation and instead preferred to invoke migration factors. Blench (2010), in particular, developed a case for language elements introduced by Austroasiatic agricultural communities that infiltrated ISEA during its pre-Austronesian period. Of central importance to his argument is the word for 'taro', which is phonologically similar between the Munda languages (Austroasiatic languages of northeast India) and the term reconstructed for Proto-Malayo-Polynesian. The implication that taro was brought to ISEA by early Austroasiatic speakers, and absorbed by early Austronesians (along with the term for taro) when they reached Kalimantan and Palawan, is strengthened by the absence of a reconstruction of the term for taro in Proto-Austronesian or Proto-Malayo-Polynesian.

From taro we move onto the issue of animal domestication. The results of several studies suggest that the early domesticated pigs and chickens originated in MSEA before being introduced to ISEA as part of a Neolithic dispersal (Dobney et al. 2008). For example, ancient and modern DNA studies have demonstrated that a unique haplotype in *Sus scrofa* known as the 'Pacific Clade' appears to have its origins in Yunnan Province, China, and/or northern Vietnam and Laos where wild progenitors of this genetic lineage have been identified (Dobney et al. 2008; Larson et al. 2010). Translocation of this haplotype can be traced south through Vietnam, probably as part of the Austroasiatic human movements around 4000 BP (see Piper, Chapter 15, this volume). The dispersal continues through Peninsula Malaysia and western Indonesia, Nusa Tenggara and into the Pacific (Larson et al. 2007). Modern chicken genetic studies have indicated multiple domestication events between South Asia and Thailand (Fumihito et al. 1996; Liu et al. 2002; Storey et al. 2013), with Haplogroup D chickens potentially being introduced to ISEA via Peninsula Malaysia and western Indonesia. The presence of different and distinctive lineages of pigs and chickens in the Philippine archipelago argues against an Austronesian introduction of these domestic animals into ISEA (Larson et al. 2007; Blench 2010), and at present it appears that of all the potential domesticated animals (pig, dog and chicken) from Taiwan/Philippines, it is only the chicken that was dispersed more widely (Thomson et al. 2014).

Results from human genetic studies also support a Neolithic connection between western Indonesian and MSEA populations. One of these studies (Tumonggor et al. 2013) shows that western and eastern Indonesians form separate clusters within a general Indonesian cluster that falls together with Asian groups, away from Oceanic populations. Among these Asian groups, Indonesians cluster most closely with populations from Vietnam and the Philippines and more distantly with Taiwan populations. A recent genetic study (Lipson et al. 2014) goes so far as recognising distinct Austroasiatic and Austronesian nuclear DNA components. Both of these are similarly pronounced in the sampled western Indonesian populations and the Manggarai of Flores, but with the Austroasiatic component absent from other eastern Indonesian and from Philippine populations.

In addition, the study by Lipson et al. (2014) identifies a distinct 'Negrito' component for populations in the Philippines and a 'Melanesian' component for populations across Indonesia and Austronesian-speaking parts of the Pacific. The presence of the latter component in Indonesia may be related to evidence for the introduction of certain crops such as sugar cane and at least some types of banana, taro and yam from New Guinea into Indonesia prior to the Austronesian expansion (O'Connor 2015).

Western Indonesia: Confluence of WRM and ERM

The perspectives from the various studies outlined above, from archaeology, linguistics, ethnography, palaeobotany and genetics, clearly suggest an early connection between the western parts of Indonesia and MSEA, one that operated separately from any connection with the Philippines and Taiwan. Both of these connections were probably realised by migrations, which brought Neolithic culture into Indonesia. If recent studies have focused more on the Eastern Route Migration (ERM) that originated in Taiwan, there is currently evidence for a Western Route of Migration (WRM) that possibly originated in Indochina, specifically northern Vietnam. The WRM might have proceeded from Vietnam through Kalimantan as proposed by some scholars (Blench 2010), but it might also have proceeded through Peninsular Malaysia to enter western Indonesia (Anderson 2005). More research is needed to assess these alternative proposals.

This new outlook offers a better understanding of the origins and development of the Neolithic in Indonesia. The WRM evidence brings to light the point that the bearers of the Neolithic to Indonesia were not only Austronesian but probably also Austroasiatic speakers. They intertwined in developing a culture unknown to the previous inhabitants of ISEA, a culture that included sedentary living, domesticated animals and plants, the use of polishing in adze production and other stone tools, pottery and bark-cloth making. A distinctive characteristic of the two migration routes is the associated pottery, in particular the cord-marked and other paddle-impressed pottery associated with the WRM and the red-slipped pottery associated with the ERM. It also seems that the Neolithic Austronesians, judging by their vast dispersal area across the archipelago and on to Oceania, were more advanced in seafaring techniques than the Austroasiatic-speaking Neolithic immigrants.

One question that this new perspective raises is why every indigenous ethnic group in present-day western Indonesia speaks an Austronesian language. A preliminary answer to this question comes from the available radiometric datings older than 4000 BP of the Neolithic sites of Gua Sireh in Sarawak and Takengon in Aceh, which suggest that the WRM occurred earlier than the ERM. Considering the onset of the Neolithic in Peninsular Malaysia dated back to around 6500 BP (Bulbeck 2014), the early arrival of the Neolithic to ISEA is reasonable. The Austronesians, who arrived in Sulawesi at *ca.* 4000 BP, continued to migrate in different directions, and those who reached the western parts of Indonesia afterward (*ca.* 3500–3000 BP or even later) enjoyed pre-eminence over the local cultures, resulting in the replacement of Austroasiatic or other languages.

To close my discussion, I would like to stress again that what I have presented here is still a preliminary insight into the Neolithic of Indonesia that needs to be enhanced by further research. Questions on how and when the western migration occurred, how far it dispersed in Indonesia, how the Austroasiatic and Austronesian groups with their linguistic differences interacted with each other in genetic and cultural terms, and how and why Austronesian languages came to dominate western Indonesia are challenges to be addressed in order to understand more on the cultural ancestors of Indonesians. A multidisciplinary approach is required to trace back the origins of the languages and biological affinities of Indonesia's ethnic groups, within the context of the Neolithic archaeology of Southeast Asia and its surrounds. In-depth research on those topics will hopefully reveal the origins of Indonesian ancestors, their regional and global interconnections, and their development from the beginning to the present day.

Acknowledgements

I wish to express my gratitude to Dr David Bulbeck from The Australian National University for his openhandedness to make suggestions and language corrections to this paper. I also would like to thank Dr Philip J. Piper for inviting me to contribute to this Festschrift.

References

Adelaar, K.A. 1995. Borneo as a cross-roads for comparative Austronesian linguistics. In P. Bellwood, J.J. Fox and D. Tryon (eds), *The Austronesians: Historical and Comparative Perspectives*, pp. 75–95. Canberra: The Australian National University.

Anceaux, J.C. 1965. Linguistic theories about the Austronesian homeland. *Bijdragen tot de Taal-, Land-en Volkenkunde* 121: 417–432. doi.org/10.1163/22134379-90002950.

Anderson, A. 2005. Crossing the Luzon Strait: archaeological chronology in the Batanes Islands, Philippines and the regional sequence of Neolithic dispersal. *Journal of Austronesian Studies* 1: 25–45.

Anggraeni, T. Simanjuntak, P. Bellwood and P.J. Piper. 2014. Neolithic foundations in the Karama valley, West Sulawesi, Indonesia. *Antiquity* 88: 740–756. doi.org/10.1017/S0003598X00050663.

Aziz, F.A. 2009. Laporan Penelitian Lolo Gedang, Kerinci. Unpublished research report. Jakarta: Pusat Penelitian Arkeologi Nasional.

Bellwood, P. 1978. *Man's Conquest of the Pacific*. Sydney: Collins.

——. 1984–1985. A hypothesis for Austronesian origins. *Asian Perspectives* 26: 107–117.

——. 1985. *The Prehistory of the Indo-Malaysian Archipelago*. Sydney: Academic Press.

——. 1997. *Prehistory of the Indo-Malaysian Archipelago*. 2nd edition. Honolulu: University of Hawaii Press.

——. 2005. *First Farmers: The Origins of Agricultural Societies*. Oxford: Blackwell.

——. 2006. Borneo as the homeland of Malay? The perspective from archaeology. In J.T. Collins and A. Sariyan (eds), *Borneo and the Homeland of the Malays: Four Essays*, pp. 45–63. Kuala Lumpur: Dewan Bahasa dan Pustaka.

Bellwood, P., J.J. Fox and D. Tryon. 1995. The Austronesians in history: Common origins and diverse transformations. In P. Bellwood, J.J. Fox and D. Tryon (eds), *The Austronesians: Historical and Comparative Perspectives*, pp. 3–13. Canberra: The Australian National University.

Bellwood, P., N. Goenadi, G. Irwin, A.W. Gunadi and D. Tanudirjo. 1998. 35,000 years of prehistory in the northern Moluccas. In G.J. Bartstra (ed.), *Bird's Head Approaches. Irian Jaya Studies – a Programme for Interdisiplinary Research*, pp. 233–275. Rotterdam: A.A. Balkema.

Blench, R. 2010. Was there an Austroasiatic presence in Island Southeast Asia prior to the Austronesian expansion? *Bulletin of the Indo-Pacific Prehistory Association* 30: 133–144.

Blust, R. 1984–1985. The Austronesian homeland: a linguistic perspective. *Asian Perspectives* 26: 45–68.

Bulbeck, F.D. 1996–1997. The Bronze-Iron Age of South Sulawesi, Indonesia: Mortuary traditions, metallurgy and trade. In F.D. Bulbeck and N. Barnard (eds), *Ancient Chinese and Southeast Asian Bronze Age Cultures*, pp. 1007–1076. Taipei: SMC Publishing Inc.

——. 2008. An integrated perspective on the Austronesian diaspora: The switch from cereal agriculture to maritime foraging in the colonisation of Island Southeast Asia. *Australian Archaeology* 67: 31–52. doi.org/10.1080/03122417.2008.11681877.

——. 2014. The chronometric Holocene archaeological record of the Southern Thai-Malay peninsula. *International Journal of Asia Pacific Studies* 10(1): 111–162.

Bulbeck, F.D. and Nasruddin. 2002. Recent insights on the chronology and ceramics of the Kalumpang site complex, South Sulawesi, Indonesia. *Bulletin of the Indo-Pacific Prehistory Association* 22: 83–100.

Chang, K.C. 1964. Prehistoric and early historic culture horizons and traditions in South China. *Current Anthropology* 5: 359–375. doi.org/10.1086/200525.

——. 1970. Prehistoric archaeology of Taiwan. *Asian Perspective*s 13: 59–77.

Childe, V.G. 1936. *Man Makes Himself.* Oxford: Oxford University Press.

Dobney, K., T. Cucchi and G. Larson. 2008. The pigs of Island Southeast Asia and the Pacific: New evidence for taxonomic status and human-mediated dispersal. *Asian Perspectives* 47: 59–74. doi. org/10.1353/asi.2008.0009.

Duff, R. 1970. *Stone Adzes of Southeast Asia: An Illustrated Typology.* Christchurch: Canterbury Museum Bulletin.

Dyen, I. 1965. A Lexicostatistical Classification of the Austronesian Languages. *International Journal of American Linguistic Memoir* 19.

Fumihito, A., T. Miyake, M. Takada, R. Shingu, T. Endo, T. Gojobori, N. Kondo and S. Ohno. 1996. Monophyletic origin and unique dispersal patterns of domestic fowls. *Proceedings of the National Academy of Sciences* 93: 6792–6795. doi.org/10.1073/pnas.93.13.6792.

Galipaud, J.-C., A. Noury and L. Illouz. 2010. *Le site archéologique de Pain Haka, District de Florès Timur, province de Nusa Tenggara Timur, Indonésie.* Rapport d'évaluation du potential archéologique. Paris: Institut de recherche pour le développement.

Heekeren, H.R. van. 1950. Rapport over de ontgraving te Kamasi, Kalumpang (West Centraal Celebes). *Oudheidkundig Verslag Oudheidkundige Dienst in Indonesië 1949*, pp. 26–46. Bandung: A.C. Nix and Co.

——. 1972. *The Stone Age of Indonesia.* 2nd edition. Verhandelingen van het Koninklijk Instituut voor Taal-, Land- en Volkenkunde 61. The Hague: Martinus Nijhoof.

Heine-Geldern, R. von. 1945. Prehistoric research in the Netherlands Indies. In P. Honig and F. Verdoorn (eds), *Science and Scientists in the Netherlands Indies*, pp. 129–162. New York: Board for Netherlands Indies, Surinam, and Curacao.

Jaafar, Z. 2003. *Ancient Limestone Landscapes of Malaysia: An Archaeological Insight.* Kuala Lumpur: Jabatan Muzium dan Antiquiti.

Jiao, T. 2004. The Neolithic cultures in Southeast China and the search for an Austronesian homeland. In V. Paz (ed.), *Southeast Asian Archaeology. Wilhelm G. Solheim II Festschrift*, pp. 565–588. Manila: University of the Philippines Press.

Larson, G., T. Cucchi, M. Fujita, E. Matisoo-Smith, J. Robins, A. Anderson, B. Rolett, M. Spriggs, G. Dolman, T.-H. Kim, N.T.D. Thuy, E. Randi, M. Doherty, A.D. Rokus, R. Bolt, T. Djubiantono, B. Griffin, M. Intoh, E. Keane, P. Kirch, K.-T. Li, M. Morwood, L.M. Pedriña, P.J. Piper, R.J. Rabett, P. Shooter, G. Van den Burgh, E. West, S. Wickler, J. Yuan, A. Cooper and K. Dobney. 2007. Phylogeny and ancient DNA of *Sus* provides new insights into Neolithic expansion in Island Southeast Asia and Oceania. *Proceedings of the National Academy of Sciences* 104(12): 4834–4839. doi.org/10.1073/pnas.0607753104.

Larson, G., R. Liu, X. Zhao, J. Yuan, D. Fuller, L. Barton, K. Dobney, Q. Fan, Z. Gu, Z., X-H. Liu, Y. Luo, P. Lv, L. Andersson and N. Li. 2010. Patterns of East Asian pig domestication, migration, and turnover revealed by modern and ancient DNA. *Proceedings of the National Academy of Sciences* 107(17): 7686–7691. doi.org/10.1073/pnas.0912264107.

Lipson, M., P.-R. Loh, N. Patterson, P. Moorjani, Y.-C. Ko, M. Stoneking, B. Berger and D. Reich. 2014. Reconstructing Austronesian population history in Island Southeast Asia. *Nature Communication* 5, Article no. 4689, doi: 10/1038/incomms5689.

Liu, Y.-P., G.-S. Wu, Y.-G. Yao, Y.-M. Miao, G. Luikart, M. Baig, A. Beja-Pereira, Z.-L, Ding, M. Gounder Palanichamy and Y.-P. Zhang. 2002. Multiple maternal origins of chickens: Out of the Asian jungles. *Molecular Phylogenetics and Evolution* 38: 12–19. doi.org/10.1016/j. ympev.2005.09.014.

Masanari, N. and N. Kim Dung. 2002. Excavation of An Son: A Neolithic mound site in the middle reach of the Vam Co Dong River, southern Vietnam. *Bulletin of the Indo-Pacific Prehistory Association* 22: 101–109.

Meacham, W. 1984–1985. On the improbability of Austronesian origins in South China. *Asian Perspectives* 26: 89–106.

——. 1999. Neolithic to historic in the Hong Kong region. *Bulletin of the Indo-Pacific Prehistory Association* 18: 121–127.

Noerwidi, S. 2009. Archaeological research at Kendeng Lembu, East Java, Indonesia. *Bulletin of the Indo-Pacific Prehistory Association* 29: 26–32. doi.org/10.7152/bippa.v29i0.9474.

O'Connor, S. 2015. Rethinking the Neolithic in Island Southeast Asia, with particular reference to the archaeology of Timor Leste and Sulawesi. *Archipel* 90: 15–47.

Oppenheimer, S. 1998. *Eden in the East: The Drowned Continent of Southeast Asia.* London: Weidenfeld and Nicolson.

Oppenheimer, S. and M. Richards. 2001. Fast trains, slow boats, and the ancestry of the Polynesian Islanders. *Science Progress* 84: 157–181. doi.org/10.3184/003685001783238989.

Plutniak, S., A.A. Oktaviana, B. Sugiyanto, J.-M. Chazine and F.-X. Ricaut. 2014. New Ceramic Data from East Kalimantan: The cord-marked and red-slipped sherds of Liang Abu's layer 2 and Kalimantan's pottery chronology. *Journal of Pacific Archaeology* 5(1): 90–99.

Rabett, R.J., G. Barker, H. Barton, C. Hunt, L. Lloyd-Smith, V. Paz, P.J. Piper, R. Premathilake, G. Rushworth, M. Stephens and K. Szabó. 2013. Landscape transformations and human responses *c.* 11,500–4500 years ago. In G. Barker (ed.), *Rainforest Foraging and Farming in Island Southeast Asia*, pp. 217–253. Cambridge: McDonald Institute for Archaeological Research.

Simanjuntak, T. 1992. Neolitik di Indonesia, neraca dan perspektif penelitian. *Jurnal Arkeologi Indonesia* 1: 117–130.

—— (ed.). 2008. *Austronesian in Sulawesi.* Jakarta: Center for Prehistoric and Austronesian Studies.

——. 2013. Asal usul dan diáspora penutur Austronesia. Paper presented at the seminar 'Austronesia Dispersal: Gene, Language, and Civilization', Medan.

Simanjuntak, T., R. Fauzi, J.-C. Galipaud, F.A. Aziz and H. Buckley. 2012. Prasejarah Austronesia di Nusa Tenggara. Sebuah Pandangan awal. *Amerta* 30: 73–89.

Solheim, W.G. II. 1984–1985. The Nusantao hypothesis. *Asian Perspectives* 26: 77–88.

Spriggs, M. 1989. The dating of the island Southeast Asian Neolithic: An attempt at chronometric hygiene and linguistic correlation. *Antiquity* 63: 587–613. doi.org/10.1017/S0003598X00076560.

——. 2011. Archaeology and the Austronesian expansion: Where are we now? *Antiquity* 85: 510–528. doi.org/10.1017/S0003598X00067910.

Stein Callenfels, P.V. van. 1926. Bijdrage tot de chronologie van het neolithicum in Zuid-Oost Azie. *Oudheidkundige Verslag 1926*, pp. 174–180. Batavia (Jakarta): Oudheidkundige Dienst in Nederland Indie.

Storey, A.A., D. Quiroz, N. Beavan, and E. Matisoo-Smith. 2013. Polynesian chickens in the New World: A detailed application of a commensal approach. *Archaeology in Oceania* 42(2): 101–119. doi.org/10.1002/arco.5007.

Sutayasa, I.M. 1972. Notes on the Buni pottery complex, northwest Java. *Mankind* 8: 182–184.

Tanudirjo, D.A. 2001. *Islands in Between: Prehistory of the Northeastern Indonesia Archipelago*. Unpublished PhD thesis, Department of Archaeology and Anthropology, The Australian National University, Canberra.

Tanudirjo, D.A. and T. Simanjuntak. 2004. Indonesia di tengah debat asal-usul masyarakat Austronesia. In *Polemik Tentang Masyarakat Austronesia. Fakta atau fiksi?*, pp. 11–32. Jakarta: Lembaga Ilmu Pengetahuan Indonesia.

Thomson, V.A., O. Lebrasseur, J.J. Austin, T.L. Hunt, D.A. Burney, T. Denham, N.J. Rawlence, J.R. Wood, J. Gongora, L.G. Flink, A. Linderhom, K. Dobney, G. Larson and A. Cooper. 2014. Using ancient DNA to study the origins and dispersal of ancestral Polynesian chickens across the Pacific *Proceedings of the National Academy of Sciences* 111(35): 4826–4831.

Tumonggor, M.K., T.M. Karafet, B. Hallmark, J.S. Lansing, M.F. Hammer and M.P. Cox. 2013. The Indonesian archipelago: an ancient genetic highway linking Asia and the Pacific. *Journal of Human Genetics* 58: 165–173. doi.org/10.1038/jhg.2012.154.

Wiradnyana, K. and S. Taufikurrahman. 2011. *Gayo Merangkai Identitas*. Jakarta: Yayasan Pustaka Obor Indonesia.

12

Enter the Ceramic Matrix: Identifying the Nature of the Early Austronesian Settlement in the Cagayan Valley, Philippines

Helen Heath, Glenn R. Summerhayes and Hsiao-chun Hung

This paper addresses a major gap in our knowledge: the nature of Austronesian societies associated with the spread of the Neolithic through Island Southeast Asia. It addresses this gap by presenting a pilot study on the changing nature of settlement through pottery production from the Neolithic to the Iron Age. A physico-chemical analysis of pottery from the site of Nagsabaran located in Lal-lo, Cagayan Valley, Northern Luzon, Philippines, was undertaken and the data are used to assess models of mobility and sedentism in order to understand the nature of these early Austronesian communities. The research carried out through the physico-chemical analysis suggests more mobile populations during the Neolithic in the Cagayan Valley changing through time to a more sedentary society in the Iron Age.

Introduction

The dispersal and spread of Austronesian-language speakers from Taiwan into the Philippines and onwards through Island Southeast Asia (ISEA) and the Pacific has received much attention over the last decade (see Bellwood 2013 and 2015 for updates). One of the archaeological signatures of this spread in ISEA is seen as red-slipped pottery, which has been identified in numerous excavations throughout the region (Bellwood 2015: 286–287). Yet, in modelling this spread we have little data on the nature of Austronesian society. Bellwood (2011: S363) argues that Austronesian dispersal out of Taiwan was fuelled by population growth 'and a need for new cultivation land' (Bellwood 2015: 290). He sees the spread in the context of: 1. pressure from increasing populations of southern China and Taiwan; 2. advanced technology (he refers to boat construction and carpentry); 3. a dependence on agriculture and animal domestication; and 4. a 'portable food production repertoire that allowed long distance dispersal to take place'. Bellwood (2015: 286) also notes that the pretexts for this spread are now 'well documented' with the 'documentation of a six fold or greater increase in site numbers during the course of the third millennium BCE in eastern Taiwan' (Hung 2005: 126). From Taiwan, populations of Malayo-Polynesian speakers moved into the Philippines where sites in the Batanes Islands and the Cagayan Valley in northern Luzon have produced substantial assemblages of red-slipped pottery, plain-ware and incised and stamped pottery and other material culture dating to around

4000–3500 BP (Bellwood 2015: 286). From the Philippines one branch of the diaspora appears to have involved a sea crossing of *ca.* 2,300 km to the Marianas (Hung et al. 2011; Carson et al. 2013), whilst other human populations dispersed south and southwest across ISEA, with both strands eventually ending up in the Bismarck Archipelago before proceeding on to Near and Far Oceania. The absence of substantial linguistic differentiation suggests the diaspora from the Philippines south and east into ISEA and Oceania was fairly rapid. To emphasise the expeditious maritime movements of the Malayo-Polynesian-speaking peoples, Jared Diamond (1988: 307–308) coined the term 'express train'. Archaeologists in the Pacific have long acknowledged that this expansion was never simple, but rather a complex interplay of the three 'Is': Innovation, Integration and Introduction (Green 1991, 2000, 2003).

The defining of early Malayo-Polynesian settlement patterning has been aided in the western Pacific by the identification of more than 220 Lapita sites (see Anderson et al. 2001; Summerhayes 2007; Bedford and Sand 2007), which suggest a change from high mobility during early Lapita colonisation to subsequent sedentism and permanent villages. This change has been successfully modelled based on physico-chemical analysis of present-day pottery in Melanesia and its production and distribution (Summerhayes 2000a, 2003, 2004). On the basis of the selection of both clays and mineral fillers, and comparing them to pottery form and stylistic variation/similarities, a series of pottery scenarios was defined differentiating between specialist production, household production, and mobile community production. These scenarios were used as heuristic frameworks for comparison with the production of archaeological pottery assemblages (see Summerhayes 2000a for further details).

In contrast to the intensive studies on Lapita pottery, there has been little similar research on pottery from archaeological sites in ISEA and the information ceramic analysis might provide us with regard to settlement patterning and mobility in this region. To redress this imbalance a physico-chemical analysis was undertaken on pottery from the key settlement site of Nagsabaran, located in northern Luzon, Philippines. Nagsabaran possesses a material culture repertoire with strong similarities to the Taiwan Neolithic (Bellwood and Dizon 2005), and is thus considered to represent one of the earliest settlement sites inhabited by colonists entering ISEA from Taiwan. It is a well-dated archaeological site with deep stratigraphy and chronological sequence that encompasses both the regional Neolithic (4000–2500 BP) and Iron Age (2500–1500 BP). Most importantly, it produced a substantial assemblage of decorated and plain pottery that has the potential to provide interesting new information on the nature of human habitation in some of the earliest Malayo-Polynesian settlements outside of Taiwan.

The project aimed to answer two questions: 1. What is the nature of pottery production in the Nagsabaran site; and 2. Is there a change through time from pottery production in the Neolithic to the Iron Age? These questions were addressed through a physico-chemical analysis of the ceramic assemblage within the two distinct phases of occupation at the site. The outcomes of the chemical analyses were used to develop models of mobility similar to those outlined by Summerhayes (2000a, 2000b) for the spread of Lapita in the western Pacific.

Nagsabaran – Northern Luzon

The Nagsabaran shell mound is located in the Lal-lo region of the Cagayan Valley, northeast Luzon, about 20 km inland on the south bank of Zabaran Creek/Nagsabaran Creek, to the west of the Cagayan River (Figure 12.1; Carson et al. 2013: 21).

Originally called the Alaguia shell midden in the early 1990s, the site was renamed Nagsabaran in 1996 by a Filipino-Taiwanese team who undertook initial excavations at the site a few years later, in 2000 to 2001. The excavation of eight test pits (Pits 1–8) resulted in the identification of two distinctive depositional sequences: an upper 'Metal Age' shell mound 1–3 m thick, overlying alluvial silts containing 'Neolithic' material culture between 1–2 m in depth. Sandwiched between these cultural deposits was a sedimentary horizon devoid of archaeological remains, suggesting a hiatus between the 'earlier' and 'later' phases of activity. This hiatus is especially clear within the southeast area of the site (Hung 2008). A similar 'hiatus' has been recorded on other sites in the Lal-Lo region, and Tanaka (2002) has proposed that this widespread abandonment might have been a result of flooding.

Further excavations in 2004 of Pits 9 and 10 in southeast area of Nagsabaran by archaeologists from The Australian National University and the National Museum of the Philippines confirmed the stratigraphic sequence recorded in 2000–2001, and the substantial differences between the material culture identified in the shell mound and that recorded in the underlying silt deposits (Hung 2008; Figure 12.2). Hung (2008) noted that the material culture was discontinuous between the upper shell mound deposits (with the hiatus between Spits 8 and 11) that contained black, brown or red pottery (some slipped), glass beads, glass bracelets, iron tools, fired clay pendants, jar burials with human skulls and headless extended burials, and beneath the 'hiatus' where three layers of silt sediments produced red slipped pottery (occasionally with punctate stamping and lime infill), course buff or beige pottery, spindle whorls, fired clay penannular earrings and pendants, stone flakes and adzes, and bone of pig and deer.

In 2009, another four trenches (Pits 11–14) were excavated towards the middle of the shell mound (Pit 14), close to the southeast periphery of the site near former Pits 9 and 10 (Pits 11 and 12), and yet further to the southeast (Pit 13). Although the previously documented 'three-layer' sequence of deposits was identified, much greater stratigraphic resolution was determined, especially within the shell mound. The shell mound could be differentiated into large dumps of complete or almost complete shells devoid of material culture separated by thin humic layers containing substantial amounts of pottery and bone. Numerous postholes were recorded truncating pre-existing shell mound layers (and often into the underlying silts) from the humic (occupation) layers. Some postholes measured more than 0.8 m in diameter and over 1 m in depth and contained pottery and stone used as 'post-packing' to stablise the post in the ground. These posts were clearly designed to support substantial above ground structures. Amano et al. (2013) interpreted the sequential build-ups of shell mound interspersed with habitation and construction on the mound as deliberate attempts to increase the height of the mound, and hence structures above the surrounding environment, perhaps to avoid flooding. This interpretation however is debatable.

Below the shell mound was a dark humic layer full of pottery and bone that marked the initial phases of re-occupation of the site, prior to the development of the shell mound. This layer was deposited directly on top of 0.2–0.3 m of sterile 'hiatus' deposits. Beneath this was the silty clay sediments containing high concentrations of red-slipped pottery and other material culture associated with the regional Neolithic. Some excavated postholes were assigned to this phase of activity.

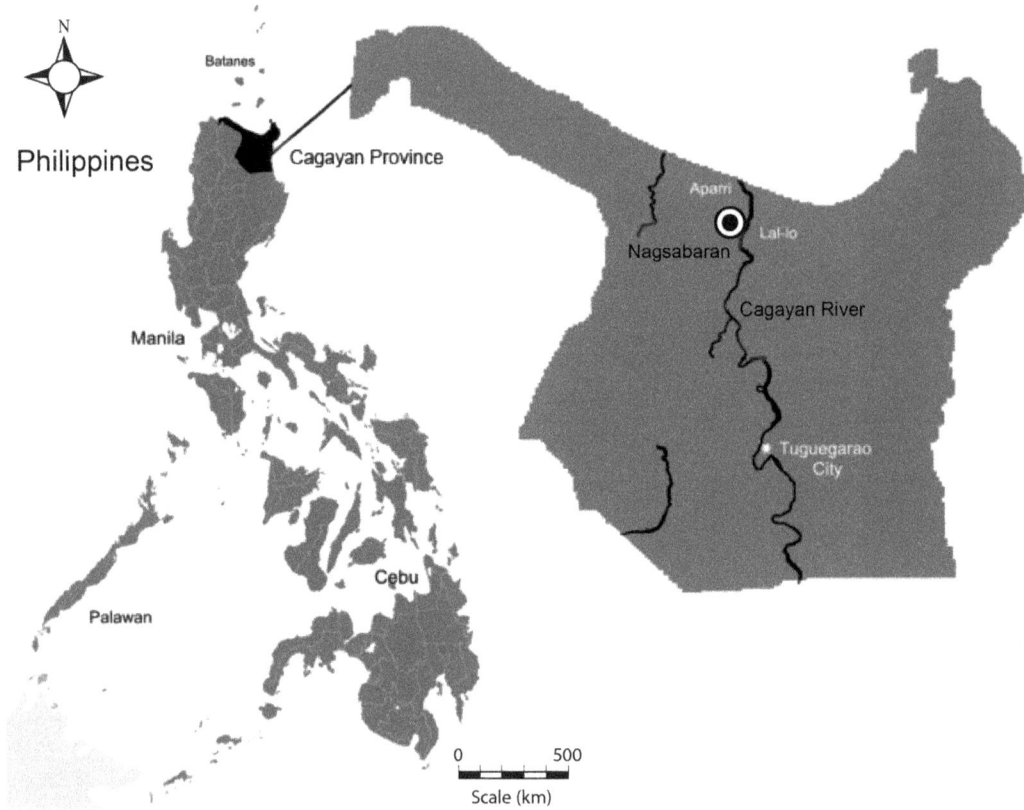

Figure 12.1 The location of Nagsabaran on the east side of the Cagayan River close to Lal-lo in northern Luzon, Philippines.

Source: After Amano et al. 2013.

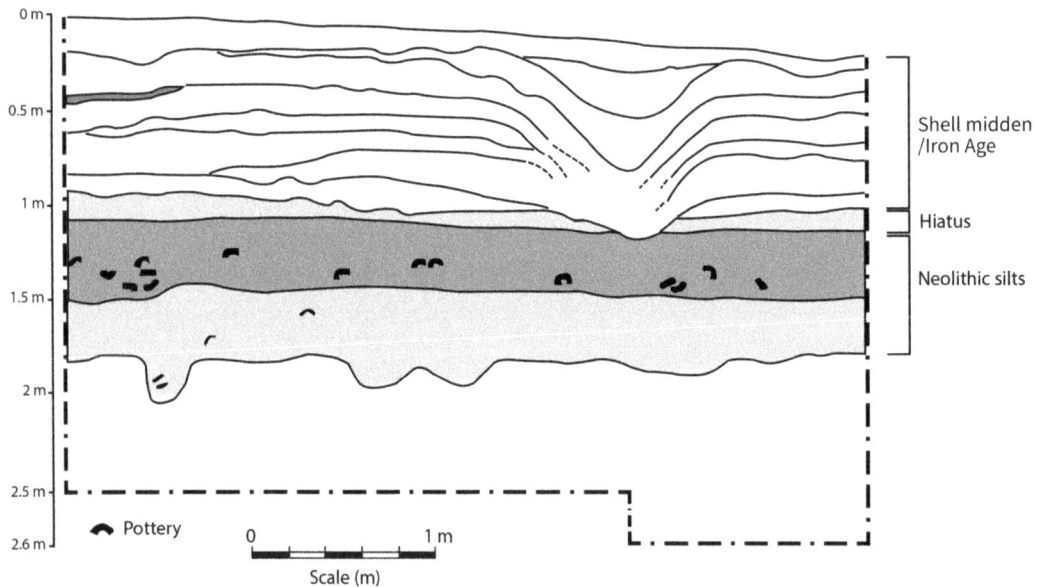

Figure 12.2 Stratigraphy of Test Pit 9 from Nagsabaran.

Source: Redrawn from Hung 2008.

The previous 31 radiocarbon dates (on charcoal, shell and bone) suggested that the occupation in the southeast area of the site was initially at 4000 through 2600 BP, and again at 2100 through 1500 BP (Hung 2008). In comparison to the gap or hiatus at 2600 through 2100 BP in the southeast portion of the site, more recent work has identified burial features dated to within this 'gap' in the central area of the site.

Studying human mobility through using physico-chemical analysis of pottery

Chemical analysis combined with other research on pottery, including morphology and design, can demonstrate potential interactions between communities. For example, if clays sourced for pottery production are local but there are design similarities across broad regions, then social, cultural and/or ideological coalesence could be invoked to account for the geographic distribution of motifs, rather than simple pottery exchange (Summerhayes 2000a: 30). Analyses can, however, go beyond identifying whether interaction occurred, and can potentially inform us about the nature of settlement patterning and mobility as well. For instance, by comparing the clays and fillers used in the production of pottery, Summerhayes (2000a, 2000b, 2003) was able to identify changing resource use and production techniques and relate these to Lapita mobility/settlement patterns within the Bismarck Archipelago. The results suggest that though Early Lapita pottery was mostly locally produced, the potters used diverse combinations of clays and tempers/fillers from various different geographic locations along river systems and beaches to produce the same vessel forms with identical decoration (Figure 12.3). In later periods, Lapita production continued to be locally based but manufacturing techniques became more conservative and standardised with only one clay source and a limited range of temper/fillers utilised in the construction of all pottery (Figure 12.4). The change in source material acquisition from Early to Late Lapita in the Bismarcks was interpreted as reflecting a change in settlement patterns, with the early production pattern resulting from higher mobility associated with the initial colonisation period and the later pattern reflecting more sedentary communities.

Neither the Early nor Late Lapita production and distribution patterns corresponded to modern specialist pottery production for exchange seen in the ethnographic past from a number of areas in Papua New Guinea. These differences are represented graphically by comparing Figures 12.3 and 12.4 with the representation of specialist production in Figure 12.5.

In contrast to Lapita studies, almost no physico-chemical studies of pottery have been attempted to explain patterns of human mobility in ISEA. However, it should be noted that a previous physico-chemical analysis on pottery from the northern Philippines was undertaken earlier by Swete Kelly (2008). Unlike the study proposed here, Swete Kelly aimed to assess human social interaction associated with Austronesian dispersals. She analysed pottery samples from two east coast Taiwan sites, three from the Batanes, two from the Cagayan Valley, and one from east Luzon (Dimolit). Yet, the analysis was to determine similarities rather than specific production issues. Thus the nature of early settlement is unknown in the valley, even though links can be drawn between sites through pottery types, decoration and petrographic analysis (Aoyagi et al. 1986; Tanaka and Orogo 2000; Ogawa 2002; Tanaka 2002; Mijares 2005; Hung 2005, 2008).

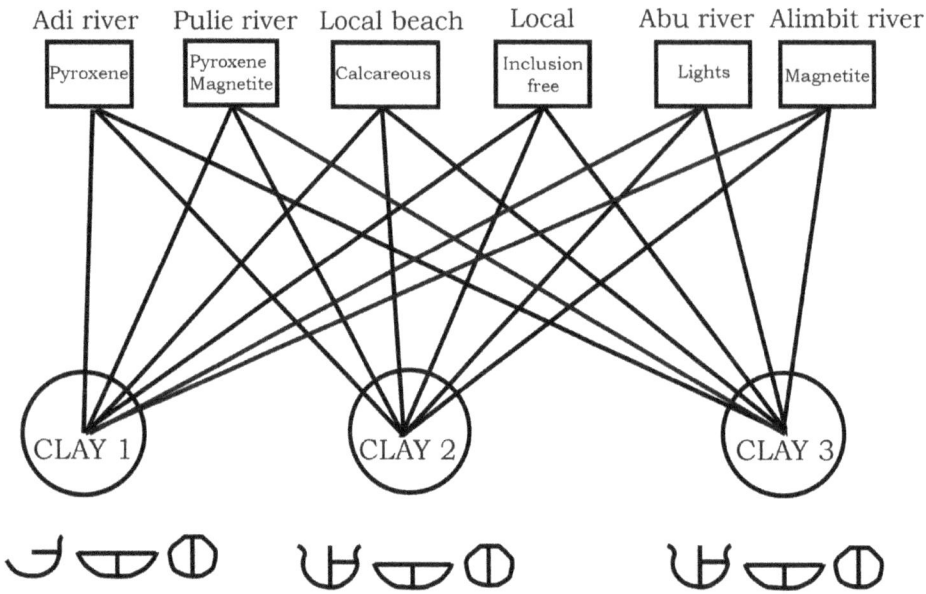

Figure 12.3 Pottery production indicating mobile settlement – selection of fabrics in the Early Lapita Arawe assemblages.

Source: G.R. Summerhayes.

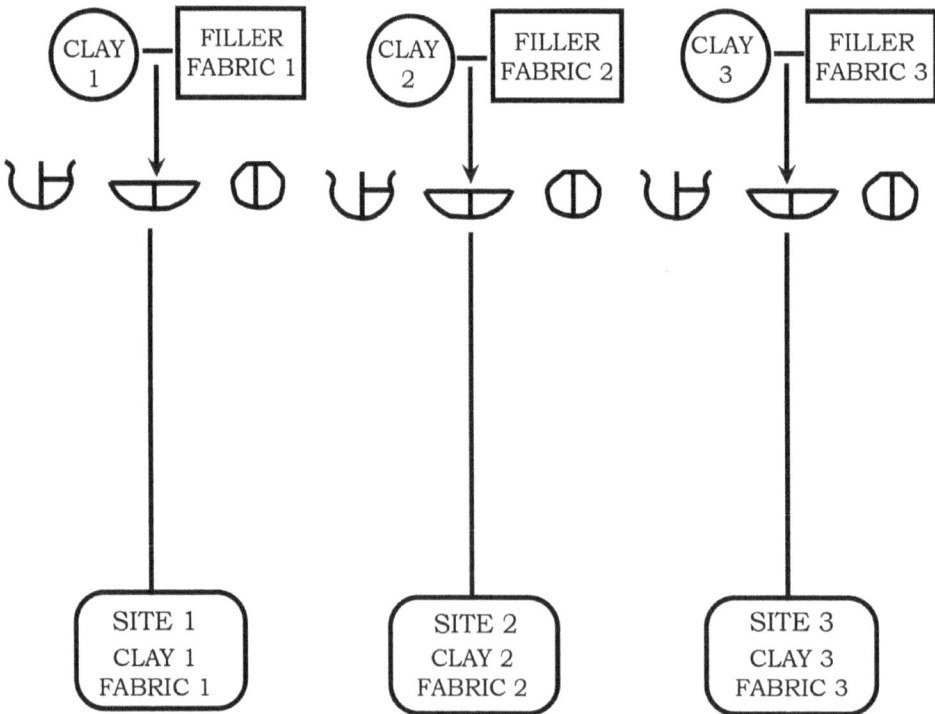

Figure 12.4 Selection of fabrics within Later Lapita assemblages: Sedentary signature.

Source: G.R. Summerhayes.

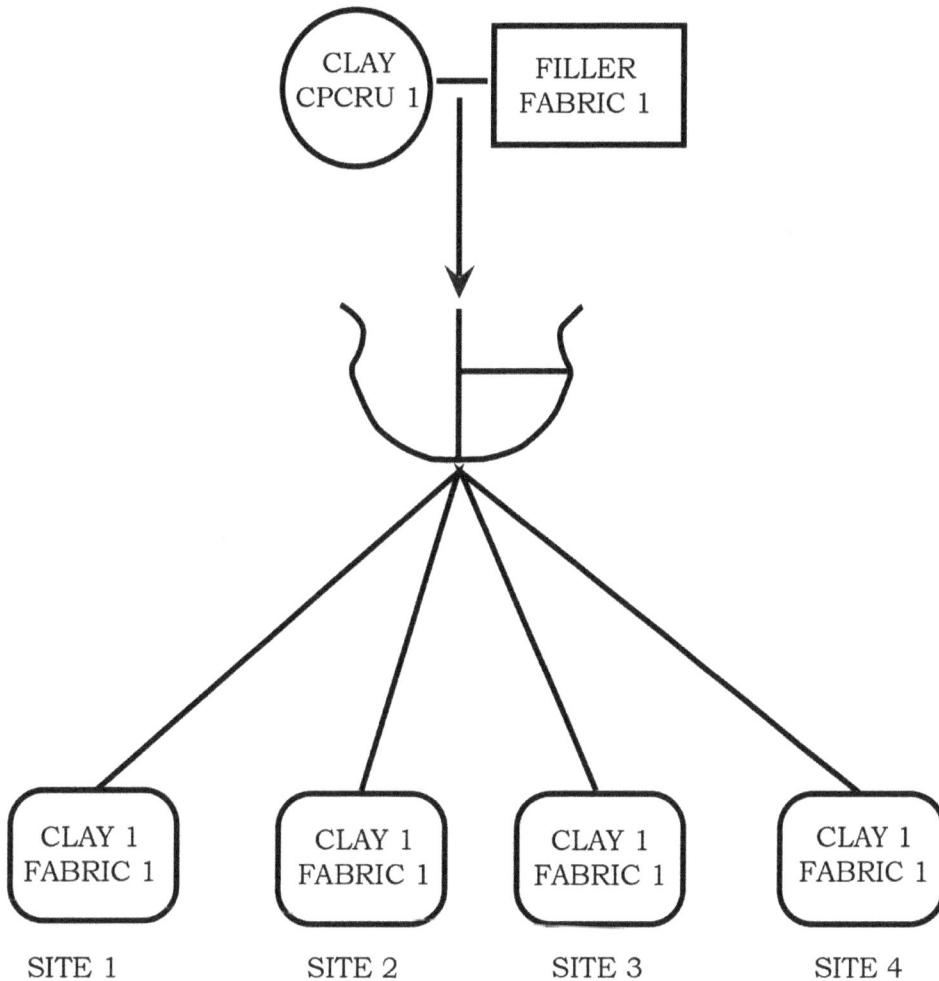

Figure 12.5 Selection of fabrics expected from specialist general production.
Source: G.R. Summerhayes.

There has been much research carried out on pottery style and decoration from Northern Luzon to the point where there is now a vast collection of recorded types of pottery (Tanaka 2002; Ogawa 2002; Hung 2008). Linking this with a physico-chemical analysis would add to an understanding of the region's past. There is much potential for a chemical analysis in the Cagayan Valley to help us understand the nature of interaction between communities, the distinction between distant and local clay sourcing as well as trade and exchange during the period.

Sample selection – Nagsabaran

For the purposes of this study, a sample of 47 sherds from throughout the stratigraphic sequence of Pits 9 and 10 (excavated in 2004) in the southeast area of Nagsabaran was selected by Hung for physico-chemical analysis (Table 12.1). Samples taken from Spits 10–18 in both pits were recovered from the lower silts and correspond to the earlier (Neolithic) phase of occupation at the site. Those from Spits 1–9 were retrieved from the sequence of shell mound deposits and all date to the Iron Age. As part of the preliminary analysis, the contextual information for each sherd was catalogued and each fragment's morphology, shape, colour and thickness were recorded. This information was useful in identifying whether form and/or function potentially played a role in the decision-making process with regard to raw material choice and manufacturing techniques.

Table 12.1 Pottery samples selected for analysis.

Spit	No. sherds
Iron Age 2500–1500 BP	
1a	1
1b	1
4	4
5	6
6	2
7	4
8	2
9	4
Neolithic 4000–3000 BP	
11	4
12	3
13	9
15	5
17	1
18	1

Source: Authors.

The Scanning Electron Microscope

This study used the Zeiss Field Emission Gun Scanning Electron Microscope (FEGSEM) to chemically characterise the raw materials used in pottery production at Nagsabaran. As the samples for FEGSEM analysis for this study were required to be in briquette form, this technique could then distinguish between and provide separate chemical analysis of the ceramic matrix and mineral inclusions, something that is not possible with techniques using crushed samples (see Summerhayes (1997, 2000a, 2000b, 2007) for more detail). The FEGSEM is also known for its remarkably high resolution imaging that allows the analyst to accurately examine fine details (Gnauck et al. 2002; Froh 2004).

Operating conditions

The FEGSM, which is housed at the Otago Centre for Electron Microscopy (OCEM), uses an XMax20 silicon drift energy dispersive X-ray (EDX) detector and AZTEC acquisition and processing software from Oxford Instruments. An image of the sample is produced by the interactions between the electron beam and the sample. The surface is scanned line by line by a focused beam of electrons. Interactions are created by the primary electrons from the beam creating the emission of secondary electrons, backscattered electrons and X-rays, which are used to identify the topography of the sample surface and are collected by a detector to be displayed on a computer. The images obtained from scanning are referred to as electron micrographs with resolutions down to about a nanometre. By looking at this image a researcher can then target a desired mineral or clay with the electron beam. The beam travels into the sample and generates several signals. Through the interaction of these signals, the elemental makeup of that minerals or clay is collected and a picture of the studied surface is fed into a computer for further analysis (Froh 2004; see Zhou et al. 2006 for more on the fundamental workings of an SEM).

Samples were made into polished briquettes and carbon coated. The elements, in oxide form, that were measured for clay analysis were as follows: magnesium, aluminium, silicon, phosphorus, potassium, calcium, titanium, and iron. Through the use of the electron microscope a statistically representative population of minerals within the temper and in the clay matrix can be identified.

Clay matrices

The data gathered for the clay matrices of the 47 samples was analysed through principal component analysis (PCA using Wrights MVARCH 1991), a statistical method commonly used in archaeological investigations (Summerhayes 2000a; Hogg 2007; Niziolek 2013). All samples were standardised using MVARCH. To evaluate the characterisation of production within the site, samples were grouped into Chemical Paste Compositional Reference Units (CPCRU). Defined by Bishop and Rands (1982; Bishop et al. 1982), CPCRUs are groupings of sherds based on their chemical similarity (see Summerhayes 2000a: Chapter 4).

Inclusions

Mineral inclusions within each sample were identified based on elemental makeup. The cataloguing of minerals was assembled within the AZTEC software so that statistically robust mineral composition data could be compiled and then analysed manually with known standard mineral compositions with the aid of the Deer et al. (1992) major text which outlines the elemental composition of all minerals.

Results

Analysis of the clay matrix

Neolithic

Five CPCRU (here called CPCRU 1 to 5) were identified in the Neolithic phase (Figure 12.6). CPCRU 1 contains the more samples (N=9) than any other CPCRU, with six identified in Spit 13, and one respectively from Spits 18, 15 and 12. The chronological spread of samples within this CPCRU (from Spits 12 to 18) suggests continual use of the same clay source region throughout much of the earlier phase of occupation at Nagsabaran. CPCRU 2 contains eight samples spread between Spits 11 to 15, and CPCRU 3 contains four samples from Spits 12 to 15. CPCRU 4 (Spit 17) and 5 (Spit 11) are outliers containing a single sample each. The available samples do not suggest any trend towards increasing or decreasing CPCRU variability over time during the Neolithic phase of occupation.

Iron Age

Of the three CPCRUs recorded for the Metal Age phase (Figure 12.7), CPCRU 1 contains 12 samples from Spits 1–8, CPCRU 2 possesses eight samples from between Spits 4 and 9 and CPCRU 3 consists of a single outlier from Spit 5.

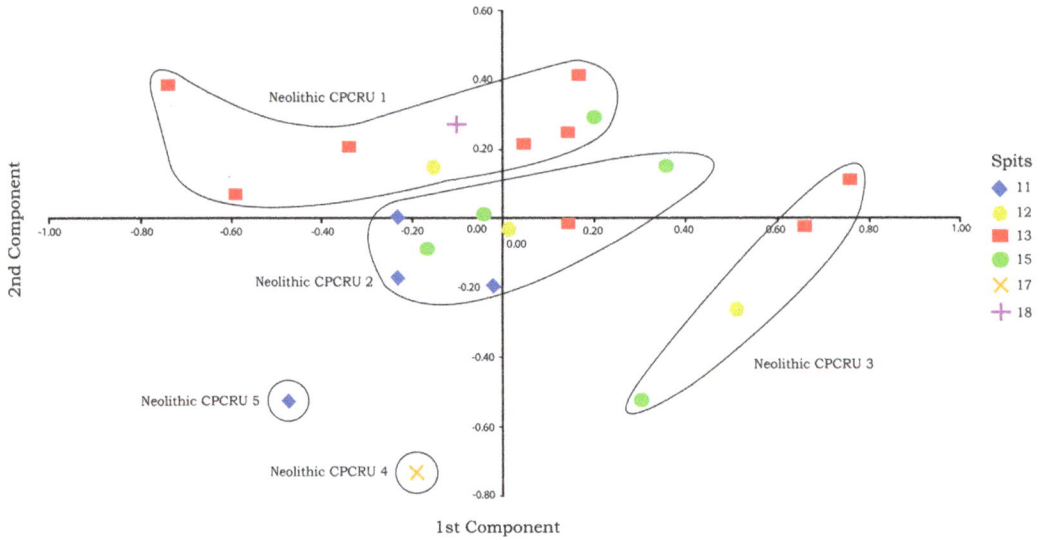

Figure 12.6 PCA plot of Neolithic showing CPCRUs.

Source: Authors.

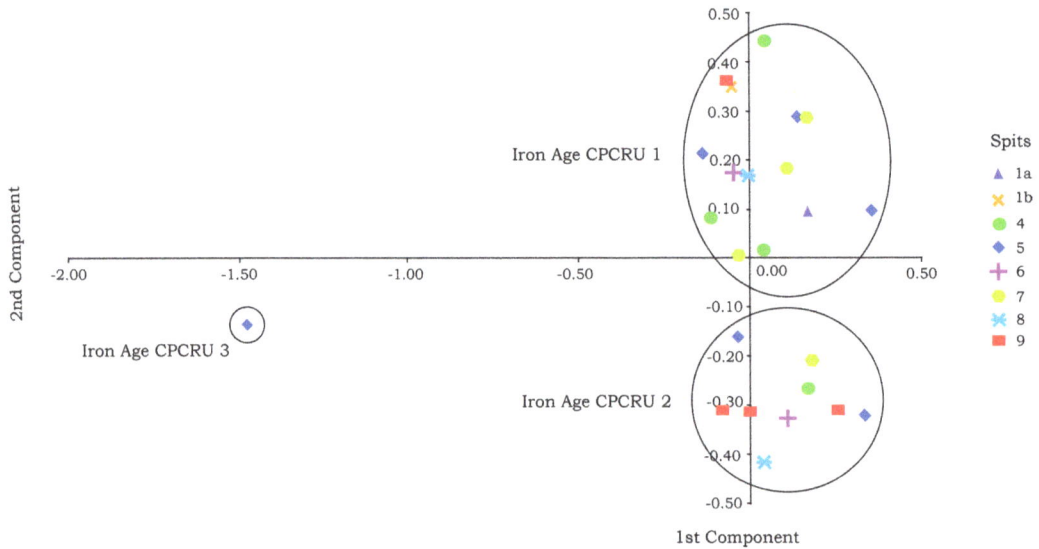

Figure 12.7 PCA plot of Iron Age showing CPCRUs.

Source: Authors.

All layers

With the exception of the two single Neolithic CPCRU samples (4 and 5), which fall within the range of the Iron Age specimens, and Iron Age sample 13 that appears to be a clear outlier, the Neolithic and Iron Age samples separate fairly neatly from each other with respect to clay matrices (Figures 12.8 and 12.9).

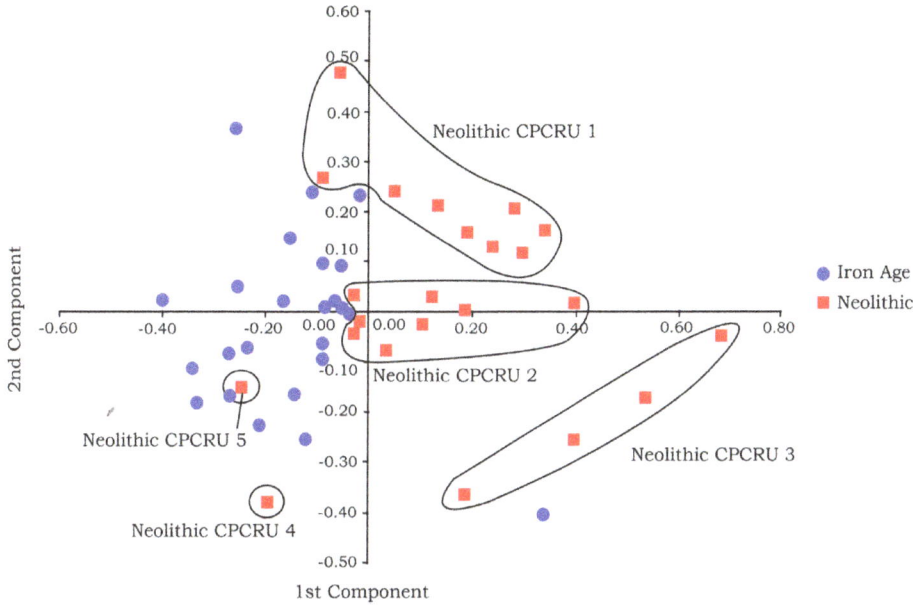

Figure 12.8 Comparison of Neolithic and Iron Age CPCRUs using components 1 and 2.
Source: Authors.

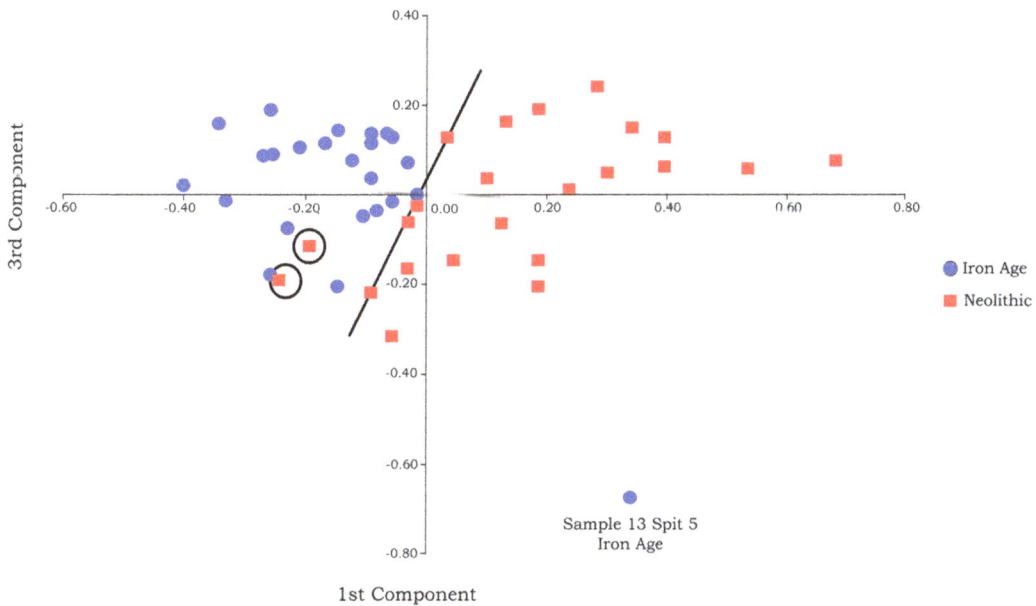

Figure 12.9 Comparison of Neolithic and Iron Age CPCRUs using components 1 and 3.
Source: Authors.

Mineral inclusions – fabrics

Plagioclase feldspars and quartz were recorded in all Neolithic (Figure 12.10) and Iron Age (Figure 12.11) samples, albeit in varying quantities. Haematite and Ilmenite were present in the majority of the Neolithic and Iron Age specimens and amphiboles were absent from just five of the tested samples. Despite clear similarities in mineral inclusions there is also some notable sample variability that suggests mineral fillers were being collected from different geographic locales, but within a region with consistent underlying geology. For example, pyroxenes were identified in only 15 of 23 Neolithic specimens and eight of 23 Iron Age samples. Similarly epidote was found in only 15 Neolithic and six Iron Age samples. Alkaline feldspars were relatively rare being found in only two Neolithic and one Iron Age samples. Other rare components in Neolithic samples were zircon (one sample, 29) and copper (two samples, 38 and 47) (see Table 12.2).

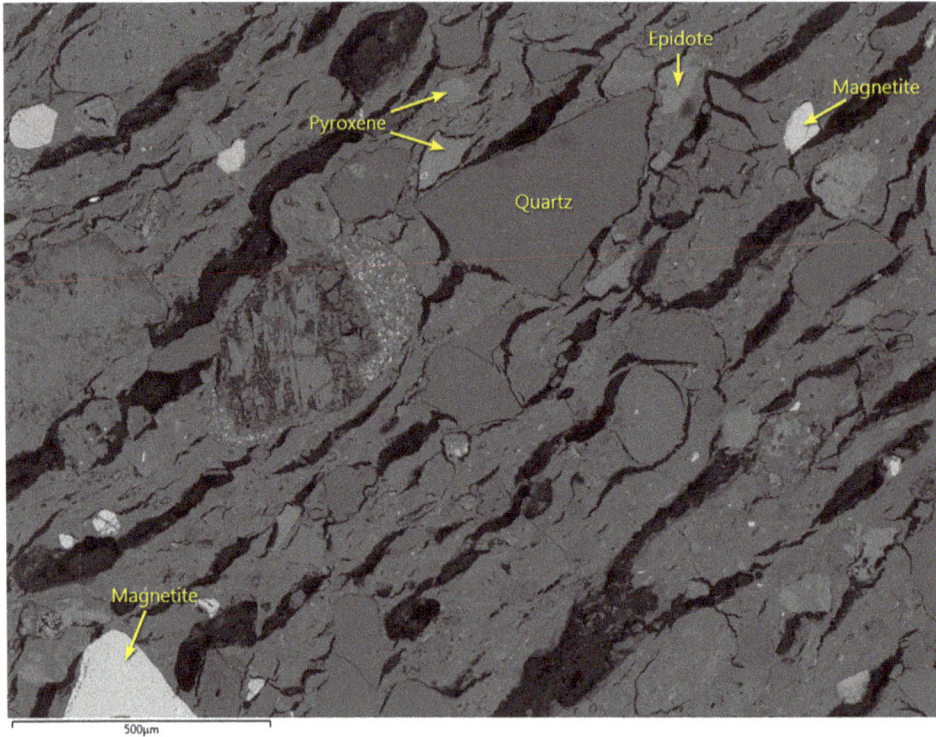

Figure 12.10 Image of pottery fabric – Neolithic at 160x magnification.
Source: Authors.

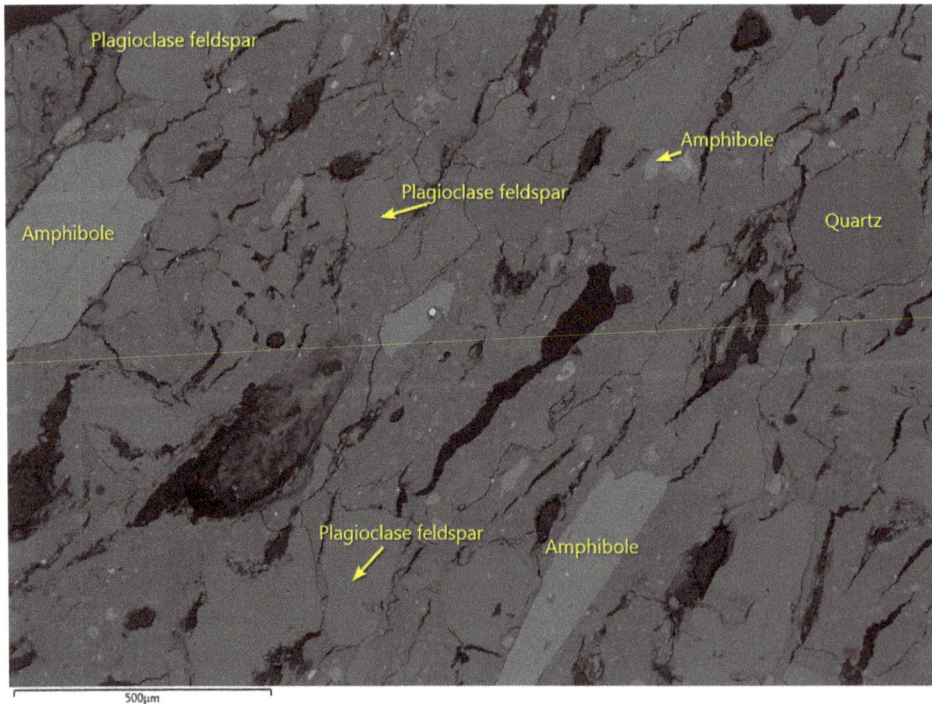

Figure 12.11 Image of pottery fabric – Iron Age at 160x magnification.
Source: Authors.

Table 12.2 Distribution of minerals in ceramic samples.

CPCRU	Sample No.	Zircon	Titanite	Epidote	Pyroxene	Amphibole	Alkali feldspar	Plagioclase feldspar	Quartz	Hematite	Ilmenite	Magnetite	Copper
Iron Age 1	1				✓	✓		✓	✓			✓	
	3					✓		✓	✓		✓		
	4			✓	✓	✓		✓	✓		✓	✓	
	5					✓		✓	✓	✓	✓	✓	
	7				✓	✓		✓	✓	✓	✓	✓	
	8			✓		✓		✓	✓	✓		✓	
	9			✓	✓	✓		✓	✓		✓	✓	
	11					✓		✓	✓	✓		✓	
	15				✓	✓	✓	✓	✓		✓	✓	
	16					✓		✓	✓			✓	
	17							✓	✓	✓	✓	✓	
	18					✓		✓	✓		✓	✓	
	21					✓		✓	✓		✓	✓	
	24				✓	✓		✓	✓			✓	
Iron Age 2	6					✓		✓	✓	✓	✓	✓	
	10				✓			✓	✓			✓	
	12							✓	✓			✓	
	14				✓	✓		✓	✓		✓	✓	
	19			✓		✓		✓	✓		✓	✓	
	20			✓		✓		✓	✓		✓		
	22					✓		✓	✓		✓		
	23			✓		✓		✓	✓		✓	✓	
	25					✓		✓	✓		✓	✓	
Iron Age 3	13			✓		✓		✓	✓				

CPCRU	Sample No.	Zircon	Titanite	Epidote	Pyroxene	Amphibole	Alkali feldspar	Plagioclase feldspar	Quartz	Hematite	Ilmenite	Magnetite	Copper
Neolithic 1	30			✓	✓	✓		✓	✓	✓		✓	
	35			✓				✓	✓	✓		✓	
	38		✓	✓	✓	✓	✓	✓	✓	✓	✓	✓	✓
	39				✓	✓		✓	✓	✓	✓	✓	
	40			✓	✓		✓	✓	✓	✓	✓	✓	
	41			✓	✓	✓		✓	✓		✓		
	42			✓	✓			✓	✓	✓			
	43				✓			✓	✓	✓	✓		
	49			✓	✓	✓		✓	✓				
Neolithic 2	26			✓	✓	✓		✓	✓			✓	
	27					✓		✓	✓		✓	✓	
	29	✓				✓		✓	✓			✓	
	32					✓		✓	✓			✓	
	37			✓	✓	✓		✓	✓	✓		✓	
	45		✓	✓	✓	✓		✓	✓			✓	
	46			✓	✓	✓		✓	✓			✓	
	47		✓	✓		✓		✓	✓			✓	✓
Neolithic 3	31			✓		✓		✓	✓	✓	✓	✓	
	34					✓		✓	✓	✓	✓	✓	
	36				✓	✓		✓	✓	✓	✓	✓	
	44			✓				✓	✓			✓	
Neolithic 4	48			✓	✓	✓		✓	✓	✓	✓	✓	
Neolithic 5	28				✓	✓		✓	✓	✓	✓	✓	

Source: Authors.

The three prevalent minerals – plagioclase feldspars, quartz and amphibole – along with rarer ones such as zircon, are common in igneous rocks formed through volcanic activity. This geology is typical of the Cagayan Valley as there is a presence of volcanic rock along the Sierra Madre Mountains (Dimalanta and Yumul 2004) and in the plains of the Cagayan River (Mijares 2005). Evidence reveals that the early potters were not using sand as a temper. Instead they were exploiting the alluvial deposits along the banks and flood plains of the Cagayan River that are rich in igneous minerals.

Discussion

The CPCRUs from the Neolithic and Iron Age clearly separate with the exception of two Neolithic samples (Figures 12.8 and 12.9). Of importance is the apparent reduction of CPCRUs from the Neolithic to the Iron Age, with potters from both periods selecting mineral fillers from the alluvium of the Cagayan Valley sediments. How do we interpret this reduction in pottery clay source selection over time?

If we compare the results to those three models seen in Figures 12.3 to 12.5 we see two correlations. Pottery production from the Neolithic fits more easily with the mobility model (Figure 12.3) with a number of CPCRUs being utilised, each containing a number of separate mineral fillers. As noted in the mobility model, technologically these potters were not conservative, using many combinations of tempers/fillers and different clays to produce similar ware (Figure 12.3). Instead of mobility, another model could involve the importation of pottery from a number of areas, each having a separate CPCRU, although the variability of mineral fillers per CPCRU argues against simple production and exchange models. From a regional perspective it can be seen that many of the Neolithic assemblages from this area are interlinked as seen by excavation and examination of assemblages in the Cagayan Valley. For example, pottery types between Bangag and Catugan share type similarities (Tanaka 2002), as is also the case comparing Pamittan and Magapit in decoration styles (Tanaka and Orogo 2000). The sites dotted along the Cagayan River are not the only areas that share similarities in cultural assemblages. Mijares (2005) found similarities in rim form, surface treatments and petrographic qualities between pottery assemblages from the Cagayan River Valley and the Peñablanca cave sites. In terms of the petrographic analysis, the temper inclusions from the cave sites were derived from the igneous mineral-rich material from the alluvial deposits along the Cagayan River. This in turn matched sherd samples from the Cagayan Valley sites of Nagsabaran, Magapit and Andarayan, as well as a modern sample from Atulu suggesting either interaction between hunter-gatherers from these upland cave sites and the early Austronesian settlers in the open valley (Mijares 2005), or indeed just the wider regional activities of the Austronesian settlers.

The evidence for links between sites throughout the valley shows that there was much interaction between groups, as supported through the chemical analysis undertaken in this research on the variability of clay sources. The early settlers were moving through the land exploiting clay sources for ceramic construction and in addition using fillers from the alluvial plains from along the river. Such movement would foster interaction with other groups resulting in trade and exchange and the cultural transmission of ideas such as pottery styles and techniques.

This differs from the later Iron Age pottery production where two CPCRUs were being utilised for all but one sample. However, the picture is more complicated as there is still a variety of mineral fillers being utilised for the Iron Age pottery. Nevertheless, they are being used with an apparent reduction in clay sources. The fewer number of clay sources could indicate a localisation in pottery manufacturing that would be indicative of a more settled community. Still, neither the Neolithic or Iron Age patterns fits the specialist trader model shown in Figure 12.5.

Conclusions

This paper aimed to shed light on the nature of Austronesian societies associated with the spread of the Neolithic through Island Southeast Asia by focusing on the changing nature of settlement through pottery production from the Neolithic to the Iron Age in the Cagayan Valley. The results suggest a change in pottery production from the Neolithic to Iron Age, which is interpreted here as a change in settlement pattern from a mobile/interactive society to a more sedentary one in the Iron Age.

Of interest is the hiatus between the Neolithic and Iron Age period pottery production. There have been major geomorphological events occurring that may partially explain the hiatus. Possible flooding obscuring the cultural transition between the Neolithic and Iron Age has been noted (Tanaka 2002). This relates to mobility in the area and change through time, as a flooding of sites along the Cagayan River would have resulted in the abandonment of these areas. This was witnessed in the stratigraphy of the Nagsabaran site with the absence of cultural material in Spit 10. After 500 years, the site was inhabited again by Iron Age peoples who were characteristically a sedentary group, compared to the Neolithic peoples who earlier inhabited the site. It is unknown who these people were, but the material culture from the Iron Age along the valley does share cultural similarities with Taiwan, especially in terms of the black pottery. This evidence suggests the establishment of continual trading connections and interactions between Taiwan and sedentary Iron Age groups in the Cagayan Valley. Connection and interaction are further supported by the theory of maritime trading networks during the Iron Age (Hung et al. 2007).

Our results agree with other evidence that the early Austronesians were highly mobile people, not only in Southeast Asia but also to the east in Micronesia. It is from ISEA that people may have colonised the Marianas for the first time (Hung et al. 2011). Hung and her colleagues (2012) do not suggest that the Marianas were directly settled from the Cagayan Valley but stress that the pottery style was shared between these two regions. The first settlements in the Marianas occurred at 3500 BP while the first Neolithic settlements in Northern Luzon occurred at 4000 BP (Hung et al. 2011) suggesting that after a period of 500 years a group of Neolithic peoples of the Northern Philippines succeeded in travelling the 2,300 km of open sea to the Marianas.

The Austronesian-speaking peoples expanded rapidly through ISEA, through the Bismarck Archipelago and into the Pacific, punctuated by stops lasting only a few hundred years. The variability of the clay sources found in the early settlement phase at Nagsabaran is consistent with other evidence for the mobile nature of early Austronesian speaking peoples.

Acknowledgements

The authors would like to thank David Prior and Kat Lilly from the Department of Geology and the Otago Microscopy Department for the use and instruction of the FEGSEM. We wish to thank the National Museum of the Philippines for permission to excavate and loan of the materials. We thank Brent Pooley for his assistance in sample making.

References

Amano, N., Piper, P., Hung, H-c., and Bellwood, P. 2013. Introduced domestic animals in the Neolithic and Metal Age of the Philippines: Evidence from Nagsabaran, Northern Luzon. *The Journal of Island and Coastal Archaeology* 8: 317–335. doi.org/10.1080/15564894.2013.781084.

Anderson, A., S. Bedford, G. Clark, I. Lilley, C. Sand, G.R. Summerhayes and R. Torrence. 2001. An Inventory of Lapita Sites containing dentate-stamped pottery. In G. Clark, A. Anderson and T. Sorovi-Vunidilo (eds), *The Archaeology of Lapita Dispersal in Oceania: Papers from the Fourth Lapita Conference, June 2000,* pp. 1–14. Terra Australis 17. Canberra: Department of Archaeology and Natural History, and Centre for Archaeology, The Australian National University.

Aoyagi, Y., M.L. Jr. Aguilera, H. Ogawa and K. Tanaka. 1986. The shell midden in the lower reaches of the Cagayan River. *The Journal of Sophia Asian Studies* 4: 45–91.

Bedford, S. and C. Sand. 2007. Lapita and Western Pacific settlement: Progress, prospects and persistent problems. In S. Bedford, C. Sand and S. Connaughton (eds), *Oceanic Explorations: Lapita and Western Pacific Settlement,* pp. 1–15. Terra Australis 26. Canberra: Department of Archaeology and Natural History and Centre for Archaeology, The Australian National University.

Bellwood, P. 2011. Holocene population history in the Pacific region as a model for worldwide food producer dispersals. *Current Anthropology* 52(S4): S363–S378. doi.org/10.1086/658181.

——. 2013. Southeast Asian Islands: archaeology. In I. Ness (ed.), *The Encyclopedia of Global Human Migration,* pp. 1–9. Oxford: Blackwell Publishing.

——. 2015. Southeast Asian Islands: archaeology. In P. Bellwood (ed.), *The Global Prehistory of Human Migration,* pp. 284–292. Chichester: Wiley Blackwell.

Bellwood, P. and E. Dizon. 2005. The Batanes Archaeological Project and the 'Out of Taiwan'. Hypothesis for Austronesian Dispersal. *Journal of Austronesian Studies* 1(1): 1–32.

Bishop, R. and R. Rands. 1982. Mayan fine paste ceramics: a compositional perspective. In J.A. Sabloff (ed.), *Analyses of Fine Paste Ceramics. Excavations at Siebal,* pp. 283–314. Cambridge: Harvard University, Memoirs of the Peabody Museum of Archaeology and Ethnology.

Bishop, R., R. Rands and G. Holley. 1982. Ceramic compositional analyses in archaeological perspective. *Archaeological Method and Theory* 5: 275–320.

Carson, T, H.-c. Hung, G.R. Summerhayes and P. Bellwood. 2013. The pottery trail from Southeast Asia to Remote Oceania. *The Journal of Island and Coastal Archaeology* 8(1): 17–36. doi.org/10.1080/1556 4894.2012.726941.

Deer, W.A., R.A. Howie and J. Zussman. 1992. *An Introduction to The Rock-Forming Minerals.* 2nd edition. Hong Kong: Longman Scientific & Technical.

Diamond, J. 1988. Express train to Polynesia. *Nature* 336: 307–308. doi.org/10.1038/336307a0.

Dimalanta, C.B. and G.P. Jr. Yumul. 2004. Crustal thickening in an active margin setting (Philippines): The whys and the hows, *Episodes* 27: 260–264.

Froh, J. 2004. Archeological ceramics studied by Scanning Electron Microscopy. *Hyperfine Interactions* 154: 159–176. doi.org/10.1023/B:HYPE.0000032074.98045.cc.

Gnauck, P. P. Hoffrogge and J. Greiser. 2002. A New CrossBeam® Inspection Tool combining an ultrahigh resolution field emission SEM and a high resolution FIB. *Metrology, Inspection, and Process Control for Microlithography* vol. 16, no. 833, viewed 27 September 2013, dx.doi.org/10.1117/12.473530.

Green, R.C. 1991. The Lapita cultural complex: Current evidence and proposed models. *Bulletin of the Indo-Pacific Prehistory Association* 11: 295–305. doi.org/10.7152/bippa.v11i0.11393.

——. 2000. Lapita and the cultural model for intrusion, integration, and innovation. In A. Anderson and T. Murray (eds), *Australian Archaeologist: Collected Papers in Honour of Jim Allen*, pp. 372–392. Canberra: Coombs Academic Publishing.

——. 2003. The Lapita horizon and traditions – Signature for one set of oceanic migrations. In C. Sand (ed.), *Pacific Archaeology: Assessments and Prospects (Proceeding of the Conference for the 50th Anniversary of the Frst Lapita Excavation. Koné-Nouméa 2002)*, pp. 95–120. Nouméa: Les Cahiers de larchéologie en Nouvelle-Calédonie 15.

Hogg, N. 2007. Settling Down: Mobility Patterns of Three Mid-Late Lapita Sites in the Anir Group, Papua New Guinea. Unpublished BA (Hons) thesis, University of Otago, Dunedin.

Hung, H.-c. 2005. Neolithic Interaction between Taiwan and Northern Luzon: The pottery and jade evidence from the Cagayan Valley. *Journal of Austronesian Studies* 1(1): 109–131.

——. 2008. Migration and Cultural Interaction in Southern Coastal China, Taiwan and the Northern Philippines, 3000 BC to AD 100: The Early History of the Austronesian-Speaking Populations. Unpublished PhD thesis, The Australian National University, Canberra.

Hung, H.-c., Y. Iizuka, P. Bellwood, K.D. Nguyen, B. Bellina, P. Silapanth, E. Dizon, R. Santiago, I. Datan and J.H. Manton. 2007. Ancient jades map 3,000 years of prehistoric exchange in Southeast Asia. *Proceedings of the National Academy of Sciences* 104(50): 19745–19750. doi.org/10.1073/pnas.0707304104.

Hung, H.-c., M.T. Carson, P. Bellwood, F.Z. Campos, P.J. Piper, E. Dizon, M.J.L.A. Bolunia, M. Oxenham and Z. Chi. 2011. The first settlement of Remote Oceania: The Philippines to the Marianas. *Antiquity* 85: 909–926. doi.org/10.1017/S0003598X00068393.

Hung, H.-c., M.T. Carson and P. Bellwood. 2012. Earliest settlement in the Marianas – a response. *Antiquity* 86(333): 910–914. doi.org/10.1017/S0003598X00048006.

Mijares, A.S. 2005. The archaeology of Penablanca Cave sites, Northern Luzon, Philippines. *Journal of Austronesian Studies* 1(2): 65–92.

Niziolek, L.C. 2013. Earthenware production and distribution in the Prehispanic Philippine polity of Tanjay: Results from laser ablation-inductively coupled plasma-mass spectrometry (LA-ICP-MS). *Journal of Archaeological Science* 40: 2824–2839. doi.org/10.1016/j.jas.2013.02.020.

Ogawa, H. 2002. *Archaeological Research on the Lower Cagayan River: Study on the Historical Process of Hunter-Gather/Farmer Interdependent Relationship*, Tokyo: Tokyo University of Foreign Studies.

Summerhayes, G.R. 1997. Losing your temper: The effect of mineral inclusions on pottery analyses. *Archaeology in Oceania* 32(1): 108–117. doi.org/10.1002/j.1834-4453.1997.tb00376.x.

——. 2000a. *Lapita Interaction*. Terra Australis 15. Canberra: Department of Archaeology and Natural History and the Centre for Archaeological Research, The Australian National University.

——. 2000b. Recent archaeological investigations in the Bismarck Archipelago, Anir-New Ireland Province, Papua New Guinea. *Bulletin of the Indo-Pacific Prehistory Association* 19(3): 167–174.

——. 2003. Modelling differences between obsidian and pottery distribution patterns in the Bismarck Archipelago In C. Sand (ed.), *Pacific Archaeology: Assessments and Prospects (Proceeding of the International Conference for the 50th Anniversary of the First Lapita Excavation. Koné-Noumé July 1952)*, pp. 139–149. Nouméa: Les Cahiers de larchéologie en Nouvelle-Calédonie 15.

——. 2004. The nature of prehistoric obsidian importation to Anir and the development of a 3,000 year old regional picture of obsidian exchange within the Bismarck Archipelago, Papua New Guinea. In V.J. Attenbrow and R. Fullagar (eds), *Archaeologist and Anthropologist in the Western Pacific: Essays in Honour of Jim Specht*, pp. 145–156. Sydney: Records of the Australian Museum Supplement 29.

——. 2007. Island Melanesian pasts – a view from archaeology. In J. Friedlaender (ed.), *Genes, Languages and Culture History in the Southwest Pacific*, pp. 10–35. New York: Oxford University Press.

Swete Kelly, M.C. 2008. Prehistoric Social Interaction and the Evidence of Pottery in the Northern Philippines. Unpublished PhD thesis, The Australian National University, Canberra.

Tanaka, K. 2002. Ceramic Chronology in Northern Luzon: Typological Analysis of the Pottery from the Lal-lo Shell-middens. Unpublished PhD thesis, University of the Philippines, Manila.

Tanaka, K., and A.B. Orogo. 2000. The archaeological excavation at the Pamittan site, Barangay Lanna, Solana, Cagayan Province, Philippines, *Journal of Environmental Studies* 8: 113–142.

Wright, R.V.S. 1991. *Doing Mulitvariate Archaeology and Prehistory: Handling Large Data Sets with MV-ARCH*. Department of Anthropology, University of Sydney.

Zhou, W., R.P. Apkarian, Z.L. Wang and D. Joy. 2006. Fundamentals of Scanning Electron Microscopy. In W. Zhou and Z.L. Wang (eds), *Scanning Microscopy for Nanotechnology: Techniques and Applications*, pp. 1–39. New York: Springer. doi.org/10.1007/978-0-387-39620-0_1.

13

Colonisation and/or Cultural Contacts: A Discussion of the Western Micronesian Case

Michiko Intoh

*Archaeology, linguistic and genetic studies have demonstrated that the history of human dispersals into Micronesia was complex. The initial population movements into Micronesia involved the western island groups. Recent studies seem to have confirmed that the Mariana Islands were settled as early as 3500 BP, possibly from the Philippine Archipelago. Although no hard evidence has been found from Palau equivalent to this early date, it is possible that the western Micronesian islands were also colonised from Island Southeast Asia, before the rest of the Micronesian islands were settled around 2,000 years ago from Melanesia. This paper examines the next step following the initial settlements in Micronesia, based on the archaeological findings from Fais in the Central Caroline Islands. Continuous cultural contact between Fais and Yap from the initial colonisation period was confirmed by excavated Yapese potsherds and stones, as well as black rat (*Rattus rattus*) remains. In addition, extensive cultural contacts between Fais Islanders and a number of islands within and beyond Micronesia were also detected. For resource-limited coral islanders, the significance of having frequent interactions with other islands can be seen as one of their survival strategies. However, it is not a simple process to understand the background anthropological phenomena that explain how an exotic material was transferred from one island to another. Was it associated with a migrating population? Was it transported through exchange? Or was it created on the island using an exchange of knowledge? A complex interaction history will be demonstrated for this small raised coral island.*

Human dispersals into the Western Pacific

Linguistic studies have shown that the major Austronesian movement was made from Taiwan, through the Philippine archipelago and Wallacea to the southwestern Pacific between about 4000 BP and 3000 BP. The distinctive decorated pottery tradition, called Lapita, was associated with the earliest colonists to settle in Island Melanesia and western Polynesia (Kirch 1997).

Micronesia, on the other hand, has a complex history of human dispersals (e.g. Intoh 1997; Rainbird 2004). Malayo-Polynesian speakers from the Indonesian and Philippine archipelagos likely made the first movements into western Micronesia (i.e. the Marianas and Palau). The earliest dates of 3500 BP obtained from the Marianas (Bellwood 2011) are older than the earliest Lapita sites in Melanesia reported so far (Kirch 1997). Palau seems to have been settled later, possibly around 3000 BP (Clark 2005) followed by Yap, though the date of initial colonisation is still unclear (cf. Ross 1996; Dodson and Intoh 1999).

The next movements were made around 2,000 years ago from Melanesia to the central and eastern parts of Micronesia by Nuclear Micronesian speakers (Blust 1984). Archaeological evidence supporting this movement has been reported in the Marshalls, Kosrae, Pohnpei and Chuuk. Based on a few archaeological results most of the atolls in the Central Caroline Islands were likely settled around 1000 BP (Rainbird 2004).[1] The initial settlement of Fais Island was believed to have occurred during this movement. This was based on the linguistic evidence, prior to the archaeological research reported here. Polynesian-speaking peoples made a further movement to the atolls, of Nukuoro and Kapingamarangi. These are considered Polynesian outliers, as are some other Polynesian-speaking groups found in Melanesia.

Besides these major colonisation movements, there were a number of interactions among islands after initial settlement. Some of these interactions are well documented in the ethnographic records, such as the *sawei* exchange system between Yap and coral islands in the Central Caroline islands (Alkire 1965), and in the Marshall Islands (Weisler 1997).

Archaeological research on Fais Island

Fais is situated near the western end of the Central Caroline Islands extending from Ulithi to Namonuito (Figure 13.1). The nearest high island is Yap, about 180 km to the west. Fais Island is a raised coral island with a maximum height of 18 m above sea level. It is about 2.7 km in length and about 1.1 km in width and covers a land area of about 2.8 km². The soil is rich in phosphate that provides a fertile environment for land subsistence; taro (*Colocasia esculenta* and *Alocasia macrorrhiza*), sweet potato, breadfruit, coconut, banana, and even yams are grown, though in a small quantity. Fishbone analysis has indicated that rich marine resources were also exploited (Ono and Intoh 2011).

It has become evident that the habitation on Fais Island was confined to the southern coastal flat throughout its history, and this is where the current villages are located.

---

1   Recently, an archaeological excavation showed that Mwoakilloa (Mokil) atoll in Eastern Micronesia was settled as early as 1700–1500 BP (Poteate et al. 2016). This data likewise the data from this paper indicates that the timing of settling small coral islands was slightly later but not considerably later than high islands nearby.

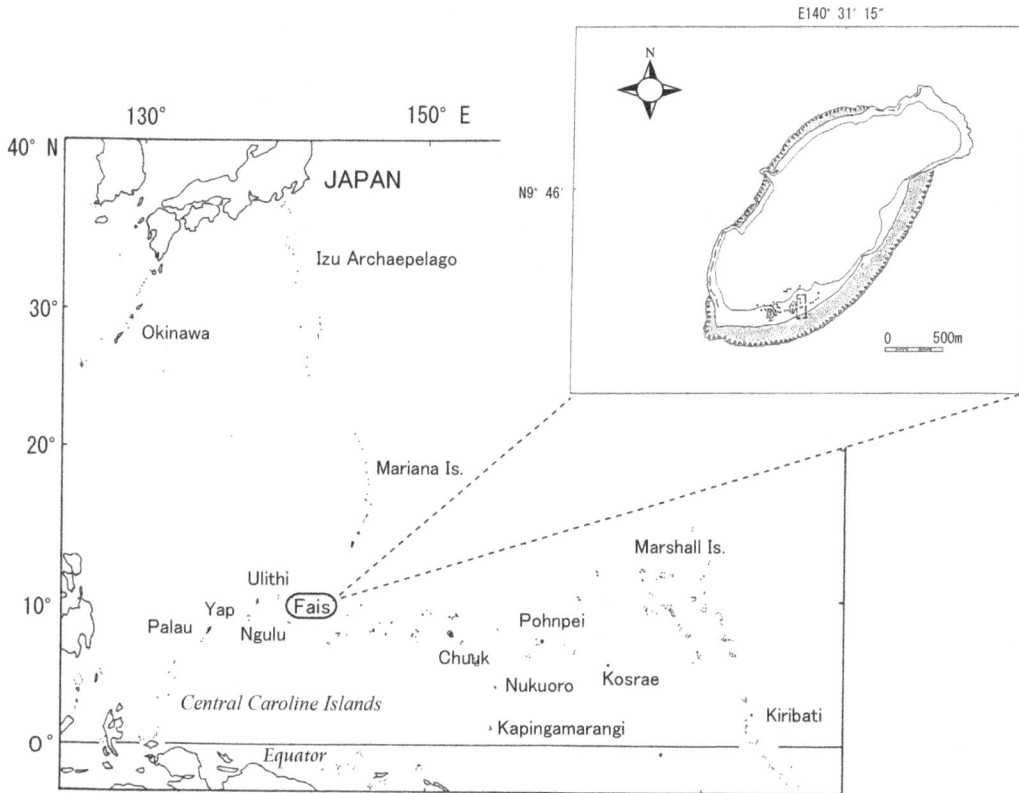

Figure 13.1 Map of Fais Island in Micronesia.
Source: M. Intoh.

Cultural sequence of Fais Island

Three seasons of archaeological excavation were undertaken on Fais. In 1991 and 2005, a deep cultural deposit, about 3.4 m, was excavated on the southern coastal flat. The continuous distribution pattern of artefacts throughout the stratigraphic and sedimentary sequence indicates that Fais Island has been constantly inhabited since initial colonisation (Intoh 2008). The stratigraphy has been anchored to a radiometric chronology by 46 ^{14}C dates obtained on charcoal samples (Ono and Intoh 2011). The earliest date of 1965–1619 cal. BP (NUTA-2167) is the oldest reported thus far from the Central Caroline Islands. The 1994 research project concentrated on the proto-contact to post-contact cemetery, and a total of 13 inhumations were excavated (Lee et al. 2009).

Four cultural phases were set out according to the dates and changes in typology of the Yapese pottery recovered (Table 13.1).

Phase 1 starts right above the sterile white beach sand and dates between 1800–1600 cal. BP (this range was based upon four ^{14}C dates). This is the first colonisation period of Fais. Excavated materials include Yapese calcareous sand tempered (CST) potsherds, small amounts of Palauan plain pottery (characteristic buff-coloured surface with dark gray core), Yapese metamorphic stones, *Tridacna* shell adzes, various shell ornaments and faunal remains of pig, dog, chicken and rat (Intoh and Dickinson 2002; Steadman and Intoh 1994; Intoh and Shigehara 2004). These items constitute the basic artefact set found through all the cultural phases (Figure 13.2). The discovery of the three domesticated animals during the initial phases of colonisation was of especial significance because no other Micronesian islands, including volcanic islands, have produced evidence for simultaneous introduction of the pig, dog and chicken during initial island colonisation (see Intoh 1986; Rainbird 2004).

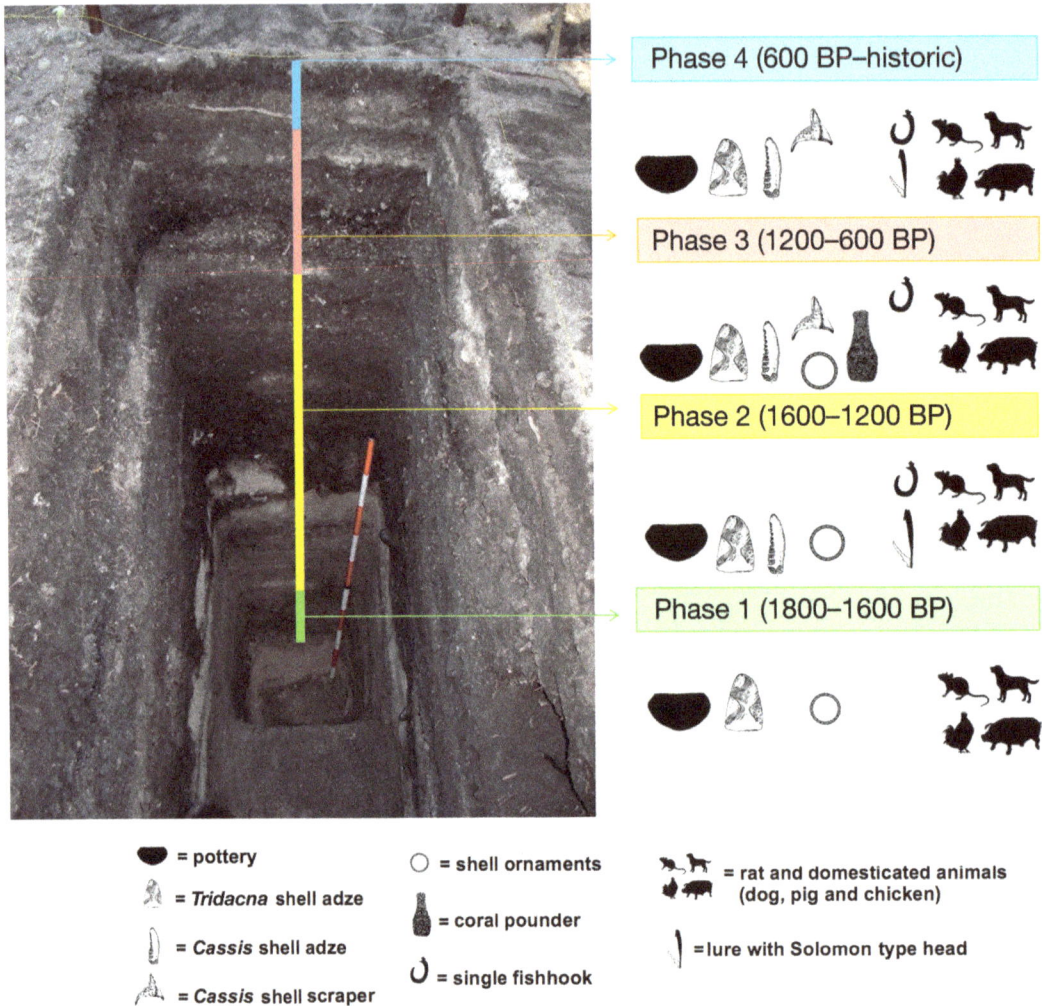

Figure 13.2 Summary diagram of excavated materials from Fais Island.
Source: M. Intoh.

From Phase 2 (1600–1200 BP), *Cassis* shell adzes and single fishhooks made of turtle carapace start to appear. A lure shank made of mother-of-pearl shell found in this phase has a head type typical of those found in the Solomons and known as the Solomon-types (Beasley 1928). As pearl shell is not available around the coasts of Fais, it is likely the lure was manufactured in the Solomon Islands and either brought directly to Fais or transported via eastern Micronesia where similar lures have been found (Weisler 2000). Another feature of the archaeological record from Phase 2 onwards is the appearance of fishhooks made of turtle carapace. Although the use of turtle carapace as a raw material in fishhook production is common in Oceania, the use of turtle carapace is very rare.

In Phase 3 (1200–600 BP), in addition to other common material culture, *Cassis* shell scrapers and a coral pounder for processing vegetable foods were found. No Solomon-type lures were recovered from this phase.

In Phase 4 (600 BP to historic period) shell ornaments disappear from the archaeological record, except in the post-European-contact burial site where a number of shell ornaments were excavated in association with the inhumations. One young female, called SK-7, dated to 387±64BP (NUTA-4075), was buried with more than 300 tiny green glass beads (less than 2 mm in diameter) around her left wrist. Based on the extremely high lead content (more than 70 per cent) in the glass beads it is likely that they were manufactured in China. Beside these beads and two larger yellow Chinese lead glass beads, one unique Venetian bead (called a gooseberry bead) was also found. This particular type of Venetian bead is known to have been manufactured after seventeenth century (Smith 1983). It is reasonable to consider that these were brought from an area where glass beads of different origins co-existed, likely somewhere in Island Southeast Asia.

Table 13.1 Cultural phases of Fais Island based on radiometric dates on charcoal (cal. BP).

Cultural Phase	FSFA-2 site (1991 research)	FSPO-3,4 site (2005 research)
IV (600 BP–historic)		
III (1200–600 BP)	2 (877–665) Wk-3564	
	3 (910–693)NZ-7884	6 (750–660) Beta-213064
II (1600–1200 BP)		8 (1320–1240) Beta-213063
	4 (1491–1290) NUTA-2163	10 (1530–1340) Beta-22149
		11 (1540–1350) Beta-213062
		11 (1530–1340) Beta-237516
I (1800–1600 BP)		
	5 (1862–1544) NZ-7885	12 (1710–1530) Beta-213061
	6 (1915–1569) NUTA-2167	12 (1720–1540) Beta-213060

Source: M. Intoh.

Colonisation and interaction

Colonisation of Fais Island

The rich excavated material culture found in Phase 1 includes various imported artefacts and domestic animals from different origins. These can be divided into two groups according to the directionality of movement from point of origin to Fais.

From the west is a group of artefacts including pottery and metamorphic stones from Yap, and a small number of ceramics from Palau. It is possible that pottery was brought directly from Palau. However, the inclusion of material culture from Yap raises the possibility that the Palauan pottery was traded down the line to Fais via Yap where some Palauan potsherds have also been excavated (Intoh and Leach 1985; Intoh 1990a, 1990b).

Besides domesticated animals, rat (*Rattus* sp.) originally identified by White and Flannery (n.d.) as *R. tanezumi* was also brought to Fais. This type of rat is not found in either Melanesia or Polynesia, but is widely distributed across Southeast Asia and Micronesia. As the rat remains were found from the bottom of the earliest cultural layer together with Yapese CST potsherds, it is very likely that rats were introduced to Fais by some of the earliest colonists to arrive from Yap.

Although pigs, dogs and chickens were all introduced to the Pacific from ISEA during colonisation by Austronesian-speaking populations (Bellwood 2011), there are very few prehistoric locations where all three are found together (Cassels 1983). There are no records of the three together anywhere in Micronesia, only dogs are found in the Eastern Caroline Islands and sporadic pig remains from Palau have been reported (Intoh 1986; Masse et al. 2006). Thus, it is very likely that domesticates were introduced to Fais from outside Micronesia, possibly from Melanesia, or directly from Southeast Asia.

The archaeological evidence suggests three different colonisation scenarios: one that brought colonists from Yap, or from the Melanesian islands, or from both, to Fais. None of these proposed scenarios based on the archaeological record corresponds to the linguistic data that proposes a migration and colonisation of Fais from the east by speakers of Nuclear Micronesian (see Jackson 1986; Pawley and Ross 1995). The Fais example emphasises caution when applying contemporary linguistic evidence to understand human movements and colonisation history, especially when it occurred almost 1,800 years ago.

Active interactions

From Phase 2 onwards, changes in the morphology of imported Fais pottery reflect similar changes within the same timeframes on Yap (Intoh 1990a, 1990b). This would suggest continuing contact between Fais and Yap. Domestic animals are also continuously represented throughout the archaeological sequences. Giovas (2006) has noted that there is high probability of pig extinctions on islands, at least in Polynesia, if island size is less than 11.64 km². This is possibly due to the perceived unsustainability of maintaining pig populations on resource-impoverished islands over the long term, and pig populations were either allowed to die out or deliberately exterminated. Does this then lend itself to the possibility that pigs were introduced to Fais more than once from Melanesia? The answer is that it is unlikely, because the recent strontium isotope study of excavated pig teeth strongly indicates that pigs on Fais were not raised within a volcanic environment, such as those that exist on Yap or Pohnpei, or common in Melanesia, but rather they spent their entire lives in a coral island environment (Gakuhari et al. 2013). This would suggest that the inhabitants of Fais found some way to maintain pig populations within a small island environment.

On the other hand, studies of ancient mitochondrial DNA (mtDNA) recovered from the excavated skeletal material on Fais support the linguistic data. Shinoda and Intoh (2012) succeeded in recovering mitochondrial DNA sequences from five skeletons dated from *ca.* 500 BP to 600 BP. Two samples contained the so-called Polynesian motif (haplogroup B4a1a1a), and one sample contained its ancestral haplogroup (B4a1a1). This suggests that at least some of the late prehistoric Fais Islanders came through Melanesia, either directly, or through eastern Micronesia.

There are also several new cultural elements introduced to Fais from various directions. For example, the Solomon-type pearl shell lure suggests either direct contact between the Solomons and Fais, or indirect transmission through the Eastern Caroline Islands (see Weisler 2000).

A weaving tradition in the proto-historic period was distributed widely among the Central Caroline coral islands and Polynesian outliers in Micronesia, but did not extend as far as western Micronesia. This rather narrow geographic distribution is similar to that of other cultural traits in the region, such as kite fishing. As the distribution of these traditions in Micronesia roughly corresponds to that of Nuclear Micronesian speakers in the coral islands, it is most likely that these cultural traditions were dispersed by inter-island transactions possibly after accidental contacts with eastern Indonesia where these traditions were also practised.

Discussion and conclusion

Combining the archaeological and ancient genetic data provides an overview of the complex prehistoric interactions between Fais and surrounding islands and archipelagos. It demonstrates strong and enduring connections between Fais and Yap, from initial colonisation between 1800–1600 BP until the historic period. The archaeological record also indicates contact with Melanesia, the likely source of the domesticated pig, dog and chicken that had arrived in the region during the Austronesian expansion. In contrast, the linguistics suggests an origin for the Fais Islanders from the east where Nuclear Micronesian languages are spoken. The problem is that none of these islands are known to have possessed domesticated animals except for dogs. Historical information indicates a later introduction of some Indonesian cultural traits, possibly through interactions with other coral islanders.

Where did the original Fais islanders originate? There are three possibilities to consider:

1. The Yapese originally colonised Fais, bringing with them pottery and rats. If so, then soon after initial settlement domestic pigs, dogs and chickens were obtained from Melanesia. This would have necessitated a round-trip voyage from Fais to somewhere in Melanesia because there is currently no evidence of people on the islands in between before 1000 BP.

2. Melanesians who brought with them domesticated pigs, dogs and chickens initially colonised Fais. If so, then shortly after initial settlement members of the founding population travelled to Yap, returning with pots and rats. This pattern of contact is somewhat different from the general colonisation strategy observed in other parts of Oceania, where the colonists kept contact with their place of origin for some time until settlement was solidly established and viable on the newly colonised island.

3. Between 1800–1600 BP populations arrived from both Yap and Melanesia on Fais. If so, then these peoples would have brought with them different cultural traditions, material cultures and domestic animals. The languages first spoken on Fais by the colonists from Yap and/or Melanesia must have been replaced by Nuclear Micronesian (Ross 1996).

Currently, either 2 or 3 seem most plausible. In the archaeological excavations, however, a small amount of Yapese pottery and rat bones were recovered from greater depth, and are possibly earlier than the appearance of domestic animals in the chronological sequence of Fais. But records of pigs, dogs and chickens in Phase 1 suggest their arrival was not more than two centuries after initial colonisation. If so, it is possible that the founding population of Fais had a dual origin and language replacement occurred early in Fais history. Detailed results will be published in a few years' time.

Besides the major colonisation movements, it has clearly been shown in this study that active interactions without formal exchange relations were widely practised within and beyond Micronesia. We should be careful not to confuse such interactions with colonisation movements.

Acknowledgements

I would like to express my sincere appreciation to the people of Fais and Yap Historic Preservation Office for providing me with the opportunity to excavate their island. I owe many thanks to the following specialists and colleagues: D. Rubinstein, W. Dickinson, K. Katayama, K. Shinoda, P. White, T. Flannery, D. Steadman, A. Storey, F. Leach, J. Davidson, R. Ono, M. Yoneda, T. Gakuhari and N. Shigehara.

This study is supported in part by KAKENHI in 2011–2015 (no. 23247040) from the Japan Society for the Promotion of Science (JSPS).

References

Alkire, W.H. 1965. *Lamotrek Atoll and Inter-Island Socioeconomic Ties*. Urbana: University of Illinois Press.

Beasley, H.G. 1928. *Fishhooks*. Pacific Island Records, London: John Hewett.

Bellwood, P. 2011. Holocene population history in the Pacific region as a model for worldwide food producer dispersals. *Current Anthropology* 52(4): S363–S378. doi.org/10.1086/658181.

Blust, R. 1984. Malaita-Micronesian: A eastern Oceanic subgroup? *The Journal of the Polynesian Society* 93: 99–140.

Cassels, R. 1983. Prehistoric man and animals in Australia and Oceania. In L.J. Peel and D.E. Tribe (eds), *Domestication, Conservation and Use of Animal Resources*, pp. 41–62. Amsterdam: Elsevier.

Clark, G.R. 2005. A 3000-year culture sequence from Palau, western Micronesia. *Asian Perspectives* 44(2): 349–380. doi.org/10.1353/asi.2005.0020.

Dodson, J.R. and M. Intoh. 1999. Prehistory and palaeoecology of Yap, Federated States of Micronesia. *Quaternary International* 59: 17–26. doi.org/10.1016/S1040-6182(98)00068-8.

Gakuhari, T., M. Intoh, T. Nakano and M. Yoneda. 2013. Strontium isotope analysis of prehistoric faunal remains excavated from Fais Island in Micronesia. *People and Culture in Oceania* 29: 69–81.

Giovas, C. 2006. No pig atoll: Island biogeography and the extirpation of a Polynesian domesticate. *Asian Perspectives* 45(1): 69–95. doi.org/10.1353/asi.2006.0004.

Intoh, M. 1986. Pigs in Micronesia: Introduction or re-introduction by the Europeans. *Man and Culture in Oceania* 2: 1–26.

——. 1990a. *Changing Prehistoric Yapese Pottery Technology: A Case Study of Adaptive Transformation*. Michigan: UMI Press.

——. 1990b. Ceramic environment and technology: A case study in the Yap islands in Micronesia. *Man and Culture in Oceania* 6: 35–52.

——. 1997. Human dispersals into Micronesia. *Anthropological Science* 105: 15–28. doi.org/10.1537/ase.105.15.

——. 2008. Ongoing archaeological research on Fais island, Micronesia. *Asian Perspectives* 47: 121–138. doi.org/10.1353/asi.2008.0000.

Intoh, M. and W.R. Dickinson. 2002. Prehistoric pottery movements in western Micronesia: Technological and petrological study of potsherds from Fais island. In S. Bedford, C. Sand and D. Burley (eds), *Fifty Years in the Field: Essays in Honour and Celebration of Richard Shutler Jr.'s Archaeological Career*, pp. 123–134. Auckland: New Zealand Archaeological Association.

Intoh, M. and B.F. Leach. 1985. *Archaeological Investigations in the Yap Islands, Micronesia: First Millennium B.P. to the Present Day*. Oxford: BAR.

Intoh M. and N. Shigehara. 2004. Prehistoric pig and dog remains from Fais island, Micronesia. *Anthropological Science* 112: 257–267. doi.org/10.1537/ase.040511.

Jackson, F.H. 1986. On determining the external relationships of the Micronesian languages. In P. Garaghty, L. Carrington and S.A. Wurm (eds), FOCAL II: Papers from the Fourth International Conference on Austronesian Linguistics (PL C-94). pp. 201–238.

Kirch, P.V. 1997. *The Lapita Peoples: Ancestors of the Oceanic World*. Massachusetts: Blackwell.

Lee, A.L., K. Katayama and M. Intoh. 2009. Morphological examination of the human skeletal remains from Fais Island, Federated States of Micronesia. *People and Culture in Oceania* 25: 53–84.

Masse, W.B., J. Liston, J. Carucci, and J.S. Athens. 2006. Evaluating the effects of climate change on environment, resource depletion, and culture in the Palau Islands between AD 1200 and 1600. *Quaternary International* 151: 106–132. doi.org/10.1016/j.quaint.2006.01.017.

Ono, R. and M. Intoh. 2011. Island of pelagic fishermen: Temporal changes in prehistoric fishing on Fais, Micronesia. *Journal of Island and Coastal Archaeology* 6(2): 255–286. doi.org/10.1080/1556489 4.2010.540531.

Pawley, A. and M. Ross. 1995. The prehistory of the Oceanic languages: A current view. In P. Bellwood, J.J. Fox and D. Tryon (eds), *The Austronesians: Historical and Comparative Perspectives*, pp. 39–74. Canberra: The Australian National University.

Poteate, A.S., S.M Fitzpatrick, W.S. Ayres and A. Thompson. 2016. First radiocarbon chronology for Mwoakilloa (Mokil) Atoll, Eastern Caroline Islands, Micronesia. *Radiocarbon* 58: 169–178. doi. org/10.1017/RDC.2015.16.

Rainbird, P. 2004. *The Archaeology of Micronesia*. Cambridge: Cambridge University Press. doi. org/10.1017/CBO9780511616952.

Ross, M. 1996. Is Yapese Oceanic? In B. Nothofer (ed.), *Reconstruction, Classification, Description: Festschrift in Honor of Isidore Dyen*, pp. 121–166. Asia-Pacific Abera Network, vol. 3. Hamburg: Abera Verlag.

Shinoda, K. and M. Intoh. 2012. Analysis of the mtDNA of human skeletal remains excavated from Fais Island, Micronesia. *Anthropological Science* 120(3): 261.

Smith, M.T. 1983. Chronology from glass beads: The Spanish Period in the Southeast, 1513–1670. In C.F. Hayes III (ed.), *Proceedings of the 1982 Glass Trade Bead Conference*, pp. 147–158. Research Records 16, NY: Rochester Museum and Science Center.

Steadman, D.W. and M. Intoh. 1994. Biogeography and prehistoric exploitation of birds from Fais Island, Yap State, Federated States of Micronesia. *Pacific Science* 48: 116–135.

Weisler, M. (ed.). 1997. *Prehistoric Long-Distance Interaction in Oceania: An Interdisciplinary Approach*. Auckland: New Zealand Archaeological Association.

——. 2000. Burial artifacts from the Marshall Islands: description, dating and evidence for extra-archipelago contacts. *Micronesica* 33(1/2): 111–136.

White, J.P. and T. Flannery. n.d. Murids from Fais Island. Unpublished manuscript.

14

Integrating Experimental Archaeology, Phytolith Analysis and Ethnographic Fieldwork to Study the Origin of Farming in China

Tracey L.-D. Lu[1]

Professor Peter Bellwood is a leading scholar studying the global origin and expansion of farming, and has published extensively on this topic (e.g. Bellwood 1978, 2005). With his guidance, the author has studied the origins of agriculture in mainland China since the 1990s, and has pursued a number of different archaeological and experimental methods to try and tackle the issue since then. In this chapter, I outline some of the methods of experimental archaeology that have been applied to determine the nature of the origins and development of prehistoric agriculture onwards, summarising the outcome of experimental archaeology integrated with phytolith analysis and ethnographic fieldwork conducted. I argue that integrating cultivation experiments, use-wear analysis of tools, phytolith analysis and ethnographic information can provide novel data and inspirational ideas within the context of the natural and cultural changes involved in and caused by cultivation. Remaining questions for further study are also discussed.

Introduction

Experiments have been used in archaeological studies since the nineteenth century in Europe (Coles 1979; Forrest 2008). Early inquiries focused on the functional analysis of ancient tools, but human behaviour, processes and social systems have become the objectives of experimental archaeology since the 1960s in order to 'generate and test hypotheses to provide or enhance analogies for archaeological interpretation' (Mathieu 2002: 1), providing a much broader scope for experimental archaeology.

Cultivation experimentation is an approach within experimental archaeology. Clearly, cultivation is a crucial process for the domestication of wild plants. Generally speaking, cultivation refers to a cultivation process from broadcasting seeds or planting, to field management including watering, fertilising and weeding, to harvesting, and selecting seeds for the following years. This is a dynamic, continuous and diversified process between humans and nature, particularly in terms of plants and their environment. It is in this process that the mutations of wild plants have been selected, fixed and reproduced, and wild plants have gradually been domesticated.

---

1   Tracey Lu died on 21 March 2016 in Melbourne, Australia.

Cultivation experimentation is a pre-designed and controlled process of replicating or modelling cultivation activities for ascertained objectives. Agronomists and other scholars have used this approach since at least the early twentieth century for various purposes, ranging from increasing productivity, to producing hybrids, and assessing the impact of modern cultivation techniques on wild plants. In the 1950s, Oka and Chang (1959) conducted cultivation experiments using wild rice, and discovered that its biological characteristics could change rapidly through cultivation. However, they used relatively modern agricultural techniques such as transplanting and irrigation, and their objective was to tackle an agronomical issue instead of the archaeological issue of the origin of rice farming.

In the 1960s, some archaeologists began to use harvesting and cultivation experiments to study the origin and development of prehistoric agriculture in the Middle East. Jack Harlan conducted a pioneering wild wheat harvesting experiment in Turkey, through which he obtained novel and quantitative data for productivity. Based on this, he argued that the high productivity of wild wheat might have been a major impetus for the origin of wheat cultivation and eventually wheat domestication in the Middle East (Harlan 1967). Harvesting and systematic cultivation of wheat and barley, as well as associated pollen, use-wear analysis and ethnographic studies have been carried out by many scholars since the 1960s (Anderson 1992; Hillman and Davies 1992). Results from these cultivation experiments have illustrated that they can provide important data on many issues, including the productivity of wild and domesticated plants, the impact of different agricultural techniques, domestication rates, and the dynamics between cultivation, human cultural change and the impact upon the environment.

Inspired by the aforementioned works, cultivation experiments using green foxtail millet (*Setaria viridis* P. Beauv) and its domesticated counterpart foxtail millet (*Setaria sativa*), and perennial wild rice (*Oryza rufipogon* Griff.) and domesticated rice (*Oryza sativa*) were carried out from 1999 to 2005 and in 2012 in the middle Yellow River Valley and South China respectively (Lu 2002, 2013), associated with phytolith analysis, use-wear analysis and ethnographic studies. This paper summarises the major outcome of these works and discusses outstanding questions.

Objectives

Cultivation experiments with phytolith and use-wear analysis, and ethnographic studies constitute an integrated approach, intended to provide a multi-perspective examination of the functions of prehistoric tools, human behaviour, and the processual and other systematic changes to ancient foragers' and farmers' cultures associated with plant and other environmental alterations. The objectives of this integrated approach are as follows:

1. To understand the biological differences between wild and cultivated plants, and the impact of human cultivation on the evolutionary process from wild to domesticated plants, particularly on how water control, soil fertilisation, harvesting, seed selection and other cultivation behaviour might have selected, concentrated and reproduced wild plants with mutated genotypes, and also changed the growth cycle, productivity and reproduction of these plants, and consequently facilitated the domestication process.

2. To understand the impact of cultivation activities on human society and culture, in aspects such as cultivation and the occurrence and extension of sedentism, farming and settlement planning, the development of farming land as immovable assets, and the emergence of land ownership and the notion of private property.

3. To understand the impact of different cultivation activities on the environment, including the flora and fauna. Various agricultural techniques might have been used at different periods of time in various regions, such as the slash-and-burn method used for dry-land farming, and the fish-agriculture symbiosis in wet-rice paddy fields. Have these activities caused deforestation, land erosion and loss of soil nutrition, have they decreased water supply and reduced floral and faunal diversity and quantity, and have they altered the landscape, all of which have eventually produced significant, indeed irreversible impacts on human society and culture from the past to the present? These are important questions for archaeology.

The ultimate goal of this integrated approach is to obtain novel qualitative and quantitative data in order to understand the economic, social and ideological changes that occurred in forager and farmer lifeways in antiquity, to tackle the questions of why, how, and by whom agriculture originated and developed in mainland China, and what were the consequences of this prehistoric cultural change.

Methods

The integrated approach of the present study chose to apply methods from agronomy, palaeoethnobotany and ethnology based on their suitability for the research questions and objectives, considering also the land, water, plant seed and human resources available for the study. Data collected from cultivation experiments, use-wear analysis, and the experiences of contemporary rice and millet farmers have been used to confirm or falsify relevant hypotheses, such as lack of cultivation management as a cause for low or nil crop returns. Research findings from agronomists and biologists have also been incorporated into a background literature review.

Briefly, the following projects have been carried out:

1. Cultivation experiments on green foxtail and perennial wild rice using the most 'primitive' techniques have been conducted. Based on ethnographic data from Taiwan Aborigines, a cultivation experiment with slash-and-burn planting and harvesting green foxtail was conducted in North China in 1999–2001 (Figure 14.1) (Lu 2002). Wild-rice cultivation using seed broadcasting and water maintenance (Figure 14.2) without fertiliser or controlled irrigation was carried out from 2000 to 2005 (Lu 2013), and a comparative cultivation experiment on wild and domesticated rice was conducted in Hong Kong in 2012 (Figures 14.3 and 14.4).

2. Harvesting wild and domesticated foxtail millet and rice was conducted from 1996 to 2002 in the Yellow River Valley and South China respectively using a variety of methods to provide comparative data for the productivity of wild and domesticated plants (Lu 1998, 2006). Tools replicating Rtools of prehistoric stone flakes, ground stone sickles, bone and shell knives (Figure 14.5) were used for the harvest in order to test the efficiency of these prehistoric implements. Additionally, they were observed under a microscope in order to establish reference data for use-wear and residue analysis of prehistoric implements found in South China and Hong Kong.

3. Soil samples were collected from slash-and-burn green foxtail fields and from foxtail millet fields involving modern farming methods. The phytolith and charcoal assemblages were compared in 1999 in order to study the impact of cultivation upon soil composition and to provide reference data to assist in the search for prehistoric farmlands in China (Figures 14.6 and 14.7).

4. Ethnographic studies of contemporary rice farmers in South China and foxtail millet farmers in the middle Yellow River Valley and Taiwan have been carried out since late 1999 in order to collect data on cultivation techniques, crop productivity and the significance of rice and millet in farming societies.

5. Verbal and visual recording has been carried out during all of the aforementioned projects. The records cover daily climate, the amount of seeds broadcast and harvested, methods of cultivation and harvesting, time, labour and the materials used for manufacturing replicas, etc.

Figure 14.1 Cultivated green foxtail in the loess in North China (top left).
Source: Photo taken by the author in 1999.

Figure 14.2 Cultivated perennial wild rice in South China (top middle).
Source: Photo taken by the author in 2002.

Figure 14.3 Wild perennial rice (*Oryza rufipogon*) and domesticated rice (*Oryza sativa*) grains for the comparative cultivation experiment in 2012 (top right).
Source: Photo taken by the author in 2012.

Figure 14.4 Flowering domesticated rice (bottom left).
Source: Photo taken by the author in 2012.

Figure 14.5 Harvesting domesticated rice using shell knife (bottom right).
Source: Photo taken by Fu Xiaguo in 2000.

Various criteria have been used to control the cultivation experiments. For example, as the objective for perennial wild rice was to know the germination rate, time and productivity of the plant at the initiation of rice cultivation, the experiment did not use water control, fertiliser or other farming techniques. The cultivation of green foxtail also simulated an 'initial farming' process, and neither irrigation nor fertilising were applied (Lu 2002). The timing and methods of harvesting have also been determined by the research objectives (Lu 2002, 2006, 2013).

A detailed example is provided by the comparative cultivation, without fertiliser or irrigation, of wild and domesticated rice in 2012, in order to compare their productivity (grain output compared to grain input). Grains of perennial wild rice (*Oryza rufipogon* Griff.) and domesticated rice (*Oryza sativa*) were selected and broadcast in boxes or basins with a relatively stable amount of water. While it is essential to supply or drain out water at certain times in contemporary rice farming in order to raise productivity, these complex water control techniques were not applied in the cultivation experiment, as it requires an irrigation mechanism, which may not have been available at the beginning of rice cultivation. Results show that the domesticated rice cultivated by this 'primitive' approach could still geminate, flower and ripen (Figure 14.4), but none of the 24 perennial wild rice grains germinated. Apart from confirming the zero or negative productivity when attempting to cultivate wild rice without irrigation, the results also demonstrate the critical importance of the genotypic differences between wild and domesticated rice.

Findings

The findings from the above projects can be summarised as follows:

1. The productivity of green foxtail in its first year of cultivation is over 9.38, while the productivity of perennial wild rice in its first year of cultivation is negative 20 (or worse), as only four grains of wild rice were harvested in the autumn after 80 grains were broadcast in the spring of 1999, and no grains were harvested from the 24 grains cultivated in 2012 (Lu 2002, 2013).

    *   One of the main causal factors of this huge difference is the biological difference between green foxtail as an annual grass reproducing itself by producing large amounts of seed, and wild rice as a perennial plant reproducing itself mainly by ratooning.

    *   Amongst all of the progenitors of domesticated crops in the world, wild rice is the only potential perennial (the issue of whether perennial or annual wild rice is the direct progenitor of domesticated rice is still a question under debate). The comparative cultivation experiments using green foxtail and perennial wild rice illustrate that the return on cultivating the latter is extremely low, even negative, thus highlighting the question of whether the cultivation of wild rice originated for the purpose of increasing food supplies or for other purposes. Hayden (2003) has argued that wild rice might have been a luxury food in prehistory, used for ritual purposes. Further archaeological studies are required to address this issue.

2. It has been observed that the stem diameter of both foxtail millet and domesticated rice is significantly bigger than their wild counterparts (Lu 1998, 2002, 2006, 2013), which might have facilitated more efficient transforming and greater utilisation of nutritional elements from the soil. In other words, the evolution from wild to domesticated plants involved changes to the whole plant, not just the spikelet base. Thus it is important for archaeologists to collect and study every fragment of rice and millet, not just the spikelets, found in archaeological deposits in order to holistically study the domestication of plants and the origin and development of prehistoric agriculture.

3. The result of the comparative cultivation experiments of perennial wild rice (*Oryza rufipogon*) and domesticated rice (*Oryza sativa*) conducted in 2012 illustrates that biological characters determine the growth cycle and productivity of the two species. However, according to contemporary farmers, both foxtail millet and domesticated rice require regular management in their watering, fertilising and weeding, otherwise the productivity could become extremely low or even negative. For example, a millet farmer in the middle Yellow Valley told the author in 1999 that over 90 per cent of the foxtail millet he had planted died out in that year because he did not have time to look after the crop. Thus, it can be argued that when prehistoric people began to cultivate green foxtail or wild rice, similar management must have been necessary, which would have demanded a sedentary lifestyle of the cultivators. Based on archaeological data in mainland China to date, sedentism occurred after the occurrence of farming, and the need to manage farming lands must have played an important role.

4. There are similarities and differences in terms of cultivation techniques and crop management for green foxtail and wild rice. While the former can be cultivated on any piece of land, the latter must be cultivated in a field with constant water supply. It is hypothesised that the prehistoric farmers might have used small water ponds or land along rivers/streams to cultivate wild rice at the initial stage, but eventually prehistoric farmers had to construct paddy fields with banks to control the water level, without which it would have been impossible to successfully cultivate and gradually domesticate the wild rice (Lu 2013). Archaeologists have found rice paddy fields in the middle and lower Yangzi River Valley, the earliest dated to approximately 7,000 years ago (Zheng et al. 2009). As the creation of rice fields required labour input, and rice, millet and other crops could be produced continuously from farmed fields, fields eventually became the immovable property of farmers, who had to become more sedentary in order to ensure their access to land and manage and protect their crops. The continuous use of farming land as a productive asset must have led to formal land ownership in ancient China, and the protective walls of the Neolithic town Chengtoushan dated to approximately 6,000 years ago in the middle Yangzi River Valley might have served the need of protecting rice farming land (Lu 2013).

5. The slash-and-burn farming technique adds many charcoal grains to the soil, associated with large quantities of phytoliths from the grass family (Figures 14.6 and 14.7). This could be a useful reference point for identifying prehistoric farming land. Soil analysis has been used to identify prehistoric rice paddy fields and farming techniques in the Yangzi River Valley (e.g. Zheng et al. 2009; Hu et al. 2013), but the farming lands of millets and other crops are yet to be identified. Though the absence of diagnostic millet phytoliths remains a major obstacle in this issue, the presence of a large amount of charcoal and phytolith from Paniceae could be a useful indicator.

6. Use-wear analysis of tools used in harvesting experiments indicates that cutting grasses does produce unique use-wear patterns, but more studies are required in order to distinguish whether the implements were used for cutting crops or grasses.

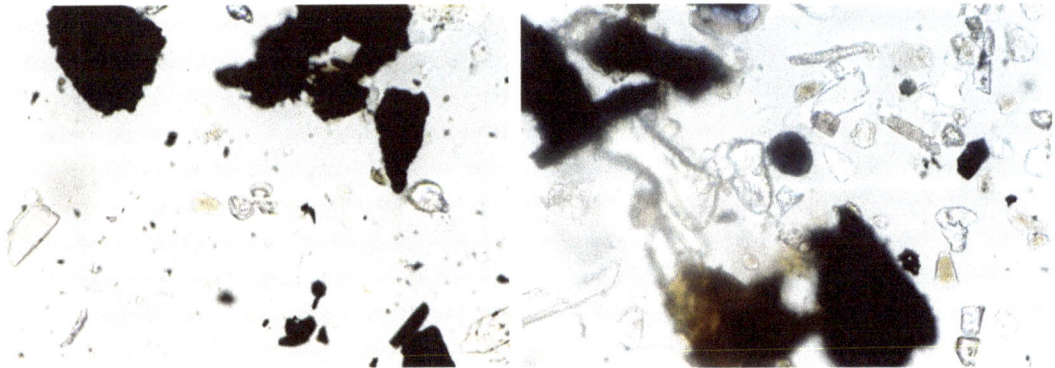

Figure 14.6 Charcoal and phytolith grains found in contemporary farming land of foxtail millet. Magnification about 400X (left).

Source: Micro-photo taken by the author in 1999.

Figure 14.7 Charcoal and phytolith grains found in contemporary farming land of green foxtail. Magnification about 400X (right).

Source: Micro-photo taken by the author in 1999.

Conclusion

The projects summarised here indicate that integrating cultivation experiments, phytolith and use-wear analyses and ethnographic studies can provide novel and useful data for studying the origin and development of farming and related cultural and natural changes in China. Through cultivating wild and domesticated plants, recording the growth cycles and the impact of farming techniques, climate and other factors upon the plants, we can understand the influence of human interventions and natural factors such as temperature and precipitation upon the evolution of plants from wild to domesticated species. Further, we can also understand how plant cultivation might have changed human behaviour and culture, such as the occurrence of sedentism, the increased importance of farming in prehistoric economic structures, and the occurrence of property and land ownership. The soils and tools used in the cultivation experiments can also be analysed to provide reference data for the study of prehistoric farming techniques, use-wear analyses and prehistoric soil analysis, etc.

However, applying ancient techniques of wet rice cultivation it takes a long time for plants to show biological changes after being cultivated by humans, and a long time for the related environmental changes to take effect, experimentation and associated studies should be a continuing and long-term program. It also requires considerable resources, including funding, stable land, sufficient grains of wild plants, a laboratory to analyse phytolith and soil samples, and most importantly, researchers who have suitable training and can remain on the experimental land to continue the work for years, even decades. The aforementioned projects and findings are very preliminary as there have not been sufficient resources to facilitate long-term and ongoing cultivation experiments and associated projects.

Further, this integrated approach requires collaborations between scholars from different disciplines. It had been hoped that the chemical elements of soil used for cultivating different crops with different techniques could have been analysed in order to provide reference data for identifying prehistoric farming land, but this could not be achieved owing to the lack of expertise. Hopefully, more scholars will engage in cultivation experiments and associated initiatives in mainland China, and more data will be generated for an improved, in-depth and holistic understanding of the origin and development of agriculture in this region.

Acknowledgements

Harvesting and cultivation experiments, and the use-wear and phytolith analyses conducted by the author from 1999 to 2000 were funded by the French Fyssen Foundation, and the author is very grateful for the financial support she has received. The author would also like to thank Professor Fu Xianguo, Institute of Archaeology, Chinese Academy of Social Sciences, Professor Li Zhen, Archaeology Team of the Guangxi Zhuang Autonomous Region, and their team members for their continuous help and support in conducting various experiments in China from 1999 to 2012.

References

Anderson, P. (ed.). 1992. *Préhistoire de l'Agriculture*. Paris: CNRS Press.

Bellwood, P. 1978. *Man's Conquest of the Pacific: The Prehistory of Southeast Asia and Oceania*. Auckland: Collins.

——. 2005. *First Farmers: The Origins of Agricultural Societies*. Malden, MA: Blackwell.

Coles, J. 1979. *Experimental Archaeology*. New York: Academic Press.

Forrest, C. 2008. The nature of scientific experimentation in archaeology: Experimental archaeology from the nineteenth to the mid twentieth century. In P. Cunningham, J. Heeb and R. Paardekooper (eds), *Experiencing Archaeology by Experiment*, pp. 61–68. Oxford: Oxbow.

Harlan, J.R. 1967. A wild wheat harvest in Turkey. *Archaeology* 20(1): 197–201.

Hayden, B. 2003. Were luxury foods the first domesticates? Ethnoarchaeological perspectives from Southeast Asia. *World Archaeology* 34: 458–469. doi.org/10.1080/0043824021000026459a.

Hillman, G.C. and M.S. Davies. 1992. Domesticated rate in wild wheat and barley under primitive cultivation: preliminary results and archaeological implications of field measurements of selection coefficient. In P.C. Anderson (ed.), *Préhistoire de l'Agriculture*, pp. 113–148. Paris: CNRS Press.

Hu, L., Z. Chao, G. Min, F. Li, L. Chen, B. Liu, X. Li, Z. Huang, Y. Li, B. Xing and J. Dai. 2013. Evidence for a Neolithic Age fire-irrigation paddy cultivation system in the lower Yangtze River Delta, China. *Journal of Archaeological Science* 40(1): 72–78. doi.org/10.1016/j.jas.2012.04.021.

Lu, T.L.-D. 1998. Some botanical characteristics of green foxtail (*Setaria viridis*) and harvesting experiments on the grass. *Antiquity* 72(278): 902–907. doi.org/10.1017/S0003598X00087548.

——. 2002. A green foxtail (*Setaria viridis*) cultivation experiment in the middle Yellow River Valley and some related issues. *Asian Perspectives* 41: 1–14. doi.org/10.1353/asi.2002.0007.

——. 2006. The occurrence of cereal cultivation in mainland China. *Asian Perspectives* 45: 129–158. doi.org/10.1353/asi.2006.0022.

——. 2013. *Daozuo yu Shiqian Wenhua Yanbian* (*Rice Farming and the Development of Prehistoric Culture*). Beijing: Science Press (in Chinese).

Mathieu, J.R. 2002. Introduction. In J.R. Mathieu (ed.), *Experimental Archaeology: Replicating Objects, Behaviors, and Processes*, pp. 1–11. Oxford: BAR International Series 1035.

Oka, H.I. and W.T. Chang. 1959. The impact of cultivation on a population of wild rice, *Oryza sativa f. spontanea*. *Phyton* 13: 105–117.

Zheng, Y., G. Sun, L. Qin, C. Li, X. Wu and X. Chen. 2009. Rice fields and modes of rice cultivation between 5000 and 2500 BC in east China. *Journal of Archaeological Science* 36: 2609–2616. doi.org/10.1016/j.jas.2009.09.026.

15

The Origins and Arrival of the Earliest Domestic Animals in Mainland and Island Southeast Asia: A Developing Story of Complexity

Philip J. Piper

Peter Bellwood's key archaeological research interests have focused on the Neolithic transition and the migration of agricultural populations from southern China southwards through Mainland and Island Southeast Asia. An important aspect of this, probably the most significant transformation in human behaviour in prehistory, was the reshaping of subsistence strategies from foraging and vegeculture/ arboriculture to crop production and animal management. When Peter initially drew together the evidence for the migration of Austroasiatic speakers across Mainland Southeast Asia and Austronesian-speaking peoples from Taiwan into Island Southeast Asia and on into the Pacific, he proposed that they transported three domestic animals with them – the pig, dog and chicken. In the almost complete absence of zooarchaeological evidence, this proposal was based primarily on linguistic reconstructions and evidence for the introduction of domestic varieties to Melanesia and the Pacific Islands. Now, and with considerably more information on the presence and/or absence of domestic/managed animals from archaeological sites in Mainland and Island Southeast Asia than was available three decades ago, I reassess the zooarchaeological evidence for domestic animal introductions with some of the earliest proposed agricultural communities in the region.

Introduction

Since the 1970s, Peter Bellwood's archaeological interests have focused particularly on investigating the emergence of agriculture in Southeast Asia (Bellwood 1976, 1997, 2001, 2005, 2013; Diamond and Bellwood 2003). Peter has been a strong advocate of the farming/ language dispersal hypothesis and has been a main proponent of the migration of agricultural populations, ultimately from southern China, through Mainland and Island Southeast Asia (ISEA) as the main mechanism explaining the geographic distribution of closely related languages and peoples across the region today (Bellwood 1996, 2005, 2013; Bellwood and Dizon 2005). He has argued that these migrating human populations brought with them new modes of sedentary settlement and agricultural life-ways for the first time, as well as a suite of new material culture.

Figure 15.1 The geographic locations of sites (in italics) where domestic animals have been recorded in the archaeological record prior to 3000 BP.

Source: P.J. Piper; Base Map: P. Bellwood, ANU Cartography.

In Mainland Southeast Asia (MSEA), the earliest such settlements were purportedly established by Austroasiatic-speaking populations in northern Vietnam, close to the confluence of the Red and Black Rivers. These settlements belong to the Phung Nguyen Culture recorded at sites such as Xom Ren and Man Bac dating from *ca.* 4000 BP onwards (Figure 15.1; Higham 2004, 2013, 2015). Connections with late Neolithic communities further up the Red River in Yunnan Province are evidenced through similarities in decorative motifs and pottery styles and specialised workshops for the production of nephrite and jadeite beads and bracelets (Rispoli 2007). From northern Vietnam (or southern China) these agricultural populations migrated south along the coast, or followed major river systems such as the Vam Co Dong and Dong Nai into the Mekong Drainage of southern Vietnam where they constructed the settlements of An Son, Loc Giang and Rach Nui, beginning around 4000 cal. BP (Bellwood et al. 2011; Oxenham et al. 2015; Piper and Oxenham 2014). They also moved west through Laos and Cambodia and into central and northern Thailand where the settlements and burial grounds of Ban Non Wat, Non Nok Tha, Ban Chiang and Ban Lum Kao record their initial arrival between *ca.* 3700–3500 cal. BP (Higham 2004; Higham and Higham 2008).

Another proposed movement brought Austronesian-speaking populations from Taiwan into the northern Philippines by *ca.* 4000 cal. BP. From the Philippines they dispersed fairly rapidly south and west into the islands of Southeast Asia (Bellwood 1979, 1997, 2005, 2013). They also moved east into the Marianas, and the Bismarck Archipelago, where the Lapita Cultural Complex developed around *ca*. 3300–3150 cal. BP. From there they travelled east into the Solomon Islands and Vanuatu, and eventually onwards further into Remote Oceania (Bellwood 2013).

Along with a variety of material culture and new modes of settlement, one of the proposed major economic components transported with these initial farming communities into MSEA and ISEA was the 'big three' of domestic pigs, dogs and chickens. When Bellwood (1975) first suggested that these domestic animals had been introduced into MSEA and ISEA by early agricultural communities it was primarily inferred, firstly by archaeological evidence of the three domesticates intermittently dispersed throughout the region, mostly recorded on islands where no native wild antecedents existed, and secondly by virtue of Proto-Austronesian lexical reconstructions (see Pawley 1966). In 1976, Peter noted of evidence for domestic pigs in ISEA:

> The archaeological evidence for pig domestication is South-east Asia is extensive, but all unfortunately of a partly circumstantial nature. No direct osteological evidence for domestication has been published. (Bellwood 1976: 262)

In reference to MSEA in particular, Bellwood (1979: 162–163) remarked that cattle bones (*Bos indicus*), almost certainly from domestic stock, had been identified associated with human burials at the Neolithic site of Non Nok Tha in northern Thailand, dated in the 1970s to 8000–6000 BP (Higham and Leach 1971, Higham 1975). The pigs and dogs, also associated with the burials, 'were presumably, but not certainly, domesticated as well' (Bellwood 1979: 162–163). In other words, the presence and timing of the appearance of domestic animals across Southeast Asia were a best estimate in the almost complete absence of any identified skeletal remains from archaeological sites.

A confounding factor in linguistic arguments for linking domestic animal translocations to the spread of Austronesian languages in ISEA was the contentious appearance of pig bones dating to 10,000–6000 BP at sites like Kafiavana, Yuku and Kiowa in the highlands of New Guinea (Bulmer 1966, 1975, 1982), and at the sites of Akari and Beri on the coast of the same island by 6000–5000 BP (Swadling et al. 1989). A recent critical reassessment of the chronological integrity of pig bones at Watinglo, Taora and Lachitu has illustrated the problems in relying on associated radiocarbon dates recovered from 'the same' stratigraphic horizons as pig bones to infer radiometric age. The study suggested a much later suid introduction into New Guinea, probably after 3000 BP, and succeeding the initial appearance of pigs in Lapita contexts (O'Connor et al. 2011).

In the decades following Peter's comments, the evidence for the introduction of the 'big three' (pigs, dogs and chickens) into SEA in the period before 3000 BP has remained rather circumstantial, and direct zooarchaeological evidence has been scarce. But for pigs to be present in Lapita period sites such as Kamgot, Babase Island, New Ireland, by 3380–2950 cal. BP (Matisoo-Smith 2007), pigs and chickens at Talepakemalai by 3500–3400 cal. BP (Kirch 1997),[1] pigs and chickens at Teouma on Vanuatu around 3100–2700 cal. BP (Storey et al. 2010, 2012; Hawkins 2015; Petchey et al. 2015) and dogs in Australia at *ca*. 3500 BP (Macintosh 1964; Milham and Thompson 1976) they must have all been transported through ISEA prior to these dates.

In this paper, I review the most recent evidence for the origins and routes of migration of the 'big three' across MSEA and ISEA prior to *ca*. 3000 BP. Two lines of evidence are drawn upon here: modern and ancient genetics, and the physical remains of domestic animals recovered from archaeological sites. I address three questions: 1. What is the likely origin of the 'big three'? 2. When do they first appear across MSEA and ISEA? and 3. What were their potential routes of translocation?

---

1   The New Ireland and Talepakemalai dates may soon need to be revised down by a few hundred years to near 3250/3100 BP (Petchey et al. 2015: 103).

Genetic evidence

Pigs

Pig domestication in MSEA is fairly complex, and further complicated by replacement of early domesticates through later translocations southwards into the region from central China (Larson et al. 2010), and what Larson and Fuller (2014: 121) term 'introgressive capture'. Introgressive capture occurs when domestic animals are translocated from one geographic location to another, where they then interbreed with their wild relatives and acquire a 'local' mitochondrial signature. This can, and has been, mistakenly identified as an independent domestication event (see Larson et al. 2005). This is almost certainly the case with the Pacific Clade of pigs, which can be traced from southern China/northern Vietnam through Laos and into Peninsular Malaysia (Larson et al. 2005, 2007). The ultimate origin of these pigs was probably in the Yangtze and Yellow River regions where pig domestication has been recorded as early as 9000 BP (Cucchi et al. 2011). Archaeological and/or modern pig samples with the Pacific Clade signature also occur in Sumatra and Java, and throughout Wallacea and Melanesia, and this has been interpreted as the potential route of migration of human populations, along with their pigs, into the Pacific (Figure 15.2; Larson et al. 2007). However, no specimens with this unique haplogroup have seemingly been found to the west in Cambodia or Thailand where similarities in material culture indicate clear connections with early agricultural communities in southern China and northern Vietnam from *ca.* 4000–3800 BP onwards (Higham 2004; Bellwood 2013). Yang et al. (2011), based on their mtDNA analyses, argued for small-scale domestication events in MSEA, including within the borders of Thailand. Contra Larson et al. (2010), they also suggested that the Pacific Clade of pigs likely had its origins in ISEA, rather than the Mainland. They based this interpretation on the fact that they found a particular haplogroup (D6 and subgroup M3) linked to the Pacific Clade in both wild and domestic pigs in ISEA populations, though they did not specify where within the islands these were recorded. Although possible, it is unlikely that the Pacific Clade was domesticated in eastern Indonesia (*Sus scrofa* is only native to the western Indonesian islands of Sumatra, Java and Bali) and transported back into MSEA. This distinctive phylogenetic grouping has been recorded in numerous wild boars in Yunnan Province of southern China, northern Vietnam and Laos where the haplotype is likely to have originated (similar to the Pacific Clade), and moved southwards as part of the Austroasiatic agricultural population migrations (Larson et al. 2010).

Lum et al. (2006) also identified a MSEA origin, possibly Vietnam, for the 'tusker' pigs of Vanuatu, and linked their introduction with the expansion of Lapita at *ca.* 3200 BP. They made a tentative connection between pig translocations and the distribution of Austronesian languages but did not specify a particular route of human migration bringing the 'tuskers' to Vanuatu.

No pigs with the Pacific Clade signature have been recorded in either Taiwan or the Philippines, precluding these islands as the point of departure eastwards into the Pacific for these domestic pigs (Larson et al. 2007). In contrast, some modern, and ancient Philippine pigs possess a unique haplotype stemming from the island of Lanyu, located between the northern Philippines and southern Taiwan (Figure 15.2; Larson et al. 2010). Though the Lanyu pigs still cluster with their relatives, Mainland East Asian *Sus scrofa*, their genetic distance would seem to indicate that they separated long enough ago to become an island native (Larson et al. 2010; Wu et al. 2007). No wild pigs exist on Lanyu nowadays (if they ever did), and only their domestic descendants remain. Interestingly, a study of modern domestic pigs in the Philippines identified several Lanyu signatures in the Cordillera region (Herrera 2010), indicating that the Lanyu haplotype had been introduced to Luzon Island sometime in the past. There is, however, no evidence yet of the expansion of this unusual haplotype beyond the Philippines during prehistory.

In ISEA, domesticated varieties of the Eurasian wild boar (*Sus scrofa*) are not the only suids to have been translocated between islands. There is genetic evidence to suggest the translocation of the Sulawesi warty pig (*S. celebensis*) from Sulawesi to offshore islands, as far as Flores, Timor, Halmahera and Roti (Groves 2007). Groves (1981, 2007) has suggested that the Sulawesi warty pig might have been deliberately introduced as a domesticate across parts of Wallacea prior to the introduction of *S. scrofa*. This raises an interesting question about the status of pig domestication in ISEA in the mid-Holocene (addressed below), and whether the Eurasian wild boar was really the first domestic pig species in the region.

Chickens

The majority of published chicken genetic research undertaken so far has focused primarily on the origins of domestic fowl in Asia and MSEA (Fumihito et al. 1996; Liu et al. 2006; Kanginakudru et al. 2008), and their routes of translocation across Oceania and on to South America (Storey et al. 2008, 2010, 2012, 2013). Less emphasis has been placed on the timing of their entry and routes of movement across ISEA, due to insufficient data to link specific modern chicken haplogroups to definitive ancient domestication centres and lineages through ISEA and into Oceania (Storey et al. 2013). There does seem to be consensus between many researchers that there were multiple domestication centres for chickens in India (Kanginaduru et al. 2008), Thailand (Fumihito et al. 1996), South and southwest China and/or surrounding areas (Liu et al. 2006), and potentially all the above (Storey et al. 2013). Storey et al. (2013) have shown that repeatable sequences on chicken bones from the 3700–3500 cal. BP Neolithic site of Ban Non Wat in Thailand are identical to those recorded in 3250–2950 cal. BP chicken remains from Teouma site on Vanuatu. This at least provides a potential point of origin for the domestic chickens of MSEA and an 'end' point of movement across ISEA in the Pacific.

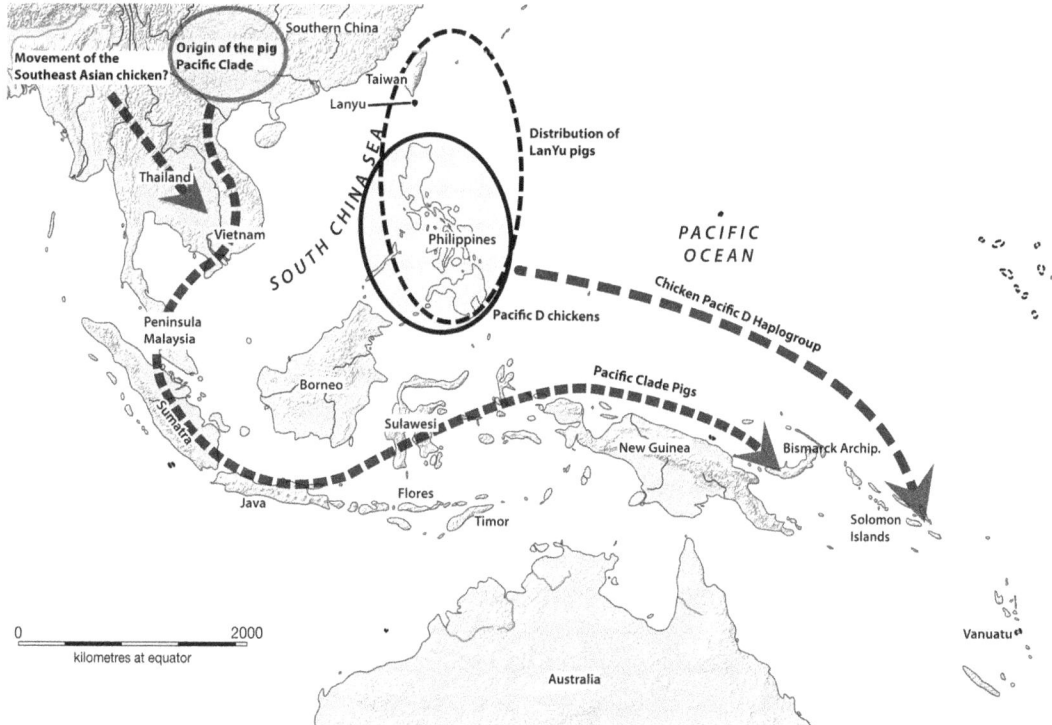

Figure 15.2 The proposed points of origin and routes of translocation of pigs and chicken across Mainland and Island Southeast Asia.

Source: P.J. Piper; Base Map: P. Bellwood, ANU Cartography.

Storey et al. (2012) originally argued that Haplogroup E chickens were the first to arrive in the Pacific, and made connections between Polynesian explorers and pre-European origins of Haplogroup E chickens in South America. More recently, Thomson et al. (2014) found that the majority of modern and all ancient chickens in the Pacific were Haplogroup D, rather than the proposed E. Furthermore, and importantly, east of the Solomon Islands the only ancient D haplotype chickens recorded are those possessing a specific signature termed the 'Pacific or Polynesian motif' (Figure 15.2). West of the Pacific Islands, Thomson et al. (2014) only found this specific D haplotype in the Philippines. This, based on the current chicken genetic evidence, and the independent spread of the Pacific D chickens east of Vanuatu, suggests an initial arrival with human populations from the Philippines into Near Oceania.

Dogs

Most modern and ancient DNA studies investigating the origins and routes of translocations of the domestic dog in MSEA and ISEA have focused on the Australian dingo (*Canis lupus dingo*). This is because archaeological research has indicated dingoes probably represent the earliest translocation of canids across ISEA and introduction to the Australasian region. This interpretation is supported by the genetic evidence, which places these relatively ancient dog breeds at the base of phylogenetic trees (Larson et al. 2012).

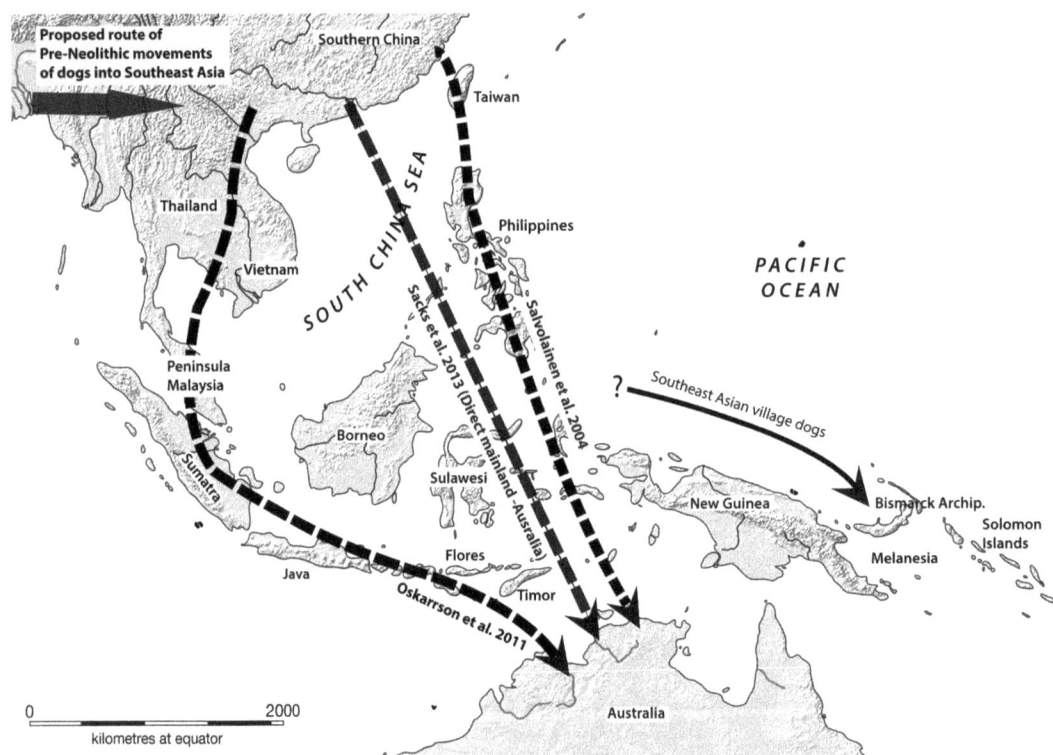

Figure 15.3 The proposed routes of translocation of dogs across Mainland and Island Southeast Asia.
Source: P.J. Piper; Base Map: P. Bellwood, ANU Cartography.

Salvolainen et al. (2004) analysed modern mtDNA from 211 dingoes, 38 Eurasian wolves and 676 dogs from all continents, as well as 19 pre-European archaeological dog samples from Polynesia. They identified a distinctive substitution (known as A29) in dingo mtDNA with a mean genetic distance that indicates an origin for the lineage at *ca.* 5000 BP. They suggested that the dingo originated from domestic dogs in East Asia, and was transported across ISEA as part of the Austronesian expansion, after 4000 BP (Figure 15.3). However, Oskarsson et al. (2011) argued that there was no evidence for the A29 substitution in any of the modern Taiwanese and Philippine dog samples they studied, and an Austronesian introduction of the dog to Polynesia was unlikely. Instead they proposed a southern Chinese origin for the dingo lineage, and a route of translocation through Southeast Asia and Indonesia, not that dissimilar to the proposed route for the Pacific Clade of pigs (Figure 15.3; see Larson et al. 2007). Other studies have also suggested a southern Chinese/MSEA origin for domestic dogs (Ding et al. 2012; Pang et al. 2009).

Sacks et al. (2013) propose a more complicated scenario, whereby the first dogs introduced into MSEA possibly came from the west, in South Asia (though no point of origin is specified) in the pre-Neolithic, and these were later replaced throughout MSEA during the expansion of farming communities across the region (Figure 15.3). Their study supports the hypothesis that ISEA dogs have their origins in MSEA, and that, contra to Oskarsson et al. (2011), Philippine dogs share their ancestry with those from Indonesia. Dingoes are also more likely to originate from the Mainland than Taiwan (though the latter location cannot be entirely discounted), but a unique haplotype, derived from (H5) observed in dingoes, but not in other ISEA modern dog populations, argues against their close relationship. Thus, Sacks et al. (2013) have proposed a direct translocation from MSEA/Taiwan of the dingo to Australia, with mutations indicating a common ancestor between the two populations at *ca*. 5000–4000 BP (Figure 15.3).

Freedman et al. (2014) also argued for a pre-agricultural origin and translocation of the dingo from the Mainland to Australia. This was primarily based on the fact that dingoes only have two copies of the starch digestion gene, and this probably meant that they were unlikely to have had any close association with cultivators of cereal crops.

One modern human genetic study has argued for considerable gene flow between Indian and Australian Aboriginal populations some 4,200 years ago, and that this coincided with introduction of the dingo and microlithic blade technologies to Australia (Pugach et al. 2013). Gollan (1980, 1984) made the same argument for an ancient connection between Indian and Australian populations based on the sudden appearance of backed blades and his morphometric study of dingo and Indian pariah dog crania.

Zooarchaeological evidence for pigs, dogs and chickens

The purported occurrence of domestic dogs in the bone assemblages of forager communities in the Yongjiang Valley in Guangxi around 7000 BP and in Dingsishan sites at 6500–5000 BP is significant in that it suggests that dogs were potentially present in southern China prior to the arrival of agriculturalists (Zhang and Hung 2010). However, close examination of the zooarchaeological data from Dingshishan indicates that dogs were only identified in the upper horizons of the site in association with rice agriculture (Lu 2010), and thus likely a later introduction than previously reported. Pigs have been described from the later layers at Tanshishan phase sites in Fujian on the southeast coast of China, opposite Taiwan, dating to *ca*. 5000–4300 BP and associated with agriculture (Hung and Carson 2014), and could have been introduced to Southeast Asia with the earliest farming communities. As far as the author is aware there are no reports of domestic chicken remains from southern China in the Neolithic as yet.

Mainland Southeast Asia

Bui Vinh (1991) has claimed the presence of domestic dogs at the late forager site of Con Co Ngua, and Patte (1932) also reported a 'dog' ulna similar in size to that of the dingo from the site of Da But, both in Thanh Hoa Province of northern Vietnam and dating to *ca.* 5500–6500 BP. Both these claims are yet to be corroborated and the specimens clearly distinguished from native wild canids.

Dogs and domesticated pigs have, however, been identified in northern Vietnam, at the transitional forager-farmer site of Man Bac dating from *ca.* 3700–3500 cal. BP onwards (Matsumura and Oxenham 2011; Sawada et al. 2011). Canid remains morphologically similar to modern domestic Vietnamese dogs were reported from Dong Dau in the earliest levels of Phung Nguyen cultural deposits dated to 3328±100 uncal. BP; Gollan 1980: 222). In the Mekong Delta region of southern Vietnam, dogs and pigs are present at the agricultural settlement sites of An Son (4000–3500 cal. BP) (Piper et al. 2014) and Loc Giang dating to *ca.* 3800–3300 cal. BP onwards (Piper et al. in press), and at Rach Nui from 3500 cal. BP onwards (Oxenham et al. 2015; Piper and Oxenham 2014). There is also a tentative identification of a chicken tarsometatarsus from a securely stratified layer at Loc Giang dating to *ca.* 3500 cal. BP (Piper et al. in press).

Domestic animals are absent from the hunter-gatherer site of Nong Nor in central Thailand, occupied around 4300 BP (Higham 2004), but dogs are present at the proposed forager site of Kok Phanom Di (KPD) after *ca.* 3700 cal. BP. Higham (2004) and Kijngam (2011) have argued that the appearance of dogs at KPD coincides with movements of rice agriculturalists into the region who brought dogs with them. There are also records of dog, pigs (possibly domesticated) and chickens from Non Nok Tha (Higham 1975) from 3400–3100 cal. BP (Higham et al. 2014), pigs and dogs from Ban Chiang (Higham et al. 1980) from 3600 BP (Higham et al. 2011), and chickens at Ban Na Di (Storey et al. 2012). In the earliest phases of Ban Non Wat, dating to 3650–3250 cal. BP, the dogs are considered to be from domestic stock, the chickens were possibly domesticated and the pigs await aDNA and geometric morphometric determinations (Higham and Higham 2008; Kijngam 2011).

Island Southeast Asia

Source populations of domestic pigs and dogs for introduction to ISEA appear to have been present across parts of MSEA from at least 4000 BP onwards, and dogs have been recorded at Nanguanli in Taiwan dating from *ca.* 4800 BP (Tsang et al. 2006). The prehistoric status of pigs in Taiwan remains unclear but there is a strong possibility they were present from at least *ca.* 4000 BP.

In the Philippines a direct C[14] determination on a pig lower fourth premolar from Nagsabaran in northern Luzon produced a date of 3940±40 BP (WK-23397) or 4499–4332 (77.4 per cent) /4568–4520 (13.2 per cent) cal. BP (all radiocarbon dates herein recalibrated using OxCal 4.2, IntCal 13; Bronk Ramsey 2015). This currently represents the earliest evidence for the introduction of domestic pigs into ISEA (Piper et al. 2009). There is no dog recorded in the early phases of Nagsabaran so far, but a dog burial at the base of the shell midden probably dates to between 2800–2500 BP (Amano et al. 2013; Piper et al. 2009). A canid 3rd left metatarsal found in Callao Cave in the Peñablanca region of northern Luzon is loosely associated with a radiocarbon date from the same stratigraphic unit of 3335±34 or 3650–3470 cal. BP (WK-17010; Mijares 2006: 39; Piper et al. 2013). There is no evidence of wild canids ever inhabiting the Philippine archipelago east of Palawan and this is almost certainly from a domestic dog. Supporting evidence for a possible mid-third millennium BC introduction of dogs to the Philippines also comes from Pasimbahan Cave on Palawan where a dog occipital fragment was recovered from a deposit with an associated radiocarbon date on charcoal of 3401±26 or 3753–3628 cal. BP (WK34844; Ochoa et al. 2014). The 'early' age determinations on associated pieces of charcoal from both Callao and Pasimbahan should be regarded with caution. At Savidug Dune Site on Sabtang in the Batanes Islands, between Taiwan and Luzon, pig is present from *ca.* 3100 cal. BP, but dogs are first recorded only in association with dates of 2500–2300 cal. BP. A single right tibiotarsus fragment from Savidug Dune site dating to *ca.* 2500–2300 cal. BP has been tentatively identified as domestic fowl (Bellwood and Dizon 2013; Piper et al. 2013).

Geometric-morphometric studies of archaeological pig teeth from Niah Cave on Borneo were inconclusive, but indicated that it was unlikely that any of the pig remains recovered within sequences securely dated to the earliest pottery phases before *ca.* 3500 BP were domestic (Cucchi et al. 2009). A few pig teeth from a single individual with domestic affinities were found at Lobang Magala E, and were considered to be of 'Neolithic' age by Medway (1973). However, the provenance of this specimen is insecure and it is highly likely to be post-Neolithic (Lloyd-Smith et al. 2013). Domestic pigs and dogs are certainly present at Niah by the early Metal Age from *ca.* 2500 BP onwards (Szabó et al. 2013).

There are two early enigmatic records of canids in ISEA. A single canine and calcaneus in the Agop Sarapad entrance to Madai Cave in Sabah (MAD2), north Borneo, are dated by freshwater shell to *ca.* 10,000–9000 BP (Bellwood 1988: 125; Cranbrook 1988a: 147, 1988b) and four bones within secure contexts date to the Terminal Pleistocene and early Holocene (10,000 BP and older) from Ille Cave, northern Palawan (Lewis et al. 2008; Piper et al. 2011). None of these remains are diagnostic enough to distinguish between *Canis* and *Cuon alpinus* (Asiatic wild dog). Cranbrook (2014) proposes that the early canid remains from Borneo and Palawan could represent remains of early domestic dogs introduced to the islands long before the Austronesian diaspora. However, both Borneo and Palawan were conjoined to the mainland during the Middle and/or Late Pleistocene (Robles et al. 2015) and the most parsimonious explanation for the presence of these canid remains at such early dates in ISEA is that they represent locally extinct populations of the Asiatic wild dog that had reached the islands across land-bridges during periods of low sea stand (Cranbrook 1988; Piper et al. 2011).

The only domestic animal reported from Indonesia west of Wallace's Line dating to greater than 2500 BP is a partial skeleton of a dog from Hoekgrot on the south coast of East Java. Storm (2001: 31) reports that this specimen had uncertain associations with two dates of 2655±60 or 2925–2544 cal. BP on 'fauna' and 3265±55 BP or 3630–3381 cal. BP on human bone (no lab codes provided).

On Sulawesi, Minanga Sipakko and Kamassi in the Kalumpang region of the Karama River Valley produced pigs, probably of domestic origin. These were recorded in some of the oldest archaeological deposits at around 3500 BP, or slightly earlier in Minanga Sipakko (Anggraeni et al. 2014). Indirect evidence for the presence of dogs at Kamassi was recorded in the form of bone gnawing and digestion from the earliest phases of occupation, but actual dog bones are only present from *ca.* 3000 BP onwards.

Glover (1986) had argued for a date as early as 5000–4000 BP for the East Timor dog remains studied by Gollan (1980). However, his East Timor chronology, which relied on extrapolation from a small number of available dates, is no longer considered reliable. A single pig tooth from Uai Bobo 2 Horizon VII, recovered from deposits dating to *ca.* 5600 BP (Glover 1986: 204), is also considered unreliable. The earliest securely dated canid remains in East Timor come from a dog burial in Matja Kuru 2 (Gonzalez et al. 2013; Veth et al. 2005). Two direct radiocarbon assays obtained on bones from the skeleton returned dates of 2967±58 or 3335–2961 cal. BP

(95.4 per cent; Wk-10051) and 2867±26 BP or 3070–2885 cal. BP (95.4 per cent; Wk-34931) (3138–2929 cal. BP, 95.4 per cent probability, X^2 test: df-1, T-2.5 (5 per cent; 3.8)) indicating the presence of dogs on the island at the end of the second millennium BC (Veth et al. 2005).

Pig bones identified as the Pacific Clade haplogroup of *S. scrofa* have been recovered from Liang Bua Cave on Flores in deposits dating to after 4000 BP, and in association with pottery and other evidence of Neolithic material culture. However, a suid tooth from the same site identified through aDNA as Sulawesi warty pig (*S. celebensis*) was recovered in association with a charcoal sample dated to *ca.* 7000 BP (Larson et al. 2007). The dog was only recorded in sub-surface layers at Liang Bua dating to within the last 500 years (van den Bergh et al. 2009). Although Meijer et al. (2013) conducted comprehensive studies on the avifauna from Liang Bua there is no mention of domestic chicken.

Numerous excavations in the Moluccas during the early 1990s produced evidence of early domesticates only from the site of Uattamdi on Kayoa Island, in association with red-slipped pottery. The earliest pig bones were recovered in layers dating between two radiocarbon dates of 3260±70 or 3693–3409 cal. BP (ANU-9323) and 2610±170 or 3211–2375 cal. BP (ANU-7775). The initial appearance of dog was recorded in slightly later deposits between 3211–2375 cal. BP and 2330±70 or 2590–2202 cal. BP (ANU-9322; Bellwood et al. 1998; Bellwood and White 2005; Flannery et al. 1998).

In the Banda group of islands, pig is recorded at the site PA1, on Ay Island, in association with a fragment of red-slipped pottery similarly incised to Lapita pottery and dated to 3150 BP (Lape 2000).

Oceania (with relevance to initial introduction from Southeast Asia)

The earliest evidence for the introduction of pig and chicken to Near Oceania is associated with the initial developments of the Lapita Cultural Complex, recently re-dated to between 3350–3300 BP (Summerhayes 2007; Kirch 2010). For example, a few pig and chicken bones have been identified in early Lapita contexts from Talepakemalai (Gosden et al. 1989; Matisoo-Smith 2007), and chicken is recorded at Etakosarai on Mussau (Matisoo-Smith 2007), and from Kainapirina on Watom the earliest reliable dates for pig is 2760–2547 cal. BP (Hawkins 2015). Direct dates on pig and chicken bones from Teouma in Vanuatu are calibrated to between *ca.* 3100–2700 cal. BP, indicating that both these domestics were introduced during the earliest phases of site occupation (Petchey et al. 2015). It is interesting to note that amongst the thousands of animal bones studied by Hawkins (2015), which included substantial records of pig and chicken, there was not a single dog bone. Chicken bones have also been recovered from Mdailu in the southeast Solomons in association with Lapita pottery, dating to after 3200 BP (McCoy and Cleghorn 1988; Storey et al. 2012). Pigs and chickens have been identified on Reef Santa Cruz (RF-2) dating between 3200–2800 BP, and sporadic reports of pig and dog bones have also been published from sites such as Apalo in the Arawe Islands (Gosden et al. 1989) and Balbalankin (pig only; 2950–2360 cal. BP) in the Anir Islands, and pigs at Lebang Halika on Nissan from 3300 BP onwards (Matisoo-Smith 2007). Kirch (1987) originally reported dog from Talepakemalai on Mussau but the identification has been questioned by Matisoo-Smith (2007), and from Tikopia (TK-4) dated to *ca.* 2800 BP (Matisoo-Smith 2007). Probably the earliest reliable dates for dog in Lapita are from Kamgot (3380–2950 cal. BP) where Summerhayes (personal communication, 2016) reports five definite dog bones from the earliest levels of the site. Although, Anderson (2009) suggests that dogs are absent from early Lapita, it seems that they were perhaps present on a few sites in Near Oceania. However, as noted for Teouma on Vanuatu, dogs do not appear to have reached Remote Oceania as early as pigs and chickens.

Australia

The arrival of the dingo into Australia is still very poorly understood. The two earliest fairly reliable dates (though it is suggested that even these 1960s dates be treated with caution) for dogs in Australia are 3450±95 (ANU-850) or 3981–3528 cal. BP from Madura cave in Western Australia (Milham and Thompson 1976), and at Fromm's Landing in South Australia where a dingo skeleton was recovered from deposits between two dates on charcoal of 3220±94 (NPL-29) or 3695–3267 cal. BP and 3000±91 (NPL-28) or 3443–2978 cal. BP (Macintosh 1964). Gollan (1984: 926) places the entry of dog to Australia at *ca.* 4200–4000 BP, and a date of between 5,000–3,000 years ago is generally accepted for the arrival of the ancestor of the Australian dingo (Crowther et al. 2014).

Discussion

Mainland Southeast Asia

There is currently no solid evidence for an association between domestic animals and hunter-gatherers in MSEA. Domestic pigs and dogs are present in the earliest phases of Phung Nguyen Culture of northern Vietnam at *ca.* 4000 cal. BP or slightly earlier as human populations apparently spread southwards from the provinces of Fujian-Guangdong and/or Guangxi into MSEA (Zhang and Hung 2008, 2010). Both pigs and dogs are present in early phases of settlement development in northern and southern Vietnam along the Red and Vam Co Dong Rivers, respectively, by *ca.* 4000 BP (Piper and Oxenham 2014; Piper et al. 2014). This distribution of domestic pigs and dogs corresponds well with the proposed origins and expansion of the Pacific Clade pigs, from southern China across parts of MSEA, likely associated with the movements of Austroasiatic-speaking populations. Domestic dogs, and possibly managed pig populations, are also present in the earliest rice agricultural settlements of Ban Non Wat, Ban Chiang and Non No Tha in northern and central Thailand. But the absence of the Pacific Clade of pigs from Thailand and Cambodia perhaps implies different origins for domestic pigs in east and west MSEA.

That east and west MSEA were on slightly different domestication trajectories is also apparent in the initial appearance of domestic cattle (*Bos* sp.) across the region. In Thailand, cattle have been recorded at Non Nok Tha by *ca.* 3500 BP (Higham and Leach 1971; Higham et al. 2014) and Ban Non Wat (Kijngam 2011) from at least *ca.* 3600 BP onwards. In northern and southern Vietnam, evidence of domestic bovines is completely absent from Neolithic sites (Sawada et al. 2011; Piper et al. 2014). The potential use of domestic cattle as traction animals for ploughs in the Neolithic of Thailand, and their absence in Vietnam, has implications for the differential timing of agricultural intensification across the region.

Bird identifications in the archaeological record are still rare across MSEA (as they are in ISEA) due to a lack of specialist study, and poor bone preservation. Thus, it is still difficult to assess the distribution of fowl across the region. However, in northern and central Thailand, a region within the natural biogeographic distribution of wild red jungle fowl (*Gallus gallus*), and where early domestication has been proposed (Fumihito et al. 1996), chicken bones are relatively common in early Neolithic sites, from *ca.* 3700 BP onwards. The deliberate inclusion of fowl in burials at sites such as Non Nok Tha and Ban Na Di (Storey et al. 2012) indicates a close relationship between domesticated chickens and people. The evidence for chicken domestication to the east is more equivocal. In southern Vietnam where domestic pigs and dogs have been reported, chickens appear to be almost completely absent from the archaeological record. A single tibiotarsus dating to *ca.* 3500 cal. BP from the settlement site of Loc Giang has been interpreted as a possible small domestic fowl. This raises the possibility that chickens were domesticated in, or introduced to, west MSEA prior to their spread south and east across the region.

Neolithic domestic animals remain unreported in the Thai-Malay Peninsula before 3000 BP, but this geographic locale is likely to be where Pacific Clade pigs passed through en route to the Pacific (see below).

Island Southeast Asia

It has been argued that the translocation of the Sulawesi warty pig from Sulawesi to surrounding islands could reflect the earliest domestication event in ISEA (van den Bergh et al. 2009). However, the early mid-Holocene timing for warty pig movements is based on a single insecure associated radiocarbon date on charcoal of 7000 BP from Liang Bua, Flores. As has been recently demonstrated with the purported early pig introduction into New Guinea (O'Connor et al. 2011), there is a possibility that the date for warty pig translocation will turn out to be considerably younger than originally reported. The enigmatic early Holocene records of a canid in Borneo and Palawan could potentially represent early introductions of domestic dogs to the region (see Cranbrook 2014). But as both islands are located within the Sundaic biogeographic region and were connected to the mainland during different periods of the Pleistocene, they could just as easily represent extinct populations of the Asiatic wild dog (*Cuon alpinus*), which is still present in Sumatra and Java. Future recovery of diagnostic anatomical elements, and/or aDNA would help resolve this issue.

Thus, on present evidence the earliest securely dated introductions of domestic animals into ISEA all date to after 4500–4200 BP.

Interestingly, Bellwood (1997: 237) considered that the *ca.* 4000 BP material culture recovered from Gua Sireh in Sarawak, Malaysian Borneo, had more in common with the Peninsular Malaysian and southern Thai Neolithic than that identified to the east in the Philippines. This correlated neatly with Adelaar's (1995) argument for an Austroasiatic substratum in Land Dayak languages of western Sarawak, and indicated a possible migration from MSEA via Peninsula Malaysia into ISEA. Recent excavations at Takongen, Silabe and Harimau caves in Sumatra support a possible Austroasiatic movement into ISEA (Simanjuntak, Chapter 11, this volume), and this might have resulted in the introduction, and then human or down-the-line movement of pigs, dogs and chickens east, where they spread out to encompass most of ISEA, with the exception of the Philippine archipelago. Unfortunately, there is currently no zooarchaeological evidence reported for any of the 'big three' in Indonesia west of Wallace's Line, prior to *ca.* 2500 BP (except the poorly dated Hoekgrot dog) in support of the Thai-Malay Peninsula route of translocation. This is a result of limited zooarchaeological study and problems in differentiating domestic from wild pigs, and chickens amongst the Phasianidae in this diverse faunal region. However, the Pacific Clade pig has been identified in *ca.* 4000 BP deposits in Liang Bua Cave, Flores, and at Uattamdi, Kayoa Island, at *ca.* 3200 cal. BP, indicating prehistoric movements through the region (though direct bone dates would be useful). The Pacific Clade of pigs was introduced to Near Oceania, perhaps during the early phases of Lapita development in the Bismarck archipelago at *ca.* 3300–3200 cal. BP, and then onwards to Vanuatu.

Based on genetic and (some) zooarchaeological evidence a second, though more enigmatic, introduction of domestic pigs, chickens and perhaps dogs occurred in the Philippines during the late third or early second millennium BC. Domestic pigs, possibly of the Lanyu haplotype, appear to have been introduced to the Batanes Islands by at least 3200 BP, and were also present in the 'open air' site of Nagsabaran in the Cagayan Valley by around *ca.* 4000 cal. BP (Piper et al. 2009, 2013). This suggests introduction during or shortly after the initial establishment of the earliest sedentary settlements associated with colonisation by Austronesian-speaking populations in the Philippines (see Hung and Carson 2015). Dogs were potentially present in the Philippines from *ca.* 4000 BP onwards but this still needs to be confirmed by more securely stratified specimens, or preferably, direct radiocarbon dates on dog bone. The physical remains of chickens are still absent from the archaeological record, but the unique Pacific D (Polynesian) haplotype with its possible origins in the Philippines suggests considerable antiquity for domestic fowl in the archipelago. This is supported by the identification of the Pacific D motif in chickens dated to *ca.* 3100–2700 cal. BP on Vanuatu (Petchey et al. 2015). A Philippine rather than Taiwan origin for the chicken also fits with the linguistic evidence in that there is no known Proto-Austronesian (Formosan) terms for domestic fowl, but they do occur in Proto-Malayo-Polynesian (Blust 1995). The absence of the Polynesian motif through eastern Indonesia suggests a possible direct introduction from the Philippines to the Solomon Islands and Vanuatu (though the aDNA research is still very limited). Furthermore, this haplotype of chickens is the only one translocated beyond Vanuatu into Remote Oceania. The presence of chickens with the 'Polynesian motif' on Vanuatu in association with the Pacific Clade of pigs from Indonesia implies staggered arrival times in Near Oceania (see also Anderson 2009).

In Sulawesi, provisional morphometric analyses of pig teeth from the deepest and oldest layers at the sites of Kamassi (Kamansi) and Minanga Sipakko in the Karama Valley suggest introduction during or shortly after the establishment of these, the oldest known 'open air' settlement sites on the island. Dog remains are absent from the earliest deposits. These settlements have been interpreted as representing those constructed by initial colonisers migrating southwards from the Philippines (Anggraeni et al. 2014). Future genetic and morphometric analyses will hopefully link the ancient domestic animal introductions either with Philippine or Indonesian lineages.

Currently, the earliest evidence for domestic dogs in ISEA is the *ca.* 3000–2800 cal. BP skeletal remains from East Timor and the early to mid-first millennium BC canid bones from Uattamdi. Biometric analysis of the well-preserved Timor dog indicates a similar stature to other prehistoric and contemporary village dogs across ISEA and the Pacific (Gonzalez et al. 2013). The 'village dogs' of eastern Indonesia and the Pacific appear to be morphologically unrelated to Australian dingoes and perhaps represent an entirely different dog introduction to ISEA, as has also been suggested through genetic analysis by Sacks et al. (2013) and Shannon et al. (2015). Thus, the zooarchaeological and genetic evidence suggests at least two different dog translocations into ISEA before 3000 BP, with dingoes reaching Australia and Southeast Asian village dogs being transported into the Pacific. The possible absence of dogs in early settlement sites in the Solomons and on Vanuatu suggests they were a later arrival in Remote Oceania than pigs and chickens.

Recently, Fillios and Taçon (2016) have argued that the dingo could have been transported first to Sulawesi and then onwards to Australia sometime prior to the arrival of Austronesian migrants, by members of the Toalean forager culture. Although the absence of evidence for pottery and other material culture associated with the Neolithic in Australia and the lack of cereal digestion genes in dingoes could indicate a pre-Neolithic movement, there is currently a lack of archaeological remains of domestic dogs anywhere in MSEA and ISEA before 4500 BP, or of a pre-3000 BP date in Sulawesi to support this hypothesis. The origins of routes of translocation across ISEA of both dog lineages proposed here currently remain unknown.

Conclusion

When Peter Bellwood initially proposed more than three decades ago that the 'big three' were first introduced to, and spread across, MSEA and ISEA by Austroasiatic- and Austronesian-speaking agriculturalists, with their ultimate origins in China, he could not have envisaged how complicated the unraveling story of animal domestication and translocation across the region would become.

Based on current evidence, none of the 'big three' was domesticated in or introduced to MSEA and ISEA prior to *ca.* 4500 BP. Thereafter, multiple translocation events probably resulted in two or more lineages of pigs, dogs and chickens originating in, or entering, MSEA and ISEA from the northeast and west. The appearance and spread of domestic pigs and dogs in early sedentary settlement sites across Vietnam supports the farming/language hypothesis and the spread of Austroasiatic-speaking agriculturalists from southern China through much of eastern MSEA. But genetic and zooarchaeological evidence also indicates a South Asian or Thailand origin for domestic chickens, and suggests a succeeding spread of fowl south and east into the Thai-Malay Peninsula and possibly Vietnam. Pigs, dogs and chickens found in ISEA all have their origins on the mainland.

Referring to comments by Pawley and Green (1975), and based on linguistic reconstructions, Bellwood wrote of the Proto-Austronesian (PAN) speakers of Taiwan: 'they kept pigs, and probably dogs and chickens, and made pottery' (Bellwood 1979: 122). Undoubtedly, the early forager-farmers of Taiwan were acquainted with pigs and dogs, with the chicken evidence remaining enigmatic. However, of the pig, dog and chicken genetic lineages with which the Proto-Austronesian and/or early Malayo-Polynesian speakers (in the Philippines) were familiar, only the chicken appears to have spread more widely, reaching Remote Oceania. The presence of both the 'Polynesian motif' chickens and Pacific Clade pigs in Near Oceania/Solomon Islands and Vanuatu suggests multiple, staggered introductions of domestic animals of different origins into Oceania. The presence of pigs in early archaeological sites in Remote Oceania suggests that suids along with chickens were transported early with the initial colonists. This argument is supported by lexical evidence that the first Oceanic speakers in Remote Oceania practised pig husbandry (see Pawley, Chapter 17, this volume). Interestingly, Valentin et al. (2015) identified the origins of the Lapita populations of Teouma on Vanuatu as Southeast Asian, and ultimately of East Asian descent. They also observed heterogeneity in the cranial morphometrics of the individuals studied and interpreted this as potentially reflecting diversity in their geographic origins. This would fit neatly with the variation observed in the likely sources of the domestic animals arriving in Oceania.

At least two lineages of dogs were apparently introduced to ISEA, the dingo and village dog, whose origins and routes of translocation across the region remain unknown. There is still a possibility that the dingo was transported across MSEA and ISEA prior to the movements of Austroasiatic- and Austronesian-speaking populations, and this would explain its unique and solo arrival in Australia. The Southeast Asian village dog was introduced more recently and was transported out into the Pacific. The lack of concrete evidence for dogs in early Lapita sites, certainly on the most westerly of the Remote Oceanic islands, suggests an introduction succeeding both pigs and chickens.

Acknowledgements

The author would like to thank all those who have helped in the zooarchaeological analysis of numerous bone assemblages and tens of thousands of bones over the last 10 years. Many thanks also to Glenn R. Summerhayes for providing up to date information on the Kamgot Lapita fauna.

This research was funded by an ARC Future Fellowship grant to the author FT100100527.

References

Adelaar, K.A. 1995. Borneo as a cross-roads for comparative Austronesian linguistics. In P. Bellwood, J.J. Fox and D. Tryon (eds), *The Austronesians: Historical and Comparative Perspectives*, pp. 75–95. Canberra: The Australian National University.

Amano, Jr N., P.J. Piper, H.-c. Hung and P. Bellwood. 2013. Introduced domestic animals in the Neolithic and Metal Age of the Philippines: evidence from Nagsabaran, Northern Luzon. *Journal of Island and Coastal Archaeology* 8: 317–335. doi.org/10.1080/15564894.2013.781084.

Anderson, A. 2009. The rat and the octopus: Initial human colonization and the prehistoric introduction of domestic animals to Oceania. *Biological Invasions* 11: 1505–1519. doi.org/10.1007/s10530-008-9403-2.

Anggraeni, T. Simanjuntak, P. Bellwood and P.J. Piper. 2014. New Research on the Karama Valley sites, West Sulawesi, Indonesia. *Antiquity* 88(341): 740–756. doi.org/10.1017/S0003598X00050663.

Bellwood, P. 1975. The prehistory of Oceania. *Current Anthropology* 16(1): 9–17. doi.org/10.1086/201515.

——. 1976. Prehistoric plant and animal domestication in Austronesia. In G. de, G. Sieveking, I.H. Longworth and K.E. Wilson (eds), *Problems in Economic and Social Archaeology*, pp. 153–168. London: Duckworth.

——. 1984. Archaeological research in the MadaiBaturong region, Sabah. *Bulletin of the Indo-Pacific Prehistory Association* 5: 38–56.

——. 1988. The Madai excavations: Sites MAD 1, MAD 2 and MAD 3. In P. Bellwood (ed.), *Archaeological Research in South-Eastern Sabah*. Sabah Museum Monograph vol. 2, pp. 97–128. Kota Kinabalu: Sabah Museum and State Archives.

——. 1996. Phylogeny vs reticulation in prehistory. *Antiquity* 70: 881–890. doi.org/10.1017/S0003598X00084131.

——. 1997. *Prehistory of the Indo-Malayan Archipelago*. Hawai'i: University of Hawaii Press.

——. 2001. Early agriculturalist population diasporas? Farming, languages and genes. *Annual Review of Anthropology* 30: 181–207. doi.org/10.1146/annurev.anthro.30.1.181.

——. 2005. *First Farmers: The Origins of Agricultural Societies*. Oxford: Blackwell.

——. 2013. *First Migrants: Ancient Migration in Global Perspective*. Chichester: Wiley-Blackwell.

Bellwood, P. and E. Dizon. 2005. The Batanes Archaeological Project and the 'Out of Taiwan' hypothesis for Austronesian dispersal. *Journal of Austronesian Studies* 1(1): 1–32.

Bellwood, P. and E. Dizon. 2013. The chronology of Batanes prehistory. In P. Bellwood, and E. Dizon (eds), *4000 Years of Migration and Cultural Exchange: Archaeology in the Batanes Islands, Northern Philippines*, pp. 67–76. Terra Australis 40. Canberra: ANU E Press.

Bellwood, P. and P. White. 2005. Domesticated pigs in Eastern Indonesia. *Science* 309: 381. doi. org/10.1126/science.309.5733.381a.

Bellwood, P., G. Nitihaminoto, G. Irwin, A. Gunadi, Waluyo and D. Tanudirjo. 1998. 35,000 years of prehistory in the northern Moluccas. In G.J. Bartstra (ed.), Bird's Head approaches: Irian Jaya studies, a program of interdisciplinary research. *Modern Quaternary Research in Southeast Asia* 15: 233–275.

Bellwood, P., M. Oxenham, C.H. Bui, T.D.K. Nguyen, A. Willis, C. Sarjeant, P.J. Piper, H. Matsumura, K. Tanaka, N. Beavan, T. Higham, Q.M. Nguyen, N.K. Dang, K.T.K. Nguyen, T.H. Vo, N.B. Van, T.K.Q. Tran, P.T. Nguyen, F. Campos, Y-I Sato, L.C. Nguyen and N. Amano. 2011. An Son and the Neolithic of Southern Vietnam. *Asian Perspectives* 50 (1&2): 144–174. doi.org/10.1353/ asi.2011.0007.

Blust, R.A. 1995. The prehistory of the Austronesian-speaking peoples: A view from language. *Journal of World Prehistory* 9(4): 453–510. doi.org/10.1007/BF02221119.

Bronk Ramsey, C. 2015. Oxcal 4.2 manual. c14.arch.ox.ac.uk/oxcal.html.

Bui, V. 1991. The Da But Culture in the Stone Age of Vietnam. *Bulletin of the Indo-Pacific Prehistory Association* 10: 127–131.

Bulmer, S. 1966. Pig bone from two archaeological sites in the New Guinea Highlands. *Journal of the Polynesian Society* 75(4): 504–505.

——. 1975. Settlement and economy in prehistoric Papua New Guinea. *Journal de la Sociétés des Océanistes* 31(46): 7–75. doi.org/10.3406/jso.1975.2688.

——. 1982. Human ecology and cultural variation in prehistoric New Guinea. In J. Gresswit (ed.), *Biogeography and Ecology of New Guinea*, pp. 169–206. The Hague, Netherlands: DR Junk. doi. org/10.1007/978-94-009-8632-9_8.

Cranbrook, E.-O. 1988a. Report on bones from the Madai and Baturong cave excavations. In P. Bellwood (ed.), *Archaeological Research in South-Eastern Sabah.* Sabah Museum Monograph vol. 2, pp. 142–154. Kota Kinabalu: Sabah Museum and State Archives.

——. 1988b. The contribution of archaeology to the zoogeography of Borneo, with the first record of a wild canid of early Holocene age. *Fieldiana Zoology* 42: 1–7.

——. 2014. Archaeology of the dog in Borneo: New evidence from the Everett Collection in the Natural History Museum, London. In K. Boyle, R. Rabett and C. Hunt (eds), *Living in the Landscape: Essays in Honour of Graeme Barker*, pp. 171–182. McDonald Institute Monographs. Cambridge: McDonald Institute for Archaeological Research.

Crowther M.S., M. Filios, N. Colman and M. Letnic. 2014. An updated description of the Australian dingo (*Canis dingo* Meyer, 1793). *Journal of Zoology* (1987) 293: 192–203. doi.org/10.1111/ jzo.12134.

Cucchi, T., M. Fujita and K. Dobney. 2009. New insights into pig taxonomy, domestication and human dispersal in Island South East Asia: Molar shape analysis of Sus remains from Niah Caves, Sarawak. *International Journal of Osteoarchaeology* 19(4): 508–530. doi.org/10.1002/oa.974.

Cucchi, T., A. Hulme-Beaman, J. Yuan and K. Dobney. 2011. Early Neolithic pig domestication at Jiahu, Henan Province, China: Clues from molar shape analyses using geometric morphometric approaches. *Journal of Archaeological Science* 38: 11–22. doi.org/10.1016/j.jas.2010.07.024.

Diamond, J. and P. Bellwood. 2003. Farmers and their languages: the first expansions. *Science* 300: 597–603. doi.org/10.1126/science.1078208.

Ding Z.-L., M. Oskarsson, A. Ardalan, H. Angleby, L-G. Dahlgren, C. Tepeli, E. Kirkness, P. Savolainen and Y-P. Zhang. 2012. Origins of domestic dog in southern East Asia is supported by analysis of Y-chromosome DNA. *Heredity* 108: 507–514. doi.org/10.1038/hdy.2011.114.

Fillios, M.A. and P.S.C. Taçon. 2016. Who let the dogs in? A review of the recent genetic evidence for the introduction of the dingo to Australia and implications for the movement of people. *Journal of Archaeological Science* 7: 782–792. doi.org/10.1016/j.jasrep.2016.03.001.

Flannery, T., P. Bellwood, J.P. White, T. Ennis, G. Irwin, K. Schubert and S. Balasubramanian. 1998. Mammals from Holocene archaeological deposits on Gebe and Morotai Islands, Northern Moluccas, Indonesia. *Australian Mammalogy* 20(3): 391–400.

Freedman, A.H., I. Gronau, R.M. Schweizer, D. Ortega-Del Vecchyo, E. Han, P.M. Silva, M. Galaverni, Z. Fan, P. Marx, B. Lorente-Galdos, H. Beale, O. Ramirez, F. Hormozdiari, C. Alkan, C. Vilà, K. Squire, E. Geffen, J. Kusak, A.R. Boyko, H.G. Parker, C. Lee, V. Tadigotla, A. Siepel, C.D. Bustamante, T.T. Harkins, S.F. Nelson, E.A. Ostrander, T. Marques-Bonet, R.K. Wayne and J. Novembre. 2014. Genome sequencing highlights the dynamic early history of dogs. *PLoS Genetics* 10(8): e1004631. doi.org/10.1371/journal.pgen.1004016.

Fumihito, A., T. Miyake, M. Takada, R. Shingu, T. Endo, T. Gojobori, N. Kondo and S. Ohno. 1996. Monophyletic origin and unique dispersal patterns of domestic fowls. *Proceedings of the National Academy of Sciences* 93: 6792–6795. doi.org/10.1073/pnas.93.13.6792.

Glover, I. 1986. *Archaeology of Eastern Timor, 1966–67.* Terra Australis 11. Canberra: Department of Prehistory, Research School of Pacific and Asian Studies, The Australian National University.

Gollan K. 1980. Prehistoric Dingo. Unpublished PhD thesis, The Australian National University, Canberra.

——. 1984. The Australian dingo: In the shadow of man. In M. Archer and G. Clayton (eds), *Vertebrate Zoogeography and Evolution in Australasia*, pp. 921–927. Perth: Haesperton.

Gonzalez, A., G. Clark, S. O'Connor and L. Matisoo-Smith. 2013. A 3000 year old dog burial in Timor-Leste. *Australian Archaeology* 76: 13–29. doi.org/10.1080/03122417.2013.11681961.

Gosden, C., J. Allen, W. Ambrose, D. Anson, J. Golson, R. Green, P. Kirch, I. Lilley, J. Specht and M. Spriggs. 1989. The Lapita sites of the Bismarck Archipelago. *Antiquity* 63(240): 561–586. doi.org/10.1017/S0003598X00076559.

Groves, C. 1981. *Ancestors for the Pigs: Taxonomy and Phylogeny of the Genus.* Sus Technical Bulletin 3. Canberra: Department of Prehistory, Research School of Pacific Studies, The Australian National University.

——. 2007. Current views on taxonomy and zoogeography of the genus *Sus*. In U. Albarella, K. Dobney, A. Ervynck and P. Rowly-Conwy (eds), *Pigs and Humans: 10,000 Years of Interaction*, pp. 15–29. Oxford: Oxford University Press.

Hawkins, S.C. 2015. Human Behavioural Ecology, Anthropogenic Impact and Subsistence Change at the Teouma Lapita Site, Central Vanuatu, 3000–2500 BP. Unpublished PhD thesis, The Australian National University, Canberra.

Herrera, M. 2010. An archaeogenetic study of the genus *Sus* in the Philippines and its propositions for understanding human translocation in Island Southeast Asia. Unpublished Master's thesis, University of the Philippines, Manila.

Higham, C.F.W. 1975. Aspects of economy and ritual in prehistoric Northeast Thailand. *Journal of Archaeological Science* 2: 245–288. doi.org/10.1016/0305-4403(75)90001-1.

——. 2004. Mainland Southeast Asia from the Neolithic to the Iron Age. In I. Glover and P. Bellwood (eds), *Southeast Asia from Prehistory to History*, pp. 41–67. London: Routledge.

——. 2013. Summary and conclusions, In C.F.W. Higham and A. Kijngam (eds), *The Origins of the Civilization of Angkor*, vol. 4, *The Excavation of Ban Non Wat: The Neolithic Occupation*, pp. 199–211. Bangkok: The Thai Fine Arts Department.

——. 2015. Southeast Asian Mainland: Archaeology. In P. Bellwood (ed.), *The Global Prehistory of Human Migration*, pp. 269–275 Chichester: Wiley-Blackwell.

Higham, C.F.W. and B.F. Leach. 1971. An early centre of bovine husbandry in Southeast Asia. *Science* 172(3978): 54–56. doi.org/10.1126/science.172.3978.54.

Higham, C. and T. Higham. 2008. A new chronological framework for prehistoric Southeast Asia, based on a Bayesian model from Ban Non Wat. *Antiquity* 83: 125–145. doi.org/10.1017/S0003598X00098136.

Higham, C., T. Higham and A. Kijngam. 2011. Cutting a Gordian Knot: the Bronze Age of Southeast Asia: origins, timing and impact. *Antiquity* 85: 583–598. doi.org/10.1017/S0003598X00067971.

Higham, C.F.W., T.F.G. Higham and K. Douka. 2014. The chronology and status of Non Nok Tha, northeast Thailand. *Journal of Indo-Pacific Archaeology* 34: 61–75. doi.org/10.7152/jipa.v34i0.14719.

Hung, H.-c. and M. Carson. 2014. Foragers, fishers and farmers: origins of the Taiwanese Neolithic. *Antiquity* 88: 1115–1131. doi.org/10.1017/S0003598X00115352.

Kanginkudru, S., M. Metta, R.D. Jakati and J. Nagaraju. 2008. Genetic evidence from Indian red jungle fowl corroborates multiple domestication and modern day chicken. *BioMed Central Evolutionary Biology* 8. doi:10.1186/1471-2148/8/174.

Kijngam, A. 2011. The mammalian fauna. In C.F.W Higham, and A. Kijngam (eds), *The Origins of the Civilization of Angkor*, vol. IV, *The Excavation of Ban Non Wat. Part II: The Neolithic Occupation*, pp. 189–197. Bangkok: The Thai Fine Arts Department.

Kirch, P.V. 1987. Lapita and Oceanic cultural origins: excavations in the Mussau Islands, Bismarck Archipelago, 1985. *Journal of Field Archaeology* 14(2): 163–180. doi.org/10.1179/009346987792208493.

Kirch, P.V. 1997. *The Lapita Peoples*. Oxford: Blackwell.

——. 2010. Peopling of the Pacific: A holistic anthropological perspective. *Annual Review of Anthropology* 39: 131–148. doi.org/10.1146/annurev.anthro.012809.104936.

Lape, P. 2000. Political dynamics and religious change in the late pre-colonial Banda Islands, eastern Indonesia. *World Archaeology* 32(1): 138–155. doi.org/10.1080/004382400409934.

Larson, G. and D.Q. Fuller. 2014. The evolution of animal domestication. *Annual Review of Ecology, Evolution and Systematics* 45: 115–136. doi.org/10.1146/annurev-ecolsys-110512-135813.

Larson. G., K. Dobney, U. Albarella, M. Fang, E. Matisoo-Smith, J. Robins, S. Lowden, H. Finlayson, T. Brand, E. Willerslev, P. Rowley-Conwy, L. Andersson and A. Cooper. 2005. Worldwide phylogeography of wild boar reveals multiple centers of domestication. *Science* 307: 1618–1621. doi.org/10.1126/science.1106927.

Larson, G., T. Cucchi, M. Fujita, E. Matisoo-Smith, J. Robins, A. Anderson, B. Rolett, M. Spriggs, G. Dolman, T.-H. Kim, T.H.T. Nguyen, E. Randi, M. Doherty, R. Awe Due, R. Bollt, T. Djubiantono, B. Griffin, M. Intoh, E. Keane, P. Kirch, K.-T. Li, M. Morwood, L.M. Pedriña, P.J. Piper, R.J. Rabett, P. Shooter, G. Van den Bergh, E. West, S. Wickler, J. Yuan, A. Cooper and K. Dobney. 2007. Phylogeny and ancient DNA of Sus provides new insights into Neolithic expansion in Island Southeast Asia and Oceania. *Proceedings of the National Academy of Sciences* 104(12): 4834–4839. doi.org/10.1073/pnas.0607753104.

Larson, G., R. Liu, X. Zhao, J. Yuan, D. Fuller, L. Barton, K. Dobney, Q. Fan, Z. Gu, Z., X.-H. Liu, Y. Luo, P. Lv, L. Andersson and N. Li. 2010. Patterns of East Asian pig domestication, migration, and turnover revealed by modern and ancient DNA. *Proceedings of the National Academy of Sciences* 107(17): 7686–7691. doi.org/10.1073/pnas.0912264107.

Larson, G., E.L.K. Karlsson, A. Perri, M.T. Webster, S.Y.W. Ho, J. Peters, P.W. Stahl, P.J. Piper, F. Lingaas, M. Fredholm, K.E. Comstock, J.F. Modiano, C. Schelling, A.I. Agoulnik, P.A. Leegwater, K. Dobney, J.-D. Vigne, C. Villa, L. Andersson and K. Lindblad-Toh. 2012. Rethinking dog domestication by integrating genetics, archaeology, and biogeography. *Proceedings of the National Academy of Sciences* 109(23): 8878–8883. doi.org/10.1073/pnas.1203005109.

Lewis, H., V. Paz, M. Lara, H. Barton, P. Piper, J. Ochoa, T. Vitales, A.J. Carlos, T. Higham, L. Neri, V. Hernandez, J. Stevenson, E. C. Robles, A. Ragragio, R. Padilla, W.S. II and W. Ronquillo. 2008. Terminal Pleistocene to mid-Holocene occupation and an early cremation burial at Ille Cave, Palawan, Philippines. *Antiquity* 82: 318–335. doi.org/10.1017/S0003598X00096836.

Liu, Y.-P., G.-S. Wu, Y.-G. Yao, Y.-W. Miao, G. Luikart, M. Baig, A. Beja-Pereira, Z.-L. Ding, M.G. Palanichamy and Y-P. Zhang. 2006. Multiple maternal origins of chickens: Out of the Asian jungles. *Molecular Phylogenetics and Evolution* 38: 12–19. doi.org/10.1016/j.ympev.2005.09.014.

Lloyd-Smith, L., G. Barker, H. Barton, J. Cameron, F. Cole, C. Doherty, C. Hunt, J. Krigbaum, H. Lewis, J. Manser, V. Paz, P.J. Piper, G. Rushworth and K. Szabó. 2013. 'Neolithic' societies *c.* 4000–2000 years ago: Austronesian farmers? In G. Barker (ed.), *Rainforest Foraging and Farming in Island Southeast Asia: The Archaeology and Environmental History of the Niah Caves, Sarawak*, Niah Cave Project Monographs Series, pp. 255–298. Cambridge: McDonald Institute for Archaeological Research.

Lu, P. 2010. Zooarchaeological Study on the Shell Middens in the Yong Valley of Guangxi. Unpublished PhD dissertation, Institute of Archaeology, of Chinese Academy of Social Sciences, Beijing (in Chinese).

Lum, K.J., J.K. McIntyre, D.L. Greger, K.W. Huffman and M.G. Vilar. 2006. Recent Southeast Asian domestication and Lapita dispersal of sacred male pseudohermaphroditic 'tuskers' and hairless pigs of Vanuatu. *Proceedings of the National Academy of Sciences* 103(46): 17190–17195. doi.org/10.1073/pnas.0608220103.

Macintosh, J.W.G. 1964. A 3,000 year old dingo skeleton from Shelter 6, In D.J. Mulvaney, G.H. Lawton and C.R. Twidale (eds), Archaeological Excavation of Rock Shelter no. 6 Fromm's Landing, South Australia. *Proceedings of the Royal Society of Victoria* 77: 479–516.

Matisoo-Smith, E. 2007. Animal translocations, genetic variation and the human settlement of the Pacific. In J.S. Friedlaender (ed.), *Genes, Language and Culture History in the Southwest Pacific*, pp. 157–170. Oxford: Oxford University Press. doi.org/10.1093/acprof:oso/9780195300307.003.0010.

Matsumura, H and M.F. Oxenham. 2011. Introduction: Man Bac biological research objectives In M.F. Oxenham, H. Matsumura and K.D. Nguyen (eds), *Man Bac: The Excavation of a Neolithic Site in Northern Vietnam*, pp. 1–8. Terra Australis 33. Canberra: ANU E Press.

McCoy, P.C. and P.L. Cleghorn. 1988. Archaeological excavations on Santa Cruz (Nendö), southeast Solomon Islands: Summary report. *Archaeology in Oceania* 23(3): 104–115. doi. org/10.1002/j.1834-4453.1988.tb00197.x.

Medway, L. 1973. The antiquity of domesticated pigs in Sarawak. *Journal of the Malaysian Branch of the Royal Asiatic Society* 46(2): 169–178.

Meijer, H.J.M., T. Sutikna, E. Wahyu Saptomo, R. Awe Due, Jatmiko, S. Wasisto, H.F. James, M.J. Morwood and M.W. Tocheri. 2013. Late Pleistocene-Holocene non-passerine avifauna of Liang Bua (Flores, Indonesia). *Journal of Vertebrate Paleontology* 33(4): 877–894. doi.org/10.1080/02724634.2 013.746941.

Mijares A.S.B. 2006. *Unearthing Prehistory. The Archaeology of Northeastern Luzon, Philippine Islands.* BAR International Series 1613. Oxford: Oxbow.

Milham, P. and P. Thompson. 1976. Relative antiquity of human occupation and extinct fauna at Madura Cave, southeastern Australia. *Mankind* 10: 175–180. doi.org/10.1111/j.1835-9310.1976. tb01149.x.

O'Connor, S., A. Barham, K. Aplin, K. Dobney, A. Fairbairn and M. Richards. 2011. The power of paradigms: examining the evidential basis for early to mid-Holocene pigs and pottery in Melanesia. *Journal of Pacific Archaeology* 2(2): 1–25.

Ochoa, J., V. Paz, H. Lewis, J. Carlos, E. Robles, N. Amano, M.R. Ferreras, M. Lara, B. Vallejo Jr., G. Velarde, S.A. Villaluz, W. Ronquillo and W. Solheim II. 2014. The archaeology and palaeobiological record of Pasimbahan-Magsanib Site, northern Palawan, Philippines. *Philippine Science Letters* 7(1): 22–36.

Oskarsson, M.C.R., C.F.C. Klütsch, U. Boonyaprakob, A. Wilton, Y. Tanabe and P. Savolainen. 2011. Mitochondrial DNA data indicate an introduction through Mainland Southeast Asia for Australian dingoes and Polynesian domestic dogs. *Proceedings of the Royal Society of London B: Biological Sciences* 279: 967–974. doi.org/10.1098/rspb.2011.1395.

Oxenham, M.F., P.J. Piper, P. Bellwood, C.H. Bui, K.T.K. Nguyen. Q.M. Nguyen, F. Campos, C. Castillo, R. Wood, C. Sarjeant, N. Amano, A. Willis and J. Ceron. 2015. Emergence and diversification of the Neolithic of southern Vietnam: insights from coastal Rach Nui. *Journal of Island and Coastal Archaeology* 10(3): 309–338. doi.org/10.1080/15564894.2014.980473.

Pang, J.F., C. Kluetsch, X.J. Zou, A-B. Zhang, L.Y Luo, H. Angleby, A. Ardalan, C. Ekstrom, A. Sköllermo, J. Lundeberg, H. Matsumura, T. Leitner, Y-P. Zhang and P. Savolainen. 2009. mtDNA data indicate a single origin for dogs south of Yangtze River, less than 16,300 years ago, from numerous wolves. *Molecular Biology and Evolution* 26: 2849–2864. doi.org/10.1093/molbev/ msp195.

Patte, E. 1932. Le Kjokkenmodding neolithique de Da But et ses sepultures. *Bulleting de la Société Géologique de l'Indochiné* 19(3): 24–35.

Pawley, A. 1966. Polynesian languages: A subgrouping based on shared innovations in morphology. *Journal of the Polynesian Society* 75: 39–64.

Pawley, A.K. and R.C. Green. 1975. Dating the dispersal of Oceanic languages. *Oceanic Linguistics* 12(1): 1–67.

Petchey, F., M. Spriggs, S. Bedford, and F. Valentin. 2015. The chronology of occupation at Teouma, Vanuatu: Use of a modified chronometric hygiene protocol and Bayesian modeling to evulate midden remains. *Journal of Archaeological Science: Reports* 4: 95–105. doi.org/10.1016/j.jasrep.2015.08.024.

Piper, P.J. and M.F. Oxenham. 2014. Of prehistoric pioneers: the establishment of the first sedentary settlements in the Mekong Delta region of southern Vietnam during the period 2000–1500 cal. BC. In K. Boyle, R. Rabett and C. Hunt (eds), *Living in the Landscape: Essays in Honour of Graeme Barker* (McDonald Institute Monographs), pp. 209–226. Cambridge: McDonald Institute for Archaeological Research.

Piper, P.J., H.-c. Hung, F.Z. Campos, P. Bellwood and R. Santiago. 2009. A 4000 year old introduction of domestic pigs into the Philippine Archipelago: implications for understanding routes of human migration through Island Southeast Asia and Wallacea. *Antiquity* 83: 687–695. doi.org/10.1017/S0003598X00098914.

Piper, P.J., J. Ochoa, E. Robles, H. Lewis and V. Paz. 2011. Palaeozoology of Palawan Island, Philippines. *Quaternary International* 233: 142–158. doi.org/10.1016/j.quaint.2010.07.009.

Piper, P.J., N. Amano, S. Yang and T.P. O'Connor. 2013. The terrestrial vertebrate remains. In P. Bellwood, and E. Dizon (eds), *4000 Years of Migration and Cultural Interaction: Archaeology in the Batanes Islands, Northern Philippines*, pp. 169–200. Terra Australis 40. Canberra: ANU E Press.

Piper, P.J., F.Z. Campos, D.N. Kinh, N. Amano, M. Oxenham, B.C. Hoang, P. Bellwood and A. Willis. 2014. Early evidence for pig and dog husbandry from the Neolithic site of An Son, Southern Vietnam, *International Journal of Osteoarchaeology* 24: 68–78. doi.org/10.1002/oa.2226.

Pugach, I., F. Delfin, E. Gunnarsdóttir, M. Kayser, M. Stoneking. 2013. Genome-wide data substantiate Holocene gene flow from India to Australia. *Proceedings of the National Academy of Sciences* 110: 1803–1808. doi.org/10.1073/pnas.1211927110.

Rispoli, F. 2007. The incised and impressed pottery style of Mainland Southeast Asia: Following the paths of neolithization. *East and West* 57(1–4): 235–304.

Robles, E., P.J. Piper, J. Ochoa, H. Lewis, V. Paz and W. Ronquillo. 2015. Late Quaternary sea level changes and the palaeohistory of Palawan Island, Philippines. *Journal of Island and Coastal Archaeology* 10(1): 76–96. doi.org/10.1080/15564894.2014.880758.

Sacks, B.N., S.K. Brown, D. Stephens, N.C. Pedersen, J.-T. Wu and O. Berry. 2013. Y chromosome analysis of dingoes and Southeast Asian village dogs suggests a Neolithic continental expansion from Southeast Asia followed by multiple Austronesian dispersals. *Molecular Biology and Evolution* 30: 1103–1108. doi.org/10.1093/molbev/mst027.

Salvolainen, P., T. Leitner, A.N. Wilton, E. Matisoo-Smith and J. Lundeberg. 2004. A detailed picture of the origin of the Australian dingo, obtained from the study of mitochondrial DNA. *Proceedings of the National Academy of Sciences* 101(33): 12387–12390. doi.org/10.1073/pnas.0401814101.

Sawada, J., K.T. Nguyen and A.T. Nguyen. 2011. Faunal remains at Man Bac. In M.F. Oxenham, H. Matsumura and K.D. Nguyen (eds), *Man Bac: The excavation of a Neolithic Site in Northern Vietnam*, pp. 105–116. Terra Australis 33. Canberra: ANU E Press.

Shannon, L.M., R.H. Boyko, M. Castelhano, E. Corey, J.J. Hayward, C. McLean, M.E. White, M.A. Said, B.A. Anita, N.I. Bondjengo, J. Calero, A. Galov, M. Hedimbi, B. Imam, R. Khalap, D. Lally, A. Masta, K.C. Oliviera, L. Perez, J. Randall, Nguyen, M.T., F.J. Trujillo-Cornejo, C. Valeriano, N.B. Sutter, R.J. Todhunter, C.D. Bustamante and A.R. Boyko. 2015. Genetic structure of village dogs reveals Central Asian domestication origin. *Proceedings of the National Academy of Sciences* 112(44): 13639–13644. doi.org/10.1073/pnas.1516215112.

Simanjuntak, T., M.J. Morwood, F.S. Intan, I. Machmud, K. Grant, N. Somba, B. Akw, D.W. Utomo. 2008. Minanga Sipakko and the Neolithic of the Karama Valley. In T. Simanjuntak (ed.), *Austronesian in Sulawesi,* pp. 57–76. Depok: Center for Prehistoric and Austronesian Studies.

Storey, A.A., T. Ladefoged and E.A. Matisoo-Smith. 2008. Counting your chickens: Density and distribution of chicken remains in archaeological sites of Oceania. *International Journal of Osteoarchaeology* 18: 240–261. doi.org/10.1002/oa.947.

Storey, A.A, M. Spriggs, S. Bedford, S.C. Hawkins, J. Robins, L. Huynen and E. Matisoo-Smith. 2010. Mitochondrial DNA from 3000-year old chickens at the Teouma site, Vanuatu. *Journal of Archaeological Science* 37: 2459–2468. doi.org/10.1016/j.jas.2010.05.006.

Storey, A.A., J.S. Athens, D. Bryant, M. Carson, K. Emery, S. deFrance, C. Higham, L. Huynen, M. Intoh, S. Jones, P.V. Kirch, T. Lagefoged, P. McCoy, A. Morales-Muñiz, D. Quiroz, E. Reitz, J. Robins, R. Walter and E. Matisoo-Smith. 2012. Investigating the global dispersal of chickens in prehistory using ancient mitochondrial DNA signatures. *PLoS One* 7(7): 1–11. doi.org/10.1371/journal.pone.0039171.

Storey, A.A., D. Quiroz, N. Beavan and E. Matisoo-Smith. 2013. Polynesian chickens in the New World: a detailed application of a commensal approach. *Archaeology in Oceania* 42(2): 101–119. doi.org/10.1002/arco.5007.

Storm, P. 2001. Resten van een hond uit de vindplaats Hoekgrot (Java). *Cranium* 18(1): 31–44 (in Dutch).

Summerhayes, G.R. 2007. The rise and transformations of Lapita in the Bismarck Archipelago, In S. Chiu and C. Sand (eds), *From Southeast Asia to the Pacific. Archaeological Perspectives on the Austronesian Expansion and the Lapita Cultural Complex,* pp. 141–184. Taipei: Academica Sinica.

Swadling, P., J. Chappell, G. Francis, N. Araho and B. Ivuyo. 1989. A Late Quaternary inland sea and early pottery in Papua New Guinea. *Archaeology in Oceania* 24: 106–109. doi.org/10.1002/j.1834-4453.1989.tb00219.x.

Szabó, K., F. Cole, L. Lloyd-Smith, G. Barker, C. Hunt, P.J. Piper and C. Doherty. 2013. The 'Metal Age' at the Niah Caves, c. 2000–500 years ago. In G. Barker (ed.), *Rainforest Foraging and Farming in Island Southeast Asia: The Archaeology and Environmental History of the Niah Caves, Sarawak,* pp. 299–340. Niah Cave Project Monographs. Cambridge: McDonald Institute for Archaeological Research.

Thomson, V.A., O. Lebrasseur, J.J. Austin, T.L. Hunt, D.A. Burney, T. Denham, N.J. Rawlence, J.R. Wood, J. Gongora, L. Girdland Flink, A. Linderhol, K. Dobney, G. Larson and A. Cooper. 2014. Using ancient DNA to study the origins and dispersal of ancestral Polynesian chickens across the Pacific. *Proceedings of the National Academy of Sciences* 111: 4826–4831. doi.org/10.1073/pnas.1320412111.

Tsang, C.H., K.T. Li and C.Y. Chu. 2006. *Footprints of Ancestors.* Tainan: Tainan County Government (in Chinese).

Valentin, F., F. Détroit, M.J.T. Spriggs and S. Bedford. 2015. Early Lapita skeletons from Vanuatu show Polynesian craniofacial shape: Implications for Remote Oceanic settlement and Lapita origins. *Proceedings of the National Academy of Sciences* 113(2): 292–297. doi.org/10.1073/pnas.1516186113.

van den Bergh, G. Rokus Due Awe, H.J.M. Meijer, K. Szabó, L.W. van den Hoek Ostende, M.J. Morwood, T. Sutikna, E.W. Saptomo, P.J. Piper and K. Dobney. 2009. The Liang Bua faunal remains: a 95kyr sequence from Flores, East Indonesia. *Journal of Human Evolution* 57: 527–537. doi.org/10.1016/j.jhevol.2008.08.015.

Veth, P., M. Spriggs and S. O'Connor. 2005. Continuity in tropical cave use: examples from East Timor and the Aru Islands, Maluku. *Asian Perspectives* 44(1): 180–192. doi.org/10.1353/asi.2005.0015.

Wu, C.Y., Y.N. Jiang, H.P. Chu, S.H. Li, Y. Wang, Y.H. Li, Y. Chang and Y.T. Ju. 2007. The type 1 Lanyu pig has a maternal genetic lineage distinct from Asian and European pigs. *Animal Genetics* 38: 499–505. doi.org/10.1111/j.1365-2052.2007.01646.x.

Yang, S., H. Zhang, H. Mao, D. Yan, S. Lu, L. Lian, G. Zhao, Y. Yan, W. Deng, X. Shi, S. Han, S. Li, X. Wang and X. Gou. 2011. The local origin of the Tibetan pig and additional insights into the origin of Asian pigs. *PLoS One* 6(12): e28215. doi.org/10.1371/journal.pone.0028215.

Zhang, C. and H.-c. Hung. 2008. The Neolithic of southern China – origin, development and dispersal. *Asian Perspectives* 47(2): 299–329. doi.org/10.1353/asi.0.0004.

——. 2010. The emergence of agriculture in southern China. *Antiquity* 84: 11–25. doi.org/10.1017/S0003598X00099737.

16

Historical Linguistics and Archaeology: An Uneasy Alliance[1]

Robert Blust

Historical linguistics and archaeology have a proven record of useful collaborative work. However, the distinctively different nature of the raw material of each discipline can easily lead researchers in the two disciplines toward different conclusions. It is important to recognise that this is perhaps inevitable, but that divergence between the conclusions of the two fields is sometimes the result of over interpretation of negative evidence, a methodological flaw that lies behind some archaeological arguments relating to the prehistory of Island Southeast Asia. Both linguistic and archaeological records will always be fragmentary, and where inferences drawn from them differ dramatically from one another, the most rational evaluation metric is the strength of each argument in terms of how successfully it competes against alternative explanations within its own discipline, not a prioritisation of the evidence of one academic discipline as against another.

Introduction

The prospects for an alliance between archaeology and historical linguistics that might strengthen the inferential basis of both disciplines were first explored at least 40 years ago in a special issue of *World Archaeology* dedicated to the topic 'Archaeology and Linguistics' (WA 8.1, June 1976). Various of the contributions to that volume showed that each discipline has resources that can illuminate aspects of the human cultural past that the other discipline lacks. In particular, archaeology can provide greater detail about material culture and settlement pattern, and has reliable methods that are not generally available to linguists for absolute dating and determining the location of prehistoric language communities. However, although it offers the possibility of inferences about non-material culture, these are normally indirect and less secure than those based on the analysis of physical artefacts. The inferences of historical linguistics, on the other hand, are not limited to those aspects of material culture that survive into the present. By identifying cognate terms with unambiguous referents, historical linguists can reconstruct a record not only of the kinds of artefacts described by archaeologists, but also of items of material culture that fail to survive in typical archaeological contexts, such as basketry, matting, traps made of wood or bamboo, and the like. In addition, the entire realm of non-material culture, including systems of kinship, marriage rules, social organisation, and ideas about the spirit world are accessible to inferences based on cognate vocabulary, but lie beyond the pale of confident archaeological

1   It is a pleasure for me to dedicate this paper to Peter Bellwood, who I first met when I held a postdoc in the Department of Linguistics at what was then the Research School of Pacific Studies at ANU from August 1974 to July 1976. At that early stage in our careers we were both trying to carve a niche for ourselves in an established field among senior scholars, and in the 40 years since then Peter has done that in spectacular fashion. Thanks go to Andy Pawley for useful feedback; any remaining errors are mine.

investigation. For a brilliant exemplification of what this approach can contribute to prehistory, in many cases filling lacunae in the archaeological record, see the landmark multivolume study *The Lexicon of Proto Oceanic*, of which five volumes have now appeared (Ross et al. 1998, 2003, 2008, 2011, 2016).

The purpose of this paper is to remind scholars in both disciplines of what can be gained by a deepened appreciation of what each has to offer the other, but at the same time to stress that the need to remain faithful to the material of one's own discipline can make this alliance an uneasy one, as will be seen in the following pages.

Converging on Taiwan

One of the great successes of convergent lines of inference originating in historical linguistics and archaeology has been the broad acceptance of the view that the movement of Austronesian (AN) languages and the related Neolithic cultures of insular Southeast Asia and the Pacific began in Taiwan, a position known for a time as the 'Bellwood-Blust hypothesis', but now more appropriately called the 'Out-of-Taiwan' (OOT) hypothesis. It is important to stress that the OOT hypothesis developed independently in each discipline. Following an earlier study (Blust 1977) in which the OOT hypothesis was implied but not stated explicitly, Blust (1984/85) argued that the AN homeland was on or near Taiwan (but not in the Philippines). At about the same time, Bellwood concluded on the basis of the earliest appearance of Neolithic cultures in insular Southeast Asia that 'the ultimate region of Austronesian origin lay in the Neolithic landscape of southern China' (1984/85: 109) with a subsequent settlement in Taiwan. In a letter written to me early in 1986, he expressed his interest that I had arrived at the same conclusion regarding the AN homeland toward which the archaeology was then driving him. Both linguistic and archaeological evidence for this claim has continued to accumulate over the 30 years since it was first put forth, and the OOT hypothesis is now all but universally accepted by linguists and archaeologists familiar with the relevant data. It is noteworthy that over the same time span no such unanimity of inference has appeared in the work of population geneticists, who have been split if not evenly then at least significantly, in either supporting or rejecting this view of AN origins.

The early invisibility of rice

Once the OOT was widely adopted as a working hypothesis, the first substantive issue that divided linguists from archaeologists was the antiquity of cereal cultivation in the AN world. As noted by Bellwood:

> remains of rice and millet were universally absent from sites of the Dabenkeng phase in Taiwan (3,500–2,500 BC) until both were found in unprecedented carbonised quantities dating to c. 2,800 BC, in hitherto unique waterlogged conditions, in the Nanguanli sites in the Tainan Science-Based Industrial Park (Tsang 2005; Tsang et al. 2004) (2011: 98).

What is striking, and one might say revealing, about this reversal relating to a major component of the archaeological record is that linguists had reported *overwhelming* evidence for rice and millet in Taiwan for more than three decades before archaeological confirmation was unearthed during Tsang's excavations from September 2002 to March 2003. Blust, for example, who located Proto-Austronesian on Taiwan, observed that '[t]he linguistic evidence for cultivation of grain crops by PAN times is abundant' (1995: 460) and supported this statement with the suite of reconstructed terms shown in (1), where the geographical distribution of reflexes in the modern languages over major regions is signalled by T = Taiwan, P = Philippines, WIN = western Indonesia, and EIN = eastern Indonesia:[2]

(1)

PAN term

1. *pajay 'riceplant, rice in the field' (T, P, WIN, EIN)
2. *beRas 'harvested, husked rice' (T, P, WIN, EIN)
3. *Semay 'cooked rice' (T, P, WIN)
4. *baCaR 'millet sp.' (T, P, WIN, EIN)
5. *beCeŋ 'millet, probably foxtail millet' (T, P, WIN, EIN)
6. *zawa 'millet sp.' (T, P, WIN)
7. *bineSiq 'seed rice' (T, P, WIN, EIN)
8. *buRaw 'chase animals from the fields' (T, P, WIN, EIN)
9. *qani 'to harvest, usually rice' (T, P, WIN)
10. *lepaw 'granary' (T, P, WIN, EIN)
11. *eRik/iRik 'thresh by trampling' (T, WIN)
12. *paspas 'thresh by beating' (T, P)
13. *lesuŋ 'mortar' (T, P, WIN, EIN)
14. *qaSelu 'pestle' (T, P, WIN, EIN)
15. *bayu 'to pound rice' (T, P, WIN, EIN)
16. *tapeS 'to winnow grains' (T, P, WIN)
17. *qeCah 'rice husk' (T, P, WIN)
18. *zaRami 'rice straw, stalks left in the field' (T, P, WIN)

It would be difficult to overemphasise the conclusiveness of this body of evidence. Whether the archaeological record showed it or not, it was obvious to well-informed AN comparativists from at least the late 1960s that speakers of PAN cultivated both rice and millet. To deny this conclusion because of negative evidence from a sister discipline would have been tantamount to rejecting the entire theoretical and methodological foundations of historical linguistics as it had developed since the first two decades of the nineteenth century, in effect denying the validity of an entire academic discipline. This is not an exaggeration: straightforward application of the comparative method that had been developed in the discovery of the Indo-European language family and tested successfully for nearly two centuries *demanded* the reconstruction of multiple terms for rice and millet in order to account for the wide geographical distribution of cognate forms. Then, with the excavation of Nanguanli the previously 'invisible' rice that clearly was

---

2   A decade earlier (Blust 1984/85: 61–62) nine of these 18 terms were cited as evidence for the same conclusion, namely that the AN homeland almost certainly included Taiwan, and that PAN speakers were sedentary cultivators of grain, root and tree crops, while continuing at the same time to hunt, fish, and gather wild foods. Nearly a decade before that (Blust 1976: 31–33), four of these terms, including the key three terms for rice (*pajay, *beRas, *Semay), were cited as evidence for PAN rice and millet agriculture, and although a Formosan homeland was not explicitly claimed it was implied in much of the discussion, where all reconstructions assigned to PAN required reflexes in at least one language from two or more of the following groups: Northern (Formosan), Western (insular Southeast Asian), and Eastern (Oceanic). Even earlier, Ferrell had noted that '[t]erms for rice in various stages (plant, unhusked grain, etc.) in Formosan languages are clearly AN, which should not have been the case if they had learned rice cultivation from Chinese' (1969: 10). In the vocabularies that accompanied his text, items relating to grain agriculture that were cognate with terms already reconstructed for 'Uraustronesisch' by Dempwolff (1934–1938) included: 1. rice (plant), 2. rice (grain), 3. rice (cooked), 4. millet, 5. mortar, and 6. pestle. Full supporting evidence for the reconstructions under (1) is given in the open-access online Austronesian Comparative Dictionary (Blust and Trussel ongoing, see www.trussel2.com/ACD).

being cultivated on Taiwan from the initial Neolithic settlement of the island, made its dramatic appearance. The old saw that 'absence of evidence is not evidence of absence' could hardly have found a better application. What is perhaps more important, however, is that evidence for PAN grain agriculture *was* available to those archaeologists who were willing to consider the data from other academic disciplines concerned with prehistory, Peter Bellwood being preeminent among them.

Radiocarbon dating and the phylogeny of Eastern Polynesian

To disarm any suspicion that I might be unfairly favouring my own discipline, I will now describe a case in which the demands of radiocarbon dating in archaeology required a rethinking of a major linguistic hypothesis that had been widely accepted for almost five decades before careful reexamination of the evidence proved it unjustified.

Polynesian languages have been recognised as a discrete group since European contact, an impression that was reinforced by the relative homogeneity of culture, at least on the high islands, and Polynesian archaeologists are equally clear in recognising a distinctive cultural sequence (Kirch and Green 2001: 53–91). While the archaeology provides a fuzzier picture of the primary schism within Polynesian, since Fiji, Tonga and Samoa evidently were settled in rapid succession, the linguistics points unambiguously to Tongic (Tongan and Niue) versus the rest (Nuclear Polynesian), a division that may reflect the relative isolation of Samoa after the roughly simultaneous Polynesian settlement of the three western archipelagos. An internal family tree for Polynesian was first proposed by Elbert (1953), based mainly on lexicostatistics and this was soon followed by more detailed qualitative studies (Pawley 1966, 1967; Green 1967). The standard phylogenetic tree for Polynesian languages, which stood virtually unchallenged for nearly half a century showed Proto-Polynesian splitting into Proto-Tongic and Proto-Nuclear Polynesian (PNP), then PNP splitting into Proto-Samoic-Outlier (PSO) and Proto-Eastern Polynesian (PEP), and then PEP splitting into Rapanui and Proto-Central-Eastern (PCE), which in turn divided into Proto-Marquesic and Proto-Tahitic (Marck 2000: 2). Apart from the Tongic: Nuclear Polynesian division, perhaps the best-supported branch within this collection of languages was Eastern Polynesian, which covers an enormous expanse that essentially defines the Polynesian Triangle from Hawai'i to Rapanui to New Zealand.

Although details of this proposed phylogeny were questioned, most notably by Wilson (1985, 2012) who drew attention to evidence that linked Eastern Polynesian (EP) languages to specific Polynesian Outliers, the internal three-way division of EP remained unchallenged. As an experiment in building cross-disciplinary bridges, from August–December 2011, Terry Hunt and I co-taught a course at the University of Hawai'i titled 'Archaeology and language in the Pacific'. An issue that continued to bother us in trying to put the archaeology and linguistics together was to find answers to the following questions: 1. Where was Proto-Eastern Polynesian spoken? 2. If Rapanui was the first language group to split off from the EP group, where was Proto-Central-Eastern Polynesian spoken? 3. How good is the evidence for Rapanui vs. Proto-Central Eastern Polynesian, and for Proto-Marquesic (the putative ancestor of Hawaiian, Marquesan and Mangarevan) versus Proto-Tahitic (the putative ancestor of Tahitian, Tuamotuan, Cook Islands Maori and New Zealand Maori, among others? Marck (2000: 3) proposed several major revisions to this model, but left the internal structure of EP intact, thus providing no answers to these questions.[3] What finally forced us to see this nearly 50-year-old phylogeny as flawed was the 'sanitised' radiocarbon chronology for eastern Polynesia proposed in Wilmshurst et al. (2011), of which Hunt was one of the contributing authors.

By restricting themselves to datable materials that provide maximum reliability, Wilmshurst et al. (2011) concluded that eastern Polynesia was settled two to five centuries later than had previously been thought. In particular, a two-phase sequence of colonisation was identified, beginning in the Society Islands AD 1025–1120 and very rapidly leading to the settlement of the rest of eastern Polynesia by AD 1190–1293. Through class discussions it became clear that if this revised chronology is valid the Pawley-Green phylogeny could not be correct; apart from the issue of identifying plausible homelands for each of the posited proto-languages, there simply was not enough time for innovations to accumulate that could distinguish Marquesic from Tahitic. Language change is inevitable, but except under the rarest circumstances it takes centuries for significant change to occur, and 100–200 years is far too short to support the scenario implied by the 'standard' model of Eastern Polynesian subgrouping.

Mary Walworth, a student in this class who was working in French Polynesia and who intended to write her dissertation on the language of Rapa in the Australs, took it upon herself to reopen the investigation of Eastern Polynesian subgrouping, and the harder she looked into the evidence presented for a Marquesic–Tahitic split the less convincing the argument became. She has now concluded that Eastern Polynesia was settled rapidly by speakers of a language with little dialect differentiation, and that the divergence of Rapanui from the rest is due to isolation after a nearly simultaneous settlement of the whole of eastern Polynesia. In other words, a reexamination of the linguistic evidence shows no well-supported internal subgrouping divisions, a pattern that is consistent with the whole of Eastern Polynesia minus Rapanui remaining an enormous interaction sphere through bidirectional sailing for at least a century after initial settlement (Walworth 2014). Although a similar idea was floated earlier in the archaeological literature by Kirch (1986), this is the first time an attempt has been made to defend a 'simultaneous settlement' view of Eastern Polynesia with evidence from both archaeology and language.

Together with the insights of Wilson (2012), it now appears likely that the Society Islands were settled directly from the northern outliers in the Solomons, and that the rest of Eastern Polynesia was peopled over a period probably not exceeding 8–10 generations, during which time contact was maintained with homeland areas and perhaps other distant locations. Following this initial period, as connections of kinship grew more distant, the interaction spheres contracted and language differentiation followed its normal course, giving rise to divergent languages and cultures. But without the prod provided by a corrected radiocarbon chronology, and its implications for language phylogeny, it is doubtful that a reevaluation of EP subgrouping would have been undertaken.[4]

---

3   Marck states that 'it is not clear from the archaeology where and when East Polynesia came to be settled' (2000: 138–139). He adds that about 500 years would be needed to account for the innovations between Proto-Ellicean (ancestral to Samoan, the Ellicean Outliers and Eastern Polynesian) and Proto-Central-Eastern Polynesian, but makes no specific claim about the location of the latter. Moreover, he is explicit in claiming that 'the divergence of Rapanui speech ... clearly preceded the differentiation of speech between the Marquesas, the Societies, the Tuamotus, the Astrals (sic), and the Cooks' (2000: 138).

4   It is only proper to add that in the years since the Wilmshurst et al. (2011) chronology was published there has been a vigorous debate of its merits within the community of Polynesian archaeologists. Much of this is summarised in Spriggs, who holds the view that the proposed settlement dates for much of Eastern Polynesia are better seen as 'when settlement is widely established in the region' (2014: 174) rather than as evidence of first contact. In either case, the fact that linguists responded to the revised chronology in an appropriate manner by re-examining the evidence for a Tahitic–Marquesic split and finding it weaker than earlier scholars thought is clear evidence that the pressures for interdisciplinary agreement that exist between historical linguistics and prehistoric archaeology are not unidirectional.

PAN 'iron' and 'rust': Making sense of undeniable lexical comparisons

The two preceding cases have shown, first, how linguistic inferences about grain agriculture preceded archaeological confirmation by decades and, second, how the demands of strictly monitored archaeological dating forced a reconsideration of the traditional internal subgrouping of Eastern Polynesian languages. Together these examples illustrate the potential benefits that each discipline can offer to the other by acting responsibly toward its own data, but simultaneously taking into account the claims of the other field.

Another insight arising from the marriage of historical linguistics and archaeology can be seen in the need to reconstruct PAN *Namat 'iron' and *diNaŋ 'rust' (Blust 2013). Words for 'iron' in AN languages have posed problems of interpretation at least since Dempwolff (1938) posited *besi 'iron', based on data from Malagasy, a few languages of western Indonesia, and a misconstrued Fijian word that no researcher today would consider cognate.

Although most previous linguistic comparisons relating to iron can now be dismissed as either flawed, or as referring to a later proto-language, the forms *Namat and *diNaŋ are unassailable. Even though reflexes of both words are restricted to Formosan languages (Taokas and Kavalan for the former, Saisiyat, Isbukun Bunun and Paiwan for the latter), these languages belong to different primary branches of the AN family, and are not now, nor do they appear to have previously been, in contact with one another. Given this distribution of apparently non-borrowed cognate linguistic forms glossed 'iron' and 'rust' in the primary sources, Blust (2013) reconstructed words with these meanings for Proto-Austronesian. Since iron-working in Taiwan developed considerably later than the initial Neolithic settlement of the island, the question arose how the meanings 'iron' and 'rust' were to be interpreted in a meaningful cultural context. An email message from Dr Hsiao-chun Hung (The Australian National University) appears to provide the answer: the earliest pottery in Taiwan was a plain red-slipped ware, and a 2005 study by Hung and the geochemist Dr Yoshiyuki Iizuka confirmed that the source of the red-slip colouring agent is hematite. Deposits of hematite are reportedly abundant in parts of Taiwan, and as the mineral form of iron oxide, its association with both iron and rust is readily understandable. What was not previously understood by linguists is that this readily decomposable mineral provided the red-slip agent for the earliest pottery in Taiwan, and that its consequent cultural importance could be reflected in linguistic forms with the generalised glosses 'iron' and 'rust', which might initially give rise to quite different culture-historical inferences.

The history of Austronesian agriculture

The later invisibility of rice

So far I have stressed that there is no single discipline that deals with human prehistory. Rather, several disciplines have developed tools for investigating the human past, including at least archaeology, population biology and historical linguistics. Some scholars in each of these disciplines appear averse to recognising the value or trustworthiness of one or more of the others. Moreover, there is a common, if often implicit, belief that the physical sciences are to be trusted more than the biological sciences, and the latter more than the social sciences. Some years ago a well-known Pacific archaeologist in Hawai'i actually began a talk that I attended (unnoticed at first) by stating that inferences in archaeology should be prioritised over those in linguistics since archaeology deals with elements of the past that are concrete and measurable (like pottery or stone tools), while linguistics only deals with 'words'. That remark in itself could trigger a long debate about the nature of science and use of the hypothetico-deductive method. More recently, an email message directed to me on 27 October 2011 by a well-known population biologist contained the following jaw-dropping statement: 'We know the methodology, the underlying assumptions, and the limitations of phylogenetic approaches. I don't think the same can always be said to hold for other approaches to reconstructing language relationships.'

Historical linguistics has foundations predating 1820, when Jakob Grimm and Rasmus Rask demonstrated that most of the languages of northern Europe derive from the same prehistoric source community as the classical languages of the Mediterranean and India, an achievement that remains today as solid as it was when it was first proposed nearly 200 years ago, and that is sometimes ranked along with the theory of evolution by natural selection as one of the two great intellectual achievements of the nineteenth century. Needless to say, this was long before either archaeology or genetics existed as academic disciplines, and any formalised set of procedures for explaining the natural or cultural world with a history this long has repeatedly been tested, and tested severely for weaknesses and inadequacies. It therefore comes as a (somewhat annoying) surprise to historical linguists to occasionally hear from social anthropologists, archaeologists, population biologists or scholars in other disciplines that we can't trust the evidence of language because historical linguistics is a novel discipline that has yet to prove its worth.

Given this perception, fostered in part by the insularity of much training in the sciences, it is refreshing to see scholars who recognise the value of interdisciplinary cooperation, a hallmark of much of Peter Bellwood's work throughout his long and productive career. Despite the unquestioned benefits of interdisciplinary approaches to common problems in prehistory there are, however, risks that come from overestimating one's understanding or command of the material of sister disciplines. An example of this inadequacy is seen in Bulbeck (2008), who argues that although Proto-Austronesian speakers on Taiwan practised cereal agriculture, they abandoned this mode of subsistence once they began to expand southward into insular Southeast Asia (ISEA), and became maritime foragers in their migrations throughout the rest of the AN world.

Bulbeck is explicit in recognising the value of a multidisciplinary approach to prehistory, but he rejects evidence that in his view is not supported by his own discipline, as seen in this passage:

> I hope it is clear from my contribution that I heartily endorse a multidisciplinary approach to ISEA prehistory, and the 'triangulation' of the linguistic, archaeological and biological evidence relevant to the Neolithic (e.g. Sagart et al. 2005). However, I have little sympathy for taking a particular interpretation of the historical linguistics, one based on idealist culture history and the assumption of an expanding Malayo-Polynesian monoculture, and using it to overwrite the archaeological and biological evidence. In my view this reduces the number of disciplines that counts to one, which is the opposite of multidisciplinary research (2008: 48).

No explanation is given for what is meant by 'a particular interpretation of the historical linguistics' or 'idealist culture history'. The 18 PAN terms relating to grain agriculture under (1) are straightforward products of application of the comparative method of linguistics. In other words, *any* well-trained historical linguist would reach the same conclusions based on the primary data that supports these inferences. There is nothing questionable or methodologically unsound about these forms; they are products of science as it is performed in any well-developed academic discipline.

As noted by the generalised distributional information in parentheses, all of these reconstructed forms are supported by data from at least one AN language of Taiwan, plus related languages in insular Southeast Asia. The material supporting these statements is publicly available online by visiting the AN Comparative Dictionary (ACD) (Blust and Trussel ongoing, see www.trussel2.com/ACD). To facilitate quick reference, (2) provides a scaled-down version of the entry for PAN *pajay 'riceplant, rice in the field' (scaled down because the full set of data would take up far too much space in this short paper):

(2)

PAN *pajay 'rice in the field; riceplant'

Taiwan:

Atayal	pagay	unhulled rice, rice in the husk
Seediq	payay	riceplant
Saisiyat	pazay	riceplant
Bunun	paað	riceplant, rice in the field
Tsou	pai	riceplant, unhusked rice
Amis	panay	rice; the harvested grain
Paiwan	paday	rice (plant, grain)

Philippines:

Ilokano	pagay	rice (unhusked)
Kapampangan	pále	rice (growing in the field)
Tagalog	pálay	riceplant
Hanunóo	páray	rice in the field
Tiruray	farey	general for rice, Oryza sativa Linn.
Tboli	halay	unhusked rice

Borneo:

Ida'an Begak	paray	paddy
Kadazan Dusun	paai	paddy
Kelabit	pade	riceplant, rice in the field
Kayan	pare	riceplant, rice in the field
Mukah Melanau	paday	riceplant, rice in the field
Iban	padi	riceplant, grain in husk

Vietnam:

Jarai	pəday	riceplant, rice in the field
Rade	mədie	riceplant, rice in the field

Thailand:

Moken	pai	paddy

Sumatra:

Karo Batak	page	riceplant, rice in the field
Nias	faxe	riceplant, cooked rice

Java-Bali:

Old Javanese	pari	riceplant, paddy
Javanese	pari	riceplant, unhulled rice
Sundanese	pare	riceplant, unhulled rice
Balinese	padi	rice in the husk

Sulawesi:

Mongondow	payoy	riceplant, unhusked rice
Bare'e	pae	riceplant, unhusked rice
Tae'	pare	rice in the field
Makasarese	pare	rice in the field
Muna	pae	rice (on the stalk)

Marianas:

Chamorro	fa?i	rice (when growing)

Lesser Sundas:

Bimanese	fare	riceplant, rice in the field
Li'o	pare	riceplant, rice in the field
Kambera	pari	riceplant
Rotinese	hade	riceplant, unhusked rice grain
Tetun	hare	rice (plant and unhusked grain)

Moluccas:

Yamdena	fase	rice
Kamarian	hala	rice (in general)
Buruese	pala	rice (in general)
Kowiai	fasa	cooked rice, husked rice
Numfor	fas	rice (in general)

This is not the place for a mini-course in historical linguistics, but let me at least point out that a borrowing explanation for the distribution of these terms will not work because the sound correspondences, particularly those affecting *j, are both phonetically diverse and almost invariably regular, something that would be possible with loanwords only if they had been borrowed before any of these languages had differentiated from a common ancestor. Since this ancestor would have been PAN, diffusion becomes meaningless as an alternative to recognising that rice agriculture in the Tapenkeng (TPK) culture of Taiwan was continued by speakers of PMP, and then by many of its descendant communities in ISEA to the present day. Far from the empirically inadequate scenario that Bulbeck defends, what the linguistic evidence shows unambiguously is a continuation of rice (and millet) agriculture, with reflexes of PAN *pajay, *beRas and *Semay retained in the languages of the Philippines and western Indonesia, but terminological distinctions (and hence presumably importance) reduced in eastern Indonesia/ West New Guinea, where sago assumes greater prominence as a staple carbohydrate, until rice finally disappears in the Pacific. The one exception to this general statement is, of course, the Marianas, which were settled directly from the central or northern Philippines by AN settlers who failed to transport the pig, water buffalo, and apparently chicken, but succeeded in taking rice, sugarcane, betel nut and a few other cultigens in what was probably a single one-way journey undertaken prior to 3500 BP (Blust 2000).[5]

Bulbeck insists that favouring the linguistic evidence at the expense of what he represents as the archaeological record violates the principle of multidisciplinary research. This may be narrowly true, but given the robustness of the linguistic evidence for PAN rice and millet agriculture and its continuation throughout ISEA to the present, it is impossible to accept the claims based on negative evidence from the archaeological record without abandoning faith in the basic principles of historical linguistics. For years archaeologists were convinced that the founding Neolithic TPK culture in Taiwan was devoid of rice agriculture. The linguistic record unambiguously contradicted this inference, and the archaeological record itself has now shown that the linguists had good reason to adopt the position they did. In short, what matters in assessing the strength of an argument is not whether the argument is based on evidence from physical science, biological science or social science, but rather how successful it is in excluding competing alternatives within its own discipline. With grain agriculture in Neolithic Taiwan there was no plausible alternative to the conclusion reached by linguists, while there obviously were other explanations for the null evidence from archaeology.

There is a general lesson in this example for how scientific method works in any field of inquiry: arguments based on negative evidence can *never* be conclusive because there is no logical imperative that absence of evidence provides evidence of absence. Ultimately this is equivalent to what philosophers of science have called 'Hume's problem', or 'the problem of induction', namely that in science (unlike mathematics) it is always possible for new and unexpected observations to alter one's previous position (Popper 1968: 28ff). Naturally, if there is no evidence of any kind for some proposition then we can say with confidence that there is no reason to believe in its validity until evidence is presented. But in the present case evidence *has* been presented, and the only reason that can be found for the skepticism with which it has been treated outside the community of knowledgeable historical linguists is the implicit belief that there is a hierarchy of trustworthiness in the sciences in which the physical sciences rank highest, followed by the biological sciences, and last of all by the social sciences.

Bulbeck (2008) appears not to have learned this lesson, as his interpretation of the AN diaspora is based in critical respects on the physical near-invisibility of rice south of northern Luzon prior to 2500 BP, ignoring not only the abundant linguistic evidence for continuity of grain agriculture in the AN expansion into equatorial insular Southeast Asia, but also the plain archaeological fact that the bulk of excavated sites in Island Southeast Asia to date have been in caves or rock shelters, where one would hardly expect to find agricultural remains. As an outsider to the archaeological enterprise one might reasonably ask: how many *village sites* prior to 3000 BP have been located and excavated in this region?

Refuting the comparative method

As already noted, linguists have good reason to dispute overinterpretations of negative evidence in archaeology that conflict with strong linguistic arguments. This is not a matter of hubris or of elevating the evidence of one academic disciple over that of another; it is a matter of collegial responsibility, and ultimately of good scientific method. Roger Blench, who is trained in African linguistics, is sufficiently aware of this issue to recognise that anyone who wishes to support

---

5   As noted in Blust (2000: 106–107) Chamorro has a native word reflecting PAN *baRiuS 'typhoon'. Since the typhoon zone extends from the central Philippines to southern Japan, with rare strikes in Mindanao and virtually none further south, and since Chamorro is clearly a Malayo-Polynesian (non-Formosan) language, a process of elimination leads us to a source in the central or northern Philippines.

Bulbeck's maritime foraging model must reconcile the negative arguments from archaeology with the positive arguments from linguistics – arguments that Bulbeck himself simply did not consider. In Blench (2012) he does this through a *tour de force* of unrestrained assertion: among other things, we are told 1) 'That the Austronesians, far from being agriculturalists, were fisher-foragers', 2) 'That the dogs, pigs and chickens supposedly characteristic of this expansion reached Island Southeast Asia through alternative routes', 3) 'That the linguistic reconstructions that appeared to support this model are in fact mosaics of loanwords', and 4) 'That the spread of Austronesian languages was due to a powerful religious/lifestyle ideology which assimilated indigenous speech communities and that this can be detected from material culture' (Blench 2012: 128).

Let me begin with points 2) and 3), since these will go a long way toward addressing point 1). Starting with the claim that the 'Pacific Clade' of pigs originated in 'Laos, Yunnan and far Northwest Vietnam' (Larson et al. 2010 and earlier work), Blench (2012: 134) concludes that AN speakers moving out of Taiwan 'would have adopted dogs, pigs and chickens from MSEA [Mainland Southeast Asia] and then carried them eastwards to Melanesia and Oceania'.

Entirely apart from the odd distinction between 'Melanesia' and 'Oceania' in this quote, which hardly instills confidence in his knowledge of the area, Blench demonstrates a remarkable ability to sweep away large quantities of conflicting linguistic data by simply declaring without evidence or argument that it is all due to borrowing. The Austronesian Comparative Dictionary (Blust and Trussel ongoing, see www.trussel2.com/ACD) is an open-access site that continues to grow on a weekly basis, but is already the largest research project ever undertaken on the AN languages (Blust and Trussel 2013). The entries for 'dog', 'pig' and 'chicken' in the ACD are: PAN *asu 'dog', PAN *babuy 'pig', PAN *beRek 'domesticated pig', and PAN *manuk 'chicken'. The first of these is currently documented by 78 forms and the second by 74 forms in attested languages, in both cases reaching from Taiwan to the Moluccas. The third reconstruction (*beRek) is documented by 26 terms reaching from Taiwan to the central Solomon Islands, and *manuk by 136 terms reaching from Taiwan to Hawai'i. Scholars who use the ACD with care know that loanwords are carefully distinguished from native forms. This is done in two distinct ways. First, apart from the main file ('Cognate sets'), which includes reconstructions and supporting evidence for over 6,600 base forms and more than 21,000 total reconstructions (bases plus affixed words) there are several separate files, including one for 'noise' (resemblances due to chance), and another for loanwords that are sufficiently widespread to introduce the danger of false reconstructions based on loan distributions, whether these be due to the diffusion of lexical innovations from particular AN languages (such as Malay), or borrowings from outside the AN language family (as widespread terms for 'papaya', 'guava', and 'pineapple'). In addition, many entries in the dictionary contain notes, and with very few exceptions forms that show irregularities in the expected sound correspondences (usually because of borrowing between related languages) are cited in the note separately from the main entry, leaving all or virtually all items in the main entry free from any problems with regard to the regularity of the sound correspondences.

Despite the care with which this material has been treated, Blench, who nowhere cites the ACD, notes that 'dogs are again conspicuous by their absence in the early archaeology of ISEA, except for Timor … Could all occurrences of the *asu root represent a semantic shift or borrowing?' (2012: 137). After acknowledging that this seems unlikely, he observes that the proto-form for 'dog' in Tai-Kadai appears to be a loanword from Hmong-Mien, and then concludes abruptly that if this could happen in Tai-Kadai 'this term may have been absent in PMP and all those occurrences of #asu are in fact loanwords reflecting early contact with Austroasiatic speakers (and the subsequent spread of the term once borrowed). Although this contradicts established wisdom in AN scholarship, it shows greater congruence with the archaeological record'

(2012: 137). To this assertion, Blench then appends the following footnote, evidently intended as a metaphorical nail in some imagined coffin: '# is a linguistic convention used here to indicate a quasi-reconstruction, a form derived from rapid inspection of cognates' (2012: 144).

At no point does Blench identify a potential Austroasiatic source for PAN *asu, nor does he mention that the word shows regular phonological developments not just in the 78 languages from which data is cited in the ACD, but from several hundred others, thus providing no empirical basis for his claim that the word has been borrowed from one AN language into another. In short, it is not 'established wisdom in AN scholarship' that he proposes to challenge, but rather the massive evidence that *asu *must* be reconstructed to explain the distributional data in daughter languages. The offhand remark that this reconstruction has been 'derived from rapid inspection of cognates', which clearly implies slipshod scholarship, is a glaring misrepresentation of the meticulous work of Otto Dempwolff (1934–1938), who laid the foundations of Austronesian comparative linguistics, and of the generations of scholars who have followed in his footsteps over the past eight decades.

It is apparent from Blench's 'wave of the hand' dismissal of fundamental products of the comparative method that his agenda is to reconcile the linguistic record with the negative evidence of archaeology by pursuing an 'absence of evidence is evidence of absence' argument, and simply sweeping the massive countervailing linguistic evidence out of sight. But, as with Bulbeck's earlier argument, Blench's use of negative evidence to rewrite AN culture history is a castle built on sand. As has already been shown with TPK in Taiwan, there simply is no logical imperative that absence of evidence is evidence of absence, and for a linguist, albeit one who is not a specialist in the AN language family, to dismiss valid linguistic evidence in order to reconcile it with zero visibility in the archaeological record is surprising, to say the least.

Blench's unfamiliarity with the comparative method is, if anything, even more evident in his treatment of *babuy and *beRek. The reader is told (Blench 2012: 137) that '[a]s with "dog" there is a widespread term in Austroasiatic (AA) which is apparently cognate either *C-liik or *C-lek'. The casual reader, particularly the non-linguist, probably will fail to notice that Blench has not, in fact, shown *any* AA form that resembles PAN *asu, let alone one that can be demonstrated by recurrent sound correspondences (hence by the comparative method) to derive from a common proto-language. With regard to 'pig', Blench also neglects to mention that the 'reconstruction' he cites is his own impromptu speculation, not the product of knowledgeable scholarship by AA specialists who have identified sound correspondences and used them to propose a PAA reconstruction, let alone a form ancestral to both AA and AN languages.[6] As with 'dog', both terms for 'pig' exhibit regular sound correspondences through many widely separated languages, showing that with very few exceptions they are directly inherited. This is particularly true of *beRek, which has distinctive reflexes of the vowels and *R that could easily give away the status of loanwords (and sometimes does), yet it is regular in its development through scores of languages reaching from Taiwan (Tsou *fraʔa*, Puyuma *varək* 'domesticated pig'), to the Philippines (Isneg *baggáʔ* 'young hog', Pangasinan *belék*, Kapampangan *abyák* 'suckling pig'), to Borneo (Paitan *vogok*, Kelabit *bərək* 'domesticated pig') to Old Javanese as recorded in palm leaf manuscripts

---

6   Referring to the late Harry L. Shorto, Paul Sidwell (email of 4 November 2014 informs me that 'Shorto proposed *liːk and *cur "pig" and *ckeʔ "boar"). *liːk is pretty solid, its in 5 branches. *cur is restricted to Eastern languages, mainly Bahnaric, and looks like a local word. *ckeʔ "boar" is in Aslian and Bahnaric. None are in Munda, apparently. I suspect that *liːk is imitative'. Note that the term 'cognate' is used here with reference to both 'dog' and 'pig', thus assuming that the Austric hypothesis is valid, and that specific Proto-Austric lexical forms can be posited, whereas for 'dog' Blench first claimed that PAN *asu is a loanword from an unidentified AA source, not a retention from Proto-Austric. These are not the only inconsistencies that will trouble linguists who read this paper. With regard to possible AA cognates of PAN *beRek, for example, Blench holds that 'The fricatives in Taiwanese may well be cognate with forms such as Pear sruːk' (Blench 2012: 139). The fact that 'Taiwanese' is a form of Minnan Chinese, not an alternative name for the Formosan aboriginal languages, seems to escape him, but more seriously, cognation refers to morphemes, not to phonemes – an elementary observation that can easily be used to distinguish someone who understands historical linguistics from someone who does not.

dating from the beginning of the ninth to the end of the fourteenth centuries (*wök* 'pig, hog, boar'), to a range of Oceanic languages, as Tigak (New Ireland) *vogo*, Wogeo (New Guinea) *boro*, and Nggela (central Solomons) *mbolo*, all glossed simply as 'pig'. Blust (1976) noted that reflexes of PAN *babuy and *beRek have different distributions that may well correlate with their distinct meanings: AN speakers introduced domesticated pigs and the name for them into the Pacific, whereas the word *babuy, which often refers to wild pigs, was lost after leaving the Moluccas, and only later reacquired in Chamorro, Yapese, and Palauan, where phonological irregularities show that the words in these three languages are loans.

Whatever merit the genetic studies of Larson et al. (2010) and others may have, they cannot be used to deny that AN speakers had terms for both domesticated and wild pigs during the initial Neolithic settlement of Taiwan and that these terms persisted during the southward migrations into insular Southeast Asia – the evidence for this is simply too strong to dismiss out of hand, and it is now up to the scientific community to try to understand why the evidence of DNA and the evidence of language appear to be at loggerheads in relation to this issue.

With regard to reconstructions relating to domesticated plants such as banana, sugarcane and taro, Blench concludes: 'When it was supposed that Austronesian was a gradual demographic expansion, it was inevitable that these subsistence terms were seen as "true" reconstructions; with our current perspective on dispersal they must now be seen as interesting fakes' (2012: 142). Again, to call such solidly supported linguistic reconstructions as PAN *beNbeN, PMP *punti 'banana', PAN *CebuS 'sugarcane', PMP *tales 'taro: *Colocasia esculenta*' 'fakes' shows little understanding of the sound correspondences, and should serve to indicate that Blench's approach to the floral evidence is identical to that for the faunal evidence: wherever the linguistic data conflicts (or appears to conflict) with the data from either archaeology or genetics the linguistics must be wrong, and decades of careful analysis and discussion are jettisoned as products of misguided scholarship.

To cap this misadventure in freewheeling imagination, Blench argues that the Austronesian diaspora was driven by 'a powerful religious/lifestyle ideology which assimilated indigenous speech communities and that this can be detected from material culture' (2012: 128, 134ff). The interested reader is hopeful that some truly convincing argument will be presented for this novel claim. In fact, all that is offered is a pedestrian reference to the ubiquity of the well-known squatting figures in traditional iconography. Blench calls these *bulul*, without stating the source of the term, but it appears to be from Ifugaw *búlul* 'wooden statue in which one of the rice culture Deities of the Underworld is believed to reside in order to guard the crops' (Lambrecht 1978: 95), *būlul* 'a rice-god idol, carved of wood and with a resident spirit … These idols are kept in a rice granary by the rich as a guardian to assure an ample supply of rice from the store. They are brought out during harvest and offered fat and blood from a sacrificed pig' (Newell 1993). Since this iconographic motif reportedly extends from the northern Philippines to Polynesia and is said to have no distributional parallels in the art of Africa or other regions, Blench opines that its spread must have been comparable to that of the iconography in world religions such as Christianity, and is thus due to a similar proselytising zeal. The only other 'arguments' offered for this conclusion are the assertions that the Pama-Nyungan expansion in Aboriginal Australia was 'associated with a new type of stone blade technology, but most importantly with a type of clan organisation and with a pattern of singing' (Blench 2012: 136), and that the Arawakan migrations from the eastern edge of the Andes (*montaña*) to the Antilles were associated with a particular style of petroglyphs in the Amazon basin. In short, what is given as support for this claim is a few lines of random observations loosely connected by something resembling free-association more than scientific argumentation. Ironically, Blench seems happily unaware that the Ifugaw *búlul* or *bûlul*, the eponymous inspiration of what we might call his 'Bulul religion', is the material residence of a rice culture deity![7]

Conclusions

In conclusion, with the growth of the ACD and the appearance of *The Lexicon of Proto Oceanic*, it is clearer now than ever that archaeology and historical linguistics in the Austronesian world need one another to reach beyond the limitations of either discipline as an independent window on the human past. As shown by the work of Bellwood, and others (e.g. Atkinson and Gray 2005; Gray et al. 2009, 2010), much can be gained from interdisciplinary cooperation between scholars in archaeology, population genetics, evolutionary biology, and historical linguistics.

At the same time caution is in order. While I feel no reservations about challenging the claims of a sister discipline if it conflicts with strong positive evidence from my own field, I would hesitate to assume the role of arbiter between competing hypotheses in archaeology or population genetics if I did not have reason to do so based on linguistic data that I control with a high level of confidence. Yet this kind of overstepping of disciplinary bounds has happened in some cases, as with Spriggs (2011: 511–514), who declared decisively, largely on the basis of a single paper (Donohue and Grimes 2008) that the Central Eastern Malayo-Polynesian node first proposed for the Austronesian family tree in Blust (1982) has been abandoned by the field, and that the AN languages of eastern Indonesia consequently constitute many primary branches of Malayo-Polynesian, thus dramatically resetting the stage with regard to implications for archaeology. Yet there are serious problems with the Donohue and Grimes proposal that were exposed promptly (Blust 2009; not noted by Spriggs).[8] A further attack on CEMP by Schapper (2011) was similarly answered in short order (Blust 2012). The reality is that the CEMP node has *not* been dismissed by knowledgeable comparativists working in the area, and one can only wonder what triggered this imaginary 'revolution'.[9]

All of this goes to show that historical linguists and archaeologists have what can be called an 'academic alliance', but owing to fundamental differences in the observational basis of the two fields it is an uneasy alliance, and one that is likely to remain this way well into the future.

References

Atkinson, Q.D. and R.D. Gray. 2005. Curious parallels and curious connections: Phylogenetic thinking in biology and historical linguistics. *Systematic Biology* 54(4): 513–526. doi. org/10.1080/10635150590950317.

Bellwood, P. 1984/85. A hypothesis for Austronesian origins. *Asian Perspectives* 26(1): 107–117.

---

7 Chen (1968: 378–405), who is not cited by Blench, devotes a fairly detailed discussion to 'Figures in squatting posture', along with numerous line drawings. Far from having associations with an aggressively proselytising religion, he argues that these figures (which also occur in the material culture of Shang and Zhou dynasty China, and on the northwest coast of North America) are naturalistic portrayals of the sitting posture that was customary before the common use of stools or chairs, namely squatting on the ground.

8 In fairness, it should be noted that Spriggs (2012) has redressed several of these shortcomings.

9 Cf. Ross, who states 'Donohue & Grimes (2008) critique Blust's PCEMP innovations and suggest that the PCEMP node is a chimera that should be done away with, with the consequence that Blust's Central MP languages would simply be treated as further western MP subgroups. Blust (2009) makes a strong response, and although some CEMP lexical innovations are not particularly convincing, first-syllable coda-loss in reduplicated monosyllables, the marsupial terms, and the remaining lexical innovations do, it seems to me, pass muster' (forthcoming, fn. 6).

——. 2011. The checkered prehistory of rice movement southwards as a domesticated cereal—from the Yangzi to the Equator. *Rice* 4: 93–103. doi.org/10.1007/s12284-011-9068-9.

Blench, R. 2012. Almost everything you believed about Austronesian isn't true. In M.L. Tjoa-Bonatz, A. Reinecke and D. Bonatz (eds), *Crossing Borders: Selected Papers from the 13th International Conference of the European Association of Southeast Asian Archaeologists*, pp. 28–48. Singapore: National University of Singapore Press.

Blust, R. 1976. Austronesian culture history: some linguistic inferences and their relations to the archeological record. *World Archaeology* 8: 19–43. Reprinted with minor additions in 1977 NUSA 3: 25–27; and in P. van de Velde (ed.), 1984 *Prehistoric Indonesia: A Reader* pp. 217–241. Dordrecht-Holland: Foris Publications. doi.org/10.1080/00438243.1976.9979650.

——. 1977. The Proto-Austronesian pronouns and Austronesian subgrouping: A preliminary report. *Working Papers in Linguistics* 9(2): 1–15. Honolulu: Department of Linguistics, University of Hawaii.

——. 1982. The linguistic value of the Wallace Line. *Bijdragen tot de Taal-, Land- en Volkenkunde* 138: 231–250.

——. 1984/85. The Austronesian homeland: A linguistic perspective. *Asian Perspectives* 26(1): 45–67.

——. 1995. The prehistory of the Austronesian-speaking peoples: a view from language. *Journal of World Prehistory* 9: 453–510. doi.org/10.1007/BF02221119.

——. 2000. Chamorro historical phonology. *Oceanic Linguistics* 39: 83–122. doi.org/10.1353/ol.2000.0002.

——. 2009. The position of the languages of eastern Indonesia: A reply to Donohue and Grimes. *Oceanic Linguistics* 48: 36–77. doi.org/10.1353/ol.0.0034.

——. 2012. The marsupials strike back: A reply to Schapper (2011). *Oceanic Linguistics* 51: 261–277. doi.org/10.1353/ol.2012.0000.

——. 2013. Formosan evidence for Early Austronesian knowledge of iron. *Oceanic Linguistics* 52: 255–264. oi.org/10.1353/ol.2013.0004.

Blust, R. and S. Trussel. 2013. The Austronesian comparative dictionary: A work in progress. *Oceanic Linguistics* 52: 493–523. doi.org/10.1353/ol.2013.0016.

——. ongoing. *Austronesian Comparative Dictionary*. Online at www.trussel2.com/ACD.

Bulbeck, D. 2008. An integrated perspective on the Austronesian diaspora: The switch from cereal agriculture to maritime foraging in the colonisation of island Southeast Asia. *Australian Archaeology* 67: 31–51. doi.org/10.1080/03122417.2008.11681877.

Chen, C.-L. 1988 [1968]. *Material Culture of the Formosan Aborigines*. Taipei: Southern Materials Center.

Dempwolff, O. 1934–1938. 3 vols. *Vergleichende Lautlehre des Austronesischen Wortschatzes*. Zeitschrift für Eingeborenen-Sprachen, Supplement 1. *Induktiver Aufbau einer Indonesischen Ursprache* (1934), Supplement 2. *Deduktive Anwendung des Urindonesischen auf Austronesische Einzelsprachen* (1937), Supplement 3. *Austronesisches Wörterverzeichnis* (1938). Berlin: Reimer.

Donohue, M. and C.E. Grimes. 2008. Yet more on the position of the languages of eastern Indonesia. *Oceanic Linguistics* 47: 114–158. doi.org/10.1353/ol.0.0008.

Elbert, S.H. 1953. Internal relationships of Polynesian languages and dialects. *Southwestern Journal of Anthropology* 9: 147–173. doi.org/10.1086/soutjanth.9.2.3628573.

Ferrell, R. 1969. *Taiwan Aboriginal Groups: Problems in Cultural and Linguistic Classification*. Monograph no. 17. Taipei: Institute of Ethnology, Academia Sinica.

Gray, R.D., A.J. Drummond and S.J. Greenhill. 2009. Language phylogenies reveal expansion pulses and pauses in Pacific settlement. *Science* 323: 479–483. doi.org/10.1126/science.1166858.

Gray, R.D., D. Bryant and S.J. Greenhill. 2010. On the shape and fabric of human history. *Philosophical Transactions of the Royal Society* 365: 3923–3933. doi.org/10.1098/rstb.2010.0162.

Green, R.C. 1967. Linguistic subgrouping within Polynesia: The implications for prehistoric settlement. *Journal of the Polynesian Society* 75: 6–38.

Kirch, P.V. 1986. Rethinking East Polynesian prehistory. *Journal of the Polynesian Society* 95(1): 9–40.

Kirch, P.V. and R.C. Green. 2001. *Hawaiki, Ancestral Polynesia: An Essay in Historical Anthropology*. Cambridge: Cambridge University Press. doi.org/10.1017/CBO9780511613678.

Lambrecht, F.H. 1978. *Ifugaw-English Dictionary*. Baguio: The Catholic Vicar Apostolic of the Mountain Province, Philippines.

Larson, G., R. Liu, X. Zhao, J. Yuan, D. Fuller, L. Barton, K. Dobney, Q. Fan, Z. Gu, Z., X-H. Liu, Y. Luo, P. Lv, L. Andersson and N. Li. 2010. Patterns of East Asian pig domestication, migration, and turnover revealed by modern and ancient DNA. *Proceedings of the National Academy of Sciences* 107(17): 7686–7691. doi.org/10.1073/pnas.0912264107.

Marck, J. 2000. *Topics in Polynesian Language and Culture History*. PL 504. Canberra: Pacific Linguistics.

Newell, L.E. 1993. *Batad Ifugao Dictionary with Ethnographic Notes*. Special Monograph Issue no. 33. Manila: Linguistic Society of the Philippines.

Pawley, A. 1966. Polynesian languages: a subgrouping based upon shared innovations in morphology. *Journal of the Polynesian Society* 75: 39–64.

——. 1967. The relationships of Polynesian Outlier languages. *Journal of the Polynesian Society* 76: 259–296.

Popper, K.R. 1968 [1935]. *The Logic of Scientific Discovery*. New York: Harper and Row.

Ross, M. forthcoming. Narrative historical linguistics: linguistic evidence for human (pre)history. In R.D. Janda, B.D. Joseph and B.S. Vance (eds), *The Handbook of Historical Linguistics* vol. 2. Oxford: Wiley-Blackwell.

Ross, M., A. Pawley and M. Osmond (eds). 1998. *The Lexicon of Proto Oceanic: The Culture and Environment of Ancestral Oceanic Society* vol. 1. *Material Culture*. PL C-152. Canberra: Pacific Linguistics.

——. 2003. *The Lexicon of Proto Oceanic: The Culture and Environment of Ancestral Oceanic Society* vol. 2. *The Physical Environment*. PL 545. Canberra: Pacific Linguistics.

——. 2008. *The Lexicon of Proto Oceanic: The Culture and Environment of Ancestral Oceanic Society* vol. 3. *Plants*. PL 599. Canberra: Pacific Linguistics.

——. 2011. *The Lexicon of Proto Oceanic: The Culture and Environment of Ancestral Oceanic Society* vol. 4. *Animals*. PL 621. Canberra: Pacific Linguistics.

——. 2016. *The Lexicon of Proto Oceanic: The Culture and Environment of Ancestral Oceanic Society* vol. 5. *Body and Mind*. Canberra: Pacific Linguistics.

Sagart, L., R. Blench and A. Sanchez-Mazas (eds). 2005. *The Peopling of East Asia: Putting together Archaeology, Linguistics and Genetics*. London and New York: RoutledgeCurzon.

Schapper, A. 2011. Phalanger facts: notes on Blust's marsupial reconstructions. *Oceanic Linguistics* 50: 258–272. doi.org/10.1353/ol.2011.0004.

Spriggs, M. 2011. Archaeology and the Austronesian expansion: Where are we now? *Antiquity* 85: 510–528. doi.org/10.1017/S0003598X00067910.

——. 2012. Is the Neolithic spread in Island Southeast Asia really as confusing as the archaeologists (and some linguists) make it seem? In M.L. Tjoa-Bonatz, A. Reinecke and D. Bonatz (eds), *Crossing Borders: Selected Papers from the 13th International Conference of the European Association of Southeast Asian Archaeologists*, pp. 109–121. Singapore: National University of Singapore Press.

——. 2014. You will never know the why of a region's history if you haven't pinned down the when: Getting the dates right in Eastern Polynesia. In I. Hoem (ed.), *Thor Heyerdahl's Kon-Tiki in New Light*, pp. 169–180. The Kon-Tiki Museum Occasional Papers, no. 14. Larvik, Norway: The Thor Heyerdahl Institute.

Tsang, C.-H. 2005. Recent discoveries at the Tapenkeng culture sites in Taiwan: implications for the problem of Austronesian origins, in L. Sagart, R. Blench and A. Sanchez-Mazas (eds), *The Peopling of East Asia: Putting Together Archaeology, Linguistics and Genetics*, pp. 63–73. London and New York: RoutledgeCurzon.

Tsang, C.-H., C.-T. Li and C.-Y. Chu. 2004. *Report on the Daoye site, Tainan Science-Based Industrial Park*. Taipei: Academia Sinica (in Chinese).

Walworth, M. 2014. Eastern Polynesian: The linguistic evidence revisited. *Oceanic Linguistics* 53(2): 257–273. doi.org/10.1353/ol.2014.0021.

Wilmshurst, J.M., T.L. Hunt, C.P. Lipo and A.J. Anderson. 2011. High-precision radiocarbon dating shows recent and rapid initial human colonization of East Polynesia. *Proceedings of the National Academy of Sciences* 108(5): 1815–1820. doi.org/10.1073/pnas.1015876108.

Wilson, W.H. 1985. Evidence for an Outlier source for the Proto-Eastern Polynesian pronominal system. *Oceanic Linguistics* 24: 85–133. doi.org/10.2307/3623064.

——. 2012. Whence the East Polynesians? Further linguistic evidence for a Northern Outlier source. *Oceanic Linguistics* 51.2: 289–359. doi.org/10.1353/ol.2012.0014.

17

Were the First Lapita Colonisers of Remote Oceania Farmers as Well as Foragers?

Andrew Pawley

Archaeological evidence indicates that the first Lapita colonisers of Remote Oceania relied heavily on foraging to sustain themselves, exploiting pristine marine and land resources. Did they also carry with them and establish a range of cultivated tubers and tree crops, as argued by Kirch (1997) and others? Noting the lack of direct evidence for horticulture in Lapita sites in this region, Anderson (2003) suggested that cultigens may not have been introduced until considerably later and then in a piecemeal fashion. This paper examines several lines of evidence that bear on this debate, with particular reference to Vanuatu, Fiji and Tonga. Micro-botanical evidence from Vanuatu indicates that yams, aroids and bananas were among the cultigens introduced very early. Comparative lexical evidence suggests the same for the greater yam, Colocasia taro, two kinds of Musa bananas and the major cultivated tree crops. Archaeological evidence shows that pigs and chickens were present in the earliest sites. Divergence of pottery styles points to loss of regular contact between Lapita communities in Near and Remote Oceania and between major regions of Remote Oceania from 2800 BP onwards, within 100–200 years of first settlement. These factors favour the conclusion that most of the typical Oceanic array of cultivated plants had already been introduced before the loss of regular contact and probably in the first generation or two of settlement.

Introduction

It is generally accepted that, as well as being skilled fishers and reef foragers, the bearers of the early Western Lapita culture in the Bismarck Archipelago practised horticulture. This is indicated by the presence in certain sites of extensive remains of nuts, seed-pods and husks from cultivated trees, and by linguistic evidence: Proto-Oceanic, the primary language of early Lapita communities in the Bismarcks, retained more than 20 Proto-Malayo-Polynesian terms for cultigens and activities associated with horticulture. However, there is less agreement about the role of horticulture in the economy of the first settlers of Remote Oceania.[1] This paper addresses two questions: (1) Did the first Lapita colonisers of Remote Oceania rely solely on foraging or were they also farmers? (2) What kinds of evidence bear on this question and how should such evidence be evaluated?

---

1   In contrast to 'Near Oceania', that part of the Southwest Pacific that comprises the closely spaced islands of New Guinea, the Bismarck Archipelago and the Solomon Islands, 'Remote Oceania' consists of the far-flung islands and island groups of the Central Pacific, chiefly those of Te Motu Province in the Solomon Islands, Vanuatu, New Caledonia-Loyalties, Fiji, Polynesia and Micronesia.

Opinions on (1) appear to differ. The following remarks by Kirch and Green represent archaeologists who support the early horticulture hypothesis:

> When Lapita populations expanded into Remote Oceania … they transported a full roster of oceanic crops, including such staples as taro, yam, bananas and breadfruit. Indeed, the very ability to transfer such systems of horticultural production was arguably an essential aspect of the successful Lapita colonization strategy (2001: 121).

Kirch makes an even stronger claim:

> Wherever they sailed in Remote Oceania, Lapita groups came fully equipped to establish permanent settlements, carrying with them domesticated animals and planting stocks of tubers, fruit, and tree crops, as well as a sophisticated knowledge of horticulture and plant manipulation (2000: 109).

Proponents of this hypothesis refer, in the first place, to (i) a sizeable array of Proto-Oceanic (POc) reconstructed terms for cultivated plants and gardening activities that have regular reflexes (continuations) widely distributed in daughter languages across Remote Oceania and which imply continuous transmission of these terms from POc to the daughter languages. They also refer to one or more of other kinds of (largely circumstantial) evidence from Remote Oceania, such as (ii) the poverty of native plant and land animal species that would have provided sufficient sources of starch and fat to sustain human colonisers for more than a short period, (iii) maintenance during the early Lapita phase of an exchange network extending from the Bismarcks to Vanuatu that would have enabled transfer of cultivated plants, (iv) deforestation and erosion associated with large-scale clearance during the early stages of settlement, (v) the presence in early Lapita sites of artefacts typically associated with horticulture, including a range of ceramic vessel types, earth ovens, and pits possibly for storage of breadfruit, taro or bananas, and of traces of substantial houses indicating permanent settlement, (vi) skeletal remains of domesticated animals – pigs and chickens – in early Lapita assemblages, and (vii) micro-fossil evidence of food crops including aroids, yam and banana in early Lapita sites in Vanuatu.

A seemingly contrary view has been taken by a number of archaeologists. Several decades ago Groube, writing about Fiji and Tonga, tentatively proposed that:

> the Lapita potters, initially at least, had a restricted maritime/lagoon economy and that … the [later] development or introduction of a more viable horticultural economy enabled them to expand and survive in Fiji and Tonga … In this conception the Lapita potters would be Oceanic 'strandloopers', who … expanded ahead of colonisation by agriculturalists (1971: 313).

He based this claim chiefly on the location of Lapita sites in Tonga and Fiji, invariably close to reef flats rich in shellfish, and on the disappearance of concentrated shellfish middens in post-Lapita sites. Groube interpreted the latter phenomenon as marking 'a shift from reef exploitation to agriculture in the latter half of the first millennium BC' (1971: 311), i.e. several hundred years after first settlement of Fiji and Tonga.

More recently, Anderson (2003) has questioned the notion that, during the initial colonisation of Remote Oceania, foraging alone could not have sustained communities for long periods in environments with few edible plants and land animals. Following Davidson and Leach (2001) he notes that alternative sources of nutrition, especially for the vital fatty acids, were present on Oceanic islands in the form of crabs, immature seabirds, eggs, turtles, lizards and dugong. 'Provided that colonization groups stayed in a 'skimming' mode, taking such resources from one island then moving to the next, non-agricultural coloniation, should have presented no insuperable difficulty. Long-term settlement probably required agriculture but it was not necessary at the beginning' (Anderson 2003: 77). He concludes that: '[a]n effectively foraging economy … still seems the most probable mode during the dispersal phase in Remote Oceania … In this matter … an hypothesis of economic discontinuity seems preferable' (2003: 78).

I referred above to 'seemingly contrary views' because the two camps have formulated their claims somewhat loosely, and they can be interpreted as making similar claims, differing merely in emphasis. Thus, proponents of the early farming hypothesis do not dispute that the first generation of Lapita colonists of Remote Oceania relied heavily on foraging. For example, Kirch writing of Polynesia says that 'in a fledgling colony's first years, transplanted cultigens could not have provided a sufficient basis for subsistence and the settling party would have to depend heavily on naturally abundant resources' (1984: 84). Conversely, proponents of the early reliance on foraging hypothesis do not categorically exclude horticulture. They simply propose that if it was present initially, it was unimportant. Neither side makes precise claims about how long it was before horticulture replaced foraging as the main source of food.

However, one can formulate a stronger version of the reliance on foraging hypothesis that is clearly distinct from the early farming hypothesis, namely that there was a delay of several generations before most of the Oceanic staple cultigens were introduced. Anderson's observation that foragers could have kept moving to new pristine locations after exhausting natural resources in their current habitat, at least in large islands and island groups, provides a model of how a mobile population could remain foragers for generations.

At any rate, whether or not Lapita colonists *could have* survived and flourished for several generations without the staple Oceanic cultivated vegetables and fruits, these questions remain: Did the first wave of colonists bring such cultigens with them and if so, which ones? And how long did the reliance on foraging last? The remainder of this paper briefly examines evidence that bears on these questions, with particular reference to Vanuatu, Fiji and Tonga.

Arguments for and against early horticulture

How long did the reliance on foraging last?

Beyond the Near Oceania/Remote Oceania divide there is a sharp diminution in the range of native plant and land animal species that would have provided food for the first human colonisers (Green 1991). However, the archaeological record shows that the pioneering Lapita colonists of islands in Remote Oceania were able to exploit an abundance of fish and shellfish, along with turtle, sea and land birds, fruit bats, and other creatures. But how long did this abundance last in any particular habitation area? The record for Vanuatu suggests what Bedford (2006), following Steadman (1998), calls the foraging 'blitzkrieg' soon reduced the abundance. Some readily procurable species became scarce or extinct or (in the case of certain shellfish) smaller. Referring to the immediately post-Lapita site at Arapus, Efate, in Vanuatu, Bedford writes that the faunal remains:

> dramatically demonstrate the subsistence strategy of a population on first arrival and how … very quickly that strategy changed following the depletion of pristine resources … The first sign of human arrival in the area is evidenced by the build-up of midden deposits directly on top of the former foreshore … This evidence gives a glimpse of a short time period, before the establishment of horticultural systems, when the population … was heavily reliant on readily procurable local marine and terrestrial resources (2006: 257).

But just how long was the 'short time period' between abundance and depletion at Arapus? Presumably depletion was a gradual process taking place over several generations or even two or three centuries. The archaeological record is probably not fine-grained enough to trace the chronology of this process more precisely than that.

Lapita sites at Nukuleka (on the northeast coast of Tongatapu) and elsewhere in Tongatapu and Ha'apai tell a similar story to Arapus. The earliest layers, dating to *ca.* 2800 BP, show an initial reliance on fish, shellfish and wild birds, including species of birds that rapidly became extinct (Shutler et al. 1994; Steadman et al. 1998). In Ha'apai sites, within a few centuries chickens replace wild birds as the most common species in middens, increasing from 24 per cent to 81 per cent of total bird bones (Steadman et al. 1998). In Tonga, the earliest *Colocasia* pollen is found in Avai'o'vuna Swamp, Vava'u Island, at about 2600 BP, less than two centuries after first human occupation of Vava'u (Fall 2010).

The oldest human skeletal remains found in the Teouma site in Vanuatu show well-marked signs of scurvy, possibly due to a high protein diet, and inadequate consumption of plant foods and/or cooking methods that destroyed the vitamin C (Buckley et al. 2014). Later skeletal remains point to improved health but it is not possible to date this improvement precisely.

Scarcity of direct evidence for horticulture in the archaeological record

Anderson writes as follows concerning the difficulties of determining the role of cultivated plants in the initial colonisation of Remote Oceania:

> Arrival of horticulture with the first colonists is not open to direct demonstration. None of the domestic tubers are yet represented clearly amongst preserved plant remains, especially of nuts, in the Western Lapita waterlogged sites, let alone further east, and, in any event, those remains beg some questions of interpretation, such as how many of them were derived merely from shoreline flotsam … There are some possible nut-processing implements but the case for tuber gardening anywhere in the early Lapita phase has yet to be made on direct evidence such as pollen, starches, or microbotanical remains …
>
> The argument has to be carried almost entirely … by linguistic reconstruction. This method has the advantage that the crops were demonstrably introduced to Remote Oceania and the names are clearly associated through numerous cognates with the species to which they refer … Thus Proto-Oceanic reconstructions for taro, yam, banana and breadfruit were retained almost unchanged into Proto-Polynesian, and much the same is true of horticultural practices. But the strength of this argument is also its weakness. If reconstructed lexemes hardly changed over long periods and across the region, they can offer little indication of the pattern of arrival. The linguistic data, alone, cannot validate the assumption that agriculture was carried by the first, early Lapita colonists of Remote Oceania. It might have arrived later in the Lapita era and never as a package (2003: 77).

Recently, micro-fossil evidence of food crops including aroids, yam and banana has been reported for early Lapita sites in Northern Vanuatu (Horrocks and Bedford 2004, 2010; Horrocks et al. 2009). Although, as Buckley et al. comment, 'it remains to be fully understood how just successful these initial communities were at establishing horticultural and aboricultural crops' (2014: 82), this is direct evidence of early horticulture. The characterisation of the materials as being 'initial' or 'early' in the sequences implies that they fall within the first century or so of settlement.

Forest clearance and erosion associated with large-scale clearance for gardening

Spriggs (1997) points to a recurrent pattern of deforestation and erosion associated with large scale clearance during the early stages of settlement in Remote Oceania, followed by 'abandonment of an area for sometimes many hundred of years and a later more conservation oriented reuse with continuing occupation'. For example, large-scale clearance of forest on Aneityum, Southern Vanuatu, is evident from around 3000–2900 BP (Hope and Spriggs 1982; Spriggs 1997). This was concentrated in the uplands because the coastal lands were swampy and prone to flooding. Although it is impossible to know whether large-scale clearing began with the first generation of settlers or later, the dates are within a century or so of earliest accepted dates for the settlement of Remote Oceania, so the delay can hardly have been a matter of centuries. A similar sequence is evident on Tikopia (Kirch and Yen 1982).

On Totoya Island in the Moala group, Fiji, Clark and Cole (1997) found evidence of forest clearance shortly after first settlement by people with Lapita ceramics, followed by the extension of grasslands and secondary forest.

Domesticated animals

Neither pigs nor chickens are native to Remote Oceania and their presence in Lapita sites there can be taken as proof of animal husbandry, normally a proxy for horticulture. Although pigs were absent from New Caledonia in prehistoric times, both pigs and chickens are present in early Lapita sites in Santa Cruz, Tikopia, and Vanuatu. There are no pig bones in Lapita sites in Tonga and no well-stratified pig bones in early sites in Fiji.

Bedford states that '[t]he archaeological record from Vanuatu indicates that pigs arrived with the earliest colonisers and it seems likely that they spread relatively quickly throughout the archipelago' (2006: 227). '[C]hicken was a consistent component of middens from the earliest layers of the sites' e.g. at Ifo, Malua Bay and Arapus, 'suggesting that it was present in some quantity from initial arrival' (2006: 231). The same applies to Tonga (see below). Chicken bones are present but scarce in Lapita sites in Fiji (Worthy and Clark 2009).

Settlement patterns and artefacts

Early Lapita settlements in Remote Oceania were typically located on sandy beach terraces close to fringing reefs and fresh water sources. The settlers built substantial wooden houses, indicative of permanent occupation. In early Lapita sites that have yielded a range of artefacts, various items associated with food preparation and cooking are found: ceramic pots for boiling, stone ovens for baking, vegetable scrapers, and pits possibly for storage and fermentation of breadfruit, taro or bananas, as well as adzes, used for clearing land for gardens (Kirch 1997). The presence of permanent settlements and such artefacts is not conclusive evidence for horticulture but it is consistent with it.

Maintenance of a trade network extending from the Bismarcks to Vanuatu during the early Lapita phase

The early Lapita colonists of Remote Oceania were capable sailors who for a time maintained long-range contacts across island groups separated by hundreds of kilometres. Their mobility is evidenced most conspicuously by their rapid expansion across the Southwest Pacific, with settlement of Reefs-Santa Cruz, Vanuatu, New Caledonia, Fiji and Tonga in the period 3100–2850 BP.

There is clear evidence that the colonists for a time maintained a long-distance trade network through which significant quantities of obsidian from Talasea on the Willaumez Peninsula in New Britain were transported to Reefs-Santa Cruz in the Eastern Solomons (Sheppard 1993), smaller but still substantial quantities to Northern and Central Vanuatu (Galipaud et al. 2014; Reepmeyer et al. 2011) and still smaller quantities to New Caledonia and Fiji. Reefs-Santa Cruz sites also contain some low-grade obsidian from the Banks Island and chert from Ulawa and Malaita in the main Solomons group (Spriggs 1997). The Northern and Central Vanuatu sites also include Banks Islands obsidian (Constantine et al. 2015; Reepmeyer et al. 2011)

Given that Proto-Oceanic speakers in the Bismarck Archipelago cultivated a wide range of crops, and given the exchange connections between the Bismarcks and Remote Oceania at the time of the Lapita dispersal, it might be expected that something as useful as staple food plants would have been carried to Remote Oceania soon after first settlement. How long it would have taken for the full set of Oceanic cultigens to be transported and become established is another matter.

Linguistic evidence

Proto-Oceanic as the primary language of early Western Lapita communities in the Bismarck Archipelago

The Oceanic subgroup comprises some 450–500 languages: all the Austronesian languages of Melanesia east of Cenderawasih Bay in New Guinea, all the languages of Micronesia except Chamorro and Palauan, and those of Polynesia. Oceanic is in turn a branch of the Malayo-Polynesian (MP) subgroup of Austronesian, which includes all Austronesian languages other than those spoken in Taiwan. The Oceanic languages have undergone a substantial number of innovations apart from the rest of the Austronesian family, pointing to a period, probably a few centuries, of compact unified development in Western Melanesia before they dispersed across the Southwest and Central Pacific. The final stages of this unified development almost certainly took place in the Bismarck Archipelago.

There is good reason to equate speakers of the Austronesian interstage known as Proto-Oceanic (POc) with bearers of the early Western Lapita culture in the Bismarck Archipelago and to equate the spread of Lapita to various parts of Remote Oceania around 3000 BP with the initial spread of Oceanic speakers to these regions. The grounds for this equation have been stated elsewhere (Green 2003; Kirch 1997; Pawley 2007, 2008; Spriggs 1997; Summerhayes 2001) and will not be elaborated here. The Lapita people who first settled Reefs-Santa Cruz, Vanuatu, Fiji and Tonga would have spoken dialects little differentiated from POc.

Dialect diversification within POc probably began with the dispersal of early Western Lapita to various parts of the Bismarcks around 3300 BP (or a bit later – there is currently a re-evaluation of early Lapita dates going on (Petchey et al. 2014: 240)). Blust (1978, 1998) has argued that the first split in Oceanic was between the Admiralties languages and the rest. If so, this would indicate that the Admiralties were not the source of the Oceanic languages of Remote Oceania. However, the decisive breakup of POc possibly did not occur until bearers of Lapita first moved beyond the Bismarcks into various parts of Remote Oceania around 3000–2900 BP.

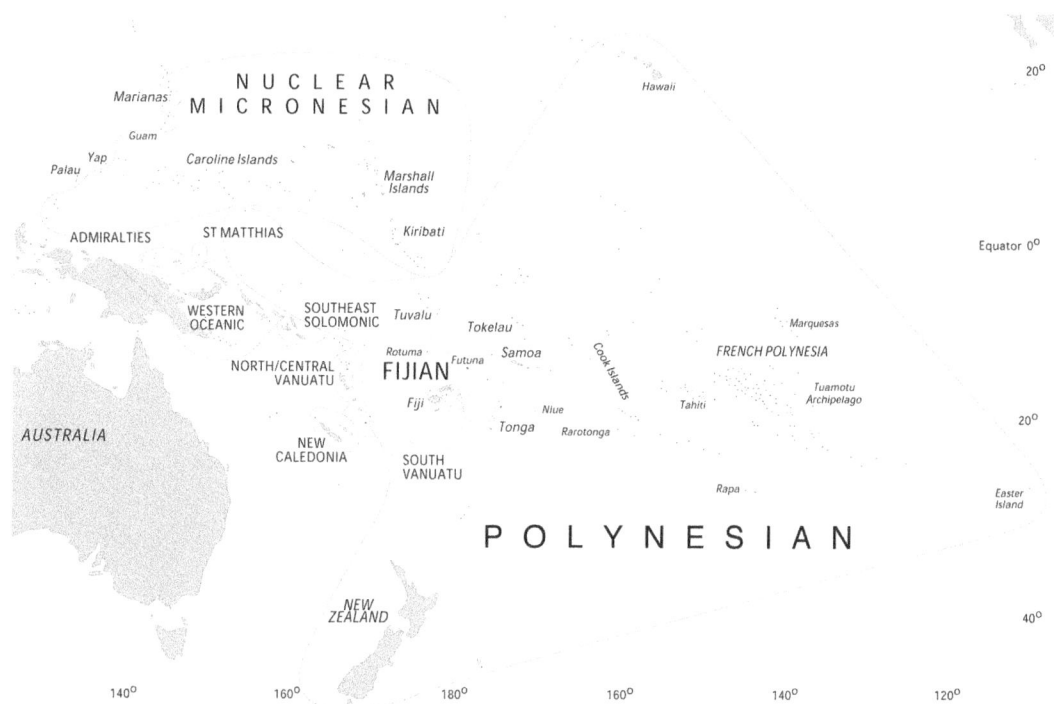

Figure 17.1 The major subgroups of Oceanic.

Source: After Ross et al. 2011, p. 11, reproduced with permission from Pacific Linguistics.

The chief high-order subgroups of Oceanic recognised here are as follows (see Figure 17.1): Admiralty Islands, Mussau, Western Oceanic (comprising the Oceanic languages of New Guinea east of the Sarmi Peninsula, New Britain, New Ireland, Bougainville and the Western Solomons), Southeast Solomonic (Guadacanal, Malaita, Makira), Te Motu (Reefs-Santa Cruz, Utupua, Vanikoro), North-Central Vanuatu, Southern Vanuatu, New Caledonia and the Loyalties, Yapese, Nuclear Micronesian (all languages of Micronesia except Palauan, Chamorro, Yapese, Nukuoro and Kapingamarangi) and Central Pacific (Fijian, Rotuman, Polynesian). The large Western Oceanic group has three major branches: North New Guinea, Papuan Tip and Meso-Melanesian. This subgrouping follows Lynch et al. (2002), Ross (1988) and Ross et al. (2011) with some modifications.

Retention of Proto-Oceanic terms for horticulture in Remote Oceanic languages

There has been extensive reconstruction of terms relating to horticulture for various stages of Austronesian. Most important for our purposes are reconstructions by Blust and Trussel (ongoing) of Proto-Austronesian (PAN), Proto-Malayo-Polynesian (PMP) and POc (see also Blust 1995) and two volumes of essays on the lexicon of POc (Ross et al. 1998, 2008).[2]

PAN and PMP had terms for a number of crops and gardening practices (Blust 1995, 2009). Terms associated with rice and millet cultivation were not preserved in POc but others were. As well as various cultivated plants, these include terms for (swidden) garden, fallow land, uncultivated land, making a garden, clearing vegetation, planting yams, weeding a garden, digging stick or dibble, and garden fence or partition. Many of these terms have regular reflexes in major subgroups of Remote Oceania, with the partial exception of Te Motu, where data are scarce, and Nuclear Micronesian, where many POc terms to do with horticulture have been lost.

---

2   Two other volumes of essays have been published in this series but the reconstructions in these do not relate to horticulture.

A selection of reconstructions with supporting cognates follows. Reflexes (inherited continuations) of each reconstructed term in daughter languages are arranged by subgroup. Where there are reflexes of a POc term in many languages only a small selection is cited, enough to roughly indicate which subgroups have reflexes. The following abbreviations are used for when citing reconstructed etyma, reflexes and sources.

Abbreviations

ACD	Austronesian Comparative Dictionary (Blust and Trussel in progress)
Adm	Admiralties
Fij	Fijian and Rotuman
Mic	Nuclear Micronesian
MM	Meso-Melanesian
N	noun
NCal	New Caledonian
PAN	Proto-Austronesian
PMP	Proto-Malayo-Polynesian
Pn	Polynesian
POc	Proto Oceanic
PPn	Proto-Polynesian
PT	Papuan Tip
PWOc	Proto Western Oceanic
SES	Southeast Solomonic
SV	Southern Vanuatu
V	verb
VT	transitive verb

Tubers

Yams

Several terms for yam taxa are reconstructable for POc: **qupi* 'Dioscorea alata, greater yam' (continuing PAn **qubi*) is found almost throughout Island Melanesia and Polynesia. Terms for other yam taxa include **pʷatika* 'D. bulbifera, potato yam', **pwasepe* 'D. alata', **udu(r,R)* 'k.o. greater yam', **mwaruqen* 'k.o. yam, wild yam (?)'. A term for *Dioscorea esculenta*, lesser yam, **kamisa* or **mamisa*, is reconstructable for PWOc but not for POc, because it lacks reflexes in Remote Oceanic languages. *D. pentaphylla* is present throughout Melanesia but no POc name can be reconstructed. Here I give only a selection of reflexes only for **qupi*.

PMP **qubi* 'yam' (ACD)

POc **qupi* 'Dioscorea alata, greater yam'; (2) 'generic for yams' (Ross et al. 1998)

Adm	Penchal	*kup*	(1) 'long yam'
NNG	Malasaga	*kui-kui*	(1) 'greater yam'; (2) 'generic'
PT	Iduna	*kuvi*	(1) 'greater yam'; (2) 'generic'
MM	Tolai	*a-up*	(1) 'greater yam'; (2) 'generic'
MM	Marovo	*uvi*	(1) 'greater yam'; (2) 'generic'
TM	Tanema	*uva*	'yam'
SES	Arosi	*uhi*	(1) 'greater yam'; (2) 'generic'
SV	Lenakel	*n-uw*	(1) 'greater yam'; (2) 'generic'

NCal	Jawe	*kuic*	(1) 'greater yam'; (2) 'generic'
Fij	Wayan	*uvi*	(1) 'greater yam'; (2) 'generic'
Pn	Tongan	*ʔufi*	(1) 'greater yam'; (2) 'generic'
Pn	Futunan	*ʔufi*	(1) 'greater yam'; (2) 'generic'

Yam-growing is a demanding enterprise, involving clearing, planting, weeding and a good understanding of the seasons. As yams are a seasonal crop, in times of shortage Oceanic yam growers relied on other staples and/or on storage of yams in storage houses.

Taro

One POc generic term for *Colocasia esculenta* continues a PMP etymon.

PMP **tales* 'taro, *Colocasia esculenta*' (ACD)

POc **talo(s)* 'taro, *Colocasia esculenta*' (Ross et al. 2008)

NNG	Manam	*taro*	'taro, *Colocasia esculenta*'
PT	Motu	*talo*	'taro, *Colocasia esculenta*'
MM	Roviana	*talo*	'taro, *Colocasia esculenta*'
SES	Lau	*alo*	'taro (generic)'
SES	Kwaio	*alo*	'taro, *Colocasia esculenta*'
NCV	S. Efate	*(n)tal*	'taro, *Colocasia esculenta*'
SV	Anejom	*n-tal*	'taro, *Colocasia esculenta*'
Fij	Bauan	*dalo*	'taro, *Colocasia esculenta*'
Pn	Samoan	*talo*	'taro, *Colocasia esculenta*'

Another term, POc **mʷapo(q)*, has widely replaced **talo(s)* as the generic for *C. esculenta* in Western Oceanic languages. Its few reflexes in Remote Oceania generally refer to a variety of *C. esculenta* and that may have been the case in POc.

Although well attested in Near Oceania, in Remote Oceania a POc term for taro seedling has known reflexes only in New Caledonian languages.

POc **up(e,a)* 'taro seedling' (Ross et al. 2008)

NNG	Tami	*uwe*	'taro seedling'
PT	Are	*ube*	'taro tops for planting'
PT	Motu	*uhe*	'the end of yam, kept for planting, any such seed'
SES	Arosi	*uha*	'taro sp.'
NCal	Pwapwa	*upe*	'taro seedling'
NCal	Yuanga	*uva*	'taro seedling'

Fruit crops

Terms for a number of cultivated fruit bearing trees and tree-like plants are reconstructable for POc (Ross et al. 2008, ch. 11) with widespread reflexes in Remote Oceania, indicating continuity as far as Fiji and Polynesia. These include terms for breadfruit and bananas (see below), **quRis* '*Spondias cytherea*, Polynesian plum', **kapika* '*Syzygium malaccense*, Malay apple', **tawan* '*Pometia pinnata*, Ocean lychee', **wai*, **waiwai* '*Mangifera* sp., mango', **molis* 'citrus fruit', **natuq* '*Burckella obovata*'. Because of space limitations, I will give cognate sets here only for breadfruit and bananas.

Breadfruit

Two well-supported terms for *Artocarpus altilis*, **kuluR* (with variant **kunuR*) and **baReko*, are attributable to POc. The first of these continues a PMP antecedent.

PMP **kuluR* 'breadfruit, *Artocarpus altilis*' (ACD)

POc **kuluR* 'breadfruit, *Artocarpus altilis*' (Ross et al. 2008)

Adm	Mussau	*ulu*	'breadfruit'
Adm	Titan	*kul*	'breadfruit'
NNG	Gedaged	*ul*	'breadfruit'
NNG	Manam	*kulu*	'breadfruit'
MM	Vitu	*kulu*	'breadfruit'
MM	Nakanai	*ulu*	'breadfruit'
NCal	Pije	*cin*	'breadfruit'
NCal	Iaai	*i-oun*	'breadfruit'
Fij	Wayan	*kulu*	'breadfruit'
Pn	Samoan	*ʔulu*	'breadfruit'

POc **baReko* 'breadfruit, *Artocarpus altilis*' (Ross et al. 2008)

PT	Tawala	*beleha*	'breadfruit'
PT	Lala	*baleʔo*	'sago palm'
MM	Tigak	*bego*	'breadfruit'
MM	Nehan	*bario*	'breadfruit'
TM	Tanema	*baleo*	'breadfruit'
SES	Gela	*baleʔo*	'pair of breadfruit tied together'
SES	Bauro	*pareʔo*	'breadfruit'
NCV	Mota	*pego*	'breadfruit'
NCV	NE Ambae	*baego*	'breadfruit'

Ross (2008: 282) notes that reflexes of **kuluR* (with variant **kunuR*) and **baReko* are almost in complementary distribution, geographically. The most widespread and frequently reflected term is **kuluR*. This has reflexes in the Admiralties and Mussau, North New Guinea, Papuan Tip, New Caledonia, Fiji and Western Polynesia. The variant **kunuR* is reflected in North New Guinea and in the Ngero-Vitiaz group of west New Britain and the Vitiaz Straits. Reflexes of **baReko* are found in New Ireland, Northwest Solomons, Southeast Solomons, Te Motu, and in both North-Central Vanuatu and Southern Vanuatu.

Ross (2008) concludes that the usual term for breadfruit in POc was **kuluR* and this was carried into Remote Oceania by the first Oceanic-speaking colonists but was later replaced by **baReko* in a block extending from New Ireland to Vanuatu. The fact that reflexes of **baReko* generally show regular sound correspondences suggests that the replacement occurred quite soon after the initial dispersal of Oceanic dialects to Remote Oceania. Matthew Spriggs (pers. comm.) suggests that the spread of **baReko* probably occurred very early, when the Lapita exchange network was still operating, because immediately after the Lapita period, Southern Vanuatu and Central and Northern Vanuatu pottery styles diverge markedly from each other (Bedford 2006).

Another generic name for breadfruit, **beta*, has replaced **kuluR* and **baReko* as the generic in certain languages of the Solomons and Vanuatu. Reflexes of yet another term for *A. altilis*, **maRi*, are limited to South Vanuatu, Polynesia and Micronesia, and cannot be attributed to POc.

Bananas

Of the two principal POc reconstructions for banana, one, *pudi*, continues a PMP etymon.

PMP *punti* 'banana' (ACD)

POc *pudi* 'banana, *Musa* cultivars' (Ross et al. 2008)

Adm	Mussau	uri	'banana'
Adm	Seimat	pudi	'*Musa* sp.'
NNG	Maenge	puri	'banana'
NNG	Gitua	pudi	'banana'
PT	Tubetube	udi	'banana'
MM	Tigak	ur	'banana'
MM	Bulu	vudi	'banana'
TM	Aiwoo	no-u	'banana'
SES	Gela	vudi	'banana'
SES	Sa'a	huti	'banana'
NCV	Uripiv	na-vij	'banana'
NCV	Port Sandwich	na-vüc	'banana'
SV	Sye	no-voh	'banana'
NCal	Pije	piji(ŋ)	'*Musa paradisica*'
NCal	Iaai	o-vic	'banana'
Mic	Mokilese	wus	'banana'
Mic	Ponapean	u:t	'banana'
Fij	Wayan	vudi	'banana'
Pn	Tongan	fusi	'banana'

POc *joRaga* 'banana, *Fe'i* (?) cultivars' (Ross et al. 2008)

NNG	Middle Watut	cok	'banana'
NNG	Patep	joŋ	'banana (generic), *Musa sapientum*'
MM	Vaghua	soga	'banana'
SES	Arosi	toraga	'banana'
NCV	Raga	hoaga	'kind of banana'
NCV	Uripiv	jok	'*Musa troglodytarum*'
Fij	Bauan	soaga	'banana, *Musa fehi*'
Pn	Samoan	soaʔa	'mountain plantain, *Musa troglodytarum*'

Several terms for varieties of banana can be attributed to POc: *sakup* 'k.o. cooking banana, with long fruit', *bwera* '*Musa* cultivar', *baqun* '*Musa* cultivar'.

Gardens and gardening activities

Aside from plant taxa, a number of POc terms relating to gardens and gardening activities can be reconstructed. Several of these, including *quma* 'a garden, work a garden', *topa* 'land cleared for a garden', *talu(n)* 'fallow land', *qutan* 'bushland', and *asok* 'dibble, plant seeds with a dibble', have PAN and/or PMP antecedents.

PAN *qumah* (N) 'swidden', (V) 'work a swidden' (ACD)

POc *quma* (N) 'garden', (V) 'to clear land for a garden' (Ross et al. 1998)

NNG	Adzera	*gum*	'garden'
NNG	Gedaged	*uma*	'garden, cultivated land'
PT	Molima	*ʔuma*	'planted garden'
PT	Motu	*uma*	'garden; enclosed, cultivated plot'
MM	Tolai	*uma*	'garden'
MM	Roviana	*uma*	'make a garden'
		in-uma	'a garden'
SES	Gela	*uma*	'clear bush in making a garden'
NCV	Mota	*umwa*	'clear growth from a garden, first stage of preparation'
NCV	Nguna	*uma*	'cut bush, clear land'
Fij	Wayan	*uma(ni)*	'turn the soil over'

PMP *talun* 'fallow land' (ACD)

POc *talu(n)* 'fallow land, land returning to secondary growth' (Ross et al. 1998)

SES	Gela	*talu*	'forest land which has been previously cultivated'
SES	Kwaio	*alu*	'garden of second or third crop'
		alu sisi	'old garden returning to secondary growth'
SES	Sa'a	*aru*	'last year's yam garden'
SES	Arosi	*aru*	'overgrown garden; land formerly used for a garden; a dug garden'
Pn	Niuean	*talu-talu*	'land out of cultivation'
Pn	Rennellese	*tagu-tagu*	'begin to be bush-covered, of a fallow garden'
Pn	Maori	*taru-taru*	'weeds, herbs'

Although the next POc term, *topa* 'garden land', has known reflexes only in Fijian languages within Oceanic, it continues a PMP etymon and so must be attributed to POc and must have been part of the vocabulary carried to Remote Oceania.

PAN *tebaS* 'clear vegetation' (ACD)

POc *topa* 'land cleared for a garden', or 'land formerly planted as a garden' (Ross et al. 1998)

Fij	Bauan	*tova*	'flat piece of land, formerly planted with yams'
Fij	Wayan	*tova-tova*	'garden plantation'

The next cognate set is included, beside the previous two, to support a three-way contrast between terms for land under cultivation (*quma*), fallow land (*talu(n)*) and bushland (*qutan*), in POc and some of its daughters.

PAN *quCaN* 'scrub-land, bush' (ACD)

POc *qutan* 'bushland, hinterland' (Ross et al. 1998)

Adm	Mussau	*utana*	'garden'
NNG	Manam	*(a)uta*	'inland'
PT	Motu	*uda*	'bush, forest'
PT	Bwaidoga	*yudana*	'forest'
SES	Tolo	*uta*	'garden'
NCV	Mota	*uta*	'bush, forest, unoccupied land; the inland country'
NCV	Nguna	*uta*	'inland'
Mic	Kosreaean	*wɔt*	'area inland or towards the mountains'

| Fij | Rotuman | *ufa* | 'land (from sea), interior (from coast)' |
| Pn | Tongan | *ʔuta* | 'land (from sea), inland (from shore) |

PMP **hasek* 'dibble, plant seeds with a dibble stick' (ACD)

POc **asok* 'plant (yams) in holes in the ground' (Ross et al. 1998)

MM	Notsi	*soka*	'plant (sweet potato etc.)'
MM	Patpatar	*soh*	'plant (sweet potato etc.)'
MM	Bali	*v-azoɣ-i*	'plant (tuber etc.)'
NNG	Malai	*p-azog-i*	'plant (tuber etc.)'
PT	Motu	*h-ado*	'plant (tuber etc.)'
SES	Sa'a:	*ato(taha)*	'throw the first yam set into the hole (of priest)'
SES	Ulawa	*ato(ni waʔa)*	'throw the yams into the holes'
SES	Arosi	*ato*	'distribute yams in holes for planting'
		atoato	'lay in rows, mark out thus, as a garden with horizontal poles'
Mic	Woleaian	*f-atox-i*	'plant s.t.'

PMP **babaw* (V) 'weed (a garden)' (ACD)

POc **papo* (V) 'weed (a garden)' (Ross et al. 1998)

NNG	Yabem	waong	'weed'
PT	Gapapaiwa	*vao*	(VT) 'grow s.t., plant s.t.'; (N) 'garden'
SES	Gela	*vavo*	(VT) 'weed s.t.'
SES	Lau	*fofo*	'weed with a knife'
SES	Sa'a	*hoho*	'cut undergrowth' (*hoho-la* 'a garden cleared for yams')
SES	Arosi	*haho*	(V) 'weed'
NCV	Mota	*wowo(r)*	(V) 'weed'
Fij	Bauan	*vovo*	'dig the ground between yam mounds'

POc **bayat* (N) 'fence, boundary marker'; (VT) **bayat-i* 'make a garden boundary'

PT	Gumawana	*bayata*	'garden boundary made by terracing rocks'
		bayas-i	'make a garden boundary'
PT	Iduna	*bai*	'stick used as garden boundary'
MM	Tolai	*bait*	(V) 'enclose with a fence'
		ba-bait	(N) 'fence'
SES	Arosi	*bai-bai*	'large logs put round a finished garden'
Fij	Bauan	*bai*	'fence around a garden or town'
Pn	E. Futunan	*pae*	'raised stone platform of house or grave'
Pn	W. Futunan	*bae*	'a stone fence'

Terms for pig

There is some lexical evidence that the first Oceanic speakers in Remote Oceania practised pig husbandry. Three terms for 'pig' are attributable to POc (Ross et al. 2011: 237–240), but only two of these are retained in Remote Oceanic languages. POc **boRok* continues PAN **beRek* 'domesticated pig' (ACD). It is reflected in all major subgroups in Near Oceania but appears in Remote Oceanic only in North-Central Vanuatu and Western Fijian. The reflexes in these languages show loss of *R and, in some cases, replacement of *b by a labiovelar or velar stop.

PAN *beRek 'domesticated pig' (ACD)

POc *boRok 'pig, *Sus scrofa*' (all reflexes glossed 'pig' unless otherwise indicated)

Adm	Seimat	*pou*	
Adm	Nyindrou	*bou*	
NNG	Manam	*boro*	
NNG	Mumeng	*bʷok*	
PT	Tubetube	*buluka*	
PT	Wedau	*poro*	
MM	Bali	*boroko*	
MM	Nakanai	*boro*	
SES	Gela	*bolo*	
NCV	Mota	*pwoe*	'pig, male pig, barrow pig'
NCV	Kiai	*poe*	
NCV	Raga	*boe*	
Fij	Wayan	*qoo*	

In some North-Central and Southern Vanuatu languages *boRok is replaced by reflexes of POc *b(o,u)kas(i) 'pig, boar'. PPn *puaka may reflect the latter term, with *bukas becoming *puka, followed by anticipatory insertion of *a*. The Polynesian term has been borrowed as *vuaka* in some Eastern Fijian dialects.

On Anderson's argument regarding delayed introduction, the lexical evidence – continuity in an extensive set of POc terms relating to horticulture – is consistent with the hypothesis that the first Lapita settlers in Vanuatu, Fiji and Western Polynesia carried with them an array of crops, including taro, yams, bananas and some tree crops. Against this, Anderson (2003) argues that the lexical evidence is also compatible with the hypothesis that some or all of these crops were introduced at a later date, because the form and meaning of many of the POc terms would have remained largely unchanged for centuries in the speech of the Lapita colonists.

His general point is well taken. However, there are a few exceptions to the generalisation. Some POc terms have undergone regular sound changes in daughter languages that probably occurred within a few centuries after the Oceanic dispersal. These sound changes provide a diagnostic for distinguishing late borrowings from retentions. For example, POc *quRis 'Polynesian plum' is reflected in Proto-Central Pacific and PPn as *wii, showing regular loss of *R and final *s and reduction of initial syllabic *u to non-syllabic *w. The Central Pacific form could not have been borrowed from, say, Vanuatu or Solomon Islands languages, which retain *R and *u in this item. A case of a somewhat different kind is the preservation of POc word initial and medial *q as glottal stop (ʔ) in Tongan and a few other Polynesian languages, in contrast to its loss in all Southeast Solomonic languages, almost all Vanuatu languages and all Fijian languages. The fact that POc *qupi 'yam, *D. alata*' is reflected in Tongan as *ʔufi*, rather than *ufi*, favours the view that the Tongan term is a direct retention from POc and not a borrowing from, say, a Vanuatu or Fijian source.

More generally, the sheer number of POc terms for cultigens and cultivation practices retained by some of the languages of Vanuatu, Fiji and Polynesia suggests to me that most of these terms, and therefore the array of crops and practices, were carried to these regions when or soon after the first Lapita colonists settled them.

There is archaeological evidence in favour of this last conclusion. The exchange network linking Lapita communities in Near and Remote Oceania did not last long – not more than a century or two after initial settlement of Remote Oceania about 3000–2900 BP. By 2700 BP, divergence in pottery styles between regions indicates loss of regular contact between Near and Remote Oceania and between regions within Remote Oceania. Fiji and Tonga drop out of contact first, along with New Caledonia, and Southern Vanuatu soon begins to diverge from Northern and Central Vanuatu (Bedford 2006; Bedford and Clark 2001). The implication is that most of the cultigens must have been transported to Vanuatu and on to New Caledonia, Fiji and Tonga *before* the Lapita exchange system broke down.

Conclusion

Is the available evidence sufficient to give a confident answer to the question: Did the first generation of Lapita colonists in Vanuatu, Fiji and Western Polynesia bring cultigens with them and, if so, which ones?

I don't think we can completely dismiss Anderson's agnosticism on this matter. But it seems to me that even though foraging was initially much the more important source of food, various lines of evidence, taken together, indicate horticulture was practised from a very early period, and probably from the beginning of settlement. The micro-botanical evidence from Vanuatu indicates that yams, aroids and bananas were among the cultigens introduced very early. The linguistic evidence suggests the same for the greater yam, *Colocasia* taro, two kinds of *Musa* bananas and the major cultivated tree crops. Then there is archaeological evidence, chiefly divergence in pottery styles, which points to loss of regular contact between Lapita communities in Near and Remote Oceania and between major regions of Remote Oceania from 2700 BP onwards, within 100–300 years of first settlement. This favours the conclusion that most of the typical Oceanic array of cultivated plants had already been introduced and established before regular contact was broken.

Does the archaeological evidence allow precise estimates of how long the early Lapita reliance on foraging lasted in Vanuatu, Fiji or Tonga? Reports for each region generally speak of a swift decline but refrain from more precise estimates. Perhaps it is wrong to frame the question so broadly. We cannot assume that the chronology was the same for all environments (in some islands resources for foraging were quite impoverished at the time of first settlement) or that there was a sharp transition. While some kinds of native fauna probably diminished quickly, e.g. turtle, land birds such as pigeons and megapodes, and fruit bats; in the case of shellfish and other reef invertebrates, it is more likely that there was a gradual decline over many generations. In any case, during the first few generations, when the human population densities were still low, people would have been able to move on to new and pristine sites.

Acknowledgements

It is a pleasure to offer this paper to Peter Bellwood and to recall that we began our careers together in the Department of Anthropology, University of Auckland, in the 1960s, before he became famous. Robert Blust, David Burley, Malcolm Ross and Matthew Spriggs provided helpful comments on a draft of this paper.

References

Anderson, A. 2003, Initial human dispersal in Remote Oceania: Pattern and explanation. In C. Sand (ed.), *Pacific Archaeology: Assessment and Prospects*, pp. 71–84. Numea: Le Cahiers de l'Archeologie en Novelle-Caledonie.

Bedford, S. 2006. *Pieces of the Vanuatu Puzzle: Archaeology of the North, South and Centre.* Terra Australis 23. Canberra: Pandanus Books, Research School of Pacific and Asian Studies, The Australian National University.

Bedford, S. and G. Clark. 2001. The rise and rise of the incised and applied relief tradition: A review and reassessment. In G.R. Clark, A.J. Anderson and T .Vunidilo (eds), *The Archaeology of Lapita Dispersal in Oceania*, pp. 61–74. Terra Australis 17. Canberra: Pandanus Books, The Australian National University.

Blust, R.A. 1978. *The Proto-Oceanic Palatals.* Auckland: Polynesian Society.

——. 1995. The prehistory of the Austronesian-speaking peoples. *Journal of World Archaeology* 9(4): 453–510.

——. 1998. A note on higher-order subgroups in Oceanic. *Oceanic Linguistics* 37(1):1 82–188.

——. 2009. *The Austronesian Languages.* Canberra: Pacific Linguistics.

Blust, R.A. and S. Trussel. ongoing. *Austronesian Comparative Dictionary.* www.trussel2.com/ACD/.

Buckley, H.R., R. Kinaston, S.E. Halcrow, A. Foster, M. Spriggs and S. Bedford. 2014. Scurvy in a tropical paradise? Evaluating the possibility of infant and adult vitamin C deficiency in the Lapita skeletal sample of Teouma, Vanuatu, Pacific Islands. *International Journal of Paleopathology* 5: 72–85. doi.org/10.1016/j.ijpp.2014.03.001.

Clark, G.R. and A.O. Cole. 1997. Environmental change and human prehistory in the Central Pacific: Archaeological and palynological investigations on Totoya Island, Fiji. Report submitted to the Fiji Museum, Suva.

Constantine, A., C. Reepmeyer, S. Bedford, M. Spriggs and M. Ravn. 2015. Obsidian distribution from a Lapita cemetery sheds light on its value to past societies. *Archaeology in Oceania* 50(2): 111–116. doi.org/10.1002/arco.5064.

Davidson, J.M. and F. Leach. 2001. The strandlooper concept and economic naivety. In G.R. Clark, A.J. Anderson and T. Vunidilo (eds), *The Archaeology of Lapita Dispersal in Oceania*, pp. 115–123. Terra Australis 17. Canberra: Pandanus Books, The Australian National University.

Fall, P.L. 2010. Pollen evidence for plant introductions in a Polynesian tropical island ecosystem, Kingdom of Tonga. In S. Haberle, J. Stevenson and M. Prebble (eds), *Altered Ecologies: Fire, Climate and Human Influence on Terrestrial Landscapes*, pp. 253–271. Terra Australis 32. Canberra: ANU E Press.

Galipaud, J.-C., C. Reepmeyer, R. Torrence, S. Kelloway and P. White. 2014. Long-distance connections in Vanuatu: new obsidian characterisations for the Makué site, Aotrie Island. *Archaeology in Oceania* 49: 110–116. doi.org/10.1002/arco.5030.

Green, R.C. 1991. Near and Remote Oceania – disestablishing 'Melanesia' in culture history. In A. Pawley (ed.), *Man and a Half: Essays in Pacific Anthropology and Ethnobiology in Honour of Ralph Bulmer*, pp. 491–502. Auckland: Polynesian Society.

——. 2003. The Lapita horizon and traditions – signature for one set of oceanic migrations. In Sand (ed.), *Pacific Archaeology: Assessments and prospects (Proceedings of the Conference for the 50th Anniversary of the First Lapita Excavation. Koné Nouméa 2002)*, pp. 95–120. Nouméa: Les Cahiers de l'archéologie en Nouvelle-Caledonie 15.

Groube, L.M. 1971. Tonga, Lapita pottery and Polynesian origins. *Journal of the Polynesian Society* 80(3): 278–316.

Hope, G. and M. Spriggs. 1982. A preliminary pollen sequence from Aneityum Island, Southern Vanuatu. *Bulletin of the Indo-Pacific Prehistory Association* 3: 88–92. doi.org/10.7152/bippa. v3i0.11194.

Horrocks, M. and S. Bedford. 2004. Microfossil analysis of Lapita deposits in Vanuatu reveals introduced Araceae(aroids). *Archaeology in Oceania* 39: 67–74.

——. 2010. Introduced *Dioscorea* spp. starch in Lapita and later deposits, Vao Island, Vanuatu. *New Zealand Journal of Botany* 48: 179–183. doi.org/10.1080/0028825X.2010.502238.

Horrocks, M., S. Bedford and M. Spriggs. 2009. A short note on banana (Musa) phytoliths in Lapita, immediately post-Lapita and modern period archaeological deposits from Vanuatu. *Journal of Archaeological Science* 36: 2048–2054. doi.org/10.1016/j.jas.2009.05.024.

Kirch, P.V. 1984. *The Evolution of the Polynesian Chiefdoms*. Cambridge: Cambridge University Press.

——. 1997. *The Lapita Peoples: Ancestors of the Oceanic World*. Oxford: Blackwell.

——. 2000. *On the Road of the Winds: An Archaeological History of the Pacific Islands before European Contact*. Berkeley, Los Angeles, London: University of California Press.

Kirch, P.V. and R.C. Green. 2001. *Hawaiki, Ancestral Polynesia: An Essay in Historical Reconstruction*. Cambridge: Cambridge University Press. doi.org/10.1017/CBO9780511613678.

Kirch, P.V. and D.E. Yen. 1982. *Tikopia: The Prehistory and Ecology of a Polynesian Outlier*. Bernice P. Bishop Museum Bulletin 238. Honolulu: Bishop Museum.

Lynch, J., M. Ross and T. Crowley. 2002. *The Oceanic Languages*. London: Curzon.

Pawley, A. 2007. The origins of early Lapita culture: The testimony of historical linguistics. In S. Bedford, S. Christophe and P.S. Connaughton (eds), *Oceanic Explorations: Lapita and Western Pacific Settlement*, pp. 17–49. Terra Australis 26. Canberra: ANU E Press.

——. 2008. Where and when was Proto Oceanic spoken? Linguistic and archaeological evidence. In A.L. Yuri and K.O. Alexander (eds), *Language and Text in the Austronesian World. Studies in Honour of Ulo Sirk*, pp. 47–71. Munich: Lincom Europa.

Petchey, F., M. Spriggs, S. Bedford, F. Valentin and H. Buckley. 2014. Radiocarbon dating of burials from the Teouma Lapita cemetery, Efate, Vanuatu. *Journal of Archaeological Science* 50: 227–242. doi. org/10.1016/j.jas.2014.07.002.

Reepmeyer, C., M. Spriggs, S. Bedford and W. Ambrose. 2011. Provenance and technology of lithic artefacts from the Teouma Lapita site, Vanuatu. *Asian Perspectives* 49(1)(for 2010): 205–225.

Ross, M. 1988. *Proto Oceanic and the Austronesian Languages of Western Melanesia.* Monograph no. 98 Canberra: Pacific Linguistics.

Ross, M., A. Pawley and M. Osmond (eds). 1998. *The Lexicon of Proto Oceanic: The Culture and Environment of Ancestral Oceanic Society* vol. 1. *Material Culture.* PL C-152. Canberra: Pacific Linguistics.

—— (eds). 2008. *The Lexicon of Proto Oceanic: The Culture and Environment of Ancestral Oceanic Society* vol. 3. *Plants.* PL 599. Canberra: Pacific Linguistics.

—— (eds). 2011. *The Lexicon of Proto Oceanic: The Culture and Environment of Ancestral Oceanic Society* vol. 4. *Animals.* PL 621. Canberra: Pacific Linguistics.

Sheppard, P.J. 1993. Lapita lithics: Trade, exchange and technology: a view from the Reefs/Santa Cruz. *Archaeology in Oceania* 28: 121–137. doi.org/10.1002/j.1834-4453.1993.tb00303.x.

Shutler, R. Jr., D.V. Burley, W.R. Dickinson, E. Nelson and A.K. Carlson. 1994. Early Lapita sites: The colonisation of Tonga and recent data from Northern Ha'apai. *Oceania* 29: 53–68.

Spriggs, M. 1997. *The Island Melanesians.* Oxford and Cambridge, Massacussetts: Blackwell.

Steadman, D.W. 1998. The Lapita extinction of Pacific Island birds: Blitzkrieg versus slow death. In J.C. Galipaud and I. Lilley (eds), *The Western Pacific 5000 to 2000 BP.* Noumea: ORSTROM.

Steadman, D.W., A. Plourde and D.V. Burley. 1998. Prehistoric butchery and consumption of birds in the Kingdom of Tonga. *Journal of Archaeological Science* 29: 571–584. doi.org/10.1006/jasc.2001.0739.

Summerhayes, G.R. 2001. Lapita in the far west: Recent developments. *Archaeology in Oceania* 36: 53–63. doi.org/10.1002/j.1834-4453.2001.tb00478.x.

Worthy, T.H. and G. Clark. 2009. Bird, mammal and reptile remains. In G. Clark and A. Anderson (eds), *The Prehistory of Early Fiji*, pp. 213–230. Terra Australis 31. Canberra: ANU E Press.

The Sa Huynh Culture in Ancient Regional Trade Networks: A Comparative Study of Ornaments

Nguyen Kim Dung

Research on the Sa Huynh culture (ca 2500–1980/1800 BP) has been ongoing for more than a century, since the Sa Huynh site was discovered and excavated by French archaeologists in 1909. Hundreds of Sa Huynh jar-burial sites have been discovered from the coastal plains to the inland highlands and offshore islands in Central and Southern Vietnam. Numerous significant ritual objects and ornaments have been recovered in association with the jar burials and provide evidence for the wide geographic distribution of trading contacts across Southeast Asia during the Sa Huynh Period. This paper focuses on a comparative study of ornaments manufactured from semi-precious stone, metals and glass recovered from Sa Huynh jar-burial sites with those from contemporary sites across Southeast Asia and demonstrates how Sa Huynh society played a significant role in regional trade networks during the Iron Age.

Introduction

During the early Iron Age (*ca.* 2500–1900/1800 BP), Vietnam was geographically divided by three well-known cultures: Dong Son in the north, Sa Huynh occupying the central regions and Oc Eo in the south. The cultural influence of Sa Huynh extended from Hue in the north to the northern fringes of the Mekong Delta in the south (Dong Nai Province and Ho Chi Minh City), and from the coastal plains to the interior highlands (Pham 2009; Lam 2011). Trade and exchange networks extended from the Sa Huynh region of influence, not only to their Dong Son and Oc Eo neighbours, but more broadly across Southeast Asia (SEA). These exchange networks are a key characteristic of the Sa Huynh culture and span the period from its early formation and development in the Bronze Age (3000–2500 BP) through to the period of Typical Sa-Huynh (*ca.* 2500–1900/1800 BP), preceding the rise of Cham society in the first millennium AD (1900–1500 BP; C.Q. Vu 1991; Lam 2008, 2009).

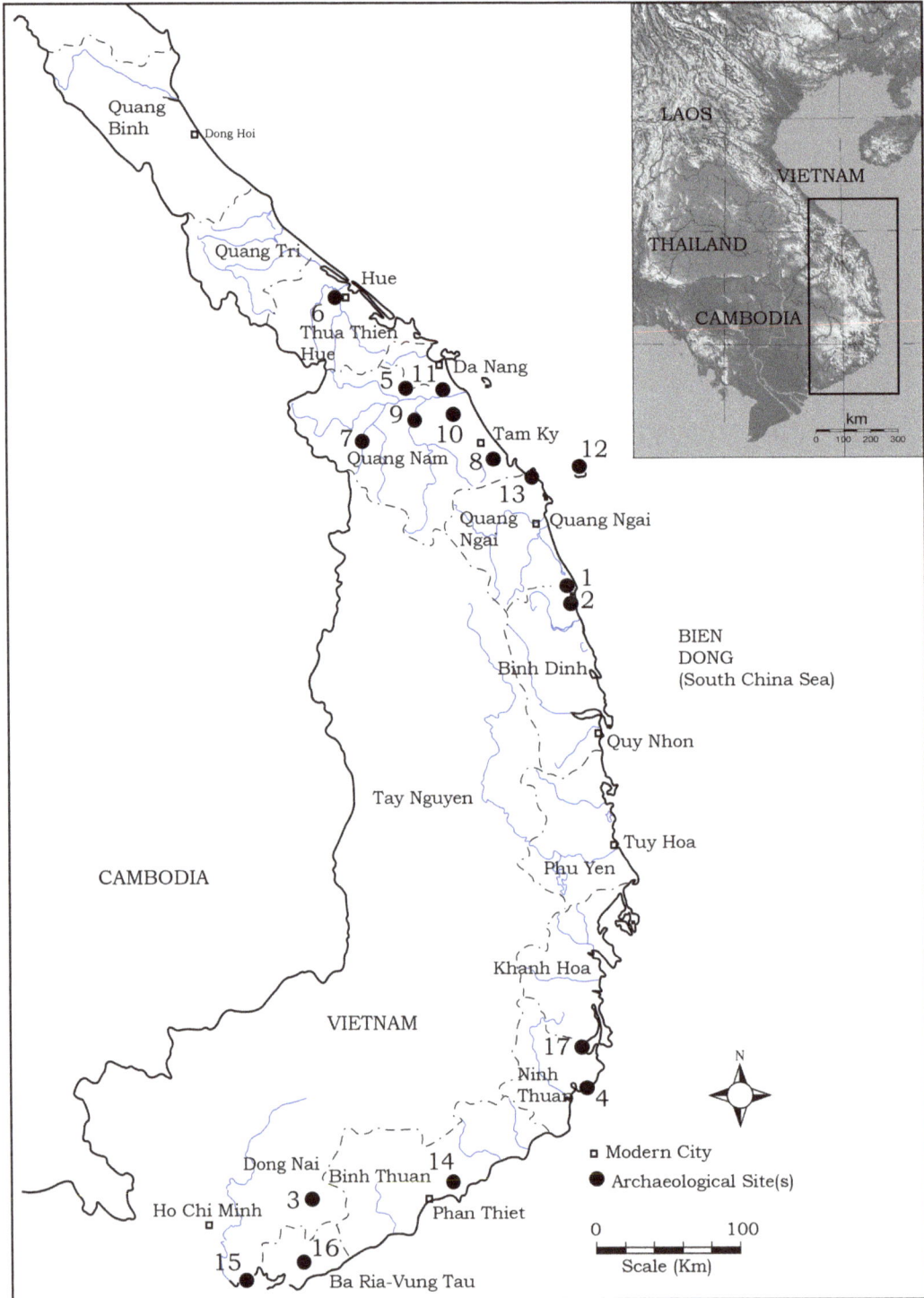

Figure 18.1 Map of Southern and Central Vietnam showing the general locations of the pre-Sa Huynh and Sa Huynh sites discussed in the text (1. Sa Huynh, Phu Khuong, Thanh Duc; 2. Long Thanh, Dong Cuom; 3. Phu Hoa, Dau Giay, Suoi Chon, Hang Gon; 4. Go Dinh, Hon Do; 5. Dai Lanh, My Tuong, Go Mun; 6. Con Rang; 7. Pa Xua; 8. Tam My; 9. Go Dua, Binh Yen, Que Loc; 10. Go Ma Voi; 11. Hua Xa I and II, Lai Nghi, An Bang; 12. Xom Oc, Suoi Chinh; 13. Go Que; 14. Hoa Vinh, Bau Hoe; 15. Giong Ca Vo, Giong Phet; 16. Giong Lon, Giong Ca Trang; 17. Hoa Diem).

Source: Redrawn by Philip Piper from an original by Hoang (2010): map of Southeast Asia (top right) modified from a Created with GMT from publicly released GLOBE data by Sadalmelik image.

Probably the most significant trade and exchange networks in SEA developed in the Bronze Age or even earlier during the Neolithic and involved maritime crossings of the South China Sea, or East Sea in Vietnamese (Ha 1998; Ngo 1987). By the beginning of the Iron Age (*ca.* 2500 BP), coastal connections became more evident as exchange intensified across the region and established the foundations for the long-distance trading networks that connected China and SEA with India and the Mediterranean.

The integration of the Sa Huynh culture within these maritime networks was first suggested by Wilhelm Solheim II who recognised the strong similarities between Sa Huynh and Kalanay pottery in the Philippines with the distinctive two-headed animal (bicephalous) ear pendants and penannular tri-projection earrings that are found both in Vietnam and across SEA (Solheim 1957, 2002). As a result, Solheim (1964, 2006) promoted the concept of the Nusantao Maritime Trading and Communication Network. Similarly, Loofs-Wissowa (1982), Higham (1989), Glover (1990), Bellwood (1997), Bellina and Glover (2004), and Hung et al. (2007, 2013) have all developed hypotheses orientated around various aspects of maritime interaction that have included the Sa Huynh culture.

The following discussion is a culmination of research on Sa Huynh material cultural remains by the author since 1995, including the excavations at Giong Ca Vo and Giong Phet (Nguyen K.D. 1995, 2001). This typological study of Sa Huynh ornamentation focuses on the geographic distribution of specific types of jewellery commonly found associated with jar burials in central Vietnam manufactured from semi-precious stone, glass and gold, with special reference to two very typical Sa Huynh ornaments: the tri-projection penannular earring and the bicephalous ear pendant (Nguyen K.D. 2010a, 2010b). The study demonstrates that societies within the Sa Huynh sphere were firmly integrated into transregional trading networks extending from China in the east, across SEA as far west as the Indian subcontinent. It illustrates that communities within the Sa Huynh culture not only imported a variety of ornaments and raw materials for their local production from a diversity of sources, but were also an important contributor to the exchange networks, not only exporting their own distinctive ornamental types but also the techniques used in their production.

Sa Huynh jar-burial sites and ornaments

One of the best known and key features of Sa Huynh, which has drawn the attention of many Vietnamese and international scholars (Solheim 1964; Loofs-Wissowa 1982; Ngo 1987; C.Q. Vu 1991; Glover 1996; Ha V.T. 1998; Bellina 2003; Yamagata 2006; Hung et al. 2007; Lam 2008; Hung and Bellwood 2010), are the hundreds of burial sites containing thousands of inhumations within large jars excavated across central and Southern Vietnam (see Figure 18.1). In addition to the burials, these sites have also produced a wide variety of other material culture that includes objects related to daily life and ritual, including bronze and iron implements, pottery and ornaments of various types, either placed within the jars (with the body) or buried adjacent to them. A diversity of imported articles is included within this burial repertoire (Nguyen K.D. 1995, 1998, 2014; Lam 2008) that includes Indo-Pacific glass beads, siliceous stone beads and metal (Hung and Bellwood 2010; Hung et al. 2013).

Ornaments were first discovered during the earliest archaeological excavations at Sa Huynh jar-burial sites by French archaeologists in the early twentieth century, at the type-site of Sa Huynh, as well as Phu Khuong and Long Thanh (Parmentier 1924: 325–343; Colani 1935; Figure 18.1), and later at Phu Hoa, Dau Giay and Suoi Chon in Dong Nai Province (Fontaine and Hoàng 1975; Figure 18.1). In total, French researchers investigated more than 20 Sa Huynh sites and identified more than 1,000 jar burials. For example, in 1903 Labarre uncovered 120 jar burials at the site of Thanh Duc (Figure 18.1), and a further 120 at Phu Khuong. In 1923, Colani excavated 55 jar burials at Long Thanh (see Parmentier 1924: 325–343) and 187 jars at Phu Khuong and Thanh Duc in 1934 (Colani 1935). Large collections of ornaments from these sites are curated and stored in the National Museum of History in Hanoi and in Ho Chi Minh City.

Over succeeding years, hundreds of Sa Huynh sites have been discovered and excavated in central Vietnam and associated ornaments have been abundantly recovered. Two of the most significant centres of Sa Huynh Culture are Quang Nam and Quang Ngai Provinces. In these provinces, Sa Huynh sites are not only located along the coast, but have also been identified inland adjacent to large rivers, and even in the mountainous highlands. The coastal provinces of Binh Dinh, Ninh Thuan and Binh Thuan have also produced many Sa Huynh jar-burial sites. These areas are also well known for their remarkable pre-Sa Huynh Period sites such as Hon Do, My Tuong and Go Dinh (Figure 18.1).

Due to the considerable number of sites excavated, and the thousands of ornaments collected, a cross-section of sites and artefacts is discussed below, with additional information presented in Tables 18.1 and 18.2. The artefacts illustrate the diversity and temporal and spatial distributions of different types of material culture associated with the Sa Huynh burials.

Table 18.1 Summary data on sites with ornaments that are discussed in the text.

Site	Location	Year(s) excavated	Excavated area	No. of jar burials	Comments	Reference
Con Rang	Hue	1993, 1995, 2004	2422 m²	243	8 ear plugs	Bui et al. 2008
Dai Lanh	Quang Nam	1977		About 100		Trinh 1982
Pa Xua	Quang Nam	1985	86 m²	60–70		Q.H. Vu 1991a
Tam My	Quang Nam	1977	About 300 m²	24		Trinh and Pham 1977
Binh Yen	Quang Nam	1999	35 m²	8		Bùi and Yamagata 2004
Go Ma Voi	Quang Nam	1998–2000	242 m²	60	1 Taiwan nephrite lingling-o	Reinecke et al. 2002
Go Dua	Quang Nam	1999	16 m²	6		Lam 2008
Lai Nghi	Quang Nam	2002–2004	192 m²	59		Nguyen T.B.H. 2012
Hua Xa 1 & II	Quang Nam	1993–1994		30		Tran 2004
Suoi Chinh	Quang Nai	2000, 2005	52 m² (2000), 28 m² (2005)	6 (2000), 3 (2005)		This contribution
Go Que	Quang Nai	2005	2,000 m²			This contribution
Dong Cuom	Binh Dinh	2003	300 m²	50		Pham 2009
Phu Hoa	Dong Nai	1971, 1972, 1975		46		Fontaine and Hoàng 1975
Hang Gon	Dong Nai	1963		62		Saurin 1963
Suoi Chon	Dong Nai	1977–1979	133 m² (1978), 50 m² (1979)	16		Q.H. Vu 1991b
Giong Ca Vo	Ho Chi Minh (HCM) City	1993–1994	255 m²	339	1 square blank, 1 discoid core	Nguyen K.D. 1995, 2001
Giong Phet	HCM City	1993	45 m²	82		Nguyen K.D. 1995, 2001
Giong Lon	Vung Tau	2003, 2005	544 m²	8	Later than Giong Ca Vo and Giong Phet	Q.H. Vu et al. 2008

Source: N. Kim Dung.

Con Rang (Figure 18.1) is a jar-burial site located in Hue City. Over 240 jar burials were identified within the *ca.* 2,400 m² area of excavation. Ornaments associated with the burials include numerous carnelian and shell beads, flat and thin (Dong Son-style) slit rings (12 pieces), five tri-projection lingling-o earrings, two bicephalous ear pendants and 40 small cylindrical beads (Bui et al. 2008).

Dai Lanh (Figure 18.1) is probably the most interesting of the 34 Sa Huynh jar-burial sites so far identified in Quang Nam Province. The site is located in Dai Lanh village, Dai Loc district. About 100 jar burials have been found in the site. The ornaments recovered include numerous carnelian, agate and glass beads and 13 small gold beads, together with three and four projection glass earrings, more than 30 tri-point lingling-os and two-headed animal earrings, Dong Son-style slit rings and many small cylindrical beads, including 25 manufactured from jade (Trinh 1982). Pa Xua (Figure 18.1) is also located away from the coast at an elevated location in Giang District. The remains of up to 70 broken jars that had been destroyed by local people searching for carnelian beads were identified within the *ca.* 100 m² excavated area. Lingling-os and bicephalous ear pendants of jade/nephrite, Dong Son-style slit rings and numerous carnelian and glass beads as well as iron implements were all recovered (Q.H. Vu 1991a).

At Tam My (Tam Ky – Quang Nam; Figure 18.1), excavated in 1977, 24 jar burials were unearthed, and associated with these were two lingling-os, three bicephalous ear pendants and six Dong Son-style slit rings, beads manufactured from a variety of raw materials and some Indo-Pacific trade beads, together with an iron implement (Trinh and Pham 1977). Jar Burial 97BYH2M1 at the site of Binh Yen (Que Phuoc, Que Son; Figure 18.1) was excavated in 1999. It produced one jade lingling-o, 30 carnelian beads, 75 glass beads and 80 Indo-Pacific beads. Associated with the inhumation in Jar 97BYH2M1a were two jade lingling-os, eight banded agate beads, 19 carnelian beads and 24 glass Indo-Pacific beads. No bicephalous ear pendants were recovered (Bùi and Yamagata 2004). The 'Typical' Sa Huynh site of Go Ma Voi in Duy Xuyen District (Figure 18.1) was excavated three times between 1998 and 2000, covering a total area of 242 m². In addition to the 60 jar burials unearthed, more than 2,000 ritual objects were discovered including pottery, ceramic bowls and lamps, and numerous bronze and iron axes. Ornamental articles included a large quantity of carnelian, glass and gold beads, several clay and three jade lingling-os, and Dong Son-style slit rings (Reinecke et al. 2002).

The site of Go Dua (Figure 18.1), in Thu Bon village, Duy Tan Commune, Duy Xuyen District is considered to be associated with the final phases of the Sa Huynh Culture in the Thu Bon River valley. A 16 m² excavation in 1999 produced six 'high jar burials', similar to those recorded at Dai Lanh and Hau Xa II (held at the Museum of Sa Huynh and Champa in Duy Xuyen district, Quang Nam Province). Besides ritual pottery, a Han Dynasty bronze mirror, bronze bowl and iron implements, several carnelian, glass and one jade lingling-o were recovered along with one flat jade Dong Son-style slit ring (Lam 2008). A rather special site within the Hoi An City area is Lai Nghi (Dien Ban District; Figure 18.1) where an excavated area of 192 m² dug between 2002–2004 produced 59 jar and six extended burials. The discovery of a collection of Eastern Han Dynasty bronze coins, a mirror and container date the site to between the third century BC and first century AD (corresponding to *ca.* 2200–1900 BP). This site produced an exceptional number of jade ornaments, including 20 jade Dong Son-style slit rings together with six complete and three fragments of lingling-os and more than 50 cylindrical beads. In addition, more than 10,000 gold, glass, carnelian and agate beads were recovered. Trading contacts with the west, including India and beyond, are evidenced through the presence of a bird pendant manufactured from crystal, a tiger pendant of carnelian, alkali-etched and gold plate glass beads, and glass collared beads (Nguyen T.B.H. 2012: 53–54). A group of 30 jar burials were found at the sites of An Bang, Hua Xa I & II and Dong Na (Figure 18.1) in Hoi An City in 1996. According to the excavation records, more than 2,121 ornaments were unearthed including 1,279 manufactured from jade, 637 of glass and several in carnelian, plus nine tri-projection earrings (four of jade and five of glass) (Tran 2004).

In Quang Ngai Province, a number of other sites have produced jade ornaments such as Long Thanh, the upper layers at Phu Khuong, Xom Oc and Suoi Chinh (Figure 18.1). So far, some 30 jade earrings have been found including bicephalous ear pendants, lingling-os, Dong Son-style slit rings and hundreds of cylindrical beads. The two largest assemblages have come from Sa Huynh itself, and Go Que (Figure 18.1). Along with typical beads and ornaments these sites have also produced four-projection circular earrings and flat, square-surfaced slit earrings.

Madeleine Colani initially excavated Dong Cuom in Binh Dinh Province in 1934, under the site name of Tang Long (Figure 18.1). More recent investigations in 2002 conducted by the National Museum of History, Hanoi, uncovered 62 burials in an area of 300 m². Included was Jar Burial 03DC.H1M20, which produced a pair of small jade lingling-os associated with 766 glass Indo-Pacific beads, and Burial 03DC.H1M21, which also contained a small jade lingling-o (Pham 2009).

The eastern part of Southern Vietnam possesses a special group of Sa Huynh Culture sites such as Bau Hoe, Hoa Vinh (Binh Thuan); Hang Gon, Dau Giay, Phu Hoa, Suoi Chon (Dong Nai Province, Figure 18.1); Giong Ca Vo, Giong Phet (Figure 18.1) and 12 other sites (Ho Chi Minh City); and Giong Lon (Ba Ria-Vung Tau, Figure 18.1). These are primarily located on low-lying landscapes in close proximity to the coast adjacent to the two most important maritime transportation routes of the Sai Gon and Dong Nai estuaries. Together the sites provide a continuous cultural sequence dating from *ca.* 2500 to 1850 BP (the first or second century AD). The archaeological sites can be divided into three phases: the Early Period (*ca.* 2500–2300 BP) represented by Suoi Chon, Phu Hoa, Hang Gon, Dau Giay; the Middle Period (*ca.* 2400–2100 BP) with Giong Ca Vo and Giong Phet; and the Late Period (*ca.* 2100–1700 BP) of Giong Lon and Giong Ca Trang (Figure 18.1). These later phase sites already have material culture characteristics typically found in succeeding Oc Eo societies.

Phu Hoa (Xuan Loc, Dong Nai) was discovered in 1961 by H. Fontaine and Hoàng, but only excavated in three seasons between 1971 and 1975. Forty-six jar burials were unearthed and produced 6,000 beads of carnelian, agate, crystal, glass and gold. Jade ornaments include two bicephalous ear pendants, six tri-projection earrings and four cylindrical bracelets. Two radiocarbon samples analysed at the Centre des Faibles Radioactivités (CFR Paris) on charcoal from Burial No. 11 and pottery from Burial No. 13 produced dates of 2400±140 BP and 2590±290 BP respectively (no lab codes; Fontaine and Hoàng 1975). The dates respectively correlate to 2778–2121 BP and 3399–1991 BP at the 95 per cent confidence interval (Oxcal 4.2; Bronk Ramsey 2015).

The site of Hang Gon (also known as Suoi Da), Xuan Loc District, Dong Nai Province produced 62 jar burials with a rich assemblage of gold earrings, a jade bicephalous ornament, small jade beads and five conical-shaped clay earrings with parallels at Giong Ca Vo. Two C¹⁴ charcoal samples analysed at CFR Paris produced dates of 2300±150 BP and 2190±150 BP (Saurin 1963), which respectively calibrate to 2738–1995 and 2700–1830 BP at the 95 per cent confidence interval (Bronk Ramsey 2015). Suoi Chon, also in Xuan Loc was excavated in 1977, 1978 (133 m²) and 1979 (50 m²). Two cultural layers were identified, with eight jar burials distributed in the upper horizon. Two typical jade lingling-os associated with a further tri-projection earring with long projections and glass bracelets were recovered (Q.H. Vu 1991b).

In the coastal regions of Ho Chi Minh City, the excavations at the Giong Ca Vo and Giong Phet jar burial sites have supplied the largest collection of ritual objects including a diverse range of pottery, iron or bronze tools and ornaments. Giong Ca Vo was first discovered and investigated in 1993 when 25 m² of the site was excavated, with a further 300 m² dug in 1994. A total of 339 jar-burials, of which 306 contained human skeletons, and 10 extended burials were unearthed. This site has also produced the largest collection of Sa Huynh ornaments (3,474 items), which includes 3,000 beads manufactured from carnelian, jade, garnet, agate, rock, crystal, tektite, glass, shell, gold and clay. There were 465 glass, 289 jade and shell and 27 bronze bracelets, a gold finger ring, gold beads and gold plate, 27 bicephalous pendants (19 of jade and eight of glass) and seven tri-projection lingling-os (Dang and Vu 1995; Dang et al. 1998). The most remarkable discoveries were the jade ornaments found in association with over 2,000 semi-precious stone and glass beads, 26 gold ornaments, and a carnelian lingling-o. In addition a square 'blank' of jade 5 cm² in area and 4 cm thick was found together with a discoid core with perforation traces at both ends, another thin broken flat blank and a jade object resembling a knife. A single C[14] sample (material not listed) produced a date of 2350±60 BP (ANU-10372), which calibrates to 2700–2161 BP at the 95 per cent confidence interval (Nguyen K.D. 1995, 2001).[1] Giong Phet, close to Giong Ca Vo and Ho Chi Minh City, was investigated in 1993. Eighty-two jar burials were identified in the 45 m² of excavation. The site produced jade bicephalous earrings, three bracelets, 55 cylindrical beads and hundreds of Indo-Pacific glass and semi-precious stone beads. A C[14] assay on charcoal returned a date of 2230±60 BP (ANU-10373; Dang et al. 1998), which calibrates to 2352–2069 BP at the 95 per cent confidence interval (Bronk Ramsey 2015).

Table 18.2 Jade ornament typology and presence of raw jade at the sites discussed in the text.

Site	Type 1	Type 2	Type 3	Type 4	Type 5	Type 6	Type 7	Raw jade
Con Rang	2	5		12		40		
Dai Lanh	42*	6	1	5	1	25	2	Present
Pa Xua	3	2		2				
Tam My	3	2				6		
Binh Yen		7		5	1			
Go Ma Voi		3		Some				
Go Dua		1		1				
Lai Nghi		9**		20	1	400		
Hua Xa 1 & II		4		3	1			
Suoi Chinh		1		2				
Go Que	Present	2	3	12	1	Some	6	
Dong Cuom		3		3		5		
Phu Hoa	2	6		30	4	Some	4	
Hang Gon	1	2				Some		
Suoi Chon	Present	2		2		Some		
Giong Ca Vo	46***	7		1****		608	28	Present
Giong Phet	2	1		3	2	5	2	
Giong Lon						Some	12	

* 17 Type 1a, 1b and 25 Type 2b ornaments.
** 6 complete and 3 broken pieces.
*** 19 Type 1a, 1b and 27 Type 2a and 2b ornaments.
**** Made of glass.
For references to sites, see Table 18.1.

Source: N. Kim Dung.

---

1   This date would appear to be the date of 2480±50 BP on charcoal published in Nguyen (2001). At around that time, The Australian National University Radiocarbon Dating Laboratory was using a slightly inaccurate method for measuring radiocarbon ages, which were corrected in recalibrated dates subsequently issued by the laboratory to the sample submitters (editors).

The site of Giong Lon (Ba Ria – Vung Tau) was discovered in 2002 and excavated twice in 2003 (344 m²) and 2005 (200 m²). The excavations produced five jar burials and 49 extended burials, and a total of 2,034 ornaments manufactured from a variety of different materials. This includes 178 gold beads, 15 gold objects (including three human faces), four gold earrings similar to those found at Lai Nghi (Quang Nam) and Prohear (Cambodia), two other earrings in different styles and 12 jade cylindrical tube bracelets. Two C¹⁴ dates (material not specified) at depths of 0.7 m and 1 m below modern ground surface produced dates of 2220±70 BP (03GL HII M1 – HNK-188/2) and 2680±55 BP (03GL HII M2 – HNK-188/1), which respectively calibrate to 2921–2734 and 2352–2045 BP (Bronk Ramsey 2015).

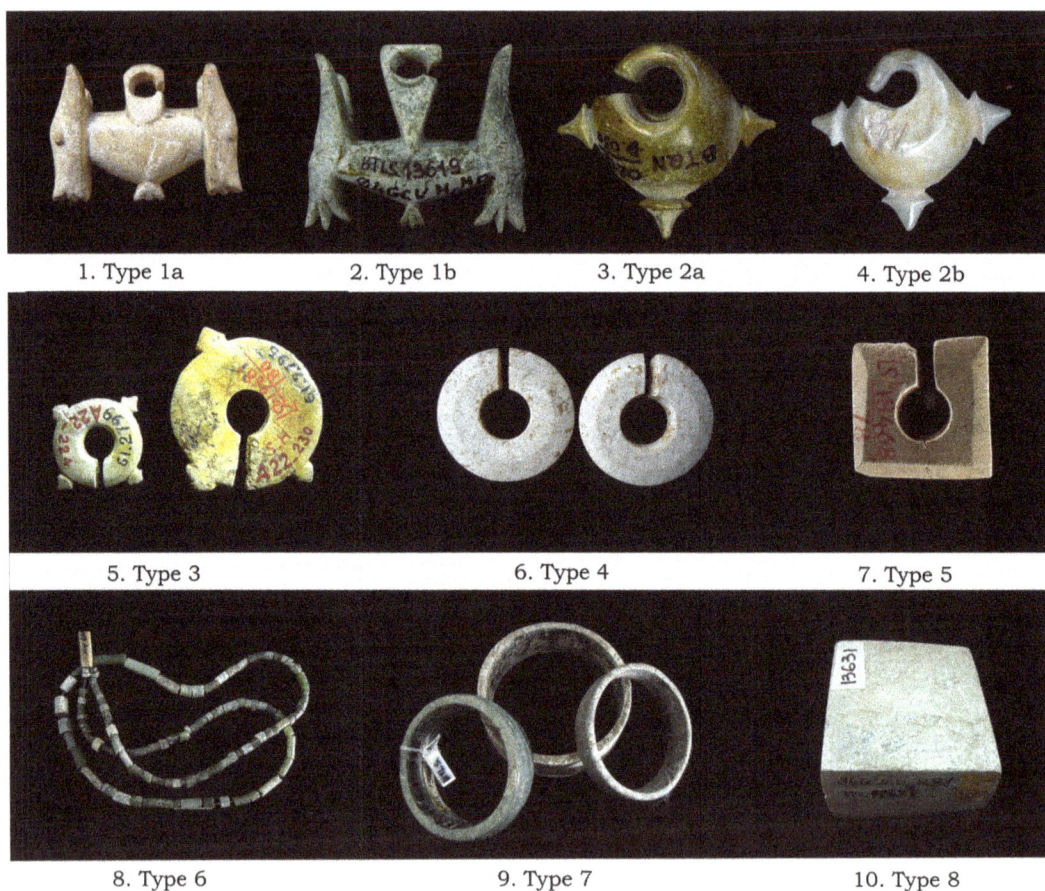

Figure 18.2 Types of jade/nephrite ornaments recovered from Sa Huynh burials.

Type 1. Two-headed (bicephalous) animal earring. Plate 1, Type 1a from Phu Hoa. Plate 2, Type 1b from Giong Ca Vo.
Type 2. Three-projection earring. Plate 3, Type 2a, from Go Ma Voi. Plate 4, Type 2b, from An Bang.
Type 3. Four-projection earring. Plate 5, from Sa Huynh.
Type 4. Dong Son-style slit ring. Plate 6, from Go Dua.
Type 5. Square-shaped earring. Plate 7, from Sa Huynh.
Type 6. Cylindrical bead. Plate 8, from Giong Ca Vo.
Type 7. Bracelet. Plate 9, from Giong Ca Vo.
Type 8. Square blank raw material. Plate 10, from Giong Ca Vo.

Source: Photographs by N. Kim Dung.

Both these dates are considered unreliable in view of a feature that makes Giong Lon distinctive from the other sites mentioned above, namely that it produced no bicephalous or tri-projection jade earrings so characteristic of Sa Huynh sites (Table 18.2). In this respect it is very similar to Hoa Diem in Khanh Hoa Province (Figure 18.1), which dates from around 1850 BP (the second century AD) onwards. Perhaps this indicates that from the second century AD, the typical jade earrings of Sa Huynh had dropped out of favour in the ancient trading networks of the region (but see Yamagata and Matsumura, Chapter 19, this volume, for a different interpretation of Hoa Diem).

Typology of Sa Huynh jade

The thousands of jade objects recovered from hundreds of Sa Huynh sites have been analysed and classified into seven types of ornament and one raw material type (Nguyen K.D. 1995, 2007a, 2014).

Ornaments

Type 1: Two types of bicephalous (animal-headed) ear pendants can be distinguished. The Type 1a (Figure 18.2, Plate 1) animal heads have a thick and fat body, short face and horns, with an almost circular-shaped eye without eyelashes. The ear fitment is curved and short. This type of earring has been recovered from sites such as Suoi Chon, Phu Hoa, Giong Ca Vo, Giong Phet and Dai Lanh. The Type 1b (Figure 18.2, Plate 2) animals have a small, thin body section and long, slightly curved horns with eyelashes carefully crafted over both eyes. The curved hook that fits to the ear is often angular. This type is represented in many sites such as Giong Ca Vo, Dai Lanh, Khuong My, Suoi Chon and Go Que.

Type 2: The penannular tri-projection lingling-o can be separated into two distinctive types. The Type 2a (Figure 18.2, Plate 3) lingling-o is large in size and relatively heavy with a round ball-shaped body and short projections. The distribution of this type seems to be limited to the sites of Go Ma Voi and Hau Xa II. The Type 2b (Figure 18.2, Plate 4) version has a flat body, and the distance from the butt end of the ear fitment to the central projection is greater than the distance from the left projection to the opposing right one. This type is sometimes called the 'pear' shaped lingling-o. Almost all Sa Huynh sites have this type. Considerable numbers have been found at Dai Lanh, Sa Huynh, Lai Nghi and Binh Yen.

Type 3: Earrings with four short pointed projections (Figure 18.2, Plate 5) are significant in that they have been recovered both in the pre-Sa Huynh sites of Long Thanh and Hon Do, and a few Sa Huynh sites such as Sa Huynh itself, Go Que and Dai Lanh.

Type 4: Dong Son-style slit rings (Figure 18.2, Plate 6) have been recovered in their hundreds across a diversity of Sa Huynh sites. Most jade slit rings found in Sa Huynh cultural sites have flat, thin cross-sections, with parallel lines incised on the body such as those unearthed at Lai Nghi, Hau Xa and Sa Huynh.

Type 5: Slit rings with square, flat surfaces and a thin section are generally very small in size (2 cm^2). They possess a narrow hole in the middle, a V-shaped cross-section and have manufacturing traces on both surfaces (Figure 18.2, Plate 7). Only about 10 of this type of jade ornament have been found, on eight sites. However, it is notable that they are found on pre-Sa Huynh sites (Long Thanh and Hon Do) as well as Sa Huynh sites (Binh Yen, Hau Xa, Lai Nghi, Que Loc (Figure 18.1), Go Que and Sa Huynh).

Type 6: Cylindrical beads (Figure 18.2, Plate 8) are often relatively small in size, measuring no more than 0.5–3.0 cm in length and 0.3–0.6 cm in diameter. They have been found on several sites such as Giong Phet, Phu Hoa, Suoi Chon, Dai Lanh, Go Que and Giong Lon, and sometimes in quite substantial numbers. For example, Giong Ca Vo yielded 608 and Lai Nghi 400 items of this type of bead. Another rare type of bead is the 'comma' shaped pendant bead. These have been unearthed at Giong Ca Vo, Binh Yen, Dai Lanh and Lai Nghi.

Type 7: Jade bracelets (Figure 18.2, Plate 9) have been found at Giong Ca Vo (28 items), Giong Phet (2), Phu Hoa (4), Go Que (6), Dai Lanh (2) and Giong Lon (12). Among these bracelets, those found at Giong Lon and Phu Hoa and some in Giong Ca Vo share the same material, shape and size. They are cylindrical with a length of 4.1–5.0 cm. Furthermore, jade bracelets found from Giong Ca Vo include another type: rectangular cross-section and D section. The thickness is about 0.2–0.4 cm, and the diameter is limited between 5.2–6.8 cm.

Raw Material

Type 8: Jade raw materials (Figure 18.2, Plate 10) consist of square blanks or discoid cores. A square blank (5.5 cm x 5.5 cm x 4.0 cm) and discoid core (diameter 4.5 cm and thickness 2.1 cm) were found at Giong Ca Vo in jar burials nos 94GCVH4M81 and 94GCV.H3M30 respectively. The presence of these raw materials strongly implies the local manufacture of jade rings at Giong Ca Vo.

The trade in Sa Huynh jade ornaments

The origin of three-pointed projections and two-headed animal earring

The manufacture of jade/nephrite earrings has a very long tradition in Vietnam. The earliest examples appear to be the Sa Huynh Type 3 with four projections and the Type 5 small slit rings with a square surface. These types have been found on pre-Sa Huynh archaeological sites such as Long Thanh dating to 3000 BP or earlier in association with clay earrings, as well as on several Sa Huynh sites on the coastal plains of central Vietnam including Vinh Tuong, Hon Do and My Tuong (Pham 2009; Nguyen K.D. 2010b). The presence of both these types of jade ornament bridging pre-Sa Huynh and Sa Huynh sites indicates that the production of jade earrings clearly has origins in Vietnam. What is currently less clear is the evolution of the penannular tri-projection earrings from earlier forms. As yet there are no intermediates that possess characteristics of the two different earring styles, though Hung et al. (2013) have suggested that a Vietnamese black nephrite lingling-o without projections from the site of Bai Coi, Ha Tinh Province, might be a prototype for the later penannular tri-projection earrings.

Beyer (1948) and Loofs-Wissowa (1982) were some of the first to note that the penannular lingling-o and bicephalous ear pendants found by researchers such as Colani (1935) in Sa Huynh burials had a much wider geographic distribution across Southeast Asia. Kano (1946: 233) also discussed the typology of earrings with three and four projections from Lanyu Island, Taiwan, and noted that they were being recovered across Southeast Asia from central Vietnam to the Philippines and Taiwan. Potential trading networks implied by the discovery of lingling-os with similar morphology found across Southeast Asia were discussed by Loofs-Wissowa (1982), and Ha and Trinh (1977) produced a paper in reference to the relationship of bicephalous ear pendants found across the same region. Over the years, most of the penannular lingling-o and bicephalous ear pendant types found beyond central Vietnam have been recorded in the Northern Philippines bordering the southern fringes of the South China Sea. For example, Fox (1970) reported on lingling-os and bicephalous ear pendants manufactured from nephrite and glass associated with jar burials from sites such as Uyaw, Duyong, Guri and Rito-Fabian (Figure 18.3, Plates 3 and 4) in central Palawan. Ille rockshelter site close to El Nido in Northern Palawan has produced penannular lingling-os manufactured from nephrite and shell (Paz pers. comm. 2012). Tri-projection lingling-os produced in shell and nephrite were identified at Arku Cave in the Peñablanca region of Northern Luzon (Thiel 1986–1987). Discarded debris produced during the manufacture of nephrite lingling-os was unearthed on Anaro, Itbayat Island in the Northern

Philippines dating to 2600–2400 BP. The raw material was sourced to Fengtian in Southeastern Taiwan, demonstrating that it was being exported from Taiwan to the Northern Philippines for ornament production (Hung and Iizuka 2013; see also below). An example of the tri-projection penannular lingling-o produced from Fengtian nephrite was found at Savidug Dune Site close to the base of a jar burial in a layer dated to 2416±30 BP, which calibrates to 2590–2390 BP (Wk-21809). Other tri-projection lingling-os have been recovered from Hengchun and Lanyu Island in Southern Taiwan (Hung and Iizuka 2013).

A single nephrite lingling-o recovered from the West Mouth of Niah Caves in Malaysian Borneo was also sourced to Fengtian (Iizuka et al. 2005). In Southeastern Thailand, a set of completed and unfinished nephrite ornaments was recovered from the port settlement of Khao Sam Kaeo dating to around 2300–2000 BP, or the fourth to first centuries BC (Figure 18.3, Plate 2; see also below). This site also produced an unfinished pre-form of a bicephalous ear pendant in the process of being carved from a square 'blank' of jade. The techniques being applied to sawing and cutting the ornament from the raw material appear to be exactly the same as the methods utilised for the same process at Giong Ca Vo, where a similar artefact in the early stages of manufacture was recovered (Nguyen K.D. 2007b; Bellina 2007; Bellina and Silapanth 2006). A bicephalous ear pendant has also been found at Ban Don Ta Phet in Kanchanaburi Province (Figure 18.3, Plate 1; Glover 1990).

Chemical analyses on the nephrite lingling-os from across Southeast Asia from Taiwan to Vietnam (including the Philippines and Thailand) have indicated that the raw material used in their production was sourced from Fengtian in Eastern Taiwan (Hung and Iizuka 2013). Hung et al. (2013) placed this raw material source in the context of the recent discovery of the production of penannular lingling-os on the Batanes Islands in the Northern Philippines and the Taiwanese islands of Lanyu and Ludao (Hung and Iizuka 2013), as well as the presence of several examples of nephrite lingling-os in Taiwan, the Philippines, Thailand, Malaysia and Cambodia, and a few two-headed animal earrings in the Philippines and Thailand (Figure 18.3, Plates 1 and 3). These led Hung et al. (2013: 390) to infer that perhaps the penannular lingling-o has its origins in Taiwan or the Philippines and it was introduced as part of trade networks linking the Austronesian world with coastal Vietnam.

However, far more nephrite/jade, glass and clay penannular lingling-os and bicephalous ear pendants have been recovered from the hundreds of Sa Huynh jar-burial sites in Central Vietnam than anywhere else. Furthermore, the outcomes of the nephrite studies reported by Hung et al. (2013) are somewhat more complicated than implied. Although the Electron Probe Micro Analysis (EPMA) conducted by Iizuka (Academia Sinica, Taipei) clearly demonstrated that some of the nephrite used in the manufacture of penannular tri-projection lingling-os from across Southeast Asia had been produced from Fengtian nephrite (Hung et al. 2007; Hung and Bellwood 2010; Iizuka et al. 2007), these studies only included a small, selective number of objects from Sa Huynh sites, and only a few of these were provenanced to Taiwan. The 18 samples analysed in Taiwan included Types 2a and 2b lingling-os from Go Ma Voi (Figure 18.2, Plates 3 and 4) and Go Dua respectively, two small broken fragments from Lai Nghi and four Type 2b fragments from other Sa Huynh sites, plus a Type 1a bicephalous ear pendant (from the collection of the Anthropological Museum of Hanoi National University), a nephrite 'blank' from Giong Ca Vo and another 10 jade objects and fragments from bicephalous earrings and beads (Figure 18.2, Types 1b and 6). Of these only the lingling-o from Go Ma Voi (Hung et al. 2007) and the jade square 'blank' from Giong Ca Vo (reported by Iizuka in January 2015 to the Hanoi University, Hue and Da Nang Museums) have been sourced to Fengtian. All the other 16 samples were probably produced from jade and nephrite sources found locally in

Vietnam (Iizuka, January 2015, pers. comm.). Potential, though unstudied, nephrite sources are well known in Vietnam, especially in the Song Ma District of Son La Province, and others are probably still to be discovered.

The interpretation of multiple sources of nephrite used in the production of Sa Huynh ornaments compares well with macroscopic observations of the ornaments by the author. Of the 28 sites studied, variations in the colour and matrices of nephrite raw materials suggest complex origins. At Giong Ca Vo and Giong Phet, for example, five differently coloured nephrite types used in the manufacture of lingling-o and bicephalous earrings were identified, while Binh Yen and Hau Xa have at least three colours and Lai Nghi two. The tri-projection lingling-o and bicephalous ear pendants are classic markers of the Sa Huynh culture. They are found extensively across the Sa Huynh region, and often with numerous examples recovered from a single site (Nguyen K.D. 2014; Table 18.2). For example, among the 18 Sa Huynh jar-burial sites studied by Nguyen K.D. (2014), 49 bicephalous animal-headed earrings were recovered from eight of the sites, and penannular lingling-os were recorded in every burial site. The bicephalous earrings also have a very distinctive geographic distribution with two major 'centres' of production identified, at Giong Ca Vo and Giong Phet (together these include 21 bicephalous ear pendants) where unfinished artefacts and square 'blanks' (the piece of Fengtian nephrite) have been recovered, and Dai Lanh (25 bicephalous ear pendants; Nguyen K.D. 1995, 2014). This clearly indicates that lingling-os and bicephalous ear pendants were being produced from a range of imported nephrite raw materials within the Sa Huynh cultural sphere. In Reinecke's (1996) detailed study of bicephalous ear pendants, he noted that Sa Huynh was almost certainly the centre for their production and utilisation where far more have been recovered than anywhere else in SEA.

Rather than considering the penannular lingling-o and bicephalous ear pendants as imports, it is perhaps more likely that the appearance of these ornaments that typify the Sa Huynh culture are coincident with its emergence and their wide geographic distribution and abundance are tangible expressions of the types of ideology that made the culture so cohesive. Sa Huynh crafts people imported raw materials from a variety of different sources and exported the technologies on how to produce them, the raw materials and the finished ornaments across Southeast Asia, and possibly even the cultural and social ideologies embedded within them. They were perhaps even itinerant.

Trade beads and pendants

Beads represent over 90 per cent of the ornaments recovered from Sa Huynh burial sites (Figure 18.4). Some sites and individual burials contained considerable numbers of beads manufactured from various materials. For example, Burial 7 at Phu Hoa produced 1,263 beads, and 1,279 beads of semi-precious stones and 637 of glass were unearthed from the 'Group of Four sites' in Ho Chi Minh City (Tran 2004). At Go Ma Voi, 40 carnelian, numerous glass and two gold beads were recovered (Reinecke 2004) and excavations at Lai Nghi produced over 7,000 beads manufactured from glass, jade, carnelian, agate, amethyst, crystal and gold, as well as tiger and bird carnelian beads (or pendants; Nguyen T.B.H. 2012; Figure 18.4, Plates 1–3 and 7). Many of the beads appear to have been imported into Vietnam from elsewhere. At the coastal site of Giong Ca Vo for instance, of the 2,916 identified beads it is possible that as many as 1,000 were trade items. These include several hundred Indo-Pacific mutisalah beads, banded beads, etched beads and collared beads made of crystal or carnelian as well as gold beads (Nguyen K.D. 1995, 2001). Burial M20 at Dong Cuom included 694 Indo-Pacific mutisalah beads together with jade/nephrite beads (Pham 2004) and Hoa Diem produced 1,280 trade beads including a number manufactured from gold (Nguyen K.D. and Bui 2012). These imports are also found far inland in the mountainous regions surrounding the Thu Bon River Valley in Quang Nam Province at sites such as Pa Xua, Dai Lanh, Binh Yen and Go Dinh which have produced Indo-Pacific mutisalah, blue glass, and carnelian and agate beads (Búi and Yamagata 2004).

Indo-Pacific glass beads are the beads found in the greatest quantities in Sa Huynh sites (Figure 18.4, Plate 9). They were manufactured using the Lada technique that originated in India. The Indian settlements of Khambhat and Arikamedu are considered as two of the largest centres of production of Indo-Pacific glass beads (including collared beads and etched beads) from the second half of the first century BC to the first or second century AD, around 2000–1850 BP (Francis 2002). However, recent investigations have produced small pieces of broken glass tube wasters (broken during drawing), black slag and tubular preforms of uncut glass beads at Giong Ca Vo (and Khao Sam Kheo, Thailand) that indicate that at least some of the glass beads were produced locally (Nguyen K.D. 1995, 2001: 109; Hirano 2008; Lankton and Dussubieux 2006) or elsewhere in Southeast Asia using imported Indian technology (Bellina 2014).

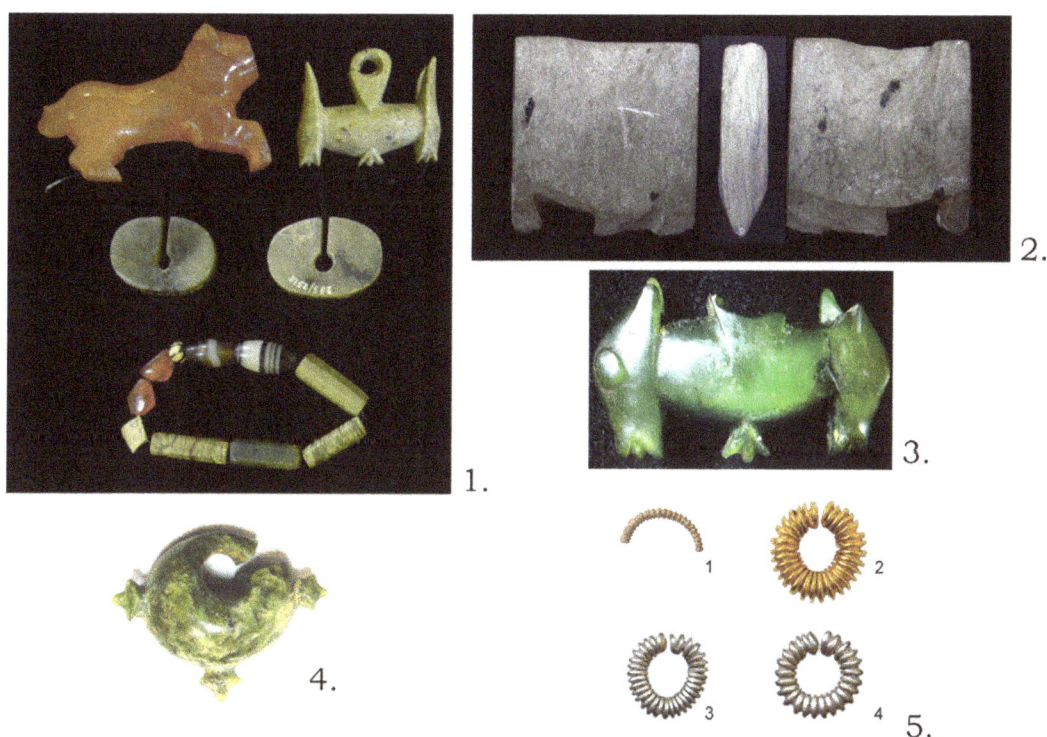

Figure 18.3 Sa Huynh Ornaments found across Southeast Asia.

1. Trading objects from Ban Don Ta Phet, Thailand (Original: Glover 1990).
2. Unfinished two headed earring (Taiwan jade) from Khao Sam Kaeo, Thailand (Reproduced with the permission of B. Bellina).
3. Two-headed animal earring (Taiwan jade) from Tabon Cave, Philippines (Original: Fox 1970).
4. Three-pointed earring (Taiwan jade) from Duyong Cave, Palawan, Philippines (Original: Fox 1970).
5. Gold earrings from Prohear (1,2) and Bit Meas (3,4) (Reinecke et al. 2009).

Source: Photographs 1–3: N. Kim Dung. 4: Hsiao-chun Hung. 5: Reinecke et al. (2009), reproduced with the permission of A. Reinecke.

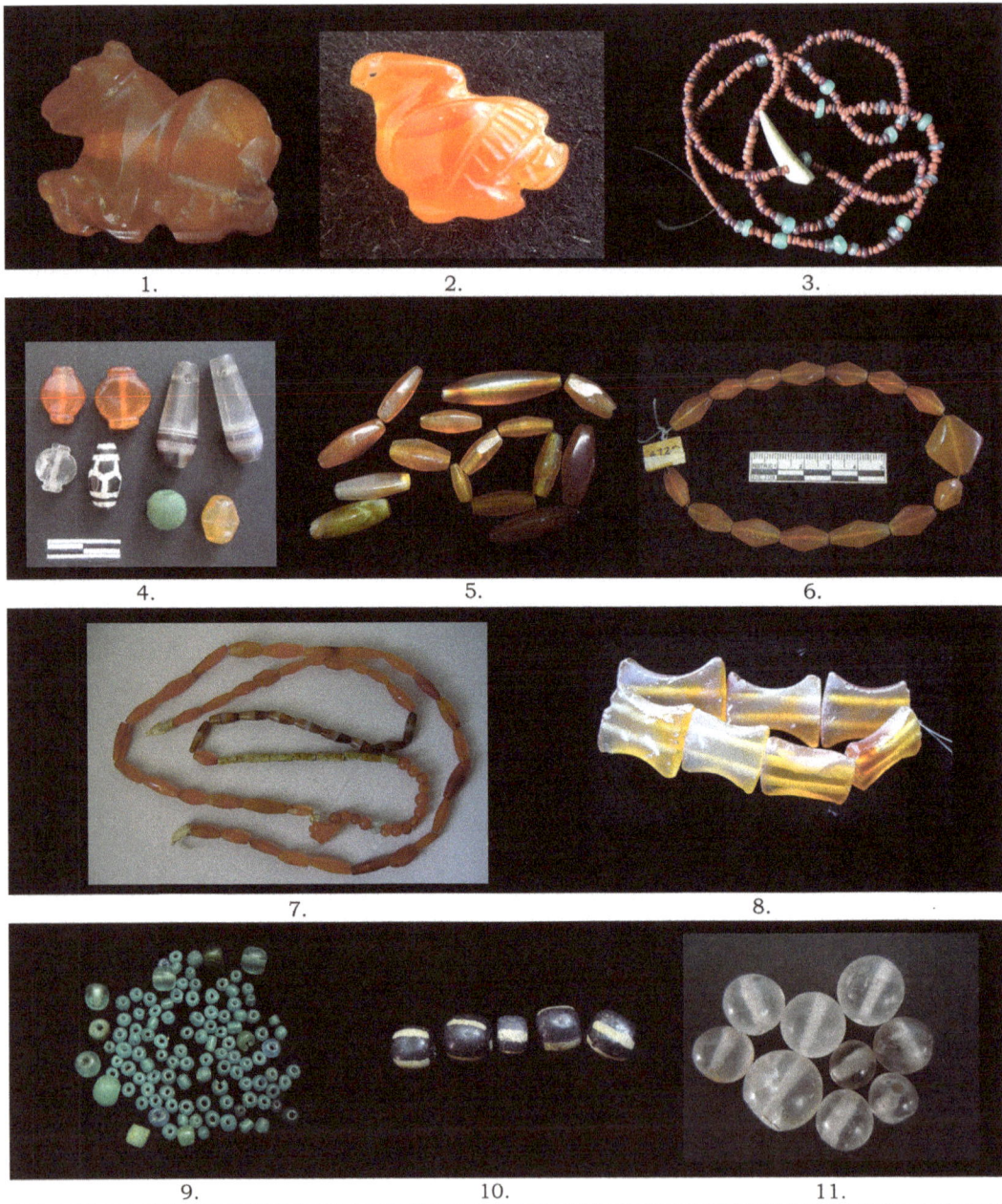

Figure 18.4 Sa Huynh beads and pendants.

1. Tiger carnelian pendant, from Lai Nghi.
2. Bird carnelian pendant, from Lai Nghi
3. Beads in different materials, from Lai Nghi.
4. Beads in different materials, from Hoa Diem.
5. Carnelian beads, from Giong Lon.
6. Beads, from Giong Ca Vo.
7. Beads, from Lai Nghi.
8. Carnelian beads, from Giong Ca Vo.
9. Indo-Pacific glass beads, from Giong Lon.
10. Glass beads, from Giong Lon.
11. Crystal beads, from Hoa Diem.

Source: Photographs 1, 3–11: N. Kim Dung, 2: Andreas Reinecke; reproduced with permission.

Indian carnelian and agate beads occur in various sizes, styles and colours. Some of them have been decorated with white lines (etched beads) or with differently coloured bands on the surface (banded agate). The tiger and bird shaped carnelian beads from Lai Nghi are particularly exquisite examples of this type of bead manufacture (Figure 18.4, Plates 1 and 2). Similar carnelian and agate beads have been unearthed at sites contemporaneous with those in Central Vietnam such as Ban Don Ta Phet, Khuan Lukpad, Phu Khao Thong and Khao Sam Kaeo in Thailand, and Halin in the Semon Valley of Myanmar (Bellina and Glover 2004; Hudson 2005; Bellina 2014; Figure 18.4, Plates 5 and 8). Glover (1990) argued that the ornaments manufactured from carnelian, agate, crystal and garnet found at Ban Don Ta Phet were produced in India, whereas those excavated from Ban Dong Phlong and Khok Charoen in Thailand had a Thai origin at Noen U-Loke (Higham and Thosarat 1998). The port site of Khao Sam Kaeo in Thailand appears to have been an important centre for the manufacture and distribution of semi-precious stone and glass beads.

Other, more technologically advanced bead types include 'alkaline-etched' and 'collared' beads were made from semi-precious stones like carnelian and agate as well as glass. These also originated in India, and were probably first introduced across Southeast Asia and into the Sa Huynh culture (found at Lai Nghi, Dai Lanh, Go Mun (Figure 18.1), Giong Ca Vo, Phu Hoa, Hoa Diem and Con Rang) in the early fourth century BC, *ca.* 2350–2300 BP (Glover 1990; Bellina 2014). Banded beads are widely distributed in Sa Huynh sites (Phu Hoa, Giong Ca Vo, Lai Nghi, Hau Xa, Con Rang and Go Mun) but only occur in small numbers.

The geographic distribution of Indo-Pacific trade beads indicates that complex trading routes had already developed widely from SEA to the Indian sub-continent, and possibly as far as the Mediterranean by the early to mid-first millennium BC (*ca.* 2350 BP). Not only were finished ornaments and raw materials traded but evidence from Thailand and Vietnam demonstrates that technological innovation and manufacturing skill were also exchanged between different cultures (Glover 1990; Nguyen K.D. 1995; Bellina and Glover 2004: 70).

Gold objects

Artefacts of gold have been recovered from numerous Sa Huynh sites including Giong Ca Vo, Giong Phet, Giong Lon, Phu Hoa, Hang Gon, Go Que, Go Ma Voi, Go Mun, Lai Nghi, Binh Yen, Con Rang and Hoa Diem (Figure 18.5). The earliest gold ornaments have been unearthed at Giong Ca Vo, Giong Phet and Go Ma Voi and probably date to the fourth century BC (*ca.* 2300 BP). Unlike most other ornament types, which are distributed in varying numbers across numerous burials, gold artefacts are generally concentrated with one or two individuals. For example, at Giong Lon four gold earrings and two masks were found in Burial 03GLHIVM1 and another two earrings and a mask in 05GLH1M1 (Figure 18.4, Plates 1–5). At Lai Nghi all four gold earrings found on the site were excavated from Burial M7 (Figure 18.5, Plate 6).

The most common gold artefact is the bead. Many of these beads have a characteristic octagonal shape and are similar to specimens recorded at Noen U-Loke in the Mun Valley of Northeast Thailand dating to the third or fourth century BC, around 2250 BP (Higham et al. 2007: 77). Some gold beads, such as examples from Giong Ca Vo, are long, narrow cylinders with five points or projections, or small shaped balls associated with gold finger rings and thin gold plate (Dang et al. 1998; Nguyen K.D. 1995). At Hoa Diem tens of very small thin beads shaped like flowers that were perhaps sewn into clothes were recovered. Also, two large polyhedral gold beads stylistically identical to examples from Khao Sam Kaeo in Thailand were unearthed (Figure 18.5, Plate 7; Nguyen K.D. and Bui 2012). Gold earrings and a finger ring have been recovered from Giong Ca Vo, Giong Phet, Phu Hoa and Giong Lon. Two different types of earring have been identified. Lai Nghi produced four examples of Type 1, while Giong Lon produced six Type 1 and two Type 2 earrings (Figure 18.5, Plates 3, 4 and 6). The latter is a form identified at no other Sa Huynh site so far (Vu et al. 2008).

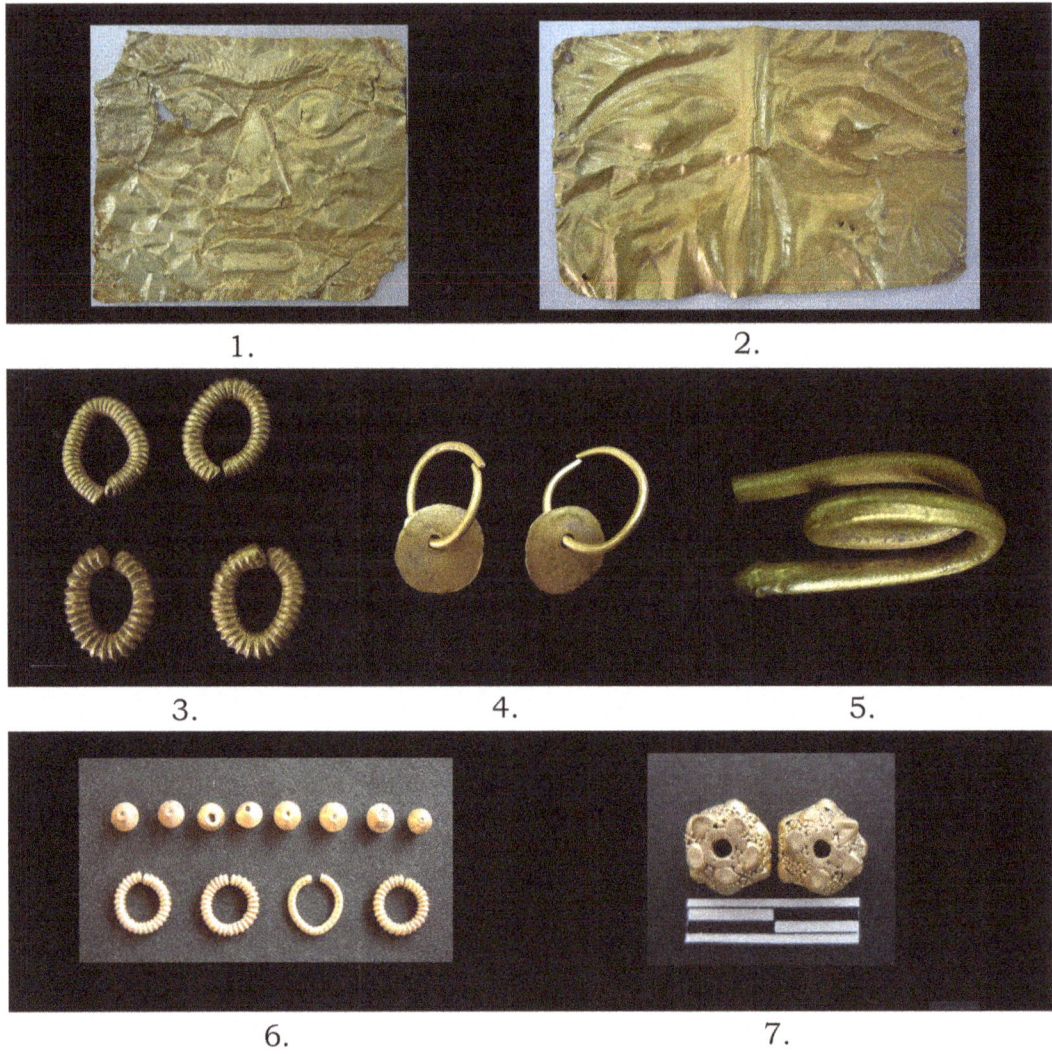

Figure 18.5 Gold objects in Sa Huynh cultural sites.

1. Gold mask from Giong Lon.
2. Gold mask from Giong Lon.
3. Gold earrings (Type 1) from Giong Lon.
4. Gold earrings (Type 2) from Giong Lon.
5. Gold in snake shape from Giong Lon.
6. Gold beads and earrings from Lai Nghi.
7. Gold beads from Hoa Diem.

Source: Photographs 1–5 and 7: N. Kim Dung 6: Andreas Reinecke, reproduced with permission.

Reinecke et al. (2009) probably undertook the most significant study of ancient gold in Vietnam. The Vietnamese samples were compared with gold earrings from various regions of the world including Cambodia, Thailand, Java, Afghanistan, Bactria and Germany. They noted that the Type 1 gold earrings found at Giong Lon and Lai Nghi had parallels at two important Iron Age sites in Cambodia, Prohear and Bit Meas (Figure 18.3, Plate 5). Analysis of the earrings indicated that among the four examples recovered from Lai Nghi, three were imported and one was locally manufactured. At Giong Lon at least four of the earrings were locally produced and two traded in.

Another remarkable example of traded gold ornaments is masks. Archaeological excavations at Giong Lon have produced three masks as well as several thin gold plates (Figure 18.5, Plates 1 and 2).

Trade and exchange during the Sa Huynh period

More than 100 archaeological sites dating to the Sa Huynh period in Central and Southern Vietnam have been excavated so far consisting primarily of jar burials dating from *ca.* 2500–1850 BP (sixth century BC to first–second centuries AD). A wide variety of ornaments manufactured from bronze, gold, jade/nephrite, semi-precious stones, glass and clay have been recovered in association with the inhumations and pottery, placed within the burial urn with the body, or adjacent to it in the excavated burial pit. These artefacts have provided a considerable amount of information with regards to domestic and ritual activities, culture, society and ideology. The broad geographic origins and diversity of identified ornaments provide important insights into the role Sa Huynh society played in these burgeoning exchange networks.

Large numbers of Indo-Pacific trade beads and other exotic items with their origins far to the west on the Indian subcontinent have been recovered from some of the earliest Sa Huynh burials in the fifth century BC (around 2500 BP). They indicate that the Sa Huynh inhabitants of Central Vietnam were already well connected to trans-regional trading networks that may have begun to develop perhaps before 3000 BP (as early as the second millennium BC). Effective internal exchange systems within the sphere of Sa Huynh influence is evidenced by the recovery of these trade beads a considerable distance from the coast along major rivers into the interior mountainous regions. There is evidence from sites such as Giong Ca Vo that not only were finished ornaments imported, so too were the knowledge and technology necessary to produce glass beads and gold earrings for the local market. In some instances, such as the unique type of gold earrings from Giong Lon, the gold smiths modified existing templates to produce jewellery specially commissioned to suit local tastes.

The geographic distribution and prevalence of the bicephalous ear pendant and penannular lingling-o are particularly informative in terms of how Sa Huynh society participated in international trading systems. These two iconic symbols of Sa Huynh have been recovered in considerable numbers across Central and Southern Vietnam. The majority were manufactured from various types of jade/nephrite, but they were also produced in clay, precious stones and glass. The emergence of the bicephalous ear pendant and penannular tri-projection earring in the early Sa Huynh phase, their ubiquity throughout the Sa Huynh cultural sphere, and their very distinctive morphologies suggest that a considerable amount of cultural, social and perhaps even religious ideology was embedded within their form. Manufacturing debris indicates that these artefacts were also being produced locally from local and imported nephrite, and glass and carnelian.

However, the bicephalous ear pendant and penannular tri-projection lingling-o have also been found in land masses encircling the South China Sea and especially on the fringing Philippine Islands where a number of lidded jar burials very similar to Sa Huynh examples have been recovered (see Fox 1970). Many of the ornaments were produced using Fengtian nephrite sourced in Southeastern Taiwan (Hung et al. 2007) including some from Sa Huynh sites. The penannular tri-projection lingling-o is particularly common in the Northern Philippines where evidence for its production has been identified in the Batanes Islands, and close by on Lanyu and Ludao, Taiwan. The production of bicephalous ear pendants has also been recorded at Khao Sam Kaeo in Southern Thailand.

Thus, the evidence suggests that Sa Huynh society played a significant role in trans-regional exchange networks. Not only were desirable exotic materials imported for local consumption, but also traders and manufacturers exported their own distinctive ornaments and the knowledge and technology of how to produce them.

Acknowledgements

I am thankful to Mariko Yamagata and Hsiao-chun Hung for their great help in my research, and to Yoshiyuki Iizuka for the chemical analyses of samples of Vietnamese nephrite ornaments.

I am also grateful to the Vietnam National Foundation for Science and Technology Development (NAFOSTED) for its generous grant number IV1.2-2011.15, which enabled me to conduct field research in Central and Southern Vietnam in 2012. Special thanks to the Museums of Hue, Quang Nam, Quang Ngai, Da Nang, Binh Dinh, Dong Nai and the Museum of History in Ho Chi Minh City. Without the help of these people and institutions, I would not have been able to complete the research contained within this manuscript. I would also like to thank Victor Paz (University of the Philippines) and Yoshiyuki Iizuka (Academica Sinica) for providing useful information on the recovery and provenance of jade/nephrite ornaments in the Philippines and Vietnam respectively.

References

Bellina, B. 2003. Social change and interaction between India and Southeast Asia. *Antiquity* 77: 285–295. doi.org/10.1017/S0003598X00092279.

———. 2007. *Cultural Exchange between India and Southeast Asia: Production and Distribution of Hard Stone Ornaments (VI c. BC–VI c. AD)*. Paris: Éditions de la Maison des Sciences de l'Homme.

———. 2014. Maritime Silk Roads' ornament industries: socio–political Practices and cultural transfers in the South China Sea. *Cambridge Archaeological Journal* 24: 345–377. doi.org/10.1017/S0959774314000547.

Bellina, B. and I.C. Glover. 2004. The archaeology of early contact with India and the Mediterranean world from the fourth century BC to the fourth century AD. In I.C. Glover and P. Bellwood (eds), *Southeast Asia: From Prehistory to History*, pp. 68–88. London: RoutledgeCurzon.

Bellina, B. and P. Silapanth. 2006. Khao Sam Kaeo and the Upper Thai Peninsula: Understanding the mechanisms of early trans-Asiatic trade and cultural exchange. In E.A. Bacus, I.C. Glover and V.C. Pigott (eds), *Uncovering Southeast Asia's Past*, pp. 379–392. Singapore: NUS Press.

Bellwood, P. 1997. *Prehistory of the Indo-Malaysian Archipelago.* 2nd edition. Honolulu: University of Hawaii Press.

Beyer, H.O. 1948. *Philippine and East Asian Archaeology and its Relation to the Origin of the Pacific Island Populations*. Bulletin 29. Manila: National Research Council of the Philippines.

Bronk Ramsey, C. 2015. Oxcal 4.2 manual. c14.arch.ox.ac.uk/oxcal.html.

Bui, C.H. and M. Yamagata. 2004. The Binh Yen site complex and Sa Huynh culture in Quang Nam. In Center for Archaeology (ed.), *Some Archaeological Achievements in Southern Vietnam*, pp. 83–123. Hanoi: Social Sciencess Publishing House (in Vietnamese).

Bui, V.L., N.Q. Nguyen and C. Nguyen. 2004. Con Rang site through three excavations: New discovery of Vietnam archaeology. *Khao Co Hoc* 2003 (2): 164–166 (in Vietnamese).

——. 2008. Con Rang site, Thua Thien Hue Province. *Khao Co Học* 2008 (5): 61–87 (in Vietnamese).

Colani, M. 1935. La céramique de Sa Huynh. Paper presented at the 2nd Congress of Far Eastern Prehistorians in Manila.

Dang, V.T. and Q.H. Vu. 1995. Excavation at Giong Ca Vo site (Ho Chi Minh City). *Khao Co Hoc* 1995(2): 3–19 (in Vietnamese).

Fontaine, H. and T.T. Hoang. 1975. Nouvelles notes sur le champ jarres funèraires de Phu Hoa avec une remarque sur la crémation au Vietnam. *Bulletin de la Société des Études indochinoises* 50.

Fontaine, H. and T.T. Hoang. 1975. Nouvelles notes sur le champ jarres funèraires de Phu Hoa avec une remarque sur la crémation au Vietnam. *Bulletin de la Société des Études indochinoises* 50(1): 7–50.

Fox, R.B. 1970. *The Tabon Caves: Archaeological Explorations and Excavations on Palawan Island, Philippines.* Monograph no. 1. Manila: National Museum.

Francis, P. 2002. *Asia's Maritime Bead Trade: 300 B.C. to the Present.* Honolulu: University of Hawai'i Press.

Glover, I.C. 1990. Ban Don Ta Phet: The 1984–5 excavation. In I.C. Glover and E. Glover (eds), *Southeast Asian Archaeology 1986, Proceedings of the First Conference of the Association of Southeast Asian Archaeologists in Western Europe,* pp. 139–183. Oxford: BAR International Series 561.

——. 1996. The Southern Silk Road: Archaeological evidence for early trade between India and Southeast Asia. In A. Srisuchat (ed.), *Ancient Trade and Cultural Contacts in Southeast Asia,* pp. 57–94. Bangkok: Office of the National Cultural Commission.

Ha, V.T. 1998. Thinking of Sa Huynh culture to and from Sa Huynh. In V.T. Ha (ed.), *Following the Trace of Vietnamese Ancient Cultures,* pp. 722–736. Hanoi: Social Sciencess Publishing House (in Vietnamese).

Ha, V.T. and D. Trinh. 1977. Two headed animal earring and Dong Son–Sa Huynh relationship. *Khao Co Học* 1977(4): 62–67 (in Vietnamese).

Higham, C. 1989. *The Archaeology of Mainland Southeast Asia.* Cambridge: Cambridge University Press.

Higham. C. and R. Thosarat. 1998. *Prehistoric Thailand from early Settlement to Sukhothai.* Bangkok: River Books.

Higham, C.F.W., A. Kijngam and S. Talbot (eds). 2007. *The Origins of the Civilization of Angkor.* vol. II. *The Excavation of Noen U-Loke and Non Muang Kao.* Bangkok: The Fine Arts Department of Thailand.

Hirano, Y. 2008. Trading and its development in Iron Age of Vietnam: A study on glass ornament. *Khao Co Hoc* 2008(4): 39–44 (in Vietnamese).

Hoàng, T.Q. 2010. Pottery from Sa Huynh culture. *Khao Co Hoc* 2010(1): 46–57 (in Vietnamese).

Hudson, B. 2005. A Pyu homeland in the Samon Valley: A new theory of the origins of Myanmar's early urban system. *Myanmar Historical Commission Conference Proceedings*, Part 2, pp. 59–79. Yangon: Universities Historical Research Centre, Myanmar.

Hung, H.-c. and P. Bellwood. 2010. Movement of raw materials and manufactured goods across the South China Sea after 500 BCE: From Taiwan to Thailand and back. In B. Bellina, E.A. Bacus, T.O. Pryce and J. Wisseman Christie (eds), *50 Years of Archaeology in Southeast Asia: Essays in Honour of Ian Glover*, pp. 235–245. Bangkok: River Books.

Hung, H.-c. and Y. Iizuka. 2013. The Batanes nephrite artefact. In P. Bellwood and E. Dizon (eds), *4000 Years of Migration and Cultural Exchange: The Archaeology of the Batanes Islands, Northern Philippines*. Terra Australis 40. Canberra: ANU Press.

Hung, H.-c., Y. Iizuka, P. Bellwood, K.D. Nguyen, B. Bellina, P. Silapanth, E. Dizon, R. Santiago, I. Datan and J.H. Manton. 2007. Ancient jades map 3000 years of prehistoric exchange in Southeast Asia. *Proceedings of the National Academy of Science* 104: 19745–19750. doi.org/10.1073/pnas.0707304104.

Hung, H.-c., K.D. Nguyen, P. Bellwood and M.T. Carson. 2013. Coastal connectivity: long-term trading networks across the South China Sea. *Journal of Island and Coastal Archaeology* 8: 384–404. doi.org/10.1080/15564894.2013.781085.

Iizuka, Y.P., P. Bellwood, I. Datan and H.-c. Hung. 2005. Mineralogical studies of the Niah West Mouth jade lingling-o. *Sarawak Museum Journal* 61 (n.s. 82): 19–29.

Iizuka, Y., H.-c. Hung and P. Bellwood. 2007. A noninvasive mineralogical study of nephrite artifacts from the Philippines and surroundings: The distribution of Taiwan nephrite and the implication for Island Southeast Asian archaeology. In J. Douglas, J. Jett and J. Winter (eds), *Scientific Research on the Sculptural Arts of Asia*, pp. 12–19. London: Archetype Publications.

Kano, T. 1946. *Tounan Ajia Minzokushi Kenkyu [Ethnography in Southeast Asia]*. Tokyo: Yajimashobo (in Japanese).

Lankton, J. and L. Dussubieux. 2006. Early glass in Asian maritime trade: a review and an interpretation of compositional analyses. *Journal of Glass Studies* 48: 121–144.

——— .2009. Sa Huynh regional and inter-regional integration in the Thu Bon Valley, Quang Nam Province, Central Vietnam. *Bulletin of the Indo Pacific Prehistoric Association* 29: 68–75.

———. 2009. Sa Huynh regional and inter-regional integration in the Thu Bon Valley, Quang Nam Province, Central Vietnam. *Bulletin of the Indo Pacific Prehistoric Association* 29: 68–75.

———. 2011. Central Vietnam during the period from 500 BCE to CE 500. In P.Y. Manguin, A. Mani and G. Wade (eds), *Early Interactions between South and Southeast Asia: Reflections on Cross-cultural Exchange*, pp. 3–15. Singapore: Institute of Southeast Asian Studies.

Loofs-Wissowa, H.E. 1982. Prehistoric and protohistoric links between the Indochinese Peninsula and the Philippines, as exemplified by two types of ear ornaments. *Journal of the Hong Kong Archaeological Society* 9: 57–76.

Ngo S.H. 1987. Origin and development of the Sa Huynh culture. *Khao Co Học* 1987(3): 37–53.

Nguyen K.D. 1995. Jewellry in jar burial sites from Can Gio District, Ho Chi Minh City, Vietnam. *Khao Co Hoc* 1995(2): 27–46 (in Vietnamese).

———. 1998. Ancient jade-manufacturing tradition in Vietnam. In T. Chung (ed.), *East Asian Jade: Symbol of Excellence*, vol. 2, pp. 383–396. Hong Kong: The Chinese University of Hong Kong (in Chinese).

——. 2001. Jewellry from late prehistoric sites recently excavated in South Vietnam. *Bulletin of the Indo Pacific Prehistoric Association* 21: 107–114.

——. 2007a. Trading contact of Sa Huynh culture with the west of Asia (India). In T.N. Pham (ed.), *Interexchange and Cultural Contact in the Early Iron Age of Southern Central Vietnam*, pp. 72–85, Hanoi: Social Sciencess Publishing House.

——. 2007b. Two headed earrings manufacturing process in Sa Huynh culture. In Institute of Archaeology (ed.), *New Discovery on Vietnam Archaeology, 2006,* pp. 301–303. Hanoi: Social Sciencess Publishing House (in Vietnamese).

——. 2010a. The manufacturing technology of jade lingling-o in Sa Huynh culture: Some discussions. In Institute of Archaeology (ed.), *New Discovery on Vietnam Archaeology, 2009,* pp. 185–188. Hanoi: Social Sciencess Publishing House (in Vietnamese).

——. 2010b. Jade slit rings in Vietnam prehistory. *Southeast Asian Archaeology*, vol. 4, pp. 147–153. Xiamen: Xiamen University Press (in Chinese).

——. 2014. Sa Huynh jade ornament: Evidence of trading contact in Southeast Asia. *Journal of Southeast Asian Archaeology* 34: 15–29.

Nguyen, K.D. and Bui C.H. 2012. A study on ornaments from Hoa Diem jar burial site, excavated 2007–2010, Khanh Hoa Province. In Institute of Archaeology (ed.), *New Discovery of Vietnam Archaeology, 2011,* pp. 156–158. Hanoi: Social Sciencess Publishing House (in Vietnamese).

Nguyen T.B.H. 2012. Collection of ornaments from Lai Nghi cemetery. *Khao Co Hoc* 2012 (3): 47–60 (in Vietnamese).

Parmentier, H. 1924. Notes d'archéologie Indochinoise, VII, Dépôts de jarres à Sa Huynh (Quang Ngai, Annam). *Bulletin de l' Ecole Française d' Extrême-Orient* 24: 325–343. Paris: l' Ecole Française d' Extrême-Orient. doi.org/10.3406/befeo.1924.3008.

Pham, T.N. 2004. Dong Cuom excavation. In Institute of Archaeology (ed.), *New Discovery of Vietnam Archaeology, 2003,* pp. 283–284. Hanoi: Social Sciencess Publishing House (in Vietnamese).

——. 2009. Socioeconomic context and cultural exchange relations of Sa Huynh people. In *Scientific Information*, pp. 40–56. Hanoi: Vietnam National Museum of History (in Vietnamese).

Reinecke, A. 1996. Bi-cephalous animal shaped ear pendants in Vietnam. *Bead Study Trust Newsletter* 28: 5–8. London: University College London.

Reinecke, A. 2004. Some remarks on Sa Huynh culture in Quang Nam Province with reference to Go Ma Voi site. In Ha Van Tan (ed.), *A Century of Vietnam Archaeology*, pp. 793–808. Hanoi: Social Sciences Publishing House (in Vietnamese).

Reinecke, A., V. Laychour and S. Sonetra. 2009. *The First Golden Age of Cambodia: Excavation at Prohear.* Bonn: Thomas Muntzer.

——. 2012. Prohear – An Iron age burial site in Southeastern Cambodia: Preliminary report after three excavations. In M.T. Bonatz, A. Reinecke and D. Bonatz (eds), *Crossing Borders in Southeast Asian Archaeology: Proceedings from the 13th International Conference of the European Association of Southeast Asian Archaeologists*, pp. 268–284. Singapore: NUS Press.

Reinecke, A., C. Nguyen, and M.D. Lam. 2002. *New Discovery on Sa Huynh Culture, Go Ma Voi Jar Burial Site and its Position in Central Vietnam (Neue Entdeckungen zur Sa Huynh Kultur).* Berlin: Linden Soft.

Saurin, E. 1963. Station prehistorique à Hang Gon près Xuan Loc (Sud Vietnam). *Bulletin de l'École Française d'Extrême Orient* 51: 433–452. doi.org/10.3406/befeo.1963.2088.

Solheim, W.G. II. 1957. The Kalanay pottery complex in the Philippines. *Artibus Asiae* 20(4): 279–288. doi.org/10.2307/3249420.

——. 1964. Further relationships of the Sa Huynh-Kalanay pottery tradition. *Asian Perspectives* 8(1): 196–211.

——. 2002. *The Archaeology of Central Philippines.* Revised edition. Diliman: University of the Philippines.

——. 2006. *Archaeology and Culture in Southeast Asia: Unraveling the Nusantao.* Quezon City: University of the Philippines Press.

Thiel, B. 1986–1987. Excavations at Arku Cave, Northeast Luzon, Philippines. *Asian Perspectives* 28(1): 61–81.

Tran, A. 2004. Ornament from Sa Huynh sites in Hoi An location. In Hoi An Committee (eds), *Sa Huynh Culture ted in the Conference of Sa Huynh Culture in Hoi An, 1995,* pp. 137–142. Hoi An: Hoi An Committee (in Vietnamese).

Trinh, C. and V.K. Pham. 1977. Tam My burial site, Quang Nam, Da Nang Province. *Science Information* 1977: 49–57. Hanoi: Vietnam National Museum of History (in Vietnamese).

Trịnh, S. 1982. Animal head earrings from Dai lanh site, Quang Nam, Da Nang Province. In Institute of Archaeology (ed.), *New Discovery of Vietnam Archaeology in 1980,* pp. 153–155. Hanoi: Social Sciences Publishing House (in Vietnamese).

Vu, C.Q. 1991. *Sa Huynh Culture.* Hanoi: The National Culture Publishing House (in Vietnamese).

Vu, Q.H. 1991a. Pa Xua jar burial site, Quang Nam, Da Nang Province. *Science Information* 1991: 167–179. Hanoi: Vietnam National Museum of History (in Vietnamese).

——. 1991b. Suoi Chon site. *Science Information* 1991: 126–138. Hanoi: Vietnam National Museum of History in Hanoi (in Vietnamese).

Vu, Q.H., D.C. Truong and V.C. Le. 2008. Giong Lon site through two excavations. *Khao Co Hoc* (5): 33–48 (in Vietnamese).

Yamagata, M. 2006. Inland Sa Huynh Culture along the Thu Bon River Valley in Central Vietnam. In E.A. Bacus, I.C. Glover and V.C. Pigott (eds), *Uncovering Southeast Asia's Past,* pp. 168–183. Singapore: National University of Singapore Press.

19

Austronesian Migration to Central Vietnam: Crossing over the Iron Age Southeast Asian Sea

Mariko Yamagata and Hirofumi Matsumura

The Sa Huynh culture, which spread over Central Vietnam during the early Metal Age, is generally associated with an Austronesian-speaking (Chamic) population. Solheim advocated the close similarity between pottery found at the Kalanay Cave in Masbate, Central Philippines, and the Sa Huynh culture in Central Vietnam. However, based on our recent archaeological research, Kalanay-type pottery is actually a feature of the jar burials at the Hoa Diem site that probably postdates Sa Huynh cultural sites. Solheim also found strikingly similar pottery from Samui Island in Southern Thailand that is quite different from Sa Huynh. The absence of a specific type of earring called lingling-o at Hoa Diem and Kalanay also suggests a chronological gap from the Sa Huynh culture. A bio-anthropological analysis of the Hoa Diem skeletons is consistent with a close affinity to insular Southeast Asians, suggesting long-distance cultural interaction and/or the demographic movement of Austronesian speakers across the South China Sea in the 1st and 2nd centuries AD.

Introduction

A focal point of Southeast Asian archaeology and anthropology has been the reconstruction of prehistoric maritime links. In prehistoric times, this area witnessed human migrations and movements that often involved major sea crossings. As Bellwood and Glover (2004: 5) described, 'Southeast Asia did not witness any truly independent development of early agriculture, urban civilisation, or literacy, but it did witness the oldest recorded maritime voyages by humans'.

Pleistocene seafarers could cross large expanses of open sea, as evidenced by the movement of early anatomically modern humans across Wallacea to Australia as far back as 50,000 years ago. Much later, Austronesian speakers (referred to simply as Austronesians from here on) based in Island Southeast Asia (ISEA) colonised the far-flung islands of the Indian Ocean and Oceania from Madagascar in the west to Easter Island in the east. Blust (1984–1985, 1996) and Bellwood (1997) reconstructed the overall linguistic and archaeological dispersal of Austronesians. A hypothesis on the homeland of Austronesian languages and the process of their dispersal was initially proposed by linguists and has significantly influenced the prehistoric archaeology of these regions. Bellwood has been working on verifying this hypothesis through archaeology and trying to reconstruct a complete history of the Austronesian dispersal that took place in various stages between 5,000 and 1,000 years ago (Bellwood 1997, 2004, 2005; Bellwood and Dizon 2005, 2008). His work suggests that the ancestors of the Austronesians originated in Southern China, and travelled to Taiwan – taking rice farming with them – probably by 5000 BP. Excavations on the Batanes Islands lying between Taiwan and Luzon identified possible evidence for the initial Neolithic dispersal out of Taiwan into the Northern Philippines by around 4000 BP (Bellwood and Dizon 2005, 2008, 2013). These Austronesians then proceeded to migrate south and east through the rest of the Philippine archipelago and into Sulawesi and Borneo before dispersing across the rest of ISEA and the Pacific.

Based on the linguistic work of Blust (1995), Bellwood described a branch of the Austronesian dispersal crossing over the South China Sea from Western Borneo to Vietnam around 2300 BP, perhaps made by people who spoke a language ancestral to Chamic (Bellwood 1997: 120–121). Chamic is actually the only Austronesian language spoken in Mainland Southeast Asia, being the language of the Chams, as well as some mountain dwellers presently living in Southern Vietnam and Cambodia.

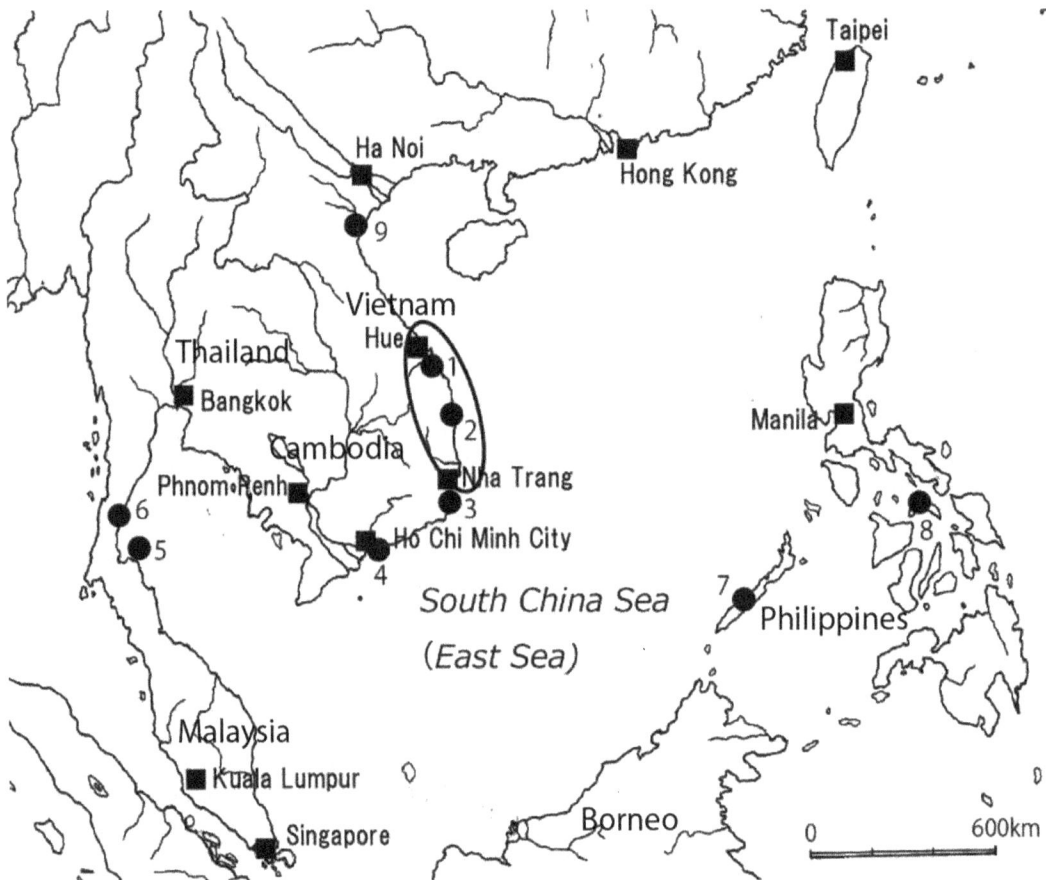

Figure 19.1 Locality map of sites relating to this chapter. Circle: Distribution sphere of the Sa Huynh culture in Vietnam.

(1) Lai Nghi, Hau Xa, An Bang, Go Ma Voi, Binh Yen; (2) Sa Huynh, Long Thanh; (3) Hoa Diem; (4) Giong Ca Vo; (5) Samui; (6) Khao Sam Kaeo; (7) Tabon; (8) Kalanay; (9) Dong Son.

Source: M. Yamagata.

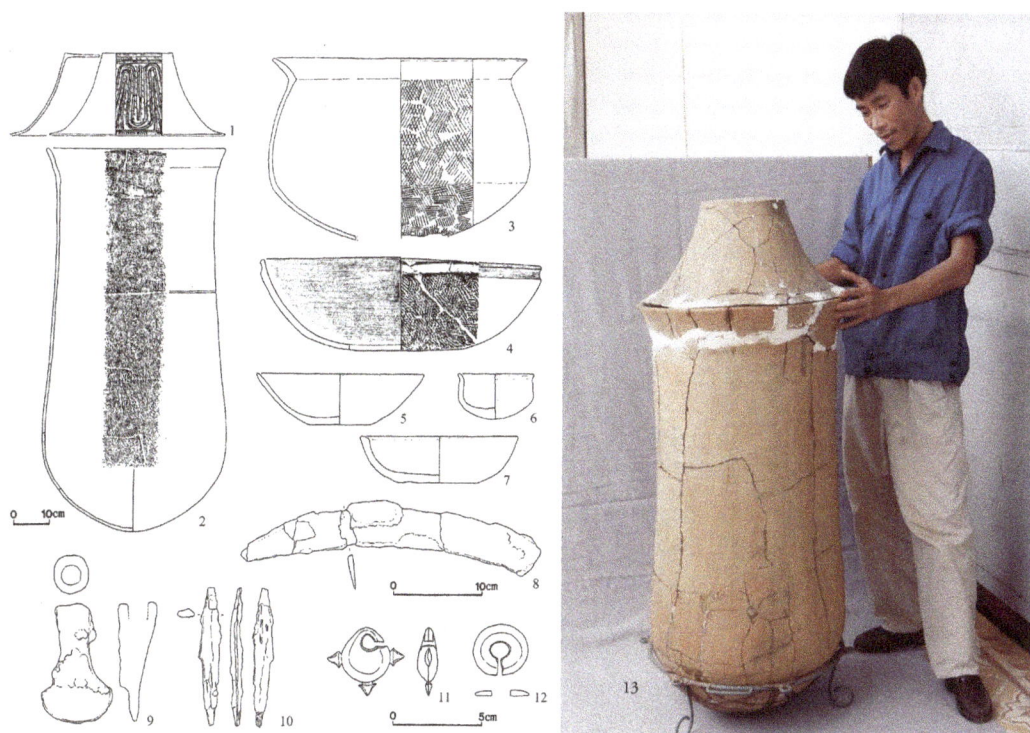

Figure 19.2 Typical jar, lid, and funerary goods of the Sa Huynh culture.

Burial No. M6 of Binh Yen (1, 13: lid; 2, 13: cylindrical burial jar; 3–7: pottery vessels; 8–10: iron tools; 11–12: stone earrings).
Source: M. Yamagata.

Bellwood thus inferred that the Iron Age Sa Huynh culture in Central Vietnam (Figure 19.1) was associated with an Austronesian-speaking (Chamic) population that had arrived in that region from either Peninsular Malaysia or Borneo, as documented archaeologically by the Sa Huynh culture itself (Bellwood 1997: 271–272).

A unique characteristic of the Sa Huynh culture is its mortuary customs, with lidded jar burials (Figure 19.2). These are associated with funerary accessory goods, such as pottery, iron and bronze implements, and earrings and beads made of agate, carnelian, jade (nephrite), and glass (see Nguyen Kim Dung, Chapter 18, this volume). The Sa Huynh cemeteries are often found on sand dunes extending along coasts or rivers on the alluvial plains. Although the Sa Huynh culture is recognised as having possibly fallen into decline in the latter half of the first century AD, the timing of its emergence still remains uncertain (Yamagata 2007a). Vietnamese archaeologists consider Champa to have emerged indigenously from local Sa Huynh (Ha 1999: 341), and that Sa Huynh populations like their Champa successors were Austronesian speakers (Ha 1984–1985).

Solheim (1984–1985, 1992, 2002, 2006) proposed a different scenario from that of Bellwood with regards to the movements of Austronesians. Solheim (2006 :60) initially coined the term 'Nusantao' or 'people of the south islands' to encompass speakers of Austronesian languages, but later used it to refer to a 'maritime-oriented trading people probably speaking an Austronesian language'. He maps the prehistoric networks of boat trading people, which he calls the Nusantao Maritime Trading and Communication Networks, extending from ISEA westward to Madagascar, northward to Korea and Japan, and eastward across the Pacific as far as Easter Island. His scenario of global-scale maritime culture evidenced through the widespread distribution of Nusantao in Southeast Asia is to some degree dependent on the accuracy of his identification of the 'Sa Huynh-Kalanay Pottery Tradition' (Solheim 1992: 201). This hypothesis developed following his excavations at Kalanay Cave in the Central Philippines in the early 1950s (Solheim 1957, 1959a, 1959b) where he found pottery forms and decoration closely resembling those recovered from Sa Huynh cultural sites in Central Vietnam (Solheim 1964, 1967). Thus, the external affinities of the Iron Age Sa Huynh culture should predominantly lie with the Central Philippines, according to Solheim's framework, rather than with Borneo or Peninsular Malaysia as proposed by Bellwood.

Since the end of the Vietnam War in 1975, a series of excavations have revealed more Sa Huynh culture sites, and the new findings have generated a more comprehensive framework for defining the Sa Huynh. Nonetheless, many researchers still tend to classify the pottery unearthed from any Iron Age site in Central and Southern Vietnam as 'Sa Huynh', despite considerable interregional dissimilarities. Given this variation, we need to refer to the 'Sa Huynh' culture more definitively in a typological sense to explore the internal and external connections of Iron Age Central Vietnam with surrounding areas in Southeast Asia.

The purpose of this paper is to review the Austronesian hypotheses as they relate to human movements across the South China Sea based on recent archaeological and anthropological discoveries from Iron Age sites in Central Vietnam. In particular, we challenge Solheim's scenario of the 'Sa Huynh-Kalanay Pottery Tradition' through comparative analysis of the two ceramic vessel types, and through our investigations of the jar burials from the site of Hoa Diem in Vietnam. The cultural and skeletal remains recovered from this Iron Age site help to refine the parameters of what is correctly assigned to 'Sa Huynh'.

What is the 'Sa Huynh' culture?

'Pre-Sa Huynh' period

Jar burials are the most diagnostic mortuary custom practised by societies belonging to the Sa Huynh culture during the Iron Age in Central Vietnam. Two 'pre-Sa Huynh' phases are recognised in Vietnamese archaeology: the Long Thanh and Binh Chau phases. The assemblages from these two phases are thought to be related ancestrally to the Sa Huynh culture (Chu and Dao 1978; Vu 1991; Ha 1999).

The site yielding the oldest jar burials found to date in Vietnam is Long Thanh, the late Neolithic cemetery situated near the Sa Huynh site. The site is located on a sand bank facing the South China Sea. In total, 15 jar burials and one pit burial with associated burial offerings were first uncovered during excavations in 1976 and 1978 (Chu and Dao 1978). The burials were associated with stone earrings with slits or four projections, bamboo-like shaped beads, and vessels with ringed feet. Radiocarbon determinations using charcoal indicate dates of 3370±40 or 3752–3599/3587–3533 cal. BP (86.8 per cent/8.6 per cent; Bln-1972) and 2875±60 or 3227–2902 cal. BP (95.4 per cent; Bln-2096; all dates herein are calibrated using OxCal 4.2 IntCal.13 (Bronk Ramsey 2014)). Another pre-Sa Huynh site is Binh Chau, located on a sand dune near the mouth of the Tra Khuc River in Quang Ngai Province that was discovered after Long Thanh. Excavation in 1978 uncovered seven pit burials associated with pottery vessels, C-shaped clay earrings, and bronze implements (Ngo 1980). Another site thought to belong to the Binh Chau phase is Xom Oc, located on Ly Son Island about 30 km northeast of the Tra Khuc River mouth, and excavated in 1997. Jar and pit burials were uncovered, associated with pottery vessels, shells, shell beads, and a bronze arrowhead (Pham 2000). The Binh Chau phase is generally regarded in Vietnamese archaeology as the immediate ancestor of the Sa Huynh culture.

Pre-Sa Huynh sites have been discovered in the highlands as well. Lung Leng, located in Kon Tum Province in the western highlands of Central Vietnam, was intensively excavated in 1999 and 2001. A total excavated area of 15,000 m² yielded 205 jar burials, some of which belong to the Neolithic period (V.L. Bui 2005). This evidence at Lung Leng led some Vietnamese archaeologists to suspect that the jar-burial tradition had originated in the highlands and then extended eastward to the coastal areas. It assimilated aspects of the existing local cultures and developed into the Long Thanh phase, and eventually the Sa Huynh culture (Ha 1999; K.S. Nguyen 2005, 2010).

Vietnamese archaeologists have thus ascribed the ultimate ancestors of the Sa Huynh culture to several local cultures of the pre-Metal period such as Xom Con, a shell midden located along Cam Ranh Bay in Khanh Hoa Province. This site has been regarded as typical of the first 'pre-Sa Huynh' phase, dating back to the latter half of the fourth millennium BP (C.B. Nguyen et al. 1993; Ha 1999; Lam 2011). However, the ultimate origins of the Sa Huynh culture and its mortuary customs remain unresolved.

Defining the Sa Huynh culture

The first Sa Huynh culture site was identified in 1909, when a French customs officer, Vinet, discovered several jar burials with some artefacts on the sand dune of Long Thanh. The Sa Huynh Site was excavated in 1923 by Labarre, and the findings were reported by Henri Parmentier (1925). During the 1930s, two notable archaeologists, Madeleine Colani and Olov Janse, conducted excavations on the same sand dune as Sa Huynh and Long Thanh, respectively (Colani 1937; Janse 1941). After the 1930s, the Sa Huynh sites received little attention from archaeologists due to World War II. It was only in the 1950s with Malleret and Solheim's investigations into the Sa Huynh culture that research was revived (Malleret 1959; Solheim 1959a, 1959b, 1959c). During the 1960s and early 1970s, French and Vietnamese archaeologists clarified the existence of jar burials along the Dong Nai River valley (Saurin 1973; Fontaine 1972; Fontaine and T.T. Hoang 1975). The Dong Nai discoveries extended the known geographic distribution of Sa Huynh culture sites south into Southeastern Vietnam.

Since the end of the Vietnam War in 1975, a large number of Sa Huynh sites have been discovered and excavated in Central Vietnam. These include Tam My, Phu Hoa, Bau Tram, Dai Lanh, Que Loc, Tabhing, Go Ma Voi, Lai Nghi, Hau Xa, An Bang, Go Dua, Binh Yen, Thach Bich, and Tien Lanh in Quang Nam (So Van Hoa Thong Tin Quang Nam – Da Nang 1985; Lam 1998, 2009; Lam et al. 2001; Reinecke et al. 2002; C.T. Nguyen et al. 2004; C.H. Bui and Yamagata 2004); Long Thanh, Binh Chau, Xom Oc, and Go Que in Quang Ngai (Chu and Dao 1978; Ngo1980; Pham 2000; Doan 2002, 2012); Dong Cuom in Binh Dinh (Dinh 2002; Pham 2014); and Con Rang and Con Dai in Thua Thien Hue (V.L. Bui et al. 2008). Furthermore, archaeological sites with numerous jar burials were also excavated in the southeastern part of Vietnam, represented by Giong Ca Vo and Giong Phet in the Can Gio District, Ho Chi Minh City (Dang and Vu 1997; Dang et al. 1998). Results of these excavations shed significant light on the Sa Huynh culture, drawing special attention to the diagnostic mortuary customs using burial jars and associated funerary goods.

Typical burial vessels of the Sa Huynh culture consist of cylindrical or egg-shaped jars with hat-shaped lids (Figure 19.2), buried vertically in the ground with grave goods. In addition to burial jars and lids, pottery vessels of the Sa Huynh culture include small jars, deep jars and shallow bowls (all of which may have pedestals), jars with wide or constricted necks, bowls, and so-called lamps (Yamagata 2009). Decorations also vary, including cord-marked impressions, incised triangular or rectangular designs filled with diagonal incised lines, paired incised lines interspersed with punctuations, coloured bands bound with paired incised lines, and horizontal V or triangular motifs of impressions made by the crenulated edge of a seashell (T.Q. Hoang 2010; Ishii 2010; Yamagata 2010). These crenulated impressions are most common among pottery of the Sa Huynh culture. These characteristic forms and decorations of Sa Huynh pottery were first presented by Parmentier (1925).

The Sa Huynh culture in the Thu Bon River valley in Quang Nam may be divided into two phases, provisionally labelled I and II by the author (MY) (Yamagata 2006, 2009, 2010). Representative sites for Phase I include Binh Yen H1 (excavation pit No. 1), Thach Binh and Go Ma Voi, while representative sites for Phase II include Binh Yen H2 and Go Dua. The differences between Phase I and II include the type of burial jars (I: egg-shaped, II: cylindrical), form and decoration of pottery (I: diverse, II: less diverse), number and type of metal objects (I: more bronze implements, II: more iron implements with a few bronze bowls and mirrors), and number of beads (increasing in II).

The Sa Huynh culture declined during the first century AD, and soon afterwards, probably in the early second century AD, the Tra Kieu and Go Cam sites were settled (K.D. Nguyen 2005; Yamagata 2007b, 2011). Neither is a burial site of the Sa Huynh culture, and Tra Kieu is generally identified as the capital of the early polity of Linyi (Champa). The indigenous society associated with the Sa Huynh culture must have been involved in the prosperous Nanhai trade connecting India and China, but at the same time was confronted by the southward expansion of the Han (Yamagata 2007b). Some jar burials of the final Phase II at the Binh Yen, Go Dua and Lai Nghi sites contained Western Han bronze mirrors (Yamagata et al. 2001).

Based on the burial jars and lids produced locally, a cylindrical or egg-shaped jar often associated with a hat-shaped lid is the most specific material for defining the Sa Huynh culture, as proposed elsewhere (Yamagata 2007a, 2010, 2013; Suzuki 2011). Given this definition, the range of the Sa Huynh culture extended from Hue in the north, in a southerly direction to Nha Trang as far as the coastal regions of Central Vietnam (Yamagata 2011, 2013; Figure 19.1).

This geographically restricted perspective on the Sa Huynh cultural sphere is shared by only a few Vietnamese archaeologists (e.g. C.H. Bui 2009). Most would also include Iron Age sites associated with jar burials in Dong Nai and Ho Chi Minh City (Ha 1983; Vu 1991; Lam 2011). Dividing Sa Huynh spatially into closely associated Northern and Southern Sa Huynh cultures has been proposed by Lam (2011).

Pottery vessels of the Sa Huynh culture

Considering the large sample of Sa Huynh pottery vessels, we are now in a position to critique earlier uses of the concept of 'Sa Huynh'. For instance, pottery locally referred to as '*binh kieu Sa Huynh*' (Sa Huynh-type vase) unearthed from Giong Ca Vo in Ho Chi Minh City (Dang et al. 1998: 163) displays a quite distinct shape. These pottery vessels have an everted rim, constricted neck, sharply angled body, and a short ring-foot. Although the excavators designate vessels characterised by these specific features as 'Sa Huynh type', such characteristics are in fact rarely seen among pottery of the Sa Huynh culture in Central Vietnam. Concerning curvilinear or rectangular scrolls and triangles decorated on '*binh kieu Sa Huynh*', some vessels of the Sa Huynh culture also bear those patterns, but only a small proportion. In the opinion of the author (MY), for the purposes of defining Sa Huynh pottery, more attention should be given to the *noi* (in Vietnamese) forms and associated decorations that constitute the modal expression, rather than assuming Sa Huynh affiliation through incidental similarities.

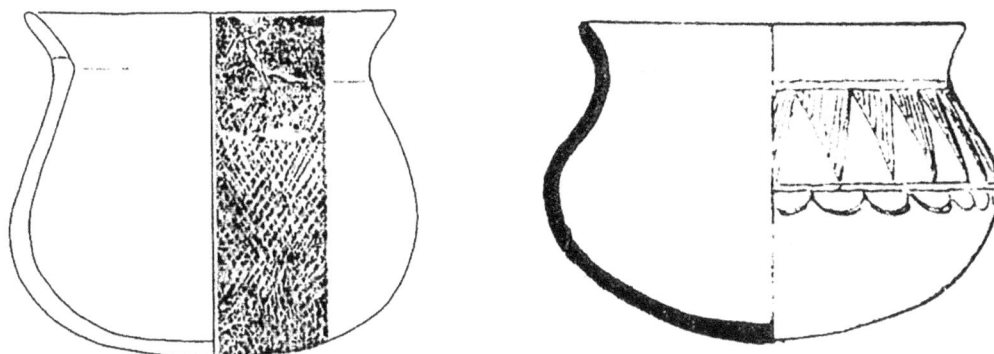

Figure 19.3 Sa Huynh pottery locally called '*noi*', found at the Sa Huynh and Thach Bich sites; (right) height: 11.0 cm; (left) height: 12.5 cm.

Source: (right) Parmentier 1925; (left) drawing by M. Yamagata.

The strong presence of *noi*, a Vietnamese term for a jar with a wide or constricted neck (Figure 19.3) can be illustrated by the following examples. From Phase I of the Go Ma Voi site, mentioned above, 86 (40 per cent) of the 215 pottery vessels are *noi*, whilst another 35 (16 per cent) pottery forms are shallow bowls with pedestals commonly known as *mam bong* or *bat bong* (Reinecke et al. 2002). Of the 125 vessels from four sites in Hoi An, 68 (54.4 per cent) were identified as *noi* and 30 (24.0 per cent) as *bat bong* (Tran et al. 2004). Likewise, at Con Rang in Hue, 354 funerary accessory pottery vessels were uncovered, 115 (32.5per cent) of which were *noi*, and 89 (25.1 per cent) are *binh*, jars with pedestals (V.L. Bui et al. 2008). Although these figures are open to influence by the criteria used to classify the pottery at each site, the modal category of Sa Huynh pottery is definitely *noi* (Ishii 2010; Yamagata 2013). Various decorations such as cord-marked impressions, impressions of a shell edge forming triangles, horizontal V or semi-circular patterns, incised triangular or rectangular designs with diagonal incised lines, paired incised lines interspersed with punctuations, and coloured bands bound with paired incised lines are commonly displayed on Sa Huynh *noi* pottery.

The pottery of Phase II, the final stage (first century BC to the first century AD) of the Sa Huynh culture in Quang Nam, shows differences in form and decoration. At the Binh Yen site H2 trench, 35 vessels were associated with seven jar burials: 21 were bowls and shallow bowls, six were small jars, and just six could be classified as *noi*. Cord-marked impressions predominate, and red and black colouring is applied to some vessels. Only two jars with foot stands bear simple incised triangles (C.H. Bui and Yamagata 2004; Yamagata 2006).

In characterising the pottery of the Sa Huynh culture, the modal category of *noi* should be emphasised, instead of regarding vessel forms that are more decorative and distinctive but fewer in number as representative of this culture.

Sa Huynh and Kalanay: Solheim's idea revised

Solheim's ponderings on the 'Sa Huynh-Kalanay Pottery Tradition' led his thinking towards a hypothesis of extensive maritime networks established by boat traders named the Nusantao Maritime Trading and Communication Networks (Solheim 1984–1985, 2006). This scenario includes four lobes of trade and communication covering a very broad area and timeframe. The Northern Lobe extended across Taiwan, Fujian, and coastal China northward to coastal Korea and the Japanese archipelago. The Eastern Lobe extended from the Moluccas in Eastern Indonesia, to the Bismarcks in Northwestern Melanesia, and across the Pacific to Easter Island.

The Western Lobe encompassed Malaysia and Western Indonesia, Sri Lanka, India and the far eastern coast of Africa, including Madagascar. The Central Lobe included eastern coastal areas of Vietnam, Southern China, and the Philippines. The Nusantao traders originated in Wallacea around 12,000 BP and developed a Pre-Austronesian language for trade communication. The network of the late Central Lobe then formed with the development of the Austronesian language, the traders' *lingua franca*, before 7000 BP.

In the scenario of Solheim's trading networks, the 'Sa Huynh-Kalanay Pottery Tradition' extended from eastern coastal Mainland Southeast Asia to insular Southeast Asia between approximately 2500 BP and 1000 BP. Solheim hypothesised that the origin and spread of the 'Sa Huynh-Kalanay Pottery Tradition' was through the agency of the Nusantao boat trading people, although not all of them made or used pottery of that tradition (Solheim 2002).

Based on his analysis of the pottery found in Kalanay Cave, which he excavated in 1951 and 1953, and of other collections in the Central Philippines, Solheim (1957, 1959b, 2002) proposed recognition of the 'Kalanay Pottery Complex' for a group of related pottery styles. In his comparison of the Kalanay Pottery Complex with the ceramic assemblage of the Sa Huynh site reported by Parmentier (1925), he concluded that a close similarity between the two ceramic traditions existed. Furthermore, he found a close cultural affiliation among local pottery complexes widely distributed throughout Island Southeast Asia (e.g. Niah Great Cave in Western Borneo and Gua Cha in Peninsular Malaysia). His observation of these pottery complexes led him to hypothesise that they were all part of a single pottery tradition that arrived at widespread locations through trading and movement of people (Solheim 1959c: 186). The concept of the Kalanay Pottery Complex thus developed into the notion of the 'Sa Huynh-Kalanay Pottery Tradition' made up of pottery complexes related to each other.

Solheim defined the following motifs as most specific in the Kalanay Pottery Complex (Solheim 2002):

1. Paired diagonals and borders.
2. Curvilinear scrolls and triangles.
3. Rectangular scrolls and triangles.
4. Emphasised punctuation field or dashes separated by incised lines.
5. Crenulations impressed with a shell edge.
6. Impressed or carved 'scallop' design.
7. Carved cutouts in ring stands.

More recent studies have shown that among these, decorations 2, 4, 5 and 7 are present on Sa Huynh pottery vessels, whilst the others are rarely seen or absent. In particular, decoration 6, which Solheim considers to be most diagnostic of the Kalanay Pottery Complex, is absent amongst Sa Huynh pottery. In addition, the Kalanay Pottery Complex lacks any cord-mark impressions that frequently appeared on Sa Huynh vessels.

The incised rectangular scrolls (motif 3) are occasionally seen on burial lids of the Sa Huynh culture, but in fact appear infrequently on funerary accessory pottery. Also, the nominal similarity between Sa Huynh and Kalanay pottery on their crenulated impressions made with a shell edge (motif 5) need not reflect true correspondence. These are very common on Sa Huynh but the actual shell-impressed decorations are different from those of the Kalanay Pottery Complex.

Thus, dissimilarities in pottery style and decoration show that Sa Huynh is not related to the Kalanay Pottery Complex. Instead, and importantly, there is remarkable similarity between Kalanay pottery and the pottery from another site called Hoa Diem in Central Vietnam that has a cultural assemblage that is not assigned to Sa Huynh.

Hoa Diem: Jar burials left by immigrants from the Philippines?

The Hoa Diem site is situated on the floodplain around Cam Ranh Bay, within the administrative district of Cam Ranh city, Khanh Hoa Province in Central Vietnam (Figure 19.1). The site is only about 400 m from the coastline. It was discovered during a reconnaissance survey by the Vietnam Institute of Archaeology in 1998, which then undertook excavations in 1999 and 2002 with the Khanh Hoa Provincial Museum (V.L. Bui et al. 2005).

What especially interested the author (MY) and her Vietnamese colleagues Bui Chi Hoang and Nguyen Kim Dung was the spherical type of burial jars used at Hoa Diem (Figure 19.4). These are distinct from cylindrical or egg-shaped burial jars commonly used within the Sa Huynh culture. Moreover, funerary accessory pottery vessels found at Hoa Diem differ significantly from those found with Sa Huynh jar burials, despite Hoa Diem's locality adjacent to the distribution area of the Sa Huynh culture. Most notable is the striking similarities of the pottery from Hoa Diem with the pottery at Kalanay Cave, Masbate Island in the Central Philippines, excavated by Solheim (1957, 1959a, 1959b) (Figure 19.5). Just as intriguingly, similar vessels are reported by Solheim (1964) to have been found on Ko Din Island near Ko Samui, Southern Thailand. Thus, Hoa Diem may be regarded as a potential site for convincing evidence supporting human movements across the South China Sea during the Iron Age.

Figure 19.4 A spherical burial jar uncovered from the site of Hoa Diem (Burial No. 07HDH1M6, max diameter: 55–59 cm; height: 42.6 cm).
Source: M. Yamagata.

Figure 19.5 Burial jars (left) and lid (right, a pedestal vessel laid upside down upon the jar) decorated with the impression of a shell edge uncovered from Hoa Diem (Burial No. 07HDH1M14, height of jar: 27.1 cm; height of lid: 23.5 cm).

Source: M. Yamagata.

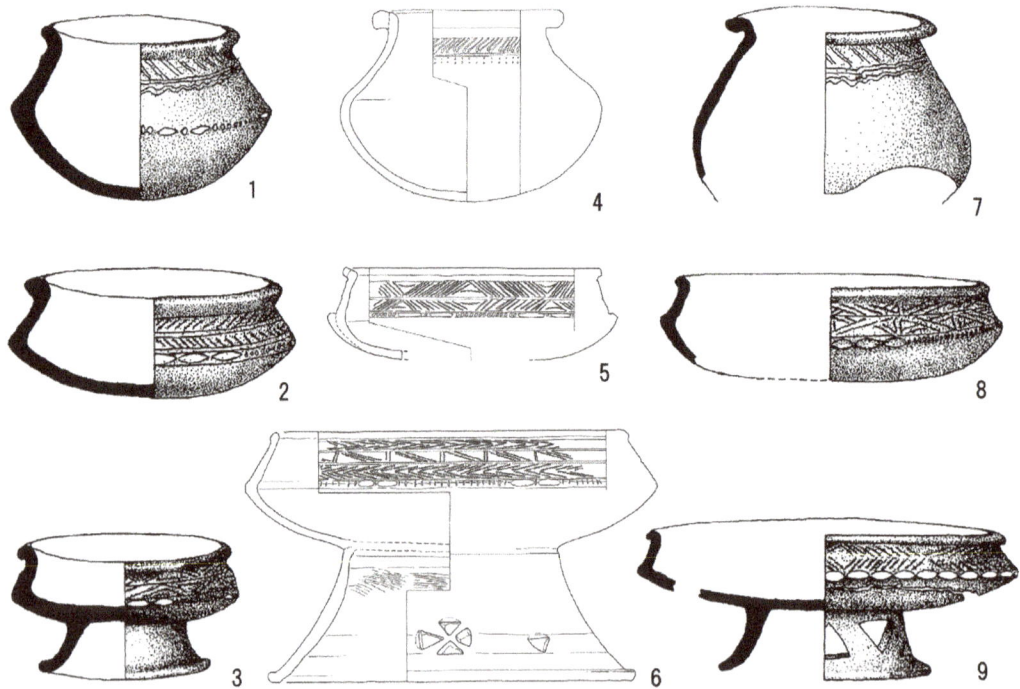

Figure 19.6 Pottery from Kalanay (7–9), Hoa Diem (4–6), Samui (1–3). Rim diameter: 4. 10.2 cm; 5. 15.0 cm; 6. 20.2 cm. Size unknown; 1–3, 7–9.

Sources: 1–3, 7–9 adapted from Solheim (1992), reproduced with the permission of White Lotus Press; 4–6 adapted from Yamagata et al. (2013), reproduced with the permission of Showa Women's University Institute of International Culture.

To undertake a more extensive investigation of Hoa Diem, especially regarding pottery and human remains, an international team of Vietnamese and Japanese archaeologists and physical anthropologists from the Southern Institute of Social Sciences, Vietnam Institute of Archaeology, Khanh Hoa Provincial Museum, and Japan conducted excavations in 2007 and 2010 (C.H. Bui et al. 2010; Yamagata et al. 2013). In 2007, a pit covering 48 m² produced 21 skeletons from 13 jar burials and two extended burials. In 2010, a further six individuals from five jar burials were recovered from a total 21 m² of excavation, and four more jar burials were identified in two test pits of a total of 15 m². All these excavation trenches were located within the area of the site known as Hoa Diem 1. Approximately 200 m to the southeast of Hoa Diem 1, two extended inhumations were found in a small test pit at Hoa Diem 2 (Yamagata et al. 2013). Besides this international project, in 2011 the National Museum of Vietnamese History conducted another excavation at Hoa Diem 1, covering an area of 51.5 m² that yielded another 26 jar burials (Le and Dinh 2013).

At Hoa Diem, most burial jars have spherical bodies (Figure 19.4). As well, one burial jar has an incised and impressed pattern on its body and rim, associated with a knobbed lid and painted patterns. Another two burial jars were decorated with impressions made with the edge of a seashell, and the pedestal vessels serve as lids that also bear the same decoration (Figure 19.5). The spherical jars are similar to those of Giong Ca Vo in Ho Chi Minh City, but other types of burial jars and lids have never been encountered before. They are completely different from those found at Sa Huynh culture sites in Central Vietnam. Many mortuary accessory pottery vessels found in these new excavations again show close affinities with the Kalanay Pottery Complex in Central Philippines (Figure 19.5). These vessels include:

1. Jars with incised parallel diagonals and borders. Some of them bear impressed 'scallop' designs at an angle around the body.
2. Shallow bowls with impressions of a shell edge. Most of them bear impressed 'scallop' designs at an angle around the body.
3. Shallow bowls with ring stand, and carved cutouts.

All of these are regarded as diagnostic characteristics of the Kalanay Pottery Complex (Figure 19.7, top and middle). Apart from these remains, a jar with eight projections like breasts and nipples is also notable at Hoa Diem (Figure 19.7, bottom). This is a type of pottery decoration that has never been discovered in Vietnam before. Interestingly, similar vessels with nipples were found on Siquijor Island in the Central Philippines (Solheim 2002: Plate 15).

Moreover, other kinds of grave goods such as beads and iron tools exhibit characteristics distinctive from those of the Sa Huynh culture. The absence of the most common earring type found in Sa Huynh burials, the lingling-o, from Hoa Diem also distinguishes the two burial traditions. Given these observations, the burial assemblage of Hoa Diem shows greater affinity with those of distant Kalanay than it does with neighbouring Sa Huynh.

A typological study of the Kalanay Pottery Complex by Tanaka (1987) divides the complex into two phases: earlier and later. The Hoa Diem complex is apparently affiliated with the later phase. Furthermore, most recent surveys done by a joint French/Thai team have discovered the Kalanay-type pottery sherds at several sites along the Isthmus of Kra in Peninsula Thailand (Favereau 2015).

Figure 19.7 Funerary accessory pottery vessels found at Hoa Diem (top: height 9.5 cm with rim diameter of 9.4 cm (outer); middle: height 4.7 cm with rim diameter of 12.5 cm; and bottom: height 15.6 cm with rim diameter of 15.1 cm).

Source: M. Yamagata.

Considering these material differences, two possible factors could explain the lack of cultural relationship between Hoa Diem and Sa Huynh: chronological separation; and cultural, social or perhaps ethnic differences between the two populations. Based on the comparative study of the material culture, the Hoa Diem cemetery with Kalanay-type pottery most likely dates from the second and third centuries AD. Thus, the authors consider temporal difference to be the most parsimonious explanation for variations in the material culture exhibited by Sa Huynh and Hoa Diem (Yamagata et al. 2013: 29–30), although the two explanations mentioned above may not be mutually exclusive. The Hoa Diem cemetery with Kalanay-type pottery was possibly in use shortly after the decline of Sa Huynh. It is then during the latter/end of Sa Huynh that a clear connection finally emerged between the Iron Age populations of the Central Philippines, Central Vietnam and Southern Thailand.

Origin of the Hoa Diem people: Bio-anthropological perspectives

From all the seasons of excavation, 49 human skeletons were recorded at Hoa Diem. Although they were poorly preserved, the bioanthropological study has indicated that most burials were primary inhumations (Figure 19.8). Multiple individuals in a jar usually consisted of a single adult and one or more infants. The adult was the primary interment, but the timing for the introduction, either with the adult of after, remains unclear.

Skeletal preservation, specific observations, and morphological data including cranial and dental measurements and nonmetric dental traits were presented in the excavation report (Matsumura and Nguyen 2013). Previous work cited in this report included preliminary comparative analyses in order to identify the craniometric affinities of the Hoa Diem populations using geographically broad population samples across Southeast/Northeast Asia and the Circum-Pacific regions. The initial study broadly showed affinities between the Hoa Diem population and some groups in Island Southeast Asia.

Here we present the results of a more substantial analysis using alternative methods applied to datasets that include newly recorded samples from the Southeast Asian region. The comparative archaeological samples are listed in Table 19.1.

Figure 19.9 presents the results from the neighbor-net split analysis (software provided by Huson and Bryant 2006) applied to distances of the Q-mode correlation coefficients based on 16 cranial measurements (Martin's method number: M1, M8, M9, M17, M43[1], M43c, M45, M46b, M46c, M48, M51, M52, M54, M55, M57, M57a). The network diagram resulting from neighbor-net split analysis branches into two major clusters at the top left and bottom right. These include: (1) East Asians and many Southeast Asians ranging from Late Neolithic to modern times; and (2) Australo-Melanesians and early Holocene Southeast Asians including the Hoabinhian and Early Neolithic series.

The jar burial assemblage with Kalanay-type pottery vessels of Hoa Diem 1 dates from the second to third century AD, corresponding with the period just after the decline of Sa Huynh culture. A C^{14} determination on a human tooth from a jar burial of Hoa Diem 1 produced a calibrated age (2α) of 1910–1898 cal. BP (2.2 per cent) and 1877–1757 cal. BP (93.2 per cent; IAAA-101437). Another C^{14} determination on a human tooth from an extended burial at Hoa Diem 2 produced a calibrated age (2α) of 2200–1951 cal. BP (95.4 per cent; IAAA-100714).

In the network tree depicted in Figure 19.9, Hoa Diem 1 (from the jar-burial group, Figure 19.8) was branched with the inhabitants of Taiwan (Bunun), Sumatra, and the Moluccas Islands, as well as other Southeast Asians including modern Cambodians, Laotians, Thais, Filipinos and

Southern Chinese. Hoa Diem 2 (one of the burials in extended position, see Figure 19.8), groups with Semang Negritos, and is relatively close to the second cluster consisting of the Australo-Melanesian and Hoabinhian samples.

Previous morphometric analyses (e.g. Matsumura and Oxenham 2014) demonstrate an apparent genetic discontinuity between pre- and post-Neolithic populations. Events occurring during the Neolithic were apparently pivotal in terms of the micro-evolutionary history of Southeast Asia. The network tree diagrams in those analyses exhibit close affinities between pre-Neolithic Hoabinhian and Australo-Melanesian samples on the one hand, and a northern source for contemporary Southeast Asians on the other. This suggests that pre-Neolithic foragers descended from the first occupants of Southeast Asia, sharing common ancestry with present-day Australian Aboriginal and Melanesian people.

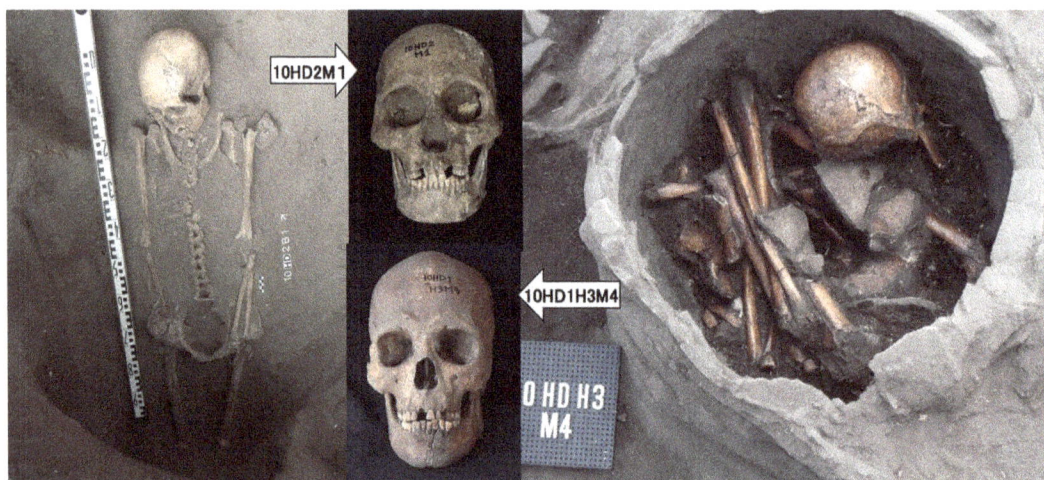

Figure 19.8 Extended burial and skull at Hoa Diem 2 (Burial No. 10HD2M1) and inhumation jar burial and skull at Hoa Diem 1 (Burial No. 10HD1H3M4).

Source: H. Matsumura.

Regarding the origin of Neolithic to post-Neolithic populations in Southeast Asia, it was widely believed they arose through a greater or lesser degree of genetic exchange between the early indigenous populations and immigrants from East Asia. Demographic transition leading to such genetic exchange was hypothetically ascribed to large-scale integration with a population-language-agriculture dispersal package originating from East Asia (e.g. Bellwood, 1997, 2005; Glover and Higham 1996; Higham 1998, 2002), ultimately contributing to the post Neolithic Southeast Asian phenotype. In terms of the Austronesian-language family, as mentioned above, linguistic and archaeological considerations suggest that Taiwan was the ultimate source of these linguistic and population dispersals (Bellwood, 1997, 2005). The Taiwan émigrés intermixed with the indigenous Australo-Melanesian stock as they diffused through Southeast Asia. The human skeleton from the Hoa Diem 2 site, which was previously buried in an extended position, may still preserve genetic traits of the early indigenous population, which perhaps implies an origin from somewhere in Island Southeast Asia. Be that as it may, the closer affinity of later jar-burial people (Hoa Diem 1) to insular Southeast Asian groups suggests an Iron Age colonisation from the Philippines across the South China Sea.

Table 19.1 Comparative population samples prehistoric of prehistoric date.

Sample	Locality	Period	Remarks
★ Pre-Neolithic Samples			
Liujinag	China	Late Pleistocene	Individual, Site in Guangxi Prov.
Lang Gao	Vietnam	Hoabinhian	Averages of two individuals (nos 17 and 19), Site in Hoa Binh Prov., N Vietnam (Cuong 2007)
Lang Bon	Vietnam	Hoabinhian (*ca.* 7000 BP)	Individual, Site in Thanh Hoa Prov., N Vietnam (Cuong 2007)
Mai Da Nuoc	Vietnam	Hoabinhian (*ca.* 8000 BP)	Individual, in Thanh Hoa Prov., N Vietnam (Cuong 1986, 2007)
Hoabinhian (average)	Vietnam	Hoabinhian (*ca.* 11000–8000 BP)	6 specimens including fragmental remains from above 4 sites and 1 from Mai Da Dieu site in Thanh Hoa Prov. (Cuong 2007)
Bac Son	Vietnam	Epi-Hoabinhian (*ca.* 8000–7000 BP)	Sites of Pho Binh Gia, Cua Git, Lang Cuom, and Dong Thuoc in N Vietnam (Mansuy and Colani 1925)
Con Co Ngua	Vietnam	Da But Culture (*ca.* 6000 BP)	Site in Than Hoa Prov., N Vietnam
Gua Cha	Malaysia	Hoabinhian (*ca.* 8000–6000 BP)	Individual Sample No. H12, Site in Kelantan Prov. (Sieveking 1954)
Tam Hang	Laos	Early Holocene	Hua Pan Province, N Laos (Mansuy and Colani 1925; Huard and. Saurin 1938; Demeter et al. 2009)
Zengpiyan	China	Mesolithic (*ca.* 8000 BP)	Site in Guangxi Prov. (IACAS et al. 2003)
◆ Neolithic Samples			
Man Bac	Vietnam	Late Neolithic (*ca.* 3800–3500 BP)	Site in Ninh Binh Prov., N Vietnam (Oxenham et al. 2011)
An Son	Vietnam	Late Neolithic (*ca.* 3800 BP)	Site in Long An Prov., S Vietnam (Nishimura and Dung 2002; Cuong 2006; Bellwood et al. 2013)
Ban Chiang	Thailand	Neolithic-Bronze Age (*ca.* 3500–1800 BP)	Site in Udon Thani Prov. (Gorman and Charoenwongsa 1976; Pietrusewsky and Douglas 2002)
Non Nok Tha	Thailand	Neolithic-Bronze Age (*ca.* 3500 3000 BP)	Site in Khok Kaen Prov. (Bayard 1971)
Weidun	China	Neolithic (*ca.* 7000–5000 BP, Majiabang Culture)	Sites in Jiangsu Prov. Central China (Nakahashi and Li 2002)
Baikal	Russia	Neolithic (*ca.* 8000–4000 BP)	Lake Baikal (Debets 1951)
Jomon	Japan	Neolithic (*ca.* 5000–2300 BP)	Over almost the entire Japanese archipelago
● Bronze–Iron Age Samples			
Anyang	China	Yin (Shan) Period (*ca.* 3500–3027 BP)	Site in Henan Prov. Central China (IHIA and CASS 1982)
Giong Ca Vo	Vietnam	Iron Age (*ca.* 2300–2000 BP)	Site in Ho Chi Minh (Dang and Vu 1997)
Go O Chua	Vietnam	Iron Age (*ca.* 2300–2000 BP)	Site in Long An Prov., S Vietnam (Francken and Wahl 2010; Cuong in press)
Hoa Diem	Vietnam	Iron Age (Hoa Diem 2=*ca.* 150 BP; Hoa Diem 1 =*ca.* 2000–1700 BP)	Site of Hoa Diem in Khanh Hoa Prov., Central Vietnam (Yamagata et al. 2013)
Dong Son	Vietnam	Dong Son Period (*ca.* 3000–1700 BP)	Sites of Dong Son Culture in N Vietnam (Cuong 1996)
Phum Snay	Cambodia	Iron Age (*ca.* 2350–1800 BP)	Site in Preah Neat Orey District, W Cambodia
Yayoi	Japan	Yayoi Period (*ca.* 2800–1700 BP)	Sites of Doigahama, Nakanohama, Kanenokuma and others in Northern Kyushu and Yamaguchi Districts, W Japan

Source: H. Matsumura.

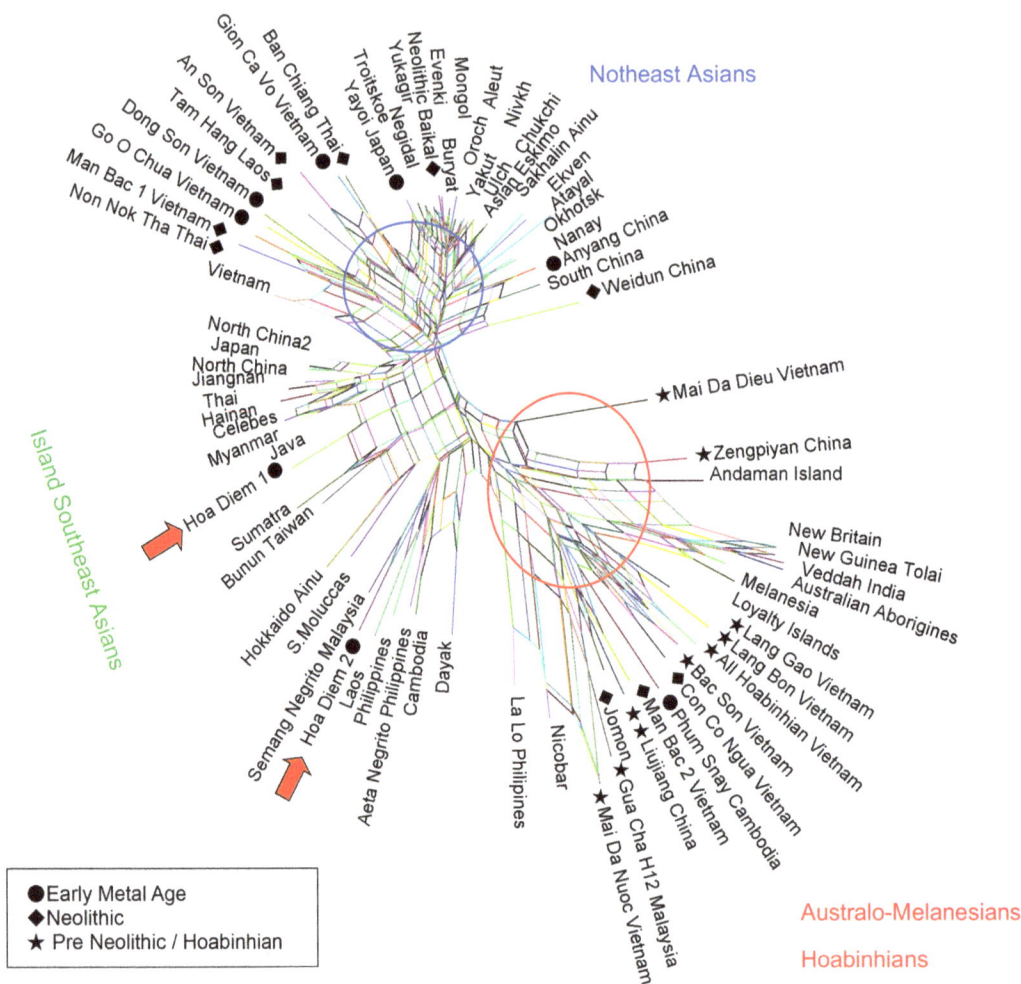

Figure 19.9 Neighbor-net tree based on 16 craniometric data sets (symbols: see Table 19.1).

Source: H. Matsumura.

Conclusions

This paper reassessed the definition of the 'Sa Huynh' culture that is currently unclear due to the considerable variation displayed in cultural assemblages by locality. It has refined the definition of what should be considered as part of the 'Sa Huynh' cultural repertoire in response to the continuing ambiguity in the spatial, temporal and material culture parameters of the tradition. The most specific and typical characteristic of the Sa Huynh culture is its mortuary practice using cylindrical or egg-shaped burial jars associated with hat-shaped lids. If adopted, this basic definition of the special distribution of Sa Huynh should be restricted to the geographic region across Central Vietnam between Hue City in the north and Nha Trang City in the south. The Sa Huynh culture emerged in the fourth or third century BC and declined at the end of the first century AD. Tra Kieu, the ancient capital of Linyi (Champa) subsequently emerged in the second century AD.

Solheim proposed a 'Sa Huynh-Kalanay Pottery Tradition' in his extensive hypothesis of the Nusantao Maritime Trade and Communication Networks. However, our study demonstrates substantial dissimilarity between the Sa Huynh and Kalanay pottery assemblages. On the other hand, our excavations of the Hoa Diem site in Khanh Hoa Province, Central Vietnam, unearthed large numbers of burial jars and funeral pottery vessels that are strikingly similar to pottery from Kalanay in the Philippines and Samui Island in Thailand – all of which is quite different from Sa Huynh pottery. The date of jar burials with Kalanay type pottery at Hoa Diem is estimated to be in the second and third centuries AD (Iron Age) and thus postdates the Sa Huynh culture. Bio-anthropological analysis using craniometric data also suggests a close affinity of the jar-burial people at Hoa Diem to insular Southeast Asians, including populations from Taiwan, Sumatra, Java and the Philippines. This finding confirms the view that the Hoa Diem site marks a colonisation of Austronesian speakers, who migrated from somewhere in ISEA across the South China Sea and settled in Central Vietnam during the Iron Age.

Acknowledgements

In this paper Vietnamese diacritics are omitted from the main text, but included in the references.

We express our sincere gratitude toward Bui Chi Hoang from the Southern Institute of Social Sciences in Vietnam; Nguyen Kim Dung and Nguyen Lan Cuong from the Vietnam Institute of Archaeology; Ian C. Glover from the Institute of Archaeology, University College London; and the staff at the Quang Nam Provincial Museum and Khanh Hoa Provincial Museum for their collaborations and providing great support to our research project in Vietnam. Acknowledgements for comparative population samples used in anthropological analyses are presented elsewhere (Matsumura and Oxenham 2014).

This study was supported in part by Japanese Society for the Promotion of Science (JSPS) KAKENHI Grant no. 18520593, no. 20520666 and no. 23247040.

References

Bayard, D.T. 1971. *Non Nok Tha: The 1968 Excavation, procedure, stratigraphy, and summary of the evidence*. University of Otago Studies in Prehistoric Anthropology, vol. 4. Dunedin: University of Otago.

Bellwood, P. 1997. *Prehistory of the Indo-Malaysian Archipelago*. 2nd edition. Honolulu: University of Hawaii Press.

——. 2004. The origins and dispersals of agricultural communities in Southeast Asia. In I. Glover and P. Bellwood (eds), *Southeast Asia from Prehistory to History*, pp. 21–40. Oxford and New York: RoutledgeCurzon.

——. 2005. *First Farmers: The Origins of Agricultural Societies*. Malden, Oxford and Victoria: Blackwell.

Bellwood, P. and I. Glover. 2004. Southeast Asia: Foundations for an archaeological history. In I. Glover and P. Bellwood (eds), *Southeast Asia from prehistory to history*, pp. 4–20. Oxford and New York: RoutledgeCurzon.

Bellwood, P. and E. Dizon. 2005. The Batanes archaeological project and the 'Out of Taiwan' hypothesis for Austronesian dispersal. *Journal of Austronesian Studies* 1(1): 1–33.

——. 2008. Austronesian cultural origins: Out of Taiwan, via Batanes Islands, and onwards to Western Polynesia. In A. Sanchez-Mazas, R. Blench, M. Ross, I. Peiros and M. Lin (eds), *Past Human Migrations in East Asia*, pp. 23–39. Oxford and New York: RoutledgeCurzon.

——. 2013. *4000 Years of Migration and Cultural Exchange: The Archaeology of the Batanes Islands, Northern Philippines*. Terra Australis 40. Canberra: ANU Press.

Blust, R. 1984–1985. The Austronesian homeland: A linguistic perspective. *Asian Perspectives* 26: 45–67.

———. 1995. The prehistory of the Austronesian-speaking peoples: A view from language. *Journal of World Prehistory* 9: 453–510. doi.org/10.1007/BF02221119.

———. 1996. Beyond the Austronesian homeland: The Austric hypothesis and its implications for archaeology. In W. Goodenough (ed.), *Prehistoric Settlement of the Pacific,* pp. 117–140. Philadelphia: American Philosophical Society.

Bronk Ramsey, C. 2014. Oxcal 4.2 Manual. c14.arch.ox.ac.uk/oxcal.html.

Buì C.H. 2009. Không gian văn hoá Sa Huỳnh: nhận thức từ di chỉ Hoa Diêm Khánh Hoà (Space of Sa Huynh culture: Awareness from Hoa Diem site, Khanh Hoa). *Khảo Cổ Học* (Archaeology) (5): 67–75.

Buì C.H. and M. Yamagata. 2004. Khu di tích Bình Yên và văn hoá Sa Huỳnh ở Quảng Nam (The Binh Yen site complex and Sa Huynh culture in Quang Nam), In Trung Tâm Nghiên Cứu Khảo Cổ Học, Viện Khoa Học Xã Hội tại Thành Phố Hồ Chí Minh (Center for Archaeology, Institute of Social Sciences in Ho Chi Minh City) (ed.), *Một số vấn đề khảo cổ học ở miền nam Việt Nam* (Some Archaeological Achievements in Southern Vietnam), pp. 83–121. Ha Noi: Nhà Xuất Bản Khoa Học Xã Hội (Social Sciences Publishing House).

Bùi C.H., M. Yamagata, K.D. Nguyen. 2010. Excavations of Hoa Diem, 2007 and 2010 seasons (with Vietnamese translation: Khai Quật Hòa Diêm năm 2007 và năm 2010). In Sở Văn Hóa, Thể Thao và Du Lịch Khánh Hòa (Khanh Hoa Culture, Sports and Tourism Office) (ed.), *Kỷ Yếu Hội Thảo Khoa Học Khảo Cổ Học Khánh Hòa* (Proceedings of Scientific Forum on Archaeology of Khanh Hoa), pp. 90–104. Nha Trang.

Bùi, V.L. 2005. Mộ táng Lung Leng (Lung Leng burials). *Khảo Cổ Học* (Archaeology) (5): 15–26.

Bùi, V.L, Đ.C. Nguyen, C.B. Nguyen and T. Nguyen. 2005. *Báo cáo khai quật di tích Hòa Diêm* (Excavation Report of the Hoa Diem Site). Hà Nội: Tư liệu Thư viện, Viện Khảo Cổ Học (Document of the Library, Institute of Archaeology).

Bùi, V.L., N.Q. Nguyen, and Đ.C. Nguyen. 2008. Di tích Cồn Ràng, Thừa Thiên Huế (The Con Rang site in Thua Thien Hue Province). *Khảo Cổ Học* (Archaeology) (5): 61–87.

Chử, V.T. and Đào L.C. 1978. Khai quật di tích Long Thạnh (Excavation of the Long Thanh site). In Viện Khoa Học Xã Hội tại Thành Phố Hồ Chí Minh (Institute of Social Sciences in Ho Chi Minh City) (ed.), *Những Phát Hiện Khảo Cổ Học ở Miền Nam* (Some Archaeological Discoveries in Southern Vietnam), pp. 196–224. Ho Chi Minh City: Viện Khoa Học Xã Hội tại Thành Phố Hồ Chí Minh (Institute of Social Sciences in Ho Chi Minh City).

Colani, M. 1937. Necropole de Sa Huỳnh. *Cahiers de l'École Française d'Extrême-Orient* 13: 8–12.

Cuong, N.L. 1986. Two early Hoabinhian crania from Thanh Hoa province, Vietnam. *Zeitschrift für Morphologie und Anthropologie* 77: 11–17.

———. 2006. About the ancient human bones at An Son (Long An) through the third excavation. *Khao Co Hoc* (Archaeology) (6): 39–51 (in Vietnamese with English title and summary).

———. 2007. Paleoanthropology in Vietnam. *Khao Co Hoc* (Archaeology) (2): 23–41.

———. in press. Địa điểm Gò Ô Chùa (Long An). In *Các Nhóm Loại Hình Nhân Chủng Ở Việt Nam Và Vấn Đề Nguồn Gốc Người Việt.* Đề Tài Khoa Học Cấp Bộ, pp. 424–467.

Đặng, V.T and Q.H. Vũ. 1997. Excavation of Giong Ca Vo site (Can Gio District, Ho Chi Minh City). *Journal of Southeast Asian Archaeology* 17: 30–44.

Đặng, V.T., Q.H. Vũ, T.H. Nguyễn, T.P. Ngô, K.D. Nguyen and L.C. Nguyen. 1998. *Khảo cổ học tiền sử và sơ sử Thành Phố Hồ Chí Minh* (Prehistoric and protohistoric archaeology of Ho Chi Minh city). Ho Chi Minh City: Nhà Xuất Bản Trẻ (The Youth Publishing House).

Debets G.F. 1951. Anthropological studies in the Kamchatka region. *Trudy Institute of Ethnography*, n.s. 17: 1–263 (in Russian).

Demeter, F.T., E. Sayavongkhamdy, Patole-Edoumba, A.S. Coupey, A.M. Bacon, J. DeVos, C. Tougard, B. Bouasisengpaseuth, P. Sichanthongtip and P. Duringer. 2009. Tam Hang rockshelter: Preliminary study of a prehistoric site in Northern Laos. *Asian Perspectives* 48: 291–308. doi.org/10.1353/asi.2009.0000.

Đình, B.H. 2002. Động Cườm – Di tích văn hoá Sa Huỳnh ở Bình Định (Dong Cuom – a site of Sa Huynh culture in Binh Dinh). *Khảo Cổ Học* (Archaeology) (2): 57–74.

Đoàn, N.K. 2002. Di tích Xóm Ốc (Cù Lao Ré – Quảng Ngãi) và di tích Bãi Ông (Cú Lao Chàm – Quảng Nam): Tư liệu và nhận thức (Xom Oc site at Cu Lao Re and Bai Ong site at Cu Lao Cham: data and perception). *Khảo Cổ Học* (Archaeology) (2): 75–100.

Đoàn, N.K. 2012. Phát hiện mới một số di tích văn hoá Sa Huỳnh tại tỉnh Quảng Ngãi (New discoveries of some Sa Huynh culture sites in Quang Ngai Province). *Những Phát Hiện Mới Về Khảo Cổ Học năm 2011* (New Discoveries of Archaeology in 2011): 278–280.

Favereau, A. 2015. *Interactions et modalités des échanges en Mer de Chine méridionale (500 avant notre ère – 200 de notre ère) : approche technologique des assemblages céramiques.* PhD thesis, Muséum National d'Histoire Naturelle, Paris, France.

Fontaine, H. 1972. Nouveau champ de jarres dans la province de Long Khanh. *Bulletin de la Société des Études Indo-Chinoises* 47(3): 398–467.

Fontaine, H. and T.T. Hoang. 1975. Nouvelle note sur le champ de jarres funéraires de Phu Hoa, avec une remarque sur la crémation au Viet Nam. *Bulletin de la Société des Études Indo-chinoises* 50(1): 7–73.

Francken, M. and J. Wahl. 2010. Reflections of a hard life – Burials from Go O Chua (Vietnam). In C. Buhl, F. Engel, L. Hartung, M. Kästner, A. Rüdell and C. W. Freiburg (eds), *Proceedings of the fourth Meeting of Junior Scientists in Anthropology*, pp. 16–23. Freiburg: University of Freiburg.

Gorman, C.F. and P. Charoenwongsa. 1976. Ban Chiang: A mosaic of impressions from the first two years. *Expedition* 18: 14–26.

Glover, I. and C.F.W. Higham. 1996. New evidence for early rice cultivation in South, Southeast and East Asia. In D.R. Harris (ed.), *The Origins and Spread of Agriculture and Pastoralism in Eurasia*, pp. 413–441. London: UCL Press.

Hà V.T. 1983. Suy nghĩ về Sa Huỳnh và từ Sa Huỳnh (Thinking about the Sa Huymh culture). Thông Báo Khoa Học Bảo Tàng Lịch Sử Việt Nam (Scientific Report, Vietnam National Museum of History) (1): 45–50.

——. 1984–1985. Prehistoric pottery in Vietnam and its relationships with Southeast Asia. *Asian Perspectives* 26(1): 135–146.

—— (ed.). 1999. *Khảo Cổ Học Việt Nam Tập II Thời Đại Kim Khí Việt Nam* (Vietnamese Archaeology vol. II. Metal Age of Vietnam). Hà Nội: Nhà Xuất Bản Khoa Học Xã Hội (Social Sciences Publishing House).

Higham, C.F.W. 1998. Archaeology, linguistics and the expansion of the East and Southeast Asian Neolithic. In R. Blench, and M. Spriggs (eds), *Archaeology and Language* II: *Archaeological Data and Linguistic Hypotheses*, pp. 103–114. London: Routledge. doi.org/10.4324/9780203202913_chapter_3.

——. 2002. *Early Cultures of Mainland Southeast Asia*. Bangkok: River Books.

Hoàng, T.Q. 2010. Đồ gốm văn hóa Sa Huỳnh (Pottery of the Sa Huynh culture). *Khảo Cổ Học* (Archaeology) (1): 57–73.

Huard, P. and E. Saurin. 1938. *État Actuel de la Craniologie Indochinoise*. Bulletin du Service Géologique de l'Indochine XXV (in French).

Huson, D.H. and D. Bryant. 2006. Application of phylogenetic networks in evolutionary studies. *Molecular Biology and Evolution* 23: 254–267. doi.org/10.1093/molbev/msj030.

IHIA (Institute of History and Institute of Archaeology) and CASS (Chinese Academy of Social Science) (eds). 1982. *Contributions to the Study on Human Skulls from the Shang Sites at Anyang*. Beijing: Cultural Relics Publishing House (in Chinese with English summary).

Institute of Archaeology, Chinese Academy of Social Science (IACAS), the Archaeological Team of the Guangxi Zhuang Municipality (ATGZM), the Zengpiyan Museum (ZM) and the Archeological Team of Guilin City (ATGC). 2003. *Zengpiyan – a Prehistoric Site in Guilin*. Archeological Monograph Series Type D No. 69. Beijing: Cultural Relics Publishing House (in Chinese with English title and abstract).

Ishii, A. 2010. Classification of the pottery of the Sa Huynh culture found in Quang Nam province, Central Vietnam: Towards new perspectives. *Sokou* 28: 1–20 (in Japanese).

Janse, O.R.T. 1941. An archaeological expedition to Indo-China and the Philippines. *Harvard Journal of Asiatic Studies* 6(2): 247–267.

Lâm, M.D. 1998. The Sa Huynh Culture in Hoi An. *Southeast Asian Archaeology 1996 Proceedings of the 6th International Conference of the European Association of Southeast Asian Archaeologists*, pp. 13–25. Hull: Centre for South-East Asian Studies.

——. 2009. Regional and inter-regional interactions in the context of Sa Huynh culture: with regards to the Thu Bon Valley in Quangnam province, Vietnam. *Bulletin of the Indo-Pacific Prehistory Association* 29: 68–75.

——. 2011. Central Vietnam during the period from 500 BCE to CE 500. In P.-Y. Manguin, A. Mani, and G. Wade (eds), *Early Interactions between South and Southeast Asia*, pp. 3–15. Singapore: Institute of Southeast Asian Studies.

Lâm, M.D., C. Nguyen and A.T. Hoàng. 2001. Khai quật Gò Dừa năm 1999 (Excavation at Go Dua in 1999). *Khảo Cổ Học* (Archaeology) (1): 68–80.

Lê, V.C., and V.M. Đinh. 2013. Khai quật Hòa Diêm năm 2011 (Excavation of Hoa Diem, 2011). *Thông Báo Khoa Học, Bảo Tàng Lịch Sử Quốc Gia Việt Nam* (Scientific Report, Vietnam National Museum of History): 18–32.

Malleret, L. 1959. Indochina. *Asian Perspectives* 3(1–2): 113–120.

Mansuy, H. and M. Colani. 1925. Contribution à l'étudede la préhistoire de l'Indochine VII. Néolithique inférieur (Bacsonien) et Néolithique supérieur dans le Haut-Tonkin. *Bulletin du Service Géologique de l'Indochine* 12: 1–45.

Matsumura, H. and M.J. Hudson. 2005. Dental perspectives on the population history of Southeast Asia. *American Journal of Physical Anthropology* 127: 182–209. doi.org/10.1002/ajpa.20067.

Matsumura, H. and L.C. Nguyen. 2013. Human skeletal remains from the Hoa Diem site. In M. Yamagata, C.H. Bùi and K.D. Nguyễn (eds), *The Excavation of Hoa Diem in Central Vietnam.* Bulletin 17. Tokyo: Showa Women's University Institute of International Culture.

Matsumura, H. and M.F. Oxenham. 2013. Population Dispersal from East Asia into Southeast Asia. In K. Pechenkina and M.F. Oxenham (eds), *Bioarchaeological Perspectives on Migration and Health in Ancient East Asia,* pp. 179–210. Florida: University of Florida Press. doi.org/10.5744/florida/9780813044279.003.0008.

——. 2014. Demographic transitions and migration in prehistoric East/Southeast Asia: through the lens of nonmetric dental traits. *American Journal of Physical Anthropology* 155: 45–65. doi.org/10.1002/ajpa.22537.

——. 2015. Eastern Asia and Japan: human biology. In P. Bellwood (ed.), *The Global Prehistory of Human Migration,* pp. 217–223 New York: Wiley-Liss.

Matsumura, H., M.F. Oxenham and L.C. Nguyen. 2015. Hoabinhian: key population with which to debate the peopling Southeast Asia. In Y. Kaifu, M. Izuho, T. Goebel, H. Sato and A. Ono (eds), *Emergence and Diversity of Modern Human Behavior in Palaeolithic Asia,* pp. 117–132. Texas: Texas A&M University Press.

Matsumura, H., M.F. Oxenham, K.T. Nguyen, L.C. Nguyen and K.D. Nguyen. 2011. The population history of mainland Southeast Asia: two layer model in the context of Northern Vietnam. In N. Enfield (ed.), *Dynamics of Human Diversity: the Case of Mainland Southeast Asia,* pp. 153–178. Canberra: Pacific Linguistics.

Nakahashi, T. and M. Li (eds). 2002. *Ancient People in the Jiangnan Region, China.* Fukuoka: Kyushu University Press.

Nishimura, M. and K.D. Nguyen 2002. Excavation of An Sơn: A Neolithic mound site in the middle reach of the Vàm Cỏ Đông river, Southern Vietnam. *Bulletin of the Indo-Pacific Prehistory Association* 22: 101–109.

Ngô, S.H. 1980. Bình Châu (Nghĩa Bình) – dạng di tích mới biết về thời đại đồng ven biển miền Trung (Binh Chau, Nghia Binh Province: a newly researched Bronze Age site located in the coastal area of Central Vietnam). *Khảo Cổ Học* (Archaeology) (1): 68–74.

Nguyen, C.B., S. Trịnh, V.C. Quang, Q.H. Vũ, V.H. Phạm and N.T. Phong. 1993. *Văn Hóa Xòm Cồn với tiền sử và sơ sử Khánh Hòa* (The Xom Con culture, with prehistory and protohistory of Khanh Hoa). Viện Bảo Tàng Lịch Sử Việt Nam – Sở Văn Hóa Thông Tin Kháng Hòa (Vietnam National Museum of History – Khanh Hoa Culture and Information Office), Nha Trang.

Nguyen, C.T., V.A. Trần, Đ.M. Nguyen and A. Trần (eds). 2004. *Văn Hóa Sa Huỳnh ở Hội An* (The Sa Huynh culture in Hoi An). Hội An: Ủy Ban Nhân Dân Thị Xã Hội An, Trung Tâm Quản Lý Di Tích Hội An (People's Committee of Hoi An, Hoi An Center for Heritage Management).

Nguyen, K.D. 2005; Di chỉ Gò Cấm và con đường tiếp biến văn hoá sau Sa Huỳnh khu vực Trà Kiệu (Go Cam site and post-Sa Huynh acculturation at Tra Kieu area). *Khảo Cổ Học* (Archaeology) (6): 35–65.

Nguyen, K.S. 2005. Di chỉ Lung Leng nhạn thức bước đầu (Lung Leng site, initial perception). *Khảo Cổ Học* (Archaeology) (5): 3–14.

——. 2010. Văn Hóa Sa Huỳnh – Văn Hóa Lung Leng những mối liên hệ (Sa Hunh and Lung Leng Cultures – relationships). *Khảo Cổ Học* (Archaeology) (5): 64–78.

Oxenham, M.F., H. Matsumura and K.D. Nguyen (eds). 2011. *Man Bac: The Excavation of a Late Neolithic Site in Northern Vietnam.* Terra Australis 33. Canberra: ANU E Press.

Parmentier, H. 1925. Dépots de jarres à Sa-Huynh (Quang-ngai, Annam). *Bulletin de l'Ecole Française d'Extrême Orient* 23: 325–343.

Pham, T.N. 2000. Recent discovery and excavation of a Sa Huynh culture sites on Ly Son Island, Central Vietnam. *Bulletin of the Indo-Pacific Prehistory Association* 19: 61–64.

——. 2014. Di tích mộ chum Động Cườm (Bình Định) – Tư liệu và nhận thức qua cuộc khai quật lần thứ 2 (The jar burial site of Dong Cuom – documents and new insights from the second excavation). *Thông Báo Khoa Học Bảo Tàng Lịch Sử Việt Nam* (Scientific Report, Vietnam National Museum of History) 2014(2): 59–77.

Pietrusewsky, M. and M.T. Douglas. 2002. *Ban Chiang, A Prehistoric Village Site in Northeast Thailand* I: *The Human Skeletal Remains.* Philadelphia: University of Pennsylvania, Museum of Archaeology and Anthropology.

Reinecke, A., C. Nguyen, and T.M.D. Lam. 2002. *Neue Entdeckungen zur Sa-Huynh-Kulter (Nhung phat hien moi ve van hoa Sa Huynh.).* Köln: Linden Soft.

Saurin, E. 1973. La champs de jarres de Hang Gon, près Xuan Loc. *Bulletin de l'Ecole française d'Extrême Orient* 60: 329–358. doi.org/10.3406/befeo.1973.5148.

Sieveking, G.G. 1954. Excavations at Gua Cha, Kelantan, Part 1. *Federation Museums Journal* 1: 75–143.

Sở Văn Hóa Thông Tin Quảng Nam – Đà Nẵng (Culture and Information Office of Quang Nam – Da Nang Province). 1985. *Những di tích thời tiền sử và sơ sử Quảng Nam – Đà Nẵng* (Prehistric and Protohistoric sites in Quang Nam – Da Nang). Quảng Nam – Đà Nẵng.

Solheim, W. 1957. The Kalanay Pottery Complex in the Philippines. *Artibus Asiae* vol. XX, 4: 279–288.

——. 1959a. Introduction to Sa-huỳnh. *Asian Perspectives* 3(1–2): 98–108.

——. 1959b. Further notes on the Kalanay Pottery Complex in the Philippines. *Asian Perspectives* 3(1–2): 157–165.

——. 1959c. Sa Huỳnh related pottery in Southeast Asia. *Asian Perspectives* 3(1–2): 177–188.

——. 1964. Further relationships of the Sa-Huỳnh-Kalanay Pottery Tradition. *Asian Perspectives* 8(1): 196–211.

——. 1967. The Sa-huynh-Kalanay Pottery Tradition: past and future research. In M.D. Zamora (ed.), *Studies in Philippine Anthropology,* pp. 151–174. Quezon City: Alemar-Phoenix Publishing House.

——. 1984–1985. The Nusantao hypothesis: the origins and spread of Austronesian speakers. *Asian Perspectives* 26(1): 77–88.

——. 1992. Nusantao traders beyond Southeast Asia. In I. Glover, P. Suchitta and J. Villiers (eds), *Early Metallurgy, Trade and Urban Centers in Thailand and Southeast Asia,* pp. 199–225. Bangkok: White Lotus.

——. 2002. (1964) *Archaeology of Central Philippines.* Revised edition. Quezon City: University of the Philippines.

——. 2006. *Archaeology and Culture in Southeast Asia: Unravelling the Nusantao.* Quezon City: University or the Philippines Press.

Suzuki, T. 2011. Typological study of a burial jar in Central Vietnam. *Bulletin of the Graduated Division of Letters, Arts and Sciences of Waseda University* 57-IV: 97–115 (in Japanese).

Tanaka, K. 1987. Rethinking the pottery found in Kalanay Cave, the Philippines: with special reference to the 'sloping-S' incised pattern. *Jōchi Shigaku* (Sophia Historical Studies) 32: 141–143 (in Japanese).

Trần, A., V.A Trần, and C.T. Nguyen. 2004. Đồ gốm trong các di tích văn hóa Sa Huỳnh ở Hội An (Pottery of the Sa Huynh cultural sites in Hoi An). In C.T. Nguyen, V.A. Trần, Đ.M. Nguyen and A. Trần (eds), *Văn Hóa Sa Huỳnh ở Hội An* (Sa Huynh Culture in Hoi An), pp. 112–127. Hội An: Ủy Ban Nhân Dân Thị Xã Hội An, Trung Tâm Quản Lý Di Tích Hội An (People's Committee of Hoi An, Hoi An Center for Heritage Management).

Vũ C.Q. 1991. *Văn Hoá Sa Huỳnh* (The Sa Huynh Culture). Hà Nội: Nhà Xuất Bản Văn Hoá Dân Tộc (National Culture Publishing House).

Yamagata, M. 2006. Inland Sa Huynh culture along the Thu Bon River Valley in Central Vietnam. In E. Bacus, I. Glover and V. Piggot (eds), *Uncovering Southeast Asia's Past,* pp. 168–183. Singapore: NUS Press.

——. 2007a. Origin of jar burials in Vietnam: a preliminary view. *Bulletin of the Graduate Division of Letters, Arts and Sciences of Waseda University* 52-IV: 97–115 (in Japanese).

——. 2007b. The early history of Lin-i viewed from archaeology. *Acta Asiatica* 92: 1–30.

——. 2009. Sa Huynh culture and the human migration hypothesis in Southeast Asia. In T. Shinkawa, and R. Takahashi (eds), *Higashi Ajia no Rekishi, Minzoku, Kōko* (History, Ethnology and Archaeology in Eastern Asia), pp. 320–354. Tokyo: Yuzankaku Shuppan (in Japanese).

——. 2010. Reconsidering the Sa Huynh – Kalanay Pottery Tradition. In K. Imamura (ed.), *Nankai wo Meguru Kōkogaku* (Archaeology around the South Seas), pp. 95–129. Tokyo: Dōseisha (in Japanese).

——. 2011. Tra Kieu during the second and third centuries CE: the formation of Linyi from an archaeological perspective. In T.K. Phuong and B.M. Lockhart (eds), *The Cham of Vietnam: History, Society and Art,* pp. 81–101. Singapore: NUS Press.

——. 2013. Some thoughts on the Sa Huynh and related pottery. In M. Yamagata, C.H. Bùi and K.D. Nguyễn (eds), *The Excavation of Hoa Diem in Central Vietnam,* pp. 261–268. Bulletin 17. Tokyo: Showa Women's University Institute of International Culture.

Yamagata, M., D.M. Pham and C.H. Bui. 2001. Western Han bronze mirrors recently discovered in Central and Southern Vietnam. *Bulletin of the Indo-Pacific Prehistory Association* 21: 91–106.

Yamagata, M., C.H. Bùi and K.D. Nguyễn (ed.). 2013. *The Excavation of Hoa Diem in Central Vietnam.* Bulletin 17. Tokyo: Showa Women's University Institute of International Culture.

20

Matting Impressions from Lo Gach: Materiality at Floor Level

Judith Cameron

In Southeast Asia, organic materials do not generally survive in the archaeological record, especially fibre-based artefacts. In this paper, I report on some rare, well-preserved impressions of floor matting discovered during the 2014 excavations at the site of Lo Gach, Long An Province, southern Vietnam, dated to ca. 2750 cal. BP. The impressions not only provide useful insights into weaving technology in the past, they also indicate that the techniques utilised more than 2,500 years ago to produce mats and winnowing trays have endured until the present day.

Introduction

Since fibres are amongst the most fragile of all organic materials, the absence of direct archaeological evidence of matting has obscured the fundamental role that this class of artefact played in prehistoric societies, not only in Southeast Asia but almost everywhere. Matting is a fibre-based artefact, intermediate between basketry and textiles woven on looms. Before the invention of furniture, all interaction took place at floor level and considerable economic expenditure would have been utilised in manufacturing mats for domestic consumption and trade. Throughout Southeast Asia, floor mats continue to provide comfort when sitting and sleeping, as well as defining space. This class of artefact also has an integral role in agricultural societies where it is used when processing and storing farm and forest products, as well as in sericulture. During mortuary rituals, mats have an important role functioning as shrouds. Given the rarity of such perishables in the archaeological record, the discovery of clay impressions of prehistoric matting and basketry embedded in clay matrices during the 2014 excavations of the late Neolithic–early Metal Age site of Lo Gach in southern Vietnam is noteworthy. Notwithstanding the obvious limitations inherent in the investigation of long vanished materials, this chapter discusses a recent investigation into the material and structural composition of these unique impressions, which not only informs us about early Metal Age materiality in this strategic part of Mainland Southeast Asia, but also provides insights into the level of technical knowledge and origins of the groups who made them more than 2,500 years ago.

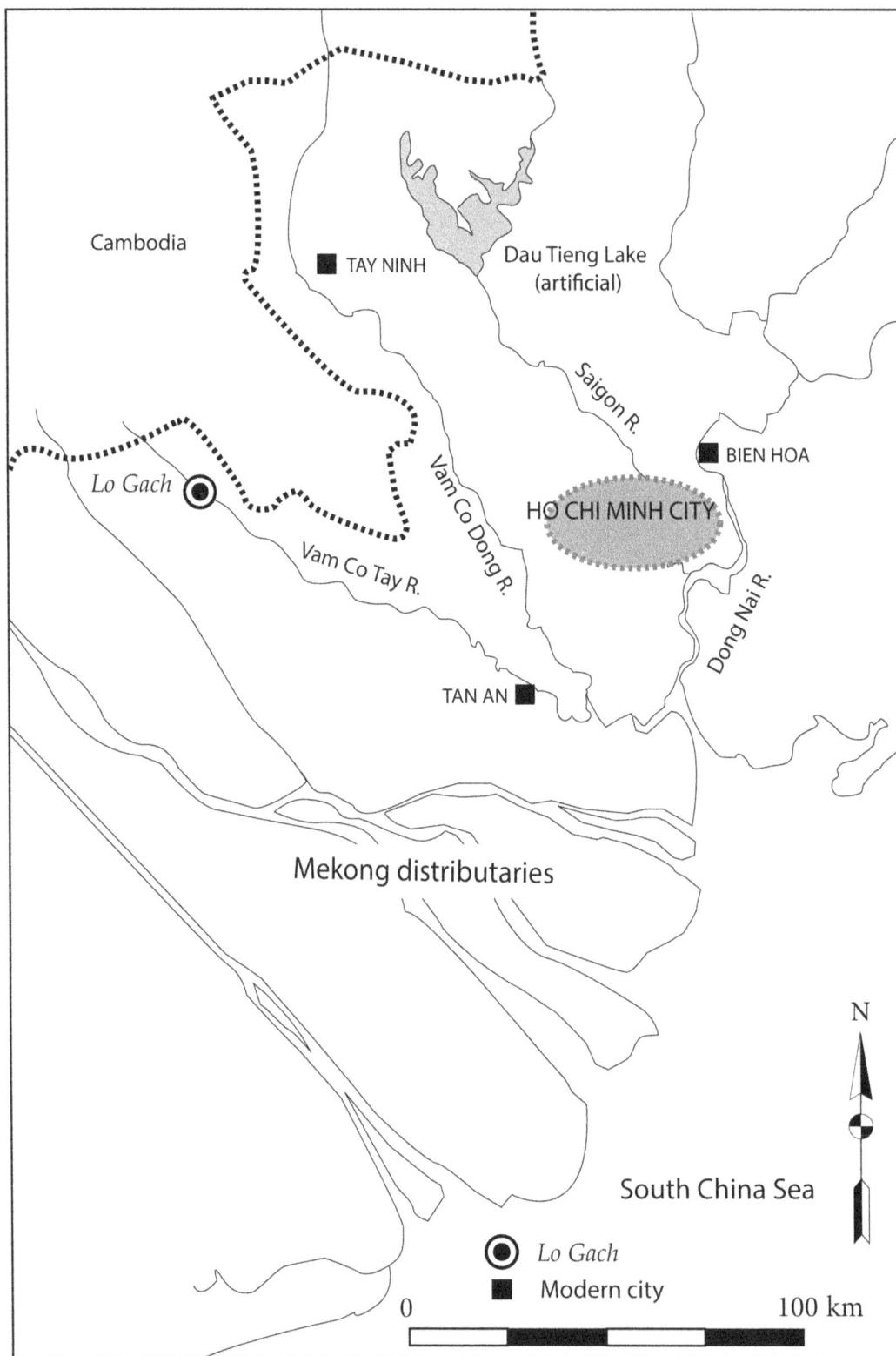

Figure 20.1 Map showing the location of the Lo Gach site.

Source: Courtesy P.J. Piper.

The site

The archaeological site of Lo Gach (105°43'50"E/10°54'58"N) lies approximately 1–2 m above sea level on the western bank of the Vam Co Tay River in Long An Province, southern Vietnam (Figure 20.1). Although the site was first discovered in 1989, initial excavations were not carried out until 2003 when Long An Provincial Museum excavated 4 m² of the site. In 2006, archaeologists from the Vietnam Institute of Archaeology in Hanoi returned to Lo Gach and excavated a further 24 m². The investigators identified 0.9–1.2 m of cultural deposit, of which the upper 0.4 m contained animal bones, broken stoneware and some early elements of the Óc Eo culture. Beneath this was a complex sequence of 'grey earth mixed with fine sand' containing concentrations of pottery, animal bone and osseous artefacts. No chronometric dating was undertaken, and based on comparisons between the material culture recovered from Lo Gach, it was determined that the settlement overlapped in chronology with other Metal Age sites in southern Vietnam such as Go Ó Chua, Co Son, Go Dinh and Rach Rung, and was likely occupied between *ca.* 2500–2200 BP (Bui Van Liem 2008: 44). In 2012, a further test excavation by members of the Department of Archaeology in the Southern Institute for Sustainable Development in Ho Chi Minh City revealed *ca.* 1.5 m of well stratified archaeological deposits, including floor surfaces and extensive midden deposits. Four radiocarbon dates on samples strategically located throughout the stratigraphic sequence from the basal layers up in Trenches 1 and 3 indicated an age of between 2800–2700 cal. BP (P.J. Piper, unpub. data).

Based on knowledge gained from previous excavations, a collaborative team from The Australian National University, the Southern Institute for Sustainable Development and Long An Provincial Museum decided to investigate Lo Gach in more detail in order to determine the nature of the settlement, the timing of its establishment and its likely function. Three trenches (Trenches 1–3) were excavated during April–May 2014. The largest, Trench 1, initially covering 12 m², was placed adjacent to the 2012 test excavation. This trench was expanded in order to remove a burial partially exposed in the northeast baulk of the trench. Trenches 2 and 3 each covered 6 m², with Trench 2 located close to the former 2006 excavations, and Trench 3 placed alongside the river where flooding has eroded away the bank exposing and destroying archaeological deposits (P.J. Piper, unpub. data). While production of a comprehensive report is still in progress, it can be said here that the excavations produced evidence for a complex sequence of well-preserved *in situ* floor and surface deposits that had developed and/or been deliberately laid sequentially on top of each other to produce the 1 m (Trench 3) to 1.5 m (Trenches 1 and 2) of deposit surviving at Lo Gach. More than 28 radiocarbon dates have confirmed that the Lo Gach settlement was primarily (though not exclusively) occupied between *ca.* 2800–2700 cal. BP. Many of the surfaces consisted of friable loamy sands or sands often with a hard-compacted surface. On excavation, several of these deposits were found to contain well-preserved plant impressions probably resulting from the compression of rapidly buried organic materials, including the impressions of fibre technology reported in this paper.

Context

All three excavated mat impressions were recovered from well-stratified and dated archaeological layers: Sample No. SA3-29 from Trench 3 in layer F3-5 (Figure 20.2a) has a radiocarbon date on charcoal of 2570±25 uncal. BP or 2807–2751 cal. BP (ANU-11790; all radiocarbon dates herein were calibrated using OxCal4.2 IntCal.13; following Bronk Ramsey et al. 2010). Figure 20.2b shows sample No. SA3-33 from layer F3-6 directly below F3-5 of the same trench and sandwiched between ANU-11790 with a associated charcoal date from the underlying Context 303 of 2575±30 or 2811–2749 cal. BP (ANU-11792). Figure 20.2c shows the sample

(SA1-70) from surface F1-32 at the northeast end of Trench 1. Layer F1-7 above F1-32 was dated on charcoal to 2560±25 or 2805–2749 cal. BP (78.8 per cent; ANU-11805), and layer F1-123 below the sample has an associated charcoal date of 2535±25 or 2796–2741 cal. BP (ANU-11802). The dating suggests that all three matting fragments were likely manufactured and utilised in the first half of the eighth century BC.

Analysis

The material and structural composition (dimensions, technique, number of elements, width of single elements, spaces, irregularities) of the impressions were measured using methodology developed for the analysis of basketry and matting by Adovasio (1977), and the results are shown in Table 20.1. However, rigidity could not be accurately measured from the impressions.

a.

b.

c.

Figure 20.2 Matting impressions remaining on the clay floor surface at Lo Gach: a. Sample SA3-29; b. Sample SA3-33; c. Sample SA1-70.

Source: Photographs courtesy P.J. Piper.

Table 20.1 Functional attributes of the Lo Gach impressions.

Sample	Context	Material	Form	Technique	Elements	Angle	Size
A3-29	F3-5	vegetable	matting	simple plaiting	2	90°	3.75
SA3-33	F3-6	vegetable	matting	simple plaiting	2	45°	3.75
SA-170	F1-7	vegetable	basketry	twill plaiting	4	45°	3.75

Source: J. Cameron.

Material composition

The uniform width of the basic elements in all three impressions indicates that the original matting was of vegetable origin. It would be difficult, albeit impossible, to cut animal skins into such uniform sized strips, whereas plant stems or leaves can be split lengthways uniformly (and easily) following the natural fibre bundles. The structural detail of SA1-70 is evident under moderately high magnification, and this clearly shows the material used to produce the basketry has a plant structure. Numerous fibre-producing plants are transformed into matting in Southeast Asia today, all of which require specific techniques to process. Informants have suggested that nipa palm (*Nipa fruticans*), which grows prolifically in estuarine habitats, could have been used to manufacture mats locally. Other botanical species traditionally employed in this region for fibre artefacts include *Pandanus* (Pandanaceae family). Sturdier fibres from bamboo (Poaceae family) and rattan (Arecaceae family) are most likely to have been used to make the third impression (SA 3-170). Positive identification could be obtained through phytoliths, i.e. siliceous particles formed within epidermal vegetable cells, which remain after the organic remains have disappeared, but that was beyond the scope of this research.

Structural composition

Form

The shape and size of two of the impressions on the clay floors (SA3-29 and SA3-33) suggest they are the remains of floor matting. Matting is one of the oldest forms of manually assembled fibre artefacts that is sometimes broadly classified as basketry although strictly speaking mats differ from baskets in that they are worked on a single plane, essentially two dimensional, whereas baskets are three dimensional (Figures 20.3a and 20.3b). The third sample (SA3-170) appears to be an impression of a basketry sieve tray. Figure 20.2c shows the artefact and fragments of the wooden frame that would have originally encircled the basket and provided the strengthening support. This type of sieve tray made from split fibre could have been used for winnowing. After harvesting, *padi* rice is spread onto a mat on the floor to dry. The grains are then winnowed, a process whereby *padi* is placed on a small flat woven tray and thrown into the air to remove the chaff while the cleaned grain falls to the back of the tray. Trays of this construction are also used in food storage, preparation and transport.

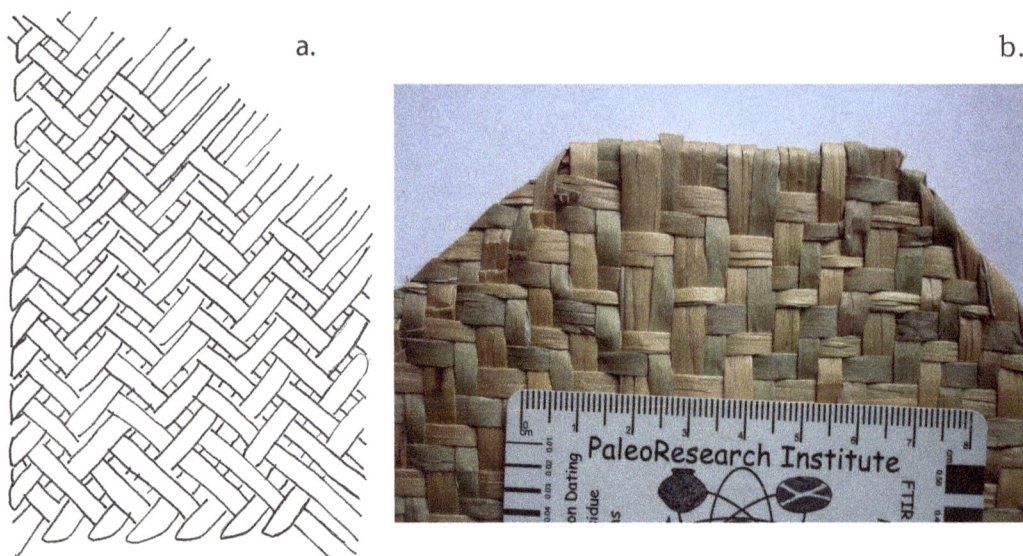

Figure 20.3 (a) Schematic diagram showing the construction of plaited matting; (b) Contemporary woven reed floor mat purchased in a market at Tan An, Long An Province in 2014.

Source: (a) J. Cameron; (b) P.J. Piper.

Techniques

Not only is matting made from stiffer fibres than those used for woven textiles, but the techniques used in construction are also different, requiring only one tool (a knife for cutting plant stems). Lengths of suitable fibres are first cut and after the shiny outer surfaces are removed, they are then rolled and stored to dry until required. The impressions remaining at Lo Gach indicate that the mats were manufactured using a technique known as plaiting, the simplest subclass of basketry in which all elements are active. Two different techniques are discernible: simple plaiting and an elaboration known as twill plaiting. Simple plaiting is evidenced in Sample SA3-29, which has single elements passing over and under each other in a 1/1 interval (Figure 20.2a, Figure 20.3). The angle of crossing of the sample was 90°. The second technique evidenced by sample SA3-33 is twill plaiting (2/2) in which one set of elements passed over and under two sets in staggered intervals (Figure 20.2b, Figure 20.3). The dimensions of the elements in all samples showed a high degree of uniformity and the usage of the same basic elements. Technological continuity is also readily discernible in the ethnographic correlate obtained from Tan An market in Long An Province where mats continue to cover the common floor areas of longhouses or are used for outside seating (Figure 20.3b; P.J. Piper, personal observations, 2014). The construction of very large mats in the lower Mekong has traditionally been a co-operative exercise, constructed by groups of mat makers (usually women) seated cross-legged on the floor using both their feet and hands in the process. As no selvedges were identified in the impressions, the size of the original mats at Lo Gach was indeterminate.

The final impression under investigation belongs to a more complex basketry construction known as a winnowing tray. It is distinguished by its rigid oval hoop rim, which was possibly made from the flexible rattan (Figure 20.2c). The main section would have been plaited from softer segments of reeds or bamboo and attached to the rim. Trays of this type are usually placed on mats where their principal function is to dry food. The fibres in the impressions appear to be rigid.

Archaeological correlates

Although both hunter-gatherers and agriculturalists made and used woven fibre mats from a wide range of locally available raw materials, as yet no archaeological fragments of matting appear to have been found at any pre-agricultural sites in Southeast Asia. Those worked plant fibres that have been unearthed from pre-agricultural sites such as Khok Phanom Di in Central Thailand (Higham and Thosarat 1987) and Gua Sireh in Borneo (Datan 1993) were the remains of bark cloth and belong to a different technological tradition that certainly is of greater antiquity in the region than matting (Cameron 2008).

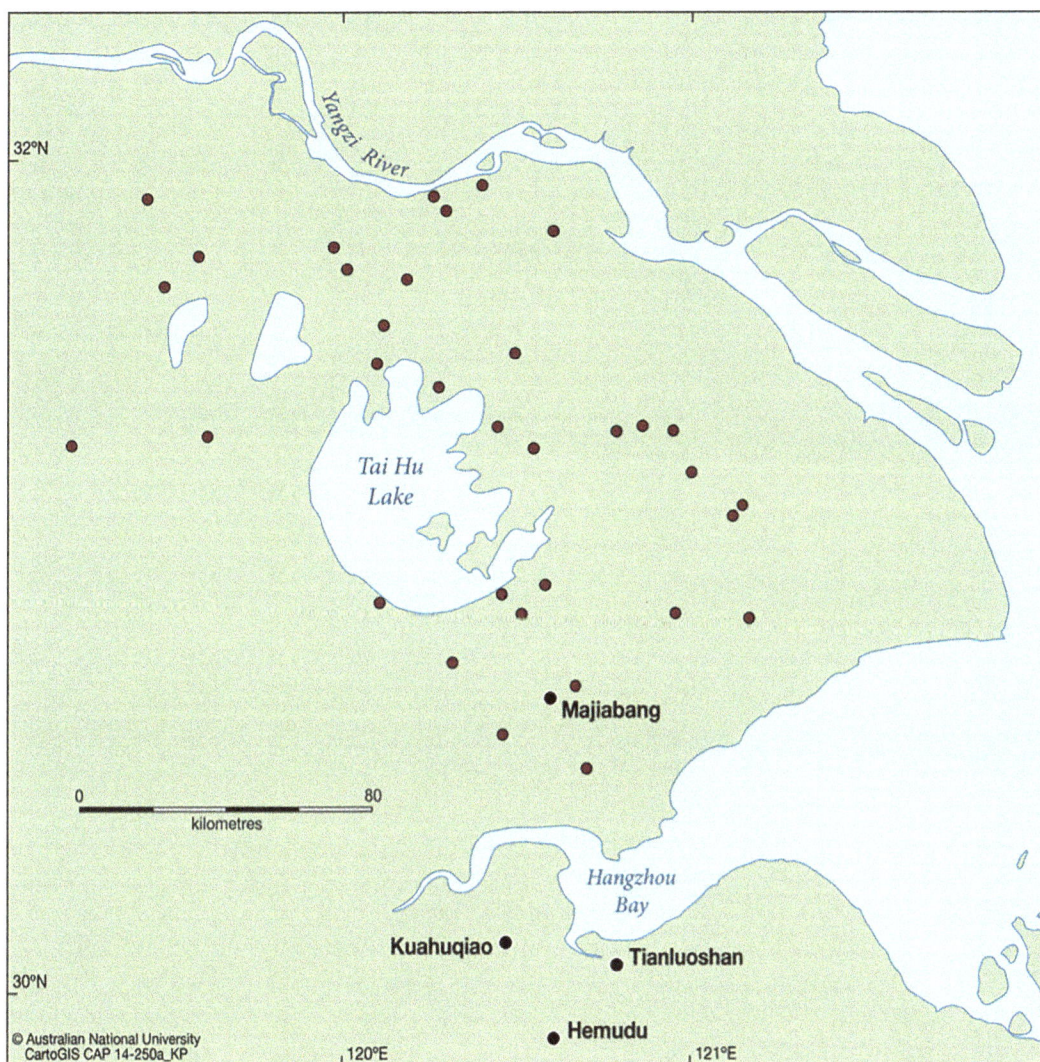

Figure 20.4 Location of Neolithic matting sites in the lower Yangzi Valley mentioned in the text.

Source: J. Cameron; Base map: ANU Cartography.

The earliest firm archaeological correlates for the Lo Gach impressions come from Early Neolithic sites in the lower Yangzi Valley where matting had several distinct functions. Key matting sites are Kuahuqiao, Tianluoshan and Hemudu, all of which cluster around Hangzhou Bay in Zhejiang Province (Figure 20.4), in an area which would have been coastal when occupied. Kuahuqiao is significant in archaeology for producing extant remains of the first canoe (possibly an outrigger), found below the water table 5–6 m beneath the surface, preserved by waterlogging. The site also produced evidence for rice and domesticated pigs. Radiocarbon dates indicate that the site was occupied 8000–7000 BP (Jiang and Liu 2004). Three strips were interworked in a 3/3 basket weave construction. Since the matting was located inside the canoe, it has been suggested that it may have functioned as a sail (Jiang and Liu 2008) although many traditional canoes in this region also feature matting canopies.

Matting was also found at the early Neolithic site of Tianluoshan (Li and Sun 2009) but here it performed an entirely different function to that at Kuahuqiao. Tianluoshan (*ca.* 8000–6800 BP) is significant in prehistory for producing the earliest known evidence for rice cultivation, thereby demonstrating that early Neolithic groups in the Yangzi Valley belonging to the Hemudu culture were gradually transitioning from hunting and gathering to settled agriculture 8,000 years ago (Fuller et al. 2009). There, matting fragments were discovered at the bottom of storage pits containing fruit and nuts. The matting inserted around the walls of the pits was almost certainly intended to stop contamination with the sand, soil and gravel, providing a moisture barrier to prevent water rising up into the stored agricultural produce thereby preventing loss through fungal and bacterial contamination. This clearly demonstrates knowledge of post-harvest handling at a surprisingly early time. In modern times, for example, we know that for long-term storage of grain, moisture content in pits is not recommended to exceed 8 per cent (B. Cameron pers. comm.).

At the better-known site assigned to the eponymous Hemudu culture, archaeologists unearthed extant remains of matting structures similar to the Lo Gach impressions (Anon. 1978). The Hemudu culture is important in Southeast Asian prehistory for its possible Austronesian connections. As Chang (1989: 91) first observed, the material remains at Hemudu and later Majiabang sites are literal transcriptions of the material culture listed in linguistic reconstructions of Proto-Austronesian. At Hemudu, matting fragments were found in layer 4, dated between 7200 and 5000 BP, amidst the wooden remains of pile dwellings. The fibres were identified as *Phragmites sp.* (reeds) (Anon. 1978). One fragment was woven using multiple warps and wefts, in a 2/2 basket weave, a technique commonly found throughout Southeast Asia for house walls, room dividers and, most importantly, flooring. Another fragment was woven using the more advanced twill technique also evidenced at Lo Gach. Twill weaves are float weaves for which a minimum of three warp groupings is essential.

Across the South China Sea, archaeological correlates have also been identified in the Niah Cave assemblages where matting was a distinguishing feature of the Neolithic/Metal Age burials in the cemetery sector and to a lesser extent at Lobang Tulang (Harrisson 1967; Barker 2013; Cameron 2016). At Niah, woven matting was identified in 48 burials of all ages and sexes. The cemetery burial matting was made using precisely the same techniques evidenced at Lo Gach, uniformly plaited in 1/1 tabby weave and 2/2 basket weave, but in Borneo these artefacts functioned as shrouds, alternatives to wooden coffins. One larger mat actually wrapped the exterior of a coffin, a practice also evidenced at later Dongson sites in Vietnam. While the usage of matting for flooring at Lo Gach and shrouds at Niah ostensibly seems incongruous, the two functions are not necessarily mutually exclusive. In traditional Island Southeast Asian societies, mats are multifunctional and when individuals die, deceased persons are wrapped in their sleeping mats, which then function as shrouds (Denison 1872; Cameron 2016).

To the north of Lo Gach, matting has also been found in burial contexts in many Bronze/Iron Age sites in the Red River plains of Northern Vietnam. A notable find was unearthed during the joint Australian/Vietnamese excavations of the Dongson site of Dong Xa in 2004 (Bellwood et al. 2007; Cameron 2009, 2012a, 2012b, 2012c) when a complete matting shroud woven from ramie (*Boehmeria nivea*) fibres was excavated. At Dong Xa, 1/1 plaited matting made from sedge was not only used to wrap the body of an adult female wearing embroidered clothing but also the wooden boat coffin itself. As mentioned above, this replicates the same mortuary practice evidenced in the cemetery sector of Niah Cave (Cameron 2016).

Conclusions

Southeast Asian archaeologists (Bellwood 1997, 2004; Higham 1989, 2014; Higham and Lu 1998) have reconstructed the expansion of Neolithic rice farmers from South China into both Mainland and Island Southeast Asia during the fifth millennium BP. Other research (Cameron 2002, 2011, 2012a, 2012b, 2012c) into the distribution of diagnostic cloth production tools established that these Neolithic agriculturalists also had fibre-based technologies (matting, basketry and cloth production) and gradually introduced these crafts into various parts of Southeast Asia during this critical period.

Recent evidence from the above-mentioned Kuahuqiao site indicates that mat-producing agriculturalists belonging to the Hemudu culture in the lower Yangzi not only domesticated pigs and rice but also had knowledge of maritime technology, which certainly would have given them the capacity to engage in inter-regional trade during the Neolithic period. Elsewhere, I (Cameron 2002, 2011, 2015) have argued that the invention of textile technology in the lower Yangzi would have provided a catalyst for the development of exchange networks that preceded the famous Maritime Silk Road of the historical period.

It is possible that the weaving technologies observed at Lo Gach, a sedentary settlement site dating to *ca.* 2800–2700 cal. BP, was first introduced to Southern Vietnam during the forager-farming transitions about 4000 BP. For example, spinning tools have been identified at An Son (Cameron 2002) and Rach Nui (Piper and Oxenham 2014; Oxenham et al. 2015), two of the earliest agricultural settlement sites in the region, as well as historical sites belonging to the Funan culture (Cameron 2002).

Elsewhere in Vietnam, firm evidence for cloth production introduced with agriculture from South China dates from the terminal Neolithic at sites assigned to the Phung Nguyen culture and continues through the Bronze and Iron Age at sites assigned to the Dong Dau, Go Mun and Dongson cultures, extending to central and southern coastal Vietnam at Proto-Historic sites assigned to the Sa Huynh culture.

Undoubtedly, the matting impressions from Lo Gach indicate that the groups who occupied the site were thoroughly familiar with plant fibres and the simple plaiting techniques used by agriculturalists to obtain the exigencies of daily life. While such heavy-duty, mundane artefacts, quickly made and discarded when worn out, are not generally afforded much attention in archaeology, they provide insights into pre-Funan material culture. At the broadest level, the data indicate levels of social and technological complexity. More specifically, the matting impressions elucidate the fundamental role of fibre artefacts in agricultural households occupying the flat deltaic terrain of the Mekong Delta and provide additional links to agricultural households who initially developed agriculture in South China.

Acknowledgements

Thanks are due to Philip J. Piper who recorded the impressions *in situ* and kindly provided the background information on the site.

References

Adovasio, J.M. 1977. *Basketry Technology*. Chicago: Aldine Publishing Company.

Anon. 1978. First season's excavations of Ho-mu-tu (Hemudu) in Yu-Yao County, Chekiang (Zhejiang) Province. *Khao Ku Hsueh Pao (Kao Gu Xue Bao)* 1: 39–94 (in Chinese).

——. 1991. A preliminary report on the excavation of the site of Keqiutou Pingtan, Fujian. *Kaogu Xuebao*: 587–589.

Barker, G. (ed.). 2013. *Rainforest Foraging and Farming in Island Southeast Asia, The archaeology of the Niah Caves, Sarawak*, vol. 1. Cambridge: McDonald Institute for Archaeological Research.

Bellwood, P. 2004. The origins and dispersals of agricultural communities in Southeast Asia. In I. Glover and P. Bellwood (eds), *Southeast Asia: from Prehistory to History*, pp. 21–40. London: RoutledgeCurzon.

——. 1997. *Prehistory of the Indo-Malaysian Archipelago*. Revised edition. Honolulu: University of Hawaii Press.

——. 1985. *Prehistory of the Indo-Malaysian Archipelago*. North Ryde: Academic Press.

Bellwood, P. and J. Cameron, Nguyen Van Viet, Bui Van Liem. 2007. Ancient boats, boat timbers, and locked mortise-and-tenon joints from Bronze/Iron-Age Northern Vietnam. *International Journal of Nautical Archaeology* 36: 2–20. doi.org/10.1111/j.1095-9270.2006.00128.x.

Bronk Ramsey, C., M. Dee, S. Lee, T. Nakagawa and R. Staff. 2010. Developments in the calibration and modeling of radiocarbon dates. *Radiocarbon* 52(3): 953–961. doi.org/10.1017/S0033822200046063.

Bui Van Liem. 2008. Di Chi Lo Gach (Long An), *Khao Co Hoc* 2008(2): 26–44 (in Vietnamese).

Cameron, J. 2002. Textile Technology in the Prehistory of Southeast Asia. Unpublished PhD thesis, The Australian National University, Canberra.

——. 2008. Trans-oceanic transfer of bark-cloth technology from South China-Southeast Asia to Mesoamerica? In G. Clark, F. Leach and S. O'Connor (eds), *Islands of Inquiry: Colonisation, Seafaring and the Archaeology of Maritime Landscapes*, pp. 203–210. Terra Australis 29. Canberra: ANU E Press.

——. 2011. Textile crafts in the Gulf of Tongking. The intersection between archaeology and history. In N. Cooke, T. Li and J.A. Anderson (ed.), *The Tongking Gulf through History*, pp. 25–38. Philadelphia: University of Pennsylvania Press.

——. 2012a. Leonard Aurousseau's hypothesis revisited: the intersection between history and archaeology. In M.L. Tjoa-Bonatz, A. Reinecke and D. Bonatz (eds), *Crossing Borders: Selected Papers from the 13th International Conference of Southeast Asian Archaeologists,* vol. 1, pp. 221–229. Singapore: NUS Press.

——. 2012b. The spinning tools. In C.F.W. Higham and A. Kijngam (eds), *The Origins of the Civilization of Angkor*. vol. V. *The Excavation of Ban Non Wat: Part Three. The Bronze Age*, pp. 497–504. Bangkok: Fine Arts Department.

——. 2012c. The spinning tools. In C.F.W. and A. Kijngam (eds), *The Origins of the Civilization of Angkor*. vol. VI. *The Excavation of Ban Non Wat: The Iron Age, Summary and Conclusions*, pp. 115–119. Bangkok: Fine Arts Department.

——. 2015. A Prehistoric Maritime Silk Road: Merchants, Boats, Cloth and Jade. In *Beyond the Silk Road: Asian Maritime History and Culture. The Collection of Papers for the 6th Session of Academic Forum (English Papers).* August 2015. Shanghai: China Maritime Museum, pp. 58–69.

——. 2016. The Archaeological Textiles from the Great Cave at Niah: Analysis and Technical Implications. In Graeme Barker (ed.), *Rainforest Foraging and Farming in Island Southeast Asia, The Archaeology of the Niah Caves, Sarawak*, vol. 2, pp. 345–362. Cambridge: McDonald Institute of Archaeological Research.

Cameron, J., P. Bellwood, Bui Van Liem, Nguyen Van Viet. 2009. Kêt Qua Nghiên Cuu Vai Trong Van Hoa Dông Son Tai Di Tich Dông Xa (Hung Yên) Trong Hop Tac Khoa Hoc Viêt Nam-Uc Lân Thu Nhât. *Khao Co Hoc* 2: 20–25 (in Vietnamese).

Chang, K.-C. 1989. Taiwan archaeology in Pacific perspectives. In K.-C. Chang, K-C. Li, A.P. Wolf and A. Yin (eds), *Anthropological Studies of the Taiwan Area: Accomplishments and Prospects*, pp. 87–98. Taipei: National Taiwan University.

Datan I. 1993. *Archaeological Excavations at Gua Sireh, Serian, and Lubang Angin, Gunung Mulu National Park, Sarawak, Malaysia*. Special Monograph no. 6. Kuching: Sarawak Museum.

Denison, N. 1872. Journal (from 29th April to 25th May, 1872) when on a trip from Sarawak to Meri, on the north-west coast of Borneo in the Brunei territory. Manuscript, National Library of Australia.

Fuller, D.Q., Q. Ling, E.L. Harvey. 2009. An evolutionary model for Chinese rice domestication: reassessing the data of the Lower Yangtze region. In S.-M. Ahn and J.-J. Lee (eds), *New Approaches to Prehistoric Agriculture*, pp. 313–345 Seoul: Sahoi Pyoungnon.

Harrisson, B. 1967. A classification of stone-age burials from Niah Great Cave, Sarawak. *Sarawak Museum Journal* 15: 126–155.

Higham, C.F.W. 1989. *The Archaeology of Mainland Southeast Asia*. Cambridge: Cambridge University Press.

Higham, C. 2014. *Early Mainland Southeast Asia: From First Humans to Angkor*. Bangkok: River Books.

Higham, C. and T.L.-D. Lu. 1998. The origins and dispersal of rice cultivation. *Antiquity* 72 (278): 867–877. doi.org/10.1017/S0003598X00087500.

Higham, C.F.W. and R. Thosarat (eds). 1987. *The Excavation of Khok Phanom Di.* vol. III (part I). *The Material Culture*. London: Society of Antiquaries.

Leping Jiang and Li Liu. 2005. The discovery of an 8000-year-old dugout canoe at Kuahuqiao in the Lower Yangzi River, China. *Antiquity* 79 (305) September: Project Gallery.

Li Anjun and Sun Guoping. 2009. *Tianluoshan Site, a new window of Hemudu Culture*. Hangzhou: Xiling Seal Society Publishing House, Hangzhou (in Chinese).

Oxenham, M.F., P.J. Piper, P. Bellwood, C. Ho. Bui, K.T.K. Nguyen, Q.M. Nguyen, F. Campos, C. Castillo, R. Wood, C. Sarjeant, N. Amano, A. Willis and J. Ceron. 2015. Emergence and diversification of the Neolithic in Southern Vietnam: insights from coastal Rach Nui. *The Journal of Island and Coastal Archaeology* 10(3): 1–30. doi.org/10.1080/15564894.2014.980473.

Piper P.J. and M.F. Oxenham. 2014. Of prehistoric pioneers: the establishment of the first sedentary settlements in the Mekong Delta region of Southern Vietnam during the period 2000–1500 cal. BC. In K. Boyle, R.J. Rabett and C.O. Hunt (eds), *Living in the Landscape: Essays in Honour of Graeme Barker*, pp. 209–226. Cambridge: McDonald Institute of Archaeological Research.

21

The Prehistoric House: A Missing Factor in Southeast Asia

Charles Higham

Excavations in Mainland Southeast Asia have yet to reveal a single complete house plan, yet the potential of residential archaeology to illuminate social change, particularly when human burials are found in association, is emphasised by recent research in other parts of the world. Non Ban Jak is a late Iron Age town in the Mun Valley of Northeast Thailand. Excavations over the past four years have revealed a sequence of domestic architecture, in which the dead were interred within houses. This paper explores the potential of this site to examine social organisation during a period when an agricultural revolution stimulated the rise of inequality at the threshold of early state formation.

Introduction

The prehistoric record of Southeast Asia from Neolithic settlement to the foundation of the first states suffers from the absence of information on where people lived. The lack of a single house plan might conceivably reflect the use of piles to raise buildings above the ground level. This should result in posthole patterns in the form of individual buildings. However, the decay of wooden posts and their replacement over time are likely to result in a palimpsest of postholes with no clear structure. Although bronze models in the Dian chiefdom of Yunnan, and images on Dong Son drums show houses raised on posts, this does not imply that it was a universal prehistoric practice. As a consequence of the dearth in archaeological research in Southeast Asia dedicated to the investigation of settlement patterning, construction techniques and function, assessments of social organisation and change rely heavily on mortuary data.

The recent literature on residential archaeology elsewhere reveals how much we are missing in Southeast Asia. Returning after an interval of over 50 years to the subject of my doctoral dissertation, the Swiss lake villages (Higham 1966), I marvel at the social information that is now available. One key, as always, is chronology, and with the precision of dendrochronology, the construction of individual houses can be dated by the year. Thus houses at Neolithic Arbon Bleiche 3 on the southern shore of Lake Constance were constructed between 5326–5334 BP (Eberschweiler et al. 2006). Houses were placed in neat rows, and each measured little more than 8 m by 4 m. New buildings constructed within a span of just eight years indicate not a growing population so much as the arrival of new members of the community from elsewhere. Ebersbach has described 'Another thrilling result of detailed spatial analyses of all kinds of remains is the observation that there are quite a lot of settlements with multi-ethnic compositions of the inhabitants' (2013: 293). Thus, again at Arbon Bleiche 3, neighbouring houses revealed distinct ceramic styles, fishing techniques and diets of the occupants (De Capitani and Leuzinger 1998; De Capitani et al. 2002). Houses did not last for long. An oak post sunk into a wet substrate has a lifespan of about six years. Hence, villages were not long lived and people moved to a new settlement several times in a lifetime. The snapshot of Arbon Bleiche, with intimate details of daily life, is but one component of millennia of social change on the alpine foreland.

Human remains are very rare in these sites, and often absent. At the Linearbandkeramik (LBK) site of Karsdorf in Central Germany, however, the conjunction of Neolithic houses with human burials has seen the deployment of aDNA to distinguish between indigenous hunter-gatherer and incoming farmer ancestry, strontium isotopes to identify those raised elsewhere, and light stable isotopes to analyse diets. One major advantage of these LBK sites is that one can excavate extensively, because the stratigraphic build up is so shallow. At Karsdorf, the excavation uncovered 51 times the area of my fieldwork at Ban Non Wat or Non Ban Jak, and 180 times that of Khok Phanom Di. Thus, 24 longhouses were mapped, set out in rows, the largest measuring 24 m by 8 m (Brandt et al. 2014). The aDNA variation indicates several maternal lineages, and close affinity with other LBK sites. A small proportion of the haplotypes evidence descent from the indigenous hunter-gatherers, but the majority reveal demic diffusion ultimately from the Near East. If only DNA survived so well in Southeast Asia. Strontium isotopes have identified two groups, which probably farmed in different soils accessible from the settlement. It is also concluded that the community was patrilocal, with women entering it from elsewhere.

The house in Southeast Asia

White and Eyre (2010) have investigated the potential of residential archaeology in Southeast Asia by suggesting that published reports on the few excavated sites in Northeast Thailand have missed a vital point: that the dead were interred in residences. Being reliant more on water than the soil for growth and maturity, rice cultivation encourages permanent settlement and sites like Ban Non Wat and Ban Chiang were occupied, and the cultural deposits accumulated, for millennia. By dovetailing long-term settlement with burial within or closely associated with domestic residences, White and Eyre argued that in Northeast Thailand house societies involved long-term occupation by heterarchic, non-violent supravillage affiliative social groupings. The problem with this proposal is the lack of archaeological evidence for houses (Higham 2015).

This void is being filled by Bellwood's fieldwork in southern Vietnam (Bellwood et al. 2013; Oxenham et al. 2015), where Neolithic Rach Nui, An Son and Loc Giang reveal superimposed floors associated with postholes that, with more extensive excavations, would doubtless illuminate house plans. These new excavation results are a reminder of a rectangular clay structure comprising a floor and walls representing the sixth mortuary phase at Khok Phanom Di. Containing three inhumation graves dating to about 3600 BP, it has been interpreted as a burial structure rather than part of a residential house (Higham and Bannanurag 1990). In 1994, excavations covering 405 m² at Bưng Bạc in Bà Rịa – Vũng Tàu Province, Southern Vietnam, uncovered the wooden piles that raised houses above the flood level, together with the planks of a wooden floor, expertly joined together with the use of dowels (Bùi et al. 2012). Structural remains dating to the late Iron Age in Northeast Thailand have also been known for some time. At Non Muang Kao, O'Reilly (1997) traced superimposed clay floors and wall foundations associated with human burials. The deposits were so hard, however, that only a very small test square was involved, and no plans of rooms, let alone houses, were mapped. Disturbed clay floors in proximity to human graves dating to the Iron Age have been identified at the nearby sites of Ban Non Wat and Noen U-Loke

(Higham and Kijngam 2012). The same pattern is also seen in Central Thailand during the Iron Age (Higham and Rispoli 2014). There is clearly a need to open very large areas of the Neolithic sites of Southern Vietnam, and Iron Age settlements of the Mun Valley in order to realise the potential of residential archaeology.

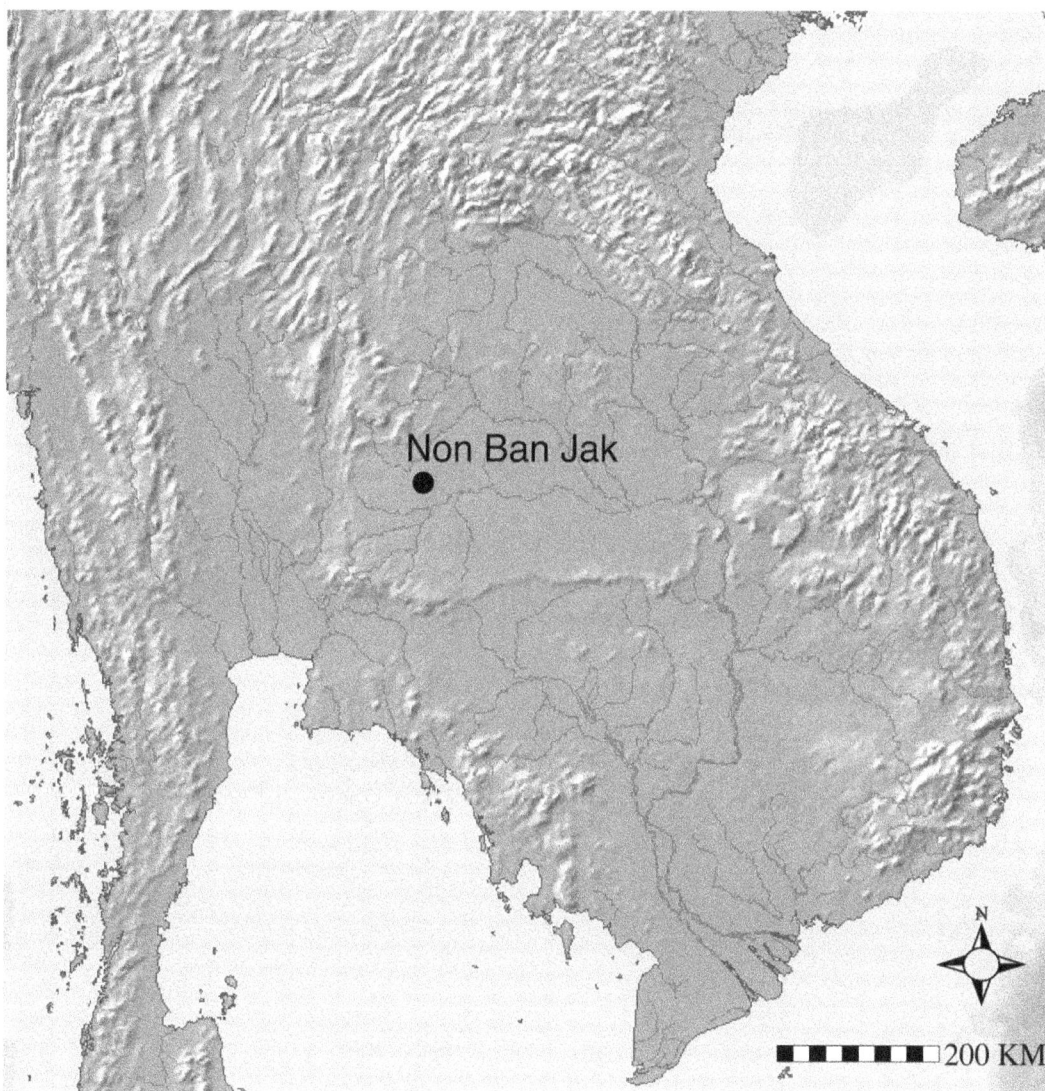

Figure 21.1 Location of Non Ban Jak in Northeast Thailand.
Source: C. Higham.

Non Ban Jak

Non Ban Jak is one of the moated, Iron Age sites that cluster densely in the upper Mun Valley on the Khorat Plateau (Figure 21.1). It covers an area of 360 m by 170 m, and is surrounded by two broad moats demarcated by banks. There is a western and an eastern mound, separated by a low-lying area that crosses the centre of the site (Figure 21.2). The first season of excavations opened an area measuring 8 m² on the eastern mound, while the following three seasons have uncovered 35 m by 10 m that began in the low-lying area and climbed onto the western mound. The radiocarbon determinations place moat construction in the fourth to fifth centuries AD

(McGrath and Boyd 2001). Over 40 C¹⁴ dates from rice, human bone and shells from occupation and mortuary contexts indicate that initial settlement took place in the third to fourth centuries AD. There are four mortuary phases that date from the fourth to at least the sixth centuries AD, with a late occupation context that incorporated Dvaravati-style pottery vessels and other artefacts. This phase ended within the period 1250–1130 BP. Non Ban Jak therefore falls into the fourth and final phase of the Iron Age in the upper Mun Valley.

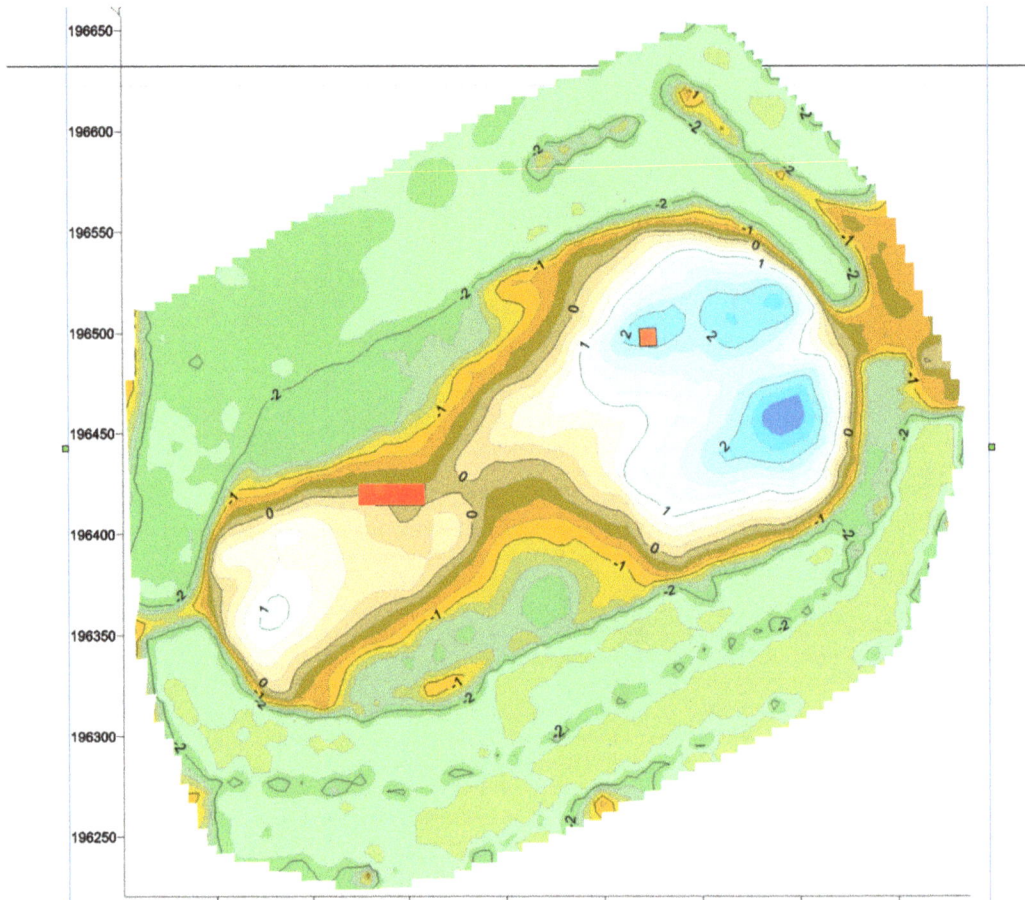

Figure 21.2 Plan of Non Ban Jak, showing the two areas excavated.
Source: Nigel Chang.

Early in the first season, we realised that Non Ban Jak had the potential for engaging with settlement archaeology. I took photographs of the surface of the excavated area at the end of each day, and downloaded and examined them in the evening. After uncovering a series of Early Historic Period Dvaravati pits filled with restorable ceramic vessels, we cleaned the newly exposed surface. The images revealed the faint traces of parallel white lines that turned right angles (Figure 21.3). Over the ensuing days, these were revealed as walls made from white clay, that enclosed rooms with smoothed clay floors. The walls contained equidistant postholes, which we presumed were structural wall supports.

Figure 21.3 The first inkling that residential structures would be found at Non Ban Jak came as white walls and a floor were revealed.

Source: C. Higham.

Our excavation on the eastern mound reached the natural substrate at a depth of 4 m below the present surface. We identified multiple building phases in which the house walls followed the same orientation, although the quality of the buildings improved over time. Manufacturing activities were undertaken in this residential area. The lowest context involved a circular ceramic kiln containing seven pots and a socketed iron ploughshare, covered by a thick layer of fragmented burnt clay that incorporated impressions of wooden supports. Kiln rake out included broken Phimai Black vessels and burnt clay, as well as carbonised rice grains. Three infant jar burials were found beside this kiln.

Houses were built over the kiln, seen in thin laterite and clay wall foundations of rooms about 3 m wide (Figure 21.4). There is a surviving area of burnt clay floor, incorporating an upright ceramic vessel, and many rice grains. The northwest part of this structure comprised a series of parallel, semi-circular impressions on the clay floor, which are probably a split bamboo foundation that end abruptly and in unison, as if they had reached the edge of an internal room within the building. A kiln lay parallel and close to the eastern wall. It contained one very large pottery vessel as well as the clay daub cover. The charred wooden wall foundations and incinerated clay floors indicate that the adjacent building had been burnt, not surprising given its close proximity to a kiln.

Figure 21.4 The surface of layer 5.2 in the eastern square showing superimposed buildings. A. is the eastern wall of the later structure. B. is the eastern wall of the earlier building, which was laid out on a different orientation. C. is the clay floor bearing what are probably bamboo impressions. D. is a ceramic kiln laid out on the same orientation as the earlier of the two structures. E. is an infant burial cut through the floor, and F. is the kitchen area. In the foreground, one can see the charcoal, ash and burnt daub of the floors and collapsed walls of the earlier building.

Source: C. Higham.

The building was replaced, but on a slightly different orientation, about 10° west of north. To the south, lay a series of pits, two of which contained intact Phimai Black ceramic vessels. There was much evidence for burning. Within, there were thin subdivisions of laterite marked by postholes that may have supported furniture or other internal features. The clay or laterite floors had been subjected to considerable heat when the structure was burnt. These floors contained concentrations of carbonised rice and broken ceramic vessels. A clay-lined hearth sitting on an incinerated kitchen floor still contained a cooking vessel and mounds of rice grains. The skeleton of a rat lay adjacent to the southern exterior wall. The structure as a whole measured 3.40 m by 6.40 m, although the walls proceeded beyond the excavation square. A laterite floor in the centre of the largest interior room sealed an oval pit that contained an infant jar burial. Since this grave also cut through an earlier laterite floor, it must date to the period when the building was in use. To the west of this building there is a clay wall foundation lying on the same orientation. A narrow gap, perhaps a lane, separates the two. The plan reveals three houses all on the same orientation, each divided from its neighbour by a narrow thoroughfare. The potential for tracing the plan of the initial Iron Age residential area is self-evident.

Following the burning of the early houses, the sequence on the eastern mound continued with the construction of new buildings, on the same orientation but with thicker wall foundations. These enclosed a solid clay floor containing a rectangular cutting of mottled fill surrounded by rows of postholes. This looked very like a further grave cut but, when opened, there were no human remains. The wall to the north of this floor had been cut into with the creation of a grave. Another structure on the eastern edge of the excavation comprised a wall foundation of white clay with a lining of grey clay enclosing superimposed grey or red clay floors and two hearths. A third ash-filled hearth was found towards the north of the room. It is evident that this room was occupied over such a period of time that re-flooring was periodically necessary.

Further superimposed floors and walls evidence yet another construction phase, but on this occasion they were accompanied by a series of clay-lined furnaces. The presence of iron slag suggests that these were smithing furnaces. A burnt red clay floor lies to the northeast of this concentration. In the northwestern quadrant, a mutilated clay floor lies adjacent to a clay wall foundation, suggesting that there was a residential complex in this part of the site. A laterite wall foundation runs just a few degrees west of due north in the central part of the square, and several postholes were dug from this depth.

Lower layer 2 incorporated a series of walls divided by town lanes or walkways. One room contained the burials of an adult, a child and an infant (Figure 21.5). The adult grave lies within two parallel rows of large postholes. A hearth is found in the southern half of this room. Mouth to mouth Phimai Black pottery vessels were placed in the three intact corners. There are also some broken pots in the southern part of the chamber. This room is separated from the building to the southeast by a narrow lane that, unlike the rooms themselves, contained occupation debris dominated by Iron Age potsherds. No further burials were found in these rooms, but a set of hearths was present in the southeastern corner room. It is possible that this complex represents a domestic dwelling incorporating a mortuary chamber.

The walls of this mortuary room were solidly built. The foundations were up to 80 cm wide, and comprise white clay of the sort that would have been available during the excavation of the moats to form the retaining banks that ring the site. The interior edge of the foundation contains a line of postholes for timbers that would have supported the walls. A narrow channel running between the posts and the wall may well have been the foundation for the interior lining of the chamber. The floor abutted the wall and one of the sets of mouth to mouth Phimai Black pots was lodged hard against the latter, sitting on the surface of the clay floor through which a grave had been cut.

Figure 21.5 Layer 2 in the eastern square, showing the mortuary chamber containing the graves of an adult, a child and an infant. A rectangular clay floor can be seen in the distance, cut by a rectangular pit. A lane between two buildings runs north–south on the left of the photograph before turning a right angle.

Source: C. Higham.

The eastern mound: Summary

Although only measuring 8 m by 8 m, the area opened on the eastern mound provided, for the first time in the Upper Mun Valley, insight into the architecture and layout of an Iron Age town, and the close relationship between residential, mortuary and manufacturing activities. Over a period of at least three centuries, houses were frequently rebuilt on the same orientation. Earlier houses were constructed with thin walls of clay or laterite, and floors of clay, fortified with bamboo foundations. A kitchen still contained a cooking vessel on its stove, and masses of rice grains on the floor, as if consumed in a conflagration. Infants had been interred within the houses, contained in ceramic vessels. These early houses were contemporary with pottery kilns, suggesting that the fashioning and firing of pots was a domestic rather than a specialised industry. The same might apply to the evidence for iron smithing being pursued in a residential part of this site. The pots remaining in these kilns had been used for both domestic and mortuary purposes.

Continuity of occupation is seen in the regular rebuilding of houses that over time became much more solidly constructed. This culminated in the final occupation phase, when walls reached a thickness of 80 cm. One room belonging to this phase contained three graves, each cut through a solid clay floor. Lidded pottery vessels had been placed in at least three of the four corners. Pots of this form were often found near inhumation graves, and this conjunction suggests that they were placed for a ritual purpose.

The western mound

The excavation on the western mound covered an area of 35 m by 10 m (Figure 21.6). Squares X and Y have little evidence for occupation, but early burials cluster on the laterite substrate. As one progresses in a westerly direction, the first structural evidence was identified in the form of a white clay wall foundation. Beyond this, in squares AA to DD, superimposed house floors and walls are found, together with human burials within these structures, and on the same orientation as the walls.

The accumulation of occupation and mortuary remains reached a maximum depth of approximately 1.8 m but in some parts of the site, little over a metre. Excavation stopped when the laterite bedrock was reached. Above this, there was a variable deposition of two naturally deposited silt layers. The earliest burial was found under this material. Occupation and mortuary remains accumulated above these, to the base of the cultivated topsoil. The latest clay floors and burials were thus encountered at a depth of only 15–20 cm. This cultural sequence has been divided into four phases on the basis of slight changes in the colour and texture of the deposits. This lack of differentiation reflects the fact that, according to the typology of the ceramics recovered, and the radiocarbon determinations, this part of the site was occupied for only a few centuries. A Bayesian analysis of the dates suggests that the initial occupation took place in the fourth century AD. The transition to layer 3 took place within the period 1490–1420 BP. Layer 2 is only marginally later. The final occupation, which incorporates historic as well as late prehistoric ceramics, ended in the eighth century AD.

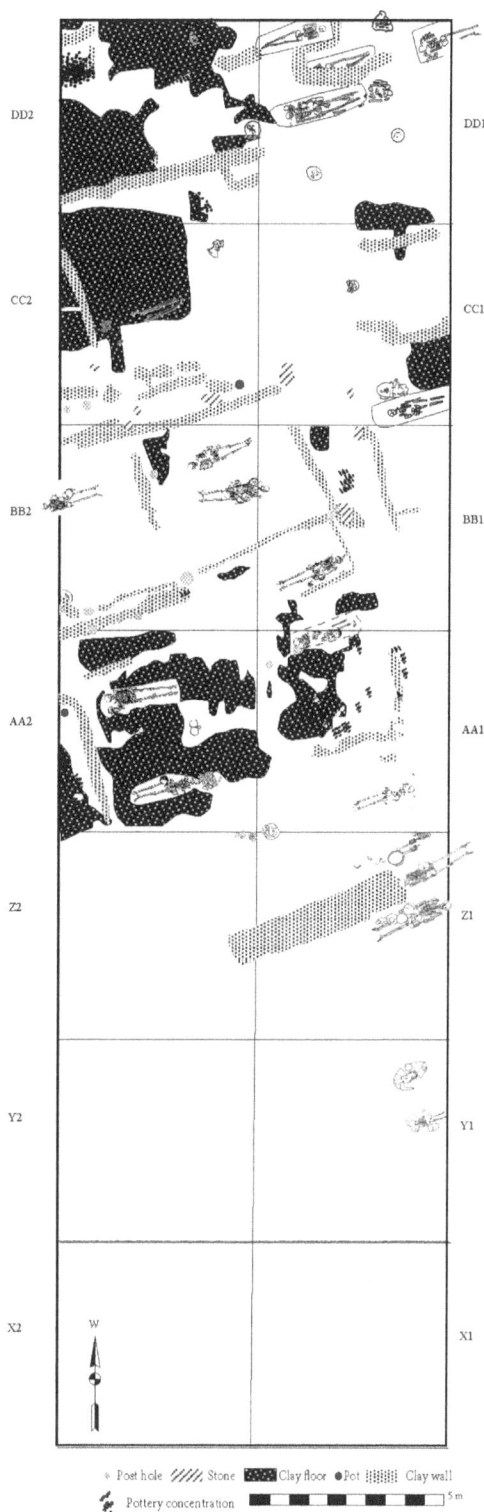

Figure 21.6 The plan of the western mound excavation showing unit numbers, and the layout of graves and structures during the third mortuary phase.

Source: C. Higham.

Figure 21.7 The western square included a wall ending with a large stone against which an infant jar burial had been interred. An adult burial had been cut through the floor and a second lay at right angles to the right. Another infant burial jar is seen in the centre of the image.

Source: C. Higham.

As with the eastern mound, superimposed house walls and floors were traced, all on the same orientation. However, at no stage were the walls as impressively finished as those in the later phases to the east. The conjunction between structures and burials is, however, equally clear. Burial 134 lay hard up against a wall, the grave having severed a floor littered with Phimai Black potsherds (Figure 21.7). The wall typically ended with a large stone foundation, against which an infant jar burial had been wedged. Burial 136 was positioned at right angles to Burial 134, and was cut through the floor to the south of the wall. Burial 137 was also placed at right angles to Burial 134, but it had been seriously disturbed. Beyond and to the south lay, on the same orientation, the complete grave of an infant. A further infant jar burial completed this nucleus of graves. This same occupation layer incorporated concentrations of hearths. Some were clay-lined, and contained deposits of ash, while others comprised a ring of stones, often with a broken pot still in place (Figure 21.8). The pots in question were of a form still used for cooking rice. Carbonised rice grains were found in one such pot that had been used as a mortuary offering.

This domestic and mortuary activity was associated with the firing of pottery vessels. One large ceramic kiln, dug down to the surface of the laterite substrate, contained a complete vessel, but lacked the concentration of rice grains found in three deep pits containing fractured pottery vessels and much charcoal and burnt daub that were encountered further to the west. It is not easy to explain the remarkable quantities of rice grains found in these but, nevertheless, the most likely interpretation is that they were also kilns. A pattern noted in the eastern mound is repeated, in that two of these kilns had infant jar burials at their uppermost edges.

Figure 21.8 Domestic activity associated with the houses is seen in the many cooking hearths.
In this instance, a set of stones surrounds ash and a broken cooking vessel.
Source: C. Higham.

Succeeding walls and floors are distributed across the excavated area, with the exception of the eastern margin. One structure incorporated a clay floor through which three burials had been cut, namely two adults and an infant (Figure 21.9). Further west, a wall and associated floors were linked to Burial 120, which was positioned at the end of the wall, and was cut through and slightly lower than the floor. Two hearths were found to the north of this grave. The tall male was interred with an impressive range of jewellery including gold earrings decorated by repoussé.

This context preceded a further a system of walls and floors, through which burials were inserted. There is also evidence for occupation in the form of pits and concentrations of pottery sherds. Burial 72 was cut through a floor, and within the corner of a clay wall. It comprises part of a row with two other burials found on the same orientation.

The postholes embedded in the walls were presumably supports for the wattle and daub superstructure. The plan suggests the presence of lanes within the settlement. In squares CC and DD, walls formed rectangular rooms with large stones placed strategically where walls ended or turned at right angles (Figure 21.7). Burial 114 at the extreme western edge of the excavated area lay within the right-angled bend of two such walls. Three radiocarbon determinations suggest that it dates to the fifth century AD, or perhaps slightly later. Structural remains and burials continued right to the present ground surface, with the latest burials being contemporary with pottery vessels characteristic of the Dvaravati Early Historic period.

Figure 21.9 Three graves were cut through the clay floor of this walled chamber in the western square.

Source: N. Chang.

The people of the western mound

Apart from the first of the four mortuary phases (MP) identified on the western mound, the dead were interred in a close relationship with the walls and floors. The MP1 burials were concentrated in the eastern part of the excavated area. Six were male, two female and one could not be assigned a sex. There are 14 infant burials representing 60 per cent of the sample, high even for the prehistoric period in Southeast Asia. The adults were interred on a northwest or southeast orientation, save for one, buried with the head directed to the east. Ornaments include agate beads and pendants, glass beads, one bimetallic iron and bronze ring, together with bronze finger and toe rings and bangles and an anklet. No individual was accompanied by more than three pottery vessels. Several had a bivalve shell. Most infants were buried in mortuary vessels. The range of offerings matched that for the adults in terms of bronze ornaments, except that an infant wore three bronze belts. There was also a marine shell pendant and an iron bangle.

Mortuary Phase 2 burials were concentrated in the central and western parts of the excavated area. There are 18 adults and 27 infants, the latter again comprising 60 per cent of the sample. Eight males have been identified, five females and five adults of unknown sex. Although rare, the first iron sickles, knives and spears were found in mortuary contexts. The ornaments worn by adults continued to include bronze rings and bangles, glass beads, and beads and pendants of agate. One man was interred with two spindle whorls. There were never more than three pottery vessels in any one adult burial. Infants had a wider range of mortuary offerings. Ornaments other than bronze rings, bangles and anklets included beads of gold, carnelian, glass and agate. One infant was associated with five pots, another with four. There were also bivalve shells, bimetallic iron and bronze rings and bangles and, with Burial 104, a bird's egg.

Mortuary Phase 3 burials are found in three clear rows that comprise the graves of men, women and infants. Ten men are represented, five women and one adult of unknown sex. There are also the graves of 18 infants, meaning that they comprise 53 per cent of the mortuary population. When burials are superimposed over the distribution of walls and floors, clear relationships are observed (Figure 21.6). There was a tangible increase in the range and quantity of mortuary offerings. Bronzes now included the two bronze belts, worn by a man, identical to those recovered from men buried at the nearby site of Noen U-Loke. There were also finger rings, bangles and earrings. Iron knives and sickles were more numerous than during MP2. One young man wore a gold finger ring another had earrings of gold. There were also bimetallic iron and bronze rings, and the man with the gold earrings also wore beads and a pendant of agate. Infants were also wealthier than hitherto, with up to five ceramic vessels, and bronze toe, ear and finger rings and bangles.

Mortuary Phase 4 burials were found just below the surface of the excavated area, and chronologically extended into the Early Historic period. However, the mortuary rituals and associated offerings remain virtually unchanged from MP3. Some burials were thus clearly related to floors and walls. Four men are represented, three women and four indeterminate adults, against five infants. The proportion of infants fell to 31 per cent of this sample. Up to four pots were found with adults. There were also gold earrings, an agate pendant and bronze ear and finger rings. Iron sickles and knives were found, along with a machete, a spear and a point. Infants were found with up to four pots, bronze earrings, bangles and glass beads.

The pseudomorphs of rice grains and fabric on the surface of iron mortuary offerings suggest that the dead were interred clothed, in a grave containing rice. There is also regularity to the mortuary offerings, seen in the placement of iron knives and sickles. Pottery vessels also follow a common theme, with at least one pot form compatible with cooking, and a bowl suited for eating therefrom. Compared with the Iron Age 3 cemetery at Noen U-Loke, however, the mortuary offerings are modest, and much more akin to those of Iron Age 4 at that site. The impression is that the western mound population included individuals who worked in the rice fields at harvest time. Some were proficient potters following a domestic mode of production. Spindle whorls evidence a weaving industry, and iron forging was also undertaken. Exotic ornaments of bronze, carnelian, agate, lead and gold, however, indicate participation in a wide exchange network.

Conclusions

Fieldwork at Non Ban Jak and the analysis of all the material and biological data are progressing, and the full interpretation of this Iron Age settlement is for the future. At present, it is easier to review the potential of the site than to draw early conclusions. A key point is the excellent preservation of the human remains. This encourages optimism when the time comes to consider evidence for demography, health and disease, stature, evidence for conflict, and physical activities reflected in bone morphology. The contrast between the quality of the later houses on the eastern mound compared with contemporary buildings to the west poses the possibility that there was an element of social inequality present in the Non Ban Jak community that might be evidenced in the human remains. Isotopic variations have not yet been studied, but identifying possible immigrants, and variations in diet over time and location in the site are planned. DNA has provided intimate insights into the population dynamics in the European sites referred to above. Most unfortunately, aDNA does not survive with any predictability in Southeast Asia, but new techniques, some centred on the dense petrous bone, offer some hope for the future.

Non Ban Jak is not currently occupied, and is open to extensive excavations. With time and resources, reconstructing the plan of a late Iron Age town is within our grasp. There is, of course, an impediment not matched in the European sites, where occupation spans were brief and stratigraphy shallow. At Non Ban Jak, houses accumulated as in a Near Eastern tell. Moreover, excavating the houses is a slow and meticulous exercise. The domestic aspect of later prehistory in the Mun Valley, if not across Southeast Asia as whole, is virtually unknown but pregnant with potential. Was there a rich suburb? Did the putative elite have a better diet? Did the less wealthy alone work in the rice fields, or labour in the construction of the moats and banks round their town site? Does the advent of residential burial signal the close bonds between corporate groups in the community and their ownership of assets? And what were the assets that generated wealth?

One of these, it is suggested, could well have been improved land for cultivating rice. The excavations at Non Ban Jak have incorporated the flotation of a sample of cultural material for organic remains. Clearly, rice dominates, but there are also weeds from species adapted to wet rice fields (Castillo 2014). A ploughshare was found in one of the eastern kilns. One of its wings was fractured and perhaps it was placed in the kiln to assist with repairs. The Mun Valley sites are ringed with broad moats. We know from remote sensing that the infrastructure of these Iron Age sites included canals and dams, as well as possible permanent rice field bunds (Parry 1992; Hawken 2011). When integrated, these have underwritten a model for an agricultural revolution involving permanent, ploughed and irrigated rice fields (Higham 2014). A second asset might well have been salt production. Many small, steeply sided mounds lie in the vicinity of the moated town sites. Excavation suggests that they accumulated through the production of salt (Rivett and Higham 2007). One potential means of obtaining wealth, the dependent production of ceramics for export, is not sustained at Non Ban Jak, where the evidence rather suggests a domestic mode for local consumption.

Summary

The first four seasons of excavation at Non Ban Jak, a moated Iron Age town in the Mun Valley of Northeast Thailand, have uncovered two residential areas. Houses were constructed of clay walls and floors, strengthened with wooden foundations and wall posts, and probably clad in wattle and daub. The dead were interred by cutting graves through the house floors. The site was occupied during the late Iron Age, and continued into the Early Historic Period. It presents the potential to reconstruct the layout of a town plan, identify modes of production, and through the excellent survival of human remains, apply established and developing analytical techniques to the prehistoric people who lived there over a period of 15 to 20 generations.

Acknowledgements

I first met Peter Bellwood in June 1966, when he stopped me in King's Parade, Cambridge, and asked if I was going to accept a lectureship at the University of Otago. When I replied yes, he said that in that case, he would take up a post at the University of Auckland. I have greatly valued his friendship and major contributions to the Southeast Asian prehistory over the past 49 years, and it is a pleasure to be able to contribute to this Festschrift.

The first three seasons of excavation at Non Ban Jak were funded by a grant from the Australian Research Council for the programme 'From Paddy to Pura: the Origins of Angkor' to Dougald O'Reilly and Louise Shewan. The fieldwork was directed by Charles Higham, Rachanie Thosarat and Nigel Chang. The fourth season was funded by a grant to Associate Professor H. Buckley and Professor C.F.W. Higham from the University of Otago. I am most grateful to the National Research Council of Thailand and the Fine Arts Department for providing the necessary research permits. I am most grateful to Sian Halcrow and Nathan Harris for their identifying the age and sex of the prehistoric dead during the course of the fieldwork.

References

Bellwood, P., M. Oxenham, C.H. Bui N.T.K. Dung, A. Willis, C. Sarjeant, P.J. Piper, H. Matsumura, K. Tanaka, N. Beavan, T. Higham, Nguyen Quoc, Manh, Dang Ngoc Kinh, Nguyen Khanh Trung Kien, Vo Thanh Huong, Van Ngoc Bich, Tran Thi Kim Quy, Nguyen Phuong Thao, F. Campos, Y.I. Sato, Nguyen Lan Cuong and N. Amano. 2013. An Son and the Neolithic of Southern Vietnam. *Asian Perspectives* 50: 144–175. doi.org/10.1353/asi.2011.0007.

Brandt, G., C. Knipper N. Nicklisch, R. Ganslmeier, M. Klamm and K.W. Alt. 2014. Settlement burials at the Karsdorf LBK site, Saxony-Anhalt, Germany. Biological ties and residential mobility. In A. Whittle and P. Bickle (eds), *Early Farmers: The View from Archaeology and Science. Proceedings of the British Academy* 198: 95–114. doi.org/10.5871/bacad/9780197265758.003.0006.

Bùi, C.H., P.C. Thân and N. K. T. Kiên. 2012. *Khảo Cổ Học Bà Rịa – Vũng Tầu Tứ Tiền Sử Dến Sơ Sử.* (Bà Rịa – Vũng Tầu. From Prehistory to History). Hà Nội: Nhà Xuất Bản Khoa Học Xã Hội.

Castillo, C.C. 2014. The botanical remains. In C.F.W. Higham, J. Cameron, N. Chang, C.C. Castillo, D. O'Reilly, S.E. Halcrow, F. Petchey and L. Shewan (eds), The excavation of Non Ban Jak, Northeast Thailand – a report on the first three seasons. *Journal of Indo-Pacific Archaeology* 34: 37–39.

De Capitani, A and U. Leuzinger. 1998. Arbon-Bleiche 3: Siedlungsgeschichte, einheimische traditionen und fremdeinflüsse im Übergangsfeld zwischen Pfyner und Horgener Kultur. *Jahrbuch der Schweizerischen Gesellschaft für Ur- und Frühgeschichte* 81: 237–249.

De Capitani, A., E. Deschler, U. Leuzinger, R. Marti-Grädel and J. Schibler. 2002. *Die Jungsteinzeiliche Seeufersiedlung Arbon Bleiche 3: Funde.* Frauenfeld: Kanton Thurgau.

Ebersbach, R. 2013. Houses, households, and settlements. Architecture and living spaces. In F. Menotti and A. O'Sullivan, (eds), *The Oxford Handbook of Wetland Archaeology* pp. 733–748. Oxford: Oxford University Press.

Eberschweiler, B., A. Hafner and C. Wolf. 2006. Unterwasserarchäeologie in der Schweiz: Bilanz un perspective aus den letzten 25 jahren. In A. Hafner, U. Niffeler and U. Ruoff (eds), *Die Neue Sicht – Unterwasserarchäeologie und Geschichtsbild. Antiqua* 40: 24–45. Basel: Multicolor Print.

Hawken, S. 2011. Metropolis of Ricefields: A Topographic Classification of a Dispersed Urban Complex. PhD thesis, University of Sydney, Sydney.

Higham C.F.W. 1966. Stock Rearing as a Cultural Factor in Prehistoric Europe. PhD thesis, University of Cambridge, Cambridge.

Higham C.F.W. 2014. From the Iron Age to Angkor: new light on the origins of a state. *Antiquity* 88: 822–835. doi.org/10.1017/S0003598X00050717.

——. 2015. From site formation to social structure in prehistoric Thailand. *Journal of Field Archaeology* 40: 383–396. doi.org/10.1179/2042458214Y.0000000010.

Higham, C.F.W. and R. Bannanurag. 1990. *The Excavation of Khok Phanom Di, a Prehistoric Site in Central Thailand.* vol. I. *The Excavation, Chronology and Human Burials.* Report no. XLVII London: Society of Antiquaries of London, Research.

Higham, C.F.W. and A. Kijngam (eds). 2012. *The Origins of the Civilization of Angkor.* vol. V. *The Excavation Ban Non Wat: The Iron Age, Summary and Conclusions.* Bangkok: The Fine Arts Department of Thailand.

Higham, C.F.W. and F. Rispoli. 2014. The Mun Valley and Central Thailand in prehistory: integrating two cultural sequences. *Open Archaeology* 1: 2–28. doi.org/10.2478/opar-2014-0002.

McGrath, R. J. and W.E. Boyd. 2001. The chronology of the Iron Age 'moats' of Northeast Thailand. *Antiquity* 75: 349–360. doi.org/10.1017/S0003598X00061007.

O'Reilly, D.J.W. 1997. The discovery of clay-lined floors at an Iron Age site in Thailand – preliminary observations from Non Muang Kao, Nakhon Ratchasima Province. *Journal of the Siam Society* 85: 133–150.

Oxenham, M, P.J. Piper, P. Bellwood, Chi Hoang Bui, Khanh Trung, Kien Nguyen, Quoc Manh Nguyen, F. Campos, C. Castillo, R. Wood, C. Sarjeant, N. Amano, A. Willis, and J. Ceron. 2015. Emergence and diversification of the Neolithic in Southern Vietnam: insights from coastal Rach Nui. *The Journal of Island and Coastal Archaeology* 10(3): 309–338. doi.org/10.1080/15564894.2014.980473.

Parry, J. 1992. The investigative role of Landsat-TM in the examination of pre- and proto-historic water management sites in Northeast Thailand. *Geocarto International* 7(4): 5–24. doi.org/10.1080/10106049209354385.

Rivett, P. and C.F.W. Higham. 2007. The archaeology of salt production. In C.F.W. Higham, A. Kijngam and S. Talbot (eds), *The Origins of the Civilization of Angkor.* vol. 2. *The Excavation of Noen U-Loke and Non Muang Kao*, pp. 589–593. Bangkok: The Fine Arts Department.

White, J.C., and C.O. Eyre. 2010. Residential burial and the metal age of Thailand. In R. L. Adams and S. M. King (eds), Residential Burial: a Multiregional Exploration. *Archaeological Papers of the American Anthropological Association* 20: 59–78. doi.org/10.1111/j.1551-8248.2011.01028.x.

www.ingramcontent.com/pod-product-compliance
Lightning Source LLC
Chambersburg PA
CBHW041432270326
41935CB00025B/1854